C000090421

1 MONTH OF
FREE
READING

at
www.ForgottenBooks.com

By purchasing this book you are eligible for one month membership to ForgottenBooks.com, giving you unlimited access to our entire collection of over 1,000,000 titles via our web site and mobile apps.

To claim your free month visit:
www.forgottenbooks.com/free965044

* Offer is valid for 45 days from date of purchase. Terms and conditions apply.

ISBN 978-0-260-70056-8
PIBN 10965044

This book is a reproduction of an important historical work. Forgotten Books uses
state-of-the-art technology to digitally reconstruct the work, preserving the original format
whilst repairing imperfections present in the aged copy. In rare cases, an imperfection in
the original, such as a blemish or missing page, may be replicated in our edition. We do,
however, repair the vast majority of imperfections successfully; any imperfections that
remain are intentionally left to preserve the state of such historical works.

Forgotten Books is a registered trademark of FB &c Ltd.
Copyright © 2018 FB &c Ltd.
FB &c Ltd, Dalton House, 60 Windsor Avenue, London, SW19 2RR.
Company number 08720141. Registered in England and Wales.

For support please visit www.forgottenbooks.com

REPORTS OF CASES

ADJUDGED IN THE

COURT OF CHANCERY

OF

UPPER CANADA,

COMMENCING DECEMBER, 1862.

BY

ALEXANDER GRANT, ESQUIRE,

BARRISTER-AT-LAW.

.VOLUME IX.

REPRINT

TORONTO AND EDINBURGH :
CARSWELL & CO., LAW BOOK PUBLISHERS.
1883.

Entered according to Act of Provincial Legislature, in the year of our Lord one thousand eight hundred and sixty-four, by Henry Rowsell, Publisher, in the Office of the Registrar of the Province of Canada.

Moore & Co., Law Printers, 20 Adelaide-street, East, Toronto.

The Hon. M. M. S. Vankoughnet, *Chancellor.*

"   J. Christie Palmer Esten, *Vice-Chancellor.*

"   J. Godfrey Spragge, *Vice-Chancellor.*

"   John S. McDonald, *Attorney-General.*

"   Adam Wilson, *Solicitor-General.*

A TABLE

OF

CASES REPORTED IN THIS VOLUME.

Versus is always put after the plaintiff's name.

B.

G.

H.

J.

M

W.

A TABLE

OF

CASES CITED IN THIS VOLUME.

GRANT IX.

REPORTS OF CASES

ADJUDGED IN THE

COURT OF CHANCERY

OF

UPPER CANADA,

COMMENCING IN JANUARY, 1862

SYKES v. THE BROCKVILLE & OTTAWA RAILWAY CO.

Railway company—Corporation— Lien of contractors on debentures authorized to be issued for constructing a railway—Parties.

By the statutes 16 Victoria, chaps. 22 and 124, and the 18 Vic. ch. 13, certain municipalities were authorized to issue debentures under by-laws of the corporations, to aid in the construction of a railroad. The contractors for building the road agreed with the company to take a certain amount of their remuneration in these debentures, and the work having been commenced certain of these debentures were issued to the company. The contractors afterwards failed to carry on the works, and disputes having arisen between them and the company, all matters in difference were left to arbitration, and an award thereunder was made in favour of the contractors for the sum of £27,645, payable by instalments. One of these instalments having become due, and been left unpaid, the contractors filed a bill to have the debentures delivered over to them in the proportion stipulated for according to the terms of the contract. *Held*, although the contractors would have been entitled to a specific lien on these debentures under their original agreement, the fact that they had referred all matters in difference to arbitration, and had obtained an award in their favour for a money payment, precluded them from now obtaining that relief; and a demurrer for want of equity was allowed.

One of several joint contractors having during the progress of the work contracted for, and a bill afterwards filed by the survivors to enforce a claim under the terms of the contract, *held*, that the personal representatives of the deceased partner should have been made parties; the rule respecting the rights of surviving partners to sue alone not applying to suits in equity.

Statement.—The bill in this case was filed by *William Sykes* and *Charles DeBergue*, against the Brockville & Ottawa Railway Company, the Corporation of the town

of Brockville, the Corporation of the township of Eliza-
bethtown, and the Corporation of the united counties
of Lanark and Renfrew, setting forth that two provincial statutes, passed in the 16th and 18th years of the
reign of her Majesty Queen Victoria, the Brockville
and Ottawa Railway Company were authorized to
construct a railroad from Brockville to Pembroke, with
a branch to Perth; and that the other defendants
agreed to aid in the enterprise; that by a by-law
passed on the 29th of July, 1853, the corporation of
the town of Brockville were authorized to loan to the
company £100,000, and for that purpose to raise the
amount on the credit of the municipal loan fund, in
cash or debentures.

That the corporation of the township of Elizabeth-
town and the united counties of Lanark and Renfrew
also in like manner authorized the issuing of debentures in aid of the undertaking; and that all these
by-laws had been duly approved and sanctioned by the
Governor-General in Council, as required by the Municipal Loan Fund Act. That in pursuance of the
said acts 16 & 18 Vic., a contract was entered into
between the plaintiffs and one *James Sykes*, deceased,
and the defendants, for the construction of the road,
which was set out at length in the bill; one stipulation being, that the company would pay 90 per cent.
of the monthly outlay, on the certificate of the engineer, 40 per cent, being payable in provincial bonds.

The bill further alleged that the several corporations
were authorized by resolutions to become parties to the
contract, and that they were accordingly made parties.
That the corporation did not execute the contract, but
they were aware of and acted upon the same. That the
plaintiffs and *James Sykes* forthwith commenced prepar-
ations for carrying on the works, but before the company could receive the debentures they were required by
the by-law to give security, which was accordingly given
by the company, and the corporations executing a mort-

gage in pursuance of the Railway Clauses Consolidation Act, and which was confirmed by an act passed in the 19th year of her Majesty's reign ; that the plaintiffs having commenced the work, some of the debentures were handed by the corporations to the company for the purpose of being paid to, and were by them paid to, the plaintiffs in pursuance of the contract.

The bill stated the death of *James Sykes*, in September, 1854, and that in 1855, after a considerable portion of the work had been done the plaintiffs suspended work in consequence of non-payment of certificates according to the contract under which a large amount was due by the company to the plaintiffs. That thereupon the company entered into a new contract with other persons for the completion of the work, without the assent, and contrary to the will of the plaintiffs ; in consequence of which they did on the 12th of September, 1857, commence an action against the company ; and on the 29th of May, 1858, all matters in difference were by rule of court referred to arbitration ; and on the same day bonds of submission were executed by the plaintiffs and the company, referring all matters in dispute as well respecting the contract as all other matters in dispute to certain parties named as arbitrators, under which the arbitration was duly proceeded with, and concluded on the 22nd of February, 1859, on which day the arbitrators made their award, whereby they directed that the company should pay to the plaintiffs £27,645, in full satisfaction of all claims and demands and differences under the contract and otherwise, by three several instalments of £9215 each, on the first day of April, 1859, the first of October following, and the first day of April, 1860, with interest ; a copy of which award was served on the company ; that the company had not paid the instalment of £9215, due on the 1st April, 1859, although often requested so to do.

The bill further stated, that a considerable amount of

debentures had been received by the defendants, but plaintiffs believe a large amount remained in the hands of the defendants ; that when plaintiffs suspended work, £10,000 and upwards had been expended by the plaintiffs ; that the mortgage is still subsisting and in force, and plaintiffs submitted they were entitled to be paid out of the debentures, and that the corporation should be restrained from delivering them to the company until the plaintiffs were paid ; or if the debentures had been exhausted, or plaintiffs not entitled to be paid out of them, that they are entitled to a lien on the property comprised in the mortgage, in preference to the corporations, under the terms of the mortgage. They further submitted that the corporations were bound by the contract, although they did not execute the same, as they were aware of its contents, and assented thereto.

The prayer of the bill was, that the plaintiffs might be declared entitled to be paid out of the debentures, and that the corporation might be enjoined from paying the same over to the company ; and the company from expending the same until plaintiffs satisfied ; that a receiver might be appointed ; or if it should appear that the debentures had been expended, or that the plaintiffs were not so entitled, that plaintiffs might be declared entitled under the terms of the mortgage, to a lien on the property comprised therein, prior to that of the corporation ; in default of payment, a sale and payment out of proceeds, and that company might be ordered to pay any deficiency.

To this bill the municipality of Brockville filed demurrers for want of equity, and for want of parties, alleging that the personal representatives of *James Sykes* ought to have been made parties.

Mr. *Brough*, Q.C., Mr. *Roaf*, and Mr. *Blake*, in support of the demurrers.

Mr. *Cameron*, Q.C., contra.

Egremont v. *Colwell*, (a) *Wrightson* v. *Bywater*, (b)
Rule v. *Bryde*, (c) *Preble* v. *Boghurst*, (d) *Gray* v.
Gwennap, (e) were referred to.

Judgment.—ESTEN, V. C.—To this bill two demurrers
have been put in; one for want of equity, the other for
want of parties. The demurrers are the demurrers of the
corporation of the town of Brockville. The first demurrer
insists that the plaintiffs are entitled to no relief against
this corporation. The question is, whether, supposing
the corporations to have in their hands, or within their
power, sufficient debentures to answer the 40 per cent.
on the £27,465, which perhaps may be intended, the
plaintiffs are or not entitled as against them to their
specific delivery. The corporations did not execute the
contract, but they assented to it, and may be considered
to be as much bound, therefore, in a court of equity, as
if they had executed it, upon the same principle that
creditors who have assented to trust deeds without
executing them, are restrained from proceeding at law,
and are declared entitled to the benefit of the trusts,
and that creditors informed of and assenting to deeds
which in the first instance are mere deeds of management, are in like manner bound and entitled. Supposing this view to be correct, the only question would
be, whether the contract in this case was or was not
founded on valuable consideration, so far as the corporations are concerned. It contains provisions for
their benefit, and it might be contended that the corporations assenting to it, and making advances under it,
all parties became bound by it, and entitled to the benefit
of its provisions, and that it became as to all parties a
contract for valuable consideration, and that it was
within the competence of the corporations, under the
by-law, to assent to it, and therefore that the corpora-

(a) 5 Beav. 620.   (b) 3 Mee. & W. 199. .
(c) 1 Ex. 151.   (d) 7 Taunt. 542.
(e) 1 B. & Ald. 106.

tions became bound in equity to give effect to its provisions in all respects as far as they were able, and became bound in particular to give effect to the provision for the payment of 40 per cent. of the amount of the monthly certificates in debentures ; and that a bill could have been filed by the contractors against the company and the corporations for an account of what was due under the contract, and for a specific delivery of debentures to the extent of 40 per cent. of the amount. Supposing this view to be correct, the question is, whether, having brought an action on the contract, instead of filing a bill, and submitted all matters in difference to arbitration, and obtain an award in their favour, they are precluded from seeking equitable relief. A party to a contract bringing an action for damages is afterwards debarred from claiming specific performance. Admitting the plaintiffs to have been entitled, when the defendants refused to make payments according to the certificates, to institute a suit in this court for an account and satisfaction, according to the terms of the contract ; they do not pursue this course, but commence an action at law, in which, had it proceeded to verdict and judgment, they would have recovered damages for the breach of the contract. At the trial, however, as I supposed, they agree to refer all matters in dispute both under the contract and otherwise, to certain gentlemen who are named, and who duly make their award, directing payment by the railway company to the plaintiff of the sum of £27,645, in satisfaction of all differences under the contract and otherwise, by certain instalments, with interest. The first instalment of the amount awarded having become due, and not having been paid, the plaintiffs claim a lien on the debentures for the amount of this and the remaining instalments of the award ; but how can they found such a claim ? Had the action proceeded, and damages been recovered, it would not have been contended that any lien existed upon these debentures for the amount of such damages. Supposing, however, the sum awarded to be not damages, but the amount due under the contract, still the difficulty arises that the arbitrators have certainly intended that it should be paid in money, and as the award is the agreement of the parties, they have agreed respectively to pay and receive the amount in money.   If the 40 per cent. is to be paid in debentures, the rest must be paid in bonds and stock; but such is not the award nor the agreement of the parties.   The court would be making a new award and agreement for the parties if it decreed such relief.   I cannot be sure that the arbitrators would have made the same award had they contemplated such a result.   The parties have in fact made a new agreement, and the plaintiffs cannot claim a lien upon what they were specifically entitled to under one agreement for the amount due to them under another agreement; I think, also, that they are not entitled to the alternative relief prayed by the bill.   It is not easy to discover the grounds upon which it is asked, but it seems to be, that as the debentures are not required for the satisfaction of the award, therefore the plaintiffs, not receiving the debentures, are to be subrogated to the rights of the municipalities *quoad* the mortgage, with this variation, that they are to be entitled to priority.   But I cannot see any reason because the plaintiffs have adopted a course which precludes them from claiming the debentures specifically, why they should become entitled in any degree to the benefit of a security, not created for their benefit, and which as to them is *res inter alios acta*.

I think also that the representatives of *James Sykes* were necessary parties to the bill.   It is true the right of action survives at law to the remaining partners, the rule is different in equity, and the representatives of *James Sykes*, if dissatisfied with the result of the present suit, might institute a fresh one on their own behalf, and the defendants would be harassed by double litigation.   It had been decided in the case of *Drake* v. *Forsyth* (a) that the personal representatives

---

(a) Ante vol. I, page 233.

of a deceased partner are necessary parties to a bill of foreclosure on a mortgage made to the firm, or for its benefit. I think both demurrers must be allowed.

ENGERSON v. SMITH.

Mortgage—Payment to mortgagee after assignment.

The holder of a mortgage security assigned the same for value on the ninth day of October,(Saturday:) on the eleventh of the same month the mortgagor, without notice of the transfer which had been made, effected an arrangement with the mortgage, one of the assignees of the mortgage being present, and concealing the fact of the assignment from the mortgagor. The mortgagor thereupon filed a bill claiming to have the mortgage discharged, alleging fraud in the transaction of the assignment. The court, under the circumstances, ordered the mortgage to be released, but refused the plaintiff his costs in consequence of his failure to prove the fraud charged.

Statement.—The facts of this case fully appear in the head-note and judgment.

Mr. *Blake*, for the plaintiff.

Mr. *Roaf*, for defendants.

Judgment—SPRAGGE, V.C—In October,1858,one *John Christie* was holder of a mortgage for £436, upon certain land in the township of Dorchester, given by the plaintiff to *Christie*. At the same time the plaintiff was the holder of a mortgage for £1100, given to him by one *Morse*, upon land in the township of Blenheim. At the above date the plaintiff and *Christie* were negotiating for the payment of the smaller mortgage, by a portion of the latter. While this was pending, *Christie* made an assignment to the defendant *Smith*, and to *John Mills*, (whose personal representatives are the defendants *Mills* and *Haight*,) of the mortgage held by him against the plaintiff, for the expressed consideration of £250, about half of which sum was satisfied to *Christie* by *Smith*, who then held securities against him ; which, with a small debt due to *Smith*, amounted to close upon that sum. This assignment it is established in evidence was made on Saturday,

the 9th of October, 1858. On the 11th of the same month
the plaintiff made some arrangement with *Christie*,
whereby, as he alleges, he satisfied and paid the same
mortgage to *Christie*, in ignorance of any assignment to
Smith and *Mills*. The arrangement was a rather com-
plicated one and is not very clearly explained in the
evidence, but it appears to have been in substance this:
the Rev. Dr. *Fuller* was the owner of lands in Iowa and
Wisconsin, and an arrangement was made through the
agency of one *Daniel McAlpine*, for the sale of certain
lands in those states to *Christie*. *McAlpine*, on behalf
of Dr. *Fuller*, paid *Christie* £550 in money, and gave a
bond to *Christie* for the conveyance of lands in the above
named states, valued at £1500, to *Christie*.

It is not quite clear from the evidence whether *Christie*
in this transaction got the benefit of the whole of the
Moore mortgage held by the plaintiff; that mortgage
was however, assigned to Dr. *Fuller* by the plaintiff;
and £350 of it, if not the whole, went in payment of the
Iowa and Wisconsin lands, and the money advanced from
Dr. *Fuller*; and in that way the plaintiff paid to that
gentleman on behalf of *Christie* a sum equal to the
mortgage held by *Christie* against him. This is clear
not only by the evidence of *Daniel McAlpine*, corroborated in some repects by that of his son, and of Mr.
Clark, a solicitor in Ingersoll; but also by the facts clearly
established that a certificate in discharge of that mortgage was at the instance of the parties prepared by Mr.
Clarke, and executed by *Christie*. The mortgage itself
was asked for in order to its being discharged, but
Christie declared that it was lost, and, it was thereupon
described as to date from the recollection of the parties:
this was erroneous, and the certificate could not be
registered.

The case then is, that on the 9th of October, *Christie*
assigned the mortgage held by him against the plaintiff
to *Smith* and *Mills*, and on the 11th of the same month

the plaintiff in ignorance of that assignment paid off
the mortgage to the mortgagee. The case of *Norrish*
v. *Marshall*, (a) establishes that a payment by the mortgagor to the mortgagee after assignment, but without
notice of the assignment, is a good payment. Here
certainly the time for giving notice was short; the assignment to *Smith* and *Mills* was on the 9th, on a Saturday,
at what time of day is not shewn; the mortgage was
paid off by the plaintiff on the Monday following, at
about 8 o'clock in the evening. It is not necessary to
decide whether it would have been a good payment if
sufficient time had not elapsed for the assignees to notify
the mortgagor of the assignment, because I think the
assignees having neglected the ordinary precaution of
communicating with the mortgagor beforehand, were
bound at least to use the most prompt diligence in notifying him afterwards; and that if they had used such
diligence they might have notified him.

It is objected that the case proved is not the case
made by the bill. The original bill, before amendment,
certainly made a different case. It charged that the
plaintiff's mortgage was satisfied by the arrangement
with Dr. *Fuller*, on the 1st of October; and that the
assignment to *Smith* and *Mills* was made on the 11th
and was without consideration, and charged fraud and
collusion between *Christie* and the assignees, for the
purpose of compelling the plaintiff to pay the mortgage
twice over. But the amended bill puts the case in the
alternative, that if it be proved that the "assignment was
executed at no earlier date than the 11th, yet it was
executed with the knowledge and fraudulent intent aforesaid, and that the said assignees never informed your
orator of the said assignment, but concealed the same
with such knowledge and fraudulent intent." I read this
as an allegation, that if in fact the assignment was before
the payment of the mortgage by the plaintiff, the

(*a*) 5 Mad. 475.

assignees did not notify the plaintiff of the assignment. It is not very distinctly put, but under the case of *Smith* v. *Kay*, (a) it is sufficient at the hearing, and after the evidence that has been taken.

With regard to costs, the charge of fraud is reiterated by the amended bill, and is not proved ; and the fact being that the assignment was on the 9th, and the satisfaction of the|mortgage on the 11th, there was no ground for charging fraud.

There is one fact in the case that it is difficult to account for, the presence of *Mills* at the satisfaction of the mortgage on the 11th, and his assisting at the arrangement without notifying the plaintiff of the previous assignment to himself and *Smith*, that would of course bar him of his share of the mortgage money; but he has by his will, for he is since dead, acquitted and released the plaintiff from the payment of it. I may add that the presence of *Mills* on the above occasion is proof that sufficient time elapsed between the assignment and the satisfaction of the mortgage by the plaintiff to notify the latter of the assignment ; it is proved that he was present at the assignment ; therefore,

DECREE,—Declare that the plaintiff's mortgage was paid and satisfied by him to the mortgagee, on the 11th of October, 1858, without notice of the assignment thereof by the mortgagee to the defendant Smith, and the testator John Mills.

Decree, that defendants release the mortgage ; and that defendant Smith do, and the other defendants, as far as they can do, re-convey the mortgaged premises. If the legal estate which passed to Mills is in some other parties, they can be made parties in the master's office ; the mortgage and title deeds, if any, to be delivered to the plaintiff. The decree to be without costs.

(a) 30 L. J. ch. 944.

Tripp v. Martin.

Marriage settlement—Bill to change trustees—Personal confidence.

By a clause in a marriage settlement it was stipulated that trustees should at their option during the life of the intended husband, permit him or the intended wife to take and use the rents, issues and profits of the trust estate to their own use; and by a subsequent clause it was provided that new trustees should be appointed in certain contingencies. Upon a bill filed by the wife to appoint a new trustee by reason of the residence of one out of the jurisdiction, *held*, that this trust was one of personal confidence, and could not be executed by a trustee appointed by the court. And it appearing that the husband had not been heard of for upwards of four years, the court, under the circumstances, appointed a new trustee, and directed him to pay one half of the rents to the plaintiff, and the other half to be invested for the benefit of the husband.

This cause come on to be heard before his Honor V.C. *Spragge*, upon bill and answer, the statements of which are clearly set forth in the judgment.

Mr. *Fitzgerald*, for plaintiff.

Mr. *R. Martin*, in person.

Judgment.—Spragge, V.C.—There are two clauses in the marriage settlement upon which more particularly this case turns. The party of the first part is *Charles Nelson Tripp*, the settlor : the party of the second part the intended wife, the plaintiff in this suit ; and the trustee, *Henry Tripp* and *Richard Martin*, both described as of the city of Hamilton, are the parties of the third part. The property settled consists of two half lots in the township of Enniskillen, as to which the trust is, as far as it is material in this suit, "during the natural life of the part of the party of the first part in trust to permit the party of the first part, or the party of the second part, at the option of the said parties of the third part, to take and use the rents, issues, and profits of the said trust property, to their own use and behoof."

The other clause material to this case, is the one providing for the appointment of new trustees, and provides, that if the trustees named in the settlement, or any future trustees to be appointed in their stead should die, or become permanently resident out of the province, or desire to be discharged, or become incapable of acting, it should be lawful for the trustees, and the survivor of them, his heirs and assigns, with the approbation of the settlor, and his intended wife, testified in writing, and signed and attested in manner therein pointed out, to appoint a new trustee or trustees."

One of the trustees, *Henry Tripp*, is now as appears in evidence, resident out of the province; and the other declares by his answer that he desires to be discharged from the execution of the trust. The husband left this province in November, 1856, leaving his wife in the province, where she has ever since resided; the husband has not been heard of since May, 1857. He is named as a defendant in this suit, but has not been served. There are no issue of the marriage.

The trust to which I have referred is clearly one of personal confidence ; and I am satisfied under the case of *Lyon* v. *Radenhurst* (a), in this court, and the cases there cited, could not be executed by a trustee appointed by this court (b).

The next point is that the trust appears by the terms of the settlement, to be exercisable only by two trustees, so that Mr. *Martin*, the only trustee in the province, would not be competent to execute it. Further, in the absence of the husband, whose concurrence is required in the appointment of a new trustee, no new trustee can be appointed without the intervention of this court.

As the discretionary power contemplated by the settlement cannot be exercised, the plaintiff, I apprehend, must be in the same position, as if from any other causes than the existing ones, it had failed to be exer-

(a), Ante vol. 5, p. 544.

(b) See also Hill on Trustees, 492, 4.

cised ; for instance, the trustees might have disagreed
as to its exercise; and for that or any other cause
have failed to exercise the power; or if the husband
was now here, he and his wife might not concur in
the appointment of a new trustee.

In all these cases the husband and wife would, I
think, be entitled to the rents and profits of the settled
property in equal shares. The point has been decided
in several cases where the question has arisen under a
will. *Brown* v. *Higgs* (*a*), and *Kemp* v. *Kemp* (*b*), are
two such cases, and *Furber* v. *Hunter* (*c*), is a case
where the like question arose under a voluntary bond
given by a certificated bankrupt for the benefit of the
wife and children of a deceased creditor.

In this case the wife, the plaintiff, it is true, does
not stand in the same position ; she is not a person
receiving bounty, but a purchaser for valuable consideration ; but still of what? Not of the whole rents and
profits of the settled property, but of the whole or
none, or possibly of a portion, at the discretion of the
trustees. I confess that if I felt that the court had a
discretion to exercise in the matter, I should be disposed, under the circumstances of the case, to give the
whole of the rents and profits to the wife.

I think this a proper case for the appointment of a
new trustee or new trustees, in the place of *Henry Tripp*,
residing without the province, and of Mr. *Martin*, who
desires to retire from the trust, but the trustee or trustees
can have only limited powers, only such as are necessary
for the management of the trust property. One half of
the rents and profits should be paid to the wife, and the
other half paid into court, to be invested for the benefit
of the husband. The defendant *Martin* is necessarily

(*a*) 4 Ves. 708; 5 Ves. 495.   (*b*) 5 Ves. 849.
(*c*) 3 Y. & J. 506.

made a defendant, and is entitled to his costs. The decree must, as usual, reserve the rights of the absent party.

NORRIS V. BELL.

Administration—Costs—Parties.

A testator devised his real estate to his widow, and in the event of her re-marriage, to his children. The widow afterwards filed a bill against the executors, charging mal-administration, which was disproved; and on the contrary, that they had benefitted the estate by their management of it; and the master having found the personal assets were insufficient to discharge the remaining liabilities, the court directed the executors to receive their costs out of the estate, that a competent portion of the real estate should be sold, and that the testator's children should be made parties to the suit in the master's office, for the purpose of re-taking the accounts, if desired by the guardian, they not being bound by the accounts already taken; and under the circumstances, refused the widow her costs.

Statement.—The widow of *John Norris* filed a bill against her deceased husband's executors, for administration and account, charging mal-administration to which the acting executors put in an answer, denying the charges. The decree, besides the usual directions, referred it to the master to enquire how the executors had dealt with the estate.

It appeared by the master's report, on the hearing on further directions, that the charge of mal-administration was disproved, and that the personal assets still undisposed of were insufficient to discharge the existing liabilities of the estate.

Mr. *Blevins* appeared for the plaintiff.

Mr. *McGregor*, for the defendants. The latter asked for a sale of a competent portion of the testator's real estate, and the defendants' costs. It was suggested that the testator's children were not necessary parties; and *Craig* v. *Templeton* (a) was referred to in support of this view.

(a) Ante vol. viii., p. 483.

Judgment.—SPRAGGE, V. C.—The bill is filed by the sole legatee and devisee under the will of the late *John Norris,* subject to a provision that she would not marry again, and in that event a devise over to children. The bill is filed against the executors, charging them with having misapplied and misappropriated the personal estate, and applied a portion thereof to their own use.

This charge wholly fails ; the master finds that personal estate came to the hands of the two executors who have acted, *Bell* and *Clarke,* to the amount of £376 4s. 8d., and that they have properly expended £398 10s. 7d., leaving them in advance to the estate £22 5s. 11d.

The master finds the available outstanding estate to be small ; the exact amount is not ascertained. He finds debts outstanding to the amount of £206. The master finds further, in regard to an enquiry directed as to the manner in which the executors had dealt with the estate, that it had been fair and just, and that they had benefitted the estate by compounding certain of the debts due by the estate.

The cause has been set down on further directions by the defendants, and they ask for a direction that a competent part of the real estate be sold to re-pay what they are in advance of the estate, and to satisfy the outstanding debts.

They ask for their costs, and are clearly entitled to them, out of the estate. A sale of real estate is shewn to be necessary, and the costs do not probably exceed what would have been incurred by the executors if they had been plaintiffs. I think the plaintiff is not entitled to her costs.

It is suggested that the children of the testator are not necessary parties, the plaintiff being devisee in fee, but I apprehend the rule laid down by Sir *J. L. Knight Bruce,* in *Goodess* v. *Williams,* (a) applies: " that where

---

(a) 2 Y. & Coll. C. C. 595, and 7 Jurist, 1123.

a person is seised in fee of an estate, having that seisin liable to be defeated by a shifting use, conditional limitation or executory devise, the inheritance is not represented here, merely by the person who has the fee, liable to be defeated." It will be necessary therefore to make the children of the testator parties : they are not bound by the account already taken. In regard to the account, the order will be the same as the court has been in the habit of making in administration suits, where, after accounts taken in the absence of those interested in the real estate, it has been found that the personality is insufficient, and that a resort to the real estate is necessary.

There appears to be a small quantity of furniture in the possession of the plaintiff, which strictly should be sold first, but there can be an enquiry whether it is not for the benefit of the children that such personal estate should not be sold. The like enquiry has been directed in other cases.

PROCTOR v. GRANT.

Crown patent—Mistake in issuing—Neglect of government agent—
Costs—Evidence—Practice—Examination of a defendant.

A locatee of the waste lands of the Crown, having settled thereon, in
preparing a portion of his land for cultivation cleared a portion of
the adjoining land. According to the usage of the Crown lands
department, any person even without settling upon lands of the
Crown, effecting a clearing thereon, was always allowed the privilege of purchasing the lot so cleared, at the price fixed upon the land
by the agent of the government. Subsequently, the government
employed a surveyor to inspect the lands in the neighbourhood of
the land so cleared upon, and in his return reported the property
on which the clearing had been made, as vacant and unimproved,
and valued it at twelve shillings and sixpence per acre. The agent
who had so inspected the lands afterwards applied for, and obtained
a patent for this lot, at the rate of eight shillings an acre, and almost
immediately after sold it to a person who had full knowledge of the
clearing which had been made. Upon a bill filed by the person who
had made the improvement on the land, the court, under the circumstances, ordered the patent to be revoked, as having been issued
in error and mistake, without costs. But, *semble*, that had the
agent of the Crown, whose conduct had created the difficulty,
been joined as a party, he would have been ordered to pay costs.

The examination of a defendant after answer, or after the time for
answering has expired, is a substitute for the discovery by answer
and a plaintiff can at the hearing read such examination, or parts of
it, in the same manner as a defendant's answer, or passages from it
could be used against him at the hearing : for this purpose it is not
necessary to examine the defendant at the examination of witnesses.

A party who had improperly obtained a patent for land from the
Crown, and conveyed the property to another, with notice was
called as a witness on behalf of his vendee, in a suit to have the
patent revoked as having been issued through error and mistake on
the part of the Crown. *Held*, that although he might be subjected to
an action at the suit of his vendee in the event of the patent being set
aside, and the land granted to another, and therefore strongly interested in defeating the suit of the plaintiff, still that he was not one
for whose immediate benefit the suit was wholly or in part defended ;
and that the objection must be to his credit, not to his competency.

Statement.—The bill in this cause was filed by *George
Proctor*, of Beaverton, in the township of Thorah, yeoman,
against *Hector Grant*, setting forth, that under the regu-
lations made for the management of the Crown lands
department, a custom existed of giving to persons who
went into possession of wild lands and made improvements thereon a privilege of pre-emption in regard to the
lands they had so improved, and such custom had become
well understood and acknowledged by the department ;
that while such custom existed, plaintiff entered into possession of the north half of lot No. 12, in the 2nd concession

of the township of Thorah, which was then vested in the Crown, and cleared up and improved seventeen acres thereof, and otherwise expended money and labour thereon : that after taking such possession, the plaintiff applied on several occasions to the Crown land agent at Toronto, to purchase this land, but was informed that it was not then in the market, but that he would have the privilege of purchasing the same when offered for sale, and that relying thereon plaintiff had continued to occupy and improve the land.   That in accordance with the custom of the office, the Crown lands department on the 15th of February, 1858, instructed one *Donald Cameron,* the then agent of the department, to inspect, among other lands, the said half lot, and to report thereon prior to the same being offered for sale ; that *Cameron* thereupon formed the design of defeating and defrauding plaintiff of his pre-emptive right, and if possible of procuring the said half lot for himself, and with that view, although well aware thereof, made no mention in his report, made on the 14th of June, 1858, to the Crown lands department, of the facts entitling plaintiff to a preference of purchasing the said land, or of the rights existing in his favour with respect thereto, but designedly and fraudulently, and in violation of his duty, left a blank in his said report under the titles, "length of occupation," and "value of improvements," thereby conveying the idea that the land was unoccupied and unimproved, while under the title, "number of acres cleared," he wrote the word, "none."   That plaintiff, under the full belief that no obstacle existed to his purchasing, applied for that purpose to the Crown lands department, when, in answer to his application, he for the first time became aware that the land had been sold to *Cameron :* that the plaintiff thereupon petitioned the department, setting forth the particulars of his possession and improvements, and praying that the sale to *Cameron* might be set aside, in order that plaintiff might be allowed to purchase in accordance with the practice of the department, in answer to which plaintiff received a letter from the Hon. the Commissioner of Crown Lands, dated the 13th of July, 1860, stating that the sale to *Cameron* had been fully carried out by a completion of the patent for the land, on the 20th day of April preceding, and that therefore the department had ceased to have any control over the land. That the Crown accordingly, in issuing the said patent, was ignorant of the claims of the plaintiff to the land—had no knowledge of the facts that the said land was not vacant, but in the occupation of the plaintiff, and improved by him; all of which had been designedly and fraudulently suppressed and concealed, or misrepresented by *Cameron* in his report.

The bill further alleged, that by indenture dated 6th of June, 1860, *Cameron* had sold and conveyed the said half lot to the defendant in fee for £105, being nearly three times the amount paid by *Cameron* to the government therefor; and charged defendant with notice, before he purchased, of plaintiff's possession and improvements, and of his claim to the said land, and of the fraud by means of which *Cameron* had obtained his patent.

The bill further stated, that plaintiff still remained in possession of the property, but that defendant threatened to institute proceedings for the purpose of ejecting him therefrom, and prayed that the patent so issued to *Cameron*, might be declared void by reason of his fraud, and of the error and mistake on the part of the Crown; and that the defendant might be decreed to deliver up such patent and conveyance to be cancelled, or that he might be declared a trustee for plaintiff, and ordered to convey to him on payment of what *Cameron* paid to the Crown.

The defendant having answered the bill, the plaintiff put the cause at issue, and evidence was taken therein before the court, and under commission. The evidence taken before the commission was that of the superintendent of Crown lands sales, in the Crown land department, who proved that the practice in the department for 15 or 20 years past, was to sell lands which are in the occupation of, or have improved by clearing and fencing, not less than five acres at a special valuation; that if a third person applies, the department will refuse to sell to him unless on production of an assignment from the person owning the improvements; and that had the department been made aware of the improvement on the half lot in question by the plaintiff, it would not have been consistent with such practice to have sold to *Cameron*; the usage of the department being to protect those who have occupied and made improvements to any important extent.

The other important facts in the case are stated in the judgment.

Mr. *Mowat*, Q.C., for plaintiff. Sufficient is admitted by the defendant to warrant the court in pronouncing a decree as asked. He was aware of plaintiff having cleared 17 or 18 acres, and does not deny that he knew also of the pre emption right acquired by such improvement.

The fact of the clearing having been effected should have been brought to the knowledge of the Crown, and the fact would have been taken into consideration; whether it would have had the effect of procuring a sale to the plaintiff is not the question now to be discussed, but looking at the statements of the officers of the land granting department, we have a right to presume that had such fact been made known to the government the patent never would have been issued to *Cameron*. It is true *Cameron* states in his evidence that he was not aware of the improvements made by plaintiff; but this he cannot be permitted to allege for his own advantage. He was the officer of government employed for the express purpose of ascertaining the improvements made on this and adjoining lands, and, as such was bound to know the facts.

Error and mistake on the part of the government is clearly shewn, if not admitted, and this is sufficient to bind *Cameron*, if even the court should not come to the conclusion that he was guilty of the fraud imputed to him; he cited *Martin* v. *Kennedy* (a), *Attorney-General McNulty* (b).

Mr. *Fitzgerald* for the defendant. The person making improvements on wild lands must do so with the intention of becoming the purchaser, to entitle him to any pre-emptive rights. Here the plaintiff is a mere speculator, and not such a person as this court will be desirous of assisting.

To warrant a decree in favour of this plaintiff, it should be made apparent that the government would *not* have granted the land to *Cameron*, and would have granted it to plaintiff. The notice alleged, he contended, was not sufficient to prevail against a registered title.

Judgment—SPRAGGE, V. C.—This bill is filed for the purpose of repealing the patent to *Donald Cameron*, granting to him the north half of lot 12, in the 2nd concession of Thorah, as issued to him in error and mistake, and of declaring the defendant a purchaser from *Cameron*, with notice a trustee for the plaintiff; and for a conveyance from him to the plaintiff.

The bill is founded on the usage of the Crown to prefer as purchasers those who have made improvements on the wild lands of the Crown; alleging that such improvements had been made by the plaintiff, who was desirous of becoming a purchaser; that *Cameron*, who was agent of the Crown, inspected the parcel of land in

---

(a) Ante vol. iv., p, 61.   (b) Ante vol. 8, p. 324.

question—had knowledge of such improvements, and fraudulently concealed the same from the Crown lands department.

Two questions are raised upon the admissibility of evidence. The plaintiff examined the defendants before the examiner, before, and not at the examination term; and now seeks to use the examination, or passages from it, as evidence against him. The defendant objects that the examination of an opposite party for the purpose of being read at the hearing, must be taken at the examination term, and says that it was so ruled by his Lordship the Chancellor in a case of *Simpson* v. *Hutchinson*. The reporter, to whom I have referred, informs me that the point did arise, and that the Chancellor's impression, as given at the time, was, that the examination so taken could not be read; but that the point was not absolutely decided. I have therefore felt bound to decide upon the admissibility of this examination upon my own judgment. I have looked carefully at the general orders under which the examination was taken, and find nothing in them to prevent its use at the hearing. Upon principle, I think, it is admissible : the examination of a defendant after answer, or after time for answering has expired, is a substitute for the discovery by answer, and as a plaintiff could at the hearing read against a defendant his answer, or passages from it, so by analogy I conceive he should be at liberty to make the like use of the examination of a defendant. As a matter of convenience, for the saving of expense, and for the furtherance of justice, I think such examination should be allowed to be read at the hearing. If the plaintiff thinks, after such examination, that he can obtain no further discovery from a defendant, it would be an inconvenient and useless proceeding to go over the same ground at the examination term, and would be attended with double expense; and further, a dishonest defendant might qualify or even deny, when examined at the examination term what he had previously said, and it would be a temptation to him to do so, if what he had previously said could not be used against him. I have addressed myself to the examination of a defendant, such an examination being the point before me; but an examination of a plaintiff by a defendant, would, I conceive, be equally admissible.

The other point upon evidence is raised by the plaintiff. He objects that *Cameron* is not a competent witness for the defendant. *Cameron* is not a party, but it is urged that the suit is in truth defended for his benefit. At most a decree repealing the patent might, if a patent were hereafter granted to the plaintiff, or to some other person, subject *Cameron* to an action at the suit of the defendant. He would therefore, no doubt, feel a strong interest in defeating the plaintiff in this suit; but he would not, I think, be one for whose immediate benefit the suit is wholly or in part defended, within the meaning of the statute or of the general orders of this court, and therefore would not fall within the disqualified class. The objection would be to his credit only, not to his competency.

As to the merits of the case—*Cameron* was employed by the Crown lands department in the year 1858, in the following service, as described by Mr. *Spragge*, an officer of the department: "He was employed by the department to inspect and value lands in the township of Thorah, and other townships, with a view to the department resuming such as should be found unoccupied and unimproved, and offering them for public sale, so as to enable the department to deal with cases of parties who, on account of occupation and improvement, were entitled to pre-emption.

At this date the plaintiff was in possession of the south-half of the lot in question, having purchased it from the government several years before. He was in occupation of it by a tenant, and had cleared a large portion of it. On the north, his clearing extended into the north-half lot in question, comprising at the above date about seventeen acres. On the west his clearing extended into lot 13, comprising about five acres. I have no doubt from the evidence that the plaintiff crossed his own lines, in clearing, by mistake.

In regard to the north-half of 12, *Cameron* did not report according to the fact. His report was, "occupant, none," "acres cleared, none."

The defendant contends that *Cameron* reported in accordance with what he believed to be the fact; and that at all events the plaintiff has no ground of complaint, inasmuch as his clearing upon the lot as he did would give him no pre-emptive right.

With regard to the defendant, it is clear from his examination that before he purchased from *Cameron*, he became acquainted with the facts that *Cameron* had inspected the land for the government; that at the date of *Cameron's* purchase, and at the date of his inspection and report the half lot was not unimproved, but that about seventeen acres of it were cleared, so that if the plaintiff has any equity as against *Cameron*, he has the same equity against the defendant.

Upon the point whether *Cameron* knew of this clearing at the date of his inspection or report, or at the date of his purchase, which seems to have been in July or August, 1858, the evidence is conflicting. Two witnesses, *Donald Ross* and *John McInnis*, are explicit and positive in their evidence upon the point of knowledge in *Cameron*, at or about the date of his inspection, certainly before the date of his purchase. It is true that it is conversations with *Cameron* that they swear to, a kind of evidence always open to comment; but the conversations were not casual, or upon a subject of indifference to the witnesses; they both of them knew of *Cameron's* official character, and enquired of him concerning the half-lot in question with a view to purchase. To each of them his answer, according to their account, was, that *Proctor*, the plaintiff, had part of his clearing upon it. To *Ross* he said that *Proctor* would not let the lot go, that he had a good part of his clearing upon it. To *McInnis* he said that *Proctor* had some improvements on it. *McInnis* told him he thought it was not much, when *Cameron* said there were some ten or twelve acres; both of these seem to have been deterred from purchasing by these answers of *Cameron*. They adhered to their account of what passed, although each of them was told that *Cameron* would be called to contradict him.

Cameron, upon being called by the defendant, denied that he had such conversation with *Ross* and *McInnis;* and denied, also, that he knew of any clearing being upon the land in question ; and said that he first discovered it, upon having the division line run, in May, 1860.

There is this in his favour, that while making his inspection he enquired of a person named *Chambers,* living on lot 13, whether any part of lot 12 was cleared, and where the line was, or where the post stood. *Chambers* gave evidence of this, and says he told *Cameron* that he did not know any of these things. It is also in *Cameron's* favour, that it was not a separate clearing from that on the south-half; and it would naturally be assumed that the owner of the south-half in making his clearing would keep within his own limits.

Still it is quite consistent with this, that *Cameron* may have ascertained the fact of clearing being upon the north-half; and if *McInnis* is to be believed, he had done this. *McInnis* says, " I knew the lot at the time. I did not know of the improvements until *Cameron* told me there were some. He said there were improvements on it—10 or 12 acres. I disputed this, and he said he was at the post, and had his compass there, and knew there were improvements on it."

Upon *Cameron* being questioned in relation to this conversation, he at first denied it; then said that he had no recollection of such conversation; then again denied it absolutely.

My brother *Esten* before whom the evidence was taken was favourably impressed by the witnesses *Ross* and *McInnis*, both as to their truthfulness and intelligence. He was not unfavourably impressed by *Cameron* but, in his evidence-book has not noted him as standing so high in his estimation as *Ross* and *McInnis*. It devolves upon me to weigh the evidence upon this point. I think it preponderates in favour of the plaintiff. Either what *Ross* and *McInnis* says is true, or they have fabricated a story, the most unusual shape in which false evidence is given. I do not think they could have been mistaken as to the land enquired of, or the time, or the answer given; the circumstances they state, only some of which I have adverted to, render this almost impossible. Then again they stand indifferent between the parties, while *Cameron* has powerful motives for denying the knowledge imputed to him; for in addition to his interest in this suit, he was, if he had such knowledge, guilty of a fraudulent dereliction of duty in making the return he did make to the public department by whom he was employed, which is not only damaging to his character, but bars the way to future employment; these considerations must be borne in mind in weighing the evidence. Still I think I should have been disposed, if the case necessarily turned upon the fact of this knowledge in *Cameron*, to grant an issue to the defendant upon this point, if he asked for it.

I think, however, that it is not necessary to bring home to *Cameron* actual knowledge of the fact of this clearing. Assuming for the present that it is a material fact, *Cameron* does not stand upon the same footing as a stanger purchasing, because it was his duty to ascertain the fact: and that it could be ascertained is

clear, for the post was there, and he might have used
his compass ; even supposing he did not use it, and the
fact had been ascertained by a previous inspector, who
had reported it.

In the case of *Martin* v. *Kennedy*, the grantee was
the object of the bounty of the Crown. He was certainly
innocent of all knowledge of the facts, upon which my
brother *Esten* thought that the patent ought to be
repealed. I do not mean now to express any opinion
whether the same principles apply in the case of a purchaser for value, as in the case of an object of the bounty
of the Crown ; but taking *Cameron* here to be purchaser
for value, and supposing him entitled to stand upon the
same footing as a purchaser for an individual, I incline
to think that he could not hold a purchase made under
the circumstances of this one.

It remains to consider whether this is an immaterial
fact. The defendant urges that the clearing was made
by mistake, and that the plaintiff is not of the class
denominated "squatters." Supposing the defendant
right upon both these points, does it follow that the fact of
this clearing being made as it was made, was immaterial,
so that the Crown in disposing of this land would not
take the circumstance into account ?

Suppose a person having a location ticket, to settle
and clear upon the wrong lot by mistake, claring say
upon lot 13, in the belief that it was lot 12, a thing quite
possible, and of which there have been several instances,
could it be said that the Crown in disposing of lot 13
would hold the circumstance immaterial? Here the
circumstance is of the same nature, only less in degree.
It seems to be assumed that a person clearing by mistake stands in a less favourable position than a "squatter." I do not understand this to be the case, or see
why it should be so, but the contrary. A squatter is in
the eye of the law a wilful intruder under the domain of

the Crown ; while a person who has rightfully acquired land from the Crown, and supposing he is exercising his right in clearing it, clears by mistake adjoining land of the Crown, occupies a position certainly entitling him to more favourable consideration. That "squatters" are not considered objects of peculiar favour is apparent from the order in Council, requiring them to purchase within a limited time ; and which order was passed, according to the evidence of Mr. *Spragge*, "with the view of deterring persons from continuing the system of squatting, which has been regarded as pernicious and attended with very great trouble to the department."

It is not for me to say that the fact of this clearing having been made by the plaintiff, ought to induce the government to grant to him the north-half of lot 12, or not to grant it to *Cameron*, or any other person. But judging from the return required to be made by inspectors in regard to clearings, and by the course of dealing on the part of the Crown, with those who have made clearings, shewing, I think, that it is the practice of the Crown to treat such persons with consideration ; I must hold the circumstance of the clearing a material fact. If the same quantity of land had been cleared by a "squatter," it is clear, I think, from the evidence, that the Crown would have preferred him to a stranger, and that a patent to a stranger in ignorance of the fact of clearing would be issued in error and mistake. Unless I have reason to think that the Crown would deal less favourably with a person making a clearing by mistake, and in the belief that he was rightfully clearing land he had purchased from the Crown, I must hold this patent issued in error and mistake.

In this case I feel that it can be done without doing wrong to *Cameron* or the defendant. *Cameron* has gotten an advantage by his own wrong ; he reported the land uncleared contrary to the fact ; and I cannot forbear alluding to another fact appearing in evidence:

he estimated this land at 12s. 6d. an acre, then got it
reduced by the estimate of another to 8s. an acre, taking
it as containing one hundred acres, when it contained
at least one-fifth more, and then sold it for about three
times what he paid for it. The defendant bought it
with knowledge of the clearing, and by whom it was
made—of the inspection by *Cameron*, and his return,
and both dealt for the land without any communication with the plaintiff, who lived in the immediate
neighbourhood.

I could not read the evidence in this case without
being struck with the impolicy of allowing inspectors
of lands, or other agents employed by the government
in the sale of lands, themselves to become purchasers.

With regard to the costs of this suit, I confess I have
some difficulty. I do not think that the defendant in
purchasing from *Cameron* believed that what is called a
pre-emption right existed in the plaintiff; he swears
that he did not. In case of "squatters" such a right
was recognized and acted upon and generally known,
and a person purchasing against such right would do
so knowingly in order to defeat it, or at least with his
eyes open as to the consequences. If *Cameron* had
been the defendant, or if he had been made defendant
for the purpose of asking costs against him, I should,
I think, have directed that he should pay the costs,
by reason of his own neglect of duty, having been the
origo mali; but I hardly think it a case for costs against
the defendant. The decree will be for the repeal of
the patent, and without costs.

GOODERHAM V. THE BANK OF UPPER CANADA.

Principal and surety.

A person became surety for another for the due discharge of his duty as agent in the purchase of wheat for a mercantile firm. Afterwards the agent and his principals entered into an agreement for partnership, and during the continuance thereof he became indebted to his co-partners in the sum of £750, and the surety having been called upon, executed a confession of judgment for the amount of his principal's indebtedness, in ignorance, as he alleged, of the fact that the agency had ceased, and a partnership been formed. Upon a bill to enforce the judgment against the surety, the court, under the circumstances, directed a reference to ascertain what, if any, portion of the debt for which the assignment was given, arose in respect of dealings during the agency, reserving further directions and costs ; or if the plaintiffs should decline this reference, then that the bill should be dismissed with costs.

Statement.—The bill in this cause, filed by *William Gooderham* and *James Gooderham Worts,* against The *Bank of Upper Canada,* was as follows :

1. " That on the 23rd day of June, A.D. 1854, your orators recovered a judgment in the Court of Queen's Bench, against *James Reeve, Salem Aldis* and *Edwin Larwill,* for the sum of £755 5s. 7d. damages, and £5 18s. 2d. costs, in an action theretofore brought by your orators against the said *James Reeve, Salem Aldis* and *Edwin Larwill,* which judgment was duly registered in the registry office of the county of Kent, on the 24th day of June, 1854, at which time the said *Edwin Larwill* had divers lands, tenements and hereditaments in the said county.

2. " That the *Bank of Upper Canada,* the above mentioned defendants, are the owners of the said lands and tenements, subject to the said judgment, having taken a conveyance of the said land, A.D. 1857.

3. " That on the 9th day of June, 1858, the said judgment was re-registered, according to the statute in such case made and provided."

The prayer was the usual one for an account ; and a sale in default of payment of the amount found due.

The defendants answered the bill, setting up that in January,1853, it was agreed upon between plaintiffs and one *James Reeve,* that they should advance to him as their agent,moneys to enable him to purchase wheat for them, at prices to be named by them from time to time, to be delivered by him on board of vessels, to be sent by them, at certain named places ; and to secure the due performance by *Reeve* of this duty, he, together with *Aldis* and *Larwill* entered into a bond, dated 11th of January, 1853, in a penal sum of £1000 ; that subsequently to the execution of such bond, and while the agreement was still subsisting, not before the recovery of the judgment by plaintiffs, it was agreed between plaintiffs and *Reeve*, without the knowledge or consent of *Larwill*, but on the contrary, with the fraudulent intent of keeping such last mentioned agreement, as it was, altogether concealed from him, that instead of their agent, that said *Reeve* should become the partner of plaintiffs in their business of wheat merchants, and in contemplation or pursuance of such concealed arrangement, the plaintiff, on the 6th of August, 1853, wrote and sent to *Reeve* a letter containing the following paragraph : "We have written to Mr. *Cusack* on the subject of your taking a share of this fall's purchases ; as he is willing to relinquish his, we have no objection to giving you the same interest he had, namely, one-third of either profit or loss." And on the 13th of the same month they wrote : "You can put your $1200 into the speculation, and we shall consider you interested to the extent of one-third in either profit or loss." And again on the 29th they wrote, "recollect we consider you one-third interested in either profit or loss." That after such partnership being entered into, and while *Larwill* supposed and believed that the original agreement for the due performance of which he had as aforesaid become surety still subsisted, and that the claim by the plaintiffs was made by them in respect of the breach of such agreement, the plaintiffs were allowed by *Larwill* to recover judgment against himself, *Aldis* and *Reeve*, and submitted that the plaintiffs' judgment having been so as aforesaid unjustly, and by fraud and concealment, obtained and registered against the lands formally belonging to *Larwill*, the same ought not to be allowed to continue as a charge or incumbrance thereon. The plaintiffs having filed a replication putting the cause at issue, evidence was taken before the court. The only two witnesses examined were *Larwill* and *Reeve*, the effect of whose evidence is fully stated in the judgment.

Mr. *McDonald* for the plaintiffs.

Mr. *Bennett* for the defendants.

Judgment.—SPRAGGE, V.C.—This case seems to turn upon a short question of fact.

In January, 1853, one *James Reeve* was, or was about to become, the agent of the plaintiffs in the purchase of wheat ; and on the 11th of that month, *Reeve*, together with *Salem Aldis* and *Edwin Larwill*, entered into a bond to the plaintiffs, which recited, that the obligees had agreed to advance to *Reeve* £500, in such sums as he might from time to time require, in the purchase of wheat for the obligees, between the date of the bond and the 15th of June following, or such other time as might thereafter be agreed upon between the obligees and *Reeve*, *Reeve* to deliver the wheat either at Chatham, Lanesville, Dresden, or Wallaceburgh, unless the same should be lost by flood or fire; the bond further recited, that *Aldis* and *Larwill* had become sureties " for the due performance of the said agreement on the part of the said *James Reeve*." The condition of the bond is in accordance with the recital.

In August, 1853 (the exact date is not shewn), the relative position of *Reeve* and the plaintiffs changed; he ceased to be their agent for the purchase of wheat, and became their partner, they continuing to supply money to him to purchase wheat, and he continuing to purchase it. He was to put in a certain sum himself, and was to be interested as a partner, receiving one-third of the profits, and bearing one-third of the losses. From this period the liability of *Aldis* and *Larwill* of course ceased, as to all but previous transactions.

An accounting took place on the 29th of January, 1854, between the plaintiffs and *Reeve*, when it was found, as he says in his evidence, that he was indebted to them to the extent of about £600.

Reeve, according to his evidence, met with several losses, one, of a schooner laden with tobacco and staves, was his individual loss; the others, which were of wheat, were, as far as I can gather the dates from his evidence, while he was a partner. Upon what footing he settled with the plaintiffs in June, 1854, does not appear; but he speaks in his evidence of all the losses as his own, and seems to have treated them as his own in his interview with the plaintiff *Worts*. He says, "I told him I wanted to secure him. I told him everything I have mentioned. The freighters would come on me, and *Worts* would not be able to get his money." The cognovit was given for £755 5s. 7d., as an amount due by *Reeve* to the plaintiffs on transactions in which *Aldis* and *Larwill* were sureties.

In part of his evidence, *Reeve* says: "In February, 1854, I shewed to *Aldis* the settlement I had made with plaintiffs on the 29th of January, which shewed that £300 was coming to me and £600 to the plaintiffs." I should understand these sums to be the profits respectively of the parties; and they are in the proportion in which they were to share the profits of the business. Yet *Reeve*, in another part of his evidence, speaks of the larger sum as an amount found due from himself to the plaintiffs. In June, when there was another accounting, and when the cognovit was given, the amount arrived at as due from *Reeve* to the plaintiffs was £775 5s. 7d. I think it can scarcely admit of a doubt that the £600 formed part of that sum, and that *Reeve's* object was to secure the plaintiffs for the amounts advanced by them, for which he was not able to account in wheat. In fact *Reeve* says as much in the part of his evidence that I have quoted.

If the parties did in truth settle upon that footing in June, 1854, it is too clear for argument that the sureties were erroneously treated as liable to the plaintiffs upon the assumed indebtedness to them of *Reeve*. It is clear from the evidence that *Aldis* and *Larwill* joined in the cognovit as being liable as sureties for the assumed debt. *Reeve* says, speaking of a mortgage for the same amount, from *Reeve* to *Aldis* and *Larwill*, and bearing date the same day as the cognovit: "I told *Aldis* and *Larwill* that I wanted to secure them against loss." Again, "I gave *Aldis* and *Larwill* this mortgage to protect them from the debt due to the plaintiffs, as my sureties."

If any part of this amount was due in respect of the purchase of wheat by *Reeve*, as agent for the plaintiffs, for that *Aldis* and *Larwill* were liable as sureties. But they were certainly liable for nothing beyond that; and I think before the court should hold them fixed with liability beyond that, it should be made very clearly to appear that they gave this cognovit with full knowledge of the change in the relative position of *Reeve* and the plaintiffs.

It is *Larwill's* land that has been sold, and it is with his knowledge of the fact that we have to do. *Reeve* says in his evidence, that he gave full information upon the point to *Aldis;* but he is much less positive and explicit as to what he told *Larwill*, all that he says, is, "I have no doubt I told *Larwill* of the new arrangement with the plaintiffs : I kept nothing a secret from them." "In June, 1854, when I gave the mortgage I think *Larwill* must have known of the new arrangement with plaintiffs, that I was buying for one-third." *Larwill* was called as a witness, and denied that he knew of the new arrangement at the time of the giving of the cognovit

in June, 1854, or until Christmas, 1860 ; he does not
give a very good reason for signing the cognovit, he
says, "I signed the papers, being willing to do so, because *Aldis* and *Reeve* thought it was right ; and *Reeve*
was giving a mortgage on his property, which was considered an equivalent. I left it to Mr. *Aldis* altogether,
who was anxious about the matter." "I had no idea
that there was a prior mortgage on the property. I
left the matter altogether with *Aldis*. I supposed he
would look into the business and understand what he
was about. I considered that the surety bond had expired, and I said so in June, 1854, at the time of the
mortgage. I thought little about the matter, and cannot
say now precisely what actuated me to sign the
papers."

I have quoted, perhaps, more of *Larwill's* evidence
than is necessary, because my brother *Esten*, before
whom it was taken, thinks it entitled to but little
weight, not that it was given otherwise than honestly,
but that he appeared, either from irregular habits, or
from some other cause, to have lost his memory. A
portion of his evidence might lead to the conclusion,
that when he signed the cognovit he knew that he was
incurring a liability. But supposing him correct in his
recollection that he considered the surety bond had run
out, and supposing that he said so, that might easily
have been met by explaining that *Reeve* was to be the
plaintiffs' agent not only to the 15th of June, 1853, but
for such further time as they and *Reeve* might agree
upon. *Reeve*, in his evidence, seems to negative the
idea of the sureties meaning to incur a new liability.

Suppose *Larwill's* evidence discarded, and that his
denial of all knowledge in June, 1854, of the partnership
between *Reeve* and the plaintiffs, be blotted out; the
fact of knowledge in *Larwill* would then rest only upon
the evidence of *Reeve*. Now I do not understand from his
evidence that he speaks from recollection, but only from
an impression—almost a conviction perhaps, that he must

have told him. I think this falls far short of that clear evidence of knowledge in *Larwill*, in June, 1854, of the fact in question, which is necessary to fix him with this new liability. *Reeve* does not say, and probably cannot say, *when* he informed *Larwill* of his ceasing to be agent, and becoming partner. It may have been, if at all, when the change took place in August, 1853; what was the state of *Larwlll's* mind and memory before June, 1854, does not appear. Knowledge at the time of the new liability is essential, and that as I have said should be clearly proved.

There is something certainly in the circumstance that *Aldis* incurred this new liability with knowledge, as it would appear, of the change which discharged him thenceforth as a surety ; but it has not been considered material to enquire as to the circumstances under which *Aldis* signed the cognovit of June, 1854. There may have been reasons and motives of which we know nothing. No reasons or motives are even suggested in regard to *Larwill* : but his liability as a surety was assumed to exist, and the arrangement was made with the avowed object of securing him and his co-surety from loss.

The arrangement was made through the intervention of the plaintiffs' solicitor—no solicitor acting for *Aldis* and *Larwill*—and no explanation given as to how they stood. To put the case most favourably for the plaintiffs, the giving of this cognovit was mere *nudum pactum* on the part of *Larwill*, but it has not been put upon that ground, but upon the absence of knowledge of the partnership, on the part of *Larwill*. One thing appears to me to be clear upon the evidence that *Aldis* and *Larwill* gave their cognovit by reason of their supposed liability as sureties. Now supposing them to have had knowledge of the fact which in law put an end to their liability, but to have given the cognovit under the mistaken belief that their liability continued, I incline to think that the cognovit cannot be enforced against

them. A learned author on the law of suretyship, Mr.
Burge, seems to be of this opinion.

To put the case shortly, as raised by the pleadings,
Larwill was discharged at the time of his giving the
cognovit, as to all liability subsequent to the ceasing
of agency. Is it proved that he knew when he gave
the cognovit that the sum for which he gave it was not,
or that a portion of it was not, due in respect of dealings between the plaintiffs and *Reeve* while he was
their agent, not their partner ?

Upon the evidence I think that this is not proved,
and therefore that the plaintiffs' judgment can only
stand for the amount, if any, which was due in respect
of dealings during the agency.

There must be a reference to ascertain that amount,
if desired by the plaintiffs, in which case further directions and costs will be reserved. If this reference is
not taken by the plaintiffs, the bill should be dismissed
with costs.

———

FISHER v. GLASS.

Practice—Injunction to restrain action at law against officer of court
—Damages.

Proceedings under a *fi. fa.* at law having been set aside, and an action
brought against the master, in whose name the *fi., fa.* had been
sued out, an injunction was issued restraining proceedings. *Held,*
the application for an injunction in the original cause in this court
was regular; and that the officer of this court was the proper person to whom should be referred the question as to the amount of
damages sustained by the proceedings which had been set aside.

The receiver who had been appointed in this cause having made default in paying over the moneys of the estate
come to his hands, an action in the name of the master
was brought upon the bond, in which a *fi. fa.* goods had
been issued against the receiver and his sureties, under
which a levy had been made upon the goods of one of

_____

the sureties, a brewer, consisting of a large stock of ale, which became so damaged and spoiled under seizure, as to be totally unfit for sale. The writ of *fi. fa.* was afterwards set aside on the ground of irregularity, whereupon an action was commenced against the master of the court for the value of the ale. An injunction was moved for and obtained, restraining that action, and referring it to the master, of the court at Hamilton, to ascertain the damage sustained by reason of the seizure.

Mr. *A. Prince* and Mr. *Blain*, moved to dissolve this injunction, relying chiefly on the ground that the verdict of a jury was the easiest mode of ascertaining the damage, and that the court of law would be the best judge as to the regularity or irregularity in the manner of conducting the proceedings there.

Mr. *Roaf*, contra.

Judgment.—ESTEN, V. C.—In this case, a receiver having been appointed, who of course furnished security for the due execution of his office; and the master having reported a sum of over £400 due from the receiver, an application was made by the plaintiffs for liberty to put in suit the security furnished by the receiver, against himself and the sureties, one of whom was Mr. *Edward Whitney*, of Galt. Leave was accordingly given to proceed at law on the bond, furnished by the receiver and his sureties, in the name of the master of this court, to whom it was made, and an action was accordingly commenced in his name against the receiver and his sureties, and judgment obtained and execution issued upon it, under which a levy was made upon the goods of Mr. *Edward Whitney*, the sum of £547 being endorsed upon the writ, which was composed of the sum of £492, reported to be due by the master, and 1 presume interest upon it and expenses.

This action was subsequently settled by the payment by the defendant *Edward Whitney*, of a sum of £92, under peculiar circumstances, which induced the plaintiffs to accept that sum, although much less than they were entitled to demand. The judgment against Mr. *Whitney* was irregularly obtained upon a summons specially endorsed under the Common Law Procedure Act, and upon application to the Court of Common Pleas for that purpose, it was set aside with costs; whereupon Mr. *Whitney* commenced an action against Mr. *Buel*, the master of this court, alone, for the recovery of damages for the illegal seizure of his goods, made under the writ issued upon the judgment which had been set aside; and the object of this application is to dissolve the injunction which was granted. The application for the injunction was, I think, properly made in the suit of *Fisher* v. *Glass*, in which the order was made which authorised the action, the irregular conduct of which gave rise to the action sought to be restrained.

In all the cases that have occurred on this branch of the practice the applications have been by motion in the respective suits. In the case of *Astor* v. *Heron*, (a) Lord *Brougham* propounded a distinction in this branch of the practice of the court, and while he admitted the authority of the court in all cases in which proceedings were instituted against its officers for anything done in the execution of their duty, to take cognisance of the whole matter; distinguished between cases where, by the effect of the action, the orders and proceedings of the court were obstructed and resisted, in which cases he considered that the court must necessarily interfere and prohibit further litigation, and cases in which no such effect occurred, and nothing more is attempted than to complain of and seek redress for an irregular use and execution of the process of the court, in which case he held that the court would in its discretion either restrain the action or permit it to proceed as might seem most expedient. This is the first case in which any such distinction has been attempted, and although no doubt the court

(a) 1 R. & M.

may in its discretion either restrain the action against
its officer or permit it to proceed according to circumstances, yet so far as the case in question may seem to
intimate, that the court would suffer the action against
its officer to proceed, unless good reason appeared to
adopt the contrary course, I am satisfied that it rests
upon no authority whatever, since in every other case
which has occurred on the subject the court has, as a
matter of course, restrained proceedings without enquiry into the circumstances of the case. I think the
present case is within the principle upon which those
cases were decided.

The master was ordered by this court to permit his
name to be used for the purpose which has been mentioned, he being indemnified by the plaintiffs, who
sought leave to commence such proceedings. The action which was accordingly commenced in his name was
an execution of that order, and was a proceeding in the
suit, and the action which has been restrained was
brought for the recovery of damages for an irregular
conduct of that proceeding. Mr. *Whitney* has not proceeded against the plaintiff in the action, or any other
person concerned in the institution of the proceedings
which were irregularly conducted, but has selected for
that purpose the officer of the court, who has been perfectly passive in the whole matter, and only permitted
his name to be used in obedience to the order of this
court; and so far as the circumstances of the case
should influence the court in adopting any particular
course, I think this a proper case for the exercise of
the jurisdiction which is invoked. Lord *Brougham* is
considered by Mr. *Drewry*, in his valuable Treatise on
Injunctions, as intimating that a case must be stated
and shewn against its officer to induce the court to
permit the proceedings against him to continue. Of
course no case can be shewn in the present instance
against the master ; and Mr. *Whitney*, who has selected
him as the object of attack, cannot complain, if the court,
in order to protect its officer, simply acting in obedience

to its order, without having been guilty of anything
savouring of wrong, interferes to stay his proceedings.
The only circumstance that was relied upon against
the interference of the court was, that the master had
neglected to obtain the indemnity which the court had
ordered to be provided ; but this circumstance, I think,
furnishes no reason whatever why the court should re-,
fuse to interfere. The court would never order any one
to permit his name to be used without an indemnity,
but this provision made for his greater security should
not deprive the officer of the court of any other privilege which he may possess. It was said that the court
of common law is the best judge of the manner in which
its own proceedings were conducted. I admit this fact,
and would always be glad to refer such a question to
its determination. But no such question remains for
decision. The legal proceedings have been already
annulled by the court of common law, and the only
question which remains to be decided is, the quantum
of damage which has been sustained, which is the
question which always governs in these cases, and
which the officer of the court has always been deemed
competent to determine. I think the motion must be
refused with costs.

McClelan v. Jacobs.
Practice—Foreclosure—Sale.

Where a decree is sought to be changed from a sale to foreclosure, the
cause must be set down to be re-heard, and notice served on the
defendant, and that too although the bill had been taken *pro confesso*.

This was a bill of foreclosure or sale upon a mortgage, and had been taken *pro confesso* against the
defendant. At the hearing a decree for sale had been
pronounced : before it was passed, the plaintiff desired
instead to obtain a decree for foreclosure ; and

Mr. *Tremayne*, for the plaintiff, moved *ex parte* that
the registrar might be directed to issue a decree of
foreclosure instead of a sale, as pronounced at a hearing ; but

Spragge, V.C.—The decree cannot be varied in the

way proposed : for aught that we know the defendant may have instructed counsel to appear on the hearing of the cause, for the purpose of asking a sale, as he had a right to do, under the general orders ; but who, on hearing that decree asked for by the plaintiff, had remained silent. If the change now asked for by the plaintiff is of importance to him, the cause must be set down to be re-heard, and notice thereof served in the usual way upon the defendant.

———

The proceeding pointed out by his Honour was subsequently adopted by the plaintiff, and the decree varied in the manner proposed.

———

BANK OF MONTREAL V. THOMPSON.

Mortgage—Registered judgment—Sale under fi. fa. issued thereon— Certificate of registration—Form of.

* The owner of lands created two mortgages thereon, after which his interest therein was sold under a writ of *fieri facias*, issued upon a judgment registered prior to both the mortgages, for the sum of twenty shillings, all parties being under the impression that the lands were sold subject to the two mortgages; subsequently the purchaser at sheriff's sale bought up the first mortgage, whereupon the holders of the second mortgage filed a bill against him, praying a decree of redemption or foreclosure, on the ground that the purchase of the equity of redemption at sheriff's sale bound him to discharge both mortgages. The court, at the hearing, refused this relief, and dismissed the bill ; but, owing to the uncertain state of the authorities on the point as to the effect to be given to the registering of a judgment, without costs ; and with leave to file a new bill impugning the sale under the *fi. fa.* : or a decree of redemption would be pronounced upon the submission to that effect contained in the answer, if the plaintiffs desired that relief.
The ruling of the Court of Queen's Bench in Doe Dougall v. Fanning, 8 U. C. Q. B. 166, and Doe Dempsey v. Boulton, 9 U. C. Q. B. 532, that the sale by a sheriff under a writ of *fi fa.* against lands conveyed the estate held by the judgment debtor at the time of the registration of the judgment, were referred to and followed; Thirkell v. Patterson, 18 U. C. Q. B. 75, and Wales v. Bullock, 10 U. C. P. 155, remarked upon.
The certificate of judgment registered was entitled " In the Queen's Bench," not " In the Court of Queen's Bench," and concluded with "Given under my hand and seal," &c., instead of "Given under my hand and the seal of the said court," &c., and omitted any form of action in which the judgment was recovered : *held*, a sufficient compliance with the forms given in the statute 9th Victoria, ch. 34.

This was a bill by the *Bank of Montreal* against *James R. Thompson*, praying, under the circumstances appearing in the head-note and judgment of the court, that a decree might be pronounced directing *Thompson* to pay plaintiffs the amount of the principal and interest due on the mortgage held by them, or stand forclosed of all equity of redemption.

The defendant answered the bill, resisting any right on the part of the plaintiffs ; but submitting at the same time to be redeemed by them upon payment of the amount due upon his mortgage.

Mr. *Blake*, for the plaintiffs.

Mr. *Proudfoot*, for the defendant.

The cases and points mainly relied on by counsel appear in the judgment of

Judgment.—ESTEN, V.C.—The facts of this case are these : one *Shaw* made a mortgage to *Francis Gore Stanton*, and then a mortgage of the same lands to one *Gillespie*, who transferred this mortgage to the plaintiffs ; then the defendant purchased the same lands, or rather all *Shaw's* interest in them, at sheriff's sale, and afterwards acquired the first mentioned mortgage ; and the present suit has been instituted against him by the second mortgagee for redemption or foreclosure, the bill insisting that by purchasing the equity of redemption of the lands, he became liable to discharge both mortgages, and that having acquired the first mortgage, and obtained an assignment of it, he cannot raise it as a shield against the second mortgage.

The answer states that the first mortgage was made to *Stanton*, as a trustee, to secure divers judgments which it mentions ; that one of these judgments was obtained by the defendant *Thompson*, but in trust for one *Powell ;* that he obtained an assignment of another of such judgments likewise in trust for *Powell ;* that he held these

judgments in this way, at the time that he purchased
the lands from the sheriff, that after such purchase he
acquired the beneficial interest in all the judgments
secured by the first mortgage, including the judgments
which he held in trust for *Powell ;* that he then obtained
an assignment of the mortgage from *Stanton ;* that
Benner, one of the judgment creditors whose judgment
the first mortgage was intended to secure, repudiated the
trust, and proceeded on his judgment, and having issued
execution against the lands of *Shaw*, caused the lands
in question to be offered for sale, when they were purchased by the defendant. It is remarkable that the bill
does not state the date of the registration of any of the
instruments which it mentions, and that the answer,
while it states the fact and date of the registration of all
the judgments, no where states the date of the registration of the mortgage to *Stanton*, and it ends by insisting
that this mortgage must be deemed to be subsisting ; that
the defendant *Thompson* is entitled to the benefit of it,
and that he is entitled to a decree of redemption or foreclosure against the plaintiffs as second mortgages. It is
quite manifest, I think, that the defendant *Thompson*
intended to represent himself as the purchaser of the
equity of redemption. Had he intended to rely on his
title as a purchaser under a judgment registered before
the registration of the first mortgage, he would have been
careful to state when that mortgage was registered, and
he would not have insisted upon the priority of that mortgage over the plaintiffs, such contention being useless,
when both mortgages had become extinct through the
purchase of the mortgage estate under a prior registered judgment. At the hearing, however, the deeds, I presume, are produced, and shew by the registrar's endorsement upon them when they were registered. Some evidence is also offered of the registration of the judgments,
or at all events of *Benner's* judgment ; and from this
evidence it appears that this judgment was registered
before either of the mortgages. I do not know now
whether it appears otherwise than by the answer, that

any writ had been delivered to the sheriff for execution on *Benner's* judgment, or that the sale in question was effected under such a writ. Supposing it to appear that the sale was effected under a writ upon a judgment registered before the registration of the mortgages, and supposing that fact to be material, and to confer a paramount title, I think the court cannot ignore it merely because the defendant has misapprehended his rights, and has supposed himself to stand in a lower position than he really occupies. Suppose for instance the answer of a defendant to state a first mortgage with power of sale, then a' second mortgage, then a third mortgage, and that the first mortgagee had exercised his power of sale, and the defendant had purchased the estate under it, and had afterwards acquired the second mortgage, and to insist that this mortgage was subsisting and prior to the third mortgage, the court would consider that the defendant had acted foolishly, and had wholly misapprehended his rights, but could not ignore the fact that the purchase under the power of sale contained in the first mortgage, had in fact extinguished the second and third mortgages, and conferred on the defendant a title paramount to both. The facts being stated and proved, the court must recognise their legal effect, however much it may be misapprehended by the defendant himself. If the proof of the material facts is defective, I think the defendant ought to be at liberty to supply what is requisite on proper terms as to costs. This leads to the consideration of the question which has been raised and argued with much ability on both sides, namely, whether after the passing of the 9th Vic., ch. 34, and before the passing of the 24th Vic., ch. 41, the sheriff's deed conveyed the estate that the debtor had at the time of the registration of the judgment under which the sale was effected; or the estate that the debtor had at the time of delivering to the sheriff for execution the writ under which the sale was performed. Four cases were cited on this point, Doe dem. *Dougall* v. *Fanning,* (a) Doe dem. *Dempsey*

(a) 8 U. C. Q. B. 166.

v. *Boulton,* (a) *Thirkell* v. *Patterson* (b) *Wales* v. *Bullock,* (c) In the cases of Doe dem. *Dougall* v. *Fanning,* and Doe dem. *Dempsey* v. *Boulton,* the precise point arose and was decided. In both these cases judgments were registered; the deeds were executed to purchaser by the debtor, then the writ was delivered to the sheriff, and he proceeded to a sale under the judgments, and in both cases it was decided by the court of Queen's Bench, that the sheriff's deed prevailed over the deeds to the purchasers on the principle that under the 9th Victoria, ch 34, the sheriff's deed conveyed all the estate that the debtor had at the time of registration of the judgments: and that that act applied to the writ of *fieri facias* against lands introduced by the 5th Geo. II., and then in use, and did not re-introduce the writ of *elegit,* which the 5th Geo. II. is considered to have abolished, which question was expressly raised and decided in the case of Doe dem. *Dempsey* v. *Boulton.*

In the case of *Thirkell* v. *Patterson* this point did not arise at all; the only question there was whether a deed was void against a prior judgment registered before it, and it was decided that it was not, because the 8th clause of the 13 and 14 Vic, ch 63, related only to subsequent judgments; the question whether the sheriff's deed related to the date of registration, or of the delivery of the writ, did not arise, because both the registration and delivery of the writ were subsequent to the deed. Mr. Justice *Burns,* however, expressed his view generally of the operation of the several clauses of the act relating to this point. His opinion was, that the registration of the judgment created only an equitable charge, and that the sheriff's deed did not relate to the registration so as to avoid mesne conveyances but only to the delivery of the writ, although the purchaser would hold subject to the equitable charge. The case of *Wales* v. *Bullock* was considered to resemble the case of *Thirkell* v. *Paterson,*

(a) 9 U. C. Q. B. 532.   (b) 18 U. C. Q. B. 000.
(c) 10 U. C. C. P. 155.

although it differed from it in the material circumstance
of the registration of the judgment being prior to the
deed, and upon the question of the relation of the sheriff's
deed, the court followed the opinion expressed by Mr.
Justice *Burns*, in the case of *Thirkell* v. *Paterson*. The
point decided in *Thirkell* v. *Paterson* did not arise in
Wales v. *Bullock;* but the question which it really
presented had been expressly decided in the cases of *Doe
Fanning* and *Doe Boulton*, which were not cited, while
the opinion of Mr. Justice *Burns*, which, however much
it might be entitled to weight, was in this respect extra-
judicial, was followed as the rule. Under these circumstances, I should consider it my duty to follow the
decision in the cases of *Doe Dougall* v. *Fanning*, and
Dempsey v. *Boulton*, even if my opinion did not agree
with it, which however it does to the fullest extent: the
13th section of the 9th Vic., ch. 34, is combined in the
Con. Stat., with the second section of 13 & 14 Vic., ch.
63, and this juxtaposition lends some countenance to the
construction that registration creates a mere charge in
equity. But the 13th sec. of the 9 Vic., ch. 34, created no
equitable charge when it first became part of the law of
the land. The equitable charge was created for the first
time by the second section of the 13 & 14 Vic., ch. 63, four
or five years afterwards. Between the 9 Vic., ch. 34, and
the 13 & 14 Vic., ch. 63, the equitable charge did not exist.
What during this interval was the operation of the 13th
section of 9 Vic., ch. 34? Doubtless it was as decided in
the cases of *Doe Dougall* v. *Fanning*, and *Doe Dempsey* v.
Boulton, to cause the judgment to attach upon the land
from the time of registration, so as to render it liable to
execution into whatever hands it might afterwards come.
No other meaning can be attached to that clause when
it was first enacted. It created no equitable charge
whatever; it authorised the sheriff to offer for sale the
estate belonging to the debtor at the date of registration, and that was its only operation. The law
continued in this state until the passing of the 13 & 14
Vic., ch. 63, which created the equitable charge for the

first time. It did not, however, vary the operation of the
9th Vic., ch. 34. The remedy it gave was cumulative, and
it likewise subjected to the payment of debts various
interests which were not before liable to execution. The
13th section of the 9th Vic., ch. 34, enacted that registered
judgments should bind lands in this province in the
same manner as docketed judgments bound lands in
England. Now the precise effect of a docketed judgment
was to bind the lands into whosoever hands they might
afterwards pass, so that the sheriff could deliver execution of them as if the intermediate conveyances and
incumbrances did not exist; the same effect must have
resulted from registration of judgments in this province.
It is said that no such intention can be collected from
the provisions of the 9th Vic., ch. 34. But it appears
to me with great deference, that no other intention can
be attributed to the legislature than what I have
mentioned. It appears to have been considered that
such a construction would be attended with great
inconvenience. But what greater inconvenience exists
in case of a judgment than in case of a mortgage with
power of sale? Such a mortgage may remain dormant
for years during which the property may pass through
twenty hands, and the power of sale may then be exercised, and all the intermediate conveyances defeated,
some of which may be sheriff's deeds. If a judgment
be registered, it is notice to all the world. Any one
purchasing the estate affected by it, will see it paid off
out of his purchase money, or require the estate to be
released from it, and if he neglect these ordinary
precautions he must blame his own folly. I have no
doubt that while the practice of registering judgments
continued, a registered judgment bound the lands at law
from the time of registration, so that the sheriff could
deliver execution of them into whosoever hands they
might afterwards pass. In deciding this I follow the
cases of Doe dem. *Dougall* v. *Fanning* and Doe dem.
Dempsey v. *Boulton*, both because I think they were
rightly decided and because I am satisfied that the Court

of Common Pleas would have followed them in the case
of *Wales* v. *Bullock*, had they been cited; the opinion
of Mr. Justice *Burns*, expressed in the case of *Thirkell*
v. *Patterson*, although entitled to the greatest respect,
being only an exposition of his views on the general
operation of the acts, except so far as it relates to the
point then in question, and unnecessary to the decision
of that case. Supposing it to appear, therefore, in the
present case that the sheriff's sale was under *Benner's*
judgment, and that this judgment was registered before
either of the mortgages, I think the defendant acquired
a title paramount to them both. It is true that he
thought he was purchasing the estate subject to both
the mortgages; and he paid, it is said, only twenty
shillings for it, but he intended doubtless to purchase
whatever he could get, which he thought, however, was
only so much. The sheriff could sell neither more nor
less than the estate that *Shaw* had at the time of the
registration of *Benner's* judgment, and *Thompson* could
purchase neither more nor less. The sale is not
impeached, and must operate according to its legal effect
so long as it is suffered to stand. Whether it can be
maintained is another question; which it would be
premature and out of place to discuss. The learned
counsel for the plaintiffs asked leave if my judgment
should be against them to amend the bill for the purpose
of impugning the sale. But such a bill would be substantially a new bill, and I think the more proper course
is to dismiss the present bill without costs in consequence
of the uncertain state of the authorities, and without
prejudice to any other suit which the plaintiffs may be
advised to institute. I do not think the defendant at
the time that he purchased from the sheriff was a
mortgagee so as to be within the protection of the second
clause of the 14 & 15 Vic., ch. 45. This provision is a very
singular one, and not to be extended beyond its letter. It
seems to contemplate a purchase by a mortgagee from
himself; and that although he may purchase the equity
of redemption at a sheriff's sale, and pay so much less

for the estate in consequence of the existence of the mortgages, and must be deemed therefore to undertake to discharge them both, he may hold the second mortgagee at arm's-length. I certainly would not extend this provision to a person who was not a mortgagee at the time, but became so afterwards; and this was the case, I think, with the defendant *Thompson*. The protection must at any rate be confined to the judgments belonging to *Powell*, and of them he was a mere trustee. I agree entirely with the able judgment of my brother *Spragge* in the case of *Pegge* v. *Metcalf*. (a)

WARREN v. TAYLOR.

Ross v. Taylor.

Mortgage—Judgment creditor—Registration and re-registration of judgment—Foreclosure.

A party foreclosing subject to a prior mortgage cannot call the common mortgagor, if he has the equity of redemption, to give evidence as to the amount due upon the prior mortgage.

A second mortgagee, as such, cannot impeach a prior-registered mortgage as fraudulent and void against creditors, but a judgment creditor, having accepted a mortgage, does not lose his rights as a judgment creditor.

Where the usual affidavit proving a mortgage debt is made, the onus of reducing the amount lies upon the opposite party.

A judgment creditor omitted to re-register within three years, *held*, that he thereby lost his lien as to persons purchasing or becoming incumbrancers after that time, and before a re-registration was effected.

Statement.—These actions were consolidated upon the hearing. The facts are clearly set out in the judgment of his Honor Vice-Chancellor *Esten*, upon the appeal from the master's report.

The cause was originally heard before his Honor Vice-Chancellor *Spragge;* upon the enquiry there directed, the accounts between the parties were taken, and the finding of the master thereon gave rise to the appeal.

(a) Ante vol. 5, p. 628.

Mr. *Proudfoot*, for the plaintiff, *Warren*.

Mr. *Crickmore* and Mr. *M. Vankoughnet*, for defendant, *Baldwin*.

Mr. *McDonald*, for *Ross, Mitchell, & Co.*

Judgment.—SPRAGGE, V. C.—I think the most proper order to make at the present stage of the cause is simply to direct an enquiry as to the amount due upon the mortgage to *Merrick;* the master to enquire whether it was given in whole or in part for moneys then due ; or in whole or in part to cover future advances.

I think that the evidence of *Taylor* is not admissible upon the question of the amount due upon the mortgage; the equity of redemption is in him, and if his evidence could be received to cut down the amount due on *Merrick's* mortgage, it would diminish *pro tanto* the amount to be ultimately paid by himself, whatever the priority might be as between *Warren*, the present holder of the mortgage, and *Ross, Mitchell & Fisken*, and other incumbrancers. It was suggested that his evidence might be received as between *Warren* and other incumbrancers, leaving what was due upon the mortgage to *Merrick*, as between himself and *Warren*, to rest upon other evidence. He is called upon two points, one to shew that there was no consideration for the mortgage, but that being in embarrassed circumstances, it was given to hinder and delay creditors, and so is void under the 13th Elizabeth ; the other, to shew that if any amount was due it was a much smaller sum than the amount of the mortgage. The latter would properly be matter of account, but still would have its bearing upon the first point; upon the mere matter of account it is not receivable here, or indeed at all. *Taylor's* interest upon the first point, it appears to me, is to shew the conveyance not fraudulent, but to reduce the amount due upon it; for this latter purpose his evidence is not receivable. The question is; whether it is for the former as between himself and the holder of the mortgage, what must be the decree if shewn to be fraudulent, and what if not shewn to be fraudulent? In the latter case he will have a right to redeem upon payment of what may really appear to be due. In the former, he would have no right to redeem at all.

But here the question is between an innocent purchaser for value of this mortgage, for such I think, upon the evidence, *Warren* appears to be, and a subsequent incumbrancer. The assigne e of the mortgage takes it of course subject to the state of the account as between mortgagor and mortgagee; but suppose there to have been really a mortgage debt, whether for the whole amount of the mortgage, or for less, will the fraudulent purpose for which the mortgage was made affect an innocent assignee? If it could not, then *Taylor's* evidence cannot be received, for it is n ot receivable upon the question of amount, and as between *Warren* and subsequent incumbrancers the fraudulent purpose of *Taylor* and *Merrick* is immaterial. If upon further directions counsel desire to raise that question against *Warren*, it will be competent to them to do so. *Merrick's* evidence is not objected to, but I think is not to be relied upon implicitly. According to his account *Taylor's* indebtedness to him was of a very large amount. The mortgage was for $3500, and that he says was only for a portion of it, he says a portion of the contract price, whatever that may mean; but he adds: "I having received $700 from the railway company," and in his assignment to *Warren* he covenants that the whole $3500 was then due; that it is clear therefore that he claimed the two sums, so that according to his account, on the 28th of May, 1854, $420 was due to him beside a portion of the item in paper O. Then came the amount appearing in paper O., £220, which supposing it to be in New York currency, would be $550 more, making in all $4750. Now even his own evidence bears out nothing, even approaching that amount : *Fynn* and *Christian* assisted at the work; their evidence would bring the amount still lower, especially that of *Fynn*, but I thought he exhibited a desire to reduce it as low as possible.

I think it desirable, however, to say no more at present upon the question of account.

Judgment.–ESTEN, V.C.–The plaintiff *Warren* filed his bill for the foreclosure of a mortgage for $3500, made by the defendant *Taylor* to one *Merrick*, and transferred by him to *Warren*, making the defendants *Ross, Mitchell, & Fisken* parties as subsequent incumbrancers, by judgment and mortgage, who set up as a defence, that the plaintiff's mortgage was made to defraud creditors and claiming priority over it by reason of its alleged defective registration, and in the meantime filed their bill to establish their own priority, alleging the same facts as they had stated in their answers to the other bill. Evidence was entered into on both sides, and by the decree pronounced at the hearing of both causes, which were consolidated, the validity and priority of the plaintiff *Warren's* mortgage was established ; and it was referred to the master to take an account of what was due under it, and to enquire what the consideration for it was. The master received further evidence, and reported only £104 due on *Warren's* mortgage for principal and interest. Both parties have excepted to this report. *Warren*, because the whole amount mentioned in the mortgage was not allowed ; *Ross, Mitchell, & Fisken*, because the master ought to have reported nothing due the defendants *Warren* and *Merrick* to the bill of *Ross, Mitchell, & Fisken*, having alleged a different consideration for that mortgage from the one proved, and not having proved the one alleged.

The facts of the case are, that *Taylor* was the owner and master of a vessel called the "Matilda," which was wrecked in the fall of 1850, in Lake Ontario, off the defendant *Merrick's* farm, laden with 250 tons of railway iron for the Cleveland and Pittsburg Railway Company. She sank and lay in about 10 feet water, on a sandy and gravelly bottom, about half a mile from the shore, and about two miles and a half from the place where the cargo could be landed. *Taylor* returned to Canada, having given authority to *Merrick* to watch the vessel, which remained in the state I have described until the following spring, when *Taylor* returned to the place, and in the character of agent of the railway company entered into a written contract with *Merrick* to remove and land the cargo of the vessel. This contract is produced and proved. It provides that if *Merrick* should succeed in removing the water from the vessel he should receive for the work to be performed the sum of $1200; if not, that he should receive a larger sum. *Taylor* was advised, he says, and he thought that as master of the vessel he could bind the company by this contract. *Merrick* performed the contract on his part, and landed the whole cargo, but did not succeed in removing the water that was in the vessel, and was obliged to employ grapnels, and he became therefore entitled to the larger sum mentioned in the contract. The company repudiated the contract, and refused to pay more than $700, which they did pay to *Merrick*, who however held the iron as long as he could, in the endeavour to compel the company to pay a larger sum, but finally was obliged to relinquish it, and be content with the $700. *Taylor* then made the mortgage in question to secure to *Merrick* the balance of the sum he had contracted to pay him for raising and landing the cargo. The mortgage was taken by *Taylor* to Canada for the purpose of registration, and was there executed or acknowledged in the presence of one *Kelly*, on whose oath it was registered. It remained in the registry office apparently until May, 1852, when *Merrick* and *Taylor* being at the register office, were attended at their request by Mr. *Woods*, to whom the mortgage was delivered by *Merrick* in the presence of *Taylor ;* and *Merrick* also gave him instructions with respect to it, and Mr. *Woods* took a power of attorney from *Merrick* to place himself, as he says, in a proper position in the matter. The mortgage remained in Mr. *Woods'* possession until the year 1858, without any communication between him and *Merrick* with respect to it. The principal sum secured by it fell due in May, 1857 ; the interest, however, was payable in the meantime. In the year 1857 *Merrick* sold this mortgage to *Warren* for $2500, and visited Canada for the purpose of making a search for it, which he made in the registry office without success, appearing to have forgotten that he had left it in the possession of Mr. *Woods*. However, he procured a certificate of its registration, which satisfied *Warren*, and the transfer was completed. The mortgage itself was supposed to be lost, but in 1858 a Mr. *Keating* advised *Merrick* to enquire for it of Mr. *Woods*, and he immediately that application was made to him produced it, and returned it to *Merrick*. The present suit of *Warren* was then instituted for the foreclosure of this mortgage.

I may remark that Messrs. *Ross, Mitchell & Fisken,* the objection of defective registration having been overruled, could not, as mortgagees, impeach the plaintiff *Warren's* mortgage as fraudulent and void against creditors. As judgment creditors, however, they could take that ground ; and of course their acceptance of a mortgage did not prejudice or affect their rights as judgment creditors. The decree, however, established, that, whatever the mortgage, held by *Warren*, may have been as between *Taylor* and *Merrick*, in the hands of *Warren*, who was a *bona fide* purchaser without notice, it was good for whatever had been actually advanced upon it, and referred it to the master to ascertain what amount had been advanced upon it, and what remained due in respect of it, and what the consideration for it was.

Upon this enquiry, the mortgage having been produced,.

and the plaintiff having made affidavit in the usual manner, claiming the whole amount secured by it, with interest, I think the onus lay upon the defendants, *Ross, Mitchell & Fisken,* to reduce it.

Looking to the evidence which was adduced before the hearing, and in the master's office, I do not think enough is shewn to overcome the legal effect of the mortgage deed. Even supposing the contract upon which it was founded to have named, as it is supposed to have done, the sum of $3000 as the additional sum to be paid in case the water could not be removed from the vessel, I should think, looking both to the express evidence and the nature of the transaction, that enough had not been shewn to qualify or impair the legal effect of the mortgage, and that the account should be taken according to its legal import as it stands. The master thinks that it was a device either to defraud creditors, or extort from the railway company the price not only of saving the cargo, but of raising and refitting the vessel. The former hypothesis is excluded by the decree; and the latter would not affect the plaintiff's claim, for if the services stipulated for were rendered, *Taylor* would be equally bound by the mortgage to its full extent, whether an intention existed to defraud the company or not. I do not see, however, the ground of this latter supposition.

I presume the only or the main chance of raising the vessel lay in removing the water from her hold, in which case she could have been raised and refitted. But in the event only the smaller sum of $1200 would become payable, to which probably no objection would be made. The larger sum would become payable only in the event of the water being irremovable, in which case it was certainly much less probable, perhaps very improbable, that the vessel would be raised, or could be refitted. It is a remarkable circumstance, however, and appears to have escaped the notice of the solicitors on both sides, although I doubt not well known to the parties, or to some of them, that the contract names as the larger sum to be paid in case it should be found impossible to remove the water from the vessel, not three *thousand* dollars, as was supposed, but three *hundred* dollars. The word is too plain to admit of doubt.

I shall refer the case back to the master to review his report with reference to the foregoing directions, without costs, and with liberty to both parties to adduce further evidence.

As to the appeal of *Baldwin*, whose claim has been disallowed by the master on account of his neglect to re-register his judgment, I am inclined to agree with the master, and to think his construction of the act correct; but I do not see that it is necessary to decide the point, inasmuch as the plaintiff *Warren* can have no objection, but must rather desire to retain *Baldwin* as a party; and the question between *Ross, Mitchell & Co.* and *Baldwin* can be only one of priority, and so long as priority is accorded to them, they cannot complain. No doubt can be entertained that the defendants, *Ross, Mitchell & Fisken*, must be entitled to priority, inasmuch as their title accrued more than three years after the registration of *Baldwin's* judgment; and even according to the construction which has been adopted in England, their priority would be incontestable. The only person entitled to require the entire exclusion of *Baldwin* is the mortgagor *Taylor*, who makes no complaint; and if he did, I think I should grant to *Baldwin* an opportunity of re-registering his mortgage, if he desired it. If only a question of priority has arisen, I think Messrs. *Ross, Mitchell & Fisken* must have their costs of this appeal; but if their priority is conceded, and they are pressing for the entire exclusion of *Baldwin*, I think it should be without costs.

CAMERON v. BRADBURY.

Vendor and purchaser—Rescision of contract—Costs.

The vendor recovered a judgment against his vendee for a portion of
the purchase money. Afterwards he wrote the vendee a letter cancelling the agreement. *Held*, that having cancelled the contract,
he could not afterwards enforce his judgment.
Where the plaintiff's bill sought to enforce two judgments, one of which
the court held him not entitled to enforce. no costs were given to
either party up to the hearing : the rule seems to be, that where
costs are to be set off against other costs, the court will not give
costs to either party.

This was a motion before his Honor Vice-Chancellor
Spragge, for the usual references to take accounts and
for sale of lands of defendants, under the circumstances
stated in the judgment.

Mr. *G. D. Boulton,* for plaintiff.

Mr. *Fitzgerald,* contra.

Judgment.—SPRAGGE V. C.—I think the position of
the parties is not the same as to the two judgments.

To deal first with the general question : by the terms of
the agreement of sale time was expressly made of the
essence of the contract. Judgment has been recovered on
the bill of exchange given on the sale to *Hyatt,* against both
Bradbury and *Hyatt ;* and judgment has been recovered
against *Bradbury,* and a second instalment of purchase
money had fallen due when the letter of the 22nd of
July, 1858, was written.   The terms of it are : " As
there seems no prospect of any payments being made by
you, the only course that I can pursue is to conceal the
agreement existing between us, for non-performance
according to its terms.   You will therefore take this as
a notice to that effect."   In making this notification, Mr.
Cameron, I should say, acted under the clause of the
agreement making time of the essence of the contract,
because without such clause he was not entitled to give
the notice.

The two parties seem to have understood this notification differently. Mr. *Cameron*, in his affidavit, denies that it was written with the intention, or that it had the effect of, cancelling the agreement, except from the date of the letter; or that it had, or was intended to have, a retrospective effect in cancelling the agreement, or releasing the judgments recovered. Mr. *Bradbury*, on the other hand, in his affidavit, stated that he fully understood and believed that Mr. *Cameron* had intended to rescind the agreement, and that the parties should be in the same position as if it had not been made except as to the moneys already paid thereunder; and that he has ever since acted upon the faith and belief that such was Mr. *Cameron's* intention in writing the letters.

If there had been no judgment recovered, the point, I apprehend, could admit of no question. The vendor could not *uno flatu* cancel the agreement, and require payment of arrears; because the payment of arrears would reinstate the agreement, the purchaser being then no longer in default. So again, if judgment had been recovered for the whole of the arrears, the effect must necessarily have been the same. The vendor's position by this bill is, that he is entitled to enforce his judgment in this court. But his judgment, or the amount recovered, is still unpaid purchase money; and I cannot see that the circumstance of judgment having been recovered for it alters its character, or the rights of the parties in respect to it. The vendor takes back the land; he cannot do that and at the same time ask for purchase money; the very essence of such a transaction is, that the vendor keeps the land, and the purchaser the purchase money.

The judgment recovered against *Hyatt* and *Bradbury* stands upon a different footing. In that case the vendor does not get back his land. *Bradbury* made a contract of sale of a parcel of land to *Hyatt*, and procured *Cameron* to make a conveyance to *Hyatt* of that parcel; a portion of the purchase money payable by

Hyatt being paid by a bill of exchange to which *Bradbury* was a party, and *Cameron* taking a mortgage from, *Hyatt* for the whole purchase money.. The judgment against *Hyatt* and *Bradbury* is upon the bill of exchange, and I do not see how the cancellation of the contract of sale as to the other land sold can affect the vendor's right upon that bill of exchange. As to the parcel sold to *Hyatt* there was no cancellation, for it no longer rested in contract. *Hyatt* is still owner of the parcel conveyed to him ; and *Bradbury's* position is at least that of surety for the payment of purchase money.

I think the plaintiff entitled to a charge upon the judgment recovered against *Bradbury* and *Hyatt;* and not upon the judgment recovered against *Bradbury* only. As to the costs, the plaintiff's would be those as upon a bill upon the former judgment only ; and the defendant's those occasioned by the plaintiffs seeking to enforce the latter judgment also. These might be set one against the other, but the course of the court in such a case is to give costs to neither party. A late case upon this point is that of *Scholefield* v. *Templer,(a)* in which Sir *W. Page Wood* said : " I think that up to the hearing there ought to be no costs at all, because if I went strictly into it there would be certain costs to be set off against each other." The plaintiff in this cause will have the costs of drawing up the decree, and the subsequent costs.

(a) 5 Jur. N. S. 619, and 622.

PROUDFOOT v. LOUNT.

Judgment—Registration—Misnomer—Seal of Court.

A judgment was recovered against " *Charles Westley Lount*," which was the correct name of the defendant. The registration was of a judgment against " *Charles Wesley Lount*." *Held*, sufficient.

The certificate of registration of a judgment given by the clerk of the Queen's Bench, expressed it to be under " my hand and seal," and it being objected that it should have been expressed to be under the seal of the court, leave was given to the judgment creditor to produce an affidavit to shew what seal was really affixed to the certificate.

This was a motion for a decree by the assignees of a judgment recovered against the defendant.

The points involved appear in the headnote and judgment.

Mr. *McBride* for the plaintiffs.

Mr. *Blake*, for defendant.

Judgment.—SPRAGGE, V. C.—The question raised is, whether there has been an effectual registration of the judgment recovered by the plaintiffs in the name of *Edward Dudley McMahon*, against the defendant.

The defendant alleges that the certificates for registration are defective. It is a registration and a re-registration. It is pointed out as a defect in the original certificate that the style of the court is, "In the Queen's Bench," instead of "In the Court of Queen's Bench." The words in the statute are, "In the Court of   ;" another alleged defect is, the omission of the words, "in a plea of," stating the form of action. The words in the statute being "in a plea of   ." Both these points had been raised before my brother *Esten*, in another cause; (*a*) and we have since considered them together, and have come to the conclusion that the certificate is, notwithstanding, sufficient within the statute.

_____

(*a*) Bank of Montreal v. Thompson, ante p. 51.

There is but one thing to which the words "In the Queen's Bench" can apply, that is, the Court of Queen's Bench, and it is the ordinary style by which the court is designated in its pleadings and proceedings. It is not indeed the full statutory style of the court, but neither is the style given in the form of certificate given by the statute ; the full style being, "Her Majesty's Court of Queen's Bench for Upper Canada," but it is a correct designation, and describes the Court of Queen's Bench, and that only, as much as if the words "Court of," were introduced. Those words are probably inserted in the statute only to shew, that it was some court that was to be designated.

I think it must have been through inadvertence that the words " in a plea of   ," find a place in the form of certificate given by the statute, since the passing of the Common Law Procedure Act. The certificate is the act of a ministerial officer of the court; and he can only certify what appears by the records of his office. Before the passing of that act, he saw upon the face of the roll what the form of action was ; it was stated in so many words, "in a plea of debt," or "in a plea of trespass on the case upon premises," or otherwise as the case might be ; but since the passing of the act this has ceased to be the case ; and if he fills up the blank after the words, " in a plea of," he must do it by finding out in some way, what the form of action would be if expressed, or would have been but for the passing of the act. The attorney entering the judgment, on asking for the certificate, may tell him, but he could not certify from information so obtained; and as a ministerial officer he has no right to certify from conclusions formed in his own mind. In short, that is implied which in the certificates of the registrar of this court is expressed " as by my books appear ;" or upon the statutory certificate, " as by the roll of the said judgment appears."

A further objection is taken to the original certificate,

that it does not give the correct name of the defendant ; the error pointed out is in the omission of a letter in the second name; the name in the certificate being *Charles Wesley Lount*, the name in the judgment, *Charles Westley Lount*, and that being the correct name.

The object of the statute being, as Lord. *St. Leonards* says of the act of William & Mary, to enable purchasers to discover judgments by the names of the persons against whom they are entered; if the name of a defendant were falsely entered, his lordship continues, as *Compton* for *Crompton*, the judgment will be void against purchasers.

It cannot be contended, I think, that the certificate must be accurate to the very letter.   In the case referred to the true name was *Crompton ;* if it had been spelt with two *n*'s at the end instead of one, that would not, I apprehend, render the judgment void, but as it was, it was calculated to mislead.   Suppose an index containing a number of names, and the name of *Crompton* the one searched for, the person searching would not commence certainly before " *Cr*," or probably " *Cro*," and would not meet with the name *Compton* at all ; or suppose the name *Compton* searched for, the person making the search would naturally leave off after getting to the end of names beginning with " *Com*," so that to hold a purchaser bound by judgments against the one name, as affecting the lands of the other, would be manifestly dangerous and unjust.

But the question, it appears to me is, how is a purchaser bound, and why ; I apprehend it is because he is affected with notice. If so, that which would convey notice to a person of ordinary intelligence would, I think, be sufficient; either that must be the principle, or the slightest deviation in the spelling of any one of the several names which the judgment debtor may have will avoid the registration. There is no such strictness in any other civil proceeding. I may instance cases where parties have been held to bail, and where if the names are *idem sonantia*, the defendant is not discharged, and the courts have been by no means rigid in seeing that the names sound exactly alike. In —————— v. *Rennolls* (a), the affidavit to hold to bail called the defendant *Rennolls;* in the suit he was called *Rennoll;* his discharge was moved for, but the court refused it, saying that the mistake of a letter in spelling the name, was not a ground for discharging the defendant. So *Beniditto* and *Benedetto* (b), were held *idem sonantia*, on an application to discharge a defendant from arrest.

In the case before me the surname is strictly correct, so is the christian name; the intermediate name is spelt *Wesley*, instead of *Westley;* it would require more than ordinarily distinct pronunciation, and a very critical ear to distinguish any difference; the mistake certainly would not entitle a defendant to be discharged from arrest—ought it to avoid a registration of judgment ?—the register's index would direct a person searching to the right surname; but there might be judgments against several of the same surname; the christian and the second name, if any, are points of identity. Suppose the person searching to be making his searches on behalf of a person proposing to purchase from *Charles Westley Lount*, finding a judgment registered against *Charles Wesley Lount*, he would surely be wilfully blind, if he had his eyes, to the probable fact, amounting almost to certainty, that they were one and the same person ; there would at least be enough to put him upon enquiry, and the judgment roll would at once prove the identity.

If the principle be that of notice, as I think it must be, I am satisfied it is a good certificate. Suppose the case of a mortgage given by this same defendant, and an intending purchaser notified by letter from a proper quarter that *Charles Wesley Lount* had given such

---

(a) 1 Ch. Rep. 659, a.   (b) 2 Taunt. 401.

mortgage, it could not be doubted, I think, that he would be affected with notice.

The judgment in question appears to have been registered in three offices, Simcoe, York, and the city of Toronto. The error has occurred only in the registration for York; there is no question as to the registration in Simcoe and Toronto, but I think it is good also in the county of York. In this case it is the judgment debtor himself who makes the objection, not an incumbrancer or purchaser. It is objected that it does not lie with him to make it. Certainly the reasons for accuracy in his name do not apply to him; but inasmuch as registration is, or rather was, required to make the judgment a charge, I suppose it is necessary to shew against him that there is a valid registration.

There has, however, been a re-registration, and if that is sufficient it is not material as against the defendant to show the sufficiency of the former. Against this second registration it is objected (in addition to the objections common to both) that the seal affixed to the certificate is not that of the court, but of the Clerk of the Crown and Pleas; the attestation being, "In witness whereof I have hereunto set my hand and seal this," etc.

The form of certificate given by the statute contains no attestation; that is gratuitous on the part of the officer; and if it mis-describes the seal really affixed, it will not, I think, avoid the certificate. I think an opportunity should be afforded to ascertain the fact, which can be done either by an inspection of the certificate, or by an affidavit as to the identity of the seal. Probably there may be no real question as to the fact. If there is, the register, or a clerk in the Crown office can make affidavit as to its identity.

If it should appear that it is the seal of the court that is affixed to the certificate, the plaintiffs will be entitled to their decree in respect of their judgment as well as their mortgage.

McDonald v. Rodger.

Registration—Judgment creditor—Misnomer—Practice—Appeal from master.

A confession of judgment was executed in the name of "*Matthew Rodger.*" The certificate for registration was of a judgment against "*Matthew Rodgers.*" *Held*, that the mistake vitiated the registration.*

Semble, that in a certificate of judgment it is sufficient to state the amount of the true debt.

Where an incumbrancer who objected to the order of priority in which he was placed, appealed from the finding of the master, the court considered this the more convenient course to adopt, although it was open to him to have moved to discharge the master's order.

This was an appeal from the master's report, made in a foreclosure suit, on the grounds stated in the judgment of his Honour Vice-Chancellor *Esten*, before whom the appeal was argued.

Mr. *Roaf*, for the judgment creditor, who appealed, cited amongst other cases *Beavan* v. *Oxford*, (a) *Brandling* v. *Plummer*. (b)

Mr. *Blake*, contra, cited *Underwood* v. Lord *Courtown*, (c) The *Queen* v. *Registrar of Middlesex*, (d) *Sale* v. *Compton*, (e) *Ross* v. *Taylor*, (f) *McQuestien* v. *Campbell*. (g)

Judgment.—Esten, V. C.—The facts of the case are, that a judgment was entered on a confession against the defendant by the appellant *Smith*, on the 22nd of June, in the year 1854, for the sum of £200 damages, and £3 12s. 8d. costs. This judgment was registered on or about the same day, in the registry of the county of Huron, where the lands comprised in the mortgage in question in this suit are situated. The judgment was re-registered on or about the 18th of May, 1858, in the same registry. The heading of both certificates is, "In the Queen's

---

* See on this point, *Proudfoot* v. *Lount*, ante p. 70.

(a) 1 Jur. N. S. 154.
(b) 3 Jur. N. S. 40; S. C. 26 L. J. N. S. ch. 326.
(c) 2 Sch. & L. 64-5.   (d) 15 Q. B. 976.
(e) 1 Wils. 61.   (f) Ante p. 59.
(g) Ante vol. 8, p. 242.

Bench," neither of them mentions the form of action;
in both the defendant is called "*Matthew Rodgers.*" In
the year 1856 the mortgage in question was executed by
the defendant *Rodger* to the plaintiff *McDonald*, and
registered in the same year in the proper registry.
The master has placed *Smith* after the plaintiff in point
of priority; and *Smith* has preferred this appeal against
that decision. *Smith* might have applied to discharge
the master's order, but the course he has taken was, I
think, open to him, and it was more convenient than the
other. The master considered the registration of the
judgment, in 1854, invalid. The grounds of his judgment do not appear. The re-registration is impugned
on the ground that the words, "Court of," are omitted
from the heading of the certificate; that the form of
action is not mentioned; that the name is mispelled;
and that the true debt is mentioned, and not the amount
for which judgment is nominally entered. The two first
defects have been decided in this court to be insufficient
to vitiate the registration. (*a*)

With regard to the true debt being mentioned, supposing the question to be untouched by decision, I should
doubt whether the registration would be void on that
account. It would be extremely mischievous to allow an
incorrect and deceptive registration. Truth should be
the character of a registry, as the object of its institution
is to inform the public of the exact state of the title, so
that they may purchase and deal with safety and confidence At the same time it can hardly be said that a
registration according to the tenor of the judgment
would be wrong. In truth I think it would be highly
proper for the clerks to deviate slightly from the form
prescribed by the act in such cases, and mention both
the nominal amount of the judgment and the true debt.

If the master has deemed the registration in this

(*a*) Bank of Montreal v. Thompson, ante p. 51.

instance void on account of the nominal amount of the judgment not being mentioned, I should not differ from him. I think, however, this registration was void on account of the mistake in the name. It is true that the close resemblance between the two names would excite the strongest suspicion in the mind of a purchaser; but it is impossible to draw the line between different sorts of mistakes, and it is much better to require a strict adherence to the fact. According to the case of *Sale* v. *Compton*, the mistake of " *Compton*" for " *Crompton*" seems to have vitiated the judgment. I must intend the cognovit to have been signed with the true name, and then I think the mistake which has occurred in the present case would vitiate the registration. It might totally mislead intending purchasers. I also think that the registration effected in 1854 became void after the lapse of three years, and that the lien of the judgment thereupon totally ceased as to the debtor and all other persons, and that thereby the plaintiff's mortgage became accelerated. I expressed this opinion in the case of *Ross* v. *Taylor*, where the point was fully argued, and I think it was correct. It is clear also, I think, that with regard to the Francis town lots, the plaintiff would be entitled to priority as to the purchase money, and the sum of £300 agreed to be advanced: but as to future advances I do not see on what ground he could claim priority. Upon all the grounds I think the appeal should be dismissed with costs.

WOOD v. BRETT.

Insolvent debtor—Assignment for benefit of creditors—Privileged creditor.—Parties.

An assignment was made to trustees for the benefit of creditors, to which was appended a list of names who were to rank as privileged creditors. One of these parties subsequently applied to the trustees, who in concert with the debtor handed to him several notes and bills, more than sufficient to cover the claim of his firm, which he took away with him for the purpose of negociating them, his desire being, as he stated, to realize funds at once. Certain of the makers and acceptors of these notes and bills having become insolvent, a bill was filed by the firm against the assignor and his trustees for an account of the trust estate, and payment of their claim ; in answer to this bill the defendants alleged that the bills and notes had been taken in payment of their demand, not as collateral security only. The evidence on this point was contradictory : the court, under the circumstances, referred it to the master to take an account of the claim of the plaintiffs against the estate, and to enquire as to the dealings of the trustees under the assignment.

Where a bill was filed by one of several creditors of a debtor, who had assigned his estate for the benefit of his creditors, against the debtor and the trustees, seeking an account of the estate and payment, without making any other creditor a party, the court overruled an objection for want of parties, on the ground of the absence of any such creditor.

Statement.—The bill in this cause was filed by *Ross W. Wood, Alexander H. Grant,* and *Richard D. Wood,* merchants, resident in New York, and carrying on business there under the style of " *Wood & Grant,*" on behalf of themselves and the other unsatisfied creditors of *Robert H. Brett,* against *Robert H. Brett, James B. Davis, William D. Taylor,* and *William Anderson,* setting forth that *Brett* had become largely indebted to the plaintiffs in carrying on his business of a banker and broker in the city of Toronto, and that at a meeting of *Brett's* creditors it was agreed that an assignment should be executed by *Brett* for the benefit of his creditors; in pursuance whereof an indenture dated the 30th of September, 1857, was executed by *Brett* and his wife, conveying to the defendants *Davis, Taylor,* and *Anderson,* all the estate and effects of *Brett,* in trust for the benefit of his creditors, to which were annexed several schedules of creditors, shewing the nature of their several claims, and the priority in which they should rank upon the assets.

The other material statements of the bill are mentioned in the judgment. The prayer of the bill was, that the trust deed might be established ; that an account of the trust estate might be taken, and of what the same consisted, and what portions had come to the hands of the trustees, or any of them, or any person on their behalf, or which but for wilful default might have been received ; also, that a receiver might be appointed to get in the estate and effects, and for further relief.

The defendants all answered the bill. *Taylor* admitted signing the trust deed, but had never acted thereunder, *Davis* and *Anderson* having managed the affairs of the estate without any reference to him, *Taylor*, and prayed to be relieved from acting therein.

Evidence at considerable length was taken in the cause, the nature of which, as also of the defence set up by the other defendants, appear in the judgment.

Mr. *Hector* and Mr. *Patterson*, for plaintiffs.

Mr. *Turner* and Mr. *Blake* for the defendants *Brett*, *Davis* and *Anderson*.

Mr. *Roaf* for defendant *Taylor*.

On the cause coming on to be heard, counsel for *Brett* objected that some of the creditors of *Brett* ought to have been made parties in order that they might contest the claim of the plaintiffs, their interest being distinct and opposing to the others, and being so opposed, they are not in a position to file a bill on behalf of themselves and the other creditors. To enable them to do so, it should appear, that the relief sought is, in its nature, beneficial to all. *Newrton* v. *Egmont* (a), *Gray* v. *Chaplin* (b), *Attorney-General* v. *Heelis* (c), *Jones* v. *Gracia* (d), were cited.

(a) 4 Sim. 574.　　　　(b) 2 Sim. & St. 267.
(c) 2 Sim. & S. 76.　　　(d) 1 Tur. & Russ. 297.

Having taken time to consider this objection, on the following day

Judgment.—VANKOUGHNET, C.—On the plaintiffs' bill being read, the defendants suggested that the bill is improperly framed, and that the plaintiffs cannot sue on behalf of themselves and all other creditors of the estate, and that some at all events of these creditors should be made parties defendants to contest the plaintiffs' right to any inquiry or relief, and that for this purpose they are not sufficiently represented by the trustees. I think that the objection should not be sustained, although it is quite probable that on hearing read the evidence, and on the argument, the court may feel it right to order the cause to stand over for the addition of parties interested. It does not appear that any of the creditors have executed the deed.

The bill is framed as such bills ordinarily are, and prays such relief as under similar facts alleged is ordinarily given. The granting the plaintiff the inquiry he seeks, and the due administration of the trust, concludes nothing as against any creditor. The trustees may be interested in resisting an inquiry, and they do here resist it, saying in their answers (which were not however read) that the plaintiffs are paid by bills and notes, which the plaintiffs allege were received only as collateral security, and that there is due but a small balance, which they tendered them before bill filed.

That the plaintiffs were originally creditors, and are entitled to the shelter and advantages of the trust deed, is not disputed. All parties are *intra domum*, but the trustees undertook to put the plaintiffs out and shut the door on them, saying they have had all they were entitled to. If they succeed in this well and good, but I do not think it necessary, at present at all events, to summon any of the *cestui que trustent* here to aid them in that effort. If they fail, it is still open to the creditors to contest the plaintiffs' claim in the master's office, and to shew that they are paid in whole or in part. This is not like the case of a plaintiff claiming to set aside the trust deed, or to fasten on the estate an incumbrance prior to the deed; nor even the case of one seeking to be admitted as a party to the deed, and to the benefits of it, and yet in the latter case bills like the present have been sustained by decrees for the administration of the estate; the plaintiffs having been held entitled to come in under the deed, without making any of the creditors who had originally or subsequently acceded to it parties.

I refer to *Broadbent* v. *Thornton*, (a) *Johnson* v. *Kershaw*, (b) *Forbes* v. *Limond*, (c) *Lane* v. *Husband*, (d) *Nicholson* v. *Tutin*, (e) *Raworth* v. *Parker*, (f) *Weld* v. *Bonham*, (g) *Powell* v. *Wright*, (h) *Waters* v. *Jones*, (i) *Lewis* v. *Zouche*, (j) *Calvert* v. *Phipp*, (k) *Duncombe* v. *Levy*, (l) *Prosser* v. *Edmonds*, (m) *Biron* v. *Moniel*, (n) *Whitmore* v. *Turquand*. (o)

In these two last cited cases the judgment creditors appear to have intervened, and, I suppose, by the order of the court, in the exercise of its discretion, as they do not appear to have been parties to the bill. In each case a creditor who had allowed the time for assenting to the deed to elapse, sought to come in and share in proportion with the other creditors, thus reducing the fund to them. I have examined the cases and authorities cited in support of the objection, and others of the same class.

The objection as to parties having been overruled, the hearing of the cause upon the pleadings and evidence

---

(a) DeG. & Smale, 65. (b) 1 DeG. & S. 260.
(c) 4 DeG. M. & G. 298. (d) 14 Sim. 656.
(e) 2 Kay & J. 18. (f) 2 Kay & J. 163.
(g) 2 Sim. & S. 91. (h) 7 Beav. 444.
(i) 6 Jur. N. S. 530. (j) 2 Sim. 388.
(k) Madd. & G. 229. (l) 5 Hare, 232.
(m) 1 Y. & C. Ex. 481 ; 1 Ll. & G. 82 ; 5 H. L. Cas. 329.
(n) 24 Beav. 642.
(o) 1 Johns. & Hem. 444, and on appeal, 7 Jur. N. S. 327.

was proceeded with. The point mainly contested being
the question as to how the notes and bills were delivered
to, and accepted by, the plaintiff *Grant*, whether as payment, or by way of collateral security only. *Bottomley*
v. *Nuttall*, (*a*) *Goldshede* v. *Cottrell*, (*b* *Puckford* v.
Maxwell, (*c*) *Hadley* v. *Hadley*, (*d*) *Camoys* v. *Best*, (*e*)
Sharp v. *Sharp*, (*f*) were amongst other cases relied
on by counsel.

Judgment.—VANKOUGHNET, C.—This is a bill filed by
privileged creditors, under a trust deed, on behalf of
themselves and all other creditors, against the trustees and the debtor making the assignment, alleging
that he has not been paid, and that there has been
mismanagement and waste; and praying for a due
administration of the estate. An objection raised
against the frame of the suit in respect of parties has
been already disposed of.

The plaintiffs are, or were, a firm of merchants carrying on business in New York, and who were in advance
to, or under liabilities for, the debtor *Brett*, to the amount
of £5360, for which sum they rank under the deed as
privileged over the general creditors of *Brett*, and are
referred to in the deed and classed as the fifth in order
of those whose special claims are to be paid. The defendants the trustees and the debtor *Brett* allege, that with
the exception of a small sum of this privileged and preferred claim, amounting by the statement of the trustees
to $352.72, and another small sum of $355.15, which the
plaintiffs are entitled to prove for only in common with
the general creditors, and which two sums they the
trustees offered to pay the plaintiffs before bill filed, in
order to avoid the expense of a suit, the plaintiffs have
been paid or satisfied their debt in full by the delivery
to, and acceptance by them, in payment of so much
thereof, of certain bills, notes, and negotiable paper of

(*a*) 5 C. B. N. S. 122.   (*b*) 2 Mee. & W. 20.
(*c*) 6 T. R. 52.   (*d*) 5 DeG. & S. 67.
(*e*) 19 Beav. 414.   (*f*) 2 B. & Al. 405.

Brett's estate, and that to that extent therefore *their original* and preferred debt became and was extinguished. The plaintiffs allege that this paper was de·livered to them as collateral security merely, and that £1000 of it, being two notes of *Bostwick* and *McDonnell* for £500 each, having been dishonored and remaining unpaid, and having become worthless before maturity by the failure and insolvency of the makers, they are entitled to claim this sum from the estate. In this as in all other such cases the inquiry is, what was the agreement between the parties at the time of the alleged transaction, as either actually made and expressed, or to be gathered from their mode of dealing and conduct then or subsequently. I take it to be quite clear law, that a creditor may discharge the original debt by taking in satisfaction of it the note of a third party, and the varying expressions and language of the courts and of judges in the cases cited on the argument, and in many others to be readily found, can be reconciled by referring them to the particular state of facts presented to the court, in each case, and not to existing doubts or differences of opinion as to the law.

If it be proved to the satisfaction of the court that a creditor has accepted from his debtor the promissory note of a third party in satisfaction of the debt, agreeing and intending that the original debt shall be thus paid and extinguished, there can be no doubt that such an agreement will be binding, and the original debt extinguished accordingly.

The notes to the case of *Cumber* v. *Wane* (a), which case itself however must be considered as modified very much in its doctrine by *Sibree* v. *Tripp* (b), contain the principal cases on this head. The law is also very clearly expressed in two cases decided in the Supreme Court of the State of New York, viz., *James* v. *Hackley* (c),

---

(a) Smith's leading cases, 2 vol: 288.   (b) 15 M. & W. 22.
(c) 16 John's, 273,

and *Frisbie* v. *Larned* (*d*). Then what is the evidence
in this case upon which the court is asked to declare
that the privileged debt of the plaintiffs is, as against
the estate, gone?

Mr. *Brett*, immediately after his assignment, tele-
graphs the plaintiffs thereof at New York, and one of
them, *Grant*, repairs to Toronto, where he meets Mr.
Brett, and also Mr.*Davis*, one of the trustees (according
to the evidence of the latter), and *Brett*, as he swears,
states to *Grant* that his assignees held a large amount
of bills receivable, and had proposed to parties to give
them such bills, or to go on collecting them, and that
Mr. *Grant* should consider whether they would wait
till the bills were collected, or would take some that had
been allotted to them—the assignees, as I gather from
the evidence, having parcelled out certain sets of bills
for particular creditors—that *Grant* said to sustain the
plaintiffs' business, it was highly desirable to realize
from the estate at once, and he looked over a memorandum of the bills intended for him, took them up
and wished *Brett* to endorse them, which the latter refused to do, saying, "the estate might as well hold
the bills and collect them." After some further questioning *Grant* took up the bills saying he thought he
could get a number of them discounted by one of the
banks in the city, "*and he would take them*." He went
out and returned in about an hour, saying he could
not get them discounted, and that it was highly important that he should get some money to remit to New
York by post. *Brett* then mentioned that he had a bill
of exchange on London (which appears to have been
for £500 sterling), and *Grant* said "*he would take that
too*." He took it, retaining, as appears from the evidence, all the other notes besides, being thus together
in amount, several hundred pounds in excess of the
plaintiffs' claim. It is explained that the notes originally handed to *Grant*, were together in a paper wrapper,

---

(*d*) 21 Windell, 450; see also Winter v, Innes, 4 M. &'C. 101,
and Thompson v. Percival, 17 Ves. 514.

and that *Brett* forgot to have any of them returned or
withheld on the delivery of the bill of exchange, as
there was a rush that day on the bank, (meaning the
bank which *Brett* had conducted,) and much hurry and
confusion. Again *Brett* says, " I told *Grant* at the
first meeting that most of the creditors had taken notes
or bills in discharge of their debts," (this does not,
however, clearly appear,) "and then what is mentioned
above took place, but there was no express agreement
in so many words by *Grant* to take the bills in satisfaction. *Grant* went out to try to get the bills or notes
discounted to get money to send to New York." Again
Brett says, " The bill of exchange was not handed to
him at the time with the others, [meaning the notes in
the wrapper,] but several hours afterwards." On cross-
examination *Brett* says, " I am decidedly of opinion
that Mr. *Grant* understood he was not taking the notes
as collateral security, but in satisfaction ; there is no
doubt about it ; *Grant* did not ask to have them as collateral security, but the question came up when he wanted
me to endorse them, and then what I have mentioned
passed." *Davis*, one of the defendants, says of this interview on the day referred to, and at which he swears
he was present: " *Brett* introduced me to *Grant*, and
said in his presence and hearing, ' that he [meaning
Grant] was willing to take these bills for his claim ;'
Grant wanted *Brett* to endorse the country bills: *Brett*
refused ; and I said he could not endorse them to make
the estate liable. *Brett* said *Grant* must take them in
payment, or not at all. I don't recollect whether *Grant*
accepted them as payment at first, or whether he went
out and returned, and then said he would take them ; but
I am certain he said he would take them *as payment ;*
Grant readily accepted the *Bostwick & McDonnell* bills,
because he knew them, but did not know anything about
the country bills," and on the occasion of his interview
with *Grant* on his second visit to Toronto, (at which time
Grant insisted that the bills had only been taken as collateral security,) he says, " I said to *Grant* that if he

really thought he had taken them as collateral I would place him in his original position if I could, by taking the bills back; he refused this." Again he says, on cross-examination : " At the meeting when the securities were handed over *Brett* called me up, and *Anderson* (the other defendant) and I were both present; I was present when the arrangement was made ; *Grant* returned and said he would take the notes, and I told *Brett* he could carry out the arrangement;" again, "the bank was full of people;I am satisfied I was present when the arrangement was concluded; I am not sure that *Grant* had made up his mind when he went out, but when he returned he said, 'Well I have made up my mind to take the bills,' and I said to Mr. *Brett*, you can carry out the arrangement; *Grant* then a little before said he must get something convertible into cash, as he could not get the bills discounted, and it was then *Brett* gave him the bill on England, and no deduction was made at the time. It was not noticed by me ; there was much confusion—a rush upon the bank."

The only party present at these two interviews was *James Brett*, whose evidence throws no light upon the transaction.   He swears that *Grant* was several times in the office on the day referred to.   As additional evidence, the entry of the bills delivered to *Grant*, made in *Brett's* books, is now produced, and is headed "Mem. of Bills receivable given to *Wood & Grant* on the 3rd of October, 1857." *Davis* swears this was done at the time ; defendant *Brett* swears to the same thing, and to another entry on the other page, as made at the same time, viz., " Paid Mr. *Grant* on 3rd October, in bills receivable, &c., £6013 13s. 8d." *James Brett* says that he does not recollect that this entry was made on that day. The form of it would rather indicate that it was not.

I have selected all the evidence which I think is at all material, as bearing upon the delivery to, and acceptance by, *Grant* of these notes or bills, and I think

nothing is shewn in any subsequent act or conduct of
the plaintiffs which strengthens the case against them.
As between the defendants *Brett* and *Davis*, *Brett* is
more interested in making out a case against the plaintiffs, as he is not released by the composition deed.
One cannot read this evidence without being struck by
the difference between the statement of these two defendants, and the apparent confusion in their own
minds as to what really did pass between all parties on
the day on which these notes were delivered over. That
may be accounted for by the general confusion in the
bank, which prevailed at the time, as explained by
Davis. It seems certain that there were two interviews
between *Grant* and *Brett*, and (though *Brett* says nothing
of it, but merely speaks of his brother *James* being then
present, yet on *Davis's* evidence,) with *Davis* too, on this
day; and *James Brett* swears that *Grant* was in the office
several times. *Brett*, defendant, swears, that "It was
on the first interview *Grant* said he would take the
notes," yet at the same time *Grant*, whose object appears
to have been to realize quickly, and to raise some money
at once, went out to see if he could get the bills discounted, and on failing, returned, when *Brett* asked him
if there was anything he would take in preference to
the notes, offering a bill on England, which *Grant* said
he "*would take too.*" Now it is not easy to see on this
statement that when *Grant* went out to try to get the
notes discounted, that he had absolutely assumed them
as his own property. If he had, why give him the bill
of exchange either in lieu of part of, or in addition to,
the notes? It is true that the defendant *Brett* swears he
was decidedly of opinion that *Grant* understood he was
taking the notes in satisfaction; that there is (that is
in his mind at the time of his examination) no doubt
about it, but when so taken? when the notes were first
handed to him, or when the bill was taken by him "too?"
Brett does not pretend it was on this latter occasion
Grant, agreed to take them as payment, and *Grant's* expression unopposed by any from *Brett* at the time would

shew the contrary, for it was not intended to give him several hundred pounds more than his debt. And again *Brett* swears that there was no express agreement in so many words by *Grant* to take the bills in satisfaction.

If this then stood alone, and treating the transaction as only closed when *Grant* took away the notes and the bill of exchange " too," can it be said to be clear that he took them in satisfaction ? and if he was not to keep them all in satisfaction, then which of them was he to so keep ? But what does *Davis* say ? He says in one place he does not know whether it was on the first occasion when *Grant* received the bills, or on the second occasion, when he returned with them, that he said that he would take them in payment. But he is certain he did so say. *Brett* says *Grant* did not say so in so many words. Again *Davis* says that he was present when the arrangement was concluded. He is not sure that *Grant* had made up his mind when he first went out, but he says *Grant* returned and said he would take the notes, and " I then told *Brett* to carry out the arrangement." Now upon this it is to be observed, firstly, that it is not *Brett's* account of the matter ; and *Brett*, not *Davis*, appears to have been the party who arranged with *Grant*, and with whom *Grant* communicated. Secondly, that it seems strange that *Grant* should return after having found that he could not use the bills, and then say he would take them ; and thirdly, that instead of taking them as payment, he asked for, and got something else or in addition, more convertible into money, being the bill on England. It seems pretty clear from *Davis's* evidence that he did not consider that *Grant* had determined to take the bills till he found he could not use them, for he thus expresses it : "When he (*Grant*) returned, he said, ' well I have made up my mind to take the bills ;' " and yet a little further on he says, *Grant* required something convertible into cash, having failed to negotiate any of the paper.

The conduct of the plaintiffs, subsequently, does **not**

furnish any evidence, that they treated the bills as payment, but the contrary; and Mr. *Davis* himself seems
to have doubts whether *Grant* had intended them to be
so used, as on the subsequent occasion before referred to
he offered *Grant*, if the latter really believed he had
taken the notes as collateral security, to restore him, if he
could, to his original position. I do not place much, if any,
stress upon the entries in the book. If made at the time,
they were made during a scene of confusion, and the
parties who made them will not swear that it was then
done. Indeed the whole transaction appears to have
been a most hurried one ; and the account of it, as I have
shewn, is any thing but satisfactory.

What the defendants have to make out is not only that
they handed the paper over in payment and satisfaction,
but that the plaintiffs received it as such ; and this I
cannot say they have done. But were the evidence
more clear to establish this allegation, I still think that
the plaintiffs are not shut out from relief. When *Grant*
left he took away with him without objection, though, as
the defendants allege, in mistake, all the notes handed
to him at first, and the bill of exchange on England
; and, without any demand on him by the
defendants in the meantime, he returned some of the
paper to *Brett* for his endorsation to render them
negotiable, and for the purpose of being collected by
Brett. Among them was a cheque of *Taylor* and *Stevenson* for £446 8s. 9d. What does *Brett* do with this
paper ? Without the consent of the plaintiffs, and
without giving them any option—without in fact
communicating with *Grant*—he retains it for the purposes of his estate, paying the plaintiffs the difference
between it and the sterling bill of exchange.

How or when this difference was paid does not appear,
but it is contended that by accepting it, the plaintiffs
waived their right to the returned and retained paper.
I do not think so. I think it appears that the plaintiffs

always insisted upon their right to this paper, and their mere acceptance of £150 out of the £446 8s. 9d., amount of *Taylor & Stevenson's* cheque, cannot bar any claim they originally had to the residue. I think that neither *Brett* nor the trustees receiving back this paper from the plaintiffs for the use of the latter, and in good faith by them, had any right to deal with it as they did. They should at least, if they felt that by their previous remissness and error, the estate was in danger to the amount they claimed back from the plaintiffs, have given them the option of saying what paper they would return, and what hold. They had no right to choose for the plaintiffs, even if they were of opinion that the plaintiffs preferred *Bostwick* and *McDonnell's* paper.

The defendants have endeavoured to shut the plaintiffs out from all enquiry and relief, and in this I think they fail, notwithstanding the very able arguments addressed to me in their behalf. The plaintiffs are therefore, in my opinion, entitled to a decree. I have considered whether the cause should stand over to have some of the creditors made parties, and I have come to the conclusion that such a course is unnecessary, as my judgment now decides nothing more than that upon the state of facts presented to me by the defendants the plaintiffs are not out of court. It will be quite open to any and every creditor to contest their claim in the master's office upon the same or other facts, and perhaps additional evidence there will give the case another complexion. For instance, an examination of the plaintiffs' books, shewing how they dealt with the notes delivered to them, may be highly important—an inquiry as to any loss to the estate by the plaintiffs' retention of *Bostwick* and *McDonnell's* paper, may result in their being charged with it—it may appear from the state of the funds, or their application, that the plaintiffs have received more in their order than they are entitled to—that they and the trustees together have committed a breach of trust in the allocation to the plaintiffs of the portion of the estate given to them.

These and all other questions affecting the creditors *inter se*, or the conduct of the trustees, can form the subject of investigation in the master's office, and of subsequent consideration, if desired, by the court.   I send the case there without prejudice to any party.

In the view I have taken, I have not thought it necessary to notice that there is an admitted balance due to the plaintiffs, though its precise amount is not ascertained or agreed upon.   It was at one time, as to the privileged debt, supposed to be $352.73, but according to Mr. *Brett's* figures, it is much less.   The trustees should of course pay no more than is due.

As regards the defendant *Taylor*, I think he is properly made a party in the suit.   He executed the deed, and thus accepted the trust; and if he wished to escape from it, it was his duty to have informed the *cestui que trustent* of such his intention, and of any act of his to effect it, that they might know that they had no longer his responsibility and guardianship, and that they were in a position to execute the power given to them by the deed of appointing some one in his place.

MASSINGBERD v. MONTAGUE.

Sale for taxes—Sheriff's officer—Duty imposed on sheriff and his officers at sales for taxes—Costs.

At a sale of lands for wild land taxes, one of the sheriff's officers conducted the sale, at which he knocked down without any competition to another officer of the sheriff, a lot of land worth about £350, for rather less than £7 10s., which lot was subsequently, with the assent of the sheriff, entered in the sales book in the name of the party who had conducted the sale, for the purpose of enabling the person to whom it had been knocked down to cheat his creditors. Upon a bill filed to set aside the deed executed by the sheriff, it was shewn that by arrangement amongst the persons attending the sale, it was understood a lot should be knocked down to each one in turn, in pursuance of which the sale in question was effected. Under these circumstances the court set aside the sale with costs as against the person to whom the conveyance was made.

The duty imposed upon the sheriffs at sales of lands for taxes is to sell such portions of the lands offered as the sheriff may consider it most for the advantage of the owners thereof; where therefore a sheriff so neglected his duty in this respect that at a sale for taxes very valuable lots of land were knocked down for trifling amounts of taxes, in pursuance of an agreement to that effect entered into amongst the bidders, some of which lands were purchased by bailiffs in his employ, and with his knowledge, the court in dismissing the bill filed to set aside one of the sales to his bailiff, as against the sheriff, refused him his costs. It is not sufficient that the sheriff does not participate in such arrangements for his own benefit.

The bill in this cause was filed by the Reverend *Hompesh Massingberd*, against *Charles Montague*, *William Glass*, sheriff of the county of Middlesex, and *John Godbold*, praying, under the circumstances appearing in the head-note and judgment, to have a sale effected by the defendant *Glass*, as sheriff, set aside, and plaintiff let in to redeem the lands so sold to the defendant *Godbold*, on the payment to him of what he had advanced.

The cause came on to be heard before his Lordship the Chancellor.

Mr. *Roaf*, for the plaintiff, referred to *Henry* v. *Barness*, (a)

Mr. *Fitzgerald* for defendants.

(a) Ante vol. 8, p. 345.

Judgment.—VANKOUGHNET, C.—This case presents, though perhaps in a less degree than some others, one of those instances of sales of lands for arrears of taxes in which the rights of owners are sacrificed to the cupidity of bidders, who by arrangements among themselves contrive to get, for trifling sums chargeable on the property, whole lots of land, when one-twentieth, and often one-fiftieth part should suffice for payment. It would seem from the facts disclosed in this and other similar cases that persons attending such sales with an intention to purchase, consider it lawful and proper to conspire together to divide between them large quantities of land so exposed to sale ; and the officer conducting the sale appears to have considered that he has discharged his duty so long as he does not participate in such an arrangement with a view to his own profit. The law has ever required that those, whose persons or property have been by misfortune or otherwise subjected to its process, shall be dealt with fairly and without oppression, and with as little suffering and loss as possible, and it throws this duty upon the officer charged with the execution of that process. The statute regulating sales of land for taxes, recognises and enforces this duty, for it provides that, " the sheriff shall sell by public auction so much of the land as may be sufficient to discharge the taxes, and all lawful charges incurred in and about the sale and the collection of the taxes, selling in preference such part *as he may consider it most for the advantage of the owner to sell first.*" The legislature have therefore not been less careful to guard against the sacrifice of property subjected to burdens for the public, than the law has always been to protect, against wanton waste and loss, property subjected under judicial process to the claims of individuals. Nor should they have been.

Taxes are at all times onerous, and are imposed merely from public necessity, and it is the policy as well as the interest of the state that they should bear as lightly as possible on individuals, and it is the duty of

those charged with the collection of such charges, to
maintain this policy so far as is in their power. We
know that at common law, if a sheriff sells under execution, unless at the peremptory mandate of the court, the
property of the debtor at a price greatly below its value,
he is liable to damages in an action for the loss.
And in one case, *Phillipps* v. *Bacon*, (a) Lord *Ellenborough* is reported to have said in reference to an
attempt to sustain on the common count for trover a
verdict recovered against the sheriff for want of proper
care and judgment in the sale of property under a *fi. fa.*,
" If the question had arisen as at present advised, I
should have inclined very strongly, from the argument
I have heard, to have held that if the sheriff, or his
officers acting for him, depart so entirely and scandalous-
ly from their duty in making a mock sale of the goods in
the manner which' has been represented to us, it could
not be considered as a sale in obedience to the writ of
fieri facias, but rather a conspiracy to despoil the plaintiff of his property, and would bring the sale within the
principle of the six carpenters' case, and make the sheriff
a trespasser *ab initio.*"

Now is not such a sale for taxes as I have referred to
a mockery, and a conspiracy to deprive the owner of his
property ? and is the sheriff, in conducting and counte-
nancing such a sale, doing his duty, and acting in the
spirit of the statute and of the law? Such a sale, to use
a paradox, is no sale. The duty of a sheriff is not to
expose lands to it, but to adjourn the time, and then
execute the writ, giving all proper notice to ensure the'
attendance of bidders. A course similar to this he adopts
on *fi. fa.* where he returns "goods on hand for want of
bidders." It is not his fault if he cannot secure a fair
sale, and thus make the money which he is charged to
collect; but it is his fault if he permits an unfair sale,
which he has the means of checking or preventing.

(a) 9 East, p. 303.

The writ for the sale of these lands is placed in the sheriff's hands, at least three months before the time of the sale, and it is not too much to expect that during that time he shall take some pains to make himself acquainted with the condition and value of the land about to be sold; and the machinery of his office would seem adequate for the purpose at very little trouble or cost. He can hardly excuse himself by total ignorance, when there is imposed upon him the exercise of judgment in selling first that portion of the land which he considers it most for the advantage of the owner to sell.

Now in this case there is much evidence to shew that at periods of the sale, which extended over two or three days, arrangements were made by those present not to compete for particular lots; but there is not the evidence of general combination and of determination to maintain it, which was furnished in the case of *Henry* v. *Burness*. There is abundant proof, on examining the book containing the entries of sale, that whole lots of land were, without any competition, sacrificed for trifling sums, and these too lying in well settled parts of the country, with the average value of which it is hard to believe that persons necessarily well acquainted with the county as the sheriff and his officers must have been, could have been entirely ignorant. Then what do we find in reference to this particular lot? not certainly distinct evidence of any arrangement that there was to be no competition, but we find the sheriff's officer who was conducting the sale, *Godbold* the defendant, selling it without any competition to another sheriff's officer, *Jeffrey*, the bailiff; and subsequently, to enable *Jeffrey* to cheat his creditors, entering in the sales-book, with the assent of the sheriff, the lot as sold to himself; the sale being for less than £7 10s., and the lot worth at least £350. Now can such a transaction stand? These two gentlemen have been too clever. I am not quite certain what the truth in the matter is; but by their own statement, *Jeffrey*, though he swears he bought for himself, but feared to hold the land in his own name, persuades the sheriff that he bought for *Godbold*, and gets the sheriff to treat *Godbold* as the purchaser, to whom as such, first, the certificate of sale, and afterwards the deed issued from the sheriff. We cannot, after this, allow Mr. *Jeffrey* or Mr. *Godbold* to deny that the latter was the purchaser ; and as I think he could not sell to himself, the sale and all transactions founded on it must be set aside, and a decree to that effect made, with costs, to be paid by *Godbold*. Even if the sale were to *Jeffrey*, and had remained in his name, I should think it an improper one. Considering the duties cast upon the sheriff, and how much he must necessarily rely for information upon his officers and bailiffs, I think none of them should be allowed to purchase at any sale which he in the exercise of his office is called upon to make, and that he should not permit any such purchase. He has the power in his own hands, for if any one of his employees desire to become a purchaser, he can be told by the sheriff that he must first leave his service.

I dismiss the bill as against the sheriff, but without costs, for I cannot hold him free from blame in the matter. He ought not to have allowed the sale to be entered in *Godbold's* name ; neither ought he to have allowed *Godbold* to become, as he did, the purchaser of several other lots, and the more especially so as he had heard the proposition to allow the auctioneer and his clerk to have a lot or two without opposition.

The amount of taxes paid by *Godbold*, with ten per cent., up to the filing of the bill, to be re-paid him, or be deducted from the costs.

Montreal Bank v. Baker.

Mortgage—Execution of deed in blank—Absconding debtor.

A debtor being about to leave this province for the purpose of raising funds to discharge his liabilities, signed and sealed a printed form of mortgage upon certain lands, without, however, having inserted either the name of himself or the mortgagee therein, which was also in like manner executed by the wife of the mortgagor, and by him locked up in his desk, From Halifax he wrote to his agent here introducing him to fill up the blanks as he should find necessary, which was accordingly done, and handed over to the mortgagee. *Held*, that this was a sufficient execution of the mortgage, and that the same was a valid charge upon the property embraced in the instrument.

When it is necessary for the purpose of settling the priority of incumbrancers to enquire whther a party who had been sued was or not an absconding debtor within the meaning of the act, this court will do so; and that too although the defendant in the action may not have taken any steps to set aside the attachment issued at law.

This was a suit of foreclosure brought by the *Bank of Montreal* upon two mortgages against *William Baker*, the mortgagor, and *Joseph Shuter*, The *Commercial Bank of Canada*, *Thomas Rigney* and *James Brown*, the younger, who were made parties as incumbrancers, *Shuter* ranking prior to the plaintiffs as to one of their mortgages, and in respect of which they submitted to redeem him.

The bill further stated, that the defendants The *Commercial Bank* claimed priorty over such second mortgage, bearing date the 25th May. 1857, by virtue of a judgment recovered against *Baker*, and duly registered; such judgment having been recovered in a suit wherein proceedings had been commenced by writ of attachment, and which was sued out prior to the registration of such second mortgage of the plaintiffs; but which the plaintiffs submitted the *Commercial Bank* could not properly claim, *Baker* never having been in fact an absconding debtor, or liable to such process.

All the defendants answered the bill. The *Commercial Bank* alleging that *Baker* was at the time of suing out their attachment an absconding debtor, and that such attachment never had been superseded or abandoned; and that the mortgage of the 25th of May, 1857, was

7   GRANT·IX.

never in fact executed by *Baker*, and that the same did not operate as a lien on the lands embraced therein.

The cause having been put at issue, evidence was taken therein before the court at great length, the material points of which, so far as the questions decided are concerned, appear in the head-note and judgment.

Mr. *Strong*, for the plaintiffs.

Mr. *Roaf*, for the Commercial Bank.

Mr. *A Crooks* and Mr. *Blake*, for the defendants *Rigney & Brown*.

For the plaintiffs, it was contended, that the execution of the mortgage in blank by signing the name and affixing the seal of the mortgagor thereto was sufficient, although the name of the mortgagee did not appear therein; and that the agent of the mortgagor having subsequently filled in the names and delivered the deed to the plaintiffs, under the written authority of the mortgagor, was a good delivery thereof, although such authority was not under seal. The interest of *Baker* at the time was only an equitable estate, and as such did not require a sealed instrument to charge it. An equity of redemption may be charged without seal. It may be admitted that to pass a legal estate by the grantor's attorney a seal is necessary to the instrument constituting the attorney. *Hudson* v. *Revett,* (a) *West* v. *Stewart,* (b) *Hibblewhite* v. *McMorine.* (c) and *Boomer's* Legal Maxims, 145-6, were referred to.

The proceeding to sue out an attachment with knowledge of the facts, was a most improper use of the provisions of the act of parliment. *Baker*, in the eye of the law, never was an absconding debtor: it is shewn that he left openly, with the knowledge of the community in which he resided, for the purpose of visiting Montreal,

---

(a) 5 Bing. 366.   (b) 14 M. & W. 47.
(c) 6 M. & W. 215.

Boston, or any other place in which he might consider it probable that he would succeed in raising funds to discharge his liabilities.

Counsel for *Rigney & Brown* insisted upon the same objections as were raised by the plaintiffs as to the invalidity of the proceedings under the attachment, which they also contended had been abandoned by the attaching creditors, *Baker* having been permitted to assume control of his property after his return, and to continue his business therein in the same way as he had previously done.

For the *Commercial Bank*, it was contended that the mortgage to the plaintiffs never was a valid subsisting charge at law; as a conveyance it was wholly void at law, and being void at law, would be void also in equity. No agreement is alleged or proved to execute a mortgage or create a charge by deposit of title deeds, or in fact do otherwise than was done. The delivery, if any such took place, was before the blanks were filled up, and the registration of the mortgage was effected upon the affidavit of a witness, who swore to the delivery by *Baker* himself: this alone is sufficient to shew that the plaintiffs relied alone upon the delivery by *Baker;* and *McNider*, agent of the plaintiffs, says he accepted the mortgage before the blanks were filled up.

So far as the question respecting the validity of the attachment is concerned, the only point for consideration is, whether there was fraud in the suing out of the writ as against other creditors; nothing turns upon the ground of the regularity or irregularity of that proceeding. *Baker* never having adopted any steps for setting aside that writ, this court will not now enquire into the fact whether the debtor was an absconding debtor or not.

Exp. *Hoover*, (a) *Shepherd* v. *Titley*, (b) *Chitty's*

(a) 1 Mer. 7.   (b) 2 Atk. 348.

Archbold's Practice, 588; *Shepherd's Touchstone*, 313; *Amer* v. *Best,* (a) were also cited.

Judgment.—SPRAGGE, V. C.—The principal question in this case is, whether the instrument which the plaintiffs claim to be a mortgage, and which bears date the 25th of May, 1857, was ever, and if ever, at what time, duly executed. The question is one of priority between the Montreal Bank, and the Commercial Bank, and the defendants *Rigney & Brown.*

The instrument in question, without the names of any party in the body of it, but with a space left for their insertion, was signed and sealed by the mortgagor *Baker,* and his wife, on the day of its date, and in that state attested by a subscribing witness. On the outside the words "mortgage with dower" are printed; below this the word, "to," and underneath it in pencil, in the handwriting of *Baker,* are the words, "Bank of Montreal." The instrument was not then delivered, but in the state I have described was retained by *Baker,* and locked up in his desk. This was done on the eve of his departure for Montreal, and perhaps to Halifax, with a view to obtaining money to relieve his embarrassments. At the latter place he wrote a letter of instructions, which is produced, to a Mr. *Lavis.* A mortgage with similar blanks executed in the same way, and intended for the Commercial Bank, was also left by *Baker* in his desk.

In his letter to *Lavis* he informs him of the execution of these instruments, and instructs him to procure them, and fill up the blanks, as he should find it necessary; and to deliver them respectively to the agents of the banks at Belleville, delivering the one in question first to the agent of the Montreal Bank. The one intended for the Commercial Bank was offered to the agent, and

---

(a) 1 Vermont Rep. 303.

refused, on the ground that it was invalid by reason of the blanks. The one offered to the Montreal Bank was accepted by its agent, *McNider*. It was delivered first, while in the state in which it was left, and again after the blanks had been filled up.

It is incontrovertible, I think, that the instrument in the state in which it was left by *Baker* was void ; and that as first delivered to *McNider*, it was void. The question is, whether the filling up of the blanks, and subsequent delivery, gave it validity.

If the only thing remaining to be done had been the delivery of the instrument, it would be clear, I think, that delivery being a matter in *pais*, was authorised by the letter from Halifax, and was validly done. I think it is also clear, as a matter of fact, that the filling up of the blanks was in accordance with the instructions contained in that letter. The question is, whether *Lavis*, as agent appointed by parol, could complete the execution of this imperfect instrument by any authority less than under seal.

If a re-execution of the instrument by *Baker* himself, supposing him present, and not acting by attorney, had been necessary after the blanks were filled up, it would follow that *Lavis* had no authority to complete its execution. A formal re-execution by signing and sealing, or its equivalent, acknowledging signature and seal, would not be necessary, I apprehend, but a filling up of the blanks in the *presence* of the grantor merely, would suffice under the authority of *Hudson* v. *Revett*, (a) even as read by the court in *Hibblewhite* v. *McMorine*. (b) But it is a question whether in *Hudson* v. *Revett* the court held the presence of the grantor necessary ; their language does not attach importance to that circumstance.

(a) 5 Bing. 368.　　　　　(b) 6 M. & W. 215.

The deed in question in that case was a conveyance to trustees for the benefit of creditors; the sums due to them respectively being inserted in the deed; a blank was left for a very large amount due to one of the principal creditors, which it was agreed should be ascertained by the production of vouchers; the deed was executed with this blank, which it was agreed should be filled up when the vouchers were produced. The next day the vouchers were produced by the grantor, and the blank filled up, probably in his presence, with the smaller amount, which only he alleged was due.

The omission in that deed was certainly not of so startling a character as in the case in question, nevertheless the court held that it was quite impossible that the deed could have any operation while the blank remained in it. It was therefore void, and more than void it could not be.

Then how did the court get over the difficulty that the deed was inoperative and void as first executed, and became a valid deed without any re-execution? As I understand the case, in this way : that there was not a perfect execution of the deed on the first day; and that its delivery at that time was in the nature of an escrow, though not technically as an escrow, the delivery being to the grantee himself; that taking it, that there was a delivery of the deed as a deed, it was only a delivery upon condition that something was afterwards done, and that then, and not till then, it became a perfect deed.

No stress was laid upon the circumstance that the blank was filled up in the presence of the grantor, nor was that circumstance material in the view which the court took of the case. It would indeed be only evidence of assent, which itself is matter in *pais*, and could be done as well by an agent authorised by parol, as by the grantor in person ; suppose, for instance, the grantor had given a power of attorney not under seal, to attend and have the blanks filled up with such a sum, and then to deliver the deed to the grantee, that would be a valid perfecting of the deed within the reasons of the decision; and even if the presence of the grantor had been relied upon.

Hudson v. *Revett* does not stand alone. The old case of *Zouch* v. *Claye* (*a*) is thus shortly stated in *Levinz:* "In debt upon an obligation, the case was thus: A. and B. delivered the bond to C., and after, and by the consent of all parties, the name and addition of D. was interlined, and D. also sealed the obligation, and delivered it; and if the obligation by this alteration was made void against A. and B. or not, was the question? But by *Hale,* and the whole court, adjudged that it was not; and that it is the obligation of all three.

In the still earlier case of *Markham* v. *Gonarstor* (*b*), it was at first held that the blank space left in the bond, afterwards filled up with the assent of the obligors, avoided the instrument; but this was subsequently reversed (*c*); and even when first heard, this distinction was taken by *Popham,* J.; that if it had been appointed by the obligor before the ensealing and delivering thereof that it should be afterwards filled up, it might, then, peradventure, have been good enough, and it should not have made the deed to be void; but being after, it shall avoid the deed—this distinction proceeding, I apprehend, upon the ground upon which *Hudson* and *Revett* was decided.

Zouch v. *Claye* was recognized as authority in *Watson* v. *Booth* (*d*), where a bond to the sheriff was executed by four obligors, with a space left for the name of a fifth. In that state it was left in the hands of an agent of the obligors who had executed it, by whom the name of a fifth obligor was inserted in the

(*a*) 2 Lev. 35.   (*b*) Cro. Eliz. 626.
(*c*) Moor. Rep. pl. 547.   (*d*) 5 M. & S. 223.

blank space, and the additional obligor executed the
bond, and it was delivered to the sheriff.   It was held
that before the insertion of the additional name, the
holding of the bond by the obligor's agent, was in the
nature of an escrow, and the addition having been
made with the assent of the agents, was the same as
if made with the assent of the obligors themselves, and
so within the case of *Zouch* v. *Claye;* and the bond
was held valid.

 Hibblewhite v. *McMorine* is one of several cases in
which it has been held that an assignment of shares in
incorporated companies,which assignments are required
by statute to be under the seal of the transferor, and
therefore deeds are void if the name of the transferee
be left blank.   That was the only point decided, though
the language of Lord *Wensleydale,* by whom the judgment of the court was delivered,militates against such
acts as were done in the case before me, by an agent not
appointed under seal, being sufficient to make a valid
deed.   In regard to *Hudson* v. *Revett,* he observes : "A
blank in a material part was filled up ; but having
been done in the *presence* of the party, and ratified by
him, it was held that it was evidence of re-delivery."

 Lord *Wensleydale* may have thought that the circumstance he adverts to was the proper ground upon
which to place the decision ; but according to the report of the case it was not placed upon that ground by
the learned judges by whom it was decided.   The circumstance of the blanks being filled up in *the presence*
of the grantor, is not even alluded to by the judges,
and it is not clear that the fact was so.   Sergeant
Wilde, who argued against the validity of the deed,
said, that the deed was always out of the grantor's possession after the first execution ; and the counsel who
sustained the deed put the case both ways, whether the
blanks were filled up in the grantor's presence or not.
The learned judges, I take it, must have thought the
circumstance either immaterial or not established.

Hudson v *Revett* was again referred to, in the Court of Exchequer, in *West* v. *Steward*, (a) when Baron *Alderson's* comment upon it was : " There the court considered it to have been executed originally as an escrow, and not absolutely executed until the blank was filled up."

The doctrine established by *Hudson* v. *Revett,* and *Markham* v. *Gonastor*, and *Zouche* v. *Claye*, I think is, that a deed containing blanks, executed by the grantor, although void at the time, may be perfected and rendered valid by the filling up of those blanks with the assent of the grantor; or by insertion made in pursuance of directions given at the time of its execution ; and *Watson* v. *Booth* establishes further that such assent may be by agent appointed not under seal. The ground upon which I understand this to proceed I have already explained.

To apply it to this case : the deed, in its imperfect state, was placed by the grantor in the hands of his agent *Lavis ;* not to deliver it immediately, but to hold it for a certain purpose, and then to deliver it ; it was then in the hands of *Lavis* as an escrow. It matters not, according to the cases, whether the purpose for which it was to be held before delivery was something collateral to the deed, or something to be inserted in the instrument itself; *Lavis* held it for the purpose for which it was placed in his hands ; caused that to be done in relation to it, which he was instructed to have done, and delivered it. It may be that there was no good reason why the blanks should not have been filled up by *Baker* himself; but there can be no doubt how they were to be filled up. The names of the executing parties, and the pencil endorsement clearly indicated that; in addition to which was the letter of instructions.

I cannot, in principle, distinguish this case from those

to which I have referred. *Watson* v. *Booth* resembles it in its circumstances, as well as in principle. It can make no difference, I think, that the delivery to *Lavis*, as an escrow, was not contemporaneous with the signing and sealing.

But it is objected that the deed was actually delivered by *Lavis* to the bank agent before the blanks were filled up; and that the deed having been registered upon the evidence of *Gould*, who only witnessed the execution by *Baker* himself, the bank must have rested upon that delivery. I do not think the registration upon *Gould's* affidavit can preclude the bank from insisting upon any delivery other than in his presence. Assuming that *Lavis* delivered the deed, and that *McNider* for the bank accepted it before the blanks were filled up, I think the bank may still insist upon a delivery by *Lavis* after the blanks were filled up; for the rule against a second delivery only applies when the first delivery is operative, as put by *Perkins:* (a) "It is to be known that a deed cannot have and take effect at *every delivery* as a deed; for if the first delivery take effect, the second delivery is void." And so in *Hudson* v. *Revett*, Sergeant *Wilde* did not contend that there *could* be no second delivery; but that as a matter of fact there was no re-delivery: and *Best*, C. J., held that there was no perfect delivery by the grantor, because the deed itself was inoperative by reason of the blank that was in it. So here the first delivery could not take effect for the like reason; and the second delivery which was proved was a good delivery.

Of course I do not mean to say that there has been any good execution of the deed by *Baker's* wife. But I have come to the conclusion, after some hesitation, that the cases warrant me in holding, that there has been a perfect execution by *Baker* and his wife.

Something is said in the evidence, of the mortgage to

(a) Sec. 154.

the Montreal Bank being in the possession of *Lavis* on the evening of the 18th of June, the blanks having been filled up; but I am satisfied from the evidence that it had at that time been a second time delivered by *Lavis;* and if in his possession afterwards, it could not affect the completeness and validity of the deed.

¹ Evidence has been given as to the exact time at which the mortgage was carried to the registry office for registration, and at which the attachment issued by the Commercial Bank, and under which that bank claims priority, was lodged in the sheriff's office. I incline to think that the mortgage was first in the registry office; but if not, I do not see how the attachment can prevail against it; if it was at the time perfectly executed, an unregistered deed is good against an attachment, unless there is some statutory provision on the subject which I have not seen.

In the view which I take of this case, it is unnecessary to consider some other points raised, at least so far as the plaintiffs' priority is concerned; but as between the Commercial Bank and *Rigney & Brown* it is necessary to determine as to the validity of the attachment issued by the bank on the 19th of June; *Baker's* mortgage to *Rigney & Brown* having been given on the 17th of October, and registered the same day, and the judgment of the Commercial Bank upon their attachment having been recovered on the 7th of June following.

Mr. *Roaf* contends that the only point open is, whether, in suing out the attachment, there was fraud on the part of those by whom it was sued out, as against other creditors; and that this court will not examine whether as a matter of fact *Baker* was an absconding debtor or not. If this be correct that fact cannot be ascertained in any court as between those claiming priority in virtue of it, and other incumbrancers. The Commercial Bank, and *Rigney & Brown* · are both

brought into this court as incumbrancers. The bank's
judgment is subsequent to the firm's mortgage, but the
bank claims priority by reason of the attachment. Is
it not open to *Rigney & Brown* to displace that claim,
by shewing that the supposed fact upon which it is
based had no existence. It would not be impeaching
the regularity of proceedings in another court, but removing the grounds of an assumed priority. The fact
is inquirable at law between the attaching creditor and
the debtor, for one purpose, the question of costs ; as
to the debtor, the priority of creditors is nothing ; and
the writ of attachment is a summons as well ; but he
is allowed an inquiry for a purpose material to himself ;
and the inquiry then is, not whether circumstances as
they appeared to the creditor, and those who made the
further affidavit, were not such as might lead reasonable
men to believe that the debtor was an absconding
debtor, but whether in fact he was an absconding debtor or not. If as a fact he was not, no attachment ought
to have been sued out, and the attaching creditor obtained his priority without right : and in a question of
priority only inquireable into in this court, it would be
anomalous, I think, if the fact could not be shewn, and
shewn by those who have no opportunity of shewing it.
If it were not so, other creditors better informed as to the
fact, not to say more careful and scrupulous in their proceedings, would be postponed ; because they cannot place
themselves in the same position as the attaching creditors, without taking the like proceedings, and upon the like
affidavits ; and this they could not do with a good conscience, and the result would be that a priority would be
gained by the *error* of the attaching creditor : a priority
which it is against good conscience that he should retain.

As to the facts necessary to constitute a debtor an
absconding debtor—the 43rd and 44th sections of the
Common Law Procedure Act are not quite consistent.
By the former, the debtor must depart from Upper
Canada with intent to defraud his creditors, but by the

latter section, attachments may issue upon its being shewn that he has departed with intent to defraud the plaintiff of his just dues, or to avoid being arrested or served with process : in the Consolidated Statutes the same discrepancy is continued.

I have carefully read the evidence, and am convinced that *Baker* did not leave Upper Canada either to defraud his creditors, or the Commercial Bank, or to avoid being arrested or served with process: but in good faith in order to procure moneys to pay his creditors, and among these the Commercial Bank.

I will refer to some of the prominent circumstances that lead to this conclusion. His leaving the mortgages to the Montreal and Commercial Banks, to be handed to them for their security, in the event of his failing to procure money on this side of the Atlantic; and which I have no doubt he *intended* to be valid and effectual, as in my judgment this one was, and the other would have been, if accepted. His directions to Mr. *Collis*, his Montreal agent, to apply the proceeds of consignments to meet the notes accruing due. His efforts at Montreal, Quebec, and Halifax, and in England, to raise money to pay his debts. His leaving not by stealth, but openly, and with a true object declared. His making provision for the conduct of his business during a temporary absence, with a view of resuming it upon his return, and its actual resumption and continuance as before, after his return.

If it were necessary to determine that the attachment was sued out upon affidavits made without sufficient reason for believing *Baker* to be an absconding debtor, and in the face of facts known to the bank agent, which ought to have lead to a different conclusion, I think I should have been prepared so to determine. The bank agent had been to Stirling on the 15th or 16th, and had seen *Lavis*, and the state in which *Baker* had left his business, and had been offered the mortgage before he made the affidavit for the attachment. Indeed it would apppear that the immediate motive for taking out the attachment was not so much to secure the estate of the debtor for the bank and other creditors, as thereby to obtain priority over the Montreal Bank. What took place on the evening of the 18th is evidence of this; when the bank agent and bank solicitor pressed it upon *Lavis* to keep the mortgage to the Montreal Bank in his hands till at least ten o'clock the following day, their object being in the meantime to lodge an attachment, with a view to obtaining priority. Upon the question of priority, therefore, between the Commercial Bank and *Rigney & Brown*, my opinion is, that the latter in respect to their mortgage are entitled to priority.

COLDWELL v. HALL.

Mortgage—Redemption—Annual rests—Wilful default.

In taking the accounts in the master's office it is improper to charge a mortgagee in possession with annual rests on rents received by him until he is paid off in full.

The Statute of Limitations forms no bar to a claim against a mortgagee in possession for occupation rent.

The principle upon which a mortgagee is liable to be charged with rents not actually received considered.

This was a redemption suit, and the usual accounts had been ordered to be taken before the master, who had made his report, from which the defendants appealed, on the grounds stated in the judgment.

Mr. *Cattanach*, for the defendants.

Mr. *Hodgins*, contra.

Judgment.—VANKOUGHNET, C.—This is an appeal by the defendants from the master's report, on the following grounds :

1. That the account was improperly taken against them with annual rests.

2. That the master improperly charged defendants with an occupation rent from October, 1839, to February, 1849, and that upon the evidence the amount or amounts only which the defendants actually received should be charged against them.

3. That the master improperly disallowed the claim of the defendants for proper and necessary repairs.

4. That from February, 1849, to November, 1855, the defendants should not have been charged with any more rent than was shewn, to have been received by them.

5th. That the master improperly charged defendants with an occupation rent since the year 1855, when he should have charged only the amounts actually received; and

6. That under any circumstances the master improperly charged the defendants with more than six years' arrears of rent.

It seems that the mortgagee of the premises, *Maxwell*, whose assignee defendant *Hall* is, went into possession of the premises under process in ejectment, in 1839; the master has assumed the time to be about the 1st of October, the evidence of *Maxwell*, and of the defendants, and of the plaintiffs, seems to establish this. The principal and interest were then in arrear and unpaid; there were one brick and three or four small tenements on the premises at the time, some, if not all, under rental.

The master has taken the account against the defendants with rests: this is wrong, for I take it to be the settled practice of the court, up to this time at all events, that when a mortgagee enters, his money being in arrear, he is not liable to account for the rents received by, or chargeable against him with rests, until he is paid off in full.

In this respect, then, the master's report must be corrected, and the account will be taken in the ordinary way, allowing the mortgagee his principal and interest until sufficient rents have been charged against him to pay off the amount due him; when that has been done he must account for the rents annually chargeable against him, with interest on each sum from the time it is so chargeable, as a mortgagee paid off is but a bare trustee of the estate for the mortgagor and should not continue to hold it, or, if he does, he must pay interest on the rental properly coming from it to the mortgagor. *Quarrell* v. *Beckford* (a), *Smith* v. *Pilkington* (b).

There are two modes in which a mortgagee in possession may be charged with rents; one is with rents actually received, or which but for wilful neglect and default might have been received; the other is with an occupation rent. This latter mode is only adopted, as I understand the law, when the mortgagee is in the actual occupation of the land, using and enjoying it in the place of a tenant, and then he is charged with such fair rental as a tenant might reasonably be expected to give for it, unless it can be shewn that he made a larger profit (c).

In this case, until after the fire of 1849, I do not find any clear evidence that either *Maxwell* or *Hall* was ever in the actual occupation of any portion of the premises. One witness does speak of the defendant having occupied for a short space some portion of the premises, but which portion, or for how long, I do not make out; and if it is right to charge him with an occupation rent during this time, better evidence should be furnished. Then after the fire the defendant appears to have occupied the stable and perhaps the vacant ground at times; and in the face of the evidence of *Edward Brown*, I cannot say that the occupation rent charged by the master is too high. *Brown's* evidence is unimpeached; and, if it was desired to afford to the

---

(a) 1 Madd. 269.   (b) 1 DeG. F. & J., 120.
(c) Truelock v. Roby, 18 Sim. 265 S. C. 2 Phill. 395.

master some other guide to the value, evidence for that purpose should have been furnished.   Nine pounds appears to me a high rental, but I do not feel as competent to judge of that as a master, who had the parties and witnesses before him.

It is urged that the master could not charge more than six years arrears of occupation rent, and that the Statute of Limitations (a) applies as a bar to a longer period. I do not find that the statute has ever been considered as applying to such a charge.   The defendant does not contend he is not bound to account for the rents received by him for more than six years before the institution of the suit, and why should his liability under the occupation rent be more restricted.   He is charged with an occupation rent, as or in lieu of so much received from the profits of the land, and fairly payable by him in account. In the one case he is charged with the rents actually received by him; in the other with the profits derived from the land, or with a rental in lieu of them, both equally applicable to paying off the mortgage debt, and both equally belonging to the mortgagor, after the payment of that debt.   This is not an action to recover rents, nor to enforce or recover anything chargeable on land merely as a charge.   It is an action for an account between the parties, and for payment by one to the other of what may be due, and in the taking of that account is necessarily involved the receipts by the mortgagee.   So soon as the mortgage debt was discharged, the mortgagee, as I have already said, became a bare trustee for the mortgagor, and as such, liable to him for anything he received from or out of the property, and I think as against that liability he cannot set up the limitation of six years to the account.   *Phillipo* v. *Munnings*, (b) *Gough* v. *Bult*, (c) *Hood* v *Easton*. (d)

Then as regards the rents and profits received

(a) Con. Stat. U. C., ch. 86, secs. 19 & 31.
(b) 2 M. & C. 309.   (c) 16 Sim. 323.
(d) 2 Jur. N. S. 729.

by the defendants, or which without the wilful default of either might have been received. I am not certain whether the master means to find that upon the whole evidence, he thinks, and therefore adjudges, that at least six dollars per month was received from the time *Maxwell* entered into possession up to the time of the fire, or but for wilful default might have been received; or whether the master has charged it as an occupation rent. I have already explained when an occupation rent may be charged; and it would therefore not be proper during this period, unless indeed for a brief time, so far as I can gather from the evidence. How then has the master arrived at the conclusion that six dollars per month has been received, or but for wilful default might have been received during the whole of that period?

If the master has satisfied himself it was received well and good. If he merely thinks that the defendant might have received it, then upon what consideration does he base this finding. It is not merely that the premises, if tenants could have been found for them during all that period, would have fetched the rental that would justify charging it against the defendants. The mortgagee in possession is not bound to procure tenants at all hazards, or pay the rent himself if the premises be vacant; neither is he bound to hunt up tenants, or do more than any prudent owner of property would do who had tenements to let. He should always be ready to let them if a tenant offers himself, and may be expected to use such ordinary means as any owner of property adopts to make it known that these are for lease; but he is not expected to consume his time in searching out lessees. He should not be indifferent, and thus keep the premises, as it were, out of view and notice, for such conduct would render him liable to a charge of negligence, and so of wilful default. *Hughes* v. *Williams* (a) *Wragg* v. *Denham*. (b)

(a) 12 Ves. 493. (b) 2 Y. & C. 117

Now in this case the property consisted of several small tenements poorly constructed, and only fitted for the humbler classes. Tenants, it seems, were constantly moving in and out. Sometimes the houses were all let, sometimes not. It was evidently a troublesome property to manage, and I do not see any thing on the evidence to shew that it was the fault of the defendant that the premises were at times vacant, or not entirely tenanted.

It is very difficult, if not impossible, to ascertain what rents the defendant and his assignor actually did receive, and for this they are to blame and must suffer, if in endeavouring to arrive as nearly as possible at the amount, they should really be charged with too much; for had they, as they should have done, kept accurate accounts of all that had been received, and from whom, the difficulty would have been avoided. If their accounts were questioned the parties named as having paid the rents could have been referred to, and some thing like accuracy secured. The account brought into the master's office by the defendant *Hall* is manifestly erroneous. If the master means that in his judgment six dollars per month is a fair average of the rents received year by year, I do not know that I should find fault with it. On matters of fact decided by the master who has had the witnesses and the parties before him, and especially on such a body of evidence as was given in this case, I should differ from the master with great hesitation, and only when I saw he had clearly fallen into error. There is much evidence to lead to the conclusion that during some months much more than six dollars per month was received, but whether the master has arrived at this by calculation upon the whole amount received year by year I cannot tell.

As regards the taxes, no interest should be allowed on them from the time that the rental paid off the arrears of interest or taxes, nor in any year in which the rents were sufficient to pay the accruing interest and taxes; and when insufficient, then only up to such time as the rents would cover the deficiency. With these observations upon the law and the facts, the case will go back to the master for his re-consideration.

DRAKE v. THE BANK OF TORONTO.

Pleading—Usury—Bank directors and managers—Trustees, &c.

The rule of the court that a person seeking to impeach a security on the ground of usury, must offer to pay the amount actually advanced and interest, applies equally to the assignee of the debtor, although ignorant of the terms on which the security was effected.

The plaintiff in a bill to impeach a security held by an incorporated bank, stated that the notes held by the bank, and respect of which the bank claimed a lien under their charter upon certain stock, had been "discounted for the said G., R. & H. upon an illegal and corrupt agreement, whereby and by reason whereof the said bank should and did receive from G., R. & H. upon the discount of the said promissory notes a much larger and greater rate of interest than at the rate of 7 per cent. per annum, and that it was only through and by reason of such discount upon such illegal and usurious consideration that the said bank became and now is holder of the said promissory notes." *Held*, a sufficient allegation of the usury as between a stranger and a party to the transaction to let in the evidence of the usury.

Semble.—The directors and managers of incorporated banks are *quasi* trustees for the general body of stockholders, and if any loss should accrue to the bank by their infringing the statute against usury, they would be liable individually to make good the loss to the bank.

Statement.—The bill in this case was filed by *Elijah Drake* and *William Henry Bull*, against the *Bank of Toronto*, *William B. Phipps*, *Frederick W. Jarvis*, sheriff of York and Peel, and *Henry A. Joseph*, setting forth that about the 17th of November, 1860, *Bull*, acting on behalf of his co-plaintiff, received for a valuable consideration from the co-partnership firm of *Gillyatt, Robinson & Hall*, carrying on business in Toronto, their promissory note for $1500, payable at 27 days after date, to *Drake*, or order; and that by way of securing this as well as other notes, the firm deposited with *Bull* a certificate of stock or scrip of the Bank of Toronto, for twenty shares of the capital thereof, of $2000 value, and which stock had been fully paid up, accompanied by a memorandum in the words following:

"We have this day deposited with *Elijah Drake* the

annexed, Bank of Toronto scrip, for twenty shares of the capital stock of said Bank of Toronto, amounting to $2000, as security for the payment of our note this day given, for $1500, 27 days after date, with full authority to sell said shares of said stock at public or private sale, on the non-payment at maturity of our aforesaid note, and in case said shares of said stock shall not bring sufficient to pay said note, we agree to pay whatever sum may be remaining due after said sale, and we have this day appointed *H. R. Forbes* our attorney, to transfer said shares of said stock. Said *Elijah Drake* is further authorised to hold said shares of said stock as security for any notes, obligations, or indebtedness of ours, either as makers or endorsers, given to or held by him, or to *W. H. Bull*, or to *W. H. Bull & Co.*, and in case of non-payment thereof to sell and transfer at his option said shares of said stock."

And at the same time the firm delivered to *Bull* the power of attorney to said *Forbes* therein referred to ; that *Bull* on the 20th of November became the holder of another note of the firm for $800, payable in 12 days after date ; which not being paid at maturity, *Bull* requested *Forbes* to transfer the stock to *Drake* or *Bull*, in order to perfecting their security, but that the bank, acting through their cashier or manager, refused to allow such transfer to be effected, alleging as grounds for such refusal, that the power of attorney to *Forbes* was executed by *Gillyatt, Robinson & Hall* in their partnership name, and not by the partners individually, although such stock stood in their partnership name and style of *Gillyatt, Robinson & Hall*. Also, that the firm were liable to the bank as endorsers of promissory notes endorsed by, and by the bank discounted for the firm, which were then current, and in respect of which the bank under its charter claimed to hold a lien or security on such stock.

The bill further alleged that the plaintiffs had been informed that the promissory notes so held by the bank, and in respect of which they set up such lien on the stock had been discounted by the bank upon an usurious consideration, and in contravention of the statute in that behalf. The bill then enumerated five notes so held by the bank, amounting in all to $2391.91, all payable to the order of the firm, and endorsed by them, which said notes the plaintiffs alleged were by "The Bank of Toronto discounted for the said *Gillyatt, Robinson, & Hall,* upon an illegal and corrupt agreement, whereby and by means whereof the said bank should and did receive from *Gillyatt, Robinson, & Hall,* upon the discount of the said promissory notes, a much higher and greater rate of interest than at the rate of 7 per cent. per annum, and that it was only through and by reason of such discount upon such illegal and usurious consideration that the said bank became and now is the holder of the said promissory notes;" and charged that the notes in the hands of the bank were utterly void, and in respect thereof the bank had no lien or claim upon the stock.

It appeared that *Gillyatt, Robinson, & Hall* had made an assignment in trust for the benefit of creditors, to the defendant *Joseph,* and that *Phipps* had recovered judgment against the firm, and sued out execution thereon, which he had placed in the hands of the defendant *Jarvis* as such sheriff, and under which it was alleged he was about to proceed to sell the stock in question.

The bill, amongst other things, prayed, that under the circumstances, the plaintiffs might be declared entitled to the stock in preference to the bank ; that the bank might be ordered to suffer a transfer thereof to be made, or that a sale thereof might be made, and the proceeds applied in payment of plaintiffs, in preference to the bank.

The bank answered the bill, denying all knowledge of the transactions in question, and that the notes were discounted on usurious consideration, and submitted "that the pretended usury is so vaguely, generally, and indifferently pleaded and alleged in the bill that the plaintiffs are not entitled to give any evidence thereof."

The cause having been put at issue, was set down for the examination of witnesses before the court. In the course of the examination of the witness *Robinson*, a question was put for the purpose of obtaining an answer establishing the usury alleged in the bill, when it was objected by

Mr. *Strong*, for the *Bank of Toronto*.—That under the statements in the bill the plaintiffs were not at liberty to prove the fact of usury, it not having been alleged with sufficient certainty as to time, the amount of money lent and foreborne, and the amount of the excess of interest charged. The rule, he contended, being, that these facts must be alleged and proved with as much distinctness in this court as in a court of law. The allegation, as it stands, is a mere general allegation of usury, this, as in the case of a general charge of fraud, is insufficient, as the defendants are in reality ignorant of the case to be made, and are unprepared to meet it.

Mr. *A. Crooks*, for the plaintiffs.—The statements in the bill follow substantially the words of the act, (*a*) which is sufficient; the particularity insisted on by the other side, is only required where the parties to the transaction are themselves the litigants, not where the objection is taken by strangers.

Willes on pleading, page 172; *Bond* v. *Bell*, (*b*) *Mansfield* v. *Ogle*, (*c*) *Thibault q. t.* v. *Gibson*, (*d*) *James* v. *Rice*, (*e*) were amongst other cases referred to.

The court having taken time to look into the authorities, on a subsequent day——

(*a*) 22 Vic., ch. 58.   (*b*) 4 Drew. 157.
(*c*) 7 D. M. & G. 181.   (*d*) 12 M. & W. 88.
(*e*) 1 Kay, 231.

ESTEN, V. C.—I think as between a stranger and a party to the transaction the usury is stated with sufficient particularity, and that the evidence ought to be received.

Afterwards the evidence was proceeded with, the principal witnesses being *Robinson*, and the manager of the bank. *Robinson*, in his evidence, after enumerating several notes discounted by his firm at the bank, and the amount of discount charged on each, stated that the bank still held one of these notes, that the funds of the note were placed to his credit by the bank, the rest having been retired; that the proceeds were placed to his credit by the bank. With a portion of them he purchased a draft on New York for $1000, from the bank, at 1 per cent. premium; that he had no occasion to purchase the draft—did not desire to remit funds to New York—that he believed Mr. *Cameron*, the cashier, was aware of this fact. Mr. *Cameron* always told him that it did not pay them to discount at 7 per cent; that they would not do so. It was thoroughly understood between Mr. *Cameron* and him that he should take drafts on New York, or Montreal, on the discount of bills or notes, and the draft in question was taken in pursuance of the general understanding. "When I presented bills for discount at the bank Mr. *Cameron* frequently told me that it did not pay them to discount at 7 per cent." Mr. *Cameron* stated this frequently, but that it came to be understood between them that the firm should take drafts on discounts; it was commonly done, Mr. *Cameron* always reminding witness that he must take drafts on his applying for discounts. Mr. *Cameron* instructed the book-keeper what premium to charge; had no voice in fixing the rate of exchange. When the discount in question took place the understanding had been thoroughly established, and the draft was taken in pursuance of the general course of dealing. Sometimes these drafts were re-deposited at par, sometimes he sold them on the street. The witness further stated that on the 17th of October, 1860, the firm obtained a discount

from the bank, the proceeds of which, $1483.40, were
placed to their credit, with which proceeds they purchased a draft on Montreal for $1500, for which they
paid ¾ per cent. premium, viz., $11.85, the ordinary
rate of exchange on Montreal about that time at the
bank being ¼ per cent. as witness knew, from having
purchased drafts for cash at about the same time. That
on the 31st of October, 1860, they obtained a discount
from the bank, and with the proceeds purchased a
draft on Montreal for $1600, at ¾ per cent., which wit-
ness believed he re-deposited at par on the same day,
on which day there was a large amount at the credit
of the witness; about the same time the witness believed he purchased drafts from the bank at ¼ per cent.
premium. This witness stated other transactions much
to the same effect, and during all this time the firm
had purchased drafts from the bank on New York and
Montreal, as they needed them for cash at ½ per cent.
on New York, and ¼ per cent. on Montreal.

The manager of the bank in his evidence swore, that
one of the directors stated to him and the president of
the bank that *Gillyatt, Robinson, & Hall* had large
transactions in the States, and would require in the
course of their business a large amount of New York
funds, and on this representation agreed to take their
account and paper that would be satisfactory; that
Robinson confirmed this statement afterwards, and
stated to witness that they would require a large amount
of New York funds to pay for their purchases in Boston;
that this was the inducement to taking their account.
He denied any arrangement with *Robinson* or his firm
that they should take drafts on New York or Montreal,
on discounts, otherwise than the bank understood they
would require drafts on New York and Montreal in the
conduct of their business; that the rate of exchange on
those cities is regulated by the supply and demand; that
there is no fixed rate—it varies sometimes daily. The
banks charge different rates constantly in the day;

that *Robinson* was generally charged ¾ per cent. for
drafts on Montreal, although all the customers of the
bank were not charged that rate ; the rate charged each
individual depending entirely upon the nature and state
of his account; that the bank had different rates for
different parties ; a stranger buying would be charged
the rate marked on the counter, which is so marked for
the day ; sometimes for the hour. A customer requiring heavy discounts might be charged a higher or lower
rate than marked on the counter, according to the
state of his account. The other evidence materially
bearing on the case is stated in the judgment.

At the hearing of the cause,

Mr. *A. Crooks* and Mr. *Blake*, for the plaintiffs.

The error into which the other side has fallen, is in
treating this suit as one for redemption, this it clearly is
not, but simply one to compel the perfecting of the title
of the plaintiffs to the bank stock held by them as
security. The rule that a mortgagor in coming to impeach a mortgage for usury, is bound to tender the
principal sum advanced and legal interest, does not
apply when the same relief is sought by a second mortgagee. *Belcher* v. *Vardon*, (a) *Fitch* v. *Rockport*, (b)
Cole v. *Savage*. (c)

As to the fact of the usury having been committed, it
is not necessary to prove a direct contract or agreement;
that in many instances could never be proved. When
parties contemplate entering into such an agreement
some devise or cloak is invariably resorted to, and the
question for the court to decide is, whether a jury, looking at all the circumstances of the case, would or not say
that usury was intended. By the statute the bank
cannot take a higher rate of premium for its drafts when

(a) 2 Coll. 162.   (b) 1 McN. & G. 184.
(c) 10 Page, 583.

a discount is required to purchase than when cash is
paid—this would clearly be in violation of their charter,
and the act is equally violated by their requiring a draft
to be taken when not wanted by the party, as when a
draft is wanted, by their demanding a rate higher than
that usually asked. When goods were furnished in
whole or part the onus of proving that the goods
were sold at the market value was upon the lender,
here drafts were taken by the firm which they did not
require at an increased premium; in other words, goods
were sold to them above their market value.

Harris v. *Boston*, (a) *Lowe* v. *Waller*, (b) *Pratt* v.
Wiley, (c) *Harrison* v. *Hannel*. (d)

Mr. *Mowat*, Q. C., and Mr. *Strong*.—The rule with
respect to the necessity for a party seeking to impeach
a security on the grounds of usury tendering the amount
of principal and legal interest is greatly strengthened by
the recent alteration of the law regarding usury, for if
that rule prevailed at a time when usury was viewed with
so much disfavour, still more will such a rule be upheld
and allowed to prevail now that the law has been so
much relaxed ; and here it is contended that the bank
has a lien, and it is immaterial how that lien is created,
whether by law or act of the parties, the same rules will
apply. The *Upper Canada Building Society* v. *Rowell*, (e)
Commercial Bank v. *Cameron*, (f) shew that the courts
will take into account the fact of the relaxation of the
usury laws, although in strictness it might be thought
that the particular transaction might have been an
evasion of the law.

The evidence in the case does not establish that when
the particular discounts now impeached were made, the
firm should take drafts for the proceeds of such dis-

(a) 2 Camp. 348.

(c) 1 Esp. 40

(e) 19 U. C. Q. B. 124.

(b) 2 Doug. 736.

(d) 5 Taunt. 780.

(f) 9 U. C. C. P. 378.

counts.; it was never made a condition of their obtaining a discount, that drafts should be purchased by them, nor was any agreement made that they should pay more than the current rate of premium, nor that a draft should be taken when not required by the parties. The evidence shews that the drafts purchased were not for the same amounts as the discounts, and not purchased on the same day.

It was also objected that this court had not the power to compel the bank to allow the transfer to be made ; the proper proceeding being by mandamus.

Judgment.—ESTEN, V. C.—The facts of this case are, that a mercantile firm of *Gillyat, Robinsan & Hall*, being indebted to the plaintiffs on a promissory note for $1500, deposited with them scrip for 20 shares of the capital stock of the Bank of Toronto, belonging to them, as collateral security for that note, and any other note or debt which they might owe to the plaintiff *Drake*, or to *Henry Bull*, or *Henry Bull & Company*, and delivered to the plaintiff a power of attorney to one *Forbes*, signed with the partnership name, authorising him to transfer the stock in the books of the bank into the name of the plaintiff so soon as default should be made in payment of any of the debts for which it was to be held as security. *Henry Bull* afterwards became possessed of a note for $800, on which *Gillyatt, Robinson & Hall* were liable, and default being made in payment of this note, and afterwards of the note for $1500, the defendant, the Bank of Toronto, which is a corporate body, established for the purpose of conducting the business of bankers, was required to permit a transfer to be made of the stock in question in its books into the name of the plaintiffs, which it refused, on the ground, first, that the power of attorney was null and void, being signed only with the partnership name ; and second, that *Gillyatt, Robinson & Hall* were indebted to them on several promissory notes of third parties, endorsed by the firm, and discounted for them

by the defendants, and that the defendants had a lien
on the stock in question for this indebtedness by virtue
of the 21st clause· of the act by which the bank was
, established.   Meanwhile *Gillyatt, Robinson & Hall*
had made·an assignment of all·their property to the
defendant *H. A. Joseph*, upon the usual trusts, for the
benefit of their creditors; after which, however, the creditors accepted a composition, and released their debts,
the composition being secured or guaranteed by Mr.
Joseph, who thereupon became·entitled to the estate for
his own benefit, and *Gillyatt, Robinson & Hall* have
no longer any interest in it.   Pending these proceedings
Mr. *Joseph* applied to the bank to renew in part a note
of one *Vandell*,· being·one of ·the notes upon ;which
Gillyatt, Robinson & Hall were endorsers, as before
mentioned,· telling·them· that if that course·was not
adopted *Vandell* would·fail,·and his note would become
a,loss, and offering,·if the bank would comply·with his
proposal, to guarantee the payment of the rest of· the
paper, held by the bank, of *Gillyatt, Robinson & Hall*,
which offer the bank declined, declaring that they relied
on their lien on the stock, and were indifferent·as to the
payment of the notes.   The plaintiffs, upon learning the
claim advanced by ·the bank, applied through their
attorney Mr. *Boyd*, to pay to the bank what was due
upon the notes, upon having the notes delivered to him,
and the stock transferred into their name; but the bank
refused to accept this offer; and thereupon the present
suit was instituted, in which in addition to the facts
before stated the plaintiffs insist that the notes held by
the bank, and for which they claim a lien on the stock,
were discounted by them upon an usurious contract;
that consequently no indebtedness existed to them on
the part of *Gillyatt, Robinson & Hall*, and they had no
lien on the stock in question, which it was their duty to
allow to be transferred as requested, and praying that
they might be declared entitled to the stock in preference to the bank, and that the bank might be ordered
to permit a transfer of it to be made into the name of

the plaintiffs; or that a sale might be made of it, and the plaintiffs paid their debt in preference to the bank; or in case of any loss, that the bank should make it good, or that the plaintiffs might be allowed to redeem the stock, and the notes, or that they should be marshalled, or that if any loss should have happened on the notes by reason of the refusal of the bank to deliver them to the plaintiffs, that the bank should make it good.

It should be mentioned that the bill contains a sort of minor case against another defendant of the name of *Phipps* who had obtained judgment against *Gillyatt, Robinson & Hall*, and had threatened to proceed to a sale of the stock under execution, and the bill prays that he may be restrained from so acting. The defendants, the Bank of Toronto, answered the bill, denying the alleged usury, but insisting that the plaintiffs must at all events pay what was really advanced, with legal interest, and relying upon their lien on the stock. The bill was taken *pro confesso* against *Phipps*.

The sheriff of York and Peel is also a party to the bill, and *H. A. Joseph*, the assignee of *Gillyatt, Robinson & Hall*, as interested in the equity of redemption of the stock and notes. Evidence was entered into on both sides, and the case was argued fully with much ability. The first point discussed was whether, supposing the transaction to be usurious, the plaintiffs were bound, as a condition of obtaining relief from this court, to tender the principal sum advanced and legal interest. It was contended that the bank had no lien on shares of stock for any debt due to it from the holder of them, under any circumstances; that when the debt or liability claimed by it against such holder, was tainted with usury and void, the bank could not prevent a transfer of the shares; that the equitable doctrine respecting the payment of the sum really advanced, and legal interest, did not extend to a subsequent incumbrancer or purchaser from the mortgagor, and that the bill did not in the first place pray redemption, but sought to compel the performance of a duty incumbent on the bank. The 21st clause of the act was certainly intended to give to the bank a sort of security on the shares of its stock held by its debtors, for the amount of their debts. No transfer can be made until all debts are paid. This must be intended as a security. The mere retention of the stock until payment operated as security; and I apprehend that the dividends accruing in the meantime can be applied by way of set-off in satisfaction of the debt. On the final arrangement of the affairs of the bank all debts would be deducted from the stock before its avails would be paid to the holder. If, in addition to these rights, the stock is to be considered as the property of the debtor, so that the bank could proceed to a sale under execution upon a judgment obtained against him, in preference to all intermediate sales and dispositions either by the owner or under legal process, the security is greatly augmented. But under any circumstances it is a security of considerable importance, and whether it is created by the act of the party or the operation of law can be of no importance to the application of the equitable doctrine which has been mentioned. It is said, however, that where there is no legal debt there is no security. But the same remark is applicable to an usurious mortgage. If the mortgage were tainted with usury it was a nullity. No estate passed to the mortgagee; the mortgage-deed was a mere piece of paper: no debt existed. The court, however, would not lend its aid to destroy it, but upon terms which it considered equitable. So in the present case, to compel a transfer of the stock would be to annihilate the security, and if the aid of the court be wanted for that purpose, it must as appears to me be on the same terms. Such would be my judgment if the relief were sought by *Gillyatt, Robinson & Hall:* but it can make no difference that the party seeking relief is not the mortgagor, but an incumbrancer claiming under him. How can he stand in a better position than the person under 'whom he claims ? at all events as a plaintiff seeking relief.

I have examined all the cases cited · by Mr. *Crooks*, and they all appear to me to recognize the doctrine in question, and no distinction is made between the mortgagor and a purchaser or incumbrancer claiming under him. Even the case of *Belcher* v. *Vardon*, recognizes the doctrine ; if it had not, relief would have been given without even proving the debt under the fiat. The case in 10 *Paige* (*a*) recognizes the doctrine expressly; and the case in 1 *Johnson* (*b*) in effect; the case of Lord *Mansfield* v. *Ogle* is distinguishable, and so are the cases in bankruptcy. My opinion, therefore, is, that if the aid of this court is required to destroy this security, whatever it may be, and however imperfect it may be, it must be upon the terms of paying to the bank what they would have been entitled to receive upon a legitimate discount of the notes in question, supposing the actual transaction occurred to have deviated from that standard.

This consideration introduces the second question, whether the transaction in question was not in fact usurious; which, however, in·consequence of my determination on the·first point, becomes of little practical importance. My sole concern is with the four transactions which form the subject of this suit ; and which occurred respectively on the 26th of September, the 17th of October, the 31st of October, and the 16th of November, 1860. The three first transactions involved purchases of drafts on New York and Montreal respectively, and the usury imputed to them consists in an alleged charge of one-half per cent. for these drafts respectively over and above the market price prevailing at the times of the respective purchases ; three-fourths per cent. being charged for the drafts on Montreal, the market price being one-fourth per cent.; and one per

---

(*a*) Cole v. Savage.   (*b*) Rogers v. Rathbun, 1 J. C. C. 367.

cent. being charged for the drafts on New York, the market price being one-half per cent. I have no doubt that if upon a discount of bills or notes the borrower should be paid wholly or in part with a draft charged at a rate beyond the market price for cash at the time, it would be usury. .

The cases reported in 2 *Campbell*, 348, and 375, and other cases of that class place this beyond doubt. A bank choosing to discount paper receives the rate of interest allowed by law, which must be deemed a sufficient remuneration, and exercises care in securing responsible endorsers, so as to guard against all risk, and must pay cash, or what is equivalent to cash, to the borrower. It may pay wholly or in part in a draft, but it must be at the market price of the day, for cash, and any departure from this rule would be usury. If the market price only were charged, it would not seem to render the transaction objectionable that the borrower did not require a draft, and that it was in a measure for cedon him, provided the sale was upon such terms that he could realize what he paid upon a re-sale. The question is, whether upon the three transactions I have mentioned the purchase of drafts was upon terms exceeding the market price for cash prevailing on the days on which they occurred respectively. The evidence on the subject is that of Messrs. *Cassels*, *Robinson*, and *Cameron*. Mr. *Cassels* proves that during a period embracing the times of these purchases, the rates of exchange on Montreal and New York respectively were one-half and one-quarter per cent. He says, however, that no agreement existed amongst the banks on the subject, but that for the most part the larger banks adopted the same rate. He shews, however, that at one time when the bank of which he is manager was charging one per cent. for drafts on New York, the Bank of Upper Canada was charging one-half per cent., adding that he believed a particular reason existed for it. *Robinson* states in his evidence that it

was an understood thing between him and Mr. *Cameron*,
that upon every discount obtained by his firm from the
bank, a draft should be purchased on New York or
Montreal ; that Mr. *Cameron* fixed the rate without consulting him, or allowing him a voice in the matter; and
that the rates charged upon discounts were three-fourths
per cent. for drafts on Montreal, and one per cent. for
drafts on New York ; that during the six months ending
on the 31st of October, 1860, his firm obtained discounts
to the amount of $22,000 and upwards, and purchased
drafts on Montreal and New York to the amount of
over $23,000 at the respective rates of three-fourths
and one per cent., while during the same period they
purchased drafts to a large amount, for cash, on the same
places, at the respective rates of one-quarter and one-
half per cent.; that Mr. *Cameron* frequently said to him
that it did not remunerate them to discount at 7 per
cent. ; that it came to be understood that whenever he
obtained a discount he must purchase a draft ; that this
understanding was thoroughly established at the time of
the transactions in question ; that he purchased a draft
on New York at one per cent. in connexion with the
discount which occurred on the 26th of September, and
re-sold it on the street at par ; that this was in pursuance of the understanding in question: that he purchased
drafts on the 17th and 31st of October, at the rate of
three-fourths per cent. on Montreal, and one per cent.
on New York out of the proceeds of discounts which occurred on those days respectively. Mr. *Cameron* in his
evidence stated that there was no fixed rate of exchange
on Montreal or New York ; that it varied from day to
day, and from hour to hour; that it was regulated by
circumstances, amongst which he instanced the state
of their funds at the places on which they drew at the
time ; the state of the account of the party with whom
they were dealing ; the nature of the funds in which they
were paid ; that a party purchasing a draft on a discount would be charged a higher rate than a party
paying cash and maintaining a good balance in the bank.

That a rate was always exhibited on the counter for the day, and sometimes for the hour; and that a stranger purchasing exchange for cash would be charged according to this rate.

Mr *Cameron* heard *Robinson's* evidence given, and did not contradict many particulars stated by *Robinson* in his evidence. Upon this whole evidence I should hesitate, if I were on a jury, to affix to these trans- actions the character of usury, whatever suspicion I might entertain. It is possible, consistently with this evidence, that on the days on which these transactions occurred the defendants, the Bank of Toronto, might have charged the same rates for cash as were charged to this firm on these discounts. There is nothing in the evidence to shew that this was not the case. *Robinson* purchased no drafts for cash on those days, nor does he prove any transaction of this nature between the bank and any other person on those days, nor what the cur- rent rates on those days respectively were. It is true that during the six months ending on 31st of October, he purchased in connexion with discounts at the above mentioned rates drafts to a greater amount than he obtained discounts. This fact, however, would not prove that the discounts in question in this cause involved the purchase of drafts at all; much less would it shew that drafts were purchased at more than the current rates. In short it is not shewn that in these transactions drafts were purchased by this firm at more than the cur- rent rates for cash, or that they were forced on them against their will. I dare say some such understanding existed as *Robinson* mentions; but it might exist legally. I dare say also, that *Robinson* purchased the drafts in question in pursuance of this understanding, and perhaps without requiring them; but it may have been done voluntarily, and without the bank being aware that he did not require them, and without their charging him more than the current rates. What I mean is, that the understanding may have been nothing more than this,

namely, that the bank preferred those customers who
required exchange ; that they would not continue the
accounts of those who did not require exchange, although
they would never force a draft upon any one, or charge
more than the current rates ; and it is possible that the
knowledge of this fact may have induced *Robinson* sometimes to purchase drafts when he did not require them,
but of his own accord, and without being required so to
do by the bank. It is possible, consistently with this
evidence, that the transactions in question may have been
legally conducted, and I should not therefore, if I were
on a jury, ascribe the character of usury to them, and I
think I must arrive at the same conclusion acting as a
judge of the law and fact.

The third point discussed was as to the right of the
plaintiff to have these securities marshalled, so that if
the bank exhausted the stock they might stand in its
place *quoad* the promissory notes. I should think the
doctrine would apply to such a case, and that relief of
this sort would be given ; but it appears to be of no
practical importance under the circumstances of the case,
as the plaintiffs must pay the bank what is due to it, and
will then be entitled to a transfer of the stock, and a
delivery of the securities. The bank cannot be compelled
a priori to take its satisfaction out of one fund more than
out of the other, although if the funds should be realized,
it would be thrown upon that which was not common to
both parties. This is what I understand by the doctrine
of marshalling.

The fourth point argued, was, whether the bank should
be charged with the amount of *Vandell's* note, lost, as
is alleged, through their refusal to accept Mr. *Joseph's*
offer ; but the answer to this claim is, that the bank was
not bound to accept that offer, and *Joseph*, if he desired
to preserve *Vandell's* note, should have paid the amount
due to the bank, and dealt with the note as he should
think fit. As to *Phipps*, there is no doubt that he must

be enjoined from selling the stock. He can stand in
no better position than the judgment debtor; and a
decree may be pronounced against him with costs of
this part of the suit. The sheriff seems to me an
unnecessary party, and must have his costs. As to
the main subject of the suit, the usual decree must be
pronounced for redemption and foreclosure or sale.

I may add, that I have been unable to trace the
supposed defect in the fourth discount, occurring on
the 16th of November. With regard to the offer made
through Mr. *Boyd*, if the amount due to the bank had
been actually tendered, and they had refused to receive
it or deliver the securities or transfer the stock, and
thereby rendered a suit necessary, they might have
been charged with the costs of it; but it does not
appear that the money was actually offered to the
bank, and it cannot be doubted that if any such offer
had been made it would have been accepted.

The plaintiffs being dissatisfied with this decision of
his Honour, brought the cause on to be re-heard before
the full court. On the re-hearing.

Mr. *A. Crooks* and Mr. *Blake* again appeared as
counsel for the plaintiffs.

Mr. *Strong*, for the defendants.

After taking time to look into the authorities,

Judgment.—VANKOUGHNET, C.—Although a perusal
of the whole evidence in this cause cannot fail to
impress one with a strong feeling that in the dealings
of this bank with the firm of *Gillyatt, Robinson &
Hall*, an attempt has been made to elude the provisions of the recent statute of this province, pro-
hibiting the taking by any bank of more than seven
per cent. per annum for the loan and forbearance
of money, I do not think the evidence here is of that

clear and conclusive character to warrant relief being granted to the plaintiffs on that ground. When the legislature was repealing the laws restricting the amount of interest to be taken by private persons for the use of money, it saw fit to retain those restrictions in their full force, so far as the banking institutions of the country are concerned; feeling, no doubt, that as there are conceded to those bodies vast and important privileges and advantages in the conduct of their business, they ought to be restricted in the amount of interest they should be permitted to charge; and there can be no doubt as regards them the laws against usury remain in force, and in a proper case will be applied with the utmost rigour. And while on this point, it may be well to direct attention to the position which gentlemen having the control and management of the moneyed institutions of the country occupy; for I have no doubt that should at any time a serious loss be sustained by a bank in consequence of the managers or directors attempting to evade the usury laws, those gentlemen may be held personally bound as trustees for the general body of the stockholder to make good such loss.

In the present case, if the plaintiffs had succeeded in clearly establishing the alleged usury, relief could have been granted to them only on condition of submitting to pay the sum actually advanced, together with legal interest. I think the decree pronounced by my brother *Esten* must be affirmed, and the present re-hearing dismissed with costs, to be taxed by the master.

ESTEN, and SPRAGGE, V.CC., concurred.

SUTHERLAND V. BUCHANAN.

Lessor and lessee—Right of purchaser—Computation of time.

By the terms of a lease it was provided that the lessee should have the
right of purchasing the leasehold property upon his desiring to do
so, " within the period of two years after the date of the commence-
meet of the term," (the 1st of April, 1852.) On the 1st of April,
1854, the desire of purchasing was declared, and a tender of the
purchase money made. *Held*, that the tender was within time, the
day of the commencement of the term (1st of April, 1852) being
exclusive.

Statement.—The bill in this cause was filed by Donald
Sutherland, against William Buchanan, Septimus
Tyrwhitt, Featherstone L. Osler, and Robert Cathcart,
setting forth that in the year 1850 Cathcart was owner
in fee of certain lands in the township of King, and had
contracted with one Tench to sell the same to him, in pursuance whereof Tench entered into possession of the
premises, where he continued some years, when he
agreed with Buchanan to sell the same lands to him for
£1,125, the full value thereof; and for the purpose of
carrying such agreement into effect, Tench executed
an instrument in the form of a lease, to Buchanan, for
a term of years, at a certain rent, and covenanted that
on payment of the purchase money he would convey, or
cause to be conveyed, the said premises in fee; in pursuance whereof Buchanan entered into possession of the
said premises, and cultivated and improved the same as
the owner, and still continued in possession thereof;
that Tyrwhitt and Osler subsequently became possessed
of and entitled to all the estate and interest of Tench in
the premises, subject to such agreement for sale to
Buchanan; and that Buchanan in 1857 being pressed
for payment of a debt of £125, applied to plaintiff to
assist him in paying off the same, in order to prevent his
crops, &c., being sold, the effect of which would be to
disable him from paying the rent reserved by the agreement with Tench, by the terms of which a default in
payment of the rent would work a forfeiture of his right
to obtain a conveyance, to prevent which plaintiff paid
off the debt, and subsequently made advances from time

to time to *Buchanan,* to the amount (in all) of £250,
who on the 30th of July, 1858, conveyed and assigned
all his estate and interest in the said lands and premises
to the plaintiff, and authorized him to take all necessary
steps and proceedings to obtain a conveyance thereof;
and also assigned all his chattel property to plaintiff,
including his crops on the premises; upon the condition
that plaintiff should re-convey the same to *Buchanan*
upon payment by him in six months of the amount of
such advances, which agreement was communicated by
plaintiff to *Tyrwhitt* about one month afterwards, who
answered, that all he and *Osler* required was payment
of the money due to them, upon payment of which they
would cause the land to be conveyed.

The bill also stated, that it was agreed that plaintiff
should advance £600 on account of the purchase money
of the premises—receive a deed thereof from *Cathcart*
and execute a mortgage securing the balance in one and
two years—to which arrangement *Buchanan* assented;
but afterwards objected, and forbade *Tyrwhitt* and *Osler*
from carrying it into effect; whereupon plaintiff offered
to pay down the whole amount due, as well as that due
to them as to *Cathcart,* which offer was declined, and
the claim of plaintiff was treated as invalid; that he
had made several other advances to *Buchanan,* amounting in all to £400, which he would not have made but
for the assurance that his security was good; but that
Buchanan, Tyrwhitt and *Osler* absolutely refused to
carry out the agreement, and *Cathcart* in consequence
refused to make a conveyance of the premises to plaintiff.

The prayer was, that plaintiff might be declared
entitled to hold the said land as a security for the
amount due him by *Buchanan,* and a reference to take
an account of what was due under the said contract for
purchase—plaintiff submitting to pay the same—and
that upon payment, a conveyance might be ordered to
be made to plaintiff, he submitting to execute a proper

instrument, giving *Buchanan* a right to a conveyance on payment of the amount due plaintiff; and what he should be obliged to pay the other defendants; or that the premises might be conveyed to *Buchanan*, and he ordered to execute to plaintiff a mortgage to secure him.

The defendants, *Tyrwhitt*, *Osler*, and *Cathcart*, answered the bill, not varying materially the statements thereof, but objecting that by reason of his transferring his claim, *Buchanan* had forfeited his interest under the lease from *Tench*. The other facts appear clearly in the judgment.

The cause was heard by way of motion for decree.

Mr. *Morphy*, for the plaintiff.

Mr. *Hodgins*, for *Cathcart*.

Mr. *G. D. Boulton*, for defendant *Buchanan*.

Judgment.—SPRAGGE, V. C.—The plaintiff claims as assignee by way of security from *Buchanan* to himself. The title is traced as follows: contract contained in lease, *Cathcart* to *Tench*: The lease dated 25th of June, 1850, for ten years from the 26th of December, in the same year, at £21 a year, with liberty to *Tench* to purchase at any time during the term for £350.

By indenture of 20th of July, 1852, *Tench* leased the premises to *Buchanan* and one *Liddell*, for eight years from the 1st of April, in the same year, with liberty to *Buchanan* to purchase upon his desiring to do so, "within the period of two years after the date of the commencement of the term," *i.e.*, the 1st of April, 1852, for the sum of £1,125.

By deed-poll of the 15th of November, 1852, *Tench*,

in consideration of £650, assigned all his interest in the property to defendants *Tyrwhitt* and *Osler*, as trustees and executors of the will of *Wm. Tyrwhitt*, deceased. The assignment under which the plaintiff claims from *Buchanan*, is dated 30th of July, 1858, and the plaintiff is thereby authorised to take all necessary proceedings for the purpose of obtaining a conveyance of the premises.

The plaintiff rests his claim upon two grounds; first, that *Buchanan* duly exercised his right to purchase within the time prescribed by the agreement with *Tench*. Second, that plaintiff entered into an agreement with *Tyrwhitt* and *Osler* in November, 1859, whereby the right of *Buchanan*, and his assignee, to purchase, was recognised as still subsisting, and terms for the payment of the purchase money were arranged. Upon the first point, the question turns upon whether *Buchanan* was within the time in exercising his right. He made a tender of money, which it is not denied was correct in amount. It is questioned, indeed, whether the tender was made on his behalf, but Mr. *Cameron*, who had acted professionally in making the tender, says that it was. It is not denied that the tender was made to an authorised agent of the parties entitled to receive, that is, *Tyrwhitt* and *Osler*. It is not quite clear from the evidence on what day the tender was made; but the parties seem agreed that it was on the 1st of April, 1854, and that conclusion seems warranted by the evidence.

The question then is, whether the date of the commencement of the term is to be reckoned inclusively or exclusively of the time within which *Buchanan* was privileged to exercise his right. The English cases upon this point are somewhat conflicting, but I think that in this case the first day may be held exclusive without conflicting with any of them.

In the *King* v. *Adderley*, (a) and in *Glassington* v. *Rawlins*, (b) it was held that when time was to be computed from an act done, the day of the act being done was inclusive; the latter case was decided upon the authority of the former, and against the view first taken by Mr. Justice *Lawrence* at *nisi prius*.

In *Ex parte Fallon*, (c) the question arose upon the enrollment of a deed granting an annuity, which by the statute is required to be enrolled within twenty days of its execution. The court held the first day exclusive, and Lord *Ellenborough* said: " Suppose the direction of the act had been to enroll the memorial within one day, after the granting of the annuity, could it be pretended that that meant the same as if it were said that it should be done on the same day on which the act was done."

Lord *Manners*, upon the authority of this last case, held in *Dowling* v. *Foxall*, (d) where a bill was filed to redeem a lease after writ of *habere* executed, that the date of the execution of the *habere* was exclusive.

It may be questioned, perhaps, whether this decision is in accordance with the weight of authority; but when the computation of time is not from an act done, but from a date, where, as in this case, within a certain period after a date, the day of the date will be held exclusive, and that whether the words be after the date, or after the day of the date. In the old case of *Thomas* v. *Popham*, (e) the question arose upon the statute for the enrollment of deeds, which requires the enrollment to be " within six months next after the date of the same indenture." The date of the indenture was held to be exclusive; and Lord *Ellenborough* held the case

---

(a) Doug. 468.

(b) 3 East. 407.

(c) 5 T. R. 283.

(d) 1. B. & B. 193.

(e) Dyer. 218 b.

to be expressly in point in *Watson* v. *Pears*, (a) which was an action on the case for the infringement of a patent. The patent bore date the 10th of May, 1808, and contained the usual proviso that a specification should be enrolled "within one calendar month next and immediately after the date thereof." The specification was enrolled on the 10th of June following. Lord *Ellenborough* held that the day on which the patent bore date was not to be reckoned, and that the month began to run on the following day.

It may be doubted whether even where the computation of time is from the doing of an act, the day of the act being done, or as put by Sir *William Grant*, in *Lester* v. *Garland*, (b) the happening of an event is always to be reckoned. But however that may be, *Thomas* v. *Popham*, and *Watson* v. *Pears*, to which I may add *Puyh* v. The *Duke of Leeds*, (d) are sufficient authority for the decision of this case. The language is almost identical—the meaning manifestly the same. If there is any difference, it is in favour of the instrument in question, for the words "after the date of the commencement of the term," must mean after the day of the date.

There is another ground upon which I apprehend the full two years should be given beyond the date of the commencement of the term, because any other consideration would operate to divest a right, and the rule is, that the construction should be liberal when any other would work a forfeiture or divest a right.

The plaintiff is, of course, entitled to the benefit of this exercise of right to purchase by *Buchanan*, and holding the opinion I do upon that point, it is not necessary that I should go upon the second: upon which I will only observe that no objection appears to have been taken on the score of delay.

(a) 2 Camp. N. P. 294.   (b) 15 Ves. 248.
(d) Cowp. 714.

As to costs, the plaintiff succeeding in his suit, and being entitled to what he asks, is entitled to his costs as against the defendants *Tyrwhitt* and *Osler;* as to the costs of defendant *Cathcart,* he would have been entitled to his costs if he had submitted to convey in pursuance of his contract, but he insists by his answer that the time had expired, and that he is not bound to convey, and that at all events he is entitled to the full value of the land, also rents and interest. If the 10 years had been from the date of the lease, 26th of June, he would have been right, but they are from the 26th of December, six months later. He made the same mistake upon being applied to by Mr. *Boultbee,* on behalf of the plaintiff, but corrected it on referring to his papers. I have no doubt that it was a mistake; but having resisted the plaintiff's right erroneously, I cannot give him his costs. I do not give costs against him, because if that had been the only point in the case, I am satisfied that upon the error being pointed out, Mr. *Cathcart* would have submitted to convey, as he did to Mr. *Boultbee.*

As between the plaintiff and *Buchanan,* the assignment to the plaintiff seems to contemplate a conveyance being made to him. The decree, therefore, should be in the first alternative of the prayer of the bill.

BANK OF MONTREAL v. WOODCOCK.

Judgment creditor—Registration.

Where a bill has been filed prior to the 18th of May, 1861, *all* judgment creditors who had their judgments duly registered, are entitled to be treated as parties to the cause, though not actually named in the bill, and not added as such in the master's office until after that date, without having placed *fi. fas.* against lands in the hands of the sheriff.

This was an appeal from the report of the master of this court at Woodstock, upon the ground that he had refused to allow the claim of a judgment creditor.

Mr. *Burton,* for the appellant.

Mr. *Leys*, for subsequent incumbrancers; contended that the appellant had no right to prove, he having omitted to sue out a *fi. fa.* against lands, as had been done by the other judgment creditors.

Mr. *Barrett*, for the plaintiffs.

Judgment.—ESTEN, V. C.—This is an appeal by a judgment creditor, whose claim has been disallowed by the master under the circumstances: the suit which is for foreclosure or sale was pending on the 18th of May, 1861, the judgment in question was registered in December, 1858. The appellant was added as a party in the master's office, and proved his claim in October, 1861, but it was rejected by the master, and excluded from his report, on the ground that at the date of it more than three years had elapsed since the registration of the judgment, and that it had not been re-registered. The appeal is on the ground that the claim ought to have been allowed, and I am of that opinion. It has been decided in this court that the effect of the 11th section of 54 Vic., ch. 41, is to preserve the charge created by a judgment registered before the 18th of May, 1861, the owner of which would be a proper party to a suit pending on that day. The charge created by this judgment was therefore preserved; and it could not be re-registered, because the 64th section of the 22 Vic., ch. 89, which provides for the re-registration of judgments was repealed by the 24 Vic., ch. 41. The charge of the judgment in question was created by its previous registration, this charge is preserved generally; the provision that it should cease at the expiration of three years without re-registration was repealed. The legislature could not have meant that the rights which it had saved should expire for want of an act which it had rendered impossible. It was ingeniously and plausibly argued, that the only effect of the 11th section of 24 Vic., ch. 41, was to leave the rights of judgment creditors, parties to suits pending on the 18th of May, 1861, in precisely the

same state in which they would have been if that act
had not passed, and as in that case the charge created
by such judgment creditor's judgment would have'expired upon the expiration of *three* years without re-
registration, the same result must follow under the 11th
section of 24 Vic., ch. 41.   If this view is correct it
must equally follow that 'this section also provided for
the re-registration of judgments, but as this cannot be
seriously, and was not in fact, contended, I think the
proposed construction of this section incorrect.   ·I rather think the intention of the legislature was to dispense with re-registration in regard to the comparatively few judgments which were saved as a charge upon
lands by the 11th section of the 24 Vic., ch. 41, and
which would diminish in number every day, and shortly become altogether extinct.   The inconvenience intended to be obviated by re-registration would in
regard to these judgments be so slight that the legislature did not think it probably worth while to re-enact
with respect to them the 64th section of 22 Vic., ch. 89.

It was also argued that the judgment creditor should
have issued his writ of execution, and delivered it to
the sheriff, and thereby preserved the lien of his judgment.   This proceeding would not have preserved the
existing lien, but created a new one.   I do not per-
ceive the bearing of this argument on the question.
The right arising from the writ against lands delivered
to the sheriff for execution, was very different from the
lien or charge preserved by the 11th section of 24 Vic.,
ch. 41.   That enabled the judgment creditor to pray
a sale of the estate in equity; the other merely enabled
the judgment creditor to redeem the estate if in mortgage.   If a judgment creditor had filed a bill for a sale
before the 18th of May, 1861, and the three years had
expired before he had prosecuted his suit to a conclusion; he could not have continued it, although he
may have delivered a writ against lands to the sheriff

before the 1st of September. The 12th section of 24
Vic., ch. 41, was only intended to regulate priority
amongst judgment creditors.

I think the exception should be allowed without costs.

McDIARMID v. McDIARMID.

*Repeal of patent—Heir and devisee commission—Contingent estate—
Statute of Frauds.*

The heir and devisee commission having reported that the heirs at
law of A. were entitled to a patent of certain lands in the Indian
reserves, Charlottenburg, the Governor in council afterwards,
upon a report of the Solicitor-General in favour of B., a brother
of A., issued a patent to B. for the lands. The heirs of A. thereupon filed a bill to have the patent set aside, and a new patent
issued to themselves, upon the grounds of the patent having been
issued to B. under an error. The court having found that there
was no error of fact, *held*, that the patent was properly issued to
B. notwithstanding the finding of the commission.

Semble, this court may, in a proper case, set aside a patent issued
upon the finding of the heir and devisee commission.

Semble, the purchase of a devisee's contingent interest in real estate
is a purchase of an interest in lands within the Statute of Frauds.

Duncan McDiarmid, the father of *Hugh* and *Finlay
McDiarmid*, was in possession of certain lands in the
Indian Reserve, in the township of Charlottenburg,
under a lease from the St. Regis Indians, for upwards
of forty years prior to his decease in 1847. He devised
one half of these lands to his son *Hugh*, and the other
half to his son *Finlay*. After the death of *Hugh*, his
heirs at law applied to the heir and devisee commission for a report in their favour, as entitled to a
patent for the half of the lands devised to *Finlay;* and
the commission certified in their favour accordingly,
but upon statements which, it afterwards appeared,
were erroneous, and without the claims of *Finlay* having
been considered by them. The latter then presented
his case to the Governor in council, who referred the
matter for inquiry to the Solicitor-General, and upon
his reporting in favour of *Finlay McDiarmid*, a patent

was issued accordingly. The heirs of *Hugh McDiarmid* then filed their bill for a declaration that this patent was issued improvidently, and through error of fact and law, charging that the finding of the commission was final, and praying that the patent to *Finlay* might be set aside, and a new patent issued to themselves.

Mr. *Hodgins*, for the plaintiff, contended that the finding of the commission was final, and referred to the Consolidated Statutes of Upper Canada, chapter 63, section, 17, and Broome's Maxims, 295, 4th ed.

Mr. *McGregor*, for the defendant *Finlay McDiarmid*, contended that there was no error in fact or law in the issuing of the patent; but that, on the contrary, the finding of the commission was clearly based on certificates issued from the Indian department, which misrepresented the facts of this case and the rights of the parties. He also contended that this court may set aside the finding of the heir and devisee commission in cases of fraud, error or mistake, as much as it sets aside a judgment at law, in analogous cases, and referred to *Jeffrey* v. *Boulton*, (a) *Scane* v. *Hartrick*, (b) Earl of *Bandon* v. *Becher* (c).

The facts of the case appear from the judgment of

Judgment.—SPRAGGE, V. C.— [Before whom the cause was heard.] —The questions raised in this cause are substantially between the heirs of the late *Hugh McDiarmid*, the plaintiffs, and the defendant *Finlay McDiarmid*; *Duncan McDiarmid*, the father of *Hugh* and *Finlay*, was occupant of certain lands in what was styled the Indian Tract or Reservation of the St. Regis Indians from the year 1801 to his death in April, 1847. He cultivated these lands as a farm ; *Hugh* for the lat-

---

(a) App. Rep. iii. (b) Ante Vol. 7, p. 161.
(c) 9 Blight. N. S. 532.

ter years of his father's life managing it for him, and
continuing the occupation after his death ; his mother,
however, living with him until his death, which occurred in February, 1858.

Very shortly after the death of *Duncan*, and in the
same year, a surveyor under instructions from the
Indian department made a survey of the tract and a
report to the department, and reported *Hugh* as in
possession of the southerly halves of lots 7, 8, 9, 10,
11, and 12, in the 9th concession of the reservation, in
the township of Charlottenburg, containing 240 acres,
and *Hugh* claimed a patent for the Crown accordingly,
desiring to purchase the same upon the terms prescribed
by the Indian department ; *Finlay* made a contra claim
as to the north halves of the above parcels as devisee
under the will of his father ; and before any patent was
issued or any decision arrived at by the Indian department or the government, *Hugh* died, and his heir
claimed before the heir and devisee commission, and
the like counter claim was made by *Finlay* before the
commissioners as had been made before the government.

In support of *Hugh's* claim a certificate of Mr.
Chesley, of the Indian department, was put in ; he certified the report of the surveyor to which I have referred ; that *Hugh* was occupant and possessor, and as
such was accepted by the Indian department as the
person entitled to purchase the same under the arrangements entered into for commuting the tenure under
which the settlers on the tract held their several lots ;
that he had paid in full for the same at the rate of a
dollar an acre on the 5th of February, 1858, and that
a patent would have issued in his favour had he survived.   Upon these claims of the heirs of *Hugh* as to
the whole, and of *Finlay* as to the half, I find the following note of the decision of the commissioners : "Mr.
Jackson applies that the case may be deferred until the
next sittings : applies on affidavit of the Hon. *J. S.*

Macdonald on behalf of *Finlay McDiarmid ;* but it appears that he has no claim except as devisee of his father, who is represented to have been lessee of the St. Regis Indians; and therefore this claim goes behind the certificate from the Indian department, contesting the right of *Hugh McDiarmid.* Allowed:" that is, the claim of the heirs of *Hugh* was allowed upon the certificate from the Indian department ; and the claim of *Finlay* as devisee of his father was not adjudicated upon by reason of its going behind the certificate. The claim of *Finlay* was however pressed upon the government; at first with the view of getting a report from the Attorney-General and an order to stay the patent within thirty days from the report of the heir and devisee commission in order to a re-hearing before that tribunal, and failing that to obtain a patent to *Finlay* for the parcels devised to him by his father's will, and this was eventually successful, after a report from the Solicitor-General setting forth the principal facts of the case."

This bill is filed to repeal that patent as having been issued in error ; and the plaintiffs' first position is that the decision of the heir and devisee commission is final and conclusive to all intents and purposes. Upon this branch of the case the alleged error consists in issuing a patent to one, when the decision of the commission was in favour of another; and it is contended that this court will look no further, and that it is not open to *Finlay* to shew that the patent was rightly issued to himself; and this involves the position that this court has not jurisdiction to enquire whether or not *Finlay* was entitled to the patent. It is quite clear that but for the intervention of the commission the matters said to be concluded would have been proper subjects of investigation in this court, and that to whichever party the patent had issued, or if no patent had issued to either: the branches of jurisdiction applicable to such cases being "to decree the issue of letters patent from the Crown to rightful claimants " and "to repeal and avoid letters patent issued erroneously or by mistake, or improvidently, or through fraud."

This jurisdiction was conferred upon the Court of Chancery without making any exception in favour of patents issued upon the reports of the heir and devisee commission. In subsequent statutes touching the constitution and jurisdiction of the commission, no mention is made of ouster of the jurisdiction of the court, and in the Consolidated Statutes, where the provisions concerning this court and concerning the commission form in a sense one statute, the respective jurisdictions are left the same; and there is the principle that the jurisdiction of a superior court is not ousted except by express words or necessary implication : of express words there are none, nor can I see that such ouster of jurisdiction is necessarily implied from the language of the act or the purposes for which that tribunal was erected. Its office, according to the original act was, " to ascertain, determine, and declare, who is, or are the heir or heirs, devisee or devisees of the said nominee or nominees of the Crown to such lands," and it is the same now (although comprised in language somewhat different) as will appear by reading together section 7 and the conclusion of section 17, of cap. 80 of the Consolidated Statutes of Upper Canada. Then the 17th section provides that the report of the decision of the commission shall be final and conclusive, and that the Governor in council shall direct a patent to issue for granting the lands in question to the party who has been determined by the decision of the commissioners to be entitled to the same as representing the original nominee of the Crown. Assuming that the report concludes the Crown as to the point reported ; does it necessarily do any thing more ? It may be that the Crown cannot after such report issue a patent to any one as representing the original nominee except to the person whose title as such is affirmed by the report; but it does not follow that the Crown may not for good reasons decline to issue the patent to any one representing such original nominee, and even if the Crown were bound, could in fact only act ministerially upon such report, it by no means follows that this court, not named in reference to the report, cannot, by virtue of its general jurisdiction over the subject matter, enquire who is entitled. Suppose the commissioners to have proceeded upon a forged certificate; or the certificate, whether from the Indian department or the Crown lands department, to misstate some material fact upon which the rights of the parties turned; or that the commissioners were mistaken as to the identity of the parties in whose favour they reported; or that they proceeded upon a forged will or a forged assignment. All these things might be, consistently with the exercise of the soundest judgment on the part of the commissioners; they might merely be mistaken in their premises, and documentary evidence might be produced to this court demonstrating this. Certainly in a case not unlike this in principle, this court does exercise jurisdiction; I allude to the case of a receipt being found after recovery at law of the money, for the payment of which the receipt was given.

It is not necessary to go further and assert the jurisdiction of this court to review the grounds of a decision arrived at by the heir and devisee commissioners. It may be that this was not intended by the statute, and looking at the composition of the court there may be reason for so thinking; but on the other hand there is no limit to the value of the property that may be in question, or to the importance of the questions involved, and unless this court has such jurisdiction, the party failing is concluded by the decision of the tribunal of the first resort; while if the question were before any of the ordinary superior courts, he could carry it to the court of last resort; and would be able to do so if this court has the jurisdiction I refer to. If the decision of the commissioners could be reviewed it would of course be upon the same principles as under the statute govern the commissioners themselves. The question of jurisdiction is raised in this case in a peculiar shape: the plaintiff invokes it for one purpose, to repeal the patent, and denies it for another—the enquiry as to whether after all it was not rightly issued. If *Finlay* could have filed a bill in the event of the patent having issued to the heir of *Hugh*, he can of course shew the same matter by way of defence to this bill—the same question of jurisdiction would arise either way, and the objection necessarily goes to this extent that the decision of the commissioners is final and conclusive as to all courts and to all persons.

The person sought to be bound in this case was not a claimant before the commissioners; his rights can hardly be said to have come in question at all. The only questions decided by the commission were two: who was the original nominee of the Crown; and who were entitled as representing him; any rights or equities outside of those questions were pointedly excluded by the commissioners. Assuming *Hugh* to have been the original nominee of the Crown, a point which I will come to presently, *Finlay*, when brought into this court to defend the patent granted to him, alleges equities outside the questions decided by the commission, and upon them claims to be entitled to retain it. In this view of the case the decision of the commission is in no way impugned, and *Finlay's* position is simply this: that he has rights independently of the commissioners and of any circumstances which give the commissioners jurisdiction, and which are properly cognizable in equity; and the circumstance that the death of a rival claimant gave the commissioners jurisdiction to consider the claim of his heirs, upon which they have decided certain questions, leaving untouched his, *Finlay's*, equitable rights, cannot oust this court of its jurisdiction to give effect to those rights or deprive him of his right to have them protected in this court. . If *Hugh* had lived, the respective rights of the parties would undoubtedly have been cognizable here; he is dead, and *Finlay's* rights not having been adjudicated upon elsewhere, they surely must continue to be cognizable by this court. For these reasons I am of opinion that the decision of the heir and devisee commission is not a bar to *Finlay's* shewing in this court that the patent was rightly issued to him.

Two other objections were raised apart from the merits of the case, one that *Finlay* by appearing before the commissioners submitted to their jurisdiction, and is bound; the other that he should, within a month from the commissioners' report, have obtained from a commissioner a stay of the issue of the patent. I am against the plaintiff upon both these points; upon the first, because the rights he submitted as a reason against the claim of the heirs of *Hugh* were excluded from consideration, and no jurisdiction exercised upon them; in fact jurisdiction disclaimed, to go behind the certificate from the Indian department; upon the other, because *Finlay's* solicitor acted with promptitude and diligence, and because he is not in the position that such proceeding is intended to avert, viz., the issuing of a patent to those whose claim has been allowed by the commissioners.

Upon the merits, apart from the decision of the heir and devisee commission, the case made by the bill is that *Hugh McDiarmid* in his life-time occupied and was entitled to the several parcels of land which were claimed by his heirs; that all the rents and the full amount of the purchase money for all of them were paid by *Hugh;* and that the several instalments were received by the government after fully investigating and finally rejecting the claims of *Finlay;* and that if *Finlay* ever had any claim to, or interest in, these lands, or any portions thereof, *Hugh* in his lifetime gave him a valuable consideration therefor.

The facts as to possession and payment of rent are

not truly stated in the bill : *Duncan*, the father, and not *Hugh*, had possession and paid rent for 46 years, that is, up to his death.   He brought up his family and among them *Hugh* upon the farm, and there is no evidence to shew any change in the possession ; and as to the rents the evidence is, that they were paid by or in the name of *Duncan*.   He was a lessee of the Indians, and occupied and paid rent as such, and if the survey made by *Bruce* had been made in his life-time, no person but himself could properly have been reported as in possession.   *Hugh* was his manager, and looked forward to becoming owner, of a part at least, upon his father's death, but in no proper sense was he in possession ; the real position of *Hugh* was not truly and accurately stated either to the Indian department or to the heir and devisee commissioners.   It is plain from the instructions to the surveyor that what the government desired to be informed of was not the mere fact of what individual might happen to be in personal occupancy of land in the tract.   The government was about to grant patents in fee to settlers who had claims on its consideration as lessees from the Indians, and the instructions to the surveyor were framed accordingly.   He was directed to survey the tract and divide it into concessions and lots of such dimensions as would leave the lessees in possession of the lands they then occupied.   In relation to what is called a clashing between the tract and adjacent townships, he is directed to report whether the lands in dispute were held in possession by Indian lessees or by grantees of the Crown, and he was directed to mark upon his "plans" the position and extent of the clearing and buildings, and the names of *the lessees*.   Now *Hugh* was not a *lessee*, nor did he represent a lessee unless as a devisee under his father's will, for he was not the heir-at-law : the surveyor for a time, while making his survey, lodged in his house, where his mother also resided, and could scarcely have avoided, one would think, learning what was his true position.   But at any rate, he reported him as the person in possession of the whole farm of

which his father had died possessed. This report certainly misstated the material fact upon which it was
manifest, from the surveyor's instructions, the government desired to be informed, and enabled *Hugh* to
appear in a character to which plainly he was not entitled, that is, as nominee of the Crown—the government intending to convert those who were in possession
as lessees into nominees for patents ; and it was upon
this character, assumed without right, that the heirs of
Hugh succeeded before the heir and devisee commissioners. The surveyor might with as much justice have
reported a yearly tenant as the person in possession
within the meaning of his instructions. Except as
devisee of *Duncan*, *Hugh* was a mere stranger, who
happened to be in visible possession, but without a
shadow of claim. According to the evidence of the surveyor, he knew nothing of *Duncan* and was a stranger
to the parties ; he says that in making his survey he
asked the occupant as to his title, and acted upon his
statement. If he asked *Hugh*, as I understand him to
mean, *Hugh* must have misled him as to the facts.
Hugh himself, after his father's death, claimed to have
been forty years in possession, and his heirs in their
petition to the government stated that he had been
many years in possession. All this was at variance
with fact, and the plain object was to give them a claim
upon the government to which they were not entitled.
In few words, the lessee from the Indians is the person recognized by the Crown as entitled to be its nominee for a patent ; the lessee dies, and a younger son,
who had been his farm bailiff, sets up that he is the
person entitled. The claim was a very gross one, and
it is a matter of surprise that it should have imposed
upon the surveyor. It really will not bear examination ; it is quite impossible that such a claim can be
supported.

The plaintiffs ask the repeal of the patent upon
another ground—that *Hugh* purchased from *Finlay*
his prospective interest in the homestead. *Duncan's*

will was made many years before his death, and it seems to have been well understood in the family that he had devised one-half of the homestead to *Hugh*, the other half to *Finlay*. The plaintiff's case is, that several years before *Duncan's* death *Finlay* expressed a wish to have a lot in Kenyon instead, and that such lot was purchased for him and paid for by *Hugh*. It is proved that a lot in Kenyon was purchased for *Finlay* for £200, and that it was paid for partly in cash, and that part of the purchase mouey was lent by a brother, and a joint note by *Finlay* and *Hugh* given for it; the principal part of the purchase money was paid by the hand of *Hugh*, and all this was done with the cognizance and, as it would appear, with the approbation of the father. It is claimed that the money furnished for the payment of the purchase money was the money of *Hugh*. It may have been so, or it may not, or it may have been partly his mouey and partly his father's. He appears to have had the entire management of his father's business, and that the profits of the farm passed through his hands; these would strictly be his father's moneys, though it was probably understood that he was not to be called to account for them; but if they were wholly his moneys it would still have to be shewn, and that clearly, that *Finlay* agreed to relinquish to him for that consideration his prospective interest in the lands in question. It seems to have been thought by some members of the family that *Finlay* was to have the Kenyon lot, instead of half of the homestead, but the evidence that *Finlay* accepted it as a substitute is weak. *Thomas Waddell* is the only witness to that effect. What he says is that *Finlay* said to him that his brother *Hugh* was going to pay for the Kenyon lot, "in substitution of the homestead lot: that it would not do to divide the homestead." The evidence of this witness is shaken by his denying explicitly and repeatedly what he had previously sworn to upon affidavit. There is no evidence whatever of any actual agreement between *Hugh* and *Finlay* to the above effect, and as both were able to write it might be expected that they would have put it in writing. *John,* who appears to have had a good deal of intercourse with his father's family, says, that he never heard in his father's life-time that the Kenyon lot was in exchange for the homestead. The Kenyon lot was partly stocked from the stock of the homestead, and it was probably from the profits of the homestead that the purchase money of the Kenyon lot was paid ; and if *Finlay* did receive that lot in exchange for what he was to have under the will, the devise to him would probably have been revoked ; and this appears to have been expected by *Peter,* a brother of *Hugh* and *Finlay.* *Peter* was named as an executor in the will, and the testator, about a year before his death, handed him the will and desired him to keep it. · *Peter* asked him if he was going to make any change in it ; he said he would make no change, that what he had done he would not alter. *Peter's* idea was that it might be his father's intention to revoke the devise of half the homestead to *Finlag,* but he does not seem to have suggested it. If *Duncan* remembered the contents of his will, as *Peter* thinks he did, what passed between him and *Peter* would be evidence that he did not understand that *Finlay* had received the Kenyon lot in substitution for half the homestead, and that he intended him to have both.

There is indeed a piece of evidence the other way, that of *John,* another brother : *Hugh's* habits had become very intemperate before his father's death, and *John* says that his father in conversation with him alluded to it, and said : "Although the whole homestead had been left to *Hugh,* it would not last long." This it is contended was an affirmation by *Duncan* that he had so devised the homestead ; but even suppose *John's* recollection of the words to have been strictly accurate (which cannot be certain) they may only mean that if he had left the whole homestead to *Hugh* it would not last long—the word " altho' " being used in the same sense as " though" in the well known

passage, " *Though I give all my goods to feed the poor.*"
But supposing the words meant as an affirmation, they
could only be used to counteract the inference from
the conversation with *Peter*; they could not operate as
a revocation of the devise.

A very strong piece of evidence against the existence of such agreement as is now set up, is the conduct
of *Hugh* himself after his father's death; when the
will was read, he made no objection; when asked by
Peter and *John* if he wanted anything but what was
in the will, his answer was that he wanted nothing
but what was in the will; so far this is deposed to by
Peter only, who, as appears by his evidence, has assisted *Finlay* in the defence of this suit, and has made
a provisional contract for the purchase of the land;
but it appears by other evidence, also, that a release
or quit claim as to the land in dispute was prepared
for *Hugh's* signature, and that *Hugh*, when it was presented to him for execution, only said that he must
get advice before he signed it: not at all the answer
which a man would give if asked to release land which
he had purchased and paid for. It is also in evidence,
though resting chiefly on that of *Peter*, that after
Hugh had determined upon claiming the whole lot he
at first rested his claim only upon possession, and that
the purchase of the Kenyon lot for *Finlay* as a consideration for relinquishing the homestead was only an
after thought. It is not a very violent supposition
that the father intended *Finlay* to have half the homestead as well as the Kenyon lot, for he had many years
before purchased a lot for *Hugh*.

There is one document which, if authentic, would
seem to be conclusive against the alleged substitution of the Kenyon lot for half of the homestead.
It purports to be an account against *Finlay*, and
one of the items is, "Bought 200 acres, cost £200,"
which is the price of the Kenyon lot. Another item is

for stock. The account do doubt refers to the Kenyon lot, and if it is a genuine account made out by *Hugh* it is obviously inconsistent with the present claim. I find the document, together with what purports to be a retired note given by *Finlay* to *Hugh*, and a cancelled note joint and several, the signatures torn off, among the papers before the heir and devisee commission. The handwriting is of persons not accustomed to write, but there is nothing to prove the papers genuine, or to shew by whom they were put in, and I must therefore discard them from consideration : I only refer to them because in case the plaintiffs should desire to carry the case further, it may be well to inquire whether they are genuine, and under what circumstances, and for what purpose, they were made out.

Upon the last branch of the case it was not contended but that *Finlay* is entitled as devisee of *Duncan*, unless *Hugh* purchased his interest, the consideration being the Kenyon lot; indeed, it is assumed that he is devisee, for unless he is so, the heir of *Duncan*, not *Hugh*, would be entitled; the purchase of his prospective estate by *Hugh* is then the point to be established. It was not taken as a point in argument that the purchase set up is a purchase of an interest in lands within the Statute of Frauds, and must be proved in the way prescribed by the statute. It certainly is not so proved, and were it out of the statute, the eivdence is not such as, in my judgment, will warrant the court in adjudging for the plaintiffs. *The bill must be dismissed with costs.*

TIFFANY v. TIFFANY.

Personal representative—Remedies when a creditor against lands devised—Parties.

The personal representative may file a bill *as a creditor simply*, upon the testator's estate against a devisee of lands under the will, after the personal estate is exhausted, and obtain a decree as an ordinary creditor.

The other creditors need not be made parties to such a bill, but the heirs-at-law must.

In a suit to administer the estate of a testator the heir-at-law ought to be a party ; but when the personal representative filed such a bill against the devisee, alleging that no lands had descended, as to which the answer was silent, and the objection was not raised at the hearing, the court, under the circumstances, made a decree in the absence of the heir.

Mr. *Blake* for the plaintiff.

Mr. *Fitzgerald* for defendants.

Judgment.—SPRAGGE, V.C.—The plaintiff is administrator, with the will annexed, of the late *Gideon Tiffany*. He files his bill as a creditor, upon the testator's estate, against the defendant as devisee of one of several parcels devised by the will, alleging that of the several parcels devised, *that* one parcel was the only one of which the testator died seised, and that he died seised of no other real estate whatever ; that the personal estate was small, and was received by the defendant before plaintiff obtained letters of administration, and was applied by him in part towards payment of the funeral expenses of the testator.

Both parties agree that the land in question passed by the will to the defendant. At the date of the will the testator had conveyed the land to the plaintiff; who conveyed it back to the testator between the date of the will and his death ; the testator could not more clearly manifest his intention that it should pass by his will than by devising it specifically, he must have intended, if he had it not then, to acquire it and devise it. My opinion is, that it passed by the devise. The defendant objects to the equity upon which the plaintiff comes into court, but I think it sustainable. If that out of which he seeks to satisfy his debt were personal estate, he would have a right of retainer; being land, he must come into court that it may be realised; any other creditor might do this; and the circumstance of his being personal representative as well as creditor, can, I think, make no difference.

It is objected, that the bill, being by the personal representative he should make all creditors parties. If the bill were by him as personal representative to pass his accounts, the objection would be good; but he comes simply as a creditor, and the defendant does not ask for an administration of the estate. If the plaintiff were not himself personal representative he would necessarily make the personal representative a party defendant, as well as the devisee, but the devisee has all the advantage of a suit framed in that way, because he had the personal representative before the court as plaintiff; and the devisee can insist upon the personal estate being exhausted first.

The point in which the bill appears defective is in not making the heirs-at-law of the testator parties, inasmuch as land descended is liable to the payment of debts before lands devised; but that objection is not taken by the answer, perhaps, because the defendant may have acquiesced in the plaintiff's allegation that there were no lands descended—he is silent as to the fact—the objection was not taken at the hearing; and I do not think that the court ought to give effect to it, as there may be no foundation for it in fact. I think the plaintiff entitled to the like decree as would be obtained by an ordinary creditor.

LANNIN v. JERMYN.

Executor—Sale of real estate at instance of.

The lessee of land, with the right to purchase, devised the same to his son, if it could be paid for, and if it could not, that one-half should be sold, and the purchase money paid for the other half, which he gave to his son, an infant; the executor advanced out of his own moneys sufficient to pay the price of the land, and the lessors conveyed to the devisee. The personal estate of the testator being small, was exhausted in the payment of debts and funeral expenses, so that the executor had no means of reimbursing himself, whereupon he filed a bill in this court praying a sale of the real estate, and payment of his advances. The court, under the circumstances, directed a sale to be made of that portion of the lot which the testator desired should be sold, if it should appear upon enquiry before the master that the payment to the lessors was for the benefit of the infant.

The facts appear in the head-note and judgment.

Mr. *Fitzgerald*, for plaintiff, referred to *Tiffany* v. *Tiffany*, (a) and *Spakman* v. *Holbrook*. (b)

Mr. *Roaf*, for defendant.

Judgment.—SPRAGGE, V. C.—The testator, *Thomas Jermyn*, father of the defendant, by his will devised to the defendant the parcel of land on which he lived, in the following terms: "I give, devise, and bequeath unto my son *John Jermyn*, this fore-mentioned lot of land, being lot 31, in the 12th concession of the township of Biddulph, if it can be paid for, and given to the said *John Jermyn*, my son." The testator was a lessee of the Canada Company of the above lands, with the privilege of purchasing the land at the expiration of his term, at a stipulated sum, £125. By his will he appointed the plaintiff, and one *Eady* executors. *Eady* renounced; and the plaintiff proved and acted.

The plaintiff alleges that the personal estate was small and was exhausted in payment of the creditor's debts and funeral expenses; and that he out of his own moneys paid to the Canada Company for arrears of rent and

---

(a) Ante p. 158.   (b) 6 Jur. N. S. 881.

purchase money, the sum of £104 1s. 9d., and that unless he had paid the same the land would have been forfeited to the Canada Company. He alleges that he also expended the sum of £25 in the execution of the trusts of the will.

The matter comes before me on motion for decree; and the allegations in the will are verified by affidavit; and it is also proved by the evidence of the commissioner of the Canada Company that the plaintiff did pay arrears of rent and purchase money, as stated in his bill. A conveyance has been made by the Canada Company to the defendant.

By the will the plaintiff and *Eady* were constituted trustees for certain purposes. The plaintiff would have acted in strict accordance with the will if he had applied money of the estate in his hands in payment of the purchase money of the whole or half of the lot devised. Before account taken, it cannot be known whether it was money of his own or of the estate that he so applied. If his own, he did certainly what the will did not in strictness authorise him to do; but so does an executor who pays debts of his testator beyond the assets in his hands. If what he did was for the benefit of the infant, or of creditors of the estate, if any, it is certainly just that he should be recouped. In the case of creditors, his equity would be clear, inasmuch as they could not realise their debts out of the land without first reimbursing the representative of the estate, who made it a fund available for the payment of their debts; but even then what the plaintiff would be entitled to would be only the value of the estate as a fee simple beyond the value of the leasehold estate held by the testator. This would probably be the full sum paid by the plaintiff, but if less he would, I take it, be only entitled to the lesser sum.

With regard to the infant, if the plaintiff is to be regarded in the light of a mere stranger choosing out of

11

mere officiousness, or from whatever motive, to purchase this land from the Canada Company in pursuance of the lease, for the benefit of the infant, I do not suppose he would have any equity to come to this court: but I do not think he should be regarded in that light. At common law an action does not lie for money paid, if the debt of another be paid without request, and without legal liability or duty, but this court gives a remedy to an executor so paying money ; for money beyond assets in hand is so paid. This court looks upon it as an advance to the estate which the position of the executor justifies him in making.

The act of the plaintiff in this case was not a mere officious one ; the paying for the land was contemplated by the testator, though he could not contemplate that the plaintiff should pay out of his own funds. I have no doubt that the court may properly direct the rear half of the lot to be sold to reimburse the plaintiff, because it would be doing substantially what the will directs, selling the rear half to pay for the front half. I do not see my way clearly beyond this ; and this probably, as I judge from the pleadings and evidence, will be sufficient. It will be proper to direct an enquiry whether the payment to the Canada Company was for the benefit of the infant ; and the taking of the usual accounts, reserving further directions and costs. The guardian of the infant is in any event entitled to his costs.

BODDY v. FINLEY.

Duress—Costs.

A party, having been arrested on a charge of obtaining money under false pretences, agreed, in presence of the magistrate who had issued the warrant to execute a mortgage on his farm to secure the amount ; whereupon he was discharged, and he, together with the complainant who had sued out the warrant, went to a convey-ancer and gave instructions for the conveyances which he subsequently executed. Afterwards a bill was filed by the mortgagor to set the instrument aside as having been obtained by duress and oppression. The court, under the circumstances, refused the relief sought, but as the conduct of the defendant had been harsh and oppressive, dismissed the bill without costs.

The facts are stated in the judgment.

Mr. *Fitzgerald* for the plaintiff.

Mr. *Roaf* for defendant.

Judgment.—SPRAGGE, V. C.—The conveyance impeached in this suit was executed under the following circumstances :—the plaintiff was the owner of the west-half of lot number one, in the second concession of the township of Malahide, subject to a mortgage to one *Wilson* for $700. He sold the west-half of this parcel of land to the defendant for $400. The defendant in his answer says that he knew of *Wilson's* mortgage covering the whole half lot, but that the plaintiff represented it to be only for $242. This is not at all sustained by evidence, which establishes, I think, that the mortgage was for $700, and that this was known to the defendant. The plaintiff's avowed object in selling to the defendant was to raise money in order to its being applied on *Wilson's* mortgage. The sale was in October, 1857.

Early in 1859, the defendant seems to have been informed that the plaintiff was selling off some farm stock, and was about to leave the province, and he took a course which does appear to me to have been a very unwarrantable one under the circumstances. He caused the plaintiff to be arrested under a criminal charge of obtaining money under false pretences ; the foundation for the charge being the dealing between the parties upon the purchase of land to which I have referred. The arrest itself was made in a violent and offensive manner. The defendant and the constable went together to the house of the plaintiff, each armed with a pistol, the defendant's loaded, but as he says not exhibited ; the constable's loaded, as he says, only with powder. It was a five-barred revolver, and was produced at the arrest, and the plaintiff threatened with it. The plaintiff was handcuffed at first, but the handcuffs were afterwards removed ; and the three, the plaintiff, the defendant, and the constable, proceeded together to the house of the magistrate by whom the warrant was issued. On the way the plaintiff agreed that he would convey to the defendant the east-half of the parcel of land which he owned, by way of securing him against the *Wilson* mortgage ; and this agreement was repeated in the presence of the magistrate, who said that if the defendant was satisfied that the plaintiff would do as he had promised, he would discharge the warrant. It was suggested by the defendant that the magistrate should himself draw the necessary papers, but he observed that he might make some mistake, and advised them to go to a conveyancer. The plaintiff was not discharged until he had promised to give the security.

I observe here that there was nothing unreasonable in the defendant being indemnified against the *Wilson* mortgage, or in its being done by such instruments as were executed, though it would have been better if it had been done in one instrument.

After the plaintiff had been discharged from his arrest, he, and the defendant went together to a Mr. *Meneray*, who lived in the village of Warwick, at a distance of about two miles from the magistrate, they together gave instructions to Mr. *Meneray* for the drawing of the papers : the plaintiff then, without the defendant, went alone into the village to see a relation as he said; the defendant remained, and mentioned to *Meneray* that the plaintiff had been arrested. When plaintiff returned he executed the papers, without, as *Meneray* says, so far as he could judge, any compulsion. The defendant left first, and the plaintiff then said to *Meneray* that he, the plaintiff, from some misinformation that he had received, had been inclined to do a very rash act for which he might be sorry hereafter.

If these instruments had been given before the discharge of the plaintiff, as was the case in the cause reported in *Aleyn,* (a) I am of opinion that they could

_____

(a) Page 92.

not stand. But the plaintiff was not under duress when he executed them, and if at that time he was a free agent, I am not prepared to hold that the previous oppressive conduct of the defendant is sufficient to invalidate the deeds. The question seems to be, as put by Lord *Eldon*, (a) whether or not the mind was so subdued, that though the execution was the free act of the party, it was the act speaking the mind, not of that person but another.

I have examined the several cases cited and some others, and it seems to me the test is that put by Lord *Eldon*, and trying the case by that test, I cannot but think that the plaintiff, in executing these instruments, was his own master in mind and body. He probably executed them because he had promised to do so when under arrest, but I see no reason to suppose that he apprehended a re-arrest or any further violence if he did not fulfil his promise.

I think the bill must be dismissed but without costs. The conduct of the defendant was not only harsh and oppressive, but, as appears by the evidence, quite unjustifiable in the transaction, and I think I ought not to give him his costs.

GOTT v. GOTT.

Voluntary assignment of chose in action.

The holder of a debenture issued by the trustees of a Methodist church, transferred the same without consideration, by signing an endorsement as follows: "pay to James Gott, or order," and delivered the same to the person named in such endorsement. *Held*, that such transfer did not vest the debt in the transferree so as to prevent the claims of the creditors of the original holder of the debenture attaching upon it.

This was a suit for alimony, and a decree having been made in favour of the plaintiff, and certain payments having fallen in arrear, which the plaintiff was

---

(a) Note a to Countess of Sirathmore v. Burns, 2 B.C.C. 351.

unable to enforce, and it appearing that the defendant having been in possession of a debenture of the Wesleyan Methodist Church at Kingston, for £600, had made a voluntary assignment and transfer thereof to one *James Gott*, a motion was made for an order to pay the interest into court, and to deposit the debenture with the officer of the court, which had been done accordingly. A motion was now made for the payment and delivery out of the money and debenture to *James Gott*.

Mr. *Roaf*, in support of the application.

Mr. *James McLennan*, for the plaintiff, contra.

The cases cited are mentioned in the judgment of

Judgment.—VANKOUGHNET, C.—In this suit, in which a decree for alimony has been made, one *James Gott* makes application on notice that there may be paid out to him certain moneys paid into court, and now here under the following circumstances: the defendant having separated from his wife, and proposing to leave the country, made over to *James Gott*, his nephew, certain property as a gift, and owning or having among other things a debenture executed under seal by the trustees of the Wesleyan Methodist Church, in the city of Kingston, for the sum of six hundred pounds, payable to him or his order, with interest at six per cent. per annum, to secure the re-payment of that amount loaned by him to the trustees, handed this debenture to the said *James Gott*, with the following endorsement made by him thereon: " Pay to *James Gott* or order.—*Robert Gott*." The trustees, on being threatened with legal proceedings by *James Gott*, paid him interest on the debenture, and they have since paid it into court under an order so to do. This assignment of endorsement and delivery passed no title at law to *James Gott*, and it is impeached as having been fraudulently made with the view of escaping the payment of the alimony decreed to the plaintiff. On the argument had before me on this ground, I did not consider the evidence as to the fraudulent intent clear, and I directed the case to be argued on the question whether or not the gift by such an assignment of such an instrument, or the debt secured by it, passed any title at law or in equity, and whether the debt or debenture did not still remain the property of the defendant in accordance with the law enunciated in *Edwards* v. *Jones*. (a) This point has accordingly been argued before me, and I proceed to state the judgment which I have formed upon it.

I was of opinion when I directed this argument to be had, and am still of opinion that if *Edwards* v. *Jones* remains an authority unshaken, or at all events not overruled, it must govern this case, for it is impossible for me to distinguish the one from the other, unless in particulars too trifling to deserve judicial comment.

In a long train of cases, among which it is sufficient to commence with *Ellison* v. *Ellison*, (b) terminating with *Milroy* v. *Ford*, reported at page 806 of the current volume of the Jurist, has been again and again discussed the principle that this court will not aid a volunteer; and that principle has been upheld, and modified, and I may say departed from, in an almost equal proportion of cases. It has been laid down as a rule for guidance that if all has been done that it lay in the power of the parties to do, this court would aid the volunteer to the enjoyment of the thing, or property assigned to him, and with this qualification in some of the cases, "so that the court is not required to act in the matter against the assignor or settlor." This rule, with or without the qualification, if it had been consistently relied on would have been intelligible enough. Another rule, which seems to have been adhered to, is, that a declaration of trust in favour of a volunteer,

---

(a) 1 M. & C. 226.　　　　(b) 6 Vesey, 656.

whether the person making it thereby constitutes himself or a third party to whom he has transferred the legal estate in the property a trustee, will be enforced. This rule, too, would in itself be plain enough. Upon it has been engrafted another rule, which seems now settled by modern cases, to the effect that a *cestui que* trust of property,—for instance of stock, which can only pass at law by a particular mode of transfer—may fasten upon that property in the hands of a trustee by a proper declaration to that effect a trust in favour of a volunteer which a court of equity will give effect to. It is also clear on authority that that which was intended to pass by transfer as a gift will not as against or in the hands of the donor be clothed with a trust, in order that thereby the donee or intended donee may get the benefit of it. The difficulty of applying these rules will be found on an examination of the cases to which I have referred; and, without attempting to reconcile them, which, indeed, I find it impossible to do, I will mention a few of them by way of illustration, and as applicable to the case before me, commencing with *Edwards* v. *Jones*. We find by it that one *Mary Custane*, the obligee in a bond for securing a debt of £200, signed, but without a seal, upon the bond the following endorsement: "I, *Mary*, &c., do hereby assign and transfer the within bond or obligation, and all my right, title and interest thereto, unto and to the use of my niece *Esther*, &c., with full power and authority for the said *Esther* to sue for and recover the amount thereof, and all interest now due or hereafter to become due thereon." This bond so endorsed was delivered by *Mary* to *Esther*. *Mary* afterwards died, leaving the defendant her executor. The obligor was induced to execute a bond to the executor, who supposed the old one had been lost, the executor indemnifying him against any claim upon it. He subsequently died, and his executor paid the amount of the new bond to the defendant. These are the only facts material to the question here. The plaintiff *Esther* filed her bill setting forth these, among other facts, claiming the money received by the defendant as properly payable to her by virtue of the assignment of the bond to her, and that the defendant should be treated as a trustee of the money received for her. The Vice-Chancellor of England first, and Lord *Cottenham* on appeal, refused any relief, and dismisssd the bill. The Lord Chancellor says, "Now it is clear that this is a voluntary gift, and a gift which cannot be made effectual without the interposition of this court. The circumstances of the bond having been afterwards paid, and the money having been put into the hands of the defendants, cannot make any difference in the determination of the question, which must depend upon the same principles as if it has arisen before." Of course, if *Mary Custance* had received the money in her lifetime after the assignment and delivery of the bond to the plaintiff, the result would have been the same, and she could not have been compelled to pay it over to the plaintiff. The necessary effect of *Edwards* v. *Jones* therefore is, that an assignment of such a bond or chose in action passes no property to the assignee, who thereby obtains nothing more than a mere power or authority to receive the money, which may be revoked at any time. Upon this view the Vice-Chancellor must have acted in the case of *Sewell* v. *Moxsy* (a), where he refused to entertain, and dismissed with costs a claim precisely of the nature of the one made here by *James Gott*. In almost every case in which the principles or rules to which I have adverted have been discussed since *Edwards* v. *Jones* was decided, that case has been cited. It has never been overruled, nor, so far as I am aware, questioned as an authority, though in *Donaldson* v. *Donaldson* (b), Vice-Chancellor *Page Wood* seems to think that it has given a wrong direction to cases involving questions of trusts; and that this was checked by the decision and very elaborate opinion

(a) 2 Sim N. S. 189.   (b) Kay, 711.

expressed by the Lords Justices in *Kekewich* v. *Manning* (a), in which case *Edwards* v. *Jones* was commented upon by Lord Justice Knight Bruce, and rested on the ground that it was impossible to pass to the assignee of a bond a legal or perfect title to it. Indeed such an assignment is treated in some of the cases as a mere agreement to give the intended assignee the benefit of the bond or deed; and where voluntary, of no value, as not enforcible. *Edwards* v. *Jones* was also cited, and approved of in *Price* v. *Price* (b), and *Meek* v. *Kettlewell* (c).

Opposed to *Edwards* v. *Jones* are the cases of *Fortescue* v. *Barnett* (d), *Blakely* v. *Brady* (e), *Pearson* v. The *Amicable Life Association Company* (f). I say opposed, because I find it impossible to reconcile them with *Edwards* v. *Jones* as subsisting authorities, though up to the time of the case in 27 Beavan it was attempted to distinguish them and similar decisions, on the ground that they were cases where the judges disposing of them had found that a trust had been created in favour of the volunteer, and as such should be executed. This, if the cases warranted it, would be very satisfactory, and the Master of the Rolls attempted so to make it in his review of the different cases, up to the time, in *Bridge* v. *Bridge* (g). All the cases in apparent, if not real opposition, to *Edwards* v. *Jones*, from *Sloane* v. *Cadogan* (g), before Sir Wm. Grant down to *Bridge* v. *Bridge*, might, under the judgment in that case, have been so treated to the present time, had not the Master of the Rolls felt that he could no longer maintain such a distinction and must abandon it when the case of *Pearson* v. The *Amicable Assurance Company* was presented to him as reported in 27 Beav.; for there he throws overboard the notion of any trust

---

(a) 1 DeG. M. & G. 176.　　(b) 16 Beav. 315.
(c) 1 Hare 474, and on App. 1 Phil. 342.
(d) 3 Myl. and Keene, 36.　　(e) Drury & Walsh, 311.
(f) 27 Beav. 229.　　(g) 3 Sugd V. & P. App. 66.

declared or existing, and decrees in favour of the assignment to a volunteer of a policy of assurance, a chose in action. Indeed it seems to me, with all possible deference for opinions to the contrary, that neither *Fortesque* v. *Barnett*, nor *Blakely* v. *Brady*, can be maintained merely on the ground that a trust was in either case created, and that it cannot be successfully contended that Sir *John Leach* in the one case, or Lord *Plunket* in the other, rested or meant to rest his judgment on any such ground, though Lord *Cottenham*, in *Edwards* v. *Jones*, assumes this to be the reason of Sir *John Leach's* decision, and the Master of the Rolls, in *Bridge* v. *Bridge*, assumes the same thing as the reason for Lord *Plunket's* decision, while, on the other hand, Lord *Plunket* endeavours to dispose of the judgment in *Edwards* v. *Jones* upon facts which, in the report of the principal case, do not appear to have existed, or, if they did, were, in my opinion, unimportant in the view Lord *Cottenham* took of the case. For instance, it could be of no importance in the view of a Court of Equity, whether the assignment of a bond was or was not under seal, unless indeed it could be maintained that being under seal it would give a right of action at law against the assignor. Sir *John Leach* certainly did not proceed on the motion of a trust having been created in *Fortesque* v. *Barnett*, for he sets out with saying that the assignment of a bond to a volunteer will, in equity, be upheld; the very position which *Edwards* v. *Jones* upsets. Lord *Plunket* certainly does not pretend, in words at all events, that he is executing a mere trust ; and yet these two cases are approved of and relied upon as law in many cases, and particularly in *Kekewich* v. *Manning*. They, with the case in 27 Beaven, seem to run in direct conflict on principle with *Edwards* v. *Jones*, a recognized authority, and with *Sewell* v. *Moxsy*; and the only difference is the unsubstantial one that in *Edwards* v. *Jones* the debt sought to be assigned was evidenced by a bond, and in the other cases by policies of assurance, and by a receipt or undertaking to pay. It appears to me that

the courts, feeling the inconvenience to which the extension of the principle of the decision in *Edwards* v. *Jones*
would lead practically, have, without venturing to over-
rule it, steered all round it. I am. compelled to choose
in which of the line of cases represented respectively by
Edwards v. *Jones* and *Fortesque* v. *Barnett*, I will rank
the case before me ; and I place it in the former, not
merely because in its circumstances it falls directly
within the authority of *Edwards* v. *Jones*, but because I
think that that case marks the true principle on which
such assignments as the present should be treated. How,
in fact, can a title to a debt be assigned as a gift, and how
can such an assignee enforce it ? Suppose the creditor
or assignor sues for it after assignment, or compromises
or releases it, is there any authority to shew that a court
of law will interfere as they will in favour of an assignee
for value when the assignor gives a fraudulent release,
and it is set up by plea ? Is there any authority to shew
that a Court of Equity will interfere to prevent the assignor collecting the money for his own benefit? or to
compel him to allow the voluntary assignee to use his
name for the collection ? Would not such interference be
the action of the court to compel the assignor to perfect
his gift ? and do not numerous cases say that the courts
will not so interfere? Must not the assignor be a party to
the bill by the assignee, to enforce the claim ? Is not such
an assignment, if it can be made at all, revocable ? and,
if revocable, does not the property remain in the assignor
liable to his debts ? *Harland* v. *Binks*, (a) in my memory
at the moment, and the cases cited in it, makes this
sufficiently clear. For all the purposes of this application the defendant *Robert Gott* has revoked his
assignment to the applicant *James Gott*, for he resists
his claim, and swears that the debenture was only handed
over to him as trustee or agent. The facts connected
with this transfer are sufficiently suspicious ; and if I
were called upon to decide upon them alone, I doubt
very much if the transaction could be sustained as

(a) 15 Q. B. 713.

against creditors. A very little additional evidence, which might be supplied by the dates now wanting would probably turn the scale. I reject the application, leaving it to higher authority to put the law in a more satisfactory state than I find it. The plaintiff's costs to be paid out of the money in court, as the fund secured as the property of the defendant is more than sufficient to pay her alimony. Otherwise I would direct the applicant to pay the costs.

DANIELS V. DAVIDSON.

Mortgage with power of sale—Registration—Sale under such power—Demurrer—Parties.

The owner of land sold and conveyed one acre thereof: afterwards, and before the registration of the deed of this acre, he executed a mortgage on the whole estate, (200 acres,) which was duly registered, and subsequently the purchaser of the acre registered his deed. Default having been made in payment of the mortgage money, the assignee of the mortgagee proceeded to a sale of the estate, the whole of which, including the acre, was sold and duly conveyed. The purchaser of the acre filed a bill against the person exercising the power of sale, and his vendee, claiming a right to redeem by virtue of his interest in the one acre, and alleging want of notice of the intention to proceed to a sale under the power contained in the mortgage.

To this bill the vendor under the power put in a demurrer for want of equity; and also for want of parties, on the ground that the mortgagor was a necessary party. *Held,* that for the purpose of obtaining the relief prayed by the bill, the mortgagor was not a necessary party, although if the bill had sought for payment of the surplus (if any) of the purchase money over and above the amount due on the mortgage, it would be necessary to bring him before the court.

Held, also, that the prior registration of a mortgage with a power of sale, enabled the mortgagee in the proper exercise of such power, to sell free from the claim of a purchaser prior in point of time, but who had neglected to register his conveyance.

The bill in this cause was filed by *Alexander Daniels* against *Samuel Davidson, Thomas C. Street,* and others, setting forth that in April, 1846, plaintiff purchased from the owner in fee, one *George P. Goulding,* one acre of land, being part of lot No. 19. in the 5th concession of Maraposa, the conveyance of which he did not register until the 12th of August, 1847 ; that on the 18th of June, 1846, *Goulding* and one *Church* conveyed the whole of this lot to one *Cutler,* in fee, to secure

£1034, and interest, which conveyance was registered on the 20th of the same month, whereby plaintiff's deed became a subsequent incumbrance to the said mortgage; and that *Cutler*, on the 14th of December, 1846, assigned and transferred the mortgage to defendant *Street*, who in June, 1848, sold the mortgage estate, for default of payment of the mortgage money, to defendant *Davidson*.

The bill further alleged want of notice to plaintiff of the intended sale by *Street;* alleged receipt of rents, &c., by *Davidson*, who had gone into possession, and prayed an account and redemption.

The defendant *Street* demurred for want of equity, and for want of parties, alleging that *Goulding* and *Church* were necessary parties.

Mr. *Brough*, Q. C., in support of the demurrer, contended the bill shewed no ground for relief; the prior registration of the mortgage clearly postponed the deed; and as to the want of notice, the bill does not allege that by the terms of the mortgage deed notice was required to be given either to the mortgagors, or any one claiming under them. The mortgagors should have been made parties in order to the taking of the accounts.

Mr. *Cameron*, Q. C., contra, insisted that this case was not within the provisions of the registry acts; true, so far as the amount of mortgage money due, the plaintiff's deed was subject to it, that, however, simply bound him to pay whatever might be due in respect of the whole two hundred acres, before he could redeem his own share of it; but so far as the power of sale was concerned, that was not a conveyance which, under the law, was, by being registered, entitled to postpone or over-ride a prior deed, though unregistered. He cited *Scrafton* v. *Quincy.* (a)

As to the objection for want of parties, the plaintiff

(a) 2 Ves. 413.

being willing to redeem, by paying the face of the mortgage, less what it may be shewn has been received by the defendant, the mortgagors were not interested in any account to be taken.

Mr. *Brough,* Q. C., in reply, objected that the plaintiff was not at liberty to raise any question as to priority under the registry act, the bill being framed with a totally different aspect.

Judgment.—VANKOUGHNET, C.—The bill in effect alleges that the plaintiff having acquired a title in fee to one acre of 200 acres of land, from one *George P. Goulding,* by deed bearing date the 25th of April, 1846, the said *Goulding* and one *Church,* who had an interest in the land, subsequently mortgaged the whole 200 acres to one *Cutler,* to secure the re-payment of £1084; and that this mortgage was registered on the 20th of June, 1847, prior to the registration by the plaintiff of his deed, which took place on the 12th of August, 1847; that on the 14th of December, 1846, *Cutler* assigned this mortgage to the defendant *Thomas Clarke Street;* that in June, 1848, the assignee, acting under a power of sale contained in the mortgage, but with full notice of the plaintiff's deed, sold, and without notice to the plaintiff, the said land to the defendant *Davidson,* who has made sale of portions thereof to the other defendants.

The bill, while admitting and submitting, that by reason of the prior registration of the mortgage, the plaintiff's deed of the one acre became in respect thereof a subsequent incumbrance, insists that inasmuch as the plaintiff's deed was registered prior to the sale to *Davidson,* the latter, and all claiming under him, bought with notice of that deed, and that by reason thereof, and the want of notice to the plaintiff of the intended sale under the power, the same is as against him, inoperative; and he claims the right to redeem.

To this bill the defendant has demurred for want of

equity, and on the ground that the mortgagor ought to be a party to the bill.

On the argument, Mr. *Cameron* very properly abandoned the position assumed by the bill, that notice to the plaintiff of the sale, if it could be made at all under the mortgage, was requisite, as it does not appear that there was any stipulation for notice in the power of sale; but he strenuously and ably urged, and I was much impressed with the argument, that the deed to the plaintiff having been executed before the creation by the mortgage of the power of sale, and having been registered before the execution of the power, the sale under the latter could not have priority over the plaintiff's deed; that the registry laws did not provide for such a case—for the registration of a power—but merely for the registration of a deed which in itself operated by way of conveyance; and that the plaintiff's deed, having priority of registration over the deed executed under the power, took precedence of it.

There is great room for argument in support of this position; but on reflection I think it cannot be sustained under the law, as it has been administered and understood to exist. In the first place, it is said that the registration of a mere power, though coupled with an interest, would be ineffectual against a subsequent conveyance of the estate registered or unregistered, as the registry law, at all events as it stood in 1846, did not provide for the position of such a document, or the right given by it. Is this so clear? In the first place it is urged on the other side that a power coupled with an interest, as for instance, a mere power of sale over an estate to re-pay a loan, cannot be revoked, unless it be by force of the registry laws. Cannot it then be secured from such revocation by force of the same laws? We must look at their intent and object to consider this. The statute 9 Vic., ch. 31, in sec. 6, gives the effect therein prescribed to all deeds and conveyances "whereby any lands, &c., may be in any wise affected in law or equity." A deed is not necessarily a conveyance. It is an instrument under seal, and when executed *inter partes*, is called an indenture. Suppose an indenture whereby A. acknowledges the receipt from B. of a sum of money, covenants to re-pay it, and, in default, gives B. power to sell the land. Such a deed certainly affects the land in equity, and would be executed by this court if necessary. I am not driven to decide upon this mere naked position. In the present case, the mortgage which contains the power of sale is a conveyance, and the bill admits that the plaintiff's deed must be postponed to it, so far as it is a mortgage; but he argues, as already stated, that the power of the sale is inoperative as against him. It was I believe, conceded, and, at all events, it has been too long admitted law for me to venture to question it, that if a mortgage with a power of sale be registered, any sale made and deed executed legally under that power will cut out any deed intermediately made by the mortgagor, and registered. If this be so, it must dispose of the whole question, because it can only be by force of the registry laws that the exercise of the power of sale could have any such effect. If it is only the conveying part of the deed that by the registry laws can give priority or effect, and not the power of sale, then it would follow that a deed made and registered subsequently to such a conveyance, would cut out a deed executed afterwards under the power; and yet by universal practice and consent such has not been its effect. If the power of sale in such a conveyance can, therefore, under the registry laws, give to a deed, executed by virtue of it, priority over a deed made subsequently to such conveyance, but made and registered prior to the exercise of the power, the same effect, in my opinion, must be given to it in relation to a deed executed as here, before the conveyance containing the power, but not registered till after that conveyance.

His Lordship suggested that it might be worth the plaintiff's while to consider whether an equity did not exist to call upon *Street* to account to him for the excess of purchase money over and above the amount of principal and interest due on the mortgage, and that an opportunity would be afforded him of praying that relief. In the event of the plaintiff taking that position, it is evident the parties creating the mortgage would require to be made parties to the bill.

[The plaintiff subsequently suffered the order allowing the demurrer to go, thereby abandoning any relief as against *Street*.]

McLennan v. Heward.

Administrator de bonis non—His right to call the estate of a predecessor to account—Rests—Agent—Commission.

The principle upon which an administrator should be charged with interest on funds belonging to the estate considered and acted on.

An administrator *de bonis non* having obtained a decree against the representatives of a deceased administrator for an account of his dealings with the estate: *Held*, that he was entitled to charge the representatives with interest, &c., in the same manner, and to the same extent, as one of the next of kin might have done.

Where an administrator who had acted as agent for the intestate during his life-time, had, with the assent of the deceased, used moneys belonging to him, without any attempt at concealment as to his so using them, the court refused to take the account against the administrator with rests; and the master having allowed the estate of the administrator a commission of 5 per cent. on moneys passing through the hands of the administrator in his life-time, the court refused, on appeal, to disturb such allowance.

This was an administration suit, in which the usual reference had been directed at the hearing. The master having made his report thereunder, both parties appealed on the grounds stated in the judgment.

Mr. *McLennan*, in person.

Mr. *A. Crooks*, contra.

Judgment.—VANKOUGHNET, C.—This is an appeal by both parties from the Master's report, by which it is found that on taking an account of the estate of the late *Alexander Wood*, deceased, there is a balance due by the personal representatives of the late administrator of the deceased amounting to £4083 10s. 7d. for principal and interest. The plaintiff sues as administrator, *de bonis non*, being the second in succession in that character. The following exceptions are taken to the Master's report by the defendants.

1st. That an administrator, *de bonis non*, cannot charge his predecessor in that office with breach of trust or dereliction of duty, or claim from his estate interest upon moneys retained by him, although such interest might be properly charged at the suit or instance of the next of kin of the intestate.

2nd. That at all events, in order to make such charge, a proper case should have been set out in the bill.

3rd. That the Master should not have charged interest at all, either upon the moneys of the intestate in his life time loaned to or received by the administrator for him, as there was no agreement or understanding between them that interest should be paid, and that no account of *Crookshank's* dealings as agent, but only as administrator, is sought in this suit; or upon the moneys held by the administrator as such after the death of the intestate, or held by him between that time and the time of his appointment as such administrator, because there was not, during those periods, any person to whom the administrator could safely pay over the moneys, the right to them being in litigation in Scotland between rival claimants, and there being nothing to shew that the administrator was not at any moment ready to account and pay over the money. That he could not invest, as the period when he might be called on to pay was uncertain, depending upon the issue of the litigation; and that it does not appear that any of the parties interested ever called upon him to invest the moneys.

4th. That the defendants are not liable for interest,

since the death of the administrator, without proof of sufficient assets to meet the claim.

5th. That the Master's mode of computing interest was erroneous in deducting the payments from the receipts in each year and calculating interest on the balance from the end of the year, and that he should have calculated interest upon the receipts and payments respectively and severally from their dates.

6th. That no case is made by the pleadings or otherwise for taking the account with rests, or charging at the most more than simple interest.

7th. That a reasonable commission should be allowed to the administrator's estate, and the Master has found that 5 per cent. on the gross receipts would, in his opinion, be a fair allowance therefor.

The cross appeal claims that the account should have been taken with rests, and that the master should not have made any report about allowance as commission. The facts necessary to the determination of the questions thus raised may be shortly stated as follows:

Alexander Wood, the intestate, for many years a resident in this city, in the spring or summer of 1842, proceeded to Scotland, where he remained till his death, in the month of September, 1844. At the time of his departure from Canada he owned a large real estate in the country, and had a deposit at his credit in the Bank of Upper Canada, in Toronto, amounting to about £1383. Prior to leaving, and about the 21st of May, 1842, the intestate prepared a memorandum of instructions addressed to two of his most intimate friends, Mr. *Crookshank*, the administrator, and Mr. *Gamble*, in which, after thanking them for their kindness in having undertaken to look after his property in his absence, (which, it seems, was not intended to be permanent,) he enters into details of various matters, and among them states:—" A considerable sum of money stands at my credit in the Bank of Upper Canada, which I was or am authorized to invest, and had intended to do so in government debentures, but there are none such in the bank at present : it has to be at command on short notice, or I could have got ample security for the use of it, as money seems much wanted at present, but it is necessary that I shall have it in my power to pay it out at any time when called for, though perhaps it may be permitted, or part of it may be permitted, to lie for some time if well secured, and the interest regularly paid; but of this I am not certain. At my credit stands about £1300, and Mr. *Webster* has promised to pay Mr. *Gamble* the debt due by him as he can spare the money. Should I require the money timely notice will be given." Whether this last sentence refers to the deposit or to *Webster's* debt, or to both, is not very clear. Again, he says, " my dividends at the bank, if any are declared, will be due in July, and a special power of attorney being required for the purpose of discharging the bank, I have filled up one to Mr. *Crookshank*. These will enable you to satisfy any outlay called for on my account." Mr. *Crookshank*, and the intestate, appear to have continued on the most friendly terms to the last, and the utmost confidence seems to have been reposed by one in the other. Both were men of large properties, and appear to have been most intimate associates for years, and Mr. *Crookshank* appears to have undertaken the duty of looking after his friend's affairs in his absence from pure friendship, and not from any expectation of reward, and so far as I can see he discharged that duty most faithfully and honourably. The personal property of the intestate is alone in question here. A great many letters from the intestate to *Crookshank*, and extracts of letters, (the originals not being forthcoming) from the latter to the former, reaching down to within a month of his death, are put in. The first in date is one of the 6th September, 1842, written by the intestate, and in which, after alluding

to a previous letter of the 20th of August, he says :
" my deposit in that institution (meaning the Bank of
Upper Canada,) is too large to be lying idle, if it can
be properly placed out at interest for a time, the proceeds will aid me, for I am not without the need of it,
times are so hard here."

On the 17th of October the intestate writes : "I have
just had the pleasure of your different respected letters
of the 23rd and 26th ultimo.   Mine, despatched only
three days ago will, in a measure, have anticipated your
wish.   My deposit in the bank is idle there, and I
wished of you to take the trouble of getting it invested
so as to bring me something.   Now, as you can employ
it so as to serve you, I shall be quite pleased if you do
so to the extent you require.   It will be serving me
quite as I wish."   On the 26th of October the intestate,
after stating the receipt on the 17th of the letters already referred to, says, " on the day yours got here, I
immediately answered them in a few lines, to say that
any thing of mine in the Bank of Upper Canada is
completely at your service.   The time was short, but I
hope my previous letter would answer the purpose."   On
the 22nd of October, by the extract produced, Mr.
Crookshank appears to have written to Mr. *Wood* on a
variety of matters, and among them the Bank deposit,
and proposes to take all the intestate's funds for two or
three years, and offers a mortgage in security.   He had
not then, of course, received the letter of the seventeenth
of October, and the contents of the letters therein alluded to are not shewn, though they, or one of them,
evidently contained a proposal to take the money.   On the
24th of November, *Crookshank* appears again to have
written that it would have been an accommodation to
himself to have got the deposit, proposing several farms
and lots by way of mortgage and security, and expressing
a wish that the mortgage should not be registered, and
stating that the deposit was, £1385 2s. 11d. ; that a
dividend of £52 had been received, out of which some

small payments had been made, and that Mr. *Wood's* cheque would be required to draw the money. On the 30th of November the intestate writes: "the particular matter interesting to yourself was, I presume, satisfactorily anticipated by my former letters. I think the power I left you (meaning the memorandum of instruction) would be sufficient to enable you to draw out of the bank. Then I suppose my dividend at last time was placed at my credit, with ten pounds from Captain *Macaulay*, would be £62; the dividend on insurance stock only a few shillings." On the 19th of December, 1842, *Wood* writes: "Mr. ———'s letter does propose to borrow my funds in the bank. I have written to him that I had requested of you to invest these funds three months since. I think the power of attorney will enable you to draw out by cheque my deposit. It would be rather hazardous to enclose one in a letter from this. If I should surprise you sooner than expectation it will be necessary for me to have some funds at my command, as times here are so bad. I see you state exactly the amount at my credit in the bank when I left; of course the dividends would, and I hope will be paid. Of course any demands made, you will be so good as to discharge, though I know of none except taxes and any little matter. *Fenwick* (a servant left in charge of his house) may need to keep things a little to rights. 'The Patriot' (newspaper) of course once a year." On the fifteenth of December, 1842, *Wood* writes: "I shall be glad to hear that the business with respect to money transactions has fully answered your wishes."

On the 26th of January, 1843, the intestate writes, "I would send you a cheque on the bank if I was not sure the cashier would have no hesitation in answering your own under the power of attorney I left, for it was intended to enable you to do so in case I required a remittance. I kept an exact copy of the power." And he enclosed him a letter to Mr. *Ridout*, cashier of the bank instructing him to honour Mr. *Crookshank's* cheque for all or any part of the money standing at his credit.

On the 28th of March, 1843, the intestate writes, "my last covered a note to the cashier of the bank of Upper Canada, though I am pleased you have done without it. I do not wish any deposit in my name in the bank of Upper Canada; if you do not want it, get it invested in some other safe way to be at my call when necessary." And he asks *Crookshank* to draw a small dividend from the assurance company. On the 25th of May, 1843, the intestate writes, "I shall be glad that you have received all my deposit, as I could not afford to leave it at such risks, though this is between ourselves. Would you advise to sell out?" alluding to his bank stock. On the 29th of April, 1844, the intestate writes a long and affectionate letter on various subjects, part of them business—and expresses his wish to be again in Toronto, but fears it cannot be realized in that year. On the 13th of August, in the same style and about many matters is written the last letter from *Wood* to *Crookshank*. It contains this passage, "I also mention to Mr. *G.* that you will be remitting me money, and if any of my own remains in his hands to give it to you that one remittance may serve. I shall hereafter inform you how much I want, so if he offers you any take it." "He says, suffering it to remain, they will pay me interest for it." In the following month, as already stated, Mr. *Wood* died. Mr. *Crookshank* died in the year 1859. Had these two old fond friends lived to come together again, doubtless they would have settled all matters between them without the intervention of any third party. They have gone, and the court is employed in adjusting the same matters, and those which have naturally grown out of them, between their respective representatives. A general power of attorney, dated the 27th of December, 1844, from several persons named *Barclay*, and from some others, claiming to be next of kin, and co-heirs of the intestate, was executed in favour of Mr. *Crookshank*. What pretence of right these parties made does not appear : they were probably the rival claimants to Mrs. *Farrell*, whose title to the intestate's real property seems to have been established at the close of the year 1850. About the same time an arrangement seems to have been come to among the relatives of the deceased as to the distribution of his personal estate, though not perfected till some time afterwards. About the 27th of December, 1845, the bill alleges, and it is not denied, Mr. *Crookshank* took out letters of administration to *Wood's* estate ; upon whose request, unless under the first-mentioned power of attorney, does not appear. On the death of Mr. *Crookshank*, and about the 19th of February, 1860, the late Mr. *Ewart*, who for some years previously had been acting as agent for the heiress and next of kin obtained administration *de bonis non* at the instance of the next of kin of the intestate, and instituted the present suit, which, on his death, after decree made, was, on the 21st of December last, revived in the name of the present plaintiff as successor in the administration *de bonis non*. The Master's report was made on the 9th of May, 1862. A general power of attorney to manage all the intestate's real and personal estate, to receive rents, get in and collect debts and moneys due him, etc., and dated the 25th of March, 1846, was executed by Mrs. *Farrell*, and sent to Mr. *Crookshank*. Another power of attorney from the same claimant, dated the 14th of March, 1850, and relating exclusively to the real estate was also furnished. As I have already stated the rights of the several claimants to the intestate's real and personal estate do not appear to have been settled till the end of the year 1850; and the arrangement in regard to the personalty not completed probably till the beginning of the following year. On the 9th of November, 1850, a letter from Mr. *John Falconer* and Mr. *James Edmund*, representing, together apparently, those inter-

ested in the personal estate, is written to Mr. *Crookshank*
in the following words :

" ABERDEEN, 9th November, 1850.

" DEAR SIR—It is a long time since we last addressed
you. We have satisfaction in now communicating, that
all opposition has been withdrawn to the claims of our
clients to the estate of Mr. *Wood.* In writing together,
we write, as you are aware, with regard to the personal
estate only, and as to that property, the forms are in
progress, and will be shortly closed, for declaring the
right to it of one of our clients. In that view it will be
convenient to prepare, in other respects, for the transmission hither of the funds which are abroad. And it
will advance us a step, if you will be so good as send us
now an account of the matter, as it presently stands.
Be so good also as inform us what form of discharge
you will require, when accounting to us as the representatives of the relations on both sides of the deceased."

"We are, dear Sir,
" Yours truly,
(Signed)   " JOHN FALCONER.
(Signed)   " JAMES EDMUND."

" The Hon. GEO. CROOKSHANK,

Toronto."

Up to this time no account of the personal estate
appears to have been asked for, no inquiry in respect
of it made, no direction given. All parties seem to
have rested satisfied with Mr. *Crookshank's* management
and responsibility. About the beginning of the year
1848, as well as I can ascertain, Mr. *Crookshank*, under
the authority given him by the intestate, drew from
the bank the deposit so often referred to of £1383.
And the question of interest arises first as to it. Before,
however, expressing an opinion thereon, it may be well
to dispose of certain questions preliminary as well as
technical and formal. I think there is nothing in the
first objection that the administrator *de bonis non* cannot claim interest on such allowances as the court

will make for breach of trust in his predecessor. He is appointed in succession to act for the court, which empowers him in getting in all that properly belongs to, or can be claimed for, the intestate's estate, and which the administrator has neglected to get in. Both the administrator and his successor merely act for the court —are both accountable to it; and the one and the other can be made accountable in this court, and can seek the aid of this court in the administration. If there be any objection to the claim of the administrator *de bonis non*, it must be this, that the administrator *de bonis non* cannot call the estate of the deceased administrator to account, but that this can only be done by the court, or under the authority of the court, which has appointed him. The objection cannot be that the administrator *de bonis non* does not represent the next of kin as fully as the original administrator, for his office, his duty, his authority, his mode of appointment from the same power is precisely similar. But that objection has not been made—a decree for an account has been consented to, and were the point a debateable one I am not now at liberty to consider it, but must treat the estate of the deceased administrator as accountable at the suit of the plaintiff. The second objection and so much of the sixth as relates to the pleadings are answered by the provisions of section 13, of General Order 42, of the court, and by the decree itself. The fourth objection is displaced by the decree, which states that the defendants admit assets of the said *George Crookshank* come to their hands sufficient to pay the plaintiff's claim ; that claim being, of course, whatever the plaintiff can make himself out entitled to under the decree according to the practice and law of the court. It thus differs from the case *Davenport* v. *Stafford.* (a)

Then, as to this deposit of £1383, which, with the intestate's permission, *Crookshank* drew from the bank

---

(a) 14 Beav. 319.

and used. It was, I think, looking at the correspondence, the intention and understanding of both parties that *Crookshank* should pay interest for it, and yet the intestate never appears to have applied for or received any interest on this sum. It is doubtful whether it was his own money. His allusion to it in the memorandum of instructions would imply that it was not. He states that it must be kept on call or short notice. He refused to invest it on mortgage; and he lets *Crookshank* have it without mortgage, though the latter appears at one time to have offered him such security if he could get the money for two or three years. Still, he writes to have the money invested so as to bring him in something, though it is to be called in on short notice; and he seems rejoiced when *Crookshank* has taken the use of it, as he evidently considers it safe with him, and to produce something. Money held on call would not generally yield the same rate of interest as that borrowed for a fixed period, and yet I do not know what rate of interest other than six per cent. can be charged in the absence of any arrangement by *Crookshank* with the intestate for a lesser sum, and of any evidence shewing any other usual rate. I think he must be so charged during the intestate's life. The time at which this sum was received does not very clearly appear, nor whether in one sum or several sums. If the latter, a time should be ascertained from which interest should be charged, considering that the money was to be on call. I think that as six per centum is to be charged, it would be but fair to charge interest only from the time when the last of the sums was drawn out, if it was all taken within a short time. On the other sums received during the intestate's life-time, I think no interest should be during that period charged, for it is evident that the intestate intended *Crookshank* to hold those moneys for the discharge of any claims payable by him, and to be remitted to him at any moment he might require a remittance. Neither, of course, should any interest be

allowed on payments made during the same period
except where and on so much as they exceed the amount
in hand to meet them. This disposes of the subject of
interest down to the intestate's death, and it is now to
be considered how it is to be dealt with during the four
subsequent periods. The 1st, from that death down to
the time letters of administration were obtained by
Crookshank. The 2nd, from that period down to the
year 1851, when the rightful claimants were ascertained.
The 3rd, from that time down to the institution of this
suit. And the 4th, during the pendency of the suit
until the final order for payment shall have been made.
I have made this division of time because the learned
counsel for the defendants contended that different rules
might be applied to them respectively. On looking at
the accounts, it does not appear that the administrator
received anything from the death of the intestate until
after letters of administration were granted to him, but
he retained during that period the deposit of $1383 ;
and as I have already found that he was to pay interest
for it, he must during this period be charged still with
interest in the same way as if the debt was owing to the
intestate's estate by a third party. And so, throughout
the subsequent periods enumerated until the money was
re-funded. It is quite true as to it as well as to other
moneys received and held by the administrator during
the second of those periods that there was no one to
whom he could have paid them over, and that it was
uncertain when he might be called upon for them. An
administrator in such a case is in an awkward position,
but I have found no case which has decided that this is
a sufficient excuse for his retaining moneys in his hands
uninvested, or a good reason for not charging him with
interest on the moneys of the estate which he has used.
In England he has no difficulty in making investments,
as he can purchase government securities in the market
every day. Here there is greater difficulty, and the
only course I think which can be properly taken is when
a certain amount, such as one would think sufficient

to offer as a loan, has accumulated in his hands to allow
the administrator a reasonable time to seek a safe investment ; and if he shall not have made one, then, after
the lapse of that time, to charge him with interest unless he can shew that he has used all proper diligence to
obtain an investment, and has failed, and that he has
not himself used the money.   If, while the parties entitled to the estate are unknown, the administrator
makes investments of such a character as this court
sanctions, those parties on establishing their title cannot complain that the money is so invested and is not
in specie ready to their hand.   Looking at the position,
then, in which this estate stood, the discretion with
which, during the pendency of the litigation, Mr. *Crookshank* appears to have been intrusted by the claimants,
and the absence as already remarked of any desire
by them that any of the moneys should be hung up in
investments, and the expectation apparent in the letter
of the 8th of November, 1850, that the funds were in
a state to be transmitted so soon as all legal formalities for confirming the title of the next of kin to them
had been completed, I think the Master exercised a
fair judgment in charging the administrator with
interest from the end only of the year in which the
receipts had accumulated, after deducting the payments in that year, when such balance amounted to
a sum sufficient for an ordinary investment, which
could hardly be less than £100. When a balance equal
to at least that sum was not in hand, it might well be
carried on into the next year, and until in the receipts
of that year, a sufficient accretion had been made to call
for an investment.   From the time when the parties
entitled to the moneys were ascertained, and reasonable
time had elapsed for arranging with them what was to be
done with the estate belonging to them, and how it was to
be transmitted or invested, the estate of the administrator must be charged with interest on all moneys then in
his hands, or afterwards recovered and held by him
without the assent of the parties entitled thereto, except

for such reasonable time of course as would be necessary for their payment over, or transmission; and from the time of Mr. *Ewart's* authority to act for the next of kin, and to receive their property, being established and made known to the administrator, there could of course be no difficulty in paying over the moneys in hand, or as required from time to time. On the 4th of October, 1851, Mr. *Crookshank* transmitted to the agents in Scotland of the next of kin, a bill of exchange for £2500 sterling, amounting to upwards of £3000 currency, and as it is not certain at what time in that year the rights of these parties were finally fixed, I cannot say that there was any unreasonable delay in transmitting those moneys, chargeable, as they were, with interest. Mr. *Crookshank* may have thought and considered that this was all he owed.

He had now become an old man, and during the residue of his life was much enfeebled by age and growing infirmities, and for some time before his death was quite imbecile. It does not appear that he was engaged in business at any time, or that he was other than a gentleman of property living on the means which it afforded him. I have said already that Mr. *Crookshank* appeared to have discharged his voluntary duty to his friend, the intestate, most faithfully, and I see nothing in his dealings with the estate, after he assumed to be its administrator, from which I should infer that he intended to act otherwise, although he has rendered himself liable to charges, which from the relation in which he had stood to the intestate, and from a mistaken notion of his own obligations, he might probably have considered himself free. I have seen nothing to shew that Mr. *Crookshank* would himself have declined to account for the money which he borrowed from the estate with interest upon it. Indeed Mr. *Ewart* says that he never heard of that pretence till lately.

The defendants were not parties to the transaction,

and were ignorant of it in its inception, and cannot be said to have improperly raised the question as guardians of their testator's estate. For the delays which have occurred of late years in the not rendering of proper accounts, and the paying over of any balance which on these adjustments might be found due, though legally he, *Crookshank*, cannot be considered morally responsible. His agents, from Mr. *Ewart's* evidence, are evidently to blame; and although it may be unfortunate for the estate that the evidence of *McLean* has not been procured, still I think the master would not have been justified in further delaying his report for it. The defendants have waited taking the risk of his return to the country instead of examining him abroad, and they must abide by it.

I have not failed to consider the objection that this is a bill for an account of Mr. *Crookshank's* transactions, as administrator, and not as agent of *Wood* in his life-time; but I think the latter are necessarily involved in the other, for it was his duty as administrator to call himself to account with himself as agent.

Mr. *Crooks* insisted again at the close of the argument that the Master's mode of computing interest was wrong, and that interest should be calculated on payments and receipts from time to time; and Mr. *McLennan*, for the plaintiff, assented to it. If the defendants still wish for this mode, I will order it, though I have already stated I would not have subjected the estate, under the circumstances, to such a rigid rule. The claim for exemption from interest during the pendency of this suit cannot be maintained. An accounting party runs the risk of a report in his favour, or a balance being found against him; he ought to know the state of his own accounts, and what moneys he has in hand, and if he disputes his indebtedness he must be charged with interest on any balance found against him

I think the cross appeal must be dismissed. This is not a case for compound interest; and any calculation of the master which would charge it should be disallowed. There has been here no wasting of the funds; no trading with them; no concealment of receipts; no making of profits with them; no delaying in accounting or paying over, which can be considered the fault of the administrator himself, though legally responsible for the neglect of his agents. I think, also, it is a proper case for the allowance of a commission. In all the powers of attorney referred to, a reasonable compensation, or as the Scotch phrase used expresses it, "gratification," for the services of the administrator is guaranteed him, and I think under the 13th section of the General Order before referred to, the master was right in reporting upon it, though perhaps it will be more proper to allow the sum recommended on the hearing on further directions than now.

I have carefully considered all the cases cited on the argument, and I cannot but feel that there will be often difficulty, and sometimes great harshness in applying rigidly in this country the rules usually adopted in England. I say usually, because they meet there with frequent relaxation, and, as they should, in no case more often than when there has been a total absence of *mala fides* in the administrator.

GAMBLE V. GUMMERSON.

Specific performance—Dower—Contract for sale of land subject to.

The court refused to enforce a contract for the sale of land, which was subject to an outstanding claim for dower, until the title to dower was removed; but the defendant in his answer having set up as a defence charges of fraud which were not established, withheld from him his costs of the suit.

Chantler v. *Ince*, reported ante volume vii., page 432, observed upon; *Thompson* v. *Brunskill*, ante volume vii., page 542, approved of.

This was a suit for specific performance under the circumstances stated in the judgment of the court, and came on for hearing upon the pleadings and evidence.

Mr. *Hillyard Cameron*, Q.C., and Mr. *G. D. Boulton*, for plaintiff, referred to *Chantler* v. *Ince*, as warranting a decree as prayed.

Mr. *Hodgins*, for defendant, contended that if even the case referred to should be deemed conclusive, this is distinguishable from it, in this, that here the agreement is for an immediate sale free from incumbrances, the purchaser to give a mortgage on the other property for a portion of the purchase money.

Judgment.—ESTEN, V. C.— [Before whom the cause was heard.]—This is a suit for specific performance of an agreement to purchase certain lands situate in the township of Vaughan, for the sum of £1325. The agreement was signed on the 4th of May, 1861. The bargain had been previously entered into on the 25th of April. Upon this occasion one *Train* was present, who has been examined as a witness. The defendant was admitted into possession and continued in possession some time. The property had belonged to one *Allan*, and did still in fact belong to his heirs, and was subject to the dower of his widow. The defendant decidedly and constantly refused to accept the estate without the dower being barred. Under these circumstances, the agreement not being performed, the present suit has been instituted. It seemed to be conceded during the argument that the title to the estate, apart from this claim of dower, was good; and I suppose I may treat the case as if the master had reported in favour of the title, except that it was subject to an outstanding title of dower, and that no prospect existed of procuring a release of it.

The suit is resisted on three grounds, first, that the plaintiff fraudulently represented when the bargain was made that the dower had been barred, when in point of fact it was not, as he knew. Second, that the real agreement between the parties was different from what is contained in the written instrument signed by them.

Third, that the title is defective by reason of this outstanding title of dower. The evidence on the first point consists of the evidence given by the plaintiff himself, who was examined by the defendant, of *Train* and Mrs. *Allan*. *Train* says positively that he was present at the making of the bargain, and that the plaintiff assured the defendant three times that the dower was barred, and pointing to a tin box, said it was there. He adds, that on a subsequent conversation with the plaintiff, upon the plaintiff saying that he had not procured a release of the dower, and *Train* observing that he thought it had been barred at the time of the bargain, the plaintiff said it was, but that it was not right; that there was a mistake. The plaintiff in effect denies the facts stated by *Train*. He evidently alludes to the same occasion, and says, that although the dower was mentioned, the defendant asked no question respecting it, but it was understood that it was to be barred: that the defendant was to have a deed free from incumbrances. Mrs. *Allan* says that she never did, to her knowledge, execute any deed releasing her dower. I cannot conceive any motive for the plaintiff asserting the dower was barred, when in fact it was not. It would be telling a deliberate falsehood without any reason. However determined the defendant might be not to accept the estate subject to dower, his end would be effectually attained by providing that unless the dower should be relinquished the agreement should be at an end. It was more consistent with usage for the dower to be released at the time the estate was conveyed than beforehand. Under these circumstances I do not think the charge of fraud is established. I would rather infer that *Train* did not accurately recollect what passed at the time of making the bargain, which occurred a year before he delivered his testimony. Upon the second point, I think the evidence fails still more signally. The charge rests entirely on the evidence of *Train*, who, as already observed, was present at the making of the bargain, but whose memory is more likely to fail in detailing the several particulars of an agreement than in mentioning a single fact. I think, too, that he must be wrong as to the dates, and it is not very likely that the plaintiff would have definitely agreed to accept a mortgage about which he knew nothing but what the defendant told him. Some slight modification might have occurred between the 25th of April and the 4th of May. No doubt some conversation occurred relative to the Tecumseth mortgage. On the other hand, the plaintiff states that the terms were those stated in the agreement, and although the defendant had a duplicate of the agreement in his possession from the time it was entered into, and although *Train* himself says that he read it to him, and that he remarked it was different from what the plaintiff had read to him, yet on two subsequent occasions occurring five or six months afterwards, the plaintiff and defendant met at Mr. *Gamble's* office, and at Mr. *Cameron's* office respectively, and on the first occasion the defendant said he was prepared to perform his part of the agreement, provided the plaintiff was ready to perform his part, by giving a deed free from dower; and on the second occasion, the agreement and the dower were the subject of conversation, but on neither occasion did the defendant complain that the written instrument which had been signed did not express the real agreement of the parties. Under these circumstances I think the evidence wholly fails to establish any variance between the agreement as concluded between the parties, and as expressed in the written instrument signed by them.

The third objection is, that the plaintiff cannot make a good title to the estate, and upon this objection I think the defendant is entitled to succeed. When the estate appears to be subject to a title of dower, and no evidence is adduced before the master to shew that the consent of the party entitled to the dower to relinquish it has been obtained, the master is bound to report against the title. The case of *VanNorman* v. *Beauprie*, in this court, decided that a purchaser is not bound to accept an estate subject to a title of dower of a married woman whose husband is still alive, and with that decision I entirely agree. It is every day's practice both in England and here to require on purchases of estate that inchoate titles of dower should be extinguished. It is said that an inchoate title of dower is not an incumbrance within the meaning of the ordinary covenant against incumbrances; and the case of *Boner* v. *Bass,* mentioned in that of *Hoyt* v. *Widderfield,* (a) is cited for that position. That case must be taken by this court to shew the law on this point. In the case of *Hoyt* v. *Widderfield,* and also in the case of *Boner* v. *Bass,* the court intimated the opinion that a refusal by a married woman and her husband to release her inchoate title of dower would be no breach of a covenant for further assurance extending to the acts of all persons. The late learned Chief Justice *Macaulay* dissented from this latter opinion, and I must say that I should have been strongly disposed to agree with him. But the question is not whether the existence of an inchoate title of dower is a breach of a covenant against incumbrancers; or whether a refusal to release such a right constitutes a breach of a covenant for further assurance, but whether a court of equity will compel a purchaser to accept a title subject to such a claim ; and it is clear from the case of *VanNorman* v. *Beauprie* that such is not the rule. It would be very unreasonable that the court should adopt such a course. The jurisdiction to compel a specific performance is discretionary, and it would be very unreasonable to compel a purchaser to accept a title so circumstanced, as to expose him to disturbance, and compel him, probably, to resort to legal proceedings for indemnification. I apprehend the existence of an inchoate title of dower would be a breach of a covenant for seisin in fee, and for good right to convey as ordinarily expressed ; and I should have thought that a refusal to release would have been a breach of a covenant for further assurance. The truth

---

(a) 5 U. C. Q. B. 180.

is, the covenant against incumbrances is a branch of the
covenant for quiet enjoyment, and so long as the estate
is quietly enjoyed, the covenant may not be broken.

Mr. *Cameron* contends that the purchaser in this case
is by the terms of the contract bound to pay the $2,300,
and to accept a conveyance containing a covenant against
incumbrances. I cannot agree to this proposition. The
payment of the $2,300, and the execution of the convey-
ance and mortgage were to be contemporaneous acts.
No time is fixed for their execution; but no doubt a
reasonable time was to be allowed for the investigation of
the title, and then the transaction was to be completed by
payment of part, and a conveyance and mortgage for the
balance. This was an ordinary contract for sale and
purchase of an estate for $5,300, payable at certain ap-
pointed times, it being agreed that when $2,300 were
paid a conveyance should be executed and a mortgage
given for the balance of the purchase money. Such a
contract undoubtedly entitled the purchaser to require
a good title to be shewn. It is true that the $2,300
were to be paid, and the conveyance executed so soon as
the title should have been examined; but he depended
upon a good title being shewn, and the estate being discharged from incumbrances. A purchaser, in the
absence of a special agreement, is not bound to pay,
except as a deposit, a particle of the purchase money,
until a good title is shewn, and the estate is discharged
from incumbrances. He may insist that all incumbrances
should be discharged before he pays any part of his purchase money; and although he may apply his purchase
money in discharge of incumbrances, he is not compellable
to do so, but may require the vendor to discharge them
in the first instance. The defendant might have insisted
before he paid his $2,300, upon a good title being shewn,
and all incumbrances being discharged, and he could not
have been compelled to pay the money or accept the
conveyance until that had been effected. As long as
this outstanding title of dower subsisted, he could not

have been compelled to pay his money, or accept a conveyance ; and I apprehend the result would have been
the same at law ; for although the existence of an inchoate title of dower may not be a breach of a covenant
for quiet enjoyment, free from incumbrances, I apprehend it would have prevented the due fulfilment of the
agreement to convey the fee simple of the estate free
from incumbrances.   •

The case of *Chantler* v. *Ince*, (a) was cited for the
plaintiff. In that case the defendant had agreed for
the sale to the plainliff of some land in the village of
Newmarket, for the sum of £100, payable £25 down,
and the balance in three annual instalments, with interest, and that upon payment of the purchase money and
interest he would convey to the plaintiff the land free
from incumbrances. After the contract was entered
into the purchaser discovered an incumbrance on the
estate, and he objected to pay any more of his purchase
money until it was discharged. It consisted of a mortgage which had become due. The defendant commenced
an action against him for the recovery of the instalments
due, and he instituted a suit in this court to restrain proceedings in the action until the incumbrance should be
discharged ; or that he might be allowed to apply his
purchase money to that purpose. An injunction was
granted, which was afterwards dissolved by the Chancellor, who thought that as the defendant had only undertaken to convey the estate free from incumbrances at the
expiration of three years, he could not be compelled
to discharge any incumbrances in the meantime, nor
to submit to the application of the purchase money
to that purpose. That case may have been rightly
decided upon its circumstances ; but if it is to be
considered as establishing a general rule that where
the purchase money is payable by instalments, and the
vendor engages, on payment of it, to convey the estate

(a) Ante vol. vii., p. 432.

free from incumbrances, the purchaser is compellable to
pay his purchase money without a good title being shewn,
and although incumbrances may remain undischarged
I do not agree to it. The agreement to convey free
from incumbrances on payment of the purchase money,
does not, I apprehend, give the vendor all the time
during which the purchase money is payable to discharge the incumbrances. The expression "free
from incumbrances," merely indicates the manner in
which the estate is to be conveyed. The agreement
would be equally forcible without them, for it would
oblige the seller to convey the estate without incumbrance, and they are in fact inoperative. It would
be extremely mischievous to hold that where the purchase money is to be paid by instalments, and when
it is paid the estate is to be conveyed, the purchaser
could be compelled to pay all his purchase money
without having a good title shewn, and without the estate
being discharged from incumbrances. The result would
be in nine cases out of ten that when the purchase
money had been all paid and spent, the vendor would
be unable to shew a good title or discharge the incumbrances, and the purchaser would be in an unfortunate
condition. When an estate is subject to incumbrances,
the fact ought to be mentioned by the vendor, and the
purchaser will either decline to purchase, or make some
special agreement. But when an estate is offered generally for sale, the purchaser has a right to assume that
the title is good, and that it is free from incumbrances,
and he has a right to require this to be shewn before he
can be compelled to pay any part of his purchase money,
or accept a conveyance. If he is prudent he will look
into the title at once. Too often, however, purchasers
enter into possession and pay part of their purchase
money, and postpone the investigation of the title. But
they may, I apprehend, at any time, require a good
title to be shewn, and incumbrances to be discharged, and
refuse to proceed until this is done ; and I believe my
brother *Spragge* has so decided, although I do not

remember .the case. in 'which. that' decision was pro-- nounced. (a)

Where incumbrances are due they should be discharg- ed,and when they are not due,the purchase money should be retained to meet them. The vendor has a lien on the estate for his. purchase money ; and the purchaser has a lien on his purchase money for the discharge of in- cumbrances, to which he ought not to be subject. Of course a contrary agreement may be expressed or implied from the circumstances of the case,as in the case of *Tully* v. *Bradbury* (b) in this court. But in the absence of special agreement, varying the rights of the parties, I appre- hend the rule to be as I have stated. In the present case no doubt can be entertained. On the payment of the $2,300 the estate is to be conveyed in fee simple free from incumbrance, In the meantime the purchaser has a right to look into the title, and if he finds it defective, or that the estate is subject to incumbrances, to require a good title to be shewn, and the incumbrances to be re- moved before he can be called upon to pay his 'money. He has a perfect right to require this title to dower to be removed, and cannot be compelled to complete his purchase until its removal is effected. Supposing this to be impracticable, although the title may be otherwise good, the bill must be dismissed. The plaintiff may either at once submit to such a decree; or take a refer- ence as to the title, if he entertains any hope of procur- ing a release of the dower. I think in either case that each party must bear his own costs to this time. *Prima facie* if the bill be dismissed it would be with costs ; or if a reference be directed, and a good title eventually shewn, the plaintiff must pay the costs to the time at which it may be first shewn, and it has not been shewn yet. But the defendant has thought fit in the present case to advance a charge of fraud,which he has failed to substantiate, and has likewise insisted,

(a) Thompson v. Brunskill, ante vol. vii., p. 542.
(b) Ante vol. vii., p. 561.

contrary to the fact, as appears from the evidence, that the written instrument was not prepared or expressed in accordance with the real agreement, and I think, under these circumstances, he must bear his own costs to the hearing, whatever disposition may ultimately be made of this suit. Should a reference be directed, I think the purchaser may object on any ground to the title.

[The plaintiff subsequently allowed his bill to be dismissed at the instance of the defendant, in consequence of the plaintiff's failure to proceed with the enquiry as to title.]

BULLEN v. RENWICK.

Mortgage—Sale with right to re-purchase.

Where after a treaty for loan on real estate the owner thereof conveyed the same absolutely to the person to whom he had applied for such loan, receiving back a bond conditioned to re-convey the property, on payment of a certain sum at the end of two years, and made default in such payment; a bill filed, alleging the transaction to have been one of loan and security merely, and praying redemption, was dismissed with costs. On a re-hearing this decree was reversed and the deed declared to have been made as security only; the bond to re-convey containing an undertaking by the vendor to pay the stipulated amount, and it appearing that the value of the property greatly exceeded the sum paid for the alleged purchase thereof; but under the circumstances the court charged the mortgagee with such rents and profits as were actually received, or an occupation rent, if in actual possession ; not with such rents as might have been received, and allowed him for repairs and permanent improvements.

The facts of this case sufficiently appear in the report on the original hearing, *ante* volume viii., page 342. The plaintiff being dissatisfied with the decree then pronounced, set the cause down to be re-heard before the full court. On the re-hearing

Mr. *Becher,* Q. C., Mr. *Roaf,* and Mr. *Proudfoot,* for plaintiff.

Mr. *Brough,* Q. C., for defendant.

On the part of the plaintiff it was contended that the real transaction was a loan, although means had been adopted to conceal the true nature of it. Defendant in his letter of August offers to purchase or lend money, and it is improbable that the owner would willingly part with the estate absolutely for a considerable sum less than had a few days before been offered by way of loan on the security of the same estate. Here also the bond which was cotemporaneous with the deed, contains a recital that *Bullen* had agreed to pay the £512, thus clearly rendering the transaction one of loan and security for re-payment, as the defendant, had he become dissatisfied with the bargain, as he states it, could have maintained an action against the plaintiff to enforce payment.

For the defendant, it was contended that the recital in the bond simply meant that *Bullen* had agreed to pay so much purchase money, not to re-pay the £400 paid to him by the defendant. The instruments on the face of them clearly evidence a transaction of purchase with a right of re-purchase by the vendor, which right it is incumbent on the vendor to enforce strictly, or it will be lost.

Abbott v. *Stewart*, (a) *Fee* v. *Cobine*, (b) *Williams* v. *Owen*, (c) *Alderson* v. *White*, (d) *Lincoln* v. *Wright*, (e) *Perry* v. *Meddowcroft*, (f) were referred to by the counsel.

The judgment of the court was delivered by.

Judgment.—SPRAGGE, V. C.—I have considered this case a good deal, and incline to the opinion, though not without some doubt, that the transaction was in reality a loan of money. The parties, no doubt, used the words purchase, and liberty of re-purchase, and other words of the like import; but that is quite usual, or rather was quite

---

(a) 5 Jur. N. S. 317.   (b) 11 Ir. Eq. 406.
(c) 5 M. & C. 301.   (d) 2 DeG. & J. 97.
(e) 4 DeG. & J. 16.   (f) 4 Beav. 197.

usual when the bargain was for the payment of more
than legal interest. But what was the substance of the
bargain ? On the 18th of August Colonel *Renwick*
offered to purchase the property at £525, or to lend
£500 upon it; and on the 26th of September it is
alleged that he purchased for £400. £400 was the sum
paid or advanced by Colonel *Renwick* to Mr. *Bullen*.
It is quite possible, certainly, that Colonel *Renwick*, as
my brother *Esten* supposes, changed his mind, and
having offered to give £525, reduced his offer to £400,
and I should have thought it not improbable that he was
unwilling to give so much if his purchase was to be
defeasible, as if it was to be absolute and final. But
Mr. *Wilson* speaks of the proposal to make the right of
re-purchase a term of the bargain, *as after the offer of*
£400 Mr. *Wilson* certainly, in the early part of his
evidence particularly, speaks as if from a full conviction
that the transaction was a purchase, and not a loan of
money; but then his impression was that Colonel *Renwick* would not lend money upon mortgage; and he
was ignorant of, and I think, taken somewhat by surprise, by Colonel *Renwick's* letter of the 18th of
August. It may be said that if the alleged purchase
money was less than the amount first offered; so also
was the alleged loan, but I am not satisfied of that—the
loan was to be on such terms as the writer should instruct
a friend to offer—and that might mean £500, subject to
discount, and other deductions which might greatly
reduce it, even to £400 ; indeed an advance of £500
upon property of the value of £525 would not be considered a good investment.

The recital in the bond that *Bullen* "hath agreed to
pay £512," is important. I think that in none of the
cases in which the transaction has been held a purchase
with right to re-purchase, has the vendor been bound to
re-purchase, but it has been optional with him. When
he is bound to re-purchase at a sum named, I do not see
in what essential point it differs from an ordinary mort-

gage. Suppose the amount fixed, as the price to be paid upon re-purchase, the same as the purchase money, with interest, the sum called purchase money becomes at once a debt to be paid with interest, that is, the same amount is to be re-paid as in the case of any other debt.

If the sum fixed for re-purchase is larger, that cannot alter its character; if it could, it would have been the simplest way in the world of obtaining more than legal interest upon a mortgage.

It must always be a question of serious doubt, when the alleged purchase, with right of re-purchase, are co-temporaneous, whether it is not in fact a loan of money in disguise. It may be otherwise certainly, and there are cases in which it has been held to be otherwise, but in those cases the court thought that it was made to appear clearly that the transaction was in reality, and not in name only, an agreement to purchase.

There are two circumstances which have led me to doubt whether this was not in reality a purchase; one, the defendant's answer, in which he asserts it positively and explicitly; the other, the assumed right of Colonel *Renwick*, apparently acquiesed in by Mr. *Bullen*, to deal with the property as his own, upon the expiration of the two years.

With regard to the answer, it may be accounted for by the habit of men to look at the form rather than the substance of such transactions, and if they agree that it should take the shape of a purchase, with liberty to re-purchase, and be called and taken to be such between them, men are apt to consider it to be so really; while in the eye of a court of equity it is only the mode in which the parties have agreed that money shall be advanced on the one side, to be re-paid on the other.

In regard to the assumed right of Colonel *Renwick*

to deal with the property, this sometimes occurs even in cases of ordinary mortgage ; and would be more easily accounted for where the transaction took the shape which it took, in this case when a man might very well suppose that his right to redeem would be gone as soon as the time limited by the agreement had expired. In favour of the plaintiff, on the other hand, is the value of the property, for I think the weight of evidence is in favour of its being at least double the alleged purchase money ; the conclusion arrived at by Mr. *Horton*, the professional gentleman employed in the matter, for although he states no particular facts, a legal mind accustomed to such transactions will generally come to a correct conclusion as to their real nature, and from what he states as having passed, as he recollects it, I should incline to think his conclusion a correct one.

Then again the amount, not the amount offered a short time previously as purchase money, but somewhere about the amount which at the rate of interest Mr. *Horton* says, as he recollects it, was spoken of before him, was proposed to be advanced by way of loan, if such interest was deducted from the amount nominally advanced, as of course it would be, the sum to be paid by *Bullen*, not bearing interest.

And further, the agreement that *Bullen* should pay, not at his option, but absolutely, leads me almost irresistibly to the conclusion that the transaction was in substance and reality a loan of money. I think, therefore, that the plaintiff is entitled to redeem ; but under the circumstances I think the defendant should be charged only with what he received ; or with occupation rent, if he actually occupied or used the premises, not with what he might have received ; and that he should be allowed for all repairs and permanent improvements. The costs to be given as is usual on a bill to redeem, where redemption is resisted, without costs of re-hearing.

Judgment.—ESTEN, V. C.—In addition to what has been stated by my brother *Spragge,* I wish to say that the recent discussion of this case has led me to doubt the correctness of the decision given by me at the original hearing, and induces me to concur in the decision arrived at by the other members of the court.

The fact which has the most material bearing on the decision of the case, namely, the agreement to pay the amount of purchase money, as agreed between the parties, was not distinctly brought to my notice on the former hearing; had it been, it is not improbable I should have arrived at a different conclusion to what I then did.

HILL v. RUTHERFORD.

Composition deed—Effect of debtor failing strictly to fulfil terms of compromise.

The rule that the terms of competition deeds must be strictly complied with, considered, and acted upon.

The creditors of an insolvent debtor, by deed, absolute and unconditionally released their claim against him ; but it appeared by a memorandum on the instrument, that such release was intended to be in consideration of the debtor delivering to them certain endorsed notes, which, however, he stated he was unable to procure and in fact they were not delivered as had been agreed upon. *Held* that the creditors were entitled in this court to enforce payment of their original claim, notwithstanding that the debtor offered to pay the sum, for which it was stipulated by the deed of composition that the notes should be given, or to give the notes agreed upon ; and that the court of common law had held the right of the creditors to recover was gone.—[SPRAGGE, V.C., dissenting.]

The bill in this cause was filed by *Daniel Hill, Jesse W. Benedict,* and *William Vann; Benedict & Vann* being merchants residing in New York, setting forth, that on the 16th of September, 1859, defendant having become indebted to *Benedict & Vann* (for goods sold to him) in the sum of $979.76, stated the account between them by signing the following :

" $979.76   Guelph, September 16, 1859.

" Six months after date, I promise to pay to the order of *Benedict & Vann,* nine hundred and seventy-nine dollars, seventy-six cents, at the Bank of Montreal, with current rate of exchange on New York."

That *Rutherford* subsequently, and on the 9th of January, 1860, made an assignment to trustees for the benefit of his creditors, which contained a general release, unless the parties signing wrote "without release" after their signatures; that the deed was only executed by a few of defendant's creditors, and all without release; and the deed was afterwards abandoned, and a deed dated the 7th of August, 1860, was subsequently made; that in the interval, and in the month of June, defendant induced many of his creditors, and amongst them *Benedict & Vann*, to believe that he was unable to pay his liabilities in full, when it was agreed between him and his said creditors, that he should pay them five shillings in the pound, payable in two equal instalments, in six and twelve months, from the 1st of July, 1860; and that he should give his promissory notes, satisfactorily endorsed, to secure such payments. That for the purpose of carrying this arrangement out, a document was prepared by the defendant, purporting to be between his creditors of the one part, and the defendant of the other part, which instrument defendant took to his several creditors, requesting them to sign it, on the agreement and understanding that he would deliver such promissory notes, as before mentioned; upon which understanding many did sign, amongst others the plaintiffs *Benedict & Vann;* that afterwards defendant discovered he could not procure the notes to be endorsed by any one who would be satisfactory to his creditors, and thus to carry into effect in good faith the agreement for composition, and that he therefore abandoned it, and entered into a new arrangement with his creditors, which was carried into effect by an indenture, dated the 7th of August, 1860, purporting to be made between defendant, of the first part, *Ross, Mitchell & Fisken*, of the second part, the Bank of Montreal, the City Bank, and the Bank of Toronto, of the third part, and all his other creditors therein named (and among them *Benedict & Vann*) of the fourth part, which deed was transmitted by defendant to *Benedict & Vann*, at New York, in a letter of the

28th of August, 1860, wherein he stated, "in effect, that he was unable to get such satisfactory endorsers as aforesaid, and had therefore abandoned the arrangement and composition in the said paper-writing of June, 1860, referred to, and had resorted to the new arrangement contained in the said indenture of the 7th of August, 1860, and requesting the said *Benedict & Vann* to execute the said indenture, and procure other creditors of defendant, resident at New York, to execute the same."

The bill further alleged, that after the abandonment of the arrangement of June, 1860, and before receipt of the deed of the 7th of August, *Benedict & Vann*, considering the paper of the 7th of September, 1859, a promissory note, sold and delivered the same to the plaintiff *Hill*, for the sum of twenty-five per cent. on the amount thereof paid by *Hill* to them, and therefore they declined to execute the deed of the 7th of August, and returned the same to the defendant, at the same time informing him of the sale and transfer of the claim; that *Hill* being afterwards advised that this writing did not constitute in law a promissory note, and therefore could not be sued in his name, *Benedict & Vann*, authorised him to bring an action at law in their names, in which action the defendant in bad faith pleaded the release of the debt by the paper of June, 1860, and put the same in evidence, when, by consent of parties, a verdict was entered for defendant, with liberty to move to enter a verdict for the plaintiff, if the court should be of opinion, that upon the facts stated, they were entitled to recover; but the court afterwards, upon argument of a rule obtained for that purpose, refused to disturb the verdict so entered for defendant. The case at law is reported in 11 Upper Canada Common Pleas Reports, 213.

The prayer was for an injunction to restrain defendant setting up the writing of June, 1860, as a valid document ; its delivery up to be cancelled, so far as plaintiff was concerned ; an account and payment of amount found due. The defendant answered the bill at length, setting up, amongst other things, that by the deed of August, 1860, he was allowed two years to pay the compromise therein stated; but that such deed was not intended, neither did it, replace or in any manner do away with the lease of June, 1860, except as to creditors who should be willing to give him the additional time and advantage allowed by the deed of August, and who should become parties thereto ; that subsequently, and about the 18th of October, 1860, a letter was written to *Hill*, offering the security stipulated and agreed to be given, and submitted, that plaintiffs by suing at law had precluded themselves from resorting to this court for relief, and that under all the circumstances, this court had no jurisdiction in the premises. The cause having been put at issue, the defendant and one of the trustees under the deed, were examined on behalf of the plaintiffs, but the evidence did not materially vary the statements in the pleadings.

The cause was originally heard before his Honour. V. C. Esten. .

Mr. *McDonald*, for plaintiffs.

Mr. *Fitzgerald*, for defendant.

Judgment.—Esten, V.C.—The evidence shews that the plaintiffs were assenting parties to the deed of January, which operated against them as a release in equity. Then the plaintiffs join in and execute the deed of June, which cannot stand with the deed of January, but supersedes it, with regard to such of the creditors as execute it.

The plaintiffs are therefore bound by the deed of June. This deed cannot be considered as abandoned, by the making of the deed of August, or otherwise, as to creditors not executing the deed of August.

Prima facie, therefore, the plaintiffs must claim under the deed of June, but they retained the note until the security should be given, or composition paid. It must be intended that the note was so retained, in order that if the security was not given or composition with punctuality paid, the original debt might be enforced. The plaintiffs are, therefore, remitted to the deed of January, but *Rutherford* having put an end to that deed, by the one of August, they are remitted to their personal remedy for their whole debt against *Rutherford*. This, however, is the operation only in a court of equity, and a bill is, therefore, the proper course.

The decree will, therefore, be, that *Rutherford* must pay the amount of the note, and costs. *Rutherford* never was in a position to pay, having stripped himself of all his property. It would now be a breach of trust in *Moore* to pay.

Rutherford renounced the deed of January by the deed of August, and the plaintiffs choose to adopt such renunciation. In this view their action was premature, but this did not dispense with the payment or tender of composition.

What was done was not equivalent to either, for *Rutherford* never was ready with money, and the action under such circumstances was no refusal to accept payment of the composition.

The defendant feeling himself aggrieved by the decree thus pronounced, petitioned for a re-hearing of the cause before the full court : on the re-hearing,

Mr. *Proudfoot*, for the plaintiffs, contended that the decision of the Court of Common Pleas in the case of *Benedict* v. *Rutherford* did not affect in any degree the questions raised in this suit. From the statements in the pleadings and evidence it is evident that *Benedict* and *Vann* never contemplated abandoning any rights they were entitled to under their original claim, unless and until the stipulations in reference to the agreement of June, 1860, were entirely fulfilled. By the deed of June no property whatever was conveyed, and there is nothing contained in it which should prevent it subsisting with the one of January previous; while on the other hand the deed of August cannot be taken to agree with that of June, but must be considered to have superseded it; and *Benedict* and *Vann* never having executed or agreed to execute the deed of August, and default having been made in payment of the amount agreed upon by the terms of the compromise, they are remitted to their original rights under the note signed by the defendant.

The release being in the hands of the defendants and pleadable at law, this court has clearly jurisdiction to restrain him such use of it being against good faith.

Simpson v. *Lord Howden*, (a) *Flower* v. *Marten*, (b) *Gudgeon* v. *Bessett*, (c) *Hudson* v. *Revett*. (d)

Mr. *McMichael* and Mr. *Fitzgerald* for the defendant.

The general rule in equity is that the court will relieve against a forfeiture which is caused by non-payment of money. Here the defendant is ready to pay the full amount agreed to be paid as a composition, and it is established that before suit commenced he offered either to pay or deliver the notes endorsed as agreed upon. Here, then, the court will be lending its aid to work a forfeiture, for the defendant is not seeking its protection against the effects of his default in payment, as at law he

---

(a) 3 M. & C. 97.   (b) 2 M. & C. 459.
(c) 8 E. & B. 986.   (d) 5 Bing. 368.

has been declared not liable. This court no doubt would restrain the defendant from setting up the release unless he pays the 5s. in the £, but, under the circumstances of the case, that is unnecessary, as the defendant is willing and always has been to pay that. The original debt was absolutely released by the instrument of June, and the fact that the original note was allowed to remain in their hands was only to enable *Benedict* and *Vann* to enforce payment in the event of the composition not being paid. If the fact of failure to pay the composition had the effect of reviving the debt which had been released, such must be the effect at law as well as in this court, and in that view the plaintiff had no right to complain of the defendant setting up the release.

The fact that the defendant had executed the deed of August cannot possibly affect the rights of the original creditors; they might have chosen to come in under it, or they might have elected, as they did, not to come in under it, and remain under the instrument of June.

Hill, by his proceeding at law, declared his determination not to accept the notes or the stipulated composition, a tender was therefore unnecessary, and the fact that no tender was made cannot now give the plaintiff any additional right to relief. They referred to *Hockster* v. *DeLatour,* (a) *The Danube and B. Sea Co.* v. *Enos,* (b) *Black* v. *Smith,* (c) *Harding* v. *Davis,* (d) *Wallis* v. *Glynn,* (e) *Davis* v. *Thomas,* (f) *Leake* v. *Young.* (g)

Judgment.—VANKOUGHNET, C.—In this case the plaintiff *Hill* sues as assignee of his co-plaintiffs of an agreement by the defendant with them to pay them the sum of $979.76, on the 16th of March, 1860. The facts of

---

(a) 17 Jur. 972.   (b) 8 Jur. N. S. 434.
(c) Peake's Rep. 88   (d) 2 C. & P. 77.
(e) 19 Ves. 383.   (f) 1 R. & M. 506.
            (g) 5 E. & B. 955.

the case appear in the judgment of *V. C. Esten*, which comes before us on this re-hearing.

I think the deed of the 18th January, 1860, may be left out of consideration, and that the right of the plaintiffs to recover depends upon the deeds of June and August, and the circumstances connected with them. By the deed of June the defendant agreed to secure the payments in composition by his own promissory notes satisfactorily endorsed. This was executed by the plaintiffs *Benedict* and *Vann*. The defendant did not, and as he subsequently explained, could not procure his notes to be endorsed. Now it cannot be doubted that the stipulation for endorsed notes was a material one; and though it only appears in the recital to the deed, and is not the covenanting or legally operative part of the deed, and could therefore form no defence at law, yet this court would not take so restricted a view of the deed, but would hold the stipulation as part of the agreement of the parties necessary to be observed. This being so, and the defendant finding he could not comply with it, abandons, as far as he can, the deed altogether, and proposes and procures to be executed by most of the parties to the deed of June, the deed of August already referred to. The deed differs in many respects from the other deed; and of course no creditor was obliged to execute it unless he chose. The plaintiffs did not execute it. In the interval between the execution by *Benedict* and *Vann* of the deed of June and the execution by the defendant of the deed of August, the assignment to the plaintiff *Hill* of the debt now in suit was made. *Hill* then and thereafter stood in no better or worse position in regard to it than his co-plaintiffs, and the question is, were or are they bound by the deed of June after what had occurred? In my opinion clearly not. The defendant did not, and admits he could not, comply with the stipulation for endorsation; he makes an entirely different arrangement for his creditors by the deed of August as a substitution for the deed of June, which he abandons both by his acts and his declarations, and yet he says the plaintiffs must be bound by it. I think the effect of what has occurred is to leave the plaintiffs in possession of the original right to recover the full amount of the debt. It is of the essence of a composition of an existing debt that every term of the agreement for composition should be strictly observed and performed. Here not only was the stipulation in the deed of June not observed, but the defendant declares he does not intend to observe it. I do not think that the judgment of the Court of Common Pleas on the rights at law of these parties in the case presented to them raises any difficulty to the plaintiffs' right here.

The doubt I have felt is, whether the plaintiffs might not now recover at law; and whether, therefore this court should in its discretion exercise its jurisdiction in favour of *Hill*, as the assignee of a chose in action. That this court has the jurisdiction, will, I suppose, not be questioned; its exercise is a matter of discretion. In the case for instance of a bond debt and an assignment simply, the court will leave the assignee to sue at law in the name of the assignor, (there being no obstacle to its use,) as in *Hammond* v. *Messenger*. (a) Here, however, I think we may properly interpose. There is a complication of transactions affecting the debt, arising out of the acts of the defendant himself. The stipulation for endorsation could not be set up at law, and it is doubtful whether the abandonment by the parties of the deed of June, after it had gone into formal operation, would be an answer to it. There is no such difficulty in equity even when the deed may affect, or is intended to affect, the rights of a third party, a stranger to the deed. See the observations of the Master of the Rolls in *Hill* v. *Gomme*, (b) and of the Lord Chancellor, on appeal. (c)

(a) 9 Sim. 327.
(c) 5 M. & C. 254.

(b) 1 Beav. 544.

ESTEN, V. C., remained of the same opinion as expressed on the original hearing.

SPRAGGE, V. C.—The same thing was sought in the action at law as is sought in this suit, that is, the recovery of the original debt from *Rutherford* to *Benedict* and *Vann*, which debt it was the object of the several deeds of January, June and August to settle by a composition.

It is *res judicata* by the judgment of the Court of Common Pleas in *Benedict* v. *Rutherford*, (a) that the legal right to recover for the original cause of action is gone; that *Rutherford's* covenant to pay the composition was future; that the release operated as a present discharge of the old debt, and that the giving of the notes was not a condition precedent: none of these points are now open.

The plaintiffs must come into this court upon some equity independent of those points, and I understand their equity to be, that although the release is in terms absolute, unconditional, and immediate, still it was intended to be conditional upon the giving by *Rutherford* of endorsed notes for the amount of the composition; and that the endorsed notes not having been given, the plaintiffs have an equity to be remitted to their original cause of action, and that the composition deed of June was abandoned. The question is not whether if *Benedict* and *Vann* had a legal right to recover the amount of the original debt, this court would have interposed to restrict the creditor to the amount of the composition; but whether this court will interfere actively to give the creditor more than the amount of his composition. This court will ordinarily interfere to relieve from forfeiture, where it occurs from non-payment of money: but the case of composition deeds is in England an admitted exception; still I think there is no instance, certainly no case has been cited, of a court of equity *enforcing* a forfeiture even upon a composition deed.

(a) 11 U. C. C. P. 213.

It is certainly to enforce a forfeiture that the plaintiffs come to this court. Assuming that they are right in treating the release as conditional under the composition deed of June, *Rutherford's* right under that deed was to have a composition of twenty-five per cent. accepted by the creditors, parties to it, upon his giving the notes; and the plaintiffs' case is, that they forfeited the right to have the composition accepted by not giving the notes; and they come into equity asking for the whole debt by reason of that forfeiture. It is true that the assumed condition was not the payment of money but the giving of notes.

I find two English cases where notes were to be given upon a composition deed. They are both cases at law, the first, *Boothby* v. *Sowden* (a), was a *nisi prius* decision before Lord *Ellenborough*: the action was upon the original debt; the defence was that the creditor had agreed to give time, and to take the debtor's notes, payable in London, for the amount. For the plaintiff, it was contended, that the giving of the notes was a condition precedent, but Lord *Ellenborough* said: "If the plaintiff could shew that the defendant had refused to give the notes according to the terms of the agreement, they might be remitted to their original remedy, but I think that remedy is suspended by the agreement, unless an infraction of the agreement is proved by the plaintiff;" and the plaintiff was nonsuited.

Doubt is thrown upon this ruling by the case of *Crawley* v. *Hilary* (b). In that case also promissory notes were to be given; and the question was whether it was the business of the creditor to apply for them, or for the debtor to give them. It was proved that the plaintiff might have had them if he had applied for them, but there was no evidence that the defendant had given or tendered them to the plaintiff. The ac-

---

(a) 3 Camp. 75.   (b) 2 M. & S. 120.

tion was not brought until after the time at which the composition notes were to be payable; so that there was default in payment of the composition money, as well as in the giving of the notes. The court evidently leaned to the opinion that the debtor was bound to give or tender the notes. But even in that case Lord *Ellenborough* observed: "If the defendant had offered the notes at the time of action brought, it might have been a ground for staying the proceedings." Mr. Justice *Bayley* only observed upon the composition notes being past due. This case shews the reluctance with which the court, Lord *Ellenborough* especially, gave effect to the forfeiture, intimating the probability of the court exercising equitable jurisdiction if the notes had been tendered even after the time at which they ought to have been given, if not after they were due.

Again, supposing that a court of equity would interfere actively in behalf of the creditor under similar circumstances to those in which it would refuse to interfere with the legal right at the instance of the debtor, which I by no means concede, I doubt whether this is not a case in which the court would properly interfere with the enforcement of the legal right. In the English cases where the court has refused to interpose, there has been an express stipulation that upon default the original debt should revive; or at least a very plain and distinct agreement that payment should be made by a day specified. Now here there is no day specified for the giving of the notes; indeed the giving of notes at all was an afterthought; the whole composition deed is framed without reference to any notes being given, the only reference to notes being written in the margin in these words: "And for which said payments to give his promissory notes, satisfactorily endorsed, and dated on the first day of July next, and at six and twelve months respectively."

No day being named for the giving of the notes, the

cases in which the court has refused to interfere for the debtor do not in terms apply. But assuming that this court would regard an absolute refusal to pay composition money, or to give composition notes as equipollent to a default on a day named, has there been such refusal here? *Rutherford* was disappointed in getting his notes endorsed in the quarter that he expected, and thereupon proposed the composition deed of August as a substitute; and on the 28th of that month wrote to *Benedict* and *Vann*, asking them to become parties to it. In that letter all that he says about the endorsed notes is this: "I could not get the security wanted— the party that promised to become a partner drew back, so I went at once to the Bank of Montreal, they being the largest creditors, and told them; they said it was more than I could expect to get any party about here to go security, as the farmers about here are terribly afraid of being security."

Before the receipt of this letter, and I think before the deed of the 7th of August, *Benedict* and *Vann* had endorsed *Rutherford's* note to the plaintiff *Hill*. The plaintiffs put it in their bill, that *Rutherford* abandoned the composition of June, and refer to the letter of the 28th of August as evidence of it, yet say that the original note was endorsed to *Hill*, before the 28th of August, after the abandonment. It is to be noted that *Hill* purchased the note at twenty-five per cent., and that twenty-five per cent. was the amount to be paid under the composition deed of June. *Benedict* and *Vann* says that in endorsing the note to *Hill* they supposed it to be a negotiable instrument. Unless there was an abandonment of the deed of June, before the endorsement of *Hill*, of which there is no evidence, it was bad faith in *Benedict* and *Vann* to make that endorsement. It is agreed, I believe, that this original note was not a negotiable instrument; and if so, *Hill* took it subject to the equities that attached to it in the hands of *Benedict* and *Vann*.

If the note had been in the hands of *Benedict* and *Vann* at the time of the receipt from *Rutherford* of his letter of August, as *Rutherford* evidently expected it would be, their proper course was clear. The letter said not a word about abandoning the deed of June, but proposed another as a substitute; indeed, abandoning the deed of June without the consent of the parties to it, was out of the question. *Benedict* and *Vann's* proper course then would have been, if they declined the proposed substitute, to say so; and to say that they insisted upon the endorsed notes in accordance with the deed of June, and so have given *Rutherford* the opportunity of making another effort to procure them; rather than pay the original debt in full, it would have been to the interest of his other creditors to assist him in doing so. *Benedict* and *Vann* having parted with the note cannot place them in a better position; nor can *Hill's* position be better than theirs. I think the plaintiff's position may fairly be put thus: suppose *Benedict* and *Vann*, immediately upon the receipt of the letter of August, to have written to *Rutherford* to say that they would hold him to have abandoned the deed of June, surely *Rutherford* might with reason answer that he had merely made a proposal to them, which if they refused would leave it still open to him to comply with the terms of the deed of June. They should hardly be countenanced in snapping at that as an abandonment which was never intended to be such.

Rutherford's action was not very prompt with *Hill*. He probably thought, with *Benedict* and *Vann*, that the note was negotiable, and that *Hill* as the holder was entitled in law to the full amount in any event, and that he was without remedy. However, on the 18th of October following his solicitor addressed a letter to *Hill* offering to give the required security under the deed of June. This offer does not seem to have been accepted, and *Hill*, in the name of *Benedict* and *Vann*, sued upon the original note, before either of the notes to be given under the deed of June would have been payable. This seems material in reference to the language of Lord *Ellenborough* in *Crawley v. Hilary.*

I do not think that *Benedict* and *Vann's* letter of the 8th of June can make any difference in the case, so as to bring it within the rule (taking it to be the rule) that a court of equity will only decline to interfere with the legal right, when in the composition deed it is expressly stipulated that upon default the original debt shall revive. The letter was written, as its contents shew, *before* the writers had seen the composition deed, and in ignorance as to whether the amount of the composition was to be secured or not; and the event in which they said they should want to hold the original note, was only in case of the deed, not providing that security, should be given. The words are, " In reply to your proposition of 5s. in the pound, would say, that you do not state whether it is to be secured or not. If not, we should want to hold the original note until the compromise paper was paid." As a fact the original note was retained by *Benedict* and *Vann*, but it was not in pursuance of any stipulation in the composition deed or letter.

There is then, as it seems to me, nothing in the case but the original debt, and the composition deed, and the omission to give the endorsed notes ; the same case that was before the Court of Common Pleas. The deed has been construed by that court, and there cannot of course be one construction by a court of law, and another by a court of equity. Neither, I apprehend, will a court of equity give a different effect to the various provisions of an instrument than is proper according to their legal construction : will not, for instance, make one a condition precedent to another, unless they are so upon a proper construction of the instrument, or treat covenants, as dependent, when upon a proper construction they are independent covenants. A case illustrative of this was decided by the Lords Justices. *Gibson* v. *Goldsmid.* (a)

_____

(a) 5 D. M. &. G. 757.

Supposing it open to the plaintiffs to shew in this court that the giving of endorsed notes was intended to be a condition precedent to the release, or to the deed of June coming into operation, they have not shewn it. What evidence there is, that of *Laurie*, called by the plaintiff, a trustee under the deed of January, is the other way. He says: "I know no other arrangement or terms, with respect to the deed of June, than what appears on the face of the deed. I am not aware of any understanding that this deed was not to operate until the notes were given."

As to the alleged abandonment of the deed of June, I have already observed upon it ; but I may add, that it was, I apprehend, equally open to the plaintiffs to urge it at law, as in this court, and as a piece of evidence, that it was not abandoned except as to those who accepted the deed of August in lieu of it, is the fact, that *Gates*, a party to the former, but not the latter, received payments of his composition according to the deed of June; he asked, indeed, for his debt in full, but this was refused, and he received his composition.

I think the plaintiffs' case fails, and that so far from having any equity to come into this court, their conduct throughout has been harsh and inequitable. I doubt, if the legal right had been with them, whether it would not have been a proper case for relieving the debtor from the forfeiture, for this reason, in addition to the case being outside the cases decided in England, that a decree for the plaintiffs would affect others besides the defendant, namely, his creditors ; a reason which weighed with Lord *Eldon* in *McKenzie* v. *McKenzie*. (a) I may observe too, what has probably had some weight with the court in refusing relief in England, that composition deeds are not favourably regarded there, it being considered that proceedings in bankruptcy are

---

(a) 16 Ves. 372.

better for both debtor and creditor. But here, in the absence of a bankrupt law, they should be regarded favourably, and as far as possible carried out, as perhaps the only mode of making a final and equitable disposition of the effects of an embarrassed trader.

If Lord *Ellenborough's* view be correct, the defendant was in time in offering the notes in October, being two months and a half before the first would have been payable. I do not quote his lordship as an *authority* in a court of equity, but the view of so eminent a judge, as to what would have been just between the parties, is entitled to respect ; and it is to be observed, that notes given in October would have placed the creditor (if he had not parted with the original note) in as good a position as if given contemporaneously with the execution of the deed. After refusing them, I cannot see his equity to recover the original debt in full.

But apart from these considerations, growing out of the particular facts of this case, I think that by sustaining this bill the court would make a precedent in discordance with the principles upon which courts of equity proceed. It is in substance and in effect a bill to enforce a forfeiture for default in the payment of money. My own conclusion, therefore, is, with great respect to the opinions of the other members of the court, with which I have the misfortune to differ, that the bill should be dismissed. I have felt it to be due to his Lordship the Chancellor, and my brother Esten, to explain my views somewhat at large.

PROCTOR v. GRANT.

Crown lands—Repeal of patent.

The court, while affirming the general doctrine on which the decree
was pronounced in this cause, as reported ante page 27, reversed
the same on the ground of want of notice of the improper conduct
of the grantee of the Crown in obtaining the patent.—[SPRAGGE,
V. C., *dubitantc.*]

The facts of this case are fully stated in the report on
the original hearing. The cause was set down for
re-hearing at the instance of the defendant. On the
re-hearing

Mr. *Mowat*, Q. C., appeared for the plaintiff.

Mr. *McMichael* and Mr. *Fitzgerald*, for the defendant.

The judgment of the court was delivered by

Judgment.—ESTEN, V. C.—This is a suit to revoke
a patent. Assuming that such a suit may be maintained by a private individual, and that in order to
maintain such a suit it is sufficient to shew that
at the time of issuing the patent in question some fact
was unknown to the government, which, had it been
known, would it is reasonable to conclude, have prevented the grant to Mr. *Cameron*, and have induced a
grant in favour of the plaintiff, we think that enough
exists in the present case in the circumstances connected with the report, and the improvements, although
we do not think that a case of bad faith is established
against Mr. *Cameron*, to have induced the government,
had it known all that has been disclosed in the evidence to cancel the sale to Mr. *Cameron*, and probably
to make a sale to Mr. *Proctor*, but this is not enough
to entitle the plaintiff to a decree: he must also shew
that the defendant had notice at the time of completing his purchase, of the circumstances upon which
his equity rests, and the majority of the court think that
the evidence is not sufficient to establish such notice.

What the defendant really knew at the time of completing his purchase we collect from his evidence, from which it appears that he was informed by Mr. *Cameron* that the plaintiff had overrun his line, and improved about seventeen acres on the north half of the lot; that he had refused to permit *Proctor's* tenant to continue in possession of these seventeen acres, except upon the condition of his becoming his tenant, to which he had consented; and that *Cameron* had received a patent of the north half from the goverment. There was nothing in this information to lead *Grant* to make any enquiry: he was justified in concluding that *Cameron* had an undisputed title of the whole north half of the lot, and the majority of the court think, therefore, that the evidence of notice fails, and that the decree which has been pronounced should be reversed, and the bill dismissed with costs.

Judgment–SPRAGGE, V. C.–In my judgment I proceeded upon this, that *Cameron* having been employed by the government to ascertain and report for the information and guidance of the government, as to occupancy and improvements, and having reported untruly upon both points, did not stand upon the same footing as a stranger in regard to his purchase. I did not think it necessary that actual fraud should be proved as against him; but that it was his duty to ascertain the facts upon which he was to report; that he might have done so with reasonable diligence; and that he, if he had been defendant, could not have been allowed to retain an advantage obtained by his own wrong, and the defendant having, before his purchase, notice of *Cameron's* official character, of his inspection of the land in question, and of the fact that seventeen acres were cleared upon it, when it was reported as uncleared and unoccupied, must be affected with the equities which would have affected *Cameron*.

If in order to affect *Cameron* it would have been necessary to prove actual fraud, then it must be con-

15

ceded, I think, that no decree ought to have been made against *Grant,* because I do not think it proved that he knew before he purchased that *Cameron* was aware, before his own purchase, that there was in fact the clearing upon the north half of the lot.   I am convinced that *Cameron* did know it before he purchased, and probably before he made his report ; and I have my suspicion that *Grant* knew of his previous knowledge in *Cameron,* but I should not think the evidence sufficient to found a decree upon that ground.

ARNER v. McKENNA.

Statute of Limitations—Dormant equities.

A person seeking to invoke the aid of the Statute of Limitations against a claim in respect of lands, must shew that he, and those under whom he claims, have been in possession of the land, or what in law is equivalent to possession.

In 1834 a contract was made for the purchase of the easterly fifty acres of a lot of land, but through mistake the deed covered the whole north half, thus conveying the legal title to the north easterly and north westerly quarters, but the purchaser went into possession of the portion actually intended to be conveyed, and shortly after the vendee of the westerly portion went into possession of and occupied it without any disturbance of his title to assertion of right by the party to whom the conveyance had been made by mistake, (although all parties knew of the error that had occurred,)until the year 1857, when the assignee of the person holding the legal title instituted proceedings in ejectment, and recovered judgment ; the evidence of adverse possession not being sufficient to outweigh the legal effect of the deed which had been so erroneously executed. The court, upon a bill filed for the purpose, restrained the owner of the legal title from proceeding to recover possession, and ordered him to convey the legal title in the land to the plaintiff who was equitably entitled thereto, and to pay the costs of the suit.

The facts of this case sufficiently appeared in the judgment.

Mr. *Blake,* for plaintiff.

The Statute of Limitations cannot be held to have run in favour of *Stockwell,* or the defendants who claim under him; for although he discovered the mistake which had been made as early as 1835, yet he knew that it was the easterly portion that it was intended to convey, and

which he meant to purchase; and no adverse claim to
Arner's was ever raised until more than twenty years
afterwards. But whatever the view of a court of law
may be, there can be no doubt that in the eye of a court
of equity he was the rightful owner of the portion now
in dispute, and which all parties thought had been conveyed to him, and which in fact he had purchased and
paid the consideration for. It would be grossly inequitable to permit such a right as that now set up by
McKenna to prevail against the plaintiff; the fact that
he was not all the time in the actual visible possession
of the portion now claimed, is not sufficient to bar his
equity, unless the other party has been in such actual
possession.

As to the defence raised under the statute relating
to dormant equities, he contended the act did not
apply. The equity in this case was never dormant,
but actively asserted, from the time of its acquisition;
the only title which had lain dormant was the legal one
of *Stockwell*, and which had been acquired by *McKenna*
under a bargain tainted with champerty; he is in fact a
trustee for *Stockwell* if not of the entire interest, certainly
of one half of the land. This in reality is a case of
actual fraud, such fraud consisting in his obtaining from
the heir of *Lawrence*, in order to rectify the mistake
which had occurred, a conveyance of the easterly portion,
and afterwards asserting title to the north half, under
the deed which had been executed in error; so that if
even *Arner's* equity could be treated as dormant, the
act would not bar him, cases of fraud being excepted
from it. He referred to *Smith* v. *Loyd*, (a) *McDonald*
v. *McKinty*, (b) *Ketchum* v. *Mighton*. (c)

Mr. *A. Cameron*, for defendants, referred to *McKenna*
v. *Arner*, (d) and *Arner* v. *McKenna*, (e) and contended
that, before any relief could be granted to plaintiff, it must

---

(a) 9 Ex. 562.   (b) 10 Ir. C. L. 516.
(c) 14 U. C. Q. B. 99   (d) 8 U. C C. P. 373.
(e) Ib. 46.

be shewn that *Fisher* took all the land which had not been
conveyed by *Lawrence* to *Stockwell*, and that under no
circumstances could *McKenna* be compelled to convey
the northerly fifty acres until he had received a deed of
the easterly portion; that there is no such principle as
that contended for by the plaintiff, that an equitable possession follows an equitable title. *Sugden's* V. & P., section 12; *Wragg* v. *Beckitt.* (a)   But if wrong in this view,
he insisted plaintiff was bound by the Dormant Equities
Act; referring to *Attorney-General* v. *Grasett.* (b)

Judgment,—VANKOUGHNET, C.—The undisputed facts
in this case are, that in May, 1834, one *John Stockwell* contracted to purchase the easterly fifty acres of
lot No. 54, in the township of Malden, from one
Richard Lawrence, the owner of the whole lot; that
by mistake the deed from *Lawrence* to *Stockwell*
covered the northerly part of the lot, extending from
east to west, instead of the easterly part, and that
thus *Stockwell* acquired a legal title to the north easterly and west quarters of the lot, and no legal title to
the southerly half of the eastern part. That this mistake was discovered by *Stockwell* in the year 1854, when
he repaired to the heir of *Lawrence* to rectify it, and
obtained from him at once a deed for this purpose,
although ineffectual, as, in the meantime, the ancestor
had conveyed all the lot not covered by the deed to
Stockwell, to one *Fisher*.   That *Lawrence*, the elder,
Stockwell, and subsequently *Fisher*, on his purchase and
conveyance from *Lawrence*, supposed that *Stockwell* had
according to his contract a conveyance of the east part
of the lot, and acted and dealt accordingly; *Stockwell*
having entered into and continued in possession thereof
as owner, and been treated by all parties as such. That
Stockwell never entered into possession of the northerly
part of the west half, covered in mistake by his deed, and
being the portion in dispute here, and never exercised
any acts of ownership thereover, or attempted to deal

(a) Ante vol. vii., p. 220.   (b) Ante vol. viii., p. 130.

with the same as his own until the year 1857, when he conveyed it to his daughter, one of the defendants, on the understanding that if the land was recovered from the plaintiff he, *Stockwell*, was to share equally therein.

That *Lawrence*, and those claiming under him, always considered themselves entitled to this piece of land, as forming part of the 'west half of the lot, and never disputed or interfered with *Stockwell's* possession of the entire east half, though as stated, his deed did not cover the south part of it, and that by continuous undisputed occupation for upwards of twenty years, he acquired in it a statutory title: both parties thus recognising and acting upon the agreement under which *Stockwell* purchased, as if the same had been correctly carried out by the deeds which were executed. That the land in dispute being the said rear part of the west half was, until the last seven or eight years, bush land uncleared.

The evidence shews that any actual occupation of this piece of land was had by the plaintiff, and those under whom he claims, and that they always dealt with it and treated it as their own, without interruption or objection by *Stockwell*, and there is not the slightest evidence that *Stockwell* ever occupied it, or prior to 1857 asserted any right to deal with it; though he says on his examination that he knew his deed covered it, but from whom or how does not appear; and such claim as expressed, in my judgment, amounts to no more than this, that he knew that his deed, by mistake, covered it and that by setting this up he might, if he chose, establish a claim to the land. I give him credit for having been too honest or ashamed, knowing as he did, the facts, to attempt this, and it was only in later years that he was tempted or induced to put it in the power of another to make it; and make it that other did, by bringing an action of ejectment against the plaintiff, and succeeded because sufficient evidence of adverse possession had not been furnished on the trial to bar the legal title, which in

the presumption of the law carried with it the possession
of land not proved to have been in the actual or visible
occupation of an adverse holder.   At law the presumption is, that the possession follows the title, and this
presumption prevails till the contrary is shewn.

This is, however, merely a *presumption* which is made
at law, and a reasonable one too, but not required or
enforced by any statute: it merely is, that the man
legally entitled to land is in the eye of the law in possession of it, unless some one not acknowledging his title
is there.   The same reason for such a presumption at
law in regard to a legal title, should, it seems to me,
govern in equity in regard to an equitable title; and I
agree with Mr. *Blake's* argument and position in that
respect.   It is no answer to say that legal and equitable
presumption may thus come into direct conflict.   Legal
and equitable rights always do when the latter are
enforced against the former.   Now in this case, although
there was not an every day use of the land by those
equitably entitled to it, still there was use of it by
them, and such use as we may suppose people ordinarily make of such land in rear of the cleared or
improved part.   The use, such as it was, was consistent with the equitable title, and not with the
legal paper title of *Stockwell*, and I think independently
of the evidence of actual occupation, that on principle,
as well as under the provisions of the 31st section of
chapter 88, of the Con. Stat. of U. C., we should treat
the possession as accompanying the equitable title.   In
this view, then, the Statutes of Limitations, as ordinarily
called, would defeat the plaintiff's claim to relief;
and it then remains to be considered whether the statute
relating to dormant equities shuts it out.

It may be observed that this statute—as found in the
Consolidated Statutes of U. C.—is not in the acts
relating to limitation of actions, but in the act respecting the Court of Chancery, being chapter 12 of those

acts, and in sections 59 and 60 thereof. On looking at the original act, as passed, we find it entitled "An act to amend the law as to dormant equities," and the recital to the first enacting clause is in these words: "Whereas by the act to establish a Court of Chancery in Upper Canada, it was provided that the rules of decision in the said courts, shall be the same as governed the Court of Chancery in England; and whereas in regard to mortgages under which, before the passing of the said act, the estate had become absolute at law by failure in performing the condition, the said act, after reciting that from the want of an equitable jurisdiction a strict application to such cases of the rules established in England might be attended with injustice, did in effect enact, that the court so established should have power and authority to make such order and decree as to the said court might appear just and reasonable under all the circumstances of the case, subject to the appeal thereby provided: and whereas in regard to claims upon, or interest in real estate, arising before the passing of the said act, it is just to restrict the future application of the said rules of decision to cases of fraud; and in regard to other cases it is expedient to extend thereto, in manner hereinafter provided, the power and authority so given as aforesaid to the said court in cases of mortgages." The legislature evidently intended to provide against those cases of hardship which might arise from the disturbance of a legal title, *bona fide* hold, and long acquiesced in or submitted to, by the assertion against it of some equitable right, which though allowed to lie dormant, would, by the well and long recognized rules of decision in England, be admitted. After the title of the act, and the recital, the legislature proceed to say: "Therefore no title to or interest in real estate which is valid at law, shall be disturbed or otherwise affected in equity by reason of any matter, or upon any ground which arose before the 4th day of March, 1837; or for the purpose of giving effect to any equitable claim, interest, or estate, which arose before

the said date, unless there has been actual and positive
fraud in the party whose title is sought to be disturbed or affected."

There are two ways in which a man's rights, whether legal or equitable, may be actually asserted. The
one is by the enjoyment of that right undisturbed; the
other is, by obtaining, when necessary, the recognition
of it by a proper tribunal. In this case, the plaintiff,
and those under and through whom he claims, up to
1857, asserted, by the undisputed or undisturbed enjoyment of it (for I hold that to be the effect of the evidence),
their clear equitable right to the land in dispute; and
the plaintiff owning and residing on the adjoining land,
never before that time set up his legal title against it.
Which of the titles, rights or claims, then, during all
that long period, lay dormant? Was it the equitable
or the legal one? Surely the latter, for it was never
asserted or attempted to be enforced in any way. All
parties for a long time knew of the mistake—none
sought to take advantage of it. *Stockwell* was allowed
to obtain a legal title by possession without any disturbance by *Lawrence* or *Fisher*, in whom the legal paper
title vested, or those who came after them; and the equitable owner of the land in question here was equally un-
molested; and this state of things continued till the arrangement between *McKenna* and *Stockwell*. Now can
it really be imagined that the legislature meant to shut
out such an equitable right as this? That they intended
it might be defeated by a dormant legal title? That
on the one hand *Stockwell*, and on the other *Arner*,
might each be turned out of the possession of land which
they had long respectively enjoyed under clear equitable
titles, when the period of time fixed by the statute had
elapsed, by bringing into use, for the first time, dormant
legal titles which had never before been insisted upon?
It seems to me that so to hold would be working the
very mischief which the statute was intended to prevent,
and that we would be setting at naught this intention,

and the very spirit of the act, if, by adhering to the mere words of the enacting part we were to give it such an effect. *a*) It may be said that *Arner* and his predecessors in title might have shut out the legal title, as *Stockwell* did, by a continuous adverse possession of twenty years; but in the first place, every man is not bound to use, day by day, or year by year, land to which he is entitled; and it has been held that something more than being merely out of possession is required to create a discontinuance of possession, or a forfeiture of the title, though I take it that when there is clear evidence of abandonment by him who has the stronger legal title, very slight evidence of possession by another who is in, not as a trespasser, but as under a claim of right, would suffice to push the other title aside; and in the next place, I, as already stated, hold here that a vacant possession follows the equitable title as at law it does the legal.

Thus though at law *Arner* might not have been able to shew such an actual or active possession or use of the land as would shut out the legal title, no equitable title being recognized there, yet, *e converso*, here, there being no possession whatever shewn in the legal owner, the possession will be held to have followed the equitable title. But I think there is evidence here of such possession and acts of ownership by *Arner*, and those before him, as, under the circumstances, and in the total absence of any possession at any time by *Stockwell*, would, if properly shewn at law, bar the legal title there. *Stockwell*, who sets up this legal title, never went into possession under it. *Lawrence*, from whom he purchased, was at the time of the conveyance to *Stockwell* in possession, and *Stockwell* clearly defined what he meant to take possession of, by entering upon and holding the easterly fifty acres, leaving the residue to *Lawrence*, and never afterwards pretending even to occupy it.

(*a*) Podmore v. Gunning, 7 Sim. 649, 655.

Take a case which might occur, and perhaps exists at this moment, of a town lot sold and paid for, and allowed to remain vacant say for six years, the purchaser not having procured a deed. At the end of that time he builds upon it, and after having been in actual possession for fifteen years, making, say twenty-one years from the time of purchase, the person having the legal title brings ejectment and recovers, because there had only been an actual occupation for fifteen years, though from the time of sale he had never pretended to claim the land. Could it be that this court would not interfere and protect the equitable title? And is it not fraud in such a case for the owner of the legal title to thus lie by, and then set up that title ?

I am of opinion that the plaintiff here is entitled to be protected; and that the conduct of the defendants and *Stockwell.* on the arrangement being made for the sale of the land, was fraudulent, and that there should be a decree against them with costs, ordering them to convey the land in dispute to the plaintiff.

Judgment.—ESTEN, V. C.—I am inclined to think Mr. *Blake* right about the Statute of Limitations. *Stockwell* never was in possession, or asserted any effectual claim until a recent period—while *Arner* intended to purchase this piece of land, and entered into possession of the whole, that he purchased; and although his ancestor, or *Lawrence* or *Fisher* could have filed a bill immediately, yet it seems that a person cannot invoke the aid of the statute unless he, or those under whom he claims have been in possession, or what is equivalent to it.

SPRAGGE, V. C.—The following are the rules of construction resolved upon by the Barons of the Exchequer in *Hayden's* case, (a) and adopted by the learned judges whose opinion was delivered to the House of Lords in

---

(a) 3 Rep. 7.

Warburton v. *Loveland*, (a) "for the sure and true interpretation of all statutes in general :"

"1. What was the common law before the making of the act?

"2. What was the mischief and defect for which the common law did not provide?

"3. What remedy the parliament hath resolved and appointed to cure the disease of the commonwealth?

"4. The true reason of the remedy; and then the office of all the judges is always to make such construction as shall suppress the mischief and advance the remedy, and to suppress subtle innovations and evasions for continuance of the mischief, and *pro private commodo*, and to add force and life to the cure and remedy, according to the true intent of the makers of the act, *pro bono publico.*"

Applying then, in the first place, the second and fourth of these rules to the statute in question, (b) and to the case before us; the statute itself very distinctly points out the mischief and defect for which it was conceived the law as it then stood did not provide. Its object is declared by its title to be "to amend the law as to dormant equities." Dormant equities were the subject of the act, and the law in relation to them being mischievous and defective, was to be amended. The question is, whether an equity openly asserted and acted upon for a series of years, and up to a recent period, in the face of the party having the legal right, and acquiesced in by him, is within the act. The words in the enacting clauses of the statute are large enough to comprehend such an equity; but does it follow that the court is to make the statute apply to

---

(a) 2 Dow. & C. 480.   (b) 18 Vic., ch. 124.

such an equity if it sees that the mischief and defect
pointed at by the statute was the state of the law in
relation, not to such equitable rights, but to equities
of a different nature.

In construing any other written instrument, the
proper course, no doubt, is, to look at the whole of it,
and to construe the whole of it together; and it must
be admitted that the title, as a general rule, is not part
of the enactment of a statute. Nevertheless the title
is not to be disregarded, and there are several instances where it has been read as assisting in the
construction of the act, and in limiting its operation.
Some cases upon this point are collected in *Dwarris*
on Statutes, (a) and there are two others which I have
met with. One, *Monk* v. *Whittenbury*, (b) before Lords
Tenterden and *Littledale*, *Park* and *Taunton*, JJ.; the
other, *Wood* v. *Rowcliffe*, (c) before Sir *James Wigram*.
The first of these cases arose under the Factor's Act,
(d) and the question was, whether the act applied to
the case of a wharfinger and flour-factor, and it was
held not to apply. The case before Sir *James Wigram*
came up after the passing of the act 5 & 6 Vic., ch. 29,
extending the provisions of the former act. The title
of the earlier act was, "An act to alter and amend an
act for the better protection of the property of merchants and others, who may hereafter enter into contracts or agreements in relation to goods, wares, and
merchandise, intrusted to factors or agents." The
title of the latter act is, "An act to amend the law
relating to advances *bona fide* made to agents intrusted
with goods;" and it provides that any agent who should
" be intrusted with the possession of goods, or of the
document of title to goods, shall be deemed and taken to
be the owner of such goods and documents, so far as to
give validity to any contract or agreement by way of

(a) Vol. i., 501.   (b) 2 B. & Ad. 484.
(c) 6 Hare 153, 191.   (d) 6 Geo. IV., ch. 94.

pledge, lien, or security *bona fide* made by any person with such agent so entrusted as aforesaid," &c., and the question in *Wood* v. *Rowcliffe* was, whether the statute applied generally to goods, the possession of which was intrusted to an agent, or was confined to mercantile transactions. Upon this Sir *James Wigram* observed : " Now it may be true that the words of the statute, in their general signification, are wide enough to comprehend the present case. But the act has never been understood to apply to other than mercantile transactions. The first act (a) is for the ' protection of the property of merchants and others ; ' and the property referred to ' goods, wares, and merchandise,' intrusted to the agent ' for the purpose of consignment, or sale,' or shipped ; and upon a judicial construction of the act it has been held that the generality of the expressions must be restricted. Every servant of the owner of goods employed in the care or carriage of such goods is in one sense an ' agent intrusted with goods, but still he is not agent within the meaning of the statute.'—*Monk* v. *Whittenbury*. The title of the second act (b) is more general; but it appears to me to relate to ' agents,' and to ' goods and merchandise,' in a sense which is not applicable to the agency or property in this case." It cannot but be observed that Sir *James Wigram* controlled the general provision of the acts by the title of the first act recited in the second, and observed upon the title of the second being more general than the title of the first; and he evidently understood *Monk* v. *Whittenbury* to have been decided upon the words of the earlier act, limited by the title of that act, for his quotations from that act are mainly from its title.

If, indeed, a statute is to be construed according to the apparent intention of the legislature, as it certainly is, we cannot disregard the title unless it is to be held as no act of the legislature. The cases to which I have

---

(a) 6 Geo. IV., ch. 94. (b) 5 & 6 Vic., ch. 39.

referred appear to me to treat the title of acts as acts of
the legislature, otherwise I do not see how they could
use them as indicating the intention of the legislature.
But were it otherwise as a general rule, the title or heading to the provisions of the act embodied in the Consolidated Statutes, "Dormant Equities," must be taken, I
apprehend, to be part of the act.   It is not a mere title
prepared by the clerk of the house, as it is said was the
practice as to titles of acts in England; but is part of
the roll authenticated, as provided by the act of consolidation; the whole of which, with the exception of the
marginal notes, and references to former statutes, it is
enacted should come into force and effect as and by the
designation of "The Consolidated Statutes for Upper
Canada," and not only so, for it is not now the title of
an act at all, but the provisions of the former Dormant
Equities Act forms with the heading "Dormant Equities"
part of the "Act respecting the Court of Chancery."

It appears to me, therefore, not too much to say that
the use of the words "Dormant Equities," as the heading of the provisions in question, is an indication by the
legislature of the subject matter to which those provisions are intended to apply.   I am quite satisfied that
the equity of the plaintiff in this case cannot possibly
fall within the designation of a dormant equity.   The
only dormant title was, as Mr. *Blake* observes, and as
his Lordship the Chancellor has shewn, that of *Stockwell*,
who was a constructive trustee for *Arner*, acquiescing
in the equity of his *cestui que trust.*

There is another rule of construction which is applicable to this case, propounded by Sir *James Wigram*, in
Salkeld v. *Johnston*, (a) where the learned judge said:
"In construing an act of parliament, the same rules of
construction must be applied as in the construction of
other writings; and if the subject matter to which an
act of parliament applies, be such as to make a given

(a) 1 Hare, 210.

construction of its clauses impossible or irrational, I cannot for a moment doubt the right or the duty of a court to have regard to such subject matter as neces-sarily bearing upon the legal construction of the act. This is invariably done in the construction of wills and deeds ; and the same principles are correctly applica-ble to the construction of an act of parliament.   *   * Courts of law have held that the mere subject matter without any preamble may safely be relied upon for restricting the operation of general words."

When it is once ascertained that the subject matter of these provisions are dormant equities, it would be an infringement of this rule to apply them to such a case as this, however comprehensive in terms they may be.   I am prepared, therefore, to hold with the other members of the court that the equity of the plaintiff in this case is not within the act; and I am glad that we are able to come to this conclusion, for any other con-struction of the act would lead to great injustice, not only in this case but in many others.

I agree with the other members of the court in thinking that this case is not barred by the Statute of Limitations.   I think the construction put upon the act by Mr. *Blake*, and adopted by the court, is sound.

GRAHAM v. CHALMERS.

Notice—Prayer for general relief—Registered title.

In a redemption suit, upon its appearing that K., a purchaser for value, with constructive, but without actual notice, held a regis-tered title of the lands in question, as well as S., to whom he had sold, the bill was dismissed as against K., with costs: and, the plaintiff praying specifically for a re-conveyance of the mortgaged premises, *held*, that he was not entitled to personal relief, under the prayer for general relief.

This cause (reported ante vol. viii., p. 597) came on for re-hearing before the court upon the petition of the defendant *Chalmers*, praying that the decrees made in the cause should be vacated or varied.

Mr. *Hector* and Mr. *Crooks* for the petitioner *Chalmers*, contended that the bill praying specifically only for a re-conveyance of the land, or that the plaintiff should be allowed to redeem, he was not, under such a bill, entitled to personal relief against *Chalmers ;* and the latter, having given only a quit-claim deed to the defendant *Knowlson*, his vendee, no relief should be had against *Chalmers*.

Mr. *Connor*, Q. C., and Mr. *Blake*, for *Knowlson*, contended that *Knowlson* having a registered title, and having no actual, but constructive, notice, was protected by the statute equally with *Chalmers*, and at the most was liable to the plaintiff only for the difference between the purchase money which he received from *Scott*, and what the plaintiff *Graham* owed on the land.

Mr. *Roaf* for the plaintiff, in support of the decrees already made, contended that *Scott* not having paid all his purchase money when the bill was filed, was not entitled to protection ; and that the notice was sufficient to bind both *Knowlson* and *Scott*.

Mr. *McGregor*, for the defendant *Scott*, contended that the decree was right as to him, and that, even if *Scott* had had actual notice, which did not appear, the facts proved clearly showed acquiescence on the part of *Graham* in the sale to *Scott*.

The judgment of the court was delivered by

SPRAGGE, V. C.—Apart from the question whether upon the bill as framed the court can properly decree personal relief against any defendant, I incline to think the case was rightly decided upon the materials then before us, except as to one point, that there being only one conveyance after the 1st of January, 1851, proof that it was a registered title would seem to be necessary, as to which the court would grant an enquiry almost as a matter of course.   In the brief which was before us the answer of *Knowlson* setting up a registered title was omitted, and his registered conveyance, if he has one, was not produced.   Assuming this capable of proof, and proved, *Knowlson* would seem to stand on the same footing as *Scott*, inasmuch as the notice proved against him would be only constructive notice.

Upon the bill as framed, it is not, I think, open to the plaintiff to shew continued possession in *Graham* at the time of *Knowlson's* purchase ; for the bill alleges eviction by *Chalmers*, and possession, and receipt of rents and profits by him ; the only other notice would be from the circumstance of the conveyance from *Chalmers* to *Knowlson* being by what is termed a quitclaim deed ; which can be no more than constructive notice ; and we must have held it to be only cons.ructive notice, otherwise we must have held it to prevail against *Scott*, being a link in his chain of title as well as against *Knowlson*.   The distinction taken evidently was, that *Knowlson*, not having so far as we saw any registered title, was affected with constructive notice, while *Scott* was protected by registration of his conveyance from all but actual notice, of which none was proved.

It is clear that *Chalmers* had notice, and the decree is right as against him, (apart from the question of *quantum*,) if such relief can properly be given upon this bill.   Such relief is not specifically prayed, but it is urged that upon the allegations in the bill it may properly be granted under the prayer for general relief.

The rule is thus put by Sir *John Leach* in *Wilkinson* v. *Beal ; (a)* " If a party prays particular relief to which he is not entitled, he may, nevertheless, under the prayer

(a) 4 Mad. 408.

for general relief, have such relief as he is entitled to upon the case alleged and proved." It is thus put by Lord *Erskine* in *Hiern* v. *Mill:* (a) " If the bill contains charges putting points in issue that are material, the plaintiff is entitled to the relief which those facts will sustain under the general prayer ; but he cannot desert the specific relief prayed ; and under the general prayer ask specific relief of another description, unless the facts and circumstances charged by the bill, will, consistently with the rules of the court, maintain that relief."

These cases are cited by Lord *Redesdale* (b) and by *Story*, (c) in their treatises on equity pleading; and after stating that the relief must be agreeable to the case made by the bill, and not different from it, they add, and the court will not in all cases (*Story* says ordinarily) be so indulgent as to permit a bill framed for one purpose to answer another, especially if the defendant may be surprised or prejudiced.

What the plaintiff seeks by the whole frame of his bill, and by the specific prayer, is the land itself ; not any personal remedy ; and consistently with his allegation of notice to *Chalmers*, to *Knowlson* and to *Scott*, the getting back the land would be the remedy he would be entitled to upon paying his mortgage money ; a personal remedy he could not be entitled to, and a prayer for it as alternative relief would be improper, unless based upon the contingency that one of the defendants had not notice. If it were true, as alleged, that *Knowlson* and *Scott* had notice, he could not ask a personal remedy ; and it might well be a surprise upon any of the parties if a personal remedy were asked ; and it probably was a surprise, as Mr. *Crooks* suggests, for they all appeared by the same solicitor and counsel, which they might properly do if only a redemption was sought ; but not if a per-

---

(a) 13 Ves. 119. (b) Page 35.
(c) Sec. 42.

sonal remedy against any was sought, for in such case their interests would be obviously conflicting. The plaintiff, if doubtful of his ability to prove notice as alleged, should, as suggested in Lord *Redesdale's* treatise, have framed his bill with a double aspect; or upon notice being denied by answer, should have amended, stating that one defendant had not notice. Without one or the other of these courses he was not at liberty, I conceive, to adopt at the hearing what was set up by answer, and ask relief in accordance with it.—*Lindsay* v. *Lynch.* (a)

A case of *Soden* v. *Soden* is referred to by Lord *Erskine* in *Hiern* v. *Mill*, which nearly resembles this case. The defendant was a widow entitled to elect between the provisions of a will and a settlement; and the bill charged, as I understand, that not knowing the value of the properties, she had not an opportunity to elect, and therefore was not bound, or to be considered as intending to make an election. All the facts charged in the bill, and the prayer, were calculated to call upon her to make an election. I understand that a declaration was asked at the hearing that she had elected and was concluded; and Lord *Erskine* held that such a declaration could not be made under the prayer for general relief, being inconsistent with the case made by the bill, and the specific prayer that she should make her election. In that case as in this, it was only necessary to add a few words; in that case, to the effect that if it should appear that she had made her election then that the court should declare accordingly, and conclude her by its decree: in this case, that if it should appear that any of the defendants had not notice, then a personal remedy.

I think for these reasons that the decree is erroneous in decreeing a personal remedy against *Chalmers* and *Knowlson*, and that we cannot, upon the bill framed as it is, decree a personal remedy against *Chalmers* alone.

TIFFANY v. THOMPSON.

*Trustee and cestui que trust—Dormant Equities Act—Statute of Limi-
tations—Administration.*

Where lands are devised to trustees to sell and divide the proceeds
among residuary legatees, this is not a *charge upon land* within the
meaning of the 22 Vic., ch. 88, sec. 24, so as to be barred by the lapse
of 20 years, but it is the case of an express trust within the 32nd section of the same act. Following *Watson* v. *Saul*, 1 Giff. 188.

Where a trustee commits a breach of trust, the person participating in
it is not a necessary party to a suit for the general administration of
the trust estate.

One devisee of a trustee, against whose estate a suit is brought, sufficiently represents those interested in the estate.

PER VANKOUGHNET, C.—The Dormant Equities Act is not a bar in
cases of express trust.

Whether an administrator *de bonis non* can call in question the admin
istration of his predecessor in office.— *Quære.*

Mr. *Blake* and Mr. *Kerr*, for plaintiff.

Mr. *Strong*, Mr. *Proudfoot*, and Mr. *Ambrose*, for
defendants.

Leonard v. *Leonard* (a) *Broderick* v. *Broderick*, (b)
Cann v. *Cann*, (c) *Hill* on Trustees, 535, were cited.

Judgment.—VANKOUGHNET, C.—By his will, dated, the
third day of March, 1835, one *Oliver Tiffany* devised in
part as follows: "I do give, devise and bequeath to my
executors hereinafter named, all my estate, both real
and personal, *in trust*, to be sold and disposed of for the
uses and purposes hereinafter mentioned, excepting such
parts as shall be hereinafter specifically made and given.
They may sell either at auction or private sale, at their
discretion, and for the real estate execute proper deeds
of conveyance for the same, and may give such credit
for the consideration money, on good security, as they
may deem most beneficial for my legatees, hereinafter
mentioned, and the avails of such sales to be paid over
agreeably to the following legacies, to wit." The testator here makes certain specific dispositions of his

---

(a) 2 B. & B. 171.   (b) 1 P. W. 239.
(c) 1 P. W. 727.

property, and then declares " all the remainder and
residue of my property and estate of every name and
description whatsoever, as well real as personal, embracing lands, hereditaments and tenements, moneys or land,
(over payment of debts, funeral charges, and reasonable
allowance to my said executors, for their time, labour,
and expenses about the discharge of their duties under
this will,) bills, book accounts, debts on bonds, promissory notes, mortgages, and all other securities for the
payment of money, and the receipts, forming the
general fund as aforementioned, (being the general
fund for the division under this residuary clause,) I do
give, devise, and bequeath to my sister *Caty*, widow
of the late Rev. *Davenport Phelps*, deceased, to my
brother *Isaac Hall Tiffany*, to my sister *Sally*, wife of
Thomas Lawyer, Esq., and to the children of my deceased
brother *Sylvester Tiffany*, and those of my deceased
sister *Lucinda*, who was the wife and widow of *Moses
Brigham*, Esq., deceased, &c., &c.," and in regard to
the share of the children of *Sylvester* deceased, (brother
of the testator,) the testator directs that the one-fourth
part thereof be equally divided between his brothers,
George and *Gideon*, or the children of such of them as
may be deceased at the time.   And he arranges how
these different shares of his residuary estate are to be
apportioned, with certain specific directions as to some of
them. He appoints *Manuel Overfield, Thomas Hammill*,
and his nephew *George Sylvester Tiffany* his executors.
The latter alone proved the will, and obtained probate
thereof on the 15th of June, 1835. *Overfield* died without having ever in any way acted as executor or trustee.
Thomas Hammill does not appear to have acted as
executor, but the bill, which has been taken *pro confesso* against him, alleges that he acted as trustee under
the will, by joining in conveyances, and by other acts;
and he is the sole surviving trustee, and as such is made a
defendant. *George Sylvester Tiffany* assumed the active
management of the estate, but what he did with it—how
much personalty he got in—how much realty he sold—

what became of the proceeds—what debts he paid, does not appear. He does not seem to have kept any books of account, or at all events any such as would shew his dealings with the estate. He does not appear to have accounted with any of the parties interested in it, except *Sally* and *Thomas Lawyer*, with whom it seems he had a settlement in respect of their shares.

He died in 1855, having first made his will, whereby he appointed the defendants *Thompson*, *Proudfoot* and *Clark* his executors, and provided and declared : " As executor to my uncle's will, I made composition with the legatees or devisees thereunder, five in number, to pay each of them as his or her share—$2000—two of these persons have been paid or satisfied—the sums due to the three others I charge on my estate."

It does not appear that with these "three others" any composition or settlement was ever had, though attempted, by *Geo. S. Tiffany.*

The plaintiff files this bill for the administration of the estate of *Oliver Tiffany*, against the executors of *Geo. S. Tiffany*, the surviving trustee *Hammill*, and *Edward Tiffany*, one of the children and devisees of *Geo. S. Tiffany*, and he claims to represent by assignment to him the shares of the estate devised and bequeathed by *Oliver Tiffany* to *Caty Phelps* and *Sylvester Tiffany*, and his children. He also claims as administrator *de bonis non* of *Oliver Tiffany*, and as one of the next of kin, and administrator with the will annexed, of *Gideon Tiffany*. His right to an account and to administration of *Oliver Tiffany's* estate, as being the assignee of the share thereof to which *Sylvester Tiffany* and his children were entitled, and as administrator, and one of the next of kin of *Gideon Tiffany*, is not disputed if the statutory defences, hereafter to be noticed, do not form a bar.

His right as administrator *de bonis non* to the full

account claimed by him, and his right as representing the shares of *Caty Phelps*, are disputed.

It is contended that an administrator *de bonis non* cannot call in question the administration of his predecessor in office; that this can only be done by the court which empowered him to act, and to which alone he is accountable; or at all events by one of the next of kin, or a legatee or devisee of the estate of the deceased, and that the administrator *de bonis non* can only claim administration of the chattels remaining in specie unconverted and undisposed of by the executor or administrator whom he succeeds. I have given this question more consideration than perhaps it called for, and I have thereby unnecessarily delayed the judgment in this case, because after all it is not material to a decision of it. If the plaintiff is not entitled in this right to such an account as he seeks, he is so in his right of assignee of one of the legatees and devisees of the testator *Oliver Tiffany*. The right of the administrator *de bonis non*, and the extent of that right to call in question the acts of his predecessor in office, are involved in some obscurity; and an examination of the doctrines, principles, and practice on which the ecclesiastical courts acted in this respect in early times, leaves the matter in considerable doubt, which, however, as I have already stated, it is not in this case necessary to remove.

The plaintiff's title as representing *Caty Phelp's* share is by no means clear. It takes an assignment from her children, without its being shewn that they received title from her, or that any one of them was her legal personal representative. The executors of *Geo. S. Tiffany*, however, treated the plaintiff's title to this share as established, for they paid him $2000 in discharge of it, and took from him a release, which the plaintiff impeaches on the ground that it was obtained from him when in necessitous circumstances, and without giving him that full information as to the value and disposition of *Oliver Tiffany's* estate, to which as one interested in it he was entitled. I do not think it necessary to pronounce any opinion now upon the plaintiff's title to this share, as that can be made out in the master's office. It certainly is not at present sufficiently established, and therefore I also refrain from any declaration as to the validity of the release obtained from the plaintiff, as it may turn out to be of no consequence, should his interest in the legacy not be established. Both these positions can be hereafter disposed of in the master's office, or on further directions. Holding, then, that the plaintiff, as representing two of the legatees of *Oliver Tiffany* has made out a *prima facie* right to a decree, I proceed to consider the defences urged in bar to that right; and these are: 1st, the act relating to dormant equities; and 2ndly, the Statute of Limitations relating to legacies.

As to any land which has been undisposed of, it vests in the surviving trustee *Hammill*, and is applicable to the purposes of the will, he raising no question on either statute, and indeed not making any defence.

Before considering the effect on this case of either of the statutes referred to, it will be well to state the relation which I think was by the will constituted between *Geo. S. Tiffany* and the legatees, and I am of opinion it was that of trustee and *cestuis que trustent* expressly. If ever there was a will by which an executor could be expressly made a trustee for the legatees, it is this will. By it the executors are not only empowered, but are charged to sell and to convert into money the real and personal estate for the uses and purposes stated in the will. To what extent they executed by sale so much of the trust reposed in them, remains to be ascertained. If they did not sell, then their possession of the property must be considered as the possession of the *cestuis que trustent*, and if they did sell, their possession of the proceeds must be treated in the same manner. If this be so, can the Dormant Equities Act have any application? In my own opinion that act does not apply to a case of express trust, for breach of which the *cestui qne trustent* seek redress against the trustee; and in the case of such a trust as the present, in respect to which the trustee is called to account, it can form no defence to him. The first section of the act provides that "no title to, or interest in, real estate, which is valid at law, shall be disturbed or otherwise affected in equity, by reason of any matter or upon any ground which arose before the 4th day of March, A.D., 1837, or for the purpose of giving effect to any equitable claim, interest, or estate which arose before the said date, unless there has been actual or positive fraud in the party whose title is sought to be disturbed or affected." I think the rule of construction should be, that the act does not apply as between trustees and *cestuis que trustent*, to the cases of such trusts, but that exceptional cases arising upon such trusts may find protection under it. I agree with what has been so well said by the late Chancellor, and by my brother *Spragge* in *Wragg* v. *Beckett* upon the question, which I do not understand to be settled by any judgment of the Court of Appeal.

The testator, *Oliver Tiffany*, died in 1835. It was the duty of the trustees, having accepted the trust, to enter into possession of the land under the title conveyed to them by the will, and to hold under that title, and under it sell and dispose of the property, and at law, and in equity, too, such title in them was valid. It is not sought here to disturb that title, or any title which by virtue of it they conveyed, by reason of any thing which arose before the 4th day of March, A.D. 1837; nor is any breach of trust or right of action prior to that time set up. How then can this section have any application to the present case?

Then as to the remaining section of the act, I have

already stated that in my opinion the act does not apply at all as between trustee and *cestuis que trustent*, to a case of express trust, unless, perhaps, in exceptional cases in regard to particular claims, or breaches of trusts. A long train of decisions has established the possession of the trustees to be that of the *cestuis que trustent*. The trustee having the legal title in hand, or in the proceeds of its sale, where he has power to sell, has possession of the one or the other; and that possession is consistent with the title conferred upon him, and with the rights of the *cestuis que trustent*. He, at all events, will not be allowed to say that he did not hold as trustee, and for his *cestuis que trustent*, however long the time during which he has so held—the origin and existence of the trust being express and clear. In this case we find *Geo. S. Tiffany* continuing to act as executor of *Oliver Tiffany* down to his death, and admitting his liability and obligation as such, in his will, executed in 1855 ; and in a letter to the plaintiff, dated the 17th of May, 1854, he professes to give him a statement of *Oliver Tiffany's* estate, with a view to his settling with the different claimants upon it, and makes, therefor, a proposition which they reject.

Now can the rights of these claimants upon the estate, thus recognised by *Tiffany* in 1854 and 1855, and in dispute with him, be treated as " dormant equities? " What precise meaning the legislature meant to attach to that term I am unable to say; but if I am called upon to pronounce an opinion, I would say that it did not embrace rights or equities created by acts *inter partes*, but rather equities springing out of the relations of rights not recognised by contracts between the parties, and which they had not chosen to procure the recognition of through the aid of the court. I say this, because I think the most limited construction must be given to a statute which in its literal interpretation would abridge or take away rights. Give the second section of the act application to all equitable claims not embraced in the first and interpret it literally; what would be the result? Why that neither payment, acknowledgment, nor compromise, (unless in itself giving a right of action,) since 1837, would preserve a claim that had arisen before that year ; and if it is to affect claims upon land, the period as to which in equity is made by the Statute of Limitations similar to that at law ; then in equity all disabilities in the prosecution of titles are disallowed, while at law they are maintained. Now if we look at the preamble to the act, we find it reciting that, "whereas in regard to claims upon, or interests in real estate, arising before the said date (4th of March, 1837), it is just to restrict the future application of the said rules of decision to cases of fraud ; and in regard to other cases, it is expedient to extend thereto, in manner hereinafter provided, the authority so given to the court as aforesaid in cases of mortgages ;" and then if we turn to the section of the act of 1837, which gives to the court this authority in mortgage cases, we find that the court was released from following the rules of decision in England, both as to the rights of mortgagees and mortgagors ; and that while they might not permit a mortgagor to redeem though twenty years had not elapsed, yet it was quite in their discretion to permit a mortgagee to foreclosure after that period. This section, therefore, was as well an enabling provision, giving the court power to deal with, and set up claims which would otherwise have been by lapse of time extinguished. If this second section is equally with the first confined to cases affecting real estate, then it has no application here, for as to the outstanding real estate it is not pleaded by the surviving trustee in whom it is vested ; and the residue of the claim is of personalty.

In commenting upon this section in *Beckett* v. *Wragg*, (a) the present learned President of the Court of Appeal says : " I take this (the expression in regard to any

---

(a) Ante vol. vii., p. 237.

other claim or right, &c.) to mean in regard to any equitable claim or right arising before the passing of the Chancery Act, to which effect can be given by the court *without disturbing or otherwise affecting a title valid in law.* In regard in such claims or rights, I think the court is empowered to act as they may find to be just and reasonable under all the circumstances of the particular case ; and they are not prohibited from acting upon and forcing such equitable claims, even in cases in which there has been no actual or positive fraud in the defendant." If this be a correct interpretation of the section under review, then it is an enabling rather than a disabling provision, though I do not well see how it is to be confined to cases affecting real estate alone. It would rather seem to be applicable to cases other than those relating " to claims upon, or interest in, real estate," in respect of which one section of the act makes special provision. It may be said, what operation can this section have unless you hold it to be entirely restrictive ? I answer that there are many cases in which the Court of Chancery would refuse to entertain stale claims, or claims against a state of things in which they thought parties had acquiesced, or which they thought were barred by laches short of twenty years.

Of recent cases *Harcourt* v. *White,* (a) and *Bright* v. *Legerton,* (b) are instances, and illustrate what I have previously said, that exceptional cases, arising out of the management of express trusts, may occur, to which the act might be a proper defence ; but for all such cases at all events the statute has fixed the positive limitation of twenty years. But why the necessity of fixing that period, it may be asked, if the court would, without the statute, have adopted that limitation ? The same suggestion might have been made against a statute of limitations at a period when courts presumed a right

---

(a) 28 Beav. 303.　　　　(b) 30 L. J. C. 338.

after twenty years' undisturbed enjoyment of it; but
yet it was thought desirable to fix a limitation by legislative enactment. And again, if this section of the
statute be viewed as an enabling power to the court, it
would be necessary, in order to give the court jurisdiction to consider claims which a much shorter period
than twenty years would have barred. Finding it
difficult to place any satisfactory interpretation on this
section, and disposed as I am to give the most limited
operation to this act as a restrictive one, I hold it has
no application to the present case.

The Statute of Limitations in regard to legacies had
for a long time been a puzzle, but I think the true solu-
tion of it is to be found in the judgment of Vice-Chancellor *Stuart,* in the case of *Watson* v. *Saul.* (a) The
difficulty has been to reconcile the sections 25 and 40
of the English act, to which sections 24 and 32 of our
act (ch. 88 of the Consol. Stats. of U.C.) are analogous.
The distinction between a legacy *qua* legacy charged on
land, even though it were held in trust to pay that
legacy, and a charge for the payment of a debt on land
in the hands of a trustee, was recognised by the master
of the rolls in *Knox* v. *Kelly.* (b) That learned judge
admitted the almost impossibility of a distinction to
which he nevertheless felt bound to give effect; and the
result of *Knox* v. *Kelly,* if literally acted on, would be
that however express and strong the trust created for the
payment of a legacy, the time within which it could be
collected or enforced, must be regulated by the 24th,
and not by the 32nd section of our act. This seemed
altogether contrary to the spirit of our act, as
evidenced by section 32, and in various ways judges
struggled to get rid of or evade in each particular case
before them such a construction.

The cases collected by Lord *St. Leonards* in his work

(a) 1 Giffard, 188.   (b) 6 Ir. Eq. R. 279.

on the new statutes, shew this ; and that learned author does not by any suggestions of his own attempt to clear away the difficulty.   It became necessary, however, directly and distinctly to decide the question in the case of *Watson* v. *Saul*; and the Vice-Chancellor there, after a review of all the preceding decisions of any importance, declares the distinction to be, that when a beneficial interest in property is conveyed to a party charged with the payment of a legacy, that then section 24 of our act as section 40 of the English act, will govern, for then it is in reality a mere charge upon land ; but that when property is conveyed to trustees upon the express trust that out of it a legacy shall be paid, that then section 32 of our act, as section 25 of the English, removes the period of limitation.   This construction is consistent with common sense and equity, and affords the means of giving to both clauses of the act operation in regard to legacies, and I accordingly adopt it.   See also *Bright* v. *Larcher*, (a) and *Obee* v. *Bishop*. (b)

In my opinion, therefore, the defence fails, and the plaintiff is entitled to a decree for the administration of the estate of *Oliver Tiffany*, and to a declaration that the trusts of his will should be carried out. I ought to have noticed at the outset the objections raised as to want of parties.   It was argued that the arrangement by *Geo. S. Tiffany* with the *Lawyers* in respect of their legacy, was a breach of trust, and therefore the *Lawyers* were necessary parties in the suit.   This might be so if the suit had reference to this transaction alone ; but as the suit is for the administration of the estate generally, the charge of mismanagement or breach of trust in the *Lawyers'* legacy is a mere incident not material to the right to relief prayed for, and is more proper for enquiry in the master's office than at the hearing, (except, perhaps, as to the question of costs, if it were necessary now to consider it for that purpose.)   It is also objected,

---

(a) 27 Beav. 130.   (b) 1 DeG. F. & J. 137.

that the devisees of *George S. Tiffany* should be parties, as their estate may be much diminished if it shall be found responsible to the estate of *Oliver Tiffany*, by reason of the acts or omissions of *George*. I do not think this objection can be maintained. If it be necessary to have the interests of the devisees *in persona* represented here, I think enough for that purpose has been done in having made one of them, *Edward Tiffany*, a defendant.

As to the question of costs up to the hearing, there is perhaps sufficient of misconduct shewn in *Geo. S. Tiffany* to warrant the court in charging his estate with those costs, but I think it better to reserve the consideration of them, and of further directions. The executors of *Geo. S. Tiffany* cannot be held blameable for raising the defences they have made to the plaintiff's claim. Ignorant, as, according to the plaintiff's bill, they must have been, of many of the transactions of *Geo. S. Tiffany* in the estate, they cannot be held responsible for not furnishing full information in regard to it, and the legal positions which they have argued by way of defence, were fair subjects for it.

KILBORN v. WORKMAN.

Vendor and purchaser—Defective title—Payment for improvements—Costs.

A vendor who was unable to complete his contract for sale of real estate, by reason of his title being defective, had, notwithstanding, instituted proceedings at law to enforce payment of the purchase money. Thereupon the purchaser filed a bill alleging his willingness to perform the contract, if a good title could be made, but that a good title could not be made; that he had paid part of the purchase money, and made improvements on the property. Upon a reference as to title it was shewn that the vendor was unable to make a good title. On further directions, the court ordered a perpetual injunction to restrain the action at law; re-payment of the amount of purchase money paid with interest, and that the same should form a charge on defendant's interest in the land, and that the defendant should pay the costs of the suit; but refused the plaintiff any allowance in respect of the improvements made by him.

This was a bill praying the rescission of a contract for

the sale and purchase of certain lands agreed to be sold
by the defendant to the plaintiff, on the ground that the
defendant could not make out a good title. An interim
injunction had been obtained to restrain proceedings
at law to enforce payment of the purchase money; and
at the hearing a reference as to title was directed to
the master at Woodstock, who reported against the
title. On the cause coming on for further directions,

Mr. *Spencer*, for the plaintiff, cited *Hallis* v. *Edwards*, (a) *Walley* v. *Walley*, (b) *Ex parte James*, (c) to
shew that a contract being rescinded, the court was in
the habit of allowing the purchaser payment for his
improvements, made upon the faith of such contract.
He contended that plaintiff was clearly entitled to his
costs, including the reference as to title, that being
necessary to shew that the plaintiff was entitled to the
injunction asked by the bill.

Mr. *Barrett*, contra, resisted the right to payment
for improvements.

Judgment.—Spragge, V.C.—The plaintiff is the purchaser of a parcel of land, described as a village lot in
the village of Plattsville. The defendant (the vendor)
sued him at law for purchase money; and thereupon
this bill is filed, alleging the plaintiff's willingness to
pay if the defendant could give good title; and alleging
that he could not make good title. The bill alleges
that payments have been made on account of purchase
money; and that the plaintiff has made improvements
upon the land purchased, which the answer describes
as the frame of a two-story building. Upon a reference
as to title, the master reports against it, and now upon
further directions the plaintiff asks for an order for
the re-payment of the purchase money paid by him,

(a) 1 Ves. 159.   (b) Ib. 487.
(c) 8 Ves. 351.

which is conceded; and for an enquiry as to the value of
his improvements, in order to the defendant being compelled to compensate the plaintiff for them; and to the
amount being made a charge upon his interest in the land.

The right to this is denied.   I am referred to Lord
St. Leonard's work on vendors and purchasers, and to
some cases as authority for the claim; but the learned
author, in the passage to which I am referred, is not
treating of such a bill as this, but of the terms upon
which a trustee, or other person whose purchase is successfully impeached, will be compelled to give up his
purchase; and one term in such cases is, allowance for
improvements; and the cases cited are with one exception cases of that nature.   The exception is *Hallis* v.
Edwards, a case for specific performance by purchaser,
of leasehold premises, alleging a parol contract, and
the expenditure of large sums of money in repairing
the premises.   The Lord Keeper threw out an opinion
without deciding the point, that the bill might be
maintained for the value of the improvements.   The
case is referred to by Lord *St. Leonards*, but not as
authority for the point contended for.

It has been decided at law in this country that in covenant for good title, the measure of damages is the purchase money and interest, and that the purchaser cannot recover for increase in value, or for improvements ;
and the late Chief Justice of Upper Canada enters at
length into the reasons why the purchaser ought not to
recover any more.   I refer to these reasons without
repeating them; there is great force in them, and they
apply as much to such a bill as this, as to proceedings
at law; and in the case before me, it does strike me
that it would be only reasonable that the plaintiff should
have his title investigated before, instead of after, making
the improvements in question, instead of going on
making improvements in ignorance of whether his title

was good or bad. I do not say that in no case ought improvements to be allowed ; but in this case the plaintiff has not much to complain of, if they are not allowed.

There is also this difficulty in the way of allowing for improvements and making them a charge upon the land : that according to the decision in *McKinnon* and *Burrows* there is no debt in respect of them due to the plaintiff, and this court would not be giving a charge for a debt ; but would, as put by Lord *St. Leonards*, (a) *raise* a debt which does not exist, and then make it a charge upon the land ; and this is consistent with the comment put upon this passage in *Wythes* v. *Lee* (b)

For these reasons I think what is asked as to improvements should be refused, but it is reasonable, under the circumstances, that the plaintiff should be re-paid his purchase money with interest, and that such moneys should be a charge upon the defendant's interest in the land.

I think the plaintiff should have his costs. It was inequitable in the defendant to sue for purchase money when he could not make a good title ; and the investigation of title as well as the proceedings before the hearing, were necessary in order to shew the defendant wrong in proceeding at law.

McPHERSON v. DOUGAN.

Mortgagor—Mortgagee—Assignee.

A mortgage set aside under the circumstances.

The rule in equity is, that the assignee of a mortgage takes it subject not only to the state of the account between the mortgagor and mortgagee, but also to the same equities as affect it in the hands of the mortgagee.

The facts of the case are stated in the judgment.

(a) Page 245.   (3) Drew. 405.

Mr. *Roaf*, for plaintiff.

Mr. *Brouyh*, Q. C., for defendant.

Judgment.–SPRAGGE, V. C.–This bill is filed by a mortgagor against the mortgagee, and the assignees of the mortgagee. It sets out that the plaintiff made a mortgage to the defendant *Dougan*, on the 16th of October, 1858, on certain farm property of the plaintiff, expressed to secure the sum of £400, but that no sum of money was advanced, or was due from the plaintiff to *Dougan*.

The bill prays that it may be declared that nothing is due upon the mortgage, and for a re-conveyance.

It is an undisputed fact that no money was advanced; and that no money was due, unless a sum of about £100, claimed by *Dougan* on a store account, and which I think is disproved. *Dougan* sets up in his answer, that the mortgage arose out of an agreement between him and the plaintiff that they should enter into partnership; there are articles of partnership produced in which there is a provision that the same property which is comprised in the mortgage, and a half acre of land, with a tavern upon it, in the village of Mars, belonging to *Dougan*, should be considered as partnership property. That provision does not account for the mortgage, but seems inconsistent with it. *Dougan*, in his answer, sets up that he was himself in debt in the sum of about £1300; and that the plaintiff owed him about £100; and that the plaintiff consented to make the mortgage in order to raise money to pay off *Dougan's* debts. He was afterwards examined before Mr. *Hector*, and commences by stating a different consideration for the mortgage, namely, a house and lot in the village of Mars, and a book debt of about £90. In another part of his examination he gives much the same account as in his answer; and again, in other parts he states, and reiterates, that there was no other agreement between them than is contained in the written articles of partnership. I have quoted one provision from them ; there is another, added after execution, or rather two are added after execution, and there is a re-execution at the foot of them. The other provision is in these words: " that the debts now standing against *Dougan* is to be paid out of the profits of the firm." These words are squeezed in between the first signature and the other added provision, evidently after the other provision was written—in effect interlined. There is no note in regard to them, and neither of the subscribing witnesses, one of whom it is said made the addition, is called. I think this provision must be discarded. The matter then stands thus: there was no money consideration for the mortgage, and there is nothing but the answer and examination of *Dougan* to shew any other consideration. I think his account of it entitled to no weight. The only circumstance of weight is, the difficulty of accounting for the mortgage being given at all, the plaintiff himself giving no explanation of how he came to execute the paper; but he seems to have been a person of less than ordinary intelligence; and is described by one witness as not competent to transact any business.

The defendants *Reid* and *Osborne* are assignees of the mortgagee. Recent decisions seem to establish that assignees of a mortgage take it, subject to the same equities as affect it in the hands of the mortgagee, and not merely subject to the state of the account. The most recent case, I believe, is that of *Parker* v. *Clarke*, at the Rolls. The mortgage was impeached as obtained by fraud and without consideration—it had got into the hands of a depositee for value, without notice—and Sir *John Romilly* held that he could only take what his assignor could give him, and could not stand in a better situation. I think the plaintiff entitled to the decree he asks for, with costs against the defendant *Dougan*.

NEALE v. WINTER.

Practice—Costs.

When a plaintiff without proper inquiry into facts, and with undue haste filed a bill in this court, to enforce a judgment at law, in which he made charges of fraudulent practices against the defendant, the court, while granting him the relief to which he was strictly entitled, refused him his costs of the suit, and ordered him to pay the costs of the defendants.

This was a bill to enforce a judgment against the defendant in the action at law, and his wife, charging him with various fraudulent practices, in order to evade payment of this demand, all of which were distinctly denied by the answer.

The cause came on to be heard by way of motion for decree.

Mr. *Roaf* for the plaintiff.

Mr. *E. B. Wood* for defendants.

Judgment.—SPRAGGE, V. C.—I cannot give costs to the plaintiff for two reasons, one, that he charges a fraudulent assignment, of which there is not the slightest evidence, and which is explicitly denied by the answer; the other, that the bill was filed with undue haste.

The bill is filed to enforce a judgment in an action for mesne profits, for £294 13s. 3d, the greater part being for costs in ejectment. Upon a revision of taxation £129 15s. 2d. was taxed off, leaving £164 18s. 1d. Mr. *Miller* states in his affidavit that he filed his bill after order for revision obtained, and as I understand his affidavit, after re-taxation, but he demands by his bill the original amount of the judgment. I am informed at the bar that the judgment, as reduced, has been paid, and that the question that I have to decide is only as to costs.

Mr. *Miller* states that after *fi. fa.* placed in the sheriff's hands, he was informed by letter from the sheriff that the defendant had made a bill of sale of his chattel property, andthat about that time a proposition was made by the defendant's attorney " for a settlement or compromise of the judgment in the suit for mesne profits if I [he] would consent to a deduction of the amount which was included in said judgment, and which amount was overcharged in the bill of costs in the action of ejectment." Mr. *Miller* adds, " I had no authority from my client to abate any portion of the judgment in the suit for mesne profits, and I declined to make the deductions asked for." Whether this proposition was made before or after the revision of taxation, does not appear ; whichever it was, it was reasonable, and ought to have been accepted.

The defendant seems to have been anxious not to evade payment, but to have the judgment reduced to a proper amount, and as far as I can make out from the evidence before me, the bill was filed without giving him a fair opportunity of doing this, and paying the proper amount. Mr. *Miller* may have been misinformed, but there is no evidence of the defendant putting any of his property out of his hands ; and I think, under the circumstances, he has been wrongly put to costs, and therefore that his costs, as well as those of his wife, should be paid by the plaintiff.

FERRIE v. KELLY.

Married woman's estate—Sale of equitable interest under fi. fa.

A married woman, jointly with her husband, conveyed her estate absolutely to a trading company, and at the same time the company executed a covenant that they would re-convey upon certain stipulations being complied with, which they accordingly did several years afterwards ; but while the estate was vested in the company, and before the passing of the act for the relief of married women, a judgment was recovered against the husband, and duly registered. *Held*, that this registration bound the estate of the husband, and his interest being equitable, was not affected by a sale of his interest under an execution at law, at the suit of other creditors.

This was a bill by the plaintiffs *Ferrie, Freeland,*

Burton and *Sadlier*, against *Daniel Kelly and Lorinda*, his wife, praying under the circumstances therein set forth, and which are stated in the judgment, for the usual decree for sale as upon a bill by a registered judgment creditor.

The cause came on to be heard by way of motion for decree.

Mr. *Proudfoot*, for plaintiffs.

Mr. *Spinger*, for defendants.

Judgment.—SPRAGGE, V. C.—On the 22nd of December, 1849, the defendant *Lorinda Kelly*, then, and still the wife of *Daniel Kelly*, was seised in fee of a parcel of land in the city of Hamilton : there was issue of the marriage, and the husband was therefore tenant by the courtesy *initiate*.

On the above date the husband and wife made an effectual conveyance of the parcel of land to the Canada Life Assurance Company ; and by an instrument of the same date, the company covenanted, upon demand by the husband, at the expiration of ten years, and upon payment by him of one dollar, to " re-convey and re-assure" the parcel of land, in effect as of the former estate of the wife.

On the 3rd of December, 1851, plaintiffs *Burton* and *Sadlier* recovered judgment against the husband, and registered the same on the 5th of June, 1858 ; and on 23rd of June, 1860, the company re-conveyed the parcel of land to the wife in pursuance of their covenant ; this re-conveyance was after the passing of the married woman's relief act.

The question is, whether at the date of the registration of the judgment, the husband had any estate or interest at law or in equity in the parcel of land.

It matters not whether the transaction was a mortgage or a defeasible purchase, or what was its nature; so as the husband retained some estate or interest within the terms of the act for the registration of judgments. Both the bill and answer speak of the arrangement with the building society as in connection with the rents of the land conveyed; but I have no evidence of the particulars of the arrangement. I think, however, from its being with a trading company, and from the terms of the instrument, that it is to be inferred that the rents were to be received by the company for some consideration advanced. *Kelly* must certainly have had an interest at the date of the registration of the judgment; his wife had an interest unquestionably, and he had an interest in virtue of his marital right—his right had attached before the instruments were executed, and it was not absolutely divested—and if not, remained only subject to such rights as the instruments conferred upon the insurance company. The married woman's relief act, seems out of the case, as the 13th section saves rights acquired by judgment or execution before the 4th of May, 1859.

Another point made, is, that the interest of the husband, whatever it was, was sold in execution at the suit of the judgment creditor. Whatever interest the husband had was equitable, and was not an equity of redemption saleable at common law; nothing, therefore, passed by such sale; and I may add, that if such sale was effectual to pass the husband's interest, he has nothing to defend in this suit; his wife only would be interested in contesting the plaintiffs' claim.

I think the plaintiffs entitled to their decree, and of course with costs.

HENEY v. LOW.

*Mortgagor—Mortgagee—Right to dower at law and in equity—
Instantaneous seisin—Merger of charge.*

. L. purchased land from S., who conveyed to him, and immediately took
back a mortgage to secure the purchase money, in which L.'s wife
did not join. L. afterwards conveyed his equity of redemption to H.,
who subsequently conveyed to S., and S. then sold to another party.
L. having died, his widow sued at law for dower. A bill filed, praying an injunction to stay the action, and for a declaration that the
widow was, under the circumstances, not entitled to dower, was dismissed with costs. On re-hearing this decree was varied, by declaring that the mortgage was not extinguished as a charge on the purchase of the equity of redemption by S. from H., or merged in his
legal estate: but the court refused to restrain the defendant from
proceeding at law for the recovery of her dower, and declared that
the dower so to be allotted should be charged with the payment of
one-third of the interest of the mortgage money unless the defendant chose to pay off one-third of the mortgage debt; and

Per curiam, the right to dower being favoured by both common law
and equity, equity will assist a dowress by removing out of her
way a satisfied mortgage, and will allow her to redeem an
unsatisfied mortgage.

Per *Esten*, V. C.—That the question of merger is one of intention; in
the absence of evidence of intention, the court will consider that
course selected by the purchaser which was most for his benefit, and
that in this case the mortgage became merged in S.'s estate; that
plaintiff had no equity to restrain the action for dower, and that
the bill should be dismissed; and

Per *Spragge*, V. C.—That L. had in him before his conveyance to H.
the beneficial legal estate, being entitled to the value of the land,
beyond the mortgage debt, and any other incidental advantage;
that in the interval between the execution of the conveyance and
mortgage, L. was a trustee for S., but not a bare trustee.

Statement.—The bill in this cause set up that *Nicholas
Sparks* being in 1831 seised in fee of lot No. 8 on the
south side of Wellington Street, in the city of Ottawa, did,
on the 28th day of March, of that year, convey the same to
John Low, late husband of the defendant. That by
mortgage executed immediately after the conveyance.
although dated as of the following day, *Low* re-conveyed
the premises to secure the unpaid purchase money to
Sparks; and that except during the momentary interval between the execution of these two conveyances *Low*
never held the legal estate in the premises.

Low afterwards conveyed his equity of redemption in
the premises to one *Haggart*, and he soon afterwards

transferred his interest to *Sparks,* from whom *Low* had purchased. In 1841 the plaintiff purchased from *Sparks* and still holds the premises.

The bill further alleged, that no part of the sum · secured by the mortgage from *Low* had been paid; that he had died, leaving the defendant to whom he had been married prior to 1831, his widow, and that she had commenced an action against the plaintiff to recover dower out of the premises.

The bill prayed for an injunction to restrain the action, and for a declaration that the defendant was not entitled to dower.

The answer set up that the defendant's late husband had, after executing the mortgage resided for a time on the premises, and erected substantial improvements thereon; that *Sparks* purchased the equity of redemption, knowing of such improvements, and for a sum not more than equal to the excess of the value of the premises over the amount due on the mortgage, and that no right to the relief claimed by the plaintiff existed under the circumstances.

The cause was heard by way of motion for decree, before his Honor V. C. *Esten.*

Mr. *Strong,* for the plaintiff.

Mr. *Hector,* for defendant.

Judgment.—ESTEN, V. C.—The facts of this case are shortly these: *Sparks* sold and conveyed to *Low,* who was married at the time, under an agreement by which the purchase money was to be secured by mortgage; a mortgage was afterwards made, and then *Low* sold and conveyed to *Haggart* and *Haggart* to *Sparks,* and *Sparks* to *Heney,* the plaintiff; *Low* then died, and his widow is suing at law for dower, and the present suit has been instituted to restrain that action.

It has been determined that if an estate is a mortgage estate at the time of the husband's (the mortgagee's) death, his widow is not entitled to dower, although at the time of making the claim the right to redeem may have become extinct ; (a) also when a legal estate in . fee *ex parte materna* is united in the same person with an equitable estate in fee *ex parte paterna*, the equitable estate merges in the legal ; and at his death the heir *ex parte paterna* has no equity against the heir *ex parte materna*, if different persons. (b) Wherever the same persons have equal and commensurate estates in the legal and equitable interest, the equitable will merge in the legal. (c) Where the owner of a charge became owner of the estate by devise, and it was more for his advantage that they should not be extinguished, it was so held in the absence of intention. (d) So also where a person was entitled to an estate as tenant in tail, and having a charge upon that estate by the same will, and it was considered more for his interest that the charge should not merge : it was so held in the absence of evidence of intention. (e) This doctrine is clearly asserted in *Davis* v. *Barrett*, (f) but the facts appear unintelligible. There the owner of a charge acquired the fee of the estate subject to it, but it was against his interest to merge it, and it was held, therefore, that it did not merge in the absence of evidence of intention. *Forbes* v. *Moffatt* (g) was a case similar in principle ; there the owner of a mortgage acquired the equity of redemption by devise, but it was more for his advantage that the mortgage should subsist—and it was so held in absence of evidence of intention.

(a) Flack v. Longmate, 8 Beav. 420. (b) Selby v. Alston, 3 Ves. 339.
(c) Brydges v. Brydges, 3 Ves. 126.
(d) Earl of Clarendon v. Barham, 1 Y. & C. C. C. 688.
(e) Grier v. Shaw, 10 Hare, 76.
(f) 14 Beav. 542.   (g) 18 Ves. 384.

It is quite clear that the owner of a charge acquiring the estate, or the owner of the estate acquiring the charge, can merge or continue the charge at his option. If his intention be expressed, and clearly shewn, no difficulty arises. In the absence of evidence of actual intention he is presumed to have intended what was most for his advantage. In the present case the only advantage to *Sparks* was to secure payment from Mrs. *Low* during her life, of one-third of the interest of the mortgage, as he was bound to pay the principal and two-thirds of the interest. This advantage was so trivial, that coupled with the fact of the mortgage not being kept on foot, and no declaration of intention being made at the time of purchase, that it is not sufficient to rebut the presumption of merger on the union of interests : *Knight* v. *Frampton*, (a) was cited by Mr. *Strong* in argument; there *Frampton* was seised of the legal estate of the whole, he and *Knight* were tenants in common in equity. *Frampton* made a mortgage of the entirety for his own benefit, without the knowledge of *Knight*, who afterwards paid off the mortgage, and took an assignment of it; he then had the legal estate in the entirety, and an equitable estate in a moiety, and a right to hold the entirety until *Frampton* paid the whole amount of the mortgage, whereupon he would convey to him a moiety : held, that this was not such an union of the legal and equitable interest in a moiety during the coverture as to entitle *Knight's* widow to dower of the moiety. This, however, is very different from a mortgagee purchasing the equity of redemption, where the charge certainly merges, unless an intention to the contrary be shown.

It must be intended that the agreement between *Sparks* and *Low* was, that part of the purchase money should be paid, and a mortgage given to secure the balance. Consequently, that the estate should be conveyed by *Sparks* to *Low*, and that *Low* should make a mortgage back to *Sparks*. In this case *Sparks* must necessarily have known

---

(a) 4 Beav. 10.

that *Low's* wife's right of dower would attach, and if we are to consider the parties as intending what they knew to be inevitable, we must conclude that *Sparks* intended to take a mortgage subject to *Low's* wife's right of dower; and then he and those claiming under him could not object to her assertion of her legal title. Supposing, however, the true effect of the agreement to be, that *Sparks* in equity retained his mortgage, rather than took it back, so that it is equitably paramount to the title of dower, yet, undoubtedly, that title attached for every other purpose, and as against every other person. It could have been enforced against *Low's heir*. For every other purpose except to give priority to the mortgage the purchase money must be considered paid, and the estate conveyed. *Low* had no intention of preventing the title of dower from attaching. If he had paid the whole purchase money it would have attached absolutely. It attached subject only to the mortgage; and the mortgage removed, it attached absolutely. If the widow should bring her suit for dower, it could be met only by this mortgage. *Haggart* stood in this situation, and so did *Sparks* and *Heney* also. The only question then, is, whether the mortgage has become extinct. *Prima facie* when a mortgagee purchases the equity of redemption, the mortgage merges in the estate, because being bound to pay the mortgage, and being also the person to receive it, no reason can in general exist why it should not merge. The rule is settled that where the owner of a charge acquires the estate, or the owner of the estate acquires a charge, the charge will sink into the estate unless it is kept on foot, or is intended to continue. It is always a question of intention. The owner of both interests may merge the charge, or keep it on foot at his option. If he manifest his intention expressly, no difficulty can arise; but in the absence of any express evidence of intention, it depends upon which is most for his advantage, whether the charge shall sink or not. He is in fact in that case presumed to have intended what was most for his advantage. If it be perfectly indifferent to him which result follows, the charge will sink in the inheritance.

In the present case when Mr. *Sparks* purchased the equity of redemption from *Haggart*, it was competent to him to have kept the mortgage on foot, and had he desired to do so, it was natural that he should have made some arrangement on that occasion for that purpose, but he did nothing of the sort, and so far as his intention can be collected from his acts, we should be justified in assuming that he intended the mortgage to merge; for having the legal estate vested in himself under the mortgage, he took the conveyance of the equity of redemption to himself in fee, and not to a trustee, and without transferring the mortgage to a trustee. This mode of proceeding, however, not being conclusive, and there being no other express evidence of intention, we are driven to enquire what was most for his advantage, as furnishing the only clue to his presumptive intention. Now, after *Sparks* acquired the equity of redemption he became bound to pay the mortgage—it formed part of his purchase money paid for the estate. If *Sparks* had not purchased, and Mrs. *Low* had redeemed the estate in order to avail herself of her title of dower, she could instantly have filed a bill against *Haggart* to compel him to pay the whole principal of the mortgage, and two-thirds of the interest, or to stand foreclosed. *Sparks*, of course, stood in the same position with *Haggart* when he purchased, and had he kept the mortgage on foot, would have been liable to the same claim. In other words, Mrs. *Low* might have insisted upon having her title of dower enforced, subject only to the obligation of keeping down a third of the interest during her life. This advantage was so trivial that its insignificance, coupled with the fact of *Sparks* having taken the conveyance of the equity of redemption to himself, without transferring the mortgage to a trustee, warrants the presumption that he intended the mortgage to merge. This being so, he held the estate subject to Mrs. *Low's* title of dower. The only thing that could have been opposed to it was the mortgage, and that had become extinct. Mrs. *Low's* title of dower, therefore, became absolute; *Sparks*, of course, conveyed the estate to *Heney* in the same plight in which he held it himself, and therefore I think the plaintiff has no equity to restrain the defendant from enforcing her legal title; and the bill consequently must be dismissed, and I think with costs.

The plaintiff afterwards applied for and obtained an order to re-hear the decree issued upon this judgment, before the full court ; upon re-hearing the same counsel appeared for the parties respectively.

In addition to the cases previously referred to, the following authorities were cited :

Mundy v. *Mundy,* (a) *Norton* v. *Smith,* (b) *Baldwin* v. *Duignan,* (c) *Kent's* Commentaries, 39 ; *Story's* Eq. Jur. vol. i, p. 634.

*Judgment.-*VANKOUGHNET, C.-The facts of this case are set forth in the judgment of my brother *Esten,* who decreed that the plaintiff was not entitled to the relief sought, on the ground that the mortgage charge had merged when *Sparks* got in the equity of redemption. Mr. *Strong,* in an able argument for the plaintiff, contended that the defendant's right to dower never attached, inasmuch as there never was in the husband a perfect seisin in law and equity.   That although at law the wife could claim her dower, because the legal estate vested in her husband for a moment under the deed from *Sparks,* yet that that estate came to him clothed or impressed with a trust to immediately reconvey the legal estate or title to *Sparks* to secure the purchase money which stood between it and the beneficial interest or estate which as purchaser *Low* had in

---

(a) 2 Ves. 122.
(b) 20 U. C. Q. B. 213 ; on Appeal, 7 U. C. L. J. 263
(c) Ante vol. vi., p. 595.

the premises, and that so there never was in him, in the eye of a court of equity, a perfect union of the legal and beneficial interests in the property; or in other words, that he never had the beneficial legal title, inasmuch as before and when he received the legal title he was under contract to re-convey it to *Sparks*, and that a court of equity would, for all purposes, treat that as done which had been agreed to be done—a doctrine applied by Sir *Joseph Jekyl* to a right to dower in the case of *Banks* v. *Sutton*, (a) and he cited in support of his position *Knight* v. *Frampton*. That case is a remarkable instance of the technical strictness with which courts of equity require a claim to dower to be made out. Dower is of course a strictly legal right, but without any equity to aid it, it is allowed to be asserted in this court as well as at law. In *Knight* v. *Frampton*, it was asserted in equity under the following circumstances : *Frampton* and *Knight* owned in moieties an estate, but the whole legal title was in *Frampton*, he being a trustee thereof as to *Knight's* moiety. *Frampton*, in fraud of *Knight*, mortgaged the whole legal estate, and died. *Knight* discovering this, paid off the mortgage money and took an assignment of the mortgage, thus getting in the legal title. He died, and his widow claimed dower out of the moiety which he owned, and which at his death was covered by the legal title he had got it. The Master of the Rolls held that she was not entitled to dower. That she was not entitled to it in respect of the equitable title which *Knight* held in the moiety; nor in respect of the legal title which he had gotten in as mortgagee; that there never was a perfect union of those two titles in *Knight's* life-time, although *Knight* had an equity by which he might have enforced or brought about an union, but which he had never acted on. This is certainly a strong case, and where the widow here asking this court to assign her dower, it would be difficult in the face of that authority to do so, for I do not myself well see how to get over the argument that the trust in *Low* to

(a) 2 *P.* W. at p. 215.

re-convey interposed from the first and instantly between the legal title which he received from *Sparks*,.
and the beneficial interest which he acquired as purchaser, and retained as mortgagor. But I do not think
we are driven to consider this case in that aspect. It
is conceded here that the widow is entitled to dower,
the courts of law having, I understand, ruled that under
such circumstances as attended this case, the widow can
claim dower in respect of the legal estate which vested
in her husband, though but for an instant. This being
so, on what grounds should a court of equity restrain.
her from enforcing that legal right? Not, I apprehend,.
by reason of any technical difficulty such as that which
occurred in *Knight* v. *Frampton*, where she claimed the
aid of the court on her own behalf, but on the ordinary
principle upon which this court acts when it is called
upon to prevent the use of a legal right contrary to equity
and good conscience. It is not, as was asserted, a rule
of universal application that what a court of equity
refuses to give, it will restrain a party from obtaining
at law. There are many notable instances to the contrary. This court would not restrain a party from avoiding at law his contract, on the ground of usury, and yet
if he came here for relief, he must have done that which
was equitable, by restoring the money loaned to him
with legal interest. So this court will often refuse specific
performance, because of the character of the bargain, or
the conduct of the parties, but it will not as of course, for
those reasons, restrain the remedy at law, even though it
be a harsh one. What, then, is the equity as between
these parties? and first, what are the dowress's rights
in respect of mortgaged estates, the equity of redemption in which was in her husband during coverture?
That dower was a right always favoured by the common
law, and following that law, by equity, need not be told
to the student, however much sentiment in these days
may have changed or been modified in regard to it.

Equity would step in to assist the claim at law of a

dowress, by removing out of her way a satisfied mortgage; and so equity always recognized the right of a dowress to redeem an unpaid mortgage. If this be so, and the plaintiff by right in his contention, that the mortgage charge must still be considered as subsisting for his protection against the dowress, then she would be allowed to redeem it, and redeeming it, the plaintiff would have to pay her back or be foreclosed.

It is not necessary, of course, in such a case, to go through these processes to get at the ultimate rights of the parties, for the result must be that she should be allowed to take her dower, paying off one-third of the principal with interest thereon, during the period for which she obtains arrears for dower; or else she must take her dower and arrears subject to the payment of past interest during the period of the arrears, and to payment of it in the future, as is pointed out in the case of *Banks* v. *Sutton*, at page 716. It is, however, said that the mortgage charge is merged and gone; that it does not exist, and can have no resurrection, and that so the widow must have her dower free from this charge. If this must be so, speaking for myself, I should be much inclined to act upon the decision in *Knight* v. *Frampton*, and to decree that she could not have dower at all. But this would not meet the equities of the case, which alone we must consider here, the legal title of the dowress being admitted. Both parties are therefore, in one view, at all events, interested in treating the mortgage charge as subsisting; the plaintiff, that he may by use of it reduce the widow's claim at law to dower; the defendant, that she may not be deprived of her dower altogether. But it seems to me that the mortgage charge should, as between these parties, be treated as subsisting; the plaintiff could not by his own act so merge it as to prevent the dowress redeeming it, and this alone would seem to settle the question; but, unless we were, in pursuance of the authority of *Knight* v. *Frampton*, to interpose and say that the widow should be restrained from obtaining dower under any circumstances, a decree which would seem to me inequitable, I think we must hold that it is for the interest of the plaintiff as it was for *Sparks*, who got in the equity of redemption, and from whom the plaintiff took title, that the charge should not be treated as extinguished.

Forbes v. *Moffatt* (a) may, I suppose, be regarded as the governing authority on this subject, and there Sir *Wm. Grant* says: "When no intention is expressed, or the party is incapable of expressing any, I apprehend that the court considers what is most advantageous to him," that is as to the sinking or preserving of charges; again he says: "Upon looking into all the cases in which charges have been held to merge, I find nothing which shows that it was not perfectly indifferent to the party in whom the interest had united, whether the charge should or should not subsist." I am therefore of opinion that the defendant should be allowed to take her dower, but that there should be a decree (without costs) charging it with one-third of the interest of the mortgage money, as already indicated, unless indeed she chooses to pay off one-third of the principal, with arrears of interest, in which case she should have her dower free. I cannot say that an annual charge of £1 10s., which may continue for the next forty years, is too insignificant a claim for the consideration of this court.

Esten, V. C.—Retained the opinion expressed by him on the original hearing.

Judgment.—Spragge, V. C.—I understand Mr. *Strong's* first proposition to be, that by the conveyance from *Sparks* to *Low* no beneficial legal estate vested in *Low*, because he took it upon trust to re-convey the *whole legal estate* back to *Sparks*. I think upon the principle up-

---

(a) 18 Ves. 384.

on which *Quiggan* and *Fuller*, and other cases following
it have been decided in this court, that *Low* did take the
legal estate upon that trust; but I do not think it follows that no beneficial legal estate vested in *Low*.   It
is true that the trust was to re-convey the whole legal
estate, but it was not to convey it absolutely.   A beneficial estate it is clear passed by the conveyance to *Low*,
being the value of the land beyond the mortgage money,
and any other benefit that might accrue to him from its
purchase.   In the interval of time between the making
of the conveyance and the mortgage, the whole legal
estate was in *Low;* and subject to the trust, the whole
beneficial interest : *Low* was a trustee, *Sparks* a *cestui
que trust*, but *Low* was not a bare trustee, for he had
an interest beyond the trust; he had then the legal
estate as trustee, and with it a beneficial interest ; that
beneficial interest, it appears to me, was in him by reason
of the legal estate being in him, and was therefore a legal
beneficial estate.   Before the execution of the conveyance he was equitable owner, by virtue of the contract of
sale, and so had a beneficial interest which was equitable,
and that became a legal beneficial interest at the instant
of the execution of the conveyance ; the position of the
parties as to the nature of their estate became reversed.
Between the contract of sale and the execution of the conveyance, *Sparks* was legal owner, and *Low* equitable
owner ; upon the execution of the conveyance *Low* was
legal owner, subject to *Sparks'* equity to have the mortgage executed ; but only subject to that equity ; and his
interest beyond that equity was, as I think, a legal beneficial interest.   By the mortgage he pledged his legal
estate to answer so much purchase money, and his beneficial interest then became equitable, but in the interval,
my conclusion is that it was legal.

It has been decided at law that the legal estate vested
in the purchaser by the execution of the conveyance, and
that dower attached at law ; a court of law not recognis-

ing the trust to re-convey by way of mortgage; and
so at law the dower is not subject to the mortgage.;
which in this court it would be, if it attaches at all, as
I think it does.

Assuming that the mortgage did not merge upon
Sparks getting in the equity of redemption from *Haggart*,
as I incline to think it did not, upon the authority of
Forbes v. *Moffatt*, and *Richards* v. *Richards* (a), and
other cases, it still lies upon the plaintiff to shew that
it is inequitable for the widow of *Low* to maintain the
legal right that she undoubtedly has to dower. To insist upon it free from the mortgage debt(or that portion
of it which may properly fall upon her as dowress),
would, I think, be against good conscience, but that is
not the point in question between the parties; apart
from that, is it against good conscience that she should
maintain her legal right? Suppose *Haggart* had still
remained owner of the equity of redemption: *Low* after
some five years' possession, and after putting up a stone
dwelling-house and out-buildings, sold to *Haggart*, at
what price we are not informed. *Haggart* surely could
have no equity to prevent the assertion of Mrs. *Low's* legal title to dower. *Sparks* purchasing from *Haggart* could
have no better right; or in other words, her inchoate
right which existed before her husband alienated, could
not be affected by his sale to *Haggart*, or *Haggart's*
sale to *Sparks*, or again by *Sparks'* sale to the plaintiff.
Suppose *Sparks* had not alienated, and she had proceeded at law to recover her dower against him, and
assuming the mortgage not merged, she could claim
her dower not against *Sparks'* mortgagee, but against
Sparks' alienee of her husband; and I really
do not see upon what principle this court could
interpose, unless in respect to the mortgage. The
equity as to that would be, I take it, that inasmuch as her husband never had any beneficial estate
in the premises, except subject to the mortgage, so she

(a) 1 John. 474.

should be dowable only of that in which he was beneficially interested.　The result, as I should have
thought, would be that the widow should keep down
the whole interest of the mortgage debt, but *Banks* v.
Sutton is against that view, and holds her entitled to
dower on keeping down one-third of the interest.

I agree, therefore, with the Chancellor that the
plaintiff may properly have relief to the extent indicated in his judgment, though I confess I was inclined
to hold such relief a matter too insignificant for him
to come into this court.

In regard to costs, my opinion is, that the plaintiff
should pay the defendant's costs, because the relief he
obtains is not at all what he asks for, or what was
really in contest between the parties.　If he had
claimed as against the widow's dower before suit, or
by his bill, only that small annual deduction which the
decree will give him in respect of his mortgage, I can
scarcely doubt that she would have allowed it, but he
did not give her the opportunity ; and his right to it
is only worked out by a process of reasoning which
probably occurred to none of the parties.　In what
was really the matter in contest between the parties,
the widow's right to dower, the plaintiff has failed.

McLennan v. Heward.

Agent—Commission—Administrator—Costs—Surrogate court.

Where the agent, after the decease of the principal intestate, had procured letters of administration to his estate, and subsequently the person who became possessed of the assets as the personal representative of the administrator refused to account, and a bill was filed to enforce it ; the court under the circumstances, there being no evidence of any improper dealing with the estate either by the administrator or those representing him, allowed the defendants a commission of five per cent. on all moneys received and paid over or properly expended by themselves or their testator, and two and a-half per cent. on all moneys received by him or them, but not yet paid over, but refused them the costs of the suit.

This court will not refer it to the surrogate judge to settle the amount of compensation or commission to be allowed to an administrator or executor ; but having possession of the subject matter of litigation will finally dispose of the rights of all parties.

After the decision of this case as reported *ante* page 178, the plaintiff again set it down before his lordship the Chancellor, to be spoken to on the question of costs, and as to the right of the defendants under the circumstances of this case to be allowed any commission.

Mr. *Mowat*, Q. C., for plaintiff.

Mr. *A. Crooks*, for defendants.

The points relied on by counsel are stated in the judgment of

Judgment.—VANKOUGHNET, C.—The principal facts in this case were before me on the appeal from the master's report, and appear in the judgment then given. The questions debated on further directions and now to be disposed of are the allowance to the agent and administrator for commission and the costs of the suit.

I propose to dispose of the latter question first, and to do so, I have had to consider as far as one can ascertain it, the principle which has governed judges

and courts on this subject in similar cases, and in cases
not quite similar, when the case before them was purely
a case for the administration of the estate of the deceased.
And, first, what was this suit instituted for ? When the
matter of costs was mentioned to me incidentally and
without argument on a former occasion I treated and
considered the case as one of an ordinary administration,
and intimated that under the opinion formed by me of
the conduct of the administrator *Crookshank*, upon the
facts as I had found them to exist, he was, on the current of modern authority and practice, entitled to his
costs ; but after hearing the argument of Mr. *Mowat*, I
confess I think I was wrong in this somewhat hasty
conclusion. I cannot on consideration look upon this
suit as an ordinary administration suit. It is in reality
a suit instituted to compel an agent or his representative
to account; rendered necessary, as the enquiry and result
has shewn, by his having neglected (for which his agents
more than himself were to blame) to furnish proper
accounts, and by him and them contesting a liability
which the court has established against them. The
ordinary rule in such cases is, that the unsuccessful
disputant pays the costs. It is true that Mr. *Crookshank*,
on the death of his principal *Wood*, became administrator of his estate ; but, as was asserted by Mr. *Crooks*,
counsel for the defendants he only assumed this character the better to enable him to discharge his duties as
agent; and such would really seem to have been the case,
as no formal administration was ever sought for, required, or had, and all that *Crookshank*, as administrator, did
was to hold what he had received and get in such moneys
as from time to time became due to the estate. Had
correct accounts of these been rendered and the
proper liability admitted, no suit would have been
necessary, or probably, instituted. Had the intestate
Wood lived to call *Crookshank* to account, he might
have sued him at law, and would there have recovered
his costs as well as his debt ; does it make, or ought it to
make, it in this respect, any difference that his represen-

tatives are suing the representatives of *Crookshank*
here on the very same account, and as liable in the very
same capacity ? I am forced to say that it ought not;
and that the estate of *Crookshank*, having necessitated
a contest in which those representing it have failed,
must pay the costs occasioned by it.

I think the language of the Master of the Rolls in
Pearse v. *Greene* (a) very apposite in a case like the
present. There, speaking of the position and duties of
an accounting party, he says : " It was reasonable that
the managers should have a time allowed them to wind
up the concern, during which they might retain the
funds in their hands, for they were liable to all the expenses that might be incurred. "As soon as the
period (that is of payment) arrived it was an impera-
tive duty on the defendants not to postpone the payment any longer. The defendants admit that they
were called upon to render accounts, but neither of
them did, and they shift the blame interchangeably
upon one another—K. and D. imputing it to G., and
he, on the other hand, recriminating on them. But I
cannot see that it is a sufficient answer for them to
say that their neglect was occasioned by the misconduct of their agent ; if they who were appointed agents
chose to transfer their duty to another, they must be
wholly responsible for his acts. The consequence of
the contrary doctrine would be, that the immediate
agent not having done his duty himself would be constantly exonerated by saying that he had appointed
another to act for him, on whom the blame was to be
thrown;" again, " It is the first duty of an accounting
party, whether an agent, a trustee, a receiver, or an
executor, for in this respect, as was remarked by the
Lord Chancellor in *Hardwicke* v. *Vernon*, (b) they all
stand in the same situation, he must be constantly ready
with his accounts. Was that the case with these persons ? No; it is admitted that though called upon they

---

(a) 1 J. & W. 135.   (b) 14 Ves. 500.

rendered no account; it cannot then be said that in their characters of agents and managers they performed their duty." With regard to costs, he says : " The defendants by not keeping accounts have rendered the suit necessary, and they ought therefore to pay the costs."

I take this to be a true, plain exposition of the law in such cases, and to be common sense.

In regard to administration suits, as such, there is great difficulty in fixing any rule by which the disposition of the costs of the suit is to be governed. The reported decisions are almost as various and different as are the judges who have disposed of them, and I must say that some of them in our own court are at all events, on first impression, difficult to bring within the principles which are supposed to govern questions of costs, in ordinary cases where one party is admittedly in the wrong. After reading and considering a great number of these cases, I think they may be reconciled, if at all, in this way—and in this way only—that all proceedings caused or provoked by the misconduct of an executor, administrator, or trustee, shall be at his cost ; but that when in the same, or in any other suit, not rendered necessary, the administration of the estate by the court is proper, that it may be properly invoked by the administrator, or any other party seeking, and entitled to have it settled and disposed of—the administrator as to so much of the costs occasioned thereby, and not resulting from his own misconduct, is entitled to be paid them, and that as between solicitor and client.

With regard to the commission claimed, it was argued in two aspects : one, as to *Crookshank's* right to it as agent; and the other, as to the propriety of allowing it to him as administrator. Until the statute 23 Vic., ch. 93, sec. 47, no administrator as such could claim any allowance for his services. This rule in regard to persons holding such fiduciary relation was established early in courts of equity, and was inflexible, but it was a rule forged as it were, by the court itself, and which the legislature has broken. It would be but pedantry in me to state the reasons for the rule. The works of reporters and text writers of ready access furnish them. I have been asked whether in a case where the court thought it proper that an administrator or executor should receive remuneration for the discharge of his duties as such, the court would refer it to the judge of the surrogate court to fix the rates of remuneration; or going still further, the court would refer it to the judge to consider whether in a case of administration before it the administrator or executor was entitled to remuneration at all. As a rule this court does not leave its work incomplete, nor ask the aid of other tribunals to perfect it—seised of the subject matter of litigation or dispute, it disposes of it entirely, and in this particular of remuneration, almost more than any other, the court which has surveyed the conduct of the trustee, has taken the accounts, and has adjudicated upon them, is the most competent to form an opinion. Being relieved from the restriction which in this aspect it had imposed upon itself, it will not seek elsewhere for an opinion as to whether remuneration should be allowed to the trustee for his labours, or what the amount of that remuneration should be.

I agree with a great deal said by Mr. *Mowat*, as to the circumstances under which the administrator or executor should be allowed such remuneration. In considering in what cases that remuneration should be awarded under the authority of the recent statute, it is of value to bear in mind the considerations which influenced the court formerly in refusing any allowance. One, if not the principal of these was, that the trustee might not make his duty subservient to his interest—that he might not create work with which to charge and load the estate. If it was considered necessary to remove every temptation of this kind by refusing all payment for such work, it may be fairly argued that it never could have been intended by the legislature that the trustee should be paid

when he had not done the work, or had done it in such
a way as to prejudice the estate or benefit himself. The
language of the act 22 Vic., ch. 93, sec. 47, is precise,
and provides "for a fair and reasonable allowance to the
executor for his *care, pains,* and *trouble,* and his time
expended in or about the executorship, and in *adminis-
tering, disposing* of, and generally in *arranging* and *settling* the same ; and therefor the court may make an
order or *orders from time to time.*" This provision seems
to mean that for such portion of the duties as the executor, &c., has bestowed his care, pains, trouble, and time
upon, in the proper administration of the estate, he
shall receive reasonable compensation. When he has
neglected any portion of his duties, or has applied his
care and pains in mal-administration, it would scarce
be asked that in respect of it, however much trouble may
be brought upon him thereby, he should receive any
wages or reward. Mr. *Mowat* urged that it would be
very salutary to establish as a rule that when an executor
had been guilty of any misconduct he should be deprived
of any remuneration whatever, even in respect of those
partial services which had been faithfully rendered, and
that thus executors and trustees might be encouraged
and induced to act honestly and faithfully throughout.
No doubt such a rule might in that respect work beneficially; but I do not think the legislature intended it,
and looking to the large powers which this court possesses
to compel defaulting executors and trustees to make
amends for their misconduct, it would not have been
considered necessary to deprive them, any more than
any other agent, of payment for what had been well
done. The statute already quoted evidently contem-
plates, and indeed provides for payment of work from
time to time. Then in this case, should any and what
rate of commission be allowed *Crookshank* or his estate ?
I have already said that I look upon *Crookshank,* even
after he assumed the position of administrator, as still
a mere agent for *Wood's* estate ; and as expressed in
my previous judgment on the subject of the commission

found by the\ master, I think him entitled to an allowance as such.   The parties in contest as to the right
·to the real and personal estate of *Wood*, in effect in-
.vited Mr. *Crookshank* to get in and hold the estate of
Wood till the rightful owner of it was ascertained.
They, equally with the intestate *Wood*, seemed to consider everything safe with *Crookshank*, and claimed
his responsibility therefor, promising him a reasonable compensation for his trouble in respect of it.
That the retention of these moneys by *Crookshank* may
have been of great service to him is very probable, and
it has been held that the deposit by a trustee of trust
moneys to his own credit, with his banker, is such a
use of them for his own advantage, though he may not
actually employ the moneys for his own purposes, as
to warrant the court in charging him with interest
upon them while so deposited.   Here, however, *Crookshank* was asked to hold the moneys, the parties trusting to his credit therefor.

It is quite true that moneys have been received by
Crookshank, and withheld by him and his estate, to
which this court now finds the plaintiff entitled.   The
same default, however, occurred in *Landman* v. *Crooks*,
and yet the court there held that the agent was
nevertheless entitled to his commission of five per cent.
On what sums passing through the agent's hands, or
whether on sums for which he was found liable, and had
not paid over, this commission was estimated, does not
appear from the report of the case.   I think five per
cent. will generally be a fair commission to be allowed
on moneys collected and paid over, or properly applied,
and therefore I think it should be allowed him on all
moneys which *Crookshank* or his estate received and
paid over, or properly expended.   On all moneys received and only now to be paid over under the decree
of this court, however honest the contention as to liability therefor may have been, I think a different rate
or scale should be adopted, and that inasmuch as they

have only been gotten in, and not paid, or to be paid over except under the compulsion of this suit, two and one-half (2½) per cent. and no more should be allowed.

BLAIN v. TERRYBERRY.

Donatio mortis causa.

A testator having agreed to sell a portion of his real estate, had taken the note of his vendee for a sum of $900, being the amount of interest accrued due on the purchase money. This note, and the papers relating to the sale, the testator had been frequently heard to say he intended to give to his son, who was named as an executor of his will, Shortly before his death, and in anticipation of it, he directed the case containing his papers to be brought to him, and from amongst them directed certain notes to be selected, and delivered them to his wife for her own use; the rest of the papers, amongst which were the note for $900, and the papers relating to the sale, together with several notes and documents, including his will, the testator handed to his son, with a direction that if he recovered they were to be brought back; but in the event of his death then that he (the son) should keep them. *Held*, that this did not constitute a good *donatio mortis causa* of any of the securities.

The bill in this cause was filed by a legatee, under the will of her father, one *William Terryberry*, under which she was entitled to a legacy of £250, and also a share of his residuary estate which remained undisposed of, against *Jacob Terryberry*, who was the acting executor under the will, and who claimed to be entitled to certain securities by virtue of a *donatio mortis causa*, alleged to have been made to him by the testator under the following circumstances, which appeared in the evidence taken in the cause. It appeared that the testator had sold an estate to one *Cramer* for £1250, and in the year 1847 an arrear of interest had accrued due under the contract; and no part of the purchase money had ever been paid. On this occasion *Cramer* gave the testator his promissory note for the arrears of interest. In that year the testator, while laboring under a mortal disease, and about six weeks before his death, and in expectation of his decease, desired his wife to produce his papers, and from among these he directed *Jacob Terryberry* to select five notes, which he delivered to his wife for her own use ; and the rest he directed *Jacob* to take home with him, and in the event of his recovering from the disease under which he was then labouring, to bring them back to him, but in the event of his death he directed *Jacob* to keep them, and as stated by *Jacob* in his evidence, as his own property. Under these circumstances *Jacob* claimed the security for the whole purchase money arising from the sale which had been effected to *Cramer*. On the other hand, the plaintiff alleged that the whole of this fund was to be accounted for by *Jacob* as part of the personal estate of the testator; the contract for sale remaining in force at the time of the death of the testator, the fruits of it became and formed part of the personal estate. It was shewn that *Jacob* had since re-sold the estate, in consequence of *Cramer* having abandoned the purchase, and had received the proceeds of the sale. Amongst the papers delivered to *Jacob* by the testator were his will and several other documents not connected in any way with the *Cramer* property.

The evidence shewing the donation to have been made was somewhat indefinite, none of the witnesses agreeing with the statements of *Jacob Terryberry* himself, that the testator directed him, in the event of the testator's illness terminating fatally, that he (*Jacob*) should keep the papers as his own property.

The effect of the evidence is fully stated in the judgments.

The cause came on originally to be heard before his Honour V.C. *Esten*, who disallowed the claim of *Jacob Terryberry* to any thing more than the note given by *Cramer* to cover the interest due on his purchase, and declared him entitled to the note for $900, as a *donatio mortis causa*. The claim of the widow to the notes delivered to her was not questioned by either party.

Jacob Terryberry being dissatisfied with the decree

then pronounced, set the cause down to be re-heard
before the full court.

On the cause coming on to be re-heard.

Mr. *Blake* and Mr. *Spohn* for the plaintiff.

Mr. *Freeman* for *Jacob Terryberry*.

For the plaintiff it was contended that the decree
already pronounced should be varied in this, that it
ought to declare the defendant not entitled to any portion of the *Cramer* purchase, whether principal or
interest. As put by defendant, all the papers in the
box were delivered to him for his own benefit, but he
says only the *Cràmer* notes were intended to pass.
Now the box contained several other notes and securities, also the will of the testator, and no distinction is
alleged even by defendant as to any one more than
another being intended for him : being named in the
will as executor, he was the proper hand to deliver it to,
and yet it cannot be contended for a moment that it was
intended to be kept by *Jacob* as his own property.

For the defendant it was insisted that sufficient was
shewn in the evidence to indicate an intention on the
part of the testator to give the *Cramer* papers, and all
the benefits derivable under them, to *Jacob;* the witnesses agree in this respect ; and if after a lapse of so
many years one witness has forgotten what another
remembers, it is not a matter of surprise that it should
be so. It is shewn that *Jacob* immediately after the
death of the testator claimed this as a gift, and acted as
the owner of it : in this the plaintiff has always acquiesced until after a lapse of fourteen years, when the
present suit is instituted.

Ward v. *Turner,* (a) *Walter* v. *Hodge,* (b) The edi-

(a) 2 Ves. Sen., 431.   (b) 2 Swan. 92.

torial article in 6 Jur. N. S. Pt. 2, 55; *Gardner* v. *Parker* (c), *Miller* v. *Miller* (d), *Lawson* v. *Lawson* (e), *Edwards* v. *Jones* (f), were cited by counsel.

Judgment—VANKOUGHNET, C.—I think the only thing wrong in this decree, and I regret to have to come to this conclusion, is the allowance to *Jacob Terryberry* as a *donatio mortis causa* of the note for $900 made by *Cramer*. I have a very strong belief that the testator intended that *Jacob* should have the moneys payable by *Cramer* as the purchase money of the land in question. As a layman he would not be likely to have any knowledge of the doctrine by which land sold is converted into personalty; and dying intestate as to this land, the legal title in which would descend to *Jacob*, as his heir, he would naturally think that *Jacob* having that title would not and could not be compelled to part with it till he had received the purchase money secured by the papers, which, with others, he some time before his death delivered to him under the circumstances detailed in the evidence. But it requires something more than conjecture or moral certainty of conviction to sustain a *donatio mortis causa*. Not that any peculiar rule of evidence distinguishes the case of such a gift from any other, but that when it is sought to be established, the evidence must be such as to satisfy the court of the fact; and the evidence in the present case does not. The testator had made his will, of which he had appointed *Jacob* one of the executors. He calls for the papers deposited in a particular place—the sideboard—in a room where he, his wife and *Jacob* were. He speaks of the *Cramer* papers, being, as I understand the bond for the purchase money, and the note for $900, for arrears of interest. He hands these with the other papers, of which there were several, including his will, to *Jacob*, and says to him: " If I get well, bring them back; if I die, keep them;" or, "they are yours," as *Jacob*

(c) 3 Mad. 184.
(e) 1 P. W. 440.

(d) 3 P. W. 356.
(f) 1 M. & C. 226.

says. Now it is not pretended by *Jacob* that the testator intended to give him anything more than the *Cramer* papers, and yet the words used by the testator, as quoted, would be, and were, as applicable to all the other papers as to the *Cramer* papers ; and if the words be so applicable, then they are more properly treated as applicable to the position *Jacob* would hold as executor, than to any claim in his own right. We cannot apply the words for one purpose to the *Cramer* papers, and for another purpose to the others. Evidence there is of previous declarations by the testator of his intention that *Jacob* should have the moneys payable by *Cramer*, but there is no evidence that he so expressed himself subsequently to the delivery to him of the papers, and there was none such, as I have explained, at the time of that delivery. I do not think that the remark made by the testator that if *Cramer* paid in the spring $500 of the $900 note, he *Jacob*, would be able to proceed with the building of his mill, sufficient to separate that note from the rest of the papers, at the time of their delivery, and so to allocate it to *Jacob's* use. No distinction was made by the testator as to any of the papers on delivering them to *Jacob*, and they were all to be brought back to him if he survived, and so far as evidence of his previously expressed intention could prevail, it was equally strong as to the principal money secured by the bond.

The decree so far as relates to the note for $900 will be varied in accordance with this expression of opinion.

Esten, V.C.—I think the evidence of *Bennett*, Mrs. *Terryberry*, Mrs. *Reid*, and *Jacob Terryberry*, insufficient to prove the *donatio mortis causa*, unless the general expressions indicating an intention that *Jacob* should have the *Cramer* moneys, are sufficient to discriminate between the *Cramer* papers and the other papers, and to give the transaction a different character with regard to them respectively, but I think they are not. I think, therefore, that the decree should be varied to the extent of disallowing the claim of *Jacob Terryberry* to the note for $900.

SPRAGGE, V. C.—I think the interview spoken of by *Bennett* must have been before the interview or interviews spoken of by the other witnesses. Mrs. *Terryberry* and *Jacob* evidently speak of the same interview, and I think Mrs. *Reid* also. At that interview certain notes were taken out from a number of papers, and handed to and kept by Mrs. *Terryberry*, and other papers were handed to *Jacob*, and none of those handed to either were returned to the testator.

I think from the evidence that all the papers spoken of by Mrs. *Terryberry* as placed in the sideboard were handed to *Jacob*, and that among them was *Cramer's* bond ; it is certain that the will was among those handed to him ; and Mrs. *Terryberry* says, that besides the notes handed to her, there were a good many deeds and papers in the sideboard. I think, further, that all the papers handed to *Jacob* were handed to him with the same direction as to their custody ; excepting of course, the notes selected out of them for Mrs. *Terryberry*.

Jacob was named as an executor in the will, and it is obvious that the papers handed to him *might* have been handed to him in that character, and the inference would be that they were so. To rebut that inference there is what took place at the interviews with *Bennett*, and what took place at the subsequent interview at which Mrs. *Terryberry* and *Jacob*, and I think *Susan Reid*, were present. What passed at the interviews with *Bennett* can go no further than evidence of an intention on the part of the testator to give some notes to his wife, and some papers, probably some evidence of *Cramer's* debt and the *Cramer* purchase money to *Jacob*. The papers spoken of by *Bennett* must in some way have got back into the cupboard, otherwise this dilemma must arise ; either the papers then laid aside for *Jacob* were not the *Cramer* papers, or else the *Cramer* papers were not among those delivered to *Jacob* at the subsequent interview; for all those so delivered were brought from the cupboard. They were then, after the interview with *Bennett*, replaced in the cupboard, either for future disposition, or it might be urged in revocation of the testator's intention to give them to *Jacob*. At the most, what then took place is evidence of an intention to give, not then carried out.

Then at the second interview, what is there to rebut the presumption that the papers were delivered to *Jacob* as intended executor, and what in favour of that presumption? The direction given to *Jacob* by the testator in relation to the papers delivered to him, was, as stated by the wife, to take them home; and in case of his recovery, to bring them back; and in case of his death, to keep them. The testator's direction, as stated by *Jacob* himself, differs from his mother's only in this, that in the event of his father's death they were his.

In relation to the *Cramer* debt is this, as stated by Mrs. *Terryberry,* "My husband told *Jacob* if *Cramer* paid the $500 he had better go on with the mill ; and if not, he had better stop. $500 was mentioned because *Cramer* had said he was not prepared to pay any more : a great deal more was due." *Jacob,* himself, says nothing as to what his father said in relation to the *Cramer* debt ; probably because the plaintiff did not think fit to ask him any question upon it.

I cannot reconcile the evidence of Mrs. *Reid* with that of Mrs. *Terryberry* and *Jacob*. According to her evidence the *Cramer* papers were selected from the other papers, and laid on the window seat, and the direction to *Jacob* was to take those papers home, and if he got well to bring them back. If this had been the case, *Jacob* could hardly have put the direction in a way so far less favourable to himself, as he did—he, as well as his mother, in narrating what passed, say nothing about separating the *Cramer* papers from the rest, though they do speak of separating the notes intended for Mrs. *Terryberry*, a circumstance which would naturally lead them to speak of the separation of the *Cramer* papers, if it occurred. Mrs. *Reid* must, I think, refer to the same interview as Mrs. *Terryberry* and *Jacob*, not to any interview spoken of by *Bennet*, though the placing of the papers in the window seat is a point of resemblance; but it is obvious from *Bennet's* evidence that *Jacob* was not present, and probably not Mrs. *Terryberry* either; and Mrs. *Reid* does not speak even of the presence of *Bennet*, whereas at the interview spoken of by himself he took a prominent part in what was done. If she speaks of any other interview before the one spoken of by Mrs. *Terryberry* and *Jacob*, it is immaterial for any other purpose than that spoken of by *Bennet*, and for the same reason ; and there is no pretence of any subsequent interview : indeed it is impossible, for Mrs. *Terryberry* and *Jacob* both say that they kept the papers taken away by them respectively.

For these reasons I think the plaintiff's case must rest upon the evidence of *Jacob Terryberry* and Mrs. *Terryberry*. *Jacob* states the direction of the testator as to what he was to do with the papers more strongly for himself than does his mother; his mother saying that the direction was in the event of his father's death that *Jacob* should keep them ; *Jacob's* version being, that in that event they were his.

I think we should take the mother's account as more reliable, even though there were nothing but the position of the parties to turn the scale. But what *Jacob* attributes to the testator, it is perfectly certain the testator could not mean, and cannot be supposed to have said ; for it would involve the gift to him as his own

property not only of the *Cramer* papers, but of the
money, deeds, and papers, and of the will which were
handed to him.

I think, then, we must take Mrs. *Terryberry's* account
of what passed as the true one : that *Jacob*, in the event
of the testator's death, was to keep the papers handed
to him : the word " keep " being used in antithesis to
what he was to do in another event, his father's recovery, to bring them back.   Then in what sense was
he to keep them ? There are two reasons against its
being understood that he was to keep them as his own ;
one, that the same direction was given as to all ; and
it is certain he was not to keep all as his own ;
the other, that he was an executor named in the will,
which was handed to him.   In the other sense, that
he was to receive and keep them as executor, the direction was sensible and proper, that in the event of
the testator's death he was to keep all the papers
handed to him, and this is in accordance with the inference, *Jacob* being named as executor, that the papers
were handed to him in that character.

There is indeed very little to rebut that inference.
One may speculate upon the probability that the testator may have been under the idea that inasmuch as the
land sold to *Cramer*, would, if unsold, have gone to
Jacob as his heir-at-law, so as the legal estate still
remained in him, his heir could take it as he himself
held it, to convey upon receiving the purchase money ;
and this idea is countenanced by some of the expressions used by the testator.

But of *evidence* there is but little in favour of the
donatio claimed by *Jacob*. There is the intention which
we may gather from the interview with *Bennet*, and what
Mrs. *Terryberry* speaks of in relation to the $500 to be
paid by *Cramer* in the spring ; and its enabling *Jacob*

to proceed with the building of the mill. It would be assuming a good deal to infer from that, that *Jacob*, was to have the whole of the *Cramer* purchase money, close upon $6000.

The decree pronounced proceeds upon this, that the money payable by *Cramer* was divisible, and that there was sufficient evidence to shew that the $900 note given for interest, and of which the $500 to be paid in the spring was a part, was so effectually given by the testator as to enable *Jacob* to claim it as a *donatio mortis causa*.

There is perhaps some room for this distinction. *Jacob* was certainly to be at liberty to apply the $500 to his own individual use at an early day. The testator may have meant certainly that *Jacob* should receive the $500 as executor, as well as receive other moneys as executor and apply the $500 to his own use, but that is not the ordinary import of the words, and besides he was not sole executor, and the money, if paid to a co-executor, might not reach the hands of *Jacob* at all, which it was certainly contemplated that it should do.

Then the note, of which the $500 was a part, was among the papers delivered. If given by itself, with the words used, I incline to think it would be a good donation as to the whole $900. Its being among others, ought not, perhaps, to make any difference, if the court could see with a reasonable degree of certainty that a distinction was to be made, for it would certainly be competent to the testator to say upon the delivery of these papers, " out of these papers you are in the event of my death to retain the $900 note to your own use." What was done and said was however materially different.

I am quite satisfied that *Jacob* can claim nothing, at all events, beyond the $900 note. To constitute a valid *donation* there must be sufficient words of gift, and *an*

act. I think that in this case there was neither.   The
words used do not necessarily imply a gift of any thing
beyond the $900 note, if they go so far.   Nor is there
any act : for the delivery of papers not necessarily connected with the words used, and to an executor, is not
necessarily or by inference a delivery by way of donation.   My doubt is, not whether the whole of the
Cramer purchase money passed, but whether any of it
passed ; for I cannot but feel the force of Lord *Lough-*
borough's language in *Tate* v. *Hibbert,* (a) that however
fair and honest a particular case may appear to be,
" yet these cases are liable to the observations that
have been made that to make a stretch to effect gifts
made to persons surrounded by relations who give
evidence for each other, would be attended with great
inconvenience."

There is this observation applicable to the whole of
this case, that the alleged gift accompanied the actual
delivery of the will, in which, and not by mere verbal
gift, it ought properly to have found a place, so that
the deceased is made to dispose of his property *at the*
same time partly by will, and partly by verbal disposition and delivery.   This circumstance did not occur in
any of the cases that I have seen, and is in my mind
strongly against the claim set by *Jacob.*

Upon the whole, my conclusion is, that *Jacob's* claim
fails in *toto.*   I should be glad to be able to support the
decree sustaining his claim as to the $900 note; but
I think the cases and the principles upon which they
proceed do not warrant it.

(a) 2 Ves. Jur. 117.

BOULTON v. CAMERON.

Injunction—Equitable plea.

Where, upon a motion for an injunction to restrain proceedings
upon an execution at law, it was shewn that the facts upon which '
the right to the injunction was founded had been raised as a defence to the action by way of equitable plea, the court refused the
application.

Mr. *Fitzgerald* for the application.

The defendant in person, *contra*.

Judgment.—VANKOUGHNET, C.—I refuse the injunction in this case upon the ground that the same matters upon which it is sought to obtain it formed the
subject of an equitable plea by way of defence to the
action at law, in which the then plaintiff, the present
defendant, has recovered judgment, execution upon
which it is the object of the present motion to restrain.
It is true, as the plaintiff contends, that the judgment
of the Court of Common Pleas which had this equitable defence under consideration finds two material
variances between the allegations in the plea and the
proof ; and these it is urged are of no importance in
the eye of a court of equity.   This may or may not
be so, but then either a court of law exercising equitable jurisdiction ought so to have treated them, or if it be
required there that the proof should exactly correspond
with the statement even in an equitable plea, then the
defendant should either take care that he made his statement correctly ; or if he made a slip, should have applied to amend : the discretion as to which is as wide at
law as in this court.   Were any different doctrine to be
maintained the result would be, that a party without any
regard to accuracy in his statement, would raise an equitable defence at law, and failing there by reason of his
mistake or omission, would then fly to this court, thus
availing himself of the double opportunity of litigating
the same matters.   This was not the intention of the
legislature when they gave him the option, without

imposing upon him the necessity of invoking the equitable jurisdiction of a court of law. He has chosen his tribunal, of co-ordinate power, in respect of the case made here, with this court. Though the cases in England are not very decided upon the question, I decline to interfere, or sit in judgment upon the decision of another court in respect of the same matters; the injunction must therefore be refused.

The Bank of Montreal v. Baker.

Registered judgment—Notice---Absconding Debtor.

Held [affirming the decree reported ante page 95], that whether the deed there mentioned as having been executed in blank, operated as a deed or as a mere parol agreement, it created a charge upon the equitable estate of the debtor; and that a registered judgment creditor having notice thereof before the registration of his judgment would be bound thereby.

Held, also [affirming the decree], that the *bona fides* of proceedings taken against a person as an absconding debtor with a view to obtaining a priority, could be questioned in this court at the suit for a creditor or third party.

Statement.—The facts of this case appear in the former report. After that decree had been pronounced, the defendents, the Commercial Bank, obtained a re-hearing of the cause. On the re-hearing

Mr. *Strong* appeared for the plaintiffs.

Mr. *Roaf* for the Commercial Bank.

Mr. *A. Crooks* and Mr. *Blake*, for the defendants *Rigney* and *Brown*.

Judgment.—VANKOUGHNET, C.—For the decision of this case I have not found it necessary to examine the ground upon which my brother *Spragge* rested his judgment in favour of the plaintiffs, as we are of opinion that irrespective of it the plaintiffs are entitled to priority and to a decree. Whether or not the instrument of the 25th of May, 1857, delivered by *Lavis*, as the agent of and under the instructions contained in the letter of *Baker*, from Halifax, operated as a deed or as a mere parol agreement, is in our judgment immaterial, because in either shape it constituted a charge upon the equitable estate of *Baker* in the premises ; and if it required registration to give it priority over the legal proceedings adopted by the Commercial Bank to secure a preference to themselves over the plaintiffs, it was well registered before those proceedings were had ; and if by reason of its being to be treated merely as a parol instrument it could not be registered, then we are of opinion that the registered judgment could not prevail against it, as in such case the registry acts as to it could have no application. *McMaster* v. *Phipps*, (*a*) *Sumpter* v. *Cooper*. (*b*) It is, however, argued that by the deed-poll executed by *Baker* on the 11th of October, 1857, this instrument of the 25th of May, which purported to be a mortgage, was converted into a deed, and so, as a parol contract, ceased to exist, and that being thus changed in its character, it required registration to give it effect against the judgment of the Commercial Bank registered a few days afterwards. The bill alleges that this deed-poll, which is called a deed of confirmation, was registered, but there is no evidence of this furnished. It is not in fact, and could not be, a deed of confirmation. Either the instrument of the 25th of May was a deed, or it was not. If it was, it required not, and could not receive as such, confirmation. If it was not, it was as a deed void, or rather no deed, and the deed-poll of October would have no other effect than by its reference and relation to it, executing it, and for the first time making it a deed.

But admitting that this instrument of May assumed the condition of a deed in October, still the charge which was created by it did not by that higher character which it assumed cease. It only received greater efficacy, and has never been destroyed or abandoned. I was

---

(*a*) Ante vol. v. p. 253.   (*b*) 2 B. and Ad. 223.

much struck with the argument that if the instrument of May was a parol instrument, it was merged and swallowed up in the deed of October, but, on reflection, I think this is not so, because the charge which that instrument created was not destroyed, but continued, enforced and enhanced in character by the deed. The case of *Sumpter* v. *Cooper*, already referred to shews this; there one of two joint purchasers of an estate having borrowed from the other his share of the purchase money, to effect the purchase, deposited with him the title deeds as security for re-payment, thus creating, upon his share, in favour of his co-purchaser an equitable mortgage. Subsequently he conveyed his moiety to his co-purchaser by deed, in discharge of this loan, and this instrument was capable of registration. After this he became bankrupt, and the assignment of his estate from the commissioners in bankruptcy was duly registered. The co-purchaser *Cooper after* the conveyance to him by the bankrupt received the whole rents of the property, and the assignees of the bankrupt sued him to recover the moiety. The plaintiffs were nonsuited, and the late Lord *Campbell*, as counsel for the plaintiffs, moved to set aside the nonsuit, taking as a principal ground, that the equitable mortgage created by the deposit of the title deeds was merged in the subsequent conveyance executed by the bankrupt, and that as this had not been registered it was cut by the assignment to the assignees, which had been registered. After taking time to consider Lord *Tenterden*, delivering the judgment of the Court of Queen's Bench, refused a rule *nisi*.

I cannot admit that a judgment creditor has by virtue of the registration laws any higher position or rights than a purchaser for valuable consideration. What I think the legislature intended to do was to bind such interest as the defendant had at the time of, or acquired after, its registration, that he might not afterwards part with it; and but for the 3rd section of the act 13 & 14 Victoria, this would be sufficiently plain. That section, in its language, at all events, carries the effect of a registered judgment further, but while it associates registered judgments with registered conveyances, I can see nothing in it which indicates that the former are to have any better position or greater effect than the latter, and in the absence of express words declaring it, we should not give it. It is sufficiently hard to say that a creditor may sweep away that which the debtor does not own, but which honestly belongs to another, without extending the right so as to relieve a judgment creditor from the consequence of a notice which would affect the registered title of a purchaser for value.

While the act declares that registration shall be notice, it does not provide that notice of an unregistered conveyance shall not affect a registered conveyance or judgment; and we must take it that the legislature had knowledge of the doctrine of a court of equity on this head; and indeed they appear to have had it expressly under consideration, when they declared that registration should be notice. I am of opinion that a registered judgment is at least equally affected by notice with a registered conveyance, and that here the Commercial Bank, having had notice of the charge created by *Baker* in favour of the plaintiffs prior to the issuing of their writ against *Baker* as an absconding debtor, and certainly prior to its being placed in the hands of the sheriff, hold their registered judgment subject to it. (a)

Then as to the proceedings against *Baker* as an absconding debtor, with a view to determining the respective positions in priority of the Commercial Bank, and of the defendants *Rigney & Brown* : unless the Commercial Bank can sustain these proceedings, so that the judgment recovered by them against *Baker* can relate back to them, and thus gain priority over *Rigney & Brown*, it is admitted that the claim of the latter must

(a) Leneve. v. Leneve, 2 White and Tudor Lead. cases, 23.

prevail against that of the Bank. I am of opinion that the proceedings against *Baker* as an absconding debtor are wholly void or a nullity, because in the first place he never was an absconding debtor; and in the second place it is evident that the Commercial Bank abused the process of the court in treating him as such with the sole object of thereby gaining a priority, particularly over the plaintiffs. To say that a man can be made and dealt with and treated as an absconding debtor, contrary to the fact, and for the express purpose, fraudulent as it must be under such circumstances, of obtaining an undue advantage, without the process and proceedings thus had against him being questionable by a third party, a creditor, because the plaintiffs to the process have procured its issue upon affidavits which have been made honestly or dishonestly in the belief of the party making them, would be monstrous, and contrary to all principles of justice. Such process might issue with or without the connivance of the debtor, and might be maintained by his subsequent assent or inaction; and are the other parties having claims against him, or interested in his estate, because of this, to be without a remedy, and to be compelled to stand by and see his estate swept into the power of a particular creditor, under a state of facts which by law did not entitle him to it? Such proceedings could be undoubtedly questioned at law in an independent action; the only remedy which a third party might have, as he would most probably not be heard on a motion to set aside the proceedings against the debtor; (and indeed it was admitted on the argument that he could not make such a motion;) and, if at law, so of course here.

The right to issue a commission in bankruptcy, and the title of assignees under it, may be always questioned, and is an analogous case. So the right of a prior execution creditor may be questioned in an action by a subsequent execution creditor, on the ground of fraud or otherwise; and in this court we must necessarily enquire into the circumstances under which impeached judgments are recovered when they are brought before us as incumbrances. Chapter 25 of the Consolidated Statutes of Upper Canada, in section 1, provides : "If any person resident in Upper Canada indebted to any other person, departs from Upper Canada with intent to defraud his creditors, and at the time of his so departing is possessed of, &c., he shall be deemed an absconding debtor ;" and the marginal note to that section is in these words : "who to be regarded as an absconding debtor." Section 2 provides that process may issue upon affidavit : "*that any such person so departing*, &c." *Baker* never was an absconding debtor, and as his whole conduct before and on leaving, and on returning to the province proved, never intended to abscond. He went to England to endeavour to raise money to pay his creditors here, as he apprised the Commercial Bank before-hand, and failing to get it, he honestly returned and faced his creditors.

The Commercial Bank, though they issued process against him as an absconding debtor, never in reality treated him as such—never acted against his personalty —never interfered with his business—(that I believe of miller and merchant)—which went on during his absence and after his return, as usual, and in fact they openly avowed and said that all they wanted was to obtain priority of charge upon his real estate. To uphold these proceedings under such circumstances would be making the court a party to a mockery, if not fraud.

Judgment.—ESTEN, V. C.—I think there was a good equitable charge. and that the deed of confirmation did not supersede or impair the instrument of the 25th of May, 1857, which retains all the force it ever had; but I think that *Baker* was not an absconding debtor, and not therefore the object of a writ of attachment, and that the writ of attachment in this case was void, and conferred no priority on the Commercial Bank, who issued it, and that the validity of the writ may properly be questioned by third persons in collateral matters. I think, therefore, the plaintiffs are entitled to succeed on two grounds: first, that they had a good equitable charge not superseded or affected by the deed of confirmation to which the registry laws do not apply, and that on the ground of the invalidity of the attachment the defendants *Rigney & Brown* are also entitled to priority over the Commercial Bank. Even, however, if it should be held that the deed of confirmation superseded the instrument of the 25th of May, 1857, I think that this latter instrument should prevail over the judgment of the Commercial Bank, on the ground of notice had by them of the original instrument of the 25th of May, 1857.

I think it is very just and proper to apply the doctrine of notice to judgment creditors; the question must be in every case whether the registration of the judgment was with fraudulent intent. Here are two general creditors, one obtains an instrument which creates a specific lien in equity, and the other has express notice of it. Under these circumstances it would be a fraud, I think, for the latter to commence an action and register a judgment for the purpose of obtaining priority over the equitable lien; and although the instrument creating the equitable lien may have subsequently become merged with the deed of confirmation, which conferred a legal title, I think the fraud continued, and should postpone the judgment to the latter instrument. The action was commenced with a fraudulent intent, and prosecuted with that same intent, until the Commercial Bank had notice of the deed of confirmation, and did not thus, I think, become a fair proceeding, but retained its fraudulent character.

The action was commenced with a fraudulent intent; that is, the attachment was issued with such an intent, and although that particular intent was defeated, and although the instrument of the 25th of May, 1857, would not be affected by the registration of the judgment, yet fraudulent intent must be deemed to continue, should an opportunity occur of carrying it into effect, and such an opportunity did occur, when the deed of confirmation was made, absorbing the previous instrument, and duly capable of being registered; and that the suit must be deemed to have been prosecuted, and the judgment registered, with intent to gain priority over this deed, which intent must be deemed to be fraudulent. I think judgment should be postponed to the deed of confirmation, on the ground of fraud.

Judgment.—SPRAGGE, V. C., concurring—decree affirmed with costs.

HODGINS V. McNEIL.

· *Marriage with deceased wife's sister—Legitimacy of offspring—Lord Lyndhurst's Act—Administration— Costs.*

The intestate, H. M , was married in this province in 1850, to the sister of his deceased wife, by whom he had children, and died in 1856.

Held, that the marriage, though voidable during the lives of both parties to it, yet that its validity not having been called in question till after the husband's death, it must be now treated as indissoluble, and that the issue thereof are entitled as heirs.

Held, also, that Lord Lyndhurst's Act (5 & 6 W. IV., cap. 54) does not extend to the colonies.

Where the plaintiff made charges of improper conduct against the administratrix, which were not sustained in evidence, he was ordered to pay all costs other than of an ordinary administration suit.

The late *Hugh McNeil*, residing near Toronto, prior to 1846, married his first wife *Eliza Hutchinson*, who died in April of that year, leaving two children.

In December, 1850, Mr. *McNeil* married *Anne*, sister of his former wife, with whom he resided till he died intestate in March, 1856.

The issue of the second marriage was two sons, *Duncan* and *Roderick*.

Mrs. *McNeil* was appointed by the surrogate court

administratrix of her husband's estate and guardian of the children of both marriages. *George*, eldest son of Mr. *McNeil*, by his first marriage, died in 1857, having first made his will, whereby the plaintiff was appointed his executor. Besides being heir of his father's estate, *George McNeil* was, prior to his death, also entitled to property left by his mother, which had come to the hands of Mrs. *Anne McNeil*. A settlement as to the estate of his mother had been effected between *George* and his stepmother shortly after he became of age, and a release in respect of all his claims on account of his mother's estate was then executed by *George*, which, apparently by an oversight on the point of the solicitor who prepared it, was made to cover all dealings in, and claims in respect of, both estates.

This being afterwards brought to the attention of Mrs. *McNeil*, she acknowledged that the release was only intended to cover the claims in respect of *Eliza's* estate.

The plaintiff, by his bill, endeavoured to set aside this settlement and release on the ground of undue influence exercised by Mrs. *McNeil* on her stepson, then a few weeks advanced in his twenty-second year, and set out certain correspondence that had passed between the plaintiff and Mrs. *McNeil* and her solicitor, in regard to the release, and to her accounting for the estate of her late husband.

The bill prayed for an injunction and receiver, and that Mrs. *McNeil* might account for all moneys received by her, either as guardian or as administratrix, and that the estate might be administered under the direction of the court.

Mrs. *McNeil*, by her answer, set up that the release was obtained voluntarily, and after full investigation of accounts. She also claimed to be entitled to dower and thirds, and to a proper allowance in respect of her guardianship and administrator. This cause was originally heard before his honour *V. C. Spragge,* when he sustained the release so far as the administratrix claimed exemption under it, and refused to grant an injunction to stay the further acting of Mrs. *McNeil,* as administratrix, or to appoint a receiver, and made the usual administration decree, and reference to the master at Hamilton. The cause afterwards came before the court on further directions, the master having reported the facts of the intestate's marriage specially as above set forth.

In addition to the authorities mentioned in his honour's judgment, the following were referred to in the argument : *Brook* v. *Brook,* (*a* *Regina* v. *Roblin,* (*b*) The *Queen* v. *Chadwick.* (*c*)　As to costs, *Colchester* v. *Lowten,* (*d*) and *Wiard* v. *Gable.* (*e*).

Mr. *Hodgins,* plaintiff, in person.

Mr. *Hector* for Mrs. *McNeil.*

Mr. *Strong* and Mr. *Fitzgerald,* for the infant defendants.

Judgment.—Esten, V.C.,—Before 25 George II.,ch 33, (the Marriage Act,) clandestine marriages were illegal, although not void, and subjected the parties to ecclesiastical censures, *i. e.,* all marriages were required to be solemnized in *facie ecclesiac* and by bonds or license, and, if a minor, with consent of parents ; such marriages were rendered void by 26 Geo. II., ch. 33, which is generally in force here under the Constitutional Act, but probably not the eleventh clause, which makes such marriages void. They are, however, illegal, and in breach of the usual bond condition that no impediment exists.

(*a*) 4 L. T. R. 93, & 7 Jur. N. S. 422.　　(*b*) 21 U. C. Q. B. 352.
(*c*) 11 Q. B. 173.　　　　　　　　　　　(*d*) 1 Ves. & B. 226.
(*e*) Ante vol. 8, p. 458.

The 33 Geo. III., ch. 5, was said by Mr. *Hodgins* to have introduced the canon law; but in fact the canon law, so far as it was part of the law of England, had been already introduced by the Constitutional Act. The 33 Geo. III., ch. 4, authorises Presbyterian, Lutheran, and Calvinist ministers to celebrate marriage between certain persons, provided they are not under any legal disqualification. It presupposes the ecclesiastical law in force, and probably did not authorise those persons to marry a man to his wife's sister, because an unlawful marriage. 11 Geo. IV., ch. 36, confirms marriages previously celebrated of persons " not under any canonical disqualification," and authorises ministers of certain denominations to solemnize marriage between persons " not under legal disqualification," " Acts altering acts in force in colonies are themselves in force." (*a*) This seems to apply to acts extended to the colonies by the parliament when passed, not when the colonies voluntarily adopt an act not originally in force there.

The *lex loci rei sitæ* must govern in all questions of succession to real estate—*Livingstone* v. *Fenton*—(*b*) therefore it was held in this case that the ancestor of the respondent, having married his wife's sister in England, the marriage not having been annulled in the life-time of the parties, such a marriage being by the law of Scotland void, and the parties to it criminal, the respondent was to be deemed illegitimate in Scotland, and even if he should have been deemed legitimate, supposing the marriage valid in England, it was not so, but unlawful and voidable, although it could not be avoided after the death of either of the parties. Such a marriage is void in England; but after the death of either of the parties the temporal courts, which have no jurisdiction themselves, and must regard every marriage *de facto*, as good until it is declared void by the ecclesiastical courts, will not permit them to

---

(*a*) Dwarris, 526.   (*b*) 5 Jur. N. S. 1183.

declare the marriage void after the death of one of the parties, when their sentence can have no effect on the marriage itself, it being already dissolved by death, and its only effect will be to bastardize the issue. The result is, that after the death of the parties, the marriage is valid and the issue legitimate *de facto* but not *de jure*.

I think the statute 5 & 6 W. IV., ch. 54, does not extend to this province, and therefore, that the marriage in question, which I assume to have been celebrated according to the law of England, as introduced into this province by the provincial act, 32 Geo. III., ch. 1, has become, by the death of one of the parties to it, indissoluble, and the children of such marriage have become absolutely legitimate. My reasons are that the colonies are not mentioned in the act; not included by any necessary or even strong intendment; that the act is one of convenience and policy; that the law of England was not introduced into this province by the imperial legislature, but adopted by our own; that we have a local legislature competent to deal adequately with such matters; that the inconvenience intended to be remedied by the act 5 & 6 W. IV., ch. 54, is practically unfelt here; that such marriages are recognised as valid by many foreign systems, and that their being in violation of God's law, is, to say the least, extremely doubtful, although so declared by the statute law of England, and for other reasons.

No doubt the act of the 32nd of the late king introduced all the law of marriage as it existed in England at that date, excepting, perhaps, some clauses of the 26 Geo. II., ch. 33. It introduced the acts 25 Hy. VIII., ch. 22, 28 H. VIII., ch. 7, 28 Hy. VIII., ch. 16, and 32 Hy. VIII., ch. 38, so far as they remained in force, and so much of the canon law as had been adopted by the law of England. The provincial statutes, cited by Mr.

Hodgins, do not, I think, affect the question. They were passed to confirm certain void marriages, and to authorise the ministers of certain denominations of christians to solemnize matrimony. Both enactments contained the qualification that the marriages in question should have been or should be between persons under no legal or canonical disqualification; thereby meaning, no doubt, that they should not be disqualified to enter into the contract of marriage by the law as it stood: that is, by the law of England as introduced into this province, both statute law and canon law, so far as adopted into the law of England. These statutes did not mean to introduce any new law, not already introduced into the province, nor is it necessary for Mr. *Hodgins'* argument that such an effect should be attributed to them. Its only effect would be to show that this marriage was unlawful and void, but, nevertheless, it must be recognised as a marriage *de facto* by the temporal courts until annulled by sentence of the ecclesiastical courts, which could only be done during the life-time of both parties to it. But this is clearly the law of this province. It cannot be doubted that the marriage in question in this case was unlawful and void at the time of its celebration, and could have been annulled by the sentence of the ecclesiastical court at any time during the life-time of both parties. But it is equally clear that, it never having been so annulled, it has become indissoluble, and the children springing from it are to all practical purposes absolutely legitimate.

I therefore think this lady is entitled to her dower and thirds, and that her children are entitled to share the estate of the intestate with the children of the first marriage.

As to the costs, my brother *Spragge* refused to give them against the administratrix at the former hearing. He thought that she had not sought by means of the release to screen herself from accounting for the estate

of *Hugh McNeil;* that there was no pertinacious refusal to account.

It seems to me that there was no refusal to account
at all. She submitted in her answer to account for the
estate of *Hugh McNeil,* and only insisted upon the
release as a bar to an account relating to the mother's
estate. It is true that her solicitor seeing a requisition
from the plaintiff for an account, and also the release,
wrote to the plaintiff saying that he had advised his
client that she was not bound to account as she held a
general release, but this letter is almost immediately
withdrawn and an offer made to account as administratrix. In the meantime the bill had been filed, but it
would have been perfectly easy for the plaintiff to have
intimated upon receipt of that letter that the defendant
needed not answer ; that he was prepared to agree to an
administration order ; but he perseveres in the suit
obviously in order to obtain an account of the guardianship to which he was not entitled.

There was nothing up to the hearing to deprive the
administratrix of her costs, to which she is *prima facie*
entitled. The only fact insisted upon was her conduct
with respect to the release, but she had insisted upon that
only so far as she was entitled to do so ; and my brother
Spragge must therefore have reserved the costs only in
order to see if any thing would come to light in the
master's office in taking the accounts which might affect
the question of costs. Nothing of the sort seems to have
been disclosed ; her administration of the estate is not
complained of ; I think, therefore, that she is entitled to
her costs. If the general refusal to account contained
in the solicitor's letter had occasioned the suit so far as
it was proper to be instituted, it would have been
discontinued on the receipt of the letter qualifying the
refusal and confining it to the mother's estate. The
suit, however, is prosecuted, and I think, with a view

to obtain an account of the guardianship, and because it
was felt that the account of *Hugh McNeil's* estate could
not be taken satisfactorily out of court.

I think all parties should have their costs proper to
an administration suit out of the estate as between
solicitor and client ; but the plaintiff ought to pay the
costs, beyond what would have been incurred, had the
usual administration order been obtained. If the object
of the evidence was in any degree to shew a refusal to
account as administratrix it must have failed to shew it,
as my brother *Spragge* says there was no pertinacious
refusal to account ; and in fact it appears from the bill
itself that the administratrix offered to account for the
estate of her husband, and only insisted upon the release
as a bar to an account as guardian ; and the only circumstance that occurred subsequently was the letter
which was withdrawn.

BARR v. HATCH.

Specific performance—Voluntary agreement.

A person being about to effect the purchase of land, stipulated verbally
with another who had been accustomed to use a road over the
property, that in the event of the purchase being completed he
would be allowed to continue the use thereof, but afterwards refused to carry out such agreement; *held*, that this promise was
merely voluntary, and, as such, insufficient to found a bill for
specific performance.

This was a suit for specific performance. It appeared
in the cause that the plaintiff had obtained the conveyance of a right of way over certain lands, which were
afterwards about to be offered for sale. It having been
ascertained that the deed to the plaintiff was invalid,
and the defendant, intending to become the purchaser at
such sale, promised the plaintiff that, in the event of her
becoming the purchaser, she would permit him to use
the right of way as before, and also to make his title
valid. After the sale and conveyance the defendant
refused to fulfil such promise : whereupon the present
suit was instituted to compel the specific performance
of the agreement.

The defendant answered the bill, and the cause having been put at issue by filing a replication, evidence was taken therein, the effect of which is mentioned in the judgment.

Mɹ. *Barrett*, for the plaintiff.

Judgment.—ESTEN, V.C.—This case entirely fails on the evidence. There is no proof whatever of the agreement upon which the suit is founded, namely, that the plaintiff intended to purchase the property, and forebore at the request of Mrs. *Hatch*, and that she in consideration of such forbearance agreed to grant the right of way in question. The utmost that is proved, is that just before the sale she promised to allow the plaintiff, if she purchased and her son remained on the place, to use the right of way as before, and that she admitted that before the sale she had agreed to make good his deed. Such a promise would not of course support a suit, as it would be perfectly voluntary. It is not shewn that the plaintiff intended to purchase, or that Mrs. *Hatch* knew it, or that he forebore to purchase in consequence of her promise. I may remark, however, that I put very little faith in the evidence of the three witnesses who depose to the conversation in the shop. They were there accidentally; were not interested in the matter, and did not understand it, for it was explained to them by the plaintiff after Mrs. *Hatch's* departure; and it happened about sixteen months before they gave their evidence.

The bill is framed on the hypothesis that the purchase was for the benefit of *John Hatch*, but treats the purchase as *bona fide*, but *pro tanto* by Mrs. *Hatch* as an agent or trustee, or in pursuance of the alleged agreement. I think the bill should be dismissed with costs.

McNames v. Phillips.

Notice of incumbrance—Purchase for value without notice.

Although the rule in equity is that a notice to be binding "must be given by a person interested in the property, and in the course of the treaty for the purchase," still where notice of an incumbrance to an intending purchaser was given by the son, and while acting on behalf of the incumbrancer in endeavouring to effect a loan upon the security of such incumbrance, the purchaser was held bound by such notice.

Statement.—The bill in this cause was filed by *Rachael McNames*, against *Thomas Phillips* and *James Johnson*, setting forth that up to December, 1858, the plaintiff was the owner of the west half of 34 in the 1st concession of Westminster, which she conveyed to one *Towsley*, for the consideration of £500, as expressed in the conveyance; but in fact the sum of £350, part of such consideration, never was paid, but was secured by a mortgage on the same property, which mortgage plaintiff neglected to register until September, 1859. That in the meantime (in April, 1859) *Towsley* mortgaged the premises to defendant *Phillips*, to secure £402 10s., which mortgage was registered on the 14th of April, 1859; that by an assignment dated the 17th of August, 1859, *Phillips* assigned his interest in the mortgage to the other defendant, *Johnson*, as collateral security for certain notes cashed by *Johnson*. The bill charged actual notice on the part of both defendants of the mortgage held by the plaintiff, and that the same was given by *Towsley* to secure a portion of the purchase money due upon the land so conveyed; that by virtue of *Towsley's* mortgage to *Phillips*, and its prior registration, the defendants claimed that it formed an incumbrance prior to the lien of the plaintiff; that the defendants both denied notice by *Johnson* of plaintiff's mortgage, and that defendant, *Phillips*, alleged that he had assigned his mortgage to his co-defendant for the express purpose of depriving plaintiff of the equitable rights against him, *Phillips*, arising out of his knowledge of the circumstances.

The bill further alleged that *Towsley* was utterly insolvent, and had absconded from the province, the money advanced by *Johnson* to *Phillips* having been borrowed by *Phillips* for, and was by him applied in, the purchase of a lot of land in the township of London, while *Phillips* was a man of substance, and well able to indemnify the defendant *Johnson* on the covenant in the assignment of the mortgage from *Phillips*, and prayed that the mortgage made by *Towsley* to plaintiff might be declared to be a first incumbrance, and that the mortgage made to *Phillips* and the registration thereof might be decreed to be fraudulent and void as against plaintiff; or if it should appear that the mortgage to *Phillips* could not be so postponed in the hands of Johnson, then that *Phillips* might be ordered to indemnify and pay to plaintiff the amount of his mortgage, interest and costs, and that he might be ordered to pay off the notes so given by him to *Johnson*, or that the lot of land purchased by *Phillips* might be sold, and for other relief.

The defendants answered the bill separately. *Phillips*, after detailing the circumstances which led to his taking the mortgage from *Towsley*, denied that at the time he took the same he had any notice, either actual or constructive, of the mortgage to the plaintiff, or that the purchase money of the land had not been paid to her; that if he had had such notice, he never would have taken a second mortgage, the more so as he did so solely for the purpose of accommodating *Towsley*: alleged that *Johnson* had not any notice at the time he took the assignment of mortgage from *Phillips*, which assignment was made *bona fide* for valuable consideration; that is to say, as collateral security for £400, which *Johnson* advanced to him; and claimed priority for his incumbrance under the registry laws. *Johnson*, by his answer, set forth the circumstances at length, denied notice of any kind, and insisted on the protection afforded by the registry laws.

The plaintiff put the cause at issue, and evidence was taken chiefly with a view of establishing notice by *Phillips* of the mortgage held by the plaintiff before *Towsley* executed the mortgage to him. *Silas Curtis McNames*, a son of the plaintiff, was the principal witness to prove such notice. It appeared that he was a subscribing witness to the conveyances between the plaintiff and *Towsley*, $1400 being secured on the property sold, and $600 on a property called the "Huff farm." He further swore: "I knew the defendant *Phillips* first after the deeds were executed; I told him my mother had sold the land, and told him how the purchase money was payable. I told him $1400 was secured by mortgage on the place; this was not more than a week or ten days after the deeds were executed. Afterwards, and in the same month of December I saw *Phillips* again; I asked about some money I wanted to borrow; I offered to secure it on the $1400 mortgage. * * * * * I postponed the payment of money by giving a renewal note at three months from the 1st of January. Before it fell due I went to see him again about the money I wished to borrow from him. I took the two mortgages over to him; I told him I had brought them. * * * He said, 'I have a mortgage on the west-half myself.' I said, Mr. *Phillips*, you knew that my mother had a mortgage on the west half; he said yes, but *Towsley* told me he would arrange that, and take it up before it became due."

Towsley was also examined, as a witness for the plaintiff. He swore that, during a negotiation between him and *Phillips*, for the sale to him, by *Phillips*, of the east half of the lot, he told *Phillips* that he had given a mortgage to Mrs. *McNames*, for $1,400, on the west half. One Richard *Baker*, and another son of the plaintiff also gave evidence, tending strongly to establish the fact of notice by *Phillips*.

Mr. *Blake*, for the plaintiff, contended that the

evidence of notice by *Phillips* was quite sufficient to outweigh the denial in his answer.

Mr. *Fitzgerald,* for defendants, opposed a decree as prayed, on the ground that the notice proved was not sufficient, it having been made by a stranger to the transaction ; that to be good it must be given by a person interested. He referred to *Barnhart* v. *Green-shields,* (a) *LeNeve* v. *LeNeve,*(b)*Hollywood* v. *Waters.* (c)

Judgment.—SPRAGGE, V.C.—I think the evidence is sufficient to establish notice to *Phillips* of the plaintiff's mortgage, before he took a mortgage from *Towsley* upon the same premises: the evidence of *Silas McNames,* a son of the plaintiff, is explict: he proves that he informed *Phillips* of the mortgage given by *Towsley* to his mother; and that not as a matter of mere information or a piece of news or gossip, but as a matter of business upon an application by him to *Phillips,* for a loan of money upon the security of this same mortgage ; the only question can be whether the information came from a quarter which *Phillips* was bound to regard. Mr. *Fitzgerald* says that it did not, and refers to *Barnhart* v. *Green-shields,* in the Privy Council, where Lord *Kingsdown* says : "We now come to the parol evidence of notice ; upon this subject the rule is settled, that a purchaser is not bound to attend to vague rumours—to statements by mere strangers—but that a notice in order to be binding must proceed from some person interested in the property. On examining the evidence it is found to consist entirely of alleged conversations of different individuals with the respondent." The language of Lord *St. Leonards* in his treatise on Vendors and Purchasers is much to the same effect; he says, that "to constitute a binding notice it must be given by a person interested in the property, and in the course of the treaty for the purchase: vague reports from persons not interested in the

(a) 9. Moo, *P. C. C.* 35.   (b) 2 M. & Lud. 38.
(c) Ante, vol. 6, p. 329.

property will not affect the purchaser's conscience, nor
will he be bound by notice in a previous transaction
which he may have forgotten." Now I think what is
said in these authorities as to what notice will bind and
what notice will not bind, must be taken together. It
is settled by decided cases that vague rumours, statements by mere strangers, notice in a previous transaction which the purchaser may have forgotten, are not
binding upon him ; and that the notice must be of such
a nature as that it would be actual fraud to disregard
it; but it is not, as I think, settled by decided cases
as a point decided in any case that the notice must be
by a person interested, and in the course of treaty for
the purchase; if these are necessary then the plaintiff
might have carried her mortgage to *Phillips*, and asked
him to advance money upon it. *Phillips* might have
examined it—have known exactly what property it
covered, and the amount it secured—and the next day
Towsley might have asked for a loan upon the same
property, and *Phillips* might have advanced it and
taken a mortgage to secure it, and he would be held
not affected with notice.

Lord *Alvanley*, in *Jollond* v. *Stainbridge*, (a) expressed
his regret that the Statute for Registration of Deeds
had been broken in upon by the admission of parol
evidence of notice, and was unwilling to admit loose
evidence of notice. He states that he thinks "that it
must be satisfactorily proved that the person who regis-
ters the subsequent deed must have known exactly the
situation of the person having the prior deed, and, knowing that, registered in order to defraud them of that
title he knew at the time was in them. * * I agree
it is not sufficient to prove notice to assert that some
other person claims a title, yet all the evidence given
here is of that sort. * * Then the person purchasing would have had notice not only of the claim, but
what sort of claim it was, I very much doubt whether

(a) 3 Ves. 478.

that general claim is sufficient to affect a purchaser with notice of a deed of which he does not appear to have had knowledge."

These extracts shew what sort of notice the defendant in that case had—it was loose and indefinite, and not by a person who was actually cognizant of the nature of the claim. Now in this case *Phillips* received definite information upon the several points suggested by Lord *Alvanley* as necessary to affect a purchaser : he had it in a business transaction, and from the son of the holder of the mortgage, who was a female—from one who, as he knew, was personally cognizant of what he stated—he had himself purchased not long before the other half of the same lot (the east half) from the same parties, and knew that *Towsley* had purchased the west half: knowing this already, he is told under the circumstances I have stated, that *Towsley* had not paid the purchase money, and that the vendor held a mortgage upon the land sold for a portion of it. With this information recently given he sells to *Towsley* at an advance, the east half of the lot, and takes a mortgage for a portion of the purchase money, not on the land sold by him, but upon the land upon which he had recently been informed the plaintiff held a mortgage for unpaid purchase money. It must be conceded that this notice did not comply with all the conditions expressed in the definitions of the authorities I have referred to, but neither of them decide it as a point. Lord *Kingsdown* says the rule is settled, and Lord *St. Leonards* refers in his treatise to authorities, none of which, however, conclude such a case as this. It does not appear that *Silas McNames* applied to *Phillips* as the agent of his mother ; if he had it would have been clear that the notice would have bound *Phillips*, but applying as he did, he conveyed to *Phillips* information of the fact, which I cannot help thinking affected *Phillips'* conscience with knowledge of it as a fact, which made it a fraud in him to take, as he did, a mortgage on the same land and register it so as to cut out the plaintiff's prior mortgage. The evidence of *Lucian McNames*, another son of the plaintiff, is confirmatory of that of his brother, and so also is that of *Baker*. The evidence of *Towsley*, the mortgagor to both the plaintiff and *Phillips*, is clear and explicit to the point of notice ; and it complies with the strictest rule enunicated, being from a person interested in the land and in the course of the treaty. It is urged that it is improbable ; but, as *Towsley* says, he told him only what he believed he already knew, and which, as appears by the evidence, he really did know ; and besides *Towsley* was at the time believed by *Phillips* himself to be a man of means ; and he may have trusted to his engagement to provide for the plaintiff's mortgage; but whether he did or not it is probable that he supposed, as others have done, that he would be safe, provided he got his mortgage registered first. I am sensible of the danger of allowing loose or vague evidence of notice to prevail against a registered deed, or indeed any but the most satisfactory evidence of notice. The defendant *Phillips* has denied notice by his answer ; and it is necessary that notice should be proved by more than one witness. *Phillips'* examination is not satisfactory—it would by itself shake the confidence which I might otherwise place in his answer. I think the evidence of *Silas McNames* admissible upon the question of notice, as well as that of *Towsley;* and that *Phillips* is bound by the notice he received.

If *Phillips* were now the holder of the mortgage from *Towsley* to himself I should feel no difficulty in postponing it to the plaintiff, but it has been assigned to the other defendant, against whom there is no evidence of notice. It is assigned as collateral security for certain notes, only one of which has as yet fallen due. I cannot therefore decree him to remove that incumbrance.

It is suggested that *Johnson* is a proper party in order to the taking of the account due on his mortgage : he cannot be a proper party for that, for he could not be brought into court to be redeemed.   Nor does he appear to me to be a proper party, as suggested, for the purpose of declaring the assignment to him to be only by way of security, it being in terms absolute ; for the right of the plaintiff, if postponed, would be the same either way, namely, to redeem upon paying the amount due by *Towsley* upon his mortgage to *Phillips*. I think, therefore, that in the absence of notice by *Johnson* he is not a proper party, and that the bill as to him must be dismissed with costs.

Phillips is bound as far as possible to place the plaintiff in as good a position as she would be in if she had a first mortgage on the land sold by her to *Towsley*.   This might be accomplished, perhaps by giving her a first mortgage on other property of equal value ; but I do not know of such relief having been decreed.   The ordinary decree in such a case is, that the defendant pay off the mortgage which by his fraudulent conduct he has postponed.   The decree will be for that relief, with costs.

BANK OF UPPER CANADA v. BEATTY.
THE SAME v. THOMAS.

Judgment creditor—Fraudulent conveyance.

In order to retain the lien created by the registration of a judgment recovered at law it is necessary that the bill to enforce such lien should have been filed on or before the 18th day of May, 1861.

When a judgment creditor files a bill to enforce his judgment against the lands of his debtor, it must be shewn that the creditor has sued out execution on such judgment.

The agent of a bank having become indebted to his principals in a large sum of money, proceedings were taken to enforce payment thereof ; and when execution therefor was on the eve of being sued out, the agent absconded from the country ; and with the avowed object of defeating the claim of the bank, but, as the agent alleged, for the purpose of paying his other creditors, conveyed away to a person to whom he was only then introduced, a large quantity of valuable lands to be paid for in goods at long dates, returning at night for the purpose of executing the conveyances, and which were executed without any investigation of the title to the property ; and the agent subsequently assigned the agreement for the delivery of the goods to his son, taking in payment his notes payable over a period of several years.   The court, under the circumstances, set aside the sale as fraudulent against the bank.

The bill in the first mentioned cause was filed by the

Bank of Upper Canada against *James Beatty, George Thomas*, and *John Stephens*, for the purpose of having enforced the payment of a judgment recovered by the bank against *Thomas*, under the circumstances set forth in the judgment. That cause, together with a suit instituted by *Beatty* against *Stephens*, and the *Bank of Upper Canada*, came on to be heard at the same time.

Mr. *Strong* and Mr. *Crickmore*, for the *Bank*.

Mr. *Blake* and Mr. *Blain*, for the defendants.

In the suit instituted by *Beatty* the usual decree was pronounced. In the other, after taking time to look into the authorities cited, the following judgment was delivered by

Judgment.—VANKOUGHNET, C.—This is a bill to set aside a certain conveyance of lands by one of the defendants *Thomas* to one other of the defendants *Stephens* on the ground that it was made with the fraudulent intent of putting the property out of reach of the plaintiffs, and during the pendency of an action by them against the defendant *Thomas*, which resulted in a judgment at law for an amount which the plaintiffs by means of this bill seek to obtain payment of out of the property in question. The bill alleges that the conveyance to *Stephens* was voluntary and without consideration. This latter allegation is disproved. The bill prays in reference to the lands *so conveyed*, that the same, upon which the plaintiffs' judgment is a lien or incumbrance, or a competent part thereof, may be sold and the proceeds applied to the payment of the judgment. The bill also impeaches a judgment recovered by the defendant *Beatty* against *Thomas ;* but this portion of it is not material to the questions under consideration here, as *Beatty*, prior to the 18th of May, 1861, filed a bill on that judgment as a judgment creditor making the plaintiffs parties defendants to it as judgment creditors.

of *Thomas*, and has obtained since this cause was heard the ordinary judgment creditor's decree. The plaintiffs in their bill, which was filed in June, 1861, do not allege that upon their judgment they have issued any *fi. fa.* against lands, but they set up, as giving them a right to obtain the aid of this court to execution on and of their judgment, the bill filed by *Beatty* as a judgment creditor on the 14th of May, 1861, and to which as stated they were made parties defendants, and they set forth that they had put in their answer in which they claimed to be paid the judgment in question, as well as a prior judgment recovered by the Savings Bank, and assigned to them, but about which there is no dispute, as *Beatty* offers to redeem and pay it off. The plaintiffs rely upon this allegation, true in fact, as bringing them within the 11th sec. of the act 24 Vic., ch. 41, and therefore keeping alive their judgments as liens, upon the lands of *Thomas* available for the payment of his debts, and they also contend that that act did not take effect till the 1st of September, 1861, whereas the bill in this case was filed in June previously, and that so their lien is preserved. I think the plaintiffs fail to maintain either of these positions, and that they filed their bill too soon to give them the benefit of any rights which they might have acquired as judgment creditors by virtue of *Beatty's* suit. The bill simply sets up the bill filed by *Beatty*, and the answer of the defendants filed long subsequently to the 18th of May, 1861. *Beatty* might at any time have dismissed that bill. The plaintiffs' right at the time this suit was commenced to preserve their lien as judgment creditors by means of *Beatty's* suit was inchoate, and until decree they could claim no benefit of the suit. This they anticipated, and therefore have in respect of it filed their bill too soon, just as when a judgment is no lien on any specific lands the plaintiff seeks equitable execution in this court without first having issued execution on his judgment at law. *Neate* v. *Marlborough* (a), *Angell* v. *Draper* (b). Had the plain-

---

(a) 3 M. & Craig, 407. (b) 1 Vernon, 399.

tiffs' right to retain their lien matured before filing
their bill by a decree at *Beatty's* suit I should in accordance with the *Bank of Montreal* v. *Woodcock* (a),
have held that they had made out a title, so far, to ask
the aid of this court.   But as I have already said they
have been premature, neither having a decree establishing their position in this court in *Beatty's* suit, nor execution at law when they filed their bill.' As to the last
clause of the 24 Vic., ch. 41, providing " This act shall
take effect on the 1st day of September next," no doubt
some uncertainty as to the time the act is to operate
is created by it.   It was probably hurriedly inserted in
the bill after it had been introduced, but I think its
effect must be limited to keeping registered judgments
in their places or order of priority (but not as liens
per se) until the 1st of September, in order that they
may as to such priorities sustain writs of execution
which shall have been issued on them in the meantime,
and that in all other respects the act came into operation
immediately on its passing.   This view is confirmed by
the act of last session, 25 Vic., ch. 21, passed to cure
an omission in the other act relative to the registry of
certificates of discharge of mortgages.   It recites that
it is expedient "to remove all doubts as to the sufficiency
of such registrations since *the passing* of the said act"
—that is, the 24th Vic., ch. 41, and provides in its 3rd
section that every certificate of mortgage registered
since the 18th of May, 1861, which, before that date,
would have been a sufficient discharge of a mortgage,
"shall have the same effect and validity as if the
second section of this act had passed and been the 8th
sub-section of section number seven of the said act 24
Vic.," from which by an oversight in repeating the
clause of the old act for the registration of such certificates provision therefor in the future had been
omitted.   The legislature here plainly shew that they
treat the act of 24 Vic., as having come into force on
the 18th of May, 1861, the date of its being passed.

(a) 9 Ante, vol, ix., p. 141.

The objection to the plaintiffs being in a position to ask the aid of this court having been taken by the answer, I must give the defendants their costs and dismiss the bill, but without prejudice; if that leave be necessary to the plaintiffs' filing another in respect of the same matters.

After this judgment had been delivered the Bank instituted proceedings in another suit against the same parties and one *F. A. Thomas*, a son of the defendant *Thomas*, to whom his father had transferred his claim upon *Stephens*.

Evidence was taken in the suit, and the case argued before his Lordship the Chancellor at the sittings of the court at London in March and April, 1863.

Mr. *Becher*, Q. C., and Mr. *Fitzgerald*, for the plaintiffs.

Mr. *Blake* and Mr. *Blain*, for defendants.

Corlett v. *Ratcliffe*, (a) *Skarf* v. *Soulby*, (b) *Buckland* v. *Rose*, (c) *Wood* v. *Dixie*, (d) *Thompson* v. *Webster*, (e) *French* v. *French*, (f) *Hale* v. *The Saloon Omnibus Co.*, (g) *Turnley* v. *Hooper*, (h) were, amongst other cases, referred to and commented on by counsel.

Judgment.–VANKOUGHNET, C.–The bill in this case is filed by the plaintiffs to have declared void as against them, and all other creditors of *George Thomas*, one of the defendants, certain conveyances of real estate executed by him to *John Stephens*, another of the defendants, under the following circumstances: *Thomas* having for some years been agent of the plaintiffs in Chatham,

---

(a) 4 L. T. N. S. 1.
(c) Ante vol. 7, p. 440.
(e) 5 Jur. N. S. 668, S.C., on app. 7 Jur. N. S. 531.
(f) D. M. & G. 95.
(g) 4 Drew, 492,

(b) 1 M. & Gor. 364,
(d) 7 Q. B. 892.
(h) 2 Jur. N. S. 1081.

became indebted to them in about the sum of $78,000 in respect of various transactions, and to secure its payment, executed to the plaintiffs, on the first day of March, 1858, a mortgage of certain lands, estimated at the time by a gentleman employed by the plaintiffs to value them, as worth $98,000. On the 13th of November, 1858, the Toronto Savings Bank, represented by Messrs. *Henderson, Proudfoot* and *Robinson*, recovered a judgment against *Thomas* for £1798 9s. Other parties were also liable to the Savings Bank for this debt, but whether they were or are solvent or not does not appear. The Savings Bank also held as security for the debt a transfer of 7000 or 8000 acres of wild land, the title to which is still in the Crown, but one instalment, viz., one-tenth of the original purchase money having been paid; whether this security is of any value does not appear. On the 16th of November, 1858, this judgment was duly registered in the counties where the lands in question here lie, and writs of execution against the lands of the defendant *Thomas* were duly issued, and placed in the hands of the sheriffs of the said counties, and have been duly kept alive. This judgment remains unsatisfied. On the 4th of October, 1860, it was assigned to the plaintiffs, who then became, and still are, entitled to the benefit of it. *Thomas* having made default in payment of one instalment of the money payable to the plaintiffs under the mortgage to them, was in the early part of the year 1860 sued by the plaintiffs therefor. In this suit he made defence, as he says, for time to enable him to secure his other creditors, and a verdict having been rendered in it against him at the Chatham assizes, which commenced on the 16th of April, 1860, judgment was entered up upon it for the sum of £2393 17s. 4d., on the 18th of the same month, and writs of *fieri facias* against his lands duly issued and delivered to the sheriffs of the said counties, in whose hands they remain unsatisfied. On the 18th and 19th days of the same month of April, the said judgment was duly registered in the same counties. On the 6th of

June, 1862, the plaintiffs recovered judgment against *Thomas* for $64,036.65, the balance of the amount secured by the mortgage to them.

In April, 1860, the outside value of the property mortgaged by *Thomas* to the bank, appears to be $15,000. How such exaggerated value as that put upon it in March, 1858, (before which the revulsion in the value of the real estate in the country had taken place,) was arrived at by the gentleman who thus estimated it, I do not know.

On the morning of the 13th of April, 1860, *Thomas* left Chatham, and arrived on the same day in Detroit, where he has ever since remained, having returned to Canada only on the occasion of his attending as a witness in this case, under the protection of a subpœna. When *Thomas* thus absconded from Chatham he was indebted to divers parties in sums not secured by judgment or otherwise, to an amount of from £4000 to £5000. On the day of his arrival in Detroit *Thomas* met with the defendant *Beatty*, with whom for many years he had been on terms of intimate friendship.   They met in the street, and *Thomas* at once proposed to *Beatty* that he *Beatty* should buy *Thomas*'s property, given as his reasons for desiring to sell, that the plaintiffs were pressing him hard; that he thought he had sufficiently secured them, and if they succeeded against him he would not be able to pay other creditors whom he owed. *Beatty*, as he swears on his examination, was personally aware that *Thomas* had got into trouble with the bank, and had had a settlement with them, and that he had lost his position as bank agent; and he next heard, as he states, of *Thomas*'s troubles when the latter came to see him in Detroit, that is, on the occasion of the interview just mentioned.   *Beatty* declined to make the proposed purchase, not being then, as he says, in a position to buy. *Thomas* then requested *Beatty* to propose to the defendant *Stephens*, his partner in business, to become the pur-

chaser, and *Beatty* promised to do so ; subsequently, on
the same day, *Thomas* went down to the store of the
defendants *Stephens* and *Beatty*, and was introduced to
the former by the latter. What then passed between
Thomas and *Stephens* is told by the former in the
following words :

"I gave *Stephens* a list of the property I. wanted to
sell, and told him *Beatty* would explain the value to
him ; that I had put it in as low as possible, to induce a
purchase : I had put the price at $50,000 : I gave him
a list of the incumbrances, which would be deducted from
this price : my interview with him lasted five or ten
minutes : I told him that the whole amount of the
Proudfoot judgment (that is the Savings Bank) was not
to be considered as due, as they had other securities :
I put down *Beatty's* judgment among the incumbrances :
Stephens said he would take time to consider : I left him,
and returned in about an hour : I considered the incumbrances to be about one-third of the price named by me :
when I returned, *Stephens* asked me my terms for payment : I said I wanted part cash, the balance in
groceries. He said there was no use of further discussion, as he would not pay any cash : I told him I wanted
means to pay off creditors, and that next to cash I considered groceries the best thing : we then spoke of the
price to be paid. *Stephens* said he must take off one-
third of the $50,000 for the incumbrances, one-third for
taxes, and to cover any defect in title, and for profit in
the transaction : he then offered me $16,000 : I tried
to get more : *Stephens* refused it, saying I might take
that or nothing : I agreed to his offer : this interview
lasted about one quarter of an hour : *Stephens* then told
me he had determined to purchase : I met Mr. *Prince*
and Mr. *Bernard* there, (the members of the firm of
Prince & Bernard, solicitors,) the latter was to draw up
the agreement : he did draw it while I was there : then
Stephens read it over, but was not satisfied, as he said
that provision ought to be made by it against *Beatty's*

judgment, and he did not see why I should not give
him this indemnity if I felt satisfied, as I said I was,
that there was other property sufficient to pay it ; *Beatty's* judgment was not estimated among the incumbrances deducted as one-third of the price of the lands:
I then added to the paper so drawn by *Bernard* the
provision in regard to *Beatty's* judgment, and with this
Stephens was satisfied : he would not sign it till he
had got the doeds : *Bernard* said he would set his
clerks to work to prepare the deeds : *Stephens* said he
would have to be quick about it, as he was going away
in the cars that evening : *Bernard* proposed a power
of attorney. *Stephens* said he would prefer signing the
agreement himself : finally, it was determined to have
a power of attorney, in case *Stephens* was gone when
the deeds were ready : I did not see *Stephens* again
that day: he had left before the deeds were ready : I
went to Windsor at night to execute the deeds, because
they were not ready before, and I feared if left till next
day I might, if I then went over, be arrested."

Thomas also states that after the deeds were ready
for execution by him, Mr. *Bernard*, whom he had consulted, advised him that if he returned to Canada after
selling his lands, the bank, being annoyed thereby, would
probably arrest him ; that having sold his property he
remained in Detroit to look after the proceeds, and to
realize them ; that he did not think it was safe to go
back to Chatham, unless he could make some arrangement with the bank, as he feared they would capias him;
that Mr. *Bernard* advised him to cross over to Windsor
to execute the deeds, as the bank might procure his
arrest, and that he crossed over to Windsor between
10 and 11 o'clock at night, to execute the deeds to
Stephens. These deeds being those impeached in this
suit were there and then executed. On the following
morning was executed by *Beatty* for *Stephens* under
power of attorney the agreement by the latter to purchase. The deeds covered a quantity of land in the

counties of Kent, Middlesex, Essex and Lambton. The
consideration, therefore, was the agreement of *Stephens*,
which after reciting that *Thomas* was about to commence
business in Detroit, and had bargained with *Stephens*
for groceries to the amount of $16,000 to be used in
such business, he, *Stephens*, agreed to supply the same
to *Thomas* in the following manner : to the amount of
$3,000 at any time within one year thereafter, to the
amount of $3,000 at any time within the year following,
and to the amount of $2,000 within each one of the five
following years. In relation to this transaction of sale
and purchase, defendant *Beatty*, on his examination,
says that he introduced *Thomas* to *Stephens*, and left
them together, and heard nothing more of the matter
till *Stephens* brought him a list of the lands offered by
Thomas for sale, for his opinion thereon: that he valued
the lands at $50,000, deducting one-third for incum-
brances, and one-third to cover taxes and defect in title
and the probable profit in the transaction, leaving one-
third as the net price to be paid for the property ; that
the interview between him and *Stephens* on this occasion
lasted a couple of hours; that he and *Stephens* discussed
Thomas' reasons for selling, as already given. He says
he advised *Stephens* to make the purchase, and did not
consider that the matter had been carried on in a very
hasty manner. He says he never visited any of the
property except the Chatham property, and that in his
estimate of value for *Stephens*, he did not take the amount
of the rents of this Chatham property into account, as
he did not know what they were. Since he took *Stephens'* purchase off his hands he says he enquired the
value of the Chatham property, and he thinks of some
of the other lands, but he is not positive. Mr. *Prince*
swears that in this transaction of sale and purchase,
he was acting for both parties, the consideration for
the sale was, as he understood from all parties, the
setting up *Thomas* in business as a grocer in Detroit ;
that he himself was at the time acquainted with *Thomas'*
position with the bank and his creditors generally, but

he thinks *Stephens* was ignorant of it; That *Stephens* was not ignorant of it, is shewn by the evidence of *Beatty*, who also swears that he must have found out about the time he signed the agreement for *Stephens* on the following morning that *Thomas* had been over late to Windsor on the previous night to execute the deeds, and he then suspected that *Thomas* had absconded from Canada. Mr. *Prince* says he investigated the title to the lands for *Stephens*. This must have been after the execution of the deeds, for it was impossible to have done it before. The deeds, when executed, were retained by Messrs. *Prince & Bernard*, as solicitors for *Stephens* and *Bernard* procured the execution by *Beatty* for *Stephens* of the agreement of the latter. Thus, then, we have a party, five or six days before a judgment is or can be recovered against him in a pending suit, flying from Canada to the city of Detroit, in the United States, and on the very day of his arrival there introduced to a man, up to that time a stranger to him, and a resident of Detroit, and within the space of about two hours thereafter, conveying to him, without any knowledge by the latter of, or any enquiry by him, except of the defendant, *Beatty*, as to their value, and without any knowledge by him of the state of the title, a large quantity of lands, valued at the lowest rate at $50,000, and for the avowed object of defeating the Bank of Upper Canada in recovering payment of the amount for which they were then seeking judgment.

Now, as against this short statement, of what actually occurred could these conveyances so executed stand? But it is said there is something more ; while on the one hand *Thomas* desired to defeat the claim of the *Bank of Upper Canada*, on the other hand. he sought by so doing to produce the means for paying his other creditors. Let us see how far this pretence is real and *bona fide*. *Thomas*, besides this property, which he conveyed to *Stephens*, had little else left—a few lots in the town of Chatham, sufficient, he thinks, and as *Beatty* swore he thought, to satisfy the judgment which defendant *Beatty* held against him (and which had been registered) for about £1500. Its value, so far as I could gather from the evidence, was not nearly equal to this, but if it was, it would be swept away under *Beatty's* judgment, and no available property was therefore left for those other creditors whose debts, to the amount of £4000 or £5000, were not in any way secured, and which *Thomas*, as he stated, was so anxious to pay. How do he and *Stephens*, to whom *Thomas'* double object was made known by *Beatty* as the latter swears, go about it to effect this object? *Thomas* transfers himself and all his property out of the country, conveying the latter to a foreigner, resident within a foreign jurisdiction, thus putting everything out of the reach not only of the *Bank of Upper Canada*, but of all his other creditors, and in consideration of this *Stephens*, or *Stephens* and *Beatty* are to set him up in the grocery business, providing him with a supply of goods by instalments extending over a period of seven years, out of which I suppose they mean us to understand the creditors are to be paid. I am now speaking of the transaction in its inception and formal completion, without any regard to what took place subsequently, and so treating it, I cannot look upon it otherwise than as a gross fraud by *Thomas* to cheat his creditors, knowingly concurred in by both *Stephens* and *Beatty*. Knowing *Thomas'* design to hinder, delay, and defeat, if he could, the *Bank of Upper Canada*, did *Stephens* take any care to see that *Thomas'* other professed object of paying certain creditors was secured? Did he not at once put it in *Thomas'* power to cheat all his creditors indiscriminately, and thus aid him in doing so, and can he now complain that their joint action to this end should be frustrated? Fraud is not very often apparent in the transaction which it affects—it is to be gathered from many circumstances, including the conduct and demeanour of the parties to it, and every contrivance is usually resorted to to hide it and to baffle enquiry. Here there was not much

· time for contrivance, so hurried was every thing, least
the expected judgments, at the suit of the bank, should
reach the property. What need for *Stephens* to have
entered into the transaction? What inducement to
close it in so hurried a way without the very ordinary
enquiries which any man, the most ignorant, would
make before committing himself to a purchase, unless
induced to do so by *Beatty*, the friend and connection
of *Thomas*, to aid the latter in the accomplishment of
his scheme? Was there not sufficient to have aroused
the suspicion of any prudent man—to have caused
him to hesitate—to make enquiry?

Let us now look at the conduct of the parties afterwards, and see whether in it there is any thing which
will remove the grounds of fraud presented in the transaction originally. We find that *Thomas* for some time
afterwards does nothing towards establishing himself in
the grocery business, or in receiving groceries, but in the
month of September, in the same year, he proposes to
his son, the defendant, *F. A. Thomas*, a partnership in
the business, in which they should share equally, and
accordingly gives directions to Mr. *Bernard* to prepare
the articles of partnership, when he is advised by that
gentleman to sell out his interest in the agreement with
Stephens, as it would be unsafe for him to go into
business, the *Bank of Upper Canada* being determined
to push him hard. Acting on this advice the elder
Thomas sells out to his son, and assigns to him the
agreement with *Stephens*, and takes his son's notes for
$16,000, payable in instalments extending over a period
of between 8 and 9 years. *Thomas*, the son, thereupon
enters upon the grocery business in his own name, receiving groceries from time to time from *Stephens* and
Beatty, and being credited up to the present time with
$3000, and $2577 as payments due him under the agreement with his father. In October, or the beginning of
November following, *Stephens* being dissatisfied with his
bargain because, as alleged, the lands were not paying

him any thing, though how he expected them to do so,
unless by sales which he does not appear to have attempted, one does not very well see, applies to *Beatty* to
take it off his hands. On this, *Beatty* feeling, as he says,
bound in honour so to do, as having advised *Stephens* to
make the purchase, consents on the terms that he is
not to be charged with the goods delivered under the
agreement until he had realised the amount out of the
property conveyed to *Stephens*, he, *Beatty*, paying, however, to the firm ten per cent. interest in the meantime
for this delay. Accordingly on the 5th November *Beatty*,
with the assent of both the *Thomases* assumes *Stephens'*
agreement, and the latter some months afterwards executes deeds of the property to *Beatty*. These transfers
between the parties appear to have been kept secret for
some time, till they came out in evidence in 1862, in a
former suit between these parties.. The deeds from
Stephens to *Beatty* were not registered, *Beatty* says
because of *Stephen's* title being disputed, that is to say,
by the bank.

In the arrangement, such as it was, between *Stephens*
and *Beatty* either a great deal of indifference or a great
deal of confidence was felt, as nothing was said or done
about passed accrued rents, or of the lands or mortgages
which had been released by *Stephens* at the instance of
Thomas out of those conveyed to him. Altogether the
other dealings between and among all parties subsequently to the original sale to *Stephens* were not of a
character to strengthen it in any way. It is evident
that the original sale can obtain no support from
what followed after it, but, on the contrary, if it appeared in its circumstances free from taint, the subsequent acts of the parties would go far to cast dis-
credit, at least grave suspicion, upon it. I quite admit
that we are not to try men's rights upon mere suspicion, however strongly entertained, that all is not
honest, but in this case, as I have already explained,
in the view which I have taken of the facts there is
much more than suspicion ; indeed, as strong evidence

as you can ever expect in such a case of the fraud by which it has been attempted to deprive a plaintiff of the fruits of his judgment. I quite admit also that a mere transfer of property to one creditor with the intent to prefer him to another, and so hinder and defeat that other's execution, will not be invalid either by the common law, or the statute of Elizabeth, but I deny that a transfer can stand made not to a creditor to pay a debt, but as a sale to prevent the operation of an execution, although there be but one such, notwithstanding that language is to be found in *Wood* v. *Dixie*, and *Hale* v. *The Saloon Omnibus Co.*, which read literally would almost sustain that proposition. A man may commit just as great a fraud in his design of defeating one creditor as of defeating a dozen, and indeed it was not contended otherwise on the argument of this case. *Beatty*, if he ought not to stand in any worse, certainly stands in no better position than *Stephens*. He was privy to the original transaction, and any suspicion he entertained then must have been amply confirmed by what transpired afterwards, and before he purchased from *Stephens*.

I should remark that it was stated in evidence that the elder *Thomas* had paid some debts to creditors in Canada since he had lived in Detroit, but they do not appear to have amounted to $300 in all. .Though after *Beatty* had sworn that *Thomas* had given to him as one of his reasons for selling the property his desire to save it from the bank as well for himself as his other creditors, he, on his evidence being read over to him, asserted that he had not meant to say that *Thomas* proposed to save any of it for himself. Yet it seems from what has taken place that it is for himself that Mr. *Thomas* has saved it, and not for his creditors, and I should be ashamed of our jurisprudence if in such a case as this the court could not step in and wrench from the parties holding it, property which should never have been withdrawn from the reach of the creditors.

The law applicable to such cases as the present is plain enough. The only difficulty was in adjudging upon the facts to ascertain whether the conveyance has been contrived of malice, fraud, covin, or collusion to delay, hinder, or defraud creditors, or others of their just and lawful debts; and whether notwithstanding such intent in the one party the lands, etc., have been conveyed on good consideration and *bona fide* to a person not having notice of such covin, fraud, etc. Of recent cases on this subject I may refer to *Corlett* v. *Ratcliffe* (a), before the Privy Council; to *Thompson* v. *Webster* (b), and in 7 Jurist. N. S., on appeal to the House of Lords. And to *Hale* v. *Saloon Omnibus Co.*, already cited. It was contended that the whole conveyance here could not be declared void, inasmuch as it covered mortgages, and that there was no allegation that writs against goods of *Thomas* had issued so as to have entitled the plaintiffs to seize such mortgages had they remained the property of *Thomas*. The allegation in the bill is that the writs against lands were *duly* issued, and this was admitted on the hearing. Although as against a demurrer this form of allegation might not be sufficient, yet I think, coupled with the admission it enables the court on the hearing to make a decree as to the mortgages. The writs against lands could not have *duly* issued had they not been preceded by writs against goods, and the mortgages were held out of the country at the time of bill filed.

The decree must be to declare these several conveyances from *Thomas* to *Stephens* void as against the plaintiffs, with costs as against the defendants *George*, *Thomas*, *Stephens* and *Beatty*, and for the usual necessary consequential relief. I give no costs to or against the defendant *F. A. Thomas*. I think he was a proper party to the bill, but he very unnecessarily in his answer enters into a defence of his father in his affairs with the bank. If on being served

---

(a) L. Times N. S. p. 1.   (b) 5 Jurist N. S. 668 and 921.

with the bill he had disclaimed all interest in the suit and the plaintiffs had nevertheless continued proceedings against him, he would then have had a claim to his costs.

At the opening of the case I ruled that the plaintiffs could not in this suit impeach the judgment of *Beatty* v. *Thomas,* as that question had been disposed of in a former suit between the same parties, but inasmuch as the conveyances from *Thomas* stand good as between him, *Stephens,* and *Beatty,* the result is that *Beatty* cannot enforce his judgment against the property covered by those conveyances.

McCrumm v. Crawford.

Parol contract partly performed—Bond for a deed—Registration— Notice of adverse title—Costs.

In 1858 a parol contract was entered into for the sale of one acre of land, the consideration for which was paid, and the purchaser was let into possession of the property, which he occupied, improved and built upon. Afterwards, and in the same year, the vendor executed by way of security a life lease to another person of 50 acres, including the acre so sold. In 1860 a bond was executed by the vendor to the wife of the purchaser for the conveyance of the acre to her. In 1862 the lessee for life purchased the 50 acres in fee and the conveyance to him was duly registered; the bond for the conveyance of the acre never was registered. The purchaser of the acre having filed a bill for a specific performance of the parol contract, the court refused relief on that ground, the parol contract having become merged in the written contract or bond : but offered the plaintiff, at the risk of costs, permission to amend by alleging the written contract, and to give further evidence to establish direct notice of the bond, reserving the question of costs until after the enquiry ; if this refused, the bill to be dismissed without costs, the defendant having falsely asserted his title under the lease to have been absolute and not by way of security merely.

The bill in this cause was filed by *James McCrumm* and his wife, against *Thomas Crawford* and *Henry Cowan,* praying under the circumstances therein stated, and which are clearly set forth in the judgment, a declaration that they were entitled to a conveyance of one acre of land purchased by them from *Cowan,* and that a deed executed by him to the other defendant was void as against the plaintiffs; that *Crawford* might be

22   GRANT. IX.

restrained from proceeding against them by ejectment, and that the defendants might be ordered to convey the acre so purchased to the plaintiffs.

Crawford answered the bill, denying notice of the claim set up by the plaintiffs. *Cowan* had allowed the bill to be taken *pro confesso*. The plaintiff having put the cause at issue by filing replication, evidence was taken therein before his Honour V.C. *Esten*, at the sittings held at Cobourg in April, 1863, the effect of which is also stated in the judgment.

Mr. *Blake*, for the plaintiffs.

Mr. *Kirkhoffer*, for *Crawford*. The defendant *Cowan* did not appear.

Judgment.–ESTEN, V.C.–The facts of this case are, that *James McCrumm*, one of the plaintiffs, and the husband of the other plaintiff, in 1858, purchased by verbal contract the acre of ground in question in the suit from *Henry Cowan*, for the sum of £10 to be paid, as to £3, by a gun, and as to the rest, by shoemakers' work, as needed, he being a shoemaker by trade. He was let into possession under the contract by *Cowan*, and continued in possession for about two years, and made some improvements on the property, and paid the purchase money. In 1860 he removed his family to a place called Perrytown, about 24 miles distant, and continued there until the spring of 1862. In 1858, after *Mc-Crumm's* purchase, the defendant *Crawford* took a life lease of the 50 acres of which the one acre was part, to secure a debt due to him by *Cowan*, and gave a bond to *Cowan* to re-convey on payment of principal and interest. He at that time heard that *McCrumm* was in possession of the acre. In 1859 he offered to sell the 50 acres to one *Phee*, saying that he had a deed of them. *Phee* did not believe him, and asked him whether he could sell *McCrumm's* acre. *Crawford* said that *McCrumm* had a very light title, and that he would soon hurl him out of that. No bargain was made, however, and on the 22nd of February, 1862, *Crawford* purchased the fee of the 50 acres, and it was conveyed to him. In March of that year he again offered to sell the 50 acres to *Phee*, and asked him what he would give for the 49 acres, without *McCrumm's* acre. About the same time he let the property to one *Stinson;* but the day before *Stinson* went into possession. Mrs. *McCrumm* returned to the place and opposed *Stinson's* entrance; upon which *Stinson* applies to *Crawford*, who repairs to the place the next day, and complains to Mrs. *McCrumm;* whereupon Mrs. *McCrumm* says she had a bond to which *Crawford* answers that he knew she had, but he did not care for it as it was not on record; that if she had a bond he had a deed; that he had searched the register and found that the bond was not registered, and that it could not be registered. The result was, that *Stinson* departed the place and he and *Kirkpatrick*, his brother-in-law who was assisting him, were summoned before a magistrate by the *McCrumms*, *James McCrumm* having arrived some days after his wife. When the *McCrumms* vacated the premises *Cowan* proposed to let them to one *Miller*, and *McCrumm* objecting refrained; afterwards he let them to one *Herse*, at a rent of $20, for the benefit of *McCrumm*. In the year 1860 a bond was given at *McCrumm's* request by *Cowan* to Mrs. *McCrumm*, for the conveyance of the premises to his wife. The purchase money was then paid. The bond was delivered to the *McCrumms* probably upon the occasion of the departure to Perrytown, and was retained by them and in the year 1861 or 1862 deposited by them with one *Stevenson* for safe custody, and delivered by him to them about the time of the commencement of this suit.

This bond is produced and proved by the plaintiffs. It was never registered. The conveyance to *Crawford* of the 22nd of February was registered on the 28th. In 1858 or 1859 the defendant *Crawford* had been at the place in question when *McCrumm* asked him whether he had purchased it, to which he replied, that was his business, upon which *McCrumm* said that he had expected to get it. *Crawford* says in his evidence that he knew that *McCrumm* was in possession when he took the life-lease but he did not know by what title, nor did he enquire.

The sole question in this suit is, whether *Crawford*, at the time he received his conveyance and paid his money had notice of *McCrumm's* title. It is to be observed that when he took the life-lease the bond was not in existence, only the parol contract. If the life-lease was not registered, as I believe it was not, *Crawford* clearly had notice sufficient to affect that interest, because he knew that *McCrumm* was in possession, and therefore had constructive notice of his title. But the life-lease is at an end; the fee has been acquired, and the deed conveying it has been registered, and therefore has obtained priority at law over the plaintiff's contract, which might have been, but was not, registered. The bond given in 1860, I think entirely superseded and extinguished the parol contract, which could not exist with it. Constructive notice of the parol contract would have been sufficient; but this contract having become extinct in 1860, two years before the purchase of the fee by *Crawford*, and replaced by the bond, which was capable of registration, actual notice became necessary in order to maintain the priority of the bond of the plaintiffs over the defendant's conveyance. The constructive notice arising from knowledge of the plaintiff's possession was not sufficient to produce this effect. The question then is, whether *Crawford* had actual notice of the contract or bond when he took the conveyance of the fee on the 22nd of February, 1862, and paid the consideration for it.

After the best consideration I have been able to give to this case, I think the evidence is insufficient to prove such notice. The first occasion on which notice could have been received was the interview between *Crawford* and *McCrumm* at the place in question; the next, was the conversation between *Phee* and *Crawford*, in the year 1859, when *Crawford* offered to sell the 50 acres to *Phee*. I think that what passed on these occasions is insufficient to shew actual knowledge on the part of *Crawford* of the contract, for the bond did not then exist, so as to make it a fraud in *Crawford* to register his deed of the 22nd of February, 1862. The only other occasion on which anything occurred from which notice could be derived or inferred was when *Crawford* attended at the place in order to compose the quarrel between Mrs. *McCrumm* and *Stinson*. At this time *Crawford* clearly had notice of the bond to Mrs. *McCrumm*: but the question is, when he acquired that knowledge. It is consistent, I think, with all that *Kirkpatrick* relates to have occurred that *Crawford* may have taken the conveyance and paid the consideration without actual knowledge of the bond or the contract. It might have come to his knowledge after the 22nd of February, 1862, and he might then have gone to Lindsay and searched the registry, and finding no bond registered his deed. This would have been justifiable. The bill states that the bond was prepared without the knowledge or instructions of the plaintiffs. It is however produced and proved by them. It is not shewn to have been disagreed to or repudiated. It is retained by them, delivered to a third person for safe custody, and returned to them by him about the time of the commencement of this suit. It is impossible for the court to ignore this instrument. The result is that if the case be determined upon the present evidence the bill must be dismissed. The parol contract is at an end, and the bond is void as against this deed both at law and in equity. I have, however, a very strong suspicion that the defendant *Crawford* had actual knowledge of this contract and perhaps of the bond before the execution of the deed of the 22nd of February,

1862. He saw *McCrumm* in possession. *McCrumm's* enquiry and remark at the interview between them after the execution of the life-lease must have strengthened any suspicion that he previously entertained. His language to *Phee* shewed that he knew the *McCrumms* had some title. He knew of the existence of the bond at all events immediately after the execution of the conveyance to him if not before. All these circumstances raise in my mind a strong suspicion that *Crawford* had actual knowledge of the contract or bond before the execution of the conveyance. I am not satisfied that all the evidence on this subject has been elicited: that *Phee* and *Cowan* and *Crawford* himself, perhaps others, might not give material evidence not yet adduced. Should the plaintiffs desire at the risk of paying costs to have a further enquiry, I am prepared to grant it, so strong is my suspicion of notice, and so strongly am I inclined to think that the plaintiffs have been wronged. In this case, however, the record must be amended. The bill should state a case upon the bond at all events in the alternative. The husband must be struck out as a co-plaintiff and added as a defendant if the case stated in this bill be founded exclusively on the bond, in which case also it would be premature to order a conveyance, and the plaintiffs could be entitled only to a declaration establishing their title, and an injunction to protect their possession unless the bond has in the meantime matured.

If the bill be dismissed it will be without costs. The defendant has in his answer deliberately misrepresented the effect and purpose of the life-lease. He says that it was in fact as well as in form absolute and not by way of security; his attention must have been drawn to the distinction between an instrument absolute in form but intended as a security, and an instrument absolute in fact as well as in form; and he deliberately and contrary to the truth asserts this life-lease to be of this

character. Should further examination be directed
the costs will be reserved.

STERLING v. RILEY.

Practice—Mortgage—Pro confesso.

Where a reference is directed to take an account of what is due on a
mortgage, it is competent to the parties to shew the real object for
which it was made, if that is not apparent on the face of the instrument; and when the bill has been taken *pro confesso* it is incumbent on the master to require the mortgagee to shew how the
money secured by the mortgage was advanced; and *semble*, that
such a course would be desirable in all cases.

Statement.—This was a mortgage case. The defendant had applied, in a former stage of the cause, to
open publication with a view of giving evidence that
the amount advanced on the security was not that
mentioned in the instrument; that plaintiff was
indebted to defendant in various sums; also, that
other land had been conveyed to the plaintiff by the
defendant, to enable him to sell it, and apply the proceeds in paying off the debt due plaintiff by defendant,
and pay the excess, if any, to the defendant. This
application was refused, his Honour

V. C. *Esten*, before whom it was made, stating—I am
satisfied that I ought to refuse this application—the
defendant desires to produce evidence for the purpose
of establishing the following points, namely:

1st. That the mortgage was made for a greater
amount than it should have been, inasmuch as the
defendant had agreed to pay the plaintiff for the property in question £50 over and above what he had
himself paid; and that he had paid £611 or upwards,
and that the defendant was to pay, and did pay £300
down; and that the mortgage should have been for the
balance, namely, £361, and upwards, whereas it is for
£500. Upon this point I think it unnecessary for the
defendant to enter into evidence. I think that his
sworn statement in his answer will be sufficient ground

for the court at the hearing to direct an enquiry on this head, upon which enquiry the defendant will receive every benefit which he could obtain by producing evidence on this point previously to the hearing.

The second point which the defendant desires to establish is, merely that the plaintiff is indebted to him in various amounts, but it has been decided that a defendant in a foreclosure suit may avail himself in the account in the master's office of any matter of set-off which it may be in his power to shew, whether simple contract or otherwise. It is unnecessary for him therefore to go into evidence for this purpose.

The 3rd point is, that he conveyed another estate to the plaintiff for the purpose of securing to him £150, which he owed him; and that the plaintiff was to sell the estate and pay him the surplus, but that is a matter wholly unconnected with the subject of this suit, and not cognizable in it. The defendant's remedy in that case is by a bill of his own. The last and most important point is, that the defendant was induced to enter into the contract of purchase by a fraudulent misrepresentation of the plaintiff that the property was worth what he had paid for it, whereas it was worth only £140, as plaintiff knew, and the defendant asks; as relief upon this case, that the mortgage should stand as a security only for what the land was worth, this is a ridiculous notion; as if the court could make a new contract for the parties. What he should have asked is, that the contract of purchase should be vacated, and the mortgage with it, and that the £300 he had paid be re-paid to him. This relief he could not obtain if he proved his facts ever so clearly, because he has not asked it. Moreover this case is one in which the plaintiff should have an opportunity of denying or explaining the alleged fraud on oath; but if the answer is to be treated as a cross-bill, in which case the plaintiff must answer it by amending his bill, he will be deprived of that advantage. It is a case in short in which the court would direct a cross suit to be instituted ; especially considering that although the defendant has paid £300 on the contract, he has not thought it worth his while to institute such a suit, but has acquiesced until the plaintiff proceeded on his mortgage.

Mr. *Blevins*, indeed, suggested that the facts, if proved, could be used simply as a defence to this suit, so that the court might dismiss the bill with costs ; in other words, that the court would adjudge that this contract ought to be set aside without setting it aside, and would therefore refuse to give relief on the mortgage ; but I apprehend that this is a course which the court will never adopt; it will never pronounce a definite judgment that a contract ought to be set aside except for the purpose of setting it aside ; will not form and pronounce such a judgment for a merely collateral or subordinate object.

I have not adverted particularly to the affidavits, but it certainly is extremely unsatisfactory that the alleged fraud should be supported only by the affidavit of the defendant, without examining a single witness who could testify to it. Very possibly in proceeding with the examination not a title of evidence might have been offered on this head. The excuses, too, assigned by the defendant for his non-attendance appeared somewhat flimsy, I think the application should be refused with costs.

The cause subsequently came on to be heard, when

Mr. *Blake*, for the plaintiff, asked that the usual decree of foreclosure might be pronounced.

Mr. *Blevins*, for defendant, asked that the decree might contain a direction for the master to enquire as to what was the consideration for the mortgage, and what sum had been advanced thereon ; but

Judgment.—ESTEN, V.C.—I should if necessary direct an enquiry, in accordance with my judgment pronounced on a motion in this case to open publication, as to the purpose for which the mortgage was made, with a view to ascertain what was due upon it. It is unnecessary, however, to adopt this course, as I am of opinion (an opinion formed after consulting with my brother judges) that upon every reference to the master to ascertain and report what is due on a mortgage it is competent to the parties if the mortgage has not been made for the purpose apparent on the face of it, to shew the real object for which it was executed. It will be competent, therefore, in this case to adduce evidence for the purpose of shewing in the master's office the real amount, if different from the apparent amount, which this mortgage was intended to secure, and for that purpose to shew the object with which the mortgage was made ; a familiar instance of what I refer to is where a specific sum is mentioned in a mortgage, but it is in fact executed to secure a floating balance. The defendant, I think, may shew the fact whether he has mentioned it in his answer or not. I take this opportunity of stating, which I do also with the concurrence of the other judges, that it is proper for the master, and incumbent upon him in all cases where the bill has been taken *pro confesso* against the mortgagor, even if not in all cases, which, however, would be desirable, to require the plaintiff to shew how the money was advanced, and not merely what remains due. It will not be necessary to introduce any special directions into the decree, according to the views which I have stated.

BOUCHER v. SMITH.

Marshalling securities—Contribution—Notice—Defective registration.

In 1849 G. being the owner of Whiteacre and Blackacre, contracted to sell half of the former to B. by a bond which was never registered. In 1852 G. executed a mortgage covering both lots to C., which was immediately registered, but the christian name of the grantor's wife (who executed to bar dower) did not appear in the memorial. In 1853 G. gave a mortgage of Blackacre to P., who also immediately registered his conveyance. In 1855 G. sold the remaining half of Whiteacre to M., and in the following year B. conveyed his interest in the other half to S. In 1861 C. sold Blackacre under a power of sale in his mortgage, and the sale realised fully what was due thereon.

In 1862 P. filed his bill against M & S. in order that he might be subrogated to the rights of C. as against Whiteacre for the amount due him on his security. S. & H. had previously paid all their purchase money.

Held, that P. was not entitled to any relief against S., but that if C.'s mortgage was duly registered, P. was entitled to contribution against M.

Statement.—The evidence in this cause shewed that a mortgagee of two lots, one of which was covered by a second mortgage, having sold the one so encumbered, under a power of sale in his mortgage, and thus realise the amount due on his security, the second mortgagee filed his bill against the mortgagor and two subsequent purchasers of the other lot praying to be subrogated in place of the prior mortgagee *pro tanto.* It appeared that these had paid all their purchase money prior to the filing of the bill; that one of them claimed under a party who had contracted for the purchase previously to the execution of the first mortgage, but had neglected to register his contract, and that both the mortgages had been registered immediately after execution, but that there was an apparent defect in the memorial of the prior mortgage, which was not produced. It did not appear that the purchasers had actual notice of either mortgage. The facts appear more fully in the judgment of the court.

Mr. *McGregor*, for the plaintiff, contended, that as the prior mortgagee had sold the land covered by the plaintiff's security, which was registered previously to the execution of the conveyances to the purchasers of the other lot, and as the first purchaser had neglected to

register his bond as he might have done, the land held
by these purchasers should be declared subject to the
amount due to the plaintiff, which was less than that due
to the prior mortgagee. He contended that the plaintiff
took his security relying on the burden of the prior incumbrance being thrown primarily on the land not comprised in his security, upon the principle that as between
subsequent purchasers or incumbrancers of different
parts of the premises, these parts are to be sold in the
inverse order of alienation, and that wherever the prior
incumbrancer disappointed the second, the latter was
entitled to be subrogated *pro tanto*.

He referred to *Aldrich* v. *Cooper*, (a) *Kellogg* v.
Rand, (b) *Hilliard* on Mortgages, chapter xviii., sec.
57, and *Story's* Ey. Jur., section 1233 note (8th edition.)
He contended that the cases of *Hamilton* v. *Royse*, (c)
and *Averall* v. *Wade*, (d) supported this contention, and
that the subsequent cases of *Barnes* v. *Racster*, (e)
and *Bugden* v. *Bignold*, (f) which awarded contribution
only, were either not in point, or were at variance both
with previous decisions and with the broad principle laid
down in some of these cases, that an incumbrancer should
not be allowed to destroy the security he had given by
putting a purchaser from him with notice in a better
position than himself, and contending that the most
recent cases of *Handcock* v. *Handcock*, (g) and *Re
Roddy's* estate, (h) were in conformity with the older
decisions, and also with principle. He also contended
that the registration of the prior mortgage was notice
to the subsequent purchasers of the equities arising under
it, and that the prior purchaser of the half lot had
lost his right to be exempted by having failed to
register his bond.

Mr. *Blake* for the two purchasers, contended that the

(a) 8 Vesey, 382.   (b) 11 Paige, 64.
(c) 2 Sch. & Lefr. 315, 327.   (d) Ll & G. t. Sugden, 252, 268.
(e) 1 Y. & C. C. C. 401.   (f) 2 Y. & C. C. C. 377.
(g) 1 Jr. ch. 444, and 474.   (h) 11 Ir. ch. 369.

registration of the first mortgage was not notice to any person but to the mortgagee, and those claiming under him, that as the christain name of the mortgagor's wife was omitted in the memorial of the first mortgage, the registry was invalid as not complying with the requirements of the registry acts. He therefore contended that these defendants were purchasers for value without notice, and not liable even to contribution. He further contended that the first purchaser's assignee was entitled to be wholly exempted even from contribution, because his purchase was prior to the first mortgage, which was a fraud on him, and consequently he had a prior equity to the plaintiff.

On behalf of the other purchaser he contended that even if the registration of the prior mortgage were notice to him, he was bound only to contribute rateably, and he relied on *Barnes* v. *Racster*, and *Bugden* v. *Bignold*, and also referred to the latter case of *Gibson* v. *Seagrim*. (a)

The judgment of the court was delivered by

ESTEN, V. C., [before whom the examition was taken and the cause heard.]—The facts of this case are, that *James D. Goslee* in the year 1848 owned the two lots of land in question in this cause, namely, lot No. 30, in the 1st concession, and lot 8, in the 4th concession of the township of Cramahe. In 1848 he contracted for the sale of one half of lot 8, to one *Becker*, a defendant, for £556, and gave him a bond for a conveyance, in the usual form, which bond might have been, but was never, registered. *Becker*, however, was let into possession, and paid part of his purchase money, and the contract continued in force, and was never abandoned or rescinded. In the year 1852 *James D. Goslee* borrowed the sum of £500

(a) 20 Beavan. 619.

from the Trust and Loan Company, and for the purpose of securing the re-payment of it, with interest, mortgaged to that company both lots above mentioned, with a power of sale, giving no notice of the sale to *Becker*. This proceeding was undoubtedly a fraud upon *Becker* or upon the company, who had no notice of the sale to *Becker* and who very properly registered their mortgage, and thereby gained priority over *Becker*. In 1853 the mortgage was made by *James D. Goslee* to the plaintiff, upon which this suit is founded. It comprised only lot 30, and was made for securing £500 and interest, but only £400 or thereabouts was actually advanced upon it, and this was the money of Mrs. *George Goslee*, for whom Mr. *Boucher*, the plaintiff, is a mere trustee. This mortgage was duly registered. In 1855 *James D. Goslee* treated for the sale of the other half of lot 8 to the defendant *McLaughlin*, who has paid his purchase money and received his conveyance. In 1856 the defendant *Smith* purchased *Becker's* interest in the south-half of lot 8, and upon that occasion *James D. Goslee* conveyed that half of the lot to *Smith* in fee, and *Smith* having paid part of his purchase money *Becker*, executed a mortgage to him to secure the residue, with interest and he has since paid the balance of *Becker's* purchase money to *James D. Goslee*, and has procured a discharge of his own mortgage to *Becker*, so that *Smith* and *McLaughlin* respectively have acquired the absolute fee simple of the two halves of the lot, and have paid their purchase money; and no evidence is adduced of notice to them of the respective mortgages to the Trust and Loan Company, and the plaintiff, except the registration of those instruments respectively. The mortgage to the Trust and Loan Company contained a power of sale, and under it they proceeded to a sale of lot 30, in the month of June, in the year 1861, when it was purchased by Mr. *Grover*, who has been examined in the cause, for the sum of £635. It appears that in the memorial of the mortgage to the Trust and Loan

Company the christian name of Mrs. *Goslee* is omitted.

The present suit has been instituted by the plaintiff in order to subject lot No. 8, in the hands of the purchasers of the two halves of it, to the whole, or to a fair proportion of the mortgage of the Trust and Loan Company, satisfied by the proceeds of the sale of lot 30. This claim is resisted by the defendants respectively on the grounds that as to the half of the lot purchased by *Becker*, his purchase being anterior to the mortgage to the Trust and Loan Company, this half of the lot ought not as between these parties to be subject to that mortgage at all; that if the case were different the principle applicable as between these parties is not the principle of marshalling, but the principle that the two estates should bear the common burden rateably; and that at all events no relief of any sort can be given as against these defendants, who are purchasers for valuable consideration, without other notice than the registration of the two mortgages, which it is said does not amount to notice for this purpose at all, or at all events does not amount to such notice under the circumstances; and that the registration of the mortgage to the Trust and Loan Company is invalid by reason of the omission of the christian name of Mrs. *Goslee* from the memorial. When *J. D. Goslee* mortgaged the whole of lot 8 to the Trust and Loan Company without giving them notice of the sale of half the lot to *Becker*, he committed a fraud upon *Becker*. It is clear that it would be contrary to equity to subject the half lot purchased by *Becker* to any part of the mortgage of the Trust and Loan Company as against *Goslee* or any one claiming under him. Under these circumstances it is impossible that the plaintiff could enforce a claim for either exoneration or contribution against *Becker* or any one standing in his place. The only argument that could be urged in favour of the plaintiff is, that *Becker* by neglecting to register his bond, exposed the plaintiff to danger, inasmuch as he may have accepted the mortgage of lot 30, relying on lot 8 for exoneration ; and if *Becker* had registered his bond the plaintiff would have seen that he could not rely on lot 8 for this purpose, and might have declined to accept the mortgage, and that such negligence should give priority to the equity of the plaintiff over the equity of *Becker*. But I think such an argument untenable—a person neglecting to register the instrument under which he claims, pays the penalty provided by the act, in the avoidance of that instrument, as against a subsequent purchaser of the same lands. I do not think an omission on the part of *Becker* to register the bond can be urged as negligence in favour of the plaintiff, a purpose not contemplated by the act,so as to subject the half of lot 8 purchased by *Becker* to contribution, which is the utmost that could be claimed. Nor could any default on the part of *Becker* even if any such had been shewn, confer any right on the plaintiff. The mortgage of lot 30 did not impair the right of *Goslee* as to lot 8. He could maintain any contract which he had made respecting lot 8, or any part of it, notwithstanding any default. The mortgage of lot 30 conveyed to the plaintiff no right to rescind any contract made respecting any part of lot 8. I therefore think that the plaintiff cannot maintain any claim of any sort against *Becker* or *Smith* as standing in his place.

With respect to *McLaughlin* and the half of the lot purchased by him, the case is different. *McLaughlin* purchased the half of the lot after both mortgages had been executed. When the mortgage of lot 30 was executed by *Goslee* to the plaintiff, an equity accrued to the plaintiff as against *Goslee*, to exoneration out of the half of lot 8 remaining unsold ; in other words, the Trust and Loan Company having two funds, and the plaintiff having only one fund to which they could resort respectively, the company were bound as between themselves and the plaintiff to take their satisfaction out of the fund to which the plaintiff could not resort, and if they should take their satisfaction out of the fund which was common to both, the plaintiff would be entitled to stand in their place as against the other fund. But as *Goslee* had mortgaged lot 30, so he could sell the half of lot 8, and the result was as between the mortgagee of lot 30 and the purchaser of the half of lot 8, that the common burden must be borne rateably, although each would have his remedies upon his covenants against the vendor and mortgagor. *Barnes* v. *Racster*, (a) *Bugden* v. *Bignold*, (b) *Gibson* v. *Seagrim*. (c) The consequence was, that upon the sale of the half of lot 8 to *McLaughlin*, the plaintiff became entitled to claim as against him that the half of the lot 8 should bear a proportionate part of the mortgage to the Trust and Loan Company. *McLaughlin*, however, insists that he is a purchaser for valuable consideration without notice, and therefore that the court will afford the plaintiff no assistance against him.

It is admitted that no exception exists to the rule that equity will not interfere to the prejudice of a purchaser for valuable consideration without notice, unless the case of a mortgagee seeking foreclosure against a purchaser of the equity of redemption, without notice of a mortgage, is an exception. But it is contended that *McLaughlin* had notice of the plaintiff's equity by reason of the registration of the respective mortgages to the Trust and Loan Company and the plaintiff. On the other hand, it was insisted that the resignation of these mortgages did not amount to such notice.

It appears to me that registration is notice of the thing registered, for the purpose of giving effect to any equity accruing from it, but it can be noticed of any given instrument only to those who are reasonably led by the nature of the transaction in which they are engaged to

---

(a) 1 Y. & C. C. C. 401.		(b) 2 J. & C. C. C. 377.
(c) 20 Beav. 619.

examine the register with respect to it. The registration of the mortgage to the Trust and Loan Company would of course be noticed of that mortgage to all persons acquiring any interest in lot 30, or lot No. 8. On the one side it is said that it is notice of the mortgage only for the purpose of giving effect to it in favour of persons claiming under it; on the other hand, it may be contended that it is notice of the mortgage for the purpose of enforcing it against the lands comprised in it whenever it is just that they should be charged with it. Thus it is just in the abstract that as between the plaintiff and *McLaughlin* the half of lot No. 8, purchased by *McLaughlin*, should be charged with a proportionate part of the mortgage of the Trust and Loan Company. Supposing *McLaughlin* to have examined the register with respect to both mortgages, he would necessarily have notice of the plaintiff's equity to contribution resulting from them and from his own purchase. Having notice of the two mortgages, he could not but have notice of this equity which necessarily flowed from them and from the sale to himself. I should think that the registration of the two mortgages would amount to notice for this purpose to any one who might be reasonably led to examine the register with respect to both mortgages.

The question is, whether *McLaughlin* was reasonably led by the nature of his purchase to make such examination.

It was suggested by Mr. *McGregor* that if he relied upon lot 30 to exonerate lot 8 he should have examined the register in order to ascertain whether lot 30 had been alienated or incumbered: *McLaughlin* might, when he purchased, have relied on lot 30 to exonerate lot 8, but he was not necessarily led for this reason to examine the register with respect to lot 30. It may be said, however, that he was bound to examine the register in order to ascertain whether the land he was purchasing was subject to any incumbrance. The very object of registration is to give to purchasers notice of incumbrances affecting the lands they are purchasing, and therefore registration must be notice of such incumbrances. A purchaser of part of lot 8 having, as he had, notice of the mortgage to the Trust and Loan Company, and knowing that *Goslee* by a dealing with lot 30 might have subjected lot 8 to a claim for contribution in the hands of a purchaser, which would be an incumbrance, of which the register would afford information, was bound, I think, to examine the register to see if lot 8 was subject to any such incumbrance. I therefore think that *McLaughlin* had notice of the plaintiff's equity to contribution, supposing the registration of the mortgage of the Trust and Loan Company to be effectual. If it is not effectual then he had notice of nothing.

I think the omission of Mrs. *Goslee's* christian name in the memorial vitiated the registration of this mortgage, unless a similar defect existed in the deed itself.

The bill must be dismissed with costs as to *Smith* and *Becker*, and also as to *McLaughlin*, if he had no notice; in other words, if the registration of the mortgage to the Trust and Loan Company was ineffectual; if it was effectual the plaintiff is entitled to a decree for contribution against *McLaughlin*. The bill should be dismissed as to *Goslee*, who seems an unnecessary party, with costs. If any relief should be decreed against *McLaughlin*, it should be with costs proper to a suit for that purpose, unless the plaintiff should have demanded too much by his bill, in which case it may be proper not to award any costs against *McLaughlin*. I do not think the evidence as to value material. If the company in the due exercise of the power of sale has by sale of lot 30 raised only enough to satisfy their own mortgage, the estates must bear the burden rateably.

TAYLOR v. RIDOUT.

Will—Construction of.

A testator bequeathed to two of his grand-children the sum of £500
each : by a subsequent clause of his will, he directed certain bonds
and securities to be realized and invested to meet two annuities
charged on his estate, and after these annuities should cease "*to
exist then, and in that case, the money so to be invested to raise the
sum to pay these annuities shall be divided equally among my children
then living share and share alike, or in case of any of their deaths,
then to their children per stirpes, and not per capita."* At the time of
making his will his daughter, the mother of the two legatees, had
been dead for some time, *held*, that the children of such deceased
daughter did not take any interest in the residuary estate.

Statement.—The bill in the case was filed by Mary
E. S. *Taylor* and *George Taylor*, infants, and *Harriet
C. Kingston*, (wife of the defendant, *Kingston*,) by
their father and next friend against the defendants,
Ridout, Dennison, and *Wilson*, as executors of the last
will and testament of *George Taylor Dennison*, deceased,
and *Frederick Kingston*, made a party solely in respect
of his being the husband of the plaintiff *Harriet C.
Kingston*, setting forth that the testator, by his will,
dated 2nd December, 1853, after bequeathing a legacy
to one of his daughters, and another to his widow,
proceeded as follows : "My will further is, that I give
and devise to each of my grand-daughters, *Harriet* and
Mary Taylor, [two of the plaintiffs,] children of my
daughter *Mary*, each the sum of £500 Halifax currency,
to be paid to each of them as they shall attain the
full age of twenty-one years.

"And my will further is, that after all my lands shall
have been sold, which I have left for sale, that a certain
sum of money shall be invested in some sure and safe
fund, so as to be prepared to pay the two annuities, one
to my widow of £150, and the other to my daughter,
Sophia, of £35, as they shall become due. My bonds
at present in my possession are £8,500, and more; those
sums of money are to be invested in some safe funds to
pay those two annuities, and when those two annuities
shall cease to exist, then and in that case the money so

to be invested to raise the sum to pay those two annuities shall be divided equally among my children then living, share and share alike, or in case of any of their deaths, then to their children *per stirpes* and not *per capita*."

The will contained this further clause, "And my will further is, that after all the different allotments of land shall have been sold, and all my bonds and outstanding debts collected, that a regular calculation shall be made; then, in that case, it is my will that the amount which shall have been realized shall be divided among all my children equally, share and share alike, except my daughter *Sophia*, as I have left her a legacy of £35 during her life, in lieu thereof." Also the following clause, " I direct that the moneys arising from such lands, and also all other, my bonds, mortgages, credits, moneys, stock, and securities of every kind, shall be formed into a fund, and be held and invested as my said executors, or a majority of them shall think most advantageous for my estate, and shall thenceforth be distributed by my said executors, or a majority of them, according to the directions and intentions of my will."

The bill further stated, that on the 7th day of December, 1853, the testator duly made and executed a codicil to his said will, whereby he reduced the aforesaid annuity to his wife, from £150 to £125. And the codicil contained this further clause, " All the rest, residue, and remainder of all my estate, real and personal, and of every thing else which I may die seised, possessed of, or entitled to, not devised or bequeathed in and by my last will and testament, do go to my executors and trustees aforesaid, to be by them appropriated to the fund in my said will mentioned, and to be distributed and applied by them in like manner as the said fund is in my said will directed to be distributed and applied."

The plaintiffs submitted that upon the true construction of the will, they were entitled to a distributive share of the residuary estate, the same as if their mother had not died until after the death of the testator and his widow, and prayed a declaration to that effect.

The defendants, the executors, answered the bill, submitting to act in accordance with the will, upon a true construction thereof.

Mr. *A. Crooks*, for the plaintiffs.

Mr. *Brough*, Q.C., for the defendants.

Judgment.—VANKOUGHNET, C.—On the argument, I felt no doubt that the plaintiffs must fail in their claim to any share of the testator's estate, other than as to the specific legacies bequeathed to two of them, but I thought it right to examine the case of *Loring* v. *Thomas*, (a) cited by Mr. *Crooks*, before giving judgment finally in the case. *Loring* v. *Thomas* was decided upon the peculiar language of the will under consideration, and can only be authority for a case similarly circumstanced. In this case, there is nothing whatever to indicate that the testator intended the children of a pre-deceased child to take the share which the parent, if living at the date of the will, could have taken. There is nothing whatever to take the case out of the ordinary rule that the living children only are to take. We must assume that the testator knew of his daughter *Mary Taylor's* death; he provides for his remaining children by specific devises to them by name, and he gives legacies to two of the children of his pre-deceased daughter *Mary*. He disposes of the fund on which the annuities are to be secured to his children who may at the time the annuities shall fall in be living, or if they be then dead, to their issue in their stead, *per stirpes;* thus negativing the idea that he intended to provide for the issue of a pre-deceased child as if that child herself were living at the time of

---

(a) 1 Drew & Sim. 497.

making his will. There is nothing in the will to indicate any intention to place the issue of such child in the place of the child, and so provide for them; but everything in the will leads to the contrary conclusion. I cannot give the plaintiffs their costs, but as the case of *Loring* v. *Thomas* may have excited false hopes, it will, perhaps, be fair not to charge them with the costs of the suit, but to direct that the defendants shall receive their costs out of the estate.

THOMPSON V. MILLIKIN.

Specific performance—Enquiry as to title—Deed sixty years old—Taxes.

On an enquiry as to title the vendor was unable to produce one of the title deeds, or to shew that a receipt was endorsed thereon for the purchase money. *Held*, no objection to the completion of the contract. So also, that, the non-production of a certificate of no taxes in arrear, was no objection to the title.

Statement.—This was a suit for specific performance instituted by the vendor against the purchaser of real estate, and at the hearing the usual reference as to title was directed. On proceeding under this reference, the master certified against the title, on the grounds, amongst others, of one of the conveyances under which the plaintiff claimed not being produced, and the memorial, as recorded in the registry office, not shewing that any consideration was paid; also, by reason of the plaintiff having failed to produce a certificate of no taxes being due upon the property.

One of the parties through whom the vendor traced his title claimed as heir-at-law of his father, but in the affidavit proving such heirship it was sworn simply that he was such heir-at-law, not showing how he became so. An objection to this affidavit taken by the defendant was over-ruled by the master, and this with others formed the grounds of a cross-appeal by the purchaser.

Mr. *Hector*, for the plaintiff, contended that the deed which had not been produced, being upwards of sixty

years old, no objection could be taken on the ground
of no receipt for the purchase money being shewn. As
to the question of taxes, that is a mere matter of con-
veyancing, for if it is shewn that taxes are due, the purchase money can be applied *pro tanto* in their discharge.

Mr. *Blain*, contra.

Judgment.—VANKOUGHNET, C.—This case comes before me on appeal by the vendor, and cross appeal by
the purchaser, to the master's report on the reference to
him as to title. I think the exceptions taken by the
appeal to the master's finding should be allowed. I
disposed of them at the hearing with the exception of
two; the one relating to the absence of any evidence
of a valuable consideration in the deed from *Jarvis*,
the patentee of the Crown, to one *Gough;* the other,
the want of a certificate that no taxes are in arrear.

As to the 1st, the deed in question is more than 60
years old—it cannot be produced, and I think its loss
sufficiently established to let in secondary evidence of
its contents. This is furnished by the memorial of it
on record, executed by the grantor. This memorial
does not express the consideration in or for the deed
but the act providing for registration did not require it,
and therefore no presumption adverse to a consideration
having been paid, and having been stated in the deed,
arises from the absence of notice of it in the memorial.
The possession has been consistent with the deed,
throughout. No claim adverse to it has ever been
made, and as I think that a jury would, on the question being left to them, presume without hesitation that
the deed disclosed a sufficient consideration to make it
valid as a deed of bargain and sale, I may do the same
here. More violent presumptions are often made in
support of facts which seem morally certain, and are
consistent with all else material in the particular case,
and I therefore think that the deed in question should be
treated as sufficiently established in the chain of title. (a)

(a) See Lyddoll v. Weston, 2 Atk. 19; Hillary v. Waller, 12 Vesey, 239.

As to taxes in arrear the vendee has a right to ask if there are any, and to obtain the vendor's answer, and if not satisfied with that, he may push his enquiries further, and satisfy himself; but I am not aware of any practice, and none such has been shewn, which requires the vendor to furnish evidence that no taxes are in arrear, any more than he is required to give evidence to negative the existence of any other incumbrance.

Then with regard to the cross-appeal, the only objections to be allowed, are the one referred to as No. 16, which I think must prevail, as the absence or non-production of the will has not been sufficiently excused. The evidence shews that it is probably in possession of the defendant, or of Messrs. *Bell & Crowther*, or of the Messrs. *Blake*, and no search appears to have been made with or by them for it; and exception 14, which complains that the heirship of *James McCabe* is not sufficiently established. The affidavit is defective in not stating that he was the eldest son of his father; and that his father and mother were married or lived together as man and wife, and were recognized as such.

The objection that the covenants in the missing deed of sixty years old and more, and a receipt endorsed on it for the purchase money are not shewn, is of no avail; after such lapse of time there can be no cause of action on the covenants, and no claim by way of lien or otherwise for the purchase money, even if the absence of a receipt on a deed be sufficient to put a purchaser on enquiry.

FERRIS v. HAMILTON.

Gift by husband to wife—What sufficient evidence of.

After the death of a man and his wife, a sum of money was found deposited in a bank at the credit of the wife, which had been so deposited in the lifetime of the husband, but it did not appear by whom. The wife survived the husband, and after her death a question being made to whose estate the fund belonged, *held*, that it belonged to the estate of the wife.

This was an appeal from the report of the master at Hamilton, the facts of the case are fully stated in the judgment.

Mr. *McLennan,* for the appeal, cited *Carr* v. *Carr* (*a*), *Hill* v. *Foley* (*b*), *Wildman* v. *Wildman* (*c*), *Ryland* v. *Smith* (*d*), *Coppin* v. ———— (*e*), *Richards* v. *Richards* (*f*), *Gaters* v. *Madeley* (*g*), *Lucas* v. *Lucas* (*h*), *McLean* v. *Langlands* (*i*), *Walter* v. *Hodge* (*j*), *Dummer* v. *Pitcher* (*k*), *Mews* v. *Mews* (*l*), *Hayes* v. *Kinderesley* (*m*).

Mr. *Proudfoot,* contra.

Judgment.—SPRAGGE, V. C.—The deceased *William Ferris* and his wife, the late *Mary Ann Ferris* emigrated from Ireland to this country in 1847. In Ireland he had been manager of a farm for the owner, and had some education, he could read and write, and knew something of accounts. His wife was illiterate —she could not write. He died in April, 1859, without issue, having for a number of years before his death kept what the witnesses call a grocery store, in Hamilton, and having made considerable property by his business.

Since the death of his wife, which took place in 1861,

(*a*) 1 Mer. 543.
(*c*) 9 Ves. 173.
(*e*) 2 P. Wms. 496.
(*g*) 6 M. & W. 423.
(*i*) 5 Ves. 75.
(*k*) 2 M. & K, 262.
(*m*) 2 Sm. & Gif. 197.

(*b*) 1 Ph. 404.
(*d*) 1 M. & Cr. 53.
(*f*) 2 B. & Ad. 447.
(*h*) 1 Atk. 271.
(*j*) 2 Swanst. 104.
(*l*) 15 Beav. 532.

a question has arisen between the next of kin of the husband, and the next of kin of the wife, in regard to two sums of money of $800 and $1300 respectively.

In regard to the first sum, the evidence is, that it was deposited in the name of the wife in the bank of British North America at Hamilton, on the 10th of February, 1857. There is no direct evidence as to whose money it was, or by whom it was deposited ; we merely find a sum of $800 deposited at that day in the name of Mrs. *Ferris*, and that it remained so deposited with the interest accumulating upon it until after the death of *Ferris*, when, on the 25th of March, 1860, it was drawn out by the widow, with $80 of interest, which had accrued due upon it, and was re-deposited by her in the same bank on the same day. *Ferris* brought to this country about £100. His wife has stated that she had no money of her own. The money deposited was either a sum deposited by some third person for the benefit of the wife, or money to which she was in some way entitled ; or else money of the husband. It was probably the latter, and probably also derived from the profits of the business, for the widow appears to have spoken to various persons of being left well off by her husband, but never, so far as appears, has spoken of deriving means from any other source.

Mr. *Proudfoot* for the next of kin of the husband contends that the inference is, that it was money of the husband, and that it was deposited by the person in whose name it was deposited. I think, from the evidence, with Mr. *Proudfoot*, that it was probably the money of the husband : but I think that the inference is that it was deposited by him. The presumption would be, I think, that the money was in the possession of the owner of it, and that the disposition that was made of it was made by the owner. I cannot presume either that she wrongfully obtained her husband's money, or wrongfully deposited it in her own name.

It was money to which she was beneficially entitled, and was deposited in her name, and never reduced into possession by the husband, it would fall within *Gates* v. *Robinson* (a) and *Wildman* v. *Wildman*, and cases of that class, and clearly belong to the widow; but that it is so is merely a surmise, and the evidence leads me to think it improbable. I think I must take it to be money of the husband deposited by him in the name of the wife; and the question is, whether the act of the husband is sufficient to establish a gift to the wife. The opinion of the master is against the claim of the wife's next of kin.

The money deposited, immediately upon the deposit being made, ceased to be the money of the depositor or of any one but the bank. It became a debt due by the bank—a mere chose in action to those entitled to it— *Carr* v. *Carr* : in the language of Lord *Lyndhurst* in *Foley* v. *Hill*, a loan to the banker.

In *Pitcher* v. *Dummer*, and *Dummer* v. *Pitcher* it was held that a transfer of stock in the funds, by a husband into the joint names of himself and his wife, the stock standing in their joint names at the death of the husband was a good gift to the wife. It was contended in that case that there was no effectual gift, because it was in the power of the husband to re-transfer the stock into his own name. Lord *Brougham* called that contention a fallacy, observing : " The testator's powers may have continued, but in what capacity ? as husband in the exercise of his marital right. Then suppose it to be admitted that he might have reduced the stock (a chose in action) into possession by having had it re-transferred into his own name during his life-time, still the argument is not at all advanced, for it is not pretended that any thing was done after the first transfer, the stock standing in the joint names at the date of the will, and

---

(a) M. & W. 423.

at the death of the testator." This will be found
material in considering the case of *Mews* v. *Mews*, to
which I will refer presently.

Hayes v. *Kinderesley*, before Sir *John Stuart*, was
also a cause of a transfer of stock, in which the same
principle was recognised ; though the Vice-Chancellor
held that the presumption which would arise in favour
of the wife was rebutted by circumstances.

Mews v. *Mews* was a rather peculiar case, *William* and
John Mews, brothers, were farmers. The plaintiff *Harriett*
was the wife of *William*, *John* was a bachelor, they all lived
together, and *William's* wife kept the house, and super-
intended the management and sale of the butter, eggs,
and poultry. She received the proceeds of the sale of
these articles, and placed the profits to her own credit in
the hands of Messrs. *Eastman* and *Hill*. She set up
that in the part of the country where the farm was
situate it was the custom that the profits from the
sale of these articles should belong to the farmer's wife
for her separate use, and that *John Mews*, as well as
her husband, had verbally agreed that she should retain
such profits. As to the custom, it was not proved, and
there was conflicting evidence as to its being a common
practice; there was evidence, however, that the proceeds
of such sales were not entered in the family accounts,
and that when either of the brothers received the proceeds of such sales it was handed to *William's* wife. The
Master of the Rolls thought the evidence insufficient,
at the same time adopting the language of Sir *Thomas
Plumer*, in *Walter* v. *Hodge*, that in negativing the claim
he did not negative the proposition that in equity a
gift by a husband to his wife may under circumstances
be valid, and observed that if the husband had himself
deposited the money with bankers, or with *Eastman*
and *Hill* as *quasi* bankers, stating that they were to hold
it for his wife, that would probably have been sufficient.
He laid stress upon a circumstance which appeared in

the evidence, that the husband upon his death-bed treated the property as his own, desiring his son and executor to take the money out of the hands of *Eastman* and *Hill*, and place it where it should be safe, and to do the best he could with the money for his mother. Sir *John Romilly* thought this inconsistent, and irreconcileable with the notion that the husband believed he had done any act by which he had divested himself of the control of the money. I confess I find it difficult to see how this opinion of the husband, evidenced by such conduct, could affect the gift. In *Lucas* v. *Lucas* similar conduct on the part of the husband was held by Lord *Hardwicke* to make no difference. At all events the case before me differs from *Mews* v. *Mews*, and resembles *Pitcher* v. *Dummer* in that, there was no conduct on the part of the husband after the gift, or supposed gift, to indicate an opinion on his part that an effectual gift had not been made, or an intention on his part in the exercise of his marital right to make any change in it.

I cannot distinguish this case in principle from *Dummer* v. *Pitcher*. In both cases a chose in action was placed by the husband in the name of the wife. In the one case a debt from the Crown; in the other, a debt from a bank; the one being a transfer, the other a deposit, can make no difference, as the intention is equally evident from both.

I agree that the act evidencing the intention must be clear and unequivocal, but the mere transferring of a chose in action was held sufficient in *Pitcher* v. *Dummer*, was thought sufficient in *Hayes* v. *Kinderesley*; and in *Mews* v. *Mews* Sir *John Romilly* suggested that a deposit of money with bankers by a husband, and in the name of his wife, would probably be sufficient to constitute a gift for the wife. I think the evidence sufficient in this case.

I think the master's finding in regard to the other

sum of money, the $1300 is right. There is no evidence to establish it as a gift. I have no doubt that it was the profits of the business carried on by the husband—the only fact is that it was in the house when the husband died, and came into the possession of the wife—how, or whether before or after the death of the husband, does not appear. There is no evidence to establish a gift as to that sum of money.

JURY v. BURROWES.

Specific performance—Principal and agent.

The owners óf several lots of land employed an agent to sell them, and for the purpose of enabling the agent to effect sales delivered to him blank forms of agreement, signed and sealed by them, leaving it necessary for the agent to insert only the name of the purchaser, the property sold, and the amount of purchase money to be paid; at the same time verbally instructing the agent to reserve all pine timber fit for sawlogs upon effecting any such sales. The agent sold one of the lots, and, after filling in the necessary blanks, delivered to the purchaser one of the agreements, without any reservation of timber, and the vendors subsequently refused to adopt the sale without such reservation being made; and commenced felling timber upon the land. Upon a bill filed by the purchaser for a specific performance of the contract before the time limited by the instrument for its completion, the court declared that the writing so delivered to the plaintiff contained the true agreement between the parties, leaving it to the vendors to enforce any claim they might have against their agent for having acted in breach of their instructions; and ordered the defendants to pay the value of the timber cut and removed by them together with the costs of the suit.

Statement—The facts of the case appear in the head note and judgment.

Mr. *D. G. Miller*, for plaintiff.

Mr. *Strong*, Q. C., and Mr. *Richardson*, for defendants.

Judgment.—VANKOUGHNET, C.—At the close of the argument in this case I expressed my opinion that the agreement made by *Muma*, the agent of the defendants, with the plaintiffs was to sell to the latter the lot in question, without any reservation of the standing timber fit for saw-logs, and to that opinion I adhere.

The evidence of the plaintiffs' witnesses is clear upon the matter, and *Muma* himself will not swear positively that it was otherwise. The question remaining for consideration after the argument was, whether or not *Muma* as agent had authority to sell for the defendants without making this reservation. It appeared that the defendants being the owners of several lots of land, had employed Mr. *Muma* as their agent, to sell them on the best terms he could obtain, and to enable him to do this they signed printed forms of agreement for sale and purchase, and put their seals to them, leaving blank the names of the purchasers, the purchase money, and terms of payment, and the description of the land; and entrusted these to *Muma* to fill up and deliver to the purchasers on making bargains with them. By this means they put it in the power of the agent to deceive either themselves or the purchaser by exceeding any verbal instructions which he might have received from them, fettering his discretion.

One would think that in all common fairness any loss arising from this cause should fall upon the party who has enabled his agent to occasion it, and not upon the innocent purchaser dealing in good faith upon the terms of the contract he had obtained from the agent. Authority is to be found, however, for saying that the purchaser runs the risk of this excess of power by the agent; and the case of *Taylor* v. *The Great Indian Peninsula Railway Company* (a) is to this effect.

If an agent has nothing to shew but his mere verbal instructions, the party dealing with him, if he does not choose to enquire of the principal, places his confidence in the agent and must take the consequences. If the agent has written powers they of course will govern; but when the agent is entrusted with his principal's name as in this case, a layman at least may very reasonably suppose that everything has been entrusted to his discretion, or that the principal is willing and prepared to abide by his agent's act.

(a) 5 Jur. N.S. 1087.

The evidence as to the agent's authority here is furnished by himself. He says that when there was any pine timber fit for saw-logs he was to reserve it from sale for the defendants, who were owners of mills for the manufacture of logs into boards; but the instructions on this head do not appear to have been very precise, for he says again, that it was the understanding between him and the defendants that such reservation was to be made. Certainly this was a very loose arrangement, but coupled with the great power and latitude of discretion which the entrusting him with these blank agreements implied, I take and construe the evidence to mean this: that while the defendants wished the trees fit for saw-logs to be reserved, their agent *Muma* was entrusted with the discretion of saying on what lot of land it would be in his judgment proper or of importance to reserve them, and that the defendants intended to be bound by his exercise of judgment thereon; that there was no absolute prohibition to him from selling a lot on which a pine tree might be growing, but that the matter of reservation as well as of price was left to his judgment. This being so, I am to enquire what took place on the sale, and I find that the plaintiffs, or rather those acting for them, said to *Muma* that they would not buy the lot if there was a reservation of any of the standing timber; and that *Muma* in reply said that he had been over the lot; that it was pretty well cut over, and that there was little or no timber on it worth reserving, and upon this a provision previously written into the agreement, reserving the standing timber, was struck out, and thereupon the plaintiffs bought the land, and on the faith of the agreement so constituted entered into possession of it, and have been improving it. I think the defendants cannot now dispute this agreement, and that if their agent has been guilty of any negligence to their interest in not reserving timber, they must look to him to repair it, and in this way justice will be better secured than by depriving the plaintiffs of what they fairly bought.

As to the objection that the plaintiff *White* is no party to the written agreement which represents the true bargain màde at the time with the agent, it is proved in evidence that though his father executed it in his own name, he in truth did so for the son; that the latter with the other plaintiff who is a party to it, having been substituted for his mother, who also originally executed it for her son, have been in possession of the land, improving it; that it was well known to the defendants that the land was purchased by and for them; that the defendants have recognised them as the purchasers, and through their agents received payments from them as such, and that the plaintiff *White* executed in his own name with the other plaintiff what they both were untruly told was a duplicate of this agreement, and was represented to them to be intended as such at the time they signed it. I think that *White* should execute the agreement in his own name, so that the defendants may, if they wish, have their legal remedy upon it against him, and the better way will be for him and the other plaintiff to execute a duplicate of the agreement held by them and deliver it to the defendants, or deposit it in court for them. I think there should be a decree for the plaintiffs, with costs, declaring that the agreement as contained in the paper writing held by them is the true agreement between the parties, and should be executed accordingly, and that the defendants should account for all the timber cut and carried away by them since the date of that agreement, and pay the same to the plaintiffs.

LAWRASON v. FITZGERALD.

Mortgage—County court—Costs.

The act giving to county courts equitable jurisdiction, in relation to mortgages when the sum due does not exceed fifty pounds, does not apply when the defendant is resident out of jurisdiction.

This was a motion for decree in a foreclosure suit.

Mr. *Fitzgerald*, for the plaintiff, asked that the usual decree might be drawn up.

Mr. *S. Blake*, for the defendants, objected to the decree giving the plaintiff his costs of the suit, as the sum due was shewn to be only £42, and the bill should therefore have been filed in the county court.

Mr. *Fitzgerald.*—The act, (16 Vic., ch. 119 ; Con. Stat. U. C. ch. 15,) restrict proceedings in that court to defendants resident within the jurisdiction, for the second section (Con. Stat. sec. 34) provides expressly that "any person seeking equitable relief enter a claim against any person from which such relief is sought, with the clerk of the county court of the county *within which* such last-mentioned person resides." And the orders of this court for the regulation of the practice of the inferior courts do not provide any machinery whereby proceedings can be taken against a person resident out of the jurisdiction.

VANKOUGHNET, C.—Let the usual decree be drawn up ; and let an enquiry be made whether a sale or closure will be more beneficial for the infant defendants. And if it shall appear that a sale is proper, order a sale without requiring any deposit.

McAlpine v. How.

Parol evidence—Written instrument.

Parol evidence to vary the terms of a written instrument rejected
although the court considered it doubtful if the written document
contained all the terms of the agreement between the parties.

An assignment of a bond for the conveyance of land was made from
a debtor to his creditor, by a writing absolute in form, but the
creditor at the same time executed a memorandum shewing such
assignment to be by way of security only. Subsequently the debtor
executed another absolute assignment without receiving back any
such memorandum from the creditor. The court, under the circumstances, refused to act upon parol evidence that the assignor
was to be interested in the proceeds of the land over and above
his indebtedness to the assignee.

Statement.—The bill in this cause was filed by *Alexander McAlpine,* as administrator of *Duncan McAlpine,*
against *William How,* the younger, *George How* and
Edward How, praying under the circumstances stated
in the bill, and which are set forth in the judgment
of the court, a declaration that the defendants were
trustees for the estate of the intestate *Duncan McAlpine*
of the excess of the moneys realised by them under and
by virtue of the arbitration and bonds in the bill mentioned, over and above the indebtedness of the intestate.

The defendants answered the bill, denying any action
by them as trustees for the deceased *Duncan McAlpine.*

Mr. *Hodgins,* for plaintiff.

Mr. *A. Crooks,* Q. C., for defendants.

Shaw v. *Jeffrey,* (a) *Tapply* v. *Sheather* (a) *Lincoln*
v. *Wright,* (c) were referred to.

Judgment—Esten,V.C—The facts of this case are, that
the late *Duncan McAlpine* purchased the lot number 31,
in the 8th concession of the township of Erin, of *Achsa
Ann Forester,* and *Jeremiah Forester,* the executrix and

(a) 13 Moo. P. C. 432.   (b) 8 Jur. N. S. 1163.
(c) 5 Jur. N. S. 1142.

executor of *John Forester*, deceased, and received a bond
for a conveyance on payment of the purchase money—
£225. *Duncan McAlpine* paid about £150 of the purchase money, and entered into possession, and made
large improvements. He became indebted to divers
persons, and amongst others to one *Worts*, and to the
defendants, who carried on business as merchants at
Hillsburgh, in partnership. On the 2nd of November,
1857, he made an assignment of the *Foresters'* bond to
the defendants in order to secure his indebtedness to
them. The assignment was absolute in form, but it was
accompanied by a memorandum under the hands of
the defendants which shewed it to be a security. The
defendants having been advised that this assignment,
which was not under seal, was for that reason invalid,
and also that *A. A. Forester* and *Jeremiah Forester* had
no power of sale over the land comprised in it, applied to
McAlpine to affix his seal to the assignment, which he
refused. After the expiration of the nine years allowed
to *McAlpine* for payment of his purchase money, he being behind in his payments, received notice from Mrs.
Forester, the surviving executrix, that he must pay rent
or purchase money, or submit to be dispossessed. Under these circumstances he consulted the defendants;
and their father *William How*, senior, who in a great
measure managed their business, told him that a suit in
Chancery was his only remedy. *Duncan McAlpine* had
owned a clergy reserve, which he had also sold and apparently conveyed, to one *Geachern*, who had mortgaged
it to a person of the name of *Young*, to secure £81.
McAlpine held *Geachern's* notes for the purchase money,
or the balance of the purchase money, which he had
agreed to pay, to the amount of £500, and was considered to have a lien for it upon the land, in preference to
Young's mortgage. Besides these notes secured, if they
were secured by this lien, *McAlpine* had no property
but his interest in the land purchased from the *Foresters*. On the 19th of January, 1860, *McAlpine* executed a second assignment to the defendants of the

Foresters' bond,and upon the intention and effect of this assignment the whole question in this suit turns. It is absolute in form like the former one, but was accompanied by no memorandum stamping it with the character of a security. The consideration mentioned in both the assignments is the same, namely, £200, and both assignments contain a power of attorney to the defendants to proceed in the name of *McAlpine* for the recovery of what was secured by the bond, but in the first assignment it is added, "at the cost of *McAlpine*," which is omitted in the second assignment. There is a parenthesis in the second assignment immediately following the mention of the £200, to the effect that if the £200 should exceed *McAlpine's* debt to the defendants, and interest, and the costs of proceedings on the bond, the balance should be refunded to him. This parenthesis appears to me to be in a different handwriting from nearly all the rest of the assignment,and to have been inserted in a blank space left for the purpose, when the assignment was prepared. At the time of executing this assignment *McAlpine* owed the defendants£100 16s.3d. This debt was afterwards increased to £283. Proceedings were commenced in Chancery by the defendants against Mrs. *Forester*, on the bond, by a bill, which prayed a specific performance of the contract, or in default, that the moneys paid might be repaid, and compensation for the improvements. The suit was soon settled, Mrs. *Forester* agreeing on surrender of the land to repay the moneys paid and the costs of the suit, and the value of the improvements, which it was referred to arbitrators to settle. This occurred in the autumn of 1860. The arbitrators awarded $1,000 as the value of the improvements, and in the whole $168.00 was paid by Mrs. *Forester* to the defendants during the spring of 1861. *McAlpine* was a defendant in the suit, but was no party to the arbitration. He was aware of it, however, and acquiesced in it, pointing out the clearings to the arbitrators, when they went to view the property, and readily giving up possession at the time appointed, until which time he had been continually in possession. About this time *Green,* who held a note for £45, made by one of the sons of *McAlpine,* offered it to the defendants at a reduction of £10 ; they refused to receive it, but said if he would obtain an order from *McAlpine* they would take it. *McAlpine* refused to give the order. About the same time also, but after the payment of the award, the defendants paid about £30 to one *McAllister,* to the order of *McAlpine.* About the time of the arbitration *McAlpine* must have reached the limit of the £200; and at the time of the payment of the money on the award he must have owed the defendants about £27, after receiving credit for the £200, and he was afterwards permitted to increase his indebtedness to them by about £56, in addition to which they were certainly willing to pay *Green* £35 for his note, upon an order being obtained from *McAlpine,* and perhaps the £30 paid to *McAllister* was also in addition. It was also about the time of the payment of the money on the award that the conversation occurred between *Edward How* and *McMillan,* which is mentioned by that witness, and is indeed placed beyond doubt by the testimony of *Edward How* himself, and which forms perhaps the most material piece of evidence in the cause. *Parkinson* and *McKinnon* also mention a conversation with Mr. *How,* senior, which might be to some extent material.

In the course of the year 1860 three suits were instituted against the defendants by three different creditors of *McAlpine,* with the view of fastening upon the surplus of the moneys paid under the arbitration which should remain after satisfaction of the defendant's debt. In their answers to these bills the defendants represented both assignments as absolute both in form and fact, and made with the same intent ; and that the second was obtained because the first wanted a seal. Mr. *Guthrie,* the clerk of the defendants' solicitors, states that the answers were prepared from written instructions, from which, and from the form of the instruments he judges that they were made with the same intent; and that the answers were transmitted to Erin to be perfected.　In the autumn of the same year Mr. *How*, senior, at the instance of *McAlpine*, addressed a letter to *Taylor*, proposing either that *McAlpine* should pay him the £81 due to him from *Geachern*, and that he should transfer the clergy reserve to *McAlpine*, or that he should pay to *McAlpine* the amount due to him from *Geachern*, and retain the reserve.　This letter seems immaterial, and is at all events no evidence against the defendants.　In an action brought by *Worts* against *McAlpine* in this autumn, he was examined under a judge's summons before his Honour Mr. *McDonald*, the judge of the county court of the county of Wellington, as to his property.　Upon this occasion *McAlpine* handed to the judge a written statement, which had been prepared by Mr. *How*, senior.　He was also examined orally by the judge, who was satisfied from the tenor of his answers, and the statement, and from his demeanour, that he was interested in the surplus of the moneys paid under the award, and was endeavouring, in collusion with the defendants, to conceal and withhold this interest from his creditors, and he accordingly ordered a *capias ad satisfaciendum* to issue against him.　Upon this point it may also be remarked, that neither the statement of *McAlpine*, prepared by *How*, senior, nor *McAlpine's* answers to the questions, nor the conclusion of the learned judge, however well-founded, are any evidence against the defendants.

Upon these various facts and evidence the plaintiff's counsel contended with much force that the court must arrive at the conclusion that the second assignment, as well as the first, was intended by way of security, and not as an absolute sale.　With the exception of the conversation between *McMillan* and *Edward How*, I think the circumstances which are relied upon, however material they might be as corroborative of other evidence of a more decisive character, would be insufficient to reduce this instrument to a mere security. Upon the effect of this conversation I have felt much doubt and hesitation. The fact of the conversation and its tenor is placed beyond doubt by the testimony of *Edward How* himself, in addition to which *McMillan* was a witness in every way worthy of credit. It is quite certain that *Edward How* told *McMillan* in the month of February or March, 1861, when the moneys payable under the award were all, or nearly all, paid, and when *McAlpine* must have owed the defendants about £27, after receiving credit for the £200, that enough would be coming to *McAlpine* to purchase a farm, provided he would retire into one of the back townships. At this time nothing was coming to *McAlpine* of the £200 to be paid for the assignment, for he had exhausted and overstepped it. The statement cannot be reconciled with any other state of things than *McAlpine* being entitled to the surplus of the arbitration moneys, after paying the debt of the defendants. *How* does not say that he could not answer the question, as he was ignorant of the state of *McAlpine's* account. Such an answer would not have excited surprise, as the partners seem to have been ignorant of the state of the accounts generally, which were managed by their book-keeper, and perhaps their father. But the answer which he does make argues an acquaintance with the state of *McAlpine's* account. It is impossible to suppose, if he knew any thing of the state of his account, he could have imagined that enough was coming to *McAlpine* of the £200 to purchase a farm any where. The evidence afforded by this statement, which was made, *McMillan* says, not once, but many times, and probably in conversation with others or another of the defendants, and always to the same effect, and as a fact is incontestable, appears to me so strong that it has almost convinced my mind of the truth of the plaintiff's contention. Upon reflection, however, I think it insufficient to overbear the effect of the form of the transaction. I cannot imagine why if the transaction were the creation of a new security, and not a purchase, it should not have assumed that form. Upon a former occasion a memorandum was delivered to *McAlpine*, indicative of his right of redemption. The parties, therefore, were alive to the importance of such a provision. Not only is any such provision omitted in the latter transaction, but the statement with regard to the payment of the consideration is utterly incompatible with the fact of this instrument being a mere security, and the variation of phraseology as regards the cost of the proceedings agrees with this view. The amount of the consideration—£200—seems to me to exceed what the interest could be fairly considered worth. I do not think *McAlpine* could have recovered either at law or in equity the value of his improvements.

The institution of the suit was a clear stratagem, which had the effect, no doubt intended, of frightening Mrs. *Forester*, and bringing her to terms. The only way of reconciling the form of the instruments with the fact of its being a security is to suppose that it received that form in order to deceive and defraud creditors. But this is a construction which the plaintiff cannot be heard to propound. In fact it would be suicidal, and therefore it is not enunciated in the bill; nor can the plaintiffs be permitted to advance it as an answer to the inference drawn from the form of the instruments. Upon the whole, I think the safest conclusion at which I can arrive, although with much hesitation, is, that the evidence is insufficient to support the contention of the plaintiffs, and therefore, that the bill must be dismissed with costs.

The plaintiff being dissatisfied with the decree drawn up upon this judgment, set the cause down to be reheard before the full court. When, after argument, the decree was affirmed,

VANKOUGHNET, C.—Stating, upon a consideration of all the facts, I think the decree should be affirmed. It is not alleged nor shewn that the intestate was imposed upon by the form of the instrument which was signed, and the agreement on the face of it expresses that the difference between his indebtedness to the defendants and the sum of £200 as the consideration for the assignment is to be accounted for to him. It is not the case of an assignment for a certain sum merely, silent as to any trust, but the trust is expressed by the assignment itself. If there were any other understanding or agreement between the parties, and there is evidence to shew that the defendants considered there was, it was kept secret at the time, and most probable for the purpose of deceiving and defrauding creditors. *McAlpine*, and those claiming under him, cannot take advantage of this, and as against his own oath on his examination before the judge of the county court, he ought not to be now heard to say that the agreement which he signed does not express the truth.

Judgment.—ESTEN, V. C., retained the opinion expressed by him on the original hearing.

SPRAGGE, V. C.—After a good deal of hesitation and doubt in my mind as to the correctness of the defence raised by the answer in this cause, I have come to the conclusion that the proper course is to affirm the decree which has been drawn up.

Per Curiam.—Decree affirmed with costs.

HENDERSON v. DICKSON.

Specific performance—Agreement to add interest to principal.

Where, by the terms of a contract for sale and purchase of land, it was stipulated that in the event of interest on the unpaid purchase money being unpaid at the end of each year, the same should be added to the principal, and the purchaser filed a bill praying for a conveyance upon payment of the amount of principal and simple interest only : the court refused to decree specific performance, except upon the terms of payment of the interest, according to the stipulation in the agreement ; and *semble*, that he would in like manner have been bound to pay this amount, if the bill had been filed by the vendor, seeking to enforce the sale.

The bill in this case was filed by *Thomas Henderson*

against *William Dickson*, setting forth that in November, 1845, the plaintiff agreed to buy from the defendant 100 acres of land in the township of Dumfries, being the north half of lot No. 30, in the 10th concession of that township, for the sum of £268 5s. 2d., payable £50 down; and that a written bond or agreement was signed by the parties, whereby the defendant agreed to convey on payment of £218 5s. 2d., with interest at 6 per cent. per annum, from the 1st of January, 1845.

The defendant answered the bill, setting up that by a bond executed by the plaintiff, and given to the defendant, it was stipulated that in the event of the interest on the £218 5s. 2d. being unpaid as it became due, that it should be added to the principal, and form part of the purchase money of the land.

Upon the coming in of the defendant's answer, the plaintiff amended his bill, setting up that such provision for compound interest had been introduced without his knowledge or assent, he being an uneducated person, and unable to read writing; and under any circumstances he resisted such claim of the defendant, contending that the stipulation was in the nature of a penalty only, and that, as such, this court would not enforce it. The defendant, on the other hand, contended that the stipulation for such payment of compound interest was the deliberate act of the plaintiff, and that it was not to be looked on as in the nature of a penalty, from which this court would relieve the party.

Mr. *Fitzgerald* for plaintiff.

Mr. *Strong*, Q. C., for defendant.

SPRAGGE, V. C.—In this case the plaintiff, a purchaser of real estate from the defendant, files his bill for specific performance of the contract. The contract of sale consists of two instruments, one an agreement *inter partes*, reciting that the defendant had agreed to sell, upon payment of the purchase money, according to the terms of a bond of the same date, made by the plaintiff to the defendant, and agreeing upon payment of such purchase money to convey ; the other is the bond for payment of purchase money, and contains this proviso, " but if the said interest is not paid annually, then the same shall be added to the principal at the end of each year." The purchase money has, from time to time, been considerably in arrear, and the defendant claims in accordance with the provision. This the plaintiff disputes, and asks for specific performance of the agreement upon payment of the purchase money, with simple interest only. The position of the plaintiff appears to me to be open to more than one objection : in effect, the plaintiff asks that his contract be executed with a variation, and that a variation in his own favour, and which he cannot say is incapable of being performed by him. I think the principle upon which specific performance is decreed is against this. (*a*) Further, specific performance will only be decreed when the court can perform the whole contract. In the words of Lord *St. Leonards*, in *Gervais* v. *Edwards*, (*b*) "The court acts only when it can perform the very thing in the terms specifically agreed upon," (subject to the obvious qualification that the party seeking specific performance may forego stipulations for his own benefit, which the court cannot enforce.) Suppose that part of the contract which the plaintiff says ought not to be executed by him, cannot be performed, the doctrine will apply, or, on the other hand, if it can be enforced or exacted, as a condition his objection fails. The plaintiff's objection happens to be to only a comparatively small part of what he contracted to pay, but it might have been to the whole interest, or to a portion, or even the whole of the principal : as to which he might say that upon grounds of public policy, or for some other reason, it ought not to

---

(*a*) Nurse v. Lord Seymour, 13 Bea. 254.   (*b*) 2 D. & W. 80.

be exacted from him. If such a position were sustainable a party might come on the ground of hardship, and ask for specific performance, upon his performing so much of his part of the contract as might be reasonable. The plaintiff asks that one term of the contract which he has stipulated to perform should be stricken out ; and that without his performing it the other party to the contract should be decreed to perform the whole of what he contracted to perform. I think there is no precedent for such a decree. The rule which prevailed in this court that a mortgagor, where the mortgage was tainted with usury, was relieved in equity, upon payment of legal interest only, does not apply. The mortgage was absolutely void by statute, and the court might have been considered as doing rather a strong thing to restore the legal estate except upon payment of debt and legal interest: to require payment of the usurious interest, would have been practically to contravene the statute, and be at variance with the principle of the court, to protect the mortgagor from oppressive bargains.

I think, therefore, that the purchaser coming for specific performance can only obtain it by paying to the vendor all that he contracted to pay. Were the position of the parties in this court reversed, and the vendor plaintiff, I am not clear that he could not enforce payment according to the terms of the contract. The stipulation objected to is not void, and the rule against it goes, I think, no further than this, that the courts will not enforce it, where he has been made on a loan of money. *Ex parte Bevan* (a) which was a case, and I think the rule has not been enforced where the contract has been for other than a loan of money. In Mr. *Coote's* work (b) it is placed upon the principle that such an agreement is oppressive and unjust, and tending to usury ; and the learned author observes that courts of equity, in cases of mortgage, protect the debtor with peculiar jealousy, against any attempt on the part of the

---

(a) 9. Ves. 223.   (b) Page 430.

mortgagee, by taking advantage of the necessities of the mortgagor, to impose on him harsher terms than the payment of principal and interest.

But these considerations do not apply to contracts for the sale and purchase of lands, and so (as I suggested at the hearing) an agreement that purchase money may carry interest beyond the legal rate of interest is not usurious—what was called respectively principal and interest being, in fact, the stipulated purchase money (a); and in the old case of *Floyer* v. *Edwards* (b), where the question arose upon a sale of goods, a point, much the same in principle as arises in this case, was decided. The goods sold consisted of gold and silver coin ; the sale was at three months' credit, and it was agreed at the time of the sale that in case the money was not paid at the end of the three months, the defendant should pay a half-penny an ounce per month until the money was paid, and that, it was contended, was usurious, and Lord *Mansfield* expressed the opinion that if the contract was within the mischief of the Statute of Anne it would be usurious, but his lordship, and the whole court held it not usurious. His Lordship observed, " Here it appears that the whole agreement was made out first, the price of the goods fixed, and a limited credit given ; but the party considered further, that perhaps punctual payment might not be made, and provided that in that case the buyer should pay him so much more."

The cases are alike in this, that in case of default, more than simple interest was payable ; the excess took a shape different from what it takes in this case ; but a shape which, if the transaction had been a loan or forbearance of money, would have been as clearly held not sustainable as tending to usury as if it had been in the form in which it is stipulated for in the contract before me.

(a) Beete v. Bidgood, 7 B. & C. 453.   (b) 1 Cowp. 112.

It may be a question, too, whether the statute 7 William IV., chapter 3, does not apply in spirit to such a case as this. Section 20 enables a jury on the trial of an issue, or an assessment of damages, upon any debt or sum certain, payable by virtue of a written instrument at a certain time, to allow interest to the plaintiff from the time when such debt or sum becomes payable. Suppose the interest computed and stated upon the face of the instrument, it would be a sum certain within the very words of the statute, as well as the principal debt, and I do not see why a jury might not allow interest upon it, if they thought fit. Suppose, further, that the contract stipulated, as in this case, that such sum should bear interest, it could not be objectionable, as tending to usury, if a jury might, with or without such stipulation, allow interest upon it. It can, of course, make no difference in principle, whether the interest is computed and stated upon the face of the instrument or not ; *Id certum est, quod certum reddi potest.*

Upon this point I would refer to the observations of C. J. *Tindall* upon the like statute in England, in *Attwood* v. *Taylor* (a).

I think that upon this bill the plaintiff can have relief only upon payment of purchase money and interest according to the contract ; and I probably should have thought the purchaser bound to pay the same, if the bill had been filed by the vendor. In my view of the case, it will be unnecessary to direct enquiries as to the alleged settlement of accounts from time to time.

The plaintiff asks for the usual reference as to title, and I think him entitled to it ; for although he tendered a conveyance for execution, it was made under peculiar circumstances. Indeed his right to an investigation is not denied.

The defendant asks for costs up to the hearing. The

(a) 1 M. & Gr. 332.

plaintiff has, in his amended bill, made charges of fraudulent conduct against the defendant, which are unsustained by any evidence. I refer to the paragraphs numbered 17, (B) 17, (C) 17, (G) and 17, (K), especially the two first. I think the evidence and the hearing were occasioned by the ground taken by the plaintiff, and in which my opinion is against him. In any event I suppose he ought to pay those costs. But it is impossible to say now how the court may deal with the costs of enquiries in the master's office, in respect of the amount due, and as to title. The defendant claims a particular amount to be due as upon an account stated and settled, which he may establish, or upon which he may fail, for I think upon that point the plaintiff should not be concluded by the evidence already taken. I think, therefore, the proper course will be to reserve further directions and costs.

The case afterwards came on to be heard on further directions before his Lordship the Chancellor, when the plaintiff was directed to pay the costs of the suit up to and inclusive of the hearing. No costs of the reference, or subsequent costs to either party.

BELL v. MILLER.

Specific performance of award.

The finding of an arbitrator when unimpeached is treated as *res judicata* between the parties to the submission.

This court, when the relief given by the award of an arbitrator is of a nature proper to be specifically performed, will decree that relief, and that too although the court cannot specifically perform some part of the award, which is for the benefit of the plaintiff, but which portion the plaintiff consents to forego.

This was a cause heard before his Honour V. C. *Spragge*, at sittings of the court at Barrie, in April, 1863. An *ex parte* injunction had been granted before the hearing, restraining the negociation of the promissory notes mentioned in the judgment.

The facts material to the present report appear sufficiently in the judgment.

Mr. *Fitzgerald*, for the plaintiff, and the defendant *Robert Bell*.

Mr. *Strong*, Q.C., and Mr. *Osler* for the defendant *Miller*.

Baker v. *Townsend*, (a) *Petch* v. *Conlan*, (b) *Lechmere* v. *Carlisle*, (c) *Wilcox* v. *Wilcox*, (d) *Nickels* v. *Hancock*, (e) *Lewin* v. *Whitly*, (f) *Fry* on Spec. Per. 415, *Russell* on Awards, 118, 483, were referred to by counsel.

Judgment.—SPRAGGE, V.C.—The bill is primarily for the specific performance of an award, and for such relief as necessarily grows out of that which is awarded; and the first point is, whether such relief is of a nature proper for specific performance. It seems to be so. It is to restrain the negociation of promissory notes, and for security for the re-conveyance of land as awarded; or for a decree for re-conveyance itself.

The award is objected to as unreasonable—as in excess of the power of the arbitrators—and as wanting in finality and certainty, and therefore as not proper for specific performance; but whether proper or not for specific performance it may still be material as a finding of facts between the parties, which they cannot afterwards controvert; and in that sense as *res judicata*. It is so treated in *Taylor* on Evidence, sec. 1565; and *Doe* v. *Rosser* (g) is an authority for the position.

(a) 7 Taunt. 422. (b) 7 Dowl. 426.
(c) 3 P. W. 24. (d) 2 W. & Tud. 345.
(e) 7 D. M. & G. 300. (f) 4 Russ. 423.
(g) 3 East, 15.

At the time of the submission to arbitration it was a matter in controversy who was entitled to the possession of certain lots in the village of Thornbury; *David Miller* had brought ejectment to recover possession, and the plaintiffs in this suit, together with a tenant of the younger *Bell*, had filed their bill in this court to stay proceedings at law, upon substantially the same grounds as, apart from the award, are the grounds upon which relief is sought in this suit. The arbitrators awarded compensation to the younger *Bell* "for the loss of the use and rent of the buildings and lots" in Thornbury, and directed that *Miller* should pay the costs of the proceedings in ejectment and in this court, thereby adjudging in favour of *Bell* upon the question of right to the possession of the Thornbury lots, as far at least as is material to this suit. The establishment of that fact is material, upon the objection to the award, that the matter in controversy arose out of an agreement having for its object to defeat creditors, and so not proper for specific performance, being against public policy. If *Bell* was not to have possession of the lots, their conveyance to him, and the giving a mortgage by the elder *Bell* as security for their re-conveyance, taken in connexion with *Miller's* indebtedness at the time, would afford room for the presumption that it was a scheme to place the Thornbury lots beyond the reach of *Miller's* creditors; but if the younger *Bell* was to have the possession, for his own benefit for the ten years, or even for a shorter period, then the conveyance and mortgage and contemporaneous papers may have been only the mode which unskilful laymen adopted for carrying out their agreement; and certainly the elder *Bell* would be more likely to give a mortgage upon his own property where his son was beneficially interested, than gratuitously to enable a stranger to defraud his creditors. It should, I think, be quite clear, clearer certainly than it is in this case, that the object of the arrangement was to defeat creditors, before the court should oppose its maxim in relation to public policy, to the assertion of a party's equitable right.

It is next contended that the award is both unreasonable and uncertain in directing such security as it requires for the release of the mortgage. It is evidently put in the shape that it is in the award, because the mortgage is made to the son of *David Miller*, who is a minor, and no doubt at the instance of *David Miller* himself, so that the difficulty of releasing it is of his own creation, but this difficulty is obviated if the court can direct the actual release of the mortgage. By the evidence in the cause, documentary and otherwise, it is clear that the mortgage was given for no other purpose than to secure the re-conveyance of the Thornbury lots, or rather their conveyance to the infant defendant *Robert Miller*, the appointee of his father. The award directs the conveyance of these lots to the infants, and the plaintiffs submit so to convey them: the object of the mortgage will be answered upon such conveyance being made, and the court can properly decree a contemporaneous release of the mortgaged premises, and a release of the mortgage or a vesting order. The father *David Miller* submits by his answer to join in a release of the mortgage.

The direction in the award that the Thornbury lots should be conveyed to the infant and not to his father is also complained of; but that as I have said was the agreement, and was so, as I have no doubt, at the instance of the father.

I think there is nothing objectionable in my proceeding in part upon the award, and in part upon the evidence in the cause. The rule that the court will not specifically perform an award unless it can perform the whole of it, must be taken with this qualification, that the plaintiff is at liberty as in the case of any other agreement, to forego any parts of it that are for his own benefit, a position established in effect in *Martin* v. *Pycroft*, (a) and so plainly reasonable as not to need any

---

(a) 16 Jur. 1125.

case to establish it. He may in this case abandon that part of the award which directs security to be given for the future release of the mortgage ; and prove independently that he is entitled to its present discharge.

I think it was within the competence of the arbitrators to award as they did in relation to the costs at law, and in this court : the matters in controversy in both were before them, and involved the question of which party, as being in the wrong, ought to pay the costs.

It seems doubtful whether it was competent to the arbitrators to award payment of the $48 mentioned in their reward : I do not see that it was a matter in controversy, and the answer sets up that it had been a claim previously adjudged upon by a court of competent jurisdiction, a division court, adversely to the plaintiff. The award is so small as scarcely to justify a reference as to the facts. I think it will be proper for the plaintiff to abandon that part of the award.

I have abstained from considering whether the younger *Bell* was or was not entitled to the possession and use of the Thornbury lots—whether the £216 for which notes were given was the price of goods sold ; or the price of goods sold, and of such possession and use of lots, because I hold that question adjudicated upon by the arbitrators, and no longer open to controversy. I have proceeded upon that point, as established beforehand, in favour of the plaintiff, and I have not thought it proper to consider as a point for consideration whether the amount awarded for compensation for the loss of possession is a reasonable or proper sum or otherwise. The account must be taken upon the footing of that being a proper sum to be allowed against the notes. The plaintiffs are entitled to their costs up to the hearing. Further directions and costs to be reserved, the plaintiff to pay the infant defendant his costs, and to have them over with their own costs against *David Miller*. I do not see that any costs have been incurred by defendant *Robert Bell*, and I do not know why he was not made a co-plaintiff.

LARKIN v. ARMSTRONG.

Trustees—Liability for acts of co-trustee— Administration suit.

The duties and responsibilities of trustees and executors considered and acted on.

Trustees, with a power of investing in real estate, purchased at the instance of one of their number a lot of land for £1200, which, upon enquiry before the master, was found not to be worth more than £900 : the master, by his report, charged the trustees with the full sum of £1200, refusing to give them credit for the £900, on the ground of collusion on the part of one of the trustees. The court, on appeal, considered that, under the circumstances, credit should be given for the value of the land, and referred the report back to the master.

This was a suit for the administration of the estate of the testator *John P. Larkin*, and a reference had been made to the master at Hamilton, who made his report thereunder. Two of the executors and trustees appealed from the report, on the grounds, amongst others, appearing in the judgment.

Mr. *Mowat*, Q. C., and Mr. *Proudfoot*, for the appeal.

Mr. *Strong*, and Mr. *Barrett*, contra.

Judgment.—SPRAGGE, V. C.—The first objection to the master's report, is his charging the defendants *Armstrong* and *Larkin* with the sum of £776 2s. 9d., under the following head of reference: "Whether the goods sold to *Boice & Co.* were sold for full value, or for the best price that could be obtained for the same, and if not what would have been a fair price for the same."

John P. Larkin, the testator, had formerly been a retail merchant, and at the time of his death was a wholesale merchant in Hamilton. The goods in question consisted of merchandize which are classed under two heads, the one, the stock of goods which was in his establishment at the time of his death; the other, goods purchased but not yet arrived. The testator died on the 27th of August, 1852, and the sale of goods took place just one month afterwards. The testator appointed his father, *Armstrong, Wright,* and *Boice,* his executors, all of them either related, or connected by marriage. *Boice's* wife was a sister of the testator and a niece of *Armstrong. Boice* declined to prove the will as he contemplated purchasing the goods; the other three executors proved. The sale to *Boice* for *Boice & Company* was made by *Armstrong* with the assent of *Larkin,* but without the assent of, or consultation with, *Wright. Wright,* as soon as he heard of the sale, remonstrated against it, as hasty and improvident. *Armstrong* is spoken of in the evidence as a man of business, *Wright* was a medical practitioner, both resident in Toronto. *Larkin,* the other executor, the father of the testator, and of *Boice's* wife, resided in Hamilton.

The sale being made by *Armstrong* and *Larkin* to a near connexion is a reason for its being scrutinised closely, and the first enquiry naturally is, whether public competition was invited, as is usual in such cases, and whether the price offered was a good price, and the price and terms such as it was for the interest of the estate to accept. It does not appear that any such enquiries were made, and it seems that public competition was not invited by advertisement or otherwise. By thus acting the executors have imposed upon themselves the task of shewing that this sale, which we cannot but regard with suspicion, was, notwithstanding, *bona fide,* and for the advantage of the estate. There is certainly a good deal to shew that the price obtained was a good one, and were it not that a higher price was offered by a Mr. *Benedict,* a point which I will notice presently, I should say that the executors have made out a case of sale at a fair price.

The sale impeached is only of the one class of goods, that designated "the old stock;" that, as well as the goods to arrive, were sold to *Boice & Co.* The latter, upon the terms that the purchasers were to meet the liabilities of the estate in regard to them; in short, to stand in the shoes of the testator, and this arrangement is approved of by all parties. The price of these goods was £4880 ; the "old stock" was sold for £2328 8s., and that price was arrived at by deducting 25 per cent. from the amount at which they appeared, upon stock being taken by the executors, that amount being £3104 10s. For the price of the stock notes were given at one, two and three years, without interest.

Stock was taken by two persons who are called as witnesses, *Stevenson* and *Quinlan,* the same persons took stock shortly before the testator's death. A portion of the stock, of the value of about £300, was of an inferior description, and was put down at what it was estimated it would bring at auction. For the rest of it the price was arrived at by adding 50 per cent. on the cost of British goods, and 20 per cent. on the cost of American goods. Some of the goods—"many of the currency goods,"—as *Quinlan* terms them, were bought in Hamilton, and at prices higher than if bought in the foreign markets. It does not appear how these were estimated in taking stock. *Stevenson* and *Quinlan* do not quite agree in their description of the goods. *Stevenson* says, "the testator had been long in business, and the stock was well assorted," and he says he thinks the goods might have been sold for cash at the price at which they were put down by himself and *Quinlan.* *Quinlan,* on the other hand, says " the prices fixed by myself and *Stevenson,* on taking this stock, were not intended to represent the cash value." * * * * "The stock was not a good one, a portion of it had been on hand for a number of years, four or five years." *Boice,* in his evidence before the master, after the bill had been dismissed as against him, confirms this ; he says, "the stock they purchased was the remains of Mr. *Larkin's* business after several years, of purchases by him, including of course some very bad lots." * * * "I cannot say what portion of the stock sold

to us was old or damaged, but there was so large a
portion old or damaged that it was a very bad bargain for
me." *Quinlan* had been for some years in the employ of
the testator and was well acquainted with his goods.

As to the point whether the sale was at a good fair
price there are several witnesses. I think *Stevenson* is
the only witness whose evidence is against the executors upon this point, and he does not say directly that
the price was not a good one ; and when he says he
thinks the goods might have been sold for cash at the
price at which stock was taken, he may be referring to
the proposed purchase by *Benedict*, though even that
was not for cash ; but his opinion is entitled to less
weight, because he assumes the goods to have been a
well assorted stock, while *Quinlan*, from his position
and experience, a better authority, shews that they were
not ; but even in his evidence in this passage : " I now
think that I did say, after the goods had been paid for,
that it was as well they had been sold." Several witnesses speak of the price as a fair, and some as a very
good, price. *Quinlan* says, " from my knowledge of this
stock I would not have given fifteen shillings in the
pound for it ; I certainly should not have given so much.
Mr. *McInnes*, who says he has had experience in the
dry goods business twelve or thirteen years, says,
"from my knowledge of his stock I would not have
given more than 15s. in the £, and I would not have
given that if the goods had been required to be removed
off the premises. It is usual in selling an old stock in
bulk to make a reduction on the cost price ; on bad
lots this reduction is made." There is probably some
mistake in the last passage. After setting out the
terms of the whole sale, of the goods to arrive, as well
as of the old stock, he says, " I think the sale would
be a fair one." *Boice* himself, who has probably some
bias in supporting the sale, but whose evidence I should
not discard, and who has had certainly the best opportunity of forming a judgment as to the goods, says, " I

think my offer of 15s. in the £ was a fair offer, and as much
as any person could afford to give; and I have often since
thought a good deal more than I should be willing to
give again." I have already quoted a passage in his
evidence in which he says, that so much of the stock
was old or damaged that it was a very bad bargain for
him. Mr. *McKenzie* says, " it is usual on the sale of
a stock of goods, old and new, in bulk, to make a reduction
on the cost price ; an ordinary retail stock is in general
well sold at 15s. in the £ at six months, without interest."
There is also the evidence of *Benedict*, who made the
offer of 20s. in the £, he says, " he had seen the stock
before *Larkin's* death, but was not particularly acquainted with it ; that he has forgotten the terms of the offer
made by himself, but thinks a sale of the whole stock,
old and new, upon the terms of the sale in question, which
he states, a fair and reasonable sale by the executors.

Upon all this evidence, I should say, apart from
Benedict's offer, that the goods in question were sold
at their value. *Benedict's* offer remains to be considered.
He made the offer in his own name alone, intending
however to associate himself with others. *Stevenson*
intimates that it was with himself, and both think that
the offer was for the goods to arrive as well as the old
stock. *Stevenson* says that he was not in a condition
himself to give security, but thinks his brother-in-law
would have become security for him to the extent of
£1000, and that *Benedict* told him he had some real
estate, and that he had about £1000. *Benedict* himself,
however, says nothing about his own means, and made
no offer of security to *Armstrong*. He was at that time
carrying on a retail business at Hamilton. I do not
see by the evidence that *Benedict's* offer was communicated to the executor *Larkin*. If it was not, *Larkin*
certainly ought not to have been charged with the
supposed loss, for the goods were sold at a fair price,
and he did not know of any better being offered.

Benedict afterwards made an assignment for the benefit

of his creditors, and the estate of *Larkin,* among other creditors, received a dividend. The date of the failure, and the amount of the dividend, are not shewn.

The notes given by *Boice & Co.* were paid at maturity, and the liabilities in respect of the goods to arrive were also met by them.

The facts then appear to stand shortly thus: two offers were made, one at 15s. in the £ on the old stock, and of 20s. in the £ on the new; the other of 20s. in the £ on the whole. Neither party offered security, and none was given. The offer at the lower price was accepted. *Prima facie* this looks like a breach of trust.

If the only thing to be considered was the price, the conclusion that it was a breach of trust would be irresistible, if, for instance, the price was to have been paid in hand; but the ability to meet the payments was a very important consideration, and herein the business capacity, as well as the means of the proposed purchasers, was to be looked to. It was necessary to the estate not only that the old stock should be paid for, but that the estate should be protected from the liabilities to which it was subject, in respect of the goods to arrive. It being shewn in evidence that 15s. in the £ was the true value of the old stock, it is fair to assume that *Armstrong* at least, and probably *Larkin,* ascertained that such was the case, he found the one offer at the true value, another at a considerable excess over the true value; would not the natural conclusion in his mind be that he who offered the excessive price was either ignorant of the true value, or made the offer from over eagerness to get into the wholesale business formerly carried on by *Larkin.* In either view he might reasonably doubt whether this high price would ever be paid, or at any rate be paid in full. And so far as we can judge by the result, *Armstrong* seems to have exercised a sound judgment in selling to *Boice & Co.* rather than to *Benedict.* It may be that *Benedict* would

not have failed in business if he had been the purchaser; but the probabilities, with such a stock as the
old stock is shewn to be, taken in connexion with his
actual failure, are rather that he would not have been
able to meet his engagements, and in connexion with
this I would observe that, in order to charge these executors, it should be shewn with a reasonable degree
of certainty that the estate has sustained loss.   Now
this assumed loss rests only upon this, that the estate
would have been paid 20s. in the £ if *Benedict's* offer
had been accepted, and that the liabilities in respect of
the goods to arrive could have been met; this I think
has not been made out, and much is shewn against it.
As an instance of the court judging the conduct and
motives of an executor leniently and even favourably.
I would refer to the case of *Blue* v.*Marshall* (a), before
L. *Hardwicke*, and *Forshaw* v. *Higginson* (b), before
the Lords Justices.   With every disposition therefore
to scrutinize closely this sale to *Boice & Co.*, I cannot
agree with the master that any breach of trust has
been shewn.   *I must allow the objection.*

The next objection to the report is in respect of the
master's finding upon the direction to him " to enquire
and report whether the lands purchased from *Duggan*
and *Moore* were a proper investment for the benefit of
the estate of the said testator, having regard to the
trusts declared in the said will, and whether the
amount paid for the same respectively was a fair price
for the same."   The first question is whether these
purchases were proper investments at all; the second,
whether, if proper investments, the prices respectively
were fair.

The will, after directing the sale of the testator's
goods and merchandise, and the getting in of his outstanding debts, directs the executors to invest the same
and all other moneys that should come into their hands

(a) 3 P. Wm. 381.   (b) 3 Jur. N. S. 476.

in payment and completion of land purchases made by him and the purchase of real estate.

The testator devises a considerable quantity of real estate, consisting for the most part of house property in Hamilton, and declares the same trust as to all in the following terms : "And the real estate so taken, purchased, and conveyed, and that above devised shall be held by my said trustees upon the following trusts and to the following uses, that is to say, to rent and manage the same, and to collect the rents and profits thereof ; and after deducting from such rents and profits all expenses of managing the trusts hereby created, to pay the remainder unto my dear wife until my daughter *Margaret Maria* shall attain the age of 21 years, for the support and maintenance of my said wife and the maintenance and education of my said daughter." It is unnecessary to consider the various limitations of the estate. In different parts of the will the testator provides for the application of the rents and profits of the estate, and the will contains a provision enabling the trustees in their discretion to sell and convey real estate from time to time to procure means for the support of his wife, and the support and education of his daughter and her issue.

The land, the purchase of which is the subject of this objection, has been wholly unproductive, with the exception of £15 rent received from the tenant of a house on the land purchased from *Duggan*. It is contended, in the first place, that the purchase of unproductive land was not a proper investment under the trusts of the will ; was, in fact, a breach of trust ; and that the trustees or some of them should be made answerable for the funds so invested.

The first of these purchases was that from *Duggan*, and was made in July, 1855, and consisted of a parcel of land on McNab street, in the city of Hamilton, having a frontage on that street of 60 feet, with a depth of about 120 feet, and having upon it a small wooden building. For this piece of land £1200 was paid in cash, being equal to £20 per foot frontage. The purchase from *Moore* was made in March, 1856, the price was £1000 cash in hand, the property purchased being also on McNab street; but, as I gather from the evidence, in a less central part of the town; the purchase was of two lots having each a frontage of 60 feet on McNab street. The master finds the sums paid to the testator's widow, from the time of his death to the date of his report, 23rd of February, 1859, amount to £2160 3s. 5d., and he finds that a proper sum for the maintenance and support of the widow, and the maintenance, support and education of the daughter, having regard to the value of the estate, the trusts declared, and to their position in life, would not be less than £500 a year; they have received at the rate of about £350 a year. I observe in this connexion that the testator bequeaths to his wife all his household effects, *with his library, horse, carriage and harness,* for her sole and only use.

I observe in the first place that the earlier of these purchases was not made until nearly three years after the death of the testator, after the trustees had had time and opportunity to ascertain the value of the estate and its annual income. If the income of the estate at that time was smaller than was needful or proper for the support of the testator's widow and daughter in such style of living as befitted their condition, the trustees having funds in their hands to invest ought in reason so to have invested it, if they could, as to have bettered the income of the estate. The solicitude of the testator for the comfortable subsistence of his wife and daughter is shown in portions of his will to which I have referred. An investment in real estate, producing income, would have carried out the testator's intention; the investments that were made have, if the master's opinion upon the subject of proper income be correct, left them with straitened means. £2200 in cash was invested in unproductive property; for I suppose the rental from the *Duggan* lot would not save it from being unproductive, taking into account taxes and other expenses. The trustees had no funds wherewith to build and so make a return in rental, and they could not grant building leases; so that the daughter being then about seven years of age, they purchased property which they might expect to lie dead upon their hands for some fourteen years; such purchases (they can hardly be called investments) seem, on the face of them, to be extraordinary.

These purchases are open to these observations: that not only were they unproductive, but were made at a high price, without due enquiry; and the purchase of the *Duggan* lot was from the son-in-law of Mr. *Armstrong*, through whose instrumentality chiefly the purchase was made. *Wright*, a co-trustee, objected at first to this purchase being made, on the ground that it was from a near relation of *Armstrong*, but *Armstrong* persisted nevertheless, and *Wright* yielded. Such a purchase ought to be jealously examined. Its being from the son-in-law of a trustee is not of itself an objection to the purchase; but *Armstrong* should be prepared to shew that he did his whole duty to the full by the estate; that he did not forget the trustee in the family connexion.

The sale of the *Duggan* lot was made through a Mr. *Spencer*, as agent for Mr. *Duggan*, and who was another son-in-law of Mr. *Armstrong*. As evidence of value *Spencer* produced to *Armstrong* a note in writing from a Mr. *Branigan*, the owner of an adjoining lot, stating £22 10s. per foot as his price for his lot. The only person who appears to have been consulted by *Armstrong* and probably by *Larkin* also, was Mr. *Freeman*, of Hamilton. He was consulted as to the power of the trustees to invest in that particular lot, and advised that they had the power; that the lot was a valuable one, and the investment a good one, taking all things into consideration. Mr. *Freeman* says that he considered the question (the objects of the trust, as I understand) a good deal, and did not think it free from doubt; he says further that he thought that for the purpose of leasing at a ground rental the investment was a good one, not meaning, however, as he explains, to say that it was then perhaps a good investment for an immediate income; but considering the age of the infant, then about seven, he thought that when she became of age it would be found a good investment for her interest as well as that of the widow. Upon one point Mr. *Freeman* was consulted professionally—the power of the trustees under the will— and upon that he gave an opinion doubtfully, and that, assuming that the income was sufficient for the purposes indicated by the will: it is evident that he assumed this, for he looked upon it as a good *investment for the future*, so distant a future as fourteen years, rather than for the purposes of present income. If he had been informed that a present increase of income was needed, his opinion both upon the law and upon the investment being judicious might have been different.

I cannot say that in making this investment the trustees did all that it was their duty to do. I am not prepared to say that whatever the income of the estate the trustees were authorised to bury trust funds in unproductive property. I incline to think that the *cestui que trustent* had a right to have it so invested as to yield the best income that could reasonably be obtained for an investment in the purchase of real estate of a permanent character; but as it turns out the income was insufficient, and if it was not ascertained to be so at that time, it ought to have been ascertained: time enough had elapsed for the purpose, and it is not shewn or even suggested that any thing occurred to mislead the trustees upon that point. It seems indeed that they allowed the widow to overdraw to the extent of £500 beyond her income, and to retain the amount; a pretty significant proof that she held the

income insufficient, and some proof of their assent to
its being so.   Dr. *Wright's* explanation is short, and I
have no doubt true, but it is not satisfactory; he says
his opinion was that if the rents were sufficient for
the support of the family the purchases would be prudent, and he adds his opinion now that the purchases
from *Duggan* and *Moore* were not proper investments,
because knowing now the amount of rents applicable
to the maintenance of the family, which he did not
know then, he thinks them insufficient for their maintenance.   It is said that it does not appear that productive property could have been obtained; it certainly is not shewn that it could not, or that it was enquired
after; (though something is said about a property belonging to Mr. *Kennedy ;*) but in Canada, where lands
both in town and country are more plentiful than
money, it could hardly be seriously contended that
£1200 and £1000 in cash would have to lie idle for
want of productive property in which to invest it.

I think all the trustees answerable in the matter of
these purchases; they either purchased this unproductive property with the knowledge that productive property was needful to make a sufficient income, or they
made the purchases without ascertaining that material
point.   They made the purchases without due enquiry
as to the value of the land they did purchase, and
they paid too high a price.   If they had made due
enquiry, even at Hamilton, they would scarcely have
purchased at the price they did; but they were not
limited to Hamilton, or to town property anywhere.
With £1200 and £1000 cash in hand they could have
found no difficulty in investing those moneys safely
and profitably.

I have carefully read the whole of the evidence, but I
do not propose to enter minutely into the question of
value, because I think that these purchases amounted
to a breach of trust, and that the trustees are bound
to make good the trust funds employed in making them.

If I could properly make a distinction between *Armstrong* and the other trustees, I should feel inclined to do so, especially as to the *Duggan* purchase, because I think he led his co-trustees into that purchase. But I think the *cestuis que trustent* entitled to relief against all. All knew what were the trusts of the will, and all knew, or should have known, the state of the trust fund. I think that *Armstrong* was over ready in making the purchase from *Duggan*, and that *Larkin* and *Wright* too easily allowed themselves to be led.

If the trustees are to be held answerable only for the excess in value, I should not differ from the amounts fixed by the master, except that in the *Duggan* purchase I should be disposed to allow £900 as the value, the sum which the master says he should have himself allowed, but that he thought the purchase a collusion on the part of *Armstrong*. It was not collusive on the part of the other trustees, and if they are to be charged it should not be an increased amount by reason of collusion in a co-trustee, and the same amount should be charged against all. I cannot quite agree with the master upon that point, and think £900 would have been the proper sum to be allowed to the trustees upon the *Duggan* purchase.

It is not without a good deal of hesitation that I have come to the conclusion that the trustees ought to be charged with an entire misapplication of the funds in the purchase of the *Duggan* and *Moore* properties; but the more I have considered the trusts of the will and the circumstances of the purchasers, I have felt the more that it is only just to the *cestuis que trustent* that they should be so charged. However, my opinion upon that point will not conclude the defendants; the master's report is in the alternative, and the matter will come up formally upon further directions.

1. *The first objection is allowed.*

2. *Upon the second objection it will be referred back to the master to review his report as to the amount to be allowed to the trustees on the Duggan purchase, beyond that the objection is overruled.*

BLACK v. BLACK.

Agreement to devise—Specific performance—Re-hearing—Practice.

The owner of real estate having become greatly enfeebled, and unable to wait upon himself, offered to his son that if he would relinquish his own farm, and come to reside with the father, and take care of him during his life, that he would give the farm upon which he (the father) was resident, to the son. To this proposal the son acceded, and removed with his family to the residence of the father, who it was alleged subsequently made a will, devising the property to the son ; but after his decease no trace of any will could be discovered, nor was there any satisfactory account given of it. *Held*, that there had been sufficient part performance to take the case out of the statute ; and the court ordered the heirs-at-law of the father to join in conveying the property to the son.

Where a cause is re-heard by some of several defendants, and the court affirms the decree as against them, the other defendants who did not re-hear cannot obtain any relief, although they appear on the re-hearing and ask it.

Statement.—The bill in this case was filed on the 7th of September, 1858, by *William Black*, against *Charles Black*, *John Black*, *William Vader*, and *Isabella* his wife, and others, setting forth that the late *John Black*, of Sophiasburg, the father of the plaintiff and the defendants *Charles* and *John*, had advanced and settled in life the said two defendants, by conveying to each real estate, consisting of farms of considerable value, but had never made any advancement or provision for the plaintiff, who was the youngest of the three sons, and who had remained at home working the farm of the father until upwards of thirty years old. After this plaintiff having married, removed to the township of Percy, where he purchased a farm, and settled with his family, and continued to reside there until December, 1856, when in consequence of increasing age and infirmities his father requested the plaintiff to come and reside with him, and manage his farm, the father at the same time promising and agreeing with the plaintiff, that if plaintiff did so, he would devise the farm to plaintiff; and that relying upon such promise and agreement of the father, the plaintiff acceded to such, his request, and thereupon, at much loss and inconvenience, left the township of Percy, and removed with his family and furniture to Sophiasburgh, and took possession of the farm occupied by his father, and entered upon the management and superintendence thereof, and continued to do so until the death of the father. The plaintiff, under these circumstances, contended that there was a part performance of the contract sufficient to entitle him to a specific performance thereof, if even his father had not performed his part of the contract by devising the land to plaintiff. That the father died on the 19th of January, 1857, having first duly made and published his will, devising the said lands to the plaintiff, and which will was never revoked or altered. That after the death of the father the defendant *Charles* possessed himself of the will, and either destroyed the same or kept it suppressed. That the other defendants to the cause where the daughters of the testator, and their husbands, also several grand-children of the testator, all of whom claimed such interests in the property, so devised and agreed to be conveyed, as they would respectively have been entitled to had the testator died intestate. Under these circumstances the bill prayed that the will might be established against the defendants; or that the agreement between the plaintiff and his father might be specifically performed and carried into effect, and the defendants ordered to convey to the plaintiff.

The defendants *Charles* and *John* answered jointly, admitting the will of their father, as stated in the bill; but alleging that the same had been destroyed by the testator, who alleged that he had done so in consequence of the plaintiff having left the testator without any one to take care of him. They also set up laches by the plaintiff in filing the bill, and denied the destruction or suppression of the will by *Charles*, as charged in the bill.

The other defendants also answered the bill, taking substantially the same grounds of defence as alleged by *Charles* and *John*.

The plaintiff having put the cause at issue by filing replication, evidence was taken therein before his Honor V.C. *Spragge*. One of the witnesses—*Moran*—called by the plaintiff, in his evidence swore that whilst driving with the defendant *Charles*, in his sleigh, they talked of the homestead, and of *Storm*, the tenant; "I asked him what share of the rent *William* got? He said, ' Just what I have a mind to give him ;' I said, 'What has become of the will, *Charles ?*' he said, 'That is best known to myself, I have taken care of that.'" Another witness—*Gilbert*—in the course of his evidence, stated that it had been reported that the testator had destroyed the will, and that he " asked *Charles* if such was the fact, he said it was not ; he said he was not in a capacity to do so ; that he could not see or go about to keep himself. *Charles* said he had himself taken care of the will." The effect of the evidence generally is sufficiently set forth in the judgment.

Mr. *Mowat*, Q.C., and Mr. *Taylor*, for the plaintiff.

Mr. *C. Patterson* for defendants.

For the plaintiff, it was contended, that as the will set out in the bill was admitted by the defendants *John* and *Charles*, who in the event of intestacy would be equally interested with such of the defendants as do not make that admission, the devise was sufficiently established as against all, and it would be presumed that the will had been properly executed, although only one of the witnesses, *Storm*, was now alive to give evidence ; on the principle of *omnia præsumunter rite acta*. The evidence shews that the will was understood by all to have been duly executed, and the defendants, although they allege, do not prove any revocation of it, and clearly the onus of such proof was on them.　And if revoked at all, it was so at the instance and through the persuasion of *Charles ;* and he, it is shewn, has made statements altogether at variance with the fact of a revocation by the testator ; the evidence of *Moran* and *Gilbert* is distinct upon this point ; besides it would have been an actual wrong for the testator to have revoked the will ; the presumption therefore would be against such wrongful act.

But admitting that the actual devise is not suffi-ciently established, then an agreement to devise is clearly proved, and the agreement has been partly per-formed ; so far as the plaintiff is concerned, to the full extent by his leaving his own farm, and coming to reside with the father, and manage his affairs, and on the part of the father, by an actual execution of his will.　This, therefore, is a proper case in which to en-force specific performance of the contract, although it is to devise lands.

On behalf of the defendants, it was insisted that the evi-dence did not prove that the requirements of the statute as to the execution of wills had been complied with ; and the evidence as to the will ever having been admitted by *Charles* is not distinct.　*Moran's* evidence shews that it must have been one or two years after the father's death, and it was improbable that *Charles*, after diffi-culties had arisen, would have made any such admis-sions as are to be sworn to by *Moran*.　And admitting the correctness of his evidence, the language attributed to *Charles* is ambiguous ; and *Gilbert* does not prove any express admission of the will.　It was admitted that an agreement to devise may be enforced, but the part performance shewn here was not such as to entitle plaintiff to a decree, any more than payment of purchase money would create such a right.　Besides the father stipulated for, and his object in making the arrangement was to have, the personal attendance of plaintiff and his family ; this was not afforded, and plaintiff was bound either to give such attendance or abandon the contract. Under all the circumstances appearing, the only decree the court ought to make was to dismiss the bill.

Leach v. *Bates*, (a) *Jarmin* on Wills, (b) *Goilmere* v. *Battison*, (c) *Dufour* v. *Pereira*, (d) Lord *Walpole* v. Lord *Orford*, (e) *DeBeil* v. *Thompson*, (f) *Fry* on Spec. Per. secs. 385-6-7, were amongst other authorities referred to by counsel.

Judgment.—SPRAGGE, V. C.—The plaintiff's case is rested on two grounds. The one, that he is entitled to the land in question by contract, of which he asks in substance the specific performance. The other, that he is entitled to the same land by the will of the late owner *John Black*.

The plaintiff is a son of the late *John Black*; the defendants *John* and *Charles Black* are also his sons, the other defendants being also descendants of the same *John Black*. The land in question was the homestead of the father. The mother died in December, 1856 ; the father was then, and had been for some two years previously, paralytic, and almost entirely helpless. None of his sons or daughters were living with him ; and after the death of the mother it was debated among some members of the family how the old man should, for the rest of his life be cared for, and attended to ; and the name of the plaintiff appears to have been suggested. He was a married man with a family, and was living at the time some fifty odd miles from his father, and was engaged in getting out timber, having teams and about fifteen men employed.

The alleged contract between the plaintiff and his father was, that the plaintiff should go and live upon the

---

(a) 6 Notes of cases, 699. (b) Vol. 1, p. 79.
(e) 1 Ver. 48. (d) 1 Dick. 419.
(e) 3 Ves. 402. (f) 3 Beav. 469.

homestead with his family, and should manage the farm, and take care of his father as long as he lived; and that the father on his part should leave the homestead to him by will. It is alleged that the father offered these terms to the plaintiff by writing, and that he accepted and acted upon them; but the writing, if there was any, is not before me. The plaintiff goes, failing the writing, upon parol contract partly performed.

Early in the January following his mother's death, the plaintiff removed with his family to the homestead. The agreement could not be immediately carried out in all its parts, by reason of the homestead being let to a tenant by the name of *Storm*, who with a son and daughter occupied the same house as *John Black;* but it was expected that *Storm* could be induced to leave, and as it was winter that part of the arrangement was not immediately pressing. The other parts of the arrangement seem to have been carried out, at least up to a certain date; what was to be done by the plaintiff was done, and the father on his part executed, or professed to execute a will of the homestead in favour of the plaintiff. Upon this part of the case it is not material whether there was any due execution of the will or not.

I think what was done by the plaintiff were acts of such a nature as to take the case out of the statute, and to admit evidence of what the contract really was. *Foster* v. *Hall,* (a) *Dale* v. *Hamilton.* (b) There is no doubt upon the evidence that the agreement was as I have stated it.

The father lived but a short time after this. The family came down about the 8th of January, and the father died on the 19th of the same month. It is not contended, nor could it be, that the very short period during which the plaintiff and his family were called upon

---

(a) 3 Ves. 696, 712. 　　　　(b) 5 Hare, 369, 381.

to perform their part of the bargain, is any reason against their being entitled to the performance of the other side of the bargain; but it is alleged that even during that short period the plaintiff failed to perform his agreement.

On Sunday, the 11th of January, he left the homestead, temporarily, as it would appear, and went to the place where he had been getting out timber; there was nothing unreasonable in this, especially as he had been called suddenly, and as the evidence shews, unexpectedly, to take charge of his father, and the place; nor did his father complain of it; he merely observed that *William* had gone up to Percy to see about his business, and that he expected him back on Wednesday night. When about to leave, *William* requested his brother *Charles* to write to him in case of their father getting worse; he did get worse in the night of the following Friday; *Charles* did not write to the plaintiff, or in any way notify him; the father died on the following Monday; and the plaintiff did not return till after his death.

The more serious complaint of breach of the plaintiff's agreement, is in respect of the acts of the plaintiff's wife. I think the plaintiff responsible for them though absent; his agreement being that he and his family should reside with, and take care of his father. The question is, whether her absence, with that of her children, was justifiable.

The father was of an irritable, suspicious, and violent temper, and intemperate in his habits; the excuse offered for leaving him is, that his conduct drove her from the house. On the Monday, the day after the plaintiff left, the old man missed some money, and said that the plaintiff had taken it. His wife became enraged at this, as one of the witnesses says, and said she could not live there; it would break her heart. The old man also used hard language to herself; his own account of it was, that "he had scolded and jawed her more than he ought to have done." He told her also that he had destroyed the will. She left the house, and unfortunately went to the house of *Charles Black*. The father soon discovered that no money had been taken; and he sent messages to her by three or four different persons requesting her to return. She was told that the will had not been burned; and that it was discovered that no money had been taken. I think from the evidence that she would have returned but for the treacherous advice and remarks of *Charles* and his wife. She did not, however, return until Saturday, after the father had become seriously ill; and was then treated with harshness by the old man. On the Monday, when the plaintiff's wife left, a sister of the old man was in the house; she left the same evening. On Tuesday and Wednesday a son and daughter of the plaintiff were at the house attending to the wants of the old man, as I gather from the evidence. With these exceptions, he had to depend on a son and daughter of the tenant, who attended to him.

It would no doubt have been much better if the plaintiff's wife had borne with the irritability and harsh language, and even the imputation against her husband's honesty, or to have returned when he found his accusations unfounded, that the will was not destroyed, (as I am satisfied it was not at that time,) and that he wished her to come back; but there is much to excuse her. One cannot blame her for her indignation at the imputation on her husband's honesty; and she might well withhold belief as to the will not being destroyed; for the assertion that it was not burned was an assertion that he had untruly asserted that it was; and certainly, if her absence was prolonged somewhat longer than it might have been, there appears to have been only one day, or at least two, without some member of the family being with the old man, and it was his own violence and unjust suspicions that occasioned her absence at all; and during her absence he had the same attendance that he had

between his wife's death and the arrival of the plaintiff
and his family. There is no indication of an intention
on the part of the plaintiff to do otherwise than faithfully
perform his part of the agreement. His wife would
naturally look for his return from day to day; and the
early death of the old man was not looked for; and the
bedding and furniture of the plaintiff and his family do
not appear to have been removed from the homestead;
so that all that can be urged against the plaintiff is the
temporary withdrawal of his wife without his cognisance,
and that provoked by the old man himself. As regards
the defendants, they are of course in the same position
as the father would have been if he could have been
defendant; in the same position as if he had lived, and
refused after what had occured to carry out the agreement.

It is not suggested that the agreement was not a fair
and just one under the circumstances; or that it is one
not proper to be enforced in this court. *Goilmere* v.
Battison, Dufour v. *Pereira,* recognised in Lord *Walpole* v. Lord *Orford,* and *DeBeil* v. *Thompson,* are
authorities on this point. I think therefore that supposing no will properly executed, or if executed, cancelled
by the testator, the plaintiff is still entitled to a decree
upon the grounds that I have stated.

With regard to the will itself. I do not think upon
the whole of the evidence that it is proved to have been
cancelled by the testator. But I doubt whether there is
sufficient proof of its execution so as to pass real estate.
The only evidence upon the point is that of *Wm. Storm,*
a subscribing witness. He proves the execution of the
will by *Black,* and its attestation by himself; and that
the gentleman by whom it was drawn—Mr. *Stevenson*—
since deceased, was present at its execution, but he does
not know that Mr. *Stevenson* witnessed the will. If the
will were produced, with the names of *Storm* and Mr.
Stevenson, or some other subscribing witness, the court

might properly, I think, under the cases, presume that it was duly executed, even though the attestation clause were imperfect. The cases seem to have gone that length. But here the will is not forthcoming, so that there is nothing upon the view of which we can assume that it was done as it purports to have been done ; and there is no proof in any shape of execution in the presence of more than one witness. I find in the note to Mr. *Jarman's* excellent treatise on Wills, by *Wolstenholm* and *Vincent,* this passage; "The presumption of compliance with the statutory requirements, however, will only be made when the will appears on the face of it to have been duly executed, or when (the will being lost) proper evidence is adduced of its having been so executed; and the testator's own declarations of the fact are insufficient." I quote from the text, because the authority for the last proposition—*Swaby & Tristram*—is not in the library. For the other point, that when the will is lost, proper evidence must be produced of its having been executed in accordance with the statutory requirements, cases are referred to where a lost will has been admitted to probate upon such evidence, not where the question was, whether the will could be admitted to probate upon less evidence.

There is much in the evidence to show that if the will has been destroyed, it has been by *Charles Black,* and that the maxim *omnia presumunter contra spoliatorem* would apply as against him, and consequently, that the will might properly be established against him ; and I am not prepared to say that the answer of *John* and *Charles Black* does not, as against themselves, sufficiently admit the will. But if so, it would enable me to make almost a decree, as against their interest in the property in question. I think upon the first point the plaintiff is entitle to a decree as to the whole.

The decree is to be, as against *Charles Black,* with costs ; as against the other adult defendants, without costs. The infants are entitled to their costs, and the plaintiff should have them over against *Charles*.

DECLARE, that the agreement in the pleadings mentioned between *John Black*, in the pleadings named, and plaintiff, was partly performed, so as to entitle the plaintiff to have the same specifically performed and carried into execution, and that the plaintiff is entitled to stand in the same position as if the said *John Black* had devised the lands, &c., to plaintiff: Order same accordingly.

ORDER, that the defendants do execute a conveyance of the lands, &c., to plaintiff, to be settled, &c.

REFER to master to take account of rents, &c , received by *John* and *Charles Black* ; or to fix an occupation rent, if they have been in actual possession, amount to be paid by them to plaintiff.

Plaintiff to pay infant their costs and add amount to his own costs, which are to be paid by *Charles Black*.

No costs against other defendants.

After this decree had been issued *Charles Black* petitoned for and obtained an order to have the cause re-heard before the full court, and the same was accordingly re-heard before the three judges.

Mr. *Taylor*, for plaintiff.

Mr. *Hector*, and Mr. *C. Patterson*, for defendants.

After taking time to look into the authorities, the judgment of the court was delivered by

VANKOUGHNET, C—*Charles Black* alone appeals, and as against him we think the decree should stand, and this being so, the other defendants who have not presented any petition for a re-hearing, cannot have any relief, though on the argument they sought it. They must stand or fall by the appeal of *Charles*, and unless he succeeds they cannot. As regards *Charles*, I think the decree may be sustained on two grounds : 1st, that as against him the will of the testator is sufficiently established : he admits its existence at one time, and does not account for its destruction. His language after the death of his father, as proved by *Gilbert* and *Moran,* shew either that he had possession of it or destroyed it himself. 2ndly. That he contributed to bring about the alleged breach of contract by plaintiff and his wife, by advising the latter in the husband's absence to leave the old man's house, or at all events not to return to it. This at least is the view of the evidence taken by my brother *Spragge,* before whom the witnesses were examined.

HELLIWELL v. DICKSON.

Vendor's lien—Undertaking to become security.

D. having been negociating for the purchase of a large quantity of un-patented lands, and the vendee of the Crown requiring security for payment of the purchase money, agreed upon between them, D. obtained from his father a letter addressed to himself in the follow-ing words : " If you make the contemplated purchase from *Hender-son* of wild lands, amounting to sixteen thousand acres, at six dollars per acre, and deducting all amounts due or hereafter payable on the same, I will become your security for the payment of the principal on the Crown lands, and interest : and the interest on all deeded lands —*Walter H. Dickson."* And in a postscript thereto added," I will see you have two thousand pounds to pay in cash when all papers are signed.—*W. H. Dickson.*"
Held, that this letter addressed to the son was not such a promise to provide for the payment of the £2000 cash as could be enforced by the vendor : and the vendor having conveyed the lands to the son, and taking the bonds of the father for payment of the price over and above the £2000, and without any reference to it, one of which bonds was subsequently delivered up to the father upon other security being given, and a large portion of the lands to which it referred having been conveyed by the son to the father, *held, also,* that under the circumstances the vendor was not entitled to enforce his lien against those lands in the hands of the father, for the portion of the £2000 remaining unpaid ; but that his lien therefore would attach upon the lands remaining in possession of the son, and to which alone the lien must be confined.

The bill in this cause was filed on the 26th of June, 1859, by *John Helliwell,* against *William Dickson* the younger, and the honourable *Walter Hamilton Dickson,* praying, under the circumstances therein stated, and which are fully set forth in the judgment, that the defendants might be ordered to pay to the plaintiff £1500,

with interest from the 6th day of February, 1857 ; or
that defendant the Honourable *Walter Hamilton Dickson*, might pay the same in proportion to the quantity
of land conveyed to him ; and that the whole of such
money might be declared to form a lien on all the
lands conveyed to the defendants respectively.

Evidence was taken *viva voce* before his Lordship
the Chancellor.

Mr. *Mowat*, Q. C., for the plaintiff.

Mr. *Connor*, Q. C., and Mr. *Taylor*, for the defendant, the Honourable *Walter H. Dickson*.

The defendant *William Dickson* did not appear ; and
the bill as against him had been taken *pro confesso*.

Shadwell v. *Shadwell*, (a) *Jordan* v. *Money*, (b) *Hill*
v. *Gomme*, (c) *Barkworth* v. *Young*, (d) *Bond* v. *Kent*,
(e) *Price* v. *Copner*, (f) *Mackreth* v. *Symmons*, (g)
Boulton v. *Gillespie*, (h) were referred to.

Judgment.—VANKOUGHNET, C.—This bill is filed
under the following circumstances : one *James Henderson* being entitled to certain lands under purchase from
the Crown but not patented, and to certain other lands
the title to which had passed from the Crown, agreed
with the defendant *Wm. Dickson*, jr., to sell the same to
him on the terms expressed in the following letter from
Dickson to *Henderson*, dated the 4th of February, 1857 :
" I agree to give you $6 (six dollars) an acre for your
land, in all about eighteen thousand acres ; to give you
my father as security for the payment of the interest
on the whole list of lands ; to pay £2000 (two thousand

(a) 3 Law T. 628.   (b) 5 H. L. Ca. 185.
(c) 1 Beav. 554.   (d) 4 Drew. 1.
(e) 2 Vern. 281.   (f) 1 Sim. and S. 347.
(g) 15 Ves. 329.   (h) Ante vol. viii., p. 253.

pounds) down, and other matters as agreed upon can be arranged, being of minor importance."

On the 5th of February, or subsequently, a letter of that date, signed by the other defendant *Walter Dickson,* and addressed to the defendant *William Dickson, jr.,* was produced to *Henderson* in the following words : "If you make the contemplated purchase from *Henderson* of wild lands amounting to sixteen thousand acres, at six dollars per acre, and deducting all amounts due or hereafter payable on the same, I will become your security for the payment of the principal on the Crown lands and interest, and the interest on the deeded lands.— *Walter H. Dickson.*" " I will see you have the two thousand pounds to pay the cash with when all papers are executed. —*W. H. Dickson.*" Of the sum of two thousand pounds in cash therein referred to, *Wm. Dickson* paid to *Henderson* £500 in advance,—that is, before the titles and transfers to *Dickson* were completed. The residue, *Henderson,*. subsequently to the completion of these titles and trans-- fers,. and on the 11th of May, 1859, assigned to the plaintiff as a trustee, to pay off certain debts; and to recover this sum from the defendants, or to fix it as a lien on the lands sold by *Henderson* to *Wm. Dickson,* the present suit is brought. The bill alleges that *Walter Dickson* was in partnership with *William* in the purchase of the lands, and is so liable, and it charges that if this be not made out, he is yet liable under the special engagement in his letter already set out, to make good the balance of the £2000 remaining unpaid. It is as well to say at once that the allegation of partnership on a joint purchase by the defendants is not established and indeed was on the argument abandoned. A formal agreement under seal made or dated the 6th of February, 1857, was made between *Henderson* and *Wm. Dickson,*. for the sale and purchase of the lands, in accordance with the terms of *William Dickson's* letter of the 4th of February, but not one word is said in it about the £2000, or of *Walter Dickson's* undertaking to see it paid,.

while there is express stipulation for his becoming responsible for the other payments.   Delays occur redin the clearing up of *Henderson's* title, and the preparation of the necessary deeds; and it was not till December, 1857, that the contract was finally executed by him and the defendants, with the exception of the payment of the £1500, which *Henderson* appears not to have insisted on, he passing the titles to *Wm. Dickson,* and accepting the bond of *Walter Dickson* as collateral security for payment, without it and so far as I have learned, without enquiry of *William* whether he had been provided by his father with money to make the payment.   Annexed to the agreement at the time of its execution appears the letter of guarantee of the defendant *Walter Dickson.*

Two witnesses only were examined, viz.: *Henderson* and *Walter Dickson,* son of the defendant *Walter. Henderson* swears that in the negociation with *William Dickson* for the sale of the lands he wrote to him a letter stating his terms, to which *Wm. Dickson's* letter of the 4th of February was an answer, and that this latter letter with his, if it were produced, would shew the true bargain between them.   *Henderson's* letter is not produced, and, as I am told, since the evidence was closed, cannot be found, and the defendant *Wm. Dickson* does not remember ever having received it.   No notice to produce it having been given, I could not at the examination allow *Henderson* to speak, if he were able, of its contents. These, in its 'absence, we can only speculate upon. *Henderson* also swears that he never, while he held the defendant *Walter's* guarantee, called upon him for the £1500, and never spoke to him about it, or had any conversation with him on the subject, and that the reason for this was, that the defendant *William* requested him not to do so, and that he always thought *William* would pay without putting him to the necessity of troubling the other defendant, his father.   He also stated that for his convenience, in January, 1859, *Walter Dickson* settled

27

with him the sum of £8000, which by his bond as security for his son he had become responsible to pay in respect of the Crown lands purchased by the son, by giving him, *Henderson,* a mortgage on other lands of his own, (which he *Henderson,* sold,) and by conveying to him certain lands in discharge of the bond, which was then cancelled. *Henderson* swears that during this transaction or the negociatidns attending it, nothing was said about the £1500, or the giving up of the defendant *Walter's* letter of guarantee. And here it becomes important to remark upon the conversation alleged to have occurred in reference to the giving up of that paper. Both the witnesses—*Henderson,* and young *Walter Dickson*—are of unquestioned veracity and intelligence, and yet their memories singularly fail them on this subject, or perhaps were not sufficiently stimulated as to the time of the conversation referred to.

The counsel for both the plaintiff and the defendant *Walter Dickson,* in the examination of the witnesses, assumed that this conversation took place in January, 1859, when the settlement of *Walter's* bond for the £8000 was had. That this settlement took place in January, 1859, and at the defendant *Walter Dickson's* house, in the presence of his two sons, *Walter* and the defendant *William,* is sworn by *Henderson.* The witness *Walter,* whose memory as to dates and circumstances did not seem very fixed, also swears that he was present on this occasion ; at least that he was present on the occasion of a certain settlement between his father and *Henderson,* in which his father executed a document or deed, and he states having heard certain things then said which would indicate that it was at the time named by *Henderson.* He evidently has mixed up what he saw and heard with what he had been told at other times by his father or brother, or both, for he says he took no active part in the matter, and was in and out of the room while the others were talking and negociating. He, however, swears positively to this fact, that on the occasion on

which he was present, when his father then signed a
document he, his father, said to *Henderson*, "Now I
have done all I agreed to do," to which *Henderson*
replied, "Yes," when his father said, "Now I am entitled
to that piece of paper;" *Henderson* said, "Yes," and,
as he thinks, added, "that it was in Toronto;" and that
before this nothing was said about the paper; and that
on *Henderson* leaving, his father told him to remember
this conversation. He also swears positively that this
occurred before he went to England. This paper, so
far as the evidence shews, could only have been the
letter of guarantee of the 5th of February.

Now comes a fact deposed to by the witness *Walter*,
as to which he could not well be mistaken, viz.: that he
left Canada for England in August, 1858, and did not
return to Canada until May, 1859, and yet *Henderson*
swears that this payment and cancellation of the defendant *Walter's* bond took place in January, 1859, in the
presence of his two sons *William* and *Walter*, the latter
of whom was not then in the country. Are they not
both speaking of two different occasions? It is not
shewn and was not asked where the bond of the defendant *Walter* of the 22nd of December, 1857, for the
£8000, was executed, whether in Toronto, or Niagara
his home; and *Henderson* is not asked whether on this
occasion, when the contract of purchase was by this the
last requisite act completed, such a circumstance as that
detailed by the witness *Walter* took place, though he
does swear geneally that he never did agree to give up
the defendant *Walter's* guarantee.

The defendant *Walter* in his answer sets up this conversation, and alleges it to have taken place when the
bond of the 22nd of December, 1857, was executed; and
I believe him, not merely because he swears to it, and
because his son *Walter* solemnly and positively deposes
to such a conversation, (though evidently confused as to
the time of it,) but because all the circumstances render

it probable that such a conversation did occur, and at the time stated by the defendant. Both *Henderson* and the defendant *Walter* were shrewd business men, not likely to allow the one to have the advantage over the other, and particularly in land matters, to which they were both well accustomed. If it were important for the defendant *Walter* to get up his letter of guarantee, it would have been so, when, as he supposed, he had discharged it on the execution of the bond of the 22nd of December, 1857. *Henderson* says he never claimed from defendant *Walter* the payment to be made in cash, never spoke to him about it, and *Walter* might and would of course consider on the execution of this bond, that the contract on his part was executed, and, whether or not he considered himself liable for it, that the £2000 had been arranged between *Henderson* and his son, the vendee. There could be no reason for asking to give up the paper when the bond for £8000 was cancelled, because that was an independent transaction, and having no relation to the original contract, and brought about at *Henderson's* instance, and for his convenience.

I have no doubt that young *Walter*, the witness, is mistaken as to the occasion when this conversation occurred; and in reference to this, as well as to any liability of the defendant *Walter* for this £1500, the following considerations are important to a decision. In the first place, it is to be observed that it is not likely that a vendor would ask security for a payment down, *i. e.*, cash on giving his deed. If Mr. *Henderson's* letter was forthcoming, we could see whether he had demanded this. In the next place, the letter of purchase from the defendant *Wm. Dickson* (which *Henderson* does not pretend was not in accordance with his terms, or was not satisfactory to him) says nothing about the father becoming security to see that the £2000 was forthcoming. Again, the formal agreement of the 6th of February, while it provides for obtaining defendant *Walter's* security in other respects, says nothing about this cash.

payment. Again, *Henderson* accepting £500 early
after the agreement and in advance of its completion,
makes title to and executes his contract with his vendee,
the defendant *William*, without receiving this balance
of £1500, and without saying then or ever one word
to the defendant *Walter* on the subject of it, but trusting apparently to the defendant *William* to pay it.
And then both the defendant *Walter* and his son *Walter*,
swear positively that this paper or letter, having reference to the father's responsibility for his son, was
to be given up by *Henderson ;* all, to my mind, shewing
that the vendor *Henderson* did not make or execute
his contract with the defendant *William* on the faith
of any supposed liability by the father to make good
the cash payment. If I am correct in this conclusion,
the plaintiff's case necessarily fails, because it is of its
very essence, that this postscript to the defendant
Walter's letter, written, as it was, not to the vendor,
but to the vendee, should be found to contain a promise
required by the vendor *Henderson*, or given to induce
him to act, and on the faith of which he had acted. In
my opinion it contains no such promise, it was a mere
volunteer by the father to the son. Independently of
this view is the other, that the promise itself, not made
to the party now seeking to enforce it, or to his assignor, is vague and difficult, if not impossible of interpretation. What is meant by saying, " I will see that you
have the £2000 to pay in cash when all papers are executed?" Would the placing the £2000 in *Wm. Dickson's* possession, though he never applied it as a payment, be a discharge of the promise? or could that
only be performed by seeing that the money reached
the hands of the vendor? I think without evidence to
shew how such a promise was called forth, and standing alone, it would be difficult for any court to execute
it. The plaintiff must pay the costs of the defendant
Walter Dickson, and the only relief which can be given
is to order the defendant *William Dickson* to pay the

sum in dispute, and that the same shall form a lien on the lands by him purchased other than the Crown lands sold to him, a decree which the defendant *Walter Dickson* does not resist. The bill as against the defendant *William* has been taken *pro confesso*.

BARRETT v. CROSTHWAITE.

Administrator—Creditor—Amendment.

In a suit instituted by an administrator with the will annexed, upon a mortgage, the defendant produced a release for the mortgage money, given by the testator in his life-time : thereupon the plaintiff sought to be allowed to proceed against the defendant as a creditor of the estate, but as this would involve such an amendment as would create an entirely different record, the court refused such permission and dismissed the bill with costs.

This was a suit of foreclosure, and came on for the examination of witnesses and hearing before his Lordship the Chancellor at the sitting of the court held at Woodstock in the month of April, 1863.

Mr. *Strong*, for the plaintiff.

Mr. *Hodgins*, for the defendant.

Judgment—VANKOUGHNET, C—I think that the plaintiff in this suit being administrator with the will annexed, can only recover in his character as administrator, and that his claim as such is barred by the release executed by the testator. Mr. *Strong* asked that if this view were taken, the cause might stand over, to enable the plaintiff to sever his character of administrator from that of a creditor of the estate, but I do not see how this is to be effected except by a cancellation of the letters of administration, in which case an entirely different record would be necessary. The position which the plaintiff would then seek to sustain is that of equitable mortgagee, and the only evidence he offers in support of it is the production by himself of the note exhibiting the indebtedness of the testator to him, and of the mortgage and the statement of defendant himself, shewing that they were in his possession prior to his obtaining letters of administration ; but the defendant also states that the plaintiff had been doing buisness for the testator as his solicitor, and that the latter had given him an order upon the defendant for the mortgage. I do not think upon this evidence I could find that the plaintiff held the mortgage in deposit. The bill must be dismissed with costs. ·

BROWN v. FISHER.

Setting aside sale—Deterring parties from bidding.

Where out of an audience or attendance at a sale of twenty-five or thirty persons, three or four were induced to refrain from bidding, because they were informed that a person who was attending at the sale intended to buy the property for the family of the debtor ; the court refused to set aside the sale, which was made to such person at a small advance upon the upset price, although the person purchasing did so for the benefit of persons of other than the family of the debtor.

Statement.—The bill in this case was filed to set aside a sale made by a building society, under a power in their mortgage deed. The circumstances under which the sale was made, and the grounds upon which it was sought to be set aside, are stated in the judgment of the court.

Mr. *English*, for the plaintiff, contended that if it were made apparent that parties intending to be purchasers at the sale had refrained from bidding because they believed the purchaser *Thompson* was bidding for the benefit of the debtor's family, it was sufficient reason for setting aside the sale ; and that in such case the plaintiff was not bound to shew that the sale had been at an undervalue. If a fair open competition was prevented the sale would not be allowed to stand.

Mr. *Blake* for the defendants.

Watson v. *Birch*, (a) *Galton* v. *Emuss*, (b) Re *Carew's* Estate, (c) were cited by counsel.

(a) 2 Ves. Jur. 52   (b) 1 Coll. 243.
(c) 4 Jur. N. S. 1290.

Judgment.—VANKOUGHNET. C—I am of opinion that
the bill in this case should be dismissed with costs.
The most the evidence shews is, that three or four
individuals who had intended to bid for the property,
on hearing that the defendant *Thompson*, if he bid,
would buy the property for the family of the debtor, and
the other defendant *Fisher*, or rather, as it appeared,
for his son and son-in-law *Edwin Fisher*, refrained
from bidding in an audience or attendance of between
twenty-five or thirty persons, amongst whom, besides
these individuals, were wealthy men and millers, and that
the property was knocked down to *Thompson* at an advance of £5 upon the upset price of £1500.   There
is nothing to shew that *Thompson* or his co-defendant
Fisher, or *Edwin Fisher*, did anything to deter parties
from bidding, or that any of those present at the sale
were so deterred, with the exception of three or four
I have referred to, or that these acted under any influence or inducement by any one, or themselves
influenced or induced any one else upon the same or
any other consideration not to bid.   If they had
not attended the sale because they did not want to
compete with *Thompson* it would scarcely be contended
that the sale was for that cause invalid.   Their presence
there does not appear to have produced any effect more
than their absence would.

BLETCHER v. BURNS.

Replevin—Injunction—Damages.

By the statute 23 Victoria, chapter 45, the courts of common law have power to impose such terms upon the party suing out a writ of replevin as will fully indemnify the defendant in the suit from all damages he may sustain by reason of the action. Under these circumstances this court will not interfere by injunction to restrain the plaintiff suing out such writ from taking possession of, and receiving the profits derivable from, the goods so replevied; unless in a case where it could be shewn that complete security could not be obtained at law.

This was a motion to dissolve two several injunctions issued in this case; one, restraining the defendant *Burns* from removing the schooner "Jane Anne Marshall" beyond the jurisdiction of the court; the other, to restrain the other defendants, *Glassford* and *Jones*, who were added as defendants by amendment, from paying over to *Burns* the amount of freight due by them to the vessel.

Mr. *Moss*, in support of the application.

Mr. *J. Hillyard Cameron*, Q.C., contra.

Judgment.—VANKOUGHNET, C.—In this case I granted first an injunction to restrain the defendant *Burns* from removing a schooner, the property in which is in dispute between him and the plaintiff; and secondly, an injunction to restrain the other defendants Messrs. *Glassford* and *Jones*, who were added as parties to the bill, from paying over to the defendant *Burns* the value of, or charges on, cargo consigned to them. The object of both injunctions was to enforce from the defendant *Burns* security for the earnings of the ship until the disputed question could be disposed of in an action of replevin pending between him and the plaintiff, and under the writ in which *Burns* had obtained from the plaintiff, through the instrumentality of the sheriff, possession of the vessel. At the time I granted these injunctions my attention was not called to the statute 23 Vic., ch. 45, which gives a very wide power

and discretion to the judge at law to impose such
terms upon the party suing out the writ of replevin as
he may think reasonable, and also provides that in
addition to the ordinary condition of a replevin bond,
shall be superadded the condition that the plaintiff do
pay such damages as the defendant shall sustain by
the issuing of the writ of replevin. A bond to this
effect, and in a penalty of $10,000 ordered by Mr.
Justice *Hagarty* of the Queen's Bench, had been executed
by the defendant and two sureties, to the sheriff, by
whom the replevin was made. The defendant *Burns*
now moves to dissolve both injunctions, and I think
the motion must succeed. The purpose to be effected
in this suit has in my opinion already been provided
for at law, and therefore I ought not to interfere.

The most that I could do would be to order the
defendant here to give security for the earnings of the
ship, and to maintain the injunctions till he did, but
this I think he has already done. I think I must hold
that the " damages the defendant shall sustain by the
issuing of the writ of replevin" will include the
earnings which the plaintiff here might have made or
the defendant shall have made by the use of the vessel.
These damages cannot mean the mere formal damages
and costs awarded to the defendant at law with a return of the property. These, if not more, he could
recover under the old form of bond.

The court of law having therefore jurisdiction to provide for the security of such damages to the defendant
at law, and having acted in the matter, and the judge
there having fixed such a sum for security as in his
judgment was sufficient, I ought not to interfere. I do
not mean to say that this court has not the power to
interfere, and will not interfere if complete security
cannot be obtained at law; but at present I see no
necessity for its interference. If the sum fixed at law
be in the opinion of the defendant there insufficient

he can apply to a judge at law to increase it, under the very large powers given by the 4th section of the act referred to. Should the process of the common law courts be found ineffectual to enforce such additional or other security, that may form a good ground of application here.

_____

RE BABCOCK.

Will—Construction of.

Where a devise is made upon several conditions, one of which is void, the other, though good by itself, being coupled with the void one, will also be rejected.

A testator by one clause of his will devised certain of his lands to his son absolutely, and in a separate clause provided: "*And in case my son Henry shall die without issue,I hereby devise, &c.,all my real and personal estate, hereby hereinbefore devised to him, to the lawful issue of all my brothers and sisters; whether said brothers and sisters be living or dead at the time of Henry's decease:*" held, that the conditions had not the effect of cutting down the prior absolute devise to the son.

Statement.—This was a motion by way of appeal from the ruling of the master of this court at Brantford, on settling a conveyance, who required the persons interested under the devise over to be made parties to the deed.

Mr. *Morphy* for the vendor, who appeals, referred to *Lloyd* v. *Jones,* (a) *Cockburn* v. *Thompson,* (b) *Mitford* on Pleading, page 183; *Jarman* on Wills, vol. 2, page 15.

Mr. *E. B. Wood,* contra, referred to *Morris* v. *Bell,* (c) *Goodess* v. *Williams,* (d) *Beechcroft* v. *Broom,* (e) *Story's* Equity Pleadings, 147; *Jarman* on Wills, vol. 2, p. 429; *Cruise's* Dig., vol. 6, p. 373.

Judgment.—VANKOUGHNET, C.—*George Babcock,* deceased, in two distinct clauses of his will, dated the fifth day of April, 1856, devised as follows: "I also give, devise, and bequeath to my only and beloved son *Henry Babcock,* his heirs and assigns for ever, my

(a) 9 Ves. 47   (b) 16 Ves. 326.
(c) Ante. p. 23.   (d) 2 Y. & Coll. 595.
(e) 4 T. R. 441.

farm at the Mohawk village, and all my town and park lots in the town of Brantford, to hold the same for ever to his and their only use for ever." .

And in case my son *Henry* shall die intestate or without issue, I hereby devise, &c., all my real and personal estate hereby hereinbefore devised to him, to the lawful issue of all my brothers and sisters, whether said brothers and sisters be living or dead at the time of *Henry's* decease."

In the first clause an estate in fee simple is given to *Henry* the son, in language clear and precise. What difficulties there are in the case arise upon the clause secondly quoted. These, so far as they are material to the question before me, which is, "Whether or not *Henry Babcock* can execute a conveyance so as to pass the fee in the estate devised to him," are removed by certain well established rules of construction. According to the opinions expressed by Lord *Kenyon* in *Beechcroft* v. *Brown*, by Sir *Edward Sugden* in *Incorporated Society* v. *Richards*, (a) and by the Master of the Rolls in *Greated* v. *Greated*, (b) *Henry* took an estate in fee simple under the will, with an executory devise over, which latter, however, is inoperative because of one of the conditions upon which it was to take effect, viz., *his intestacy*, being repugnant and void, so that in this view he takes the estate absolutely, without any limitation over. The word " or" between the words "intestate" and "dying without issue," must be read "and," as it is only upon the happening of both events that the testator intended the estate to go over. In addition to the cases cited as authority for shewing that an attempt to make further dispositions of an estate already devised in fee in the event of the devisee dying intestate, is futile, I refer to *Barton* v. *Barton*, (c) and to *Holmes* v. *Godson* (d) before the Lord Justices. What does not seem to me so clear on reason or principle, though it

---

(a) 1 Dru. 2nd War. 282.
(c) 3 Kay & J. 512.

(b) 26 Beav. 621.
(d) 2 Jur. N. S. 383.

seems settled by authority is, that because one of the conditions or contingencies is void, therefore the other, which standing by itself would have been good, must, because coupled with the void one, be rejected also. The argument in support of this position of course is, that the testator provides for the limitation over only on both events happening, and intending that the devisee might dispose of the estate by will and that unless effect can be given to both, the executory devise must fail. But the testator is supposed to know the law, and that one of the conditions made by him is void. Why not then read the will as if it were not there at all; or rather as conferring upon the devisee a devising power merely ? Had the condition of the devise over been simply in the event of *Henry* dying without issue, then he would have taken an estate tail with a contingent remainder to the devisees over, who, it is plain from the will, are capable of being, and most probably would be, *Henry's* heirs; in which case, whenever it occurs, the words "dying without issue," are read "issue of the body." (a) If the words "without issue" were not in this case to be confined to "issue of the body," but mean an indefinite failure of issue, then the devise over would equally fail on that contingency as being too remote. It would seem to be giving more full effect to the testator's intentions to hold that *Henry* took an estate tail with a power to dispose of the whole estate by will. But even if the authorities did warrant this construction of the will, *Henry* could effectually convey the lands devised to him, so as to cut off all subsequent limitations; and those claiming under them would therefore not be necessary parties to the conveyance.

(a) Morgan v. Griffith, Cowp. 234; Doe Hatch v. Black, 6 Taunt. 485.

BRUNSKILL v. CLARKE.

Vendor and purchaser—Trustees to sell—Latent defect.

In the year 1856 a purchase was effected of certain lands from one W. and a mortgage given back by the purchaser for the greater portion of the purchase money, such purchase being effected with the view of laying the property out into building lots for the purpose of sale; which was accordingly done, and roads laid out running through the property. Several years afterwards a purchaser of one of the lots so laid out objected to complete his purchase, on the ground that W at the time he acquired his title from his vendors, the Bank of Upper Canada, was a director and the vice-president of the institution, and as such one of those entrusted to sell the real estate of the bank: which objection was sustained. W.'s vendee thereupon filed a bill to have the transaction set aside, his mortgage delivered up and discharged, and the money paid by him on account of the purchase, and expended for taxes and improvements, re-paid to him with interest. There being no evidence of any act of the vendee confirmatory of the purchase after he became aware of this defect in the title, the court decreed the relief asked, with costs.

Statement.—This was a bill filed by *Thomas Brunskill*, against *Hannah Maria Clarke* and *John Clarke*, her husband, *Adam Wilson*, and *Robert Gladstone Dalton*, the two last being the executors of the Hon. *Christopher Widmer*, deceased, setting forth that being seised in fee of certain lands in the City of Toronto, the Bank of Upper Canada in consideration of the sum of £1365, by a deed dated 2nd July, 1844, conveyed the same to the said *Christopher Widmer*, who entered into the possession thereof, and so remained until the year 1856, when the plaintiff applied to him to purchase the same for the purpose of laying it out into building lots, which intention was communicated by plaintiff to *Widmer*, whereupon a sale was made to plaintiff of the property, for the sum of £12,500; whereof £1250 was paid down in cash, and the residue was to be paid in ten years, with interest, and was secured by a mortgage on the property, which contained a covenant on the part of *Widmer* to release any portion of the premises required by the plaintiff, upon payment of a certain sum per acre. In accordance with the views and intentions of the plaintiff he procured plans of the premises to be printed ; and he laid out and constructed roads and streets on the same, and made other necessary improvements thereon ; that plaintiff had entered into contracts with various persons for the sale to them of parts of the property, and but for the circumstances connected with *Widmer's* purchase from the bank, he the plaintiff, would have been enabled to carry out his plans, pay off the mortgage, and make a large surplus profit out of the premises; that *Widmer* had died in the year 1859, having by his will appointed the defendants, *Wilson* and *Dalton*, executors thereof, and directing them to divide and apportion his estate between his two daughters; which having been done, the mortgage securing the balance of unpaid purchase money by plaintiff was apportioned to the defendant *Hannah Maria Clarke*, as part of her share of the said estate.

The bill further stated that it had recently come to the knowledge of the plaintiff that *Widmer* at the time of his purchase from the bank was one of the directors and a trustee for the bank, and was thus incapacited from making any effectual purchase of the said premises for his own benefit, and had been guilty of a breach of trust in the transaction, and that under the circumstances he had not made and could not make any effectual conveyance of the premises to the plaintiff; and that certain of the purchasers of parts of the premises having taken proceedings against the plaintiff–his title had been adjudged bad by reason of the facts stated, and their contracts had been rescinded—that this defect in the title had rendered the property wholly valueless to the plaintiff, and such defect being latent, it was the duty of *Widmer* to have pointed out the same to the plaintiff in the bargain for the purchase; that under the circumstances plaintiff was entitled to a rescission of the contract, but which the defendants, on being applied to, refused to acquiesce in; and on the contrary, had instituted proceedings against the plaintiff to enforce payment of the amount secured by the mortgage.   The bill prayed that the contract should be rescinded, and the deed cancelled; that the estate of *Widmer* might be ordered to re-pay plaintiff all sums expended in the purchase of, and upon, the premises, and an injunction to restrain the action on the mortgage.

The defendants answered the bill; the nature of the defence raised by which, as also the effect of the evidence taken in the cause, appear sufficiently in the judgment.

Mr. *Blake,* for the plaintiff.

Mr. *Hillyard Cameron,* Q.C., for the defendants *Clarke.*

Mr. *C. Patterson,* for the defendants *Wilson* and *Dalton.*

Judgment.—VANKOUGHNET, C.—I think the plaintiff in this case has made out his right to be relieved from his purchase unless it be proved that with a knowledge of the infirmity in his title he subsequently adopted it. No question arises here on the effect of the law relating to registration of title, for none such has been raised by the pleadings or the evidence. The plaintiff complains that the defect in his title arises in this wise: that the late Dr. *Widmer,* his vendor, acquired the property from the Bank of Upper Canada, while he was a director and the vice-president of the board, entrusted with the sale of its lands, and that in such position he was incapacitated from buying: that this is so, there can be no doubt. Being a trustee to sell, he could not purchase, and a stockholder in the bank has filed a bill in this court to impeach the purchase. It seems that a purchaser under *Brunskill* hearing of this defect in the title refused on that ground to complete his purchase, and the court sustained him in that position. The property was bought to be laid out as it has been, in building lots, and so to be sold. The plaintiff alleges that in this purpose he is defeated by the difficulty affecting the title. That it was a latent defect known to *Widmer,* and not to himself, and that the former should have communicated it, and that having concealed it, the plaintiff is entitled now to insist upon it, the purchase not having been completed, as the greater portion of the purchase money is unpaid, and outstanding on mortgage executed by the plaintiff to *Widmer*. This mortgage in the distribution of the estate of the latter by the defendants, the executors, was assigned to, and is the property of the defendants, *Clarke* and wife. The executors in their answer allege that *Brunskill* after he had learned *Widmer's* position at the time of the purchase by the latter from the bank, confirmed his purchase. The other defendants the *Clarkes* do not set up this defence, but rely merely on *Brunskill* having become a purchaser for value without notice. This latter defence fails, as the purchase money has not been paid. The defence raised by the executors is not sustained in evidence. The only proof of it offered is in the deposition of Mr. *Patterson*, who says that he had acted as solicitor for Dr. *Widmer* in the transfer of the property to the plaintiff; that in August, 1857, on the occasion of Mr. *Magrath* bringing to him a draft of a release of a portion of the property, to be given according to the terms of the mortgage, he, *Magrath*, mentioned to him the fact of *Widmer* having been a director of the bank at the time of his purchase, and asked him what would be the effect of it; and that this occurred before the release was executed. This is the whole evidence on this head. It does not appear for whom *Magrath* was acting—whether for the plaintiff or a purchaser under him—nor that the release was ever actually executed nor, if executed, ever acted on. The evidence is thus manifestly insufficient to support the defence of affirmation of the purchase by the plaintiff.

I think the plaintiff is entitled to a decree rescinding the contract, and cancelling the deeds founded on it, returning him his purchase money paid, and interest; recouping him for his outlay or expenditure, for taxes and improvements, and interest on that expenditure, less the profits or moneys he may have derived from the premises by sale or otherwise, and to his costs.

SCEALLY v. McCALLUM.

Municipal debenture—Liability of person negociating.

A person negociating the sale of a municipal debenture is not answerable that the municipality will pay the amount secured by the debenture. Where, therefore, a township municipality in pursuance of the Municipal Corporation Act of 1849, passed a by-law for the purpose of granting a loan of money to the Bayham, Richmond and Port Burwell Road Company, and issued debentures thereunder, which were subsequently declared to be illegal in consequence of the road company not having been properly constituted : the court, in the absence of any proof of fraud, refused to order one of the directors of the road company to refund the amount paid to him upon the sale of one of such debentures.

Statement.—The bill in this case was filed by *Anthony Sceally* against *Eliza McCallum, Heman Dodge, Shook McConnell, David Merritt* and *Sylvester Cook*, setting forth that in the year 1853-4 certain persons in Bayham agreed to form a joint-stock company, for the construction of a road in that township, under the act 16 Vic., ch. 190, who took steps to incorporate the company under the name of the "Bayham, Richmond, and Port Burwell Road Company," and that the persons so forming the company fixed the sum of £4000 as the amount necessary for the construction of the road, and *John McCallum*, deceased, the testator in the bill mentioned, was a director and the treasurer of the company, and that the municipality of Bayham believing that the company was duly constituted, passed a by-law for the purpose of loaning to the company the sum of £4000—which by-law was set out at length in the bill. This by-law the plaintiff in his bill contended was void on several grounds set forth in the bill, but which it is not necessary here to state. Nevertheless, in pursuance of the by-law so passed, the municipality issued debentures to the road company, for the £4000 so required, in sums of £500 each, and which the company sold to divers persons, amongst others, one to the plaintiff, which he purchased from *John McCallum*,

deceased, and paid therefor £400 cash ; and £10 had
been paid to plaintiff on account of the interest thereon ;
but the municipality refused to make any further payments on account of such debenture, alleging that the by-
law so passed, and under which the debenture had been
so issued, was void.   The bill further alleged, that when
plaintiff purchased such debenture he fully believed that
the debenture was a good and valid security for the sum
mentioned in it ; also, that the company was a duly incorporated company, and that he had no notice that such
debenture was void, or that the company was not duly
incorporated until long after payment of the money for
the debenture, and submitted that under the circumstances the contract for the purchase of the debenture
ought to be rescinded, and the money paid by plaintiff
refunded to him.   That the defendants *Eliza McCallum,*
Heman Dodge, and *Shook McConnell* were executrix
and executors of the last will and testament of the said
John McCallum, whose estate, it was alleged, was
bound to make good to plaintiff his purchase money so
paid for the said debenture.   The bill prayed relief
accordingly.

The defendants *McCallum, Dodge,* and *McConnell*
answered the bill, denying all improper conduct on
part of the testator in the sale and transfer of the debenture, and insisting that plaintiff took the same at his own
risk, and that under the circumstances appearing there
was not any ground for the interference of the court.

Mr. *Roaf* and Mr. *Fitzgerald* for the plaintiff.

Mr. *Blake,* for the defendants who answered.

The cases cited appear in the judgment.

Judgment.—SPRAGGE, V. C.—The cases cited by Mr.
Roaf seem to proceed upon the ground of implied representation.   When a party applies to another to give cash

for a bill of exchange or other instrument, he must be
taken to represent that it is genuine, and the dealing
being with an agent of the party to receive the money was
held to make no difference where the representation was
by the agent on his own behalf.   This point was a good
deal considered in *Gurney* v. *Womersley,* (a) in which
previous cases were reviewed. The agent in these bill
transactions is in fact the person dealt with; the principal
borrower is not dealt with by the party advancing the
money. This case differs from those cited in two respects:
one, that the instrument was genuine; the other, that
McCallum and the other directors of the road company
were only dealt with as representing the company.   It
is not unlike the case put by the Chief Justice *Gibbs* in
Jones v. *Ryde* (b) that when forged bank notes are
offered and taken, the party negociating them is not, and
does not profess to be answerable that the Bank of
England shall pay the notes; but he is answerable for
the bills being such as they purport to be.   The testator
McCallum negociated the debenture with the plaintiff,
but no special case is made against him.   The one case
is made against all the directors, which is shortly, that
the road company was not legally formed according to
the statute; and that the municipal debenture of the
township of Bayham is an invalid instrument.   It is not
charged that the directors knew that the company was
not legally formed, or that the debenture was invalid, or
that any representations were made to the plaintiff upon
either point.   The debenture was sold to the plaintiff,
and delivered to him, and he paid the purchase money,
which appears to have been applied, with all other
moneys received, towards the construction of the road;
the contract was completed; the bill asks for its rescission, the equity being simply the fact of the invalidity
of the road company and of the debenture, and the
refusal of the municipality to pay the latter.

   I find no precedent for such a bill; and the authori-

(a) 4 E. & B. 133.   (b) 5 Taunt. 494.

ties are against such an equity as that upon which the
bill is founded. If the sale had been by the defendants
in their individual capacity there would be no such
equity. *Wildè* v. *Gibson*, (a) and *Legge* v. *Croker*, (b)
cited with approbation by all the learned lords who gave
judgment in *Wilde* v. *Gibson*, were much stronger cases
for relief than this. In the case before the Lords, Lord
Campbell adverting to the distinction between a bill for
carrying into execution an executory contract, and a
bill to set aside a conveyance that had been executed,
observes: "With regard to the first, if there be in any
way whatever misrepresention or concealment which is
material to the purchaser, a court of equity will not compel him to complete the purchase ; but where the conveyance has been executed I apprehend, my lords, that
a court of equity will set aside the conveyance only on
the ground of actual fraud." This proposition was only
qualified in the subsequent case of *Slim* v. *Croucher*, (c)
which was before Lord *Campbell*, as Chancellor, to the
extent that if there is actual representation as to a fact
which the defendant had known, and had been actually
a party to, and upon the faith of which the plaintiff had
acted, his having forgotten the fact, (supposing such a
thing proved, though scarcely susceptible of proof,)
would not relieve him from his liability.

Then does the circumstance that these defendants
negociated the debentures as directors of a road company
make against them. I think they did negociate them
on behalf of the road company ; and if so the law of
principal and agent will apply to them. If they made
expressly or impliedly any representations in regard to
their principal, they will be bound by it, if untrue, and
if another has acted upon it, even though the agent
believed it to be true ; but Mr. *Story* in his book on
agency suggests this qualification, that the rule would
not, or might not apply if the want of authority was

(a) 1 H. L. C. 605.   (b) 1 B. & B. 506.
(c) 1 DeG. F. & J. 518.

known to both parties, or *unknown* to both parties; and authority is in favour of this qualification, for if the principal be dead the agent is not responsible for what he does, in the belief that he is still living. This was established in the case of *Smout* v. *Ilbery*, (a) in which case Baron *Alderson*, who delivered the judgment of, the court, observed, that in all the classes of cases in which the agent has been held personally responsible: "it will be found that he has either been guilty of some fraud—has made some statement which he knew to be false—or has stated to be true what he knew to be false; omitting at the same time to give such information to the other contracting party as would enable him equally with himself to judge as to the authority under which he proposed to act."

Tried by this test I do not think the defendants made themselves responsible. It is right to consider what is necessarily understood by parties dealing together as the plaintiffs and these defendants did; or, in other words, what was the implied representation. I do not think it can be taken to be more than this, that the debentures were genuine, and that the road company whom they represented was a road company *de facto*. Agents for a company cannot, I think, be intended to undertake for the company, or to represent that all the formalities which are necessary to its being duly constituted have been duly complied with. Neither the agent nor the party dealt with understand this; there is no such implied contract, and in the absence of bad faith there is no reason, and I think no law, to attach personal responsibility in such a case. This, too, is a registered company, and the plaintiff had therefore the same means as the defendants of judging as to its validity if he chose to act prudently. It is intimated in the case of the *Athenæum Life Insurance Company* v. *Pooley*, (b) by all the judges who decided the case, that it lies upon

---

(a) 10 M. & W. 1.　　　　(b) 28 L. J. Chy. 119.

the party buying debentures to ascertain all facts essential to their validity. Here the plaintiff either made enquiries, or assumed that everything was correct and regular when he should have enquired; and the loss ought not to fall upon parties as innocent as himself, and who in no way misled him. He seems indeed to have acted on his own judgment, for he took time to consider before he made the purchase, and if he did not ascertain for himself that the debenture was a valid security, he gave the parties reason to believe that he had satisfied himself upon that point. It seems, indeed, that he really had done so; that he had taken legal advice; and he is represented as an intelligent man.

It is agreed on both sides that the debenture is not valid, though believed to be valid at the time by the municpality as well as others, the municpality at first paid interest upon it. In the view that I take of the case it is not necessary to decide whether the road company was validly constituted, for even supposing it not to be so, I think the defendants not liable.

I think the bill should be dismissed with costs.

BROWN V. DAVIDSON.

Voluntary conveyance—Statute 13 *Elizabeth.*

In a suit brought to set aside a voluntary conveyance as void against creditors, it lies upon the parties interested in supporting the deed to shew the existence of other property in the debtor available to his creditors; but in such a case the parties having omitted to give such evidence, the court, at the hearing, directed an equiry before the master as to the indebtedness of the grantor at the date of the conveyance.

The facts are stated in the judgment.

Mr. *A. Crooks*, Q. C., for plaintiff.

Mr. *Strong*, Q. C., for defendants.

Judgment.—Spragge, V.C.—The plaintiff is a judgment creditor of the defendant *John Davidson*, upon a judgment recovered on the 7th of April, 1858. The bill impeaches a conveyance as void under statute 13th Elizabeth, made by the same *John Davidson* to his son the defendant *James Davidson*, on the 22nd of February previous. The consideration expressed is $2,400; a mortgage bearing the same date as the conveyance from *James* to his father, was made to secure payment of $2000, in sums of $400 each to five infant children of *John*, payable at various periods from 1865 to 1878. The premises consist of a village lot of small value in the township of Bayfield, and of a farm of 100 acres in the township of Stanley, the homestead of the father. It is not shewn whether the father possessed any other real property or any other means. In addition to the plaintiff's debt one *Mitchell* recovered a judgment against *John Davidson* for about £90, on the 20th of July, 1858. A writ of *fieri facias* upon the plaintiff's judgment against the goods of *John Davidson* was returned *nulla bona*, and a writ against his lands was returned lands to the value of $4 in hand for want of buyers. The father continued to reside on the homestead farm. *James* continued to reside with him until near the end of 1860, when he married and left. *John*, the father, states in evidence, given on the 6th of February, 1861, in reference to the age of his children, that *James* was then 23 years past.

The bill was taken *pro confesso* against *John Davidson* and his son *James*. The infant defendants put in the ordinary infants' answer. The two adult defendants were called as witnesses for the plaintiff, but upon its being suggested by counsel for the defendants, that the effect of their evidence, if they proved the allegations of the bill to be true, would be to expose them to the penalties of the act 13 Elizabeth and of the provincial statute 22 Victoria, they objected to give such evidence, and their objection was sustained.

The evidence for the plaintiff proves only the facts I have stated, and the question is, whether, upon those facts, a *prima facie* case is made against the infants. No evidence is given on their behalf.

A preliminary difficulty is that there is no proof as against the infants of any indebtedness by the father at the date of the impeached conveyance. The judgment roll at the suit of the plaintiff, which appears to be by *nil dicit*, states the debt as accruing on the 5th of November, 1857, but that is evidence only against the judgment debtor upon that point. However, an enquiry may be properly directed as was done in *Skarf v. Soulby,* (a) and other cases referred to in that case by the Chancellor.

Supposing the indebtedness proved, I think a *prima facie* case is made under the statute. The conveyance to *James,* and the mortgage by him were evidently one transaction; and judging of the facts as a jury properly might, I should conclude that all the children, *James* included, were appointees of the father, each to the extent of $400. The infants are clearly so, and *James* was placed upon the same footing by the difference between the consideration money expressed and the mortgage money.

It is suggested that the father may have been under some legal obligation to pay his children corresponding amounts to the mortgage moneys secured for their benefit. In the first place I incline to think that it ought to have been set up by answer: that the common infants' answer is not sufficient. The short question under the statute is, whether the conveyance impeached was made to the end, purpose and intent to delay, hinder or defraud creditors. Supposing facts proved sufficient to establish it to be so, in a case where the conveyance was voluntary, the parties, in order to

---

(a) 1 Mc. N. & G. 376.

bring themselves within the 6th section of the statute, must shew themselves to be *bona fide* purchasers; and in the case of adult defendants, I should say certainly must be set up by answer. But supposing the infants' answer sufficient, it is still, I apprehend, a defence that must be proved, a position that must be established by evidence: my inference from the facts would be that the conveyance is voluntary.

But, if voluntary, it would not necessarily be with intent to delay or defraud creditors, for the father might have had ample property besides to satisfy his debts; but who is to prove this. Is the plaintiff to prove the negative, *i. e.*, that the debtor had not other property? He has proved that his debtor had no other property in the country in which he lived which he could reach by the ordinary process of law. I think that is sufficient *prima facie*, and that it lies upon those supporting a voluntary conveyance to shew the existence of other property in the debtor available to his creditors. There is one point which was not observed upon in argument. If *John* the father is correct as to the age of *James*, *James* was under age at the date of the conveyance and mortgage. Whatever the legal consequence might be as regards the infants, the conveyance made to a minor under the circumstances looks as if made to answer a particular exigency—I think to protect the property from creditors.

There will be an enquiry as to the indebtedness of the father at the date of the conveyance; further directions and costs reserved.

HARROLD v. WALLIS.

Injunction— Receiver—Executor—Insolvency.

As a general rule an assignment for the benefit of creditors will be taken as a declaration of insolvency, and equivalent to bankruptcy in England; where, therefore, some of the legatees of a testator filed a bill against his executor and two of the legatees, charging maladministration, and alleging that the executor, subsequently to the death of the testator, had made an assignment for the benefit of his creditors, and that he was insolvent, the court, upon motion for an injunction and receiver, before answer, under the circumstances granted an interim injunction and a receiver, notwithstanding the executor denied any maladministration of the estate, or that his insolvency was the reason for his making the assignment of his estate.

Statement.—Two of the legatees of the deceased testator *Samuel Harrold* filed a bill against his executor *Wallis*, his widow, and his unmarried daughter, alleging, among other things, that the executor had been guilty of maladministration, and was insolvent, having made an assignment for the benefit of his creditors subsequently to the death of the testator. The bill prayed for an injunction and a receiver; and

Mr. *Hodgins*, for the plaintiffs, moved on affidavits, before answer, for an injunction and receiver, conformably to the prayer of the bill.

Mr. *McGregor*, for the defendants, other than formal parties, opposed the motion, on counter affidavits, denying all the material allegations of the plaintiffs, except the making of the assignment.

The facts of the case appear more fully from the judgment of the court.

Judgment.-SPRAGGE, V. C.-The bill is filed by the two sons and the three married daughters of the testator, impeaching the will, as made by undue influence exercised by his wife and by defendant *Wallis*, who is named sole executor. The defendants are his wife and *Wallis*, and the unmarried daughters of the testator, (the husbands of the married daughters are also defendants.) This application is for a receiver ; it is grounded on alleged misconduct in the administration of the estate, and upon the alleged insolvency of the executor, evidenced by his having recently, and since the death of the testator, made an assignment for the benefit of his creditors. The misconduct is denied upon affidavit ; the alleged insolvency is also denied, and an explanation is offered in regard to the assignment, that it was made to pacify creditors, who it was expected would refrain from suing, upon seeing the amount of the assets ; and it is alleged that the estate is more than sufficient to pay all the debts in full; and there is some evidence in support of this.

I think the weight of authority is in favour of granting the application. In some cases a distinction is made between cases where the personal representative is an administrator, and where he is an executor, the court interfering with more difficulty in the latter case, because an executor is the personal choice of the testator ; and mere poverty, there being no misconduct, appears not to be a sufficient ground for the appointment of a receiver. It was so held by Sir *William Grant,* (*a*) but he gave no direct answer to the suggestion, " suppose the executor was insolvent." And it was also held by Sir *Thomas Plumer* in *Howard* v. *Papera,* (*b*) that poverty alone was not sufficient ground; but *John Leach* held in a subsequent case, *Langley* v. *Hawke,* (*c*) that bankruptcy was a sufficient ground. In the early case of *Middleton* v. *Dodswell,* Lord *Erskine* (*d*) made the order on the ground of insolvency, though misconduct also was charged. In a case two years afterwards before Lord *Eldon, Gladdon* v. *Stoneman,* (*e*) the order was made on the ground of bankruptcy. The question in that case and in *Langley* v. *Hawk* appears not so much to have been whether bankruptcy was a sufficient

---

(*a*) Anm. 12 Ves. 5.   (*b*) 1 Mad. 141.
(*c*) 5 Mad. 46.   (*d*) 13 Ves. 266.
(*e*) 1 Mad. 141, n.

ground for the appointment of a receiver, as whether the circumstance of the commission of bankruptcy having issued before the death of the testator, he must not be taken to have intended to commit the administration of his estate to him, notwithstanding his bankruptcy. In *Scott* v. *Becher*, (*a*) in the Exchequer, a receiver was granted on the ground of insolvency; and in *Mansfield* v. *Shaw* (*b*) a like order was made on the same ground. *Smith* v. *Smith* (*c*) is not an authority the other way: the executor and trustee had been a bankrupt some thirty-eight years before, and the case was peculiar in its circumstances. The executor and trustee was himself interested, and the court felt that they could not usefully or properly interfere. Lord *Abinger* put it thus: "Then when the three trustees have renounced and his sister is dead, what is to be done? He is the only person who can interfere. He must do so for the benefit of others if not for his own." There are no such difficulties in this case. I think as a general rule that an assignment for the benefit of creditors must be taken as a declaration of insolvency and equivalent to bankruptcy in England. The expectation that the estate will be more than sufficient to pay the debts in full, is not in my opinion a sufficient reason for taking the case out of the rule; that was one of the grounds upon which the application was resisted in *Langley* v. *Hawk*, and proceedings had been taken to supersede the commission, but Sir *John Leach* said he must consider bankruptcy notwithstanding the petition to supersede as evidence of insolvency. This case is stronger for the interference of the court. We have the executor's own act, and to that I attach more weight than to the explanation he offers in regard to it.

There is also this in favour of the application, which is noticed in some of the cases as entitled to weight: that the interposition of the court is desired by a

---

(*a*) 4 Price, 346.   (*b*) 3 Mad. 100.
(*c*) 2 Y. & C. 353.

great majority of those interested in the estate. The affidavits are conflicting as to the fitness of the executor for his office, and as to his honesty and punctuality, but I proceed upon the grounds that I have stated. The question is whether the circumstances are such that the court ought to interfere for the protection of the fund; I have come to the conclusion that this is such a case.

MOFFATT v. NICHOLL.

Void lease—Lessee improving premises leased.

One E. was left in charge of the estate of N., who promised to leave the same by will to E. N. afterwards left this country and died abroad intestate; and E., acting on the presumption that N. had died without heirs, made a building lease in his own name of a portion of the estate, and the lessee entered into possession and erected valuable buildings thereon. Afterwards the heir of N. established his right to the estate as such, and refused to recognise the validity of the lease; whereupon a bill was filed seeking to bind the heir with this lease, or that he should pay the value of the improvements on the ground of a ratification of the lease. The court refused to grant either branch of relief asked, and the fact that the heir instituted proceedings in this court against the lessor, calling upon him for an account of the rents, &c., received by him from the estate of the intestate, was not such a proceeding as could properly be considered a ratification of E.'s acts.

Statement.–After the production of documents in the suit of *Nicholl* v. *Elliott* was ordered, as reported *ante* volume iii., page 536, that cause was brought to a hearing, and a decree for an account directed, after which the plaintiff in that action instituted proceedings at law to obtain possession of the premises in question, whereupon the present bill was filed; the object of which, and the evidence in the cause, is clearly stated in the judgment.

Mr. *Fitzgerald* for the plaintiffs.

Mr. *Crooks,* Q. C., for defendant.

Judgment.–SPRAGGE, V.C.–The plaintiffs are assignees for the benefit of creditors of one *Edward Lawson.* *Lawson* was tenant of the premises mentioned in the plead-

ings under a lease from *George Nicholl,* which expired in
August, 1850. *Nicholl* died in Detroit sometime in the
year 1849. He had for many years been a resident of
Toronto ; and one *Thomas Elliott* acted for him in the
management of his property. Upon his leaving for
Detroit he left with *Elliott* a power of attorney, which
is not produced. *Nicholl* and *Elliott* had been very
intimate for many years ; and *Nicholl,* having no near
relatives, had promised, as *Elliott* says, to leave his
property to him by will.

After the death of *Nicholl,* and after it was known
to *Elliott, Elliott* granted a building lease of these
premises to *Lawson* in his own name. It seems probable from the evidence that *Lawson* was not aware at
the time, of the death of *Nicholl. Lawson* has built
upon the premises comprised in the lease.

The defendant in this suit has established by a
decree of this court under a bill filed by him against
Elliott, his heirship to *George Nicholl ;* and has brought
ejectment to recover the premises in question.

The object of the present bill is to bind the defendant with the lease made by *Elliott ;* or, in the alternative, for compensation for improvements made by
Lawson. The evidence read I understand to be, the
examination of the defendant and the statement of
Mr. *Cooper.*

The bill makes two grounds for binding the defendant with the lease ; one, representations and promises
by *George Nicholl,* a ground which is not sustained by
any evidence ; and secondly, ratification by the defendant. I do not think there was any ratification.
The acts relied upon are, the bringing *Elliott* to account for the rents received for these premises among
others ; and as to the rents of these premises receiving
the amount paid under the lease to *Elliott ;* and the
delivery by *Elliott* to the defendant of the counterpart

of the lease held by him ; and it is put in argument
that by proceeding in this court, and not at law, the
defendant must have come into this court to bring
Elliott to account *as his agent ;* but the bill and answer
in that suit shew clearly that he did not bring him to
account as his agent ; but that *Elliott* having been
agent for his ancestor, had muniments of title in his
possession, and had received rents since his ancestor's
death, for which he was accountable to him. The
rents for these particular premises received by *Elliott*
were taken as the proper sum for which he should account, by consent of the solicitors for the parties.
Elliott could not account for less, and the plaintiff did
not ask for more ; but that amount was not fixed upon,
so far as appears, because it was named in the lease,
certainly not with any idea of confirming or adopting
the lease, but simply because *Elliott* had received so
much in the way of rental of a piece of land, for the
rents and profits of which he was decreed to account.
As to the delivery of the counterpart of the lease I
have nothing on the subject but the answer of the defendant ; his account of it is, that it was among a
number of deeds and documents delivered to his solicitor by *Elliott*.

To come now to the case of compensation. It is a
bare case of improvements made under a mistake as to
title ; that mistake not induced by any conduct of the
real owner. The defendant swears that he knew nothing of the lease or of the improvements, until after
the latter were made, and there is no evidence to contradict this. It is therefore the naked case of a building
lease made by a person without title; and the lessee building upon it. Is there any equity for the lessee to come
into this court to compel the true owner to compensate
him for the improvements; it might, as was said by Sir
James Wigram in the Master of *Clare-Hall* v. *Harding* (a), be improving a man out of his estate. The

(a) 6 Hare, 296.

nearest authority for it that I have seen is the case of *Neesom* v. *Clarkson* (a), but in that case an account of the value of the improvements was submitted to without argument, it may have been from liberality, or it may have been that counsel thought the case within *Peterson* v. *Hickman*, referred to by Lord *Ellesmere* in the Earl of *Oxford's* case (b). In both these cases there was *conduct*, a looking on without objection, while money was being expended under mistake, which was held to affect even one under disability.

In this case there is the strong circumstance of the lease being, not in the name of *Nicholl*, for whom, as *Lawson* says, he supposed *Elliott* was acting, but in the name of *Elliott* himself; and *Lawson* says he did not observe that it was so. This seems incomprehensible. It was at least most culpable negligence. The most ordinary care and attention would have prevented the difficulty into which *Lawson* brought himself. He does not say he thought that *Elliott*, as agent of *Nicholl*, could properly make the lease in his own name; but that he thought that it was in *Nicholl's* name. *Elliott* and the solicitors employed well knew of *Nicholl's* death, and ought to have communicated it to *Lawson*, and to have explained why the lease was in *Elliott's* name, viz., that he supposed he was devisee, or perhaps that no heirs of *Nicholl* would appear. Still, that a man of intelligence, a man in business as *Lawson* was, should take a lease and build houses upon the strength of it, under a mistake as to who was his lessor, seems unintelligible.

If *Lawson* had expended his money under a mistake, not fallen into through any negligence on his part, I do not see that he could sustain the claim for compensation. As it is it cannot, I think, be said, in the proper legal sense of the term, that he did so *innocently*. I think the bill wholly fails, and it must be dismissed with costs.

(a) 2 Hare, 176.   (b) 2 Wh. & Tud. 506, 519.

McDOUGALL v. BARRON.

Specific performance—Infants.

The holders of a mortgage on real estate and of a judgment recovered against the mortgagor, entered into an agreement, after the death of the mortgagor, with his widow and two of the heirs, on certain terms, for the release of the equity of redemption in the mortgaged premises,and also for the conveyance to him of another portion of the real estate in discharge of the mortgage and judgment debts. On a bill filed to enforce this agreement it appeared that other children of the mortgagor,who were infants, were interested in the estate,the court refused the relief prayed, but directed a reference to the master to enquire if it would be more for the advantage of the infants to adopt the agreement, or that a sale of the estate should be made under the decree of the court.

The facts are sufficiently stated in the head-note and judgment.

Mr. *J. McLennan,* for plaintiff.

Mr. *Mathieson,* for defendants.

Judgment.—SPRAGGE, V. C.—The bill as framed is primarily for the specific performance of an agreement; this certainly cannot be decreed, for the obvious reason that the land, which is the subject of it on the part of the defendants, was inherited from the late *William Barron* by his nine children, of whom two only (the rest being infants), and the widow as dowress, were parties to the contract.

The land consists of eight acres, comprising a mill and mill site, of which six were mortgaged by *William Barron* to one *Iredale,* of whom the plaintiff is the assignee. The bill alleges that a judgment was recovered and registered by *Iredale,*for mortgage money in arrear; that *Barron* died shortly afterwards ; and that no further payments have been made upon the mortgage, the whole of which has since fallen due. Under these circumstances the agreement mentioned in the pleadings was entered into, and it is shortly this, that the equity of redemption in the six acres,and the defendants'estate in the two acres should be conveyed to the plaintiff, he on his part conveyed to the defendants a house

and lot in the village of St. Mary's. The contract was
entered into as on behalf of the infants as well as the
adults. The court can of course only adopt this agreement in case it should appear that it will be more for
the interest of the infants than any other course that
can be taken. It may be made to appear that it is so.
It may be, that in pursuing the full rights of the holder of the mortgage and judgment, the whole of the
eight acres would probably be lost to the defendants.
On the other hand it may be, that the value so greatly
exceeds the mortgage money that it would be for the
interest of the infants that a sale should be directed,
and that the court would feel warranted in directing
such a sale, rather than adopt the agreement.

I think it will be proper to direct an enquiry upon
this point; I have not before me the materials for
forming a judgment upon it.

I understand all the adult defendants to submit to
the agreement being performed, and among them I
understand are two who were not parties to the agreement, but who have come of age since.

Further directions must be reserved. The infants
are entitled to their costs. The costs of other parties
will depend upon the result of the enquiry. If the
agreement should be adopted, I think each party should
pay his own costs, because a suit in this court to establish it, must, I suppose, have been in the contemplation of the parties, when they entered into it.
If the agreement should not be adopted, the plaintiff
will be left to his ordinary remedies upon his mortgage
and judgment, and can have those remedies in this
suit, and should in that event have the same costs as
if he had filed his bill for that purpose only; as if, in
fact, no such agreement existed.

WOOD v. BRETT.

Principal and surety—Acceptor, and drawer of bill of exchange—Composition.

The acceptance by a creditor of part of his demand against his debtor, and agreeing not to sue him, with a reservation of the creditor's rights against a surety of such debtor, will not discharge the surety: where, therefore, the holders of a bill of exchange received from the acceptor a composition of the debt, and executed a deed to that effect, but expressly reserved their rights against the drawer of the bill, *held*, that this had not the effect of discharging the drawer.

In proceeding in the master's office under the decree made in this cause, reported *ante* page 78, a claim was brought in against the estate of *Brett*, founded on a bill of exchange, which claim the master refused to allow, whereupon the claimant appealed from the ruling of the master, on the grounds stated in the judgment.

Mr. *Fitzgerald* for the appeal.

Mr. *Hector*, Q. C., contra.

Judgment—ESTEN, V.C—The facts are, that *Brett* drew bills of exchange on *Haley & Co.*, of London, England, in favour of *Taylor & Stevenson*, for value, which bills were accepted by *Haley & Co.*, and afterwards dishonoured, *Haley & Co.*, having made a composition with their creditors, and paid them 10 shillings in the pound. This composition was received by Messrs. *Overend, Gurney & Co.*, who appear to have discounted the bills on behalf of *Taylor & Stevenson*, who paid them the difference, and a deed was executed by *Overend, Gurney, & Co.*, the provisions of which do not appear. *Taylor*, who was in England at the time, and saw the clerk of *Haley & Co.*, states in his affidavit that the composition was received only in respect of the estate of *Haley & Co.*, and not in satisfaction of the claim on *Brett & Co.*, and that the rights against *Brett & Co.* were to remain wholly unaffected by it. *Brett* made an assignment for the benefit of his creditors. *Taylor & Stevenson*, or their assignee, *Mason*, acceded to it. They accordingly

claimed against the estate the balance of the bills, after
allowing credit for the composition. This claim was
disallowed, as I understand, on the ground that *Brett*
must be deemed to have had effects in the hands of
Haley & Co. when they accepted the bills, and, therefore, stood in the position of surety in the transaction,
and that the creditors, *Taylor & Stevenson,* by compounding with *Haley & Co.,* the principal debtors, discharged the surety, *Brett.* The bills being dishonoured,
Brett, the drawer became, of course, *primâ facie,* liable
to the holder, and the onus is upon him, or those representing him, to show that he or his estate has been discharged from such liability. The state of the law, as
settled by the cases of *Dean* v. *Newhall,* (a) *Hutton* v.
Eyre, (b) *Price* v. *Barker,* (c) *Kearsley* v. *Cole,* (d)
appears to be this : a release, operating as such, extin-
guishes the debt, and renders any reservation of remedies
nugatory; but a release in form, accompanied by a
reservation of remedies, may, in favour of the intention,
be construed as a covenant not to sue. A release of one
of several debtors, or of one of several co-obligors, either
joint, or joint and several, will operate as a release of
the others; but a covenant not to sue one of several joint
debtors or co-obligors, either joint, or joint and several,
does not prevent the other from being sued, and if the
covenantee be sued with the other, he cannot plead the
covenant in bar of the action, but must resort to his cross-
action ; and if the other joint debtor, &c., be sued, or
pay voluntarily, he may sue the covenantee. When, however, the relation of principal and surety exists between
the parties, it appears necessary to combine with the
covenant not to sue the principal a reservation of the
remedies against the surety, as it would seem that a
mere covenant not to sue the principal, unaccompanied
by a reservation of remedies against the surety, will discharge the surety; and that the effect of such a reservation is to preserve all the remedies of the surety, as well

(a) 8 T. R. 168.   (c) 4 A. & E. 760.
(b) 6 Taunt. 289.   (d) 16 Mees. & W. 128.

as of the creditor, for if the remedies of the surety are not preserved, he is discharged, and in order therefore to prevent his discharge, that is, to preserve the remedies of the creditor against him, *his* remedies against the principal are equally preserved; and such is the meaning and legal effect of the reservation, so that notwithstanding a covenant by the creditor not to sue the principal, the surety may the next day compel him to sue him. Such a proceeding is not a breach of the covenant, and, of course the surety, if compelled to pay, or if he pay voluntarily, may sue the principal, or may compel him, if he can, to pay the debt *a priori*, and exonerate him. To apply these principles to the present case, what do the defendants shew in order to exonerate the estate of *Brett?* Merely that a composition of 10 shillings in the pound was received; but supposing it to be proved also that a deed was executed, this is the utmost that appears. The acceptance of the composition cannot amount to more than an agreement not to sue the principal for the balance, and if a deed exists which appears not to have contained a release, and, at all events does not appear to have contained one, and if it contained a covenant not to sue, or was silent, then, certainly, it appears from the evidence of *Taylor* that it was intended to reserve all the remedies, and I must conclude upon this evidence that they were reserved, and then the very case arises similar to the case of *Price* v. *Barker*, of an agreement or covenant not to sue the principal, accompanied by a reservation of remedies against the surety, which does not discharge the surety, and, therefore, I think this appeal should be allowed without costs.

PETO v. THE WELLAND RAILWAY COMPANY.

Judgment creditor of railway company—Receiver.

Held, that a judgment creditor of a railway company, with execution against lands of the company, lodged in the hands of the sheriff, is entitled to the appointment of a receiver of the earnings of the road, the profits thereof to be applied in payment of his demand.

Statement.—The bill in this case was filed by Sir *Samuel Morton Peto*, Baronet, *Thomas Brassey*, and *Edward Sadd Betts*, against the Welland Railway Company, setting forth the recovery of a judgment against the defendants, the registration thereof, and the lodging of execution against lands in the hands of the sheriff, which remained unsatisfied. Under these circumstances, the plaintiffs prayed, 1st, a decree for payment of the amount to be found due, with costs; 2nd, in default, that a manager might be appointed, by whom the railway might be worked; 3rd, that a receiver might also be appointed of the earnings of the road, and thereout the debt due plaintiffs discharged; and for further relief. To this bill the defendants put in a general demurrer, for want of equity.

Mr. *Roaf*, in support of the demurrer, contended that if any title to relief in favour of the plaintiff existed at all it was purely a legal one, and if there was not any title at law, neither was there any in the view of a court of equity. Lands are liable to execution under *fi. fa.*, and to that proceeding the creditor must resort, they not being liable to attachment under the writ of *elegit* in this country.

He also contended that neither the judgment nor the execution thereunder affected the rolling stock of the company, or the privileges conferred upon them by their charter, although they might have been reached under the writ against goods.

Mr. *A. Crooks*, Q.C., contra. The legal remedy is inadequate for the relief of the plaintiff; the plaintiffs have a right against the lands of the company which cannot be enforced by legal process; their lands being composed of the railway itself, cannot be sold at law, as it will not allow them to be alienated from the purposes of the railway to which the act has given them; but that cannot afford any reason for holding that a railway company should enjoy an immunity from debts. *Furness* v. *The Caterham Railway Co.*, (a) *De Winton* v. *Brecon*, (b) *Fripp* v. *The Chard Railway Co.*, (c) *Legg* v. *Matthieson*, (d) were referred to by counsel.

Judgment.—ESTEN, V.C.—The bill states that the plaintiffs had obtained a judgment against the defendants on the 19th of November, 1859, for the sum of £2,034 7s. damages, and £15 5s. costs, which was registered in the counties of Lincoln and Welland, on the 28th of the same month, at which time the defendants were entitled to divers lands, called and being the Welland Railway, situate within those counties, from which the defendants derived large profits, by carrying on traffic on them; that the plaintiffs issued writs of *fi. fa.* against goods on their judgment, which had been returned *nulla bona*, and that on the 28th of August, 1861, writs against lands were issued on the judgment, and were renewed on the 16th August, 1862, and delivered to the sheriff of those counties for execution, and remain in force in his hands. The bill then insists upon the 24th Victoria, ch. 41, and that the plaintiffs are entitled to equitable execution against such lands, and the profits arising from them, and it prays that a manager or receiver may be appointed of the earnings and profits of the railway, and that thereout the plaintiffs' debt may be paid. To this bill there is a general demurrer, for want of equity. The right under the act was not insisted on in the argument, and it appears untenable. As no suit was pending on the 18th May, 1861, the lien of the judgment became extinct, according to the decisions of this court,

---

(a) 25 Beav. 614.　　　　　(b) 26 Beav. 533.
(c) 11 Hare, 241.　　　　　(d) 2 Giff. 71.

on the 1st of September, in that year. The claim, therefore, must be based on the right of a judgment creditor having an execution against lands in the sheriff's hands, under the peculiar circumstances of this case, to have equitable execution against these lands. No authority, exactly, in point has been cited, nor is it likely that such an authority exists amongst the English cases. Cases were cited in which the courts have appointed receiver of railways at the instance of mortgagees ; it being considered that when the act authorised a mortgage of the railway, it also, by implication, authorised the appointment of a receiver as necessary to give effect to the mortgage, and some of the railway and other acts provide for the appointment of a receiver by two justices. These cases and provisions show that the appointment of a receiver on a railway is not contrary to public policy, and in fact it must be obvious that as a receiver is only to receive the surplus, after defraying all the expenses of the road, which is all the time managed by the directors of the company, the appointment of such an officer cannot be contrary to public policy. The appointment of a manager may be open to different observations, and may appear to come within the reasons adduced by Sir *Knight Bruce*, in the case of *Russell* v. East Anglian Railway Company, (a) as inducing him to hesitate in that case. In fact in that case the receiver, Mr. *Seppings*, was appointed manager of several railways. In the present instance I must suppose the defendants to have had no goods at the return of the writs against goods, but to have become possessed of a plant and stock, or some interest in a plant and stock, since that time, for the writs were returned *nulla bona*, and yet the bill states that the defendants were working the road. Under the writ against the lands, the plaintiffs are entitled to proceed to a sale of the defendants' lands, including the land on which the railway is built, and the station houses and other buildings

---

(a) 6 Railway cases, 528.

erected upon it, unless some rule of law exists which
renders such a proceeding impracticable. The bill seems
to assume that the railway lands and buildings cannot
be offered for sale. I must presume that the railway
company is constituted like other railway companies by
act of parliament, authorising them to acquire lands for
the purposes of the railway. I apprehend it to be quite
clear from the authorities that the sheriff's vendee could
not exercise the powers conferred by the act of incorporation, or, in other words, conduct the railway; and I
apprehend it is equally clear that the legislature conferred those powers, and especially the power to acquire
lands for the purposes of the railway, on the understanding, and with the intent, that those lands should not be
diverted or alienated to any other purpose through a proceeding in *invitum*. The result is, that no sale of the
land and buildings of the railway can be effected under
process of execution. Is the execution to be entirely
inoperative? Is the company to reap large profits from
the use of property which the process of law cannot
reach, and refuse to pay its debts? The writ binds the
lands, and gives a power of disposition on the whole fee
simple for the satisfaction of the debt. The rents and
profits are included in the estate; if the whole estate
is given for the payment of the debt, the rents and
profits are given; and if the creditor cannot apply the
corpus of the estate to the satisfaction of his debt, he
ought at least to be able to grasp the rents and profits—
in fact any thing that can be seized and applied consistently with the intention of the legislature. It is not
the province of a court of equity to interfere under such
circumstances? No machinery exists whereby the rents
and profits of the estate can be reached at law; where
it is a sale or nothing. The judgment creditor under
the elegit received the lands of his debtor upon a certain extent, and must await the satisfaction of his
debt through the slow method of receiving the rents,
but a court of equity interfered and accelerated the

remedy, by ordering a sale, *Stileman* v. *Ashdown.* (a)
This is the converse of that case. The creditors' right
is to a sale, but a sale is impracticable, owing to the
nature of the property. The rents and profits are, however, available without interfering with the purposes of
the legislature; but no machinery exists whereby they
may be reached or applied at law. Should not equity
interfere under such circumstances,and supply the defect
in the legal remedy? The whole estate is devoted by
law to the satisfaction of the debt, and if the whole
estate is devoted, the rents and profits must be devoted
to that purpose, and I think where rules of public policy
prohibit the application of the *corpus* of the estate, but
permit recourse to be had to the rents and profits for
that purpose, and no machinery exists at law by which
their application can be effected, it is the duty of a
court of equity to interfere and supply the remedy,which
their machinery enables them to extend. I apprehend
the court would apply the same remedy as to personal
estate, so circumstanced as not to be the subject of sale ;
as, for instance, when a railway company works its
railway by means of stock hired from another company,
as sometimes happens; in which case the stock is not to
be removed from the road, and, therefore, cannot be the
object of sale, but producing by its application to the
railway large profits, I apprehend the court would not
suffer these profits to go into the pocket of the company
while they set their creditors at defiance. By the 5th
Geo. II., ch. 7, the remedies against lands are the same
as against chattels. Under such circumstances the
judgment creditor might purchase the interest in the
stock under the writ against goods, intending to obtain
a receiver under the writ against lands. No one else would
purchase such interest under such circumstances and
the benefit of the stock and road could be combined only
in this way, as the writ against goods must be returned
before the writ against lands can issue. It is objected

(a) 2 Atk. 610, Coote on Mortgages, 73.

in the present case that the writ does not affect the
stock; but the rents and profits are produced by the
application of the moveable stock and plant to the
railway; both combined constitute the source of the
profits, and the court, I apprehend, will not permit the
whole profits to go into the pocket of the company, but
will devise some apportionment at the hearing, whereby
the ends of judgment can be attained. It may be suggested that the judgment creditor purchasing the rolling stock under a writ against goods, might obtain a receiver under a writ against lands, as they may introduce
the stock upon the road, and permit the company to use
it, whose duty it is to carry on the business of the road
as long as possible. The present road is in operation,
and the court must presume that the company will perform their duty, and continue to work the road, as their
duty is, and not stop it, lest their surplus profits should
be applied in payment of their debts, and as in that
case I think the court will devise some method by which
a portion of the profits can be applied to the satisfaction of the plaintiffs' demands, I think the demurrer
should be overruled. It is true that this is a new case,
and no authority exactly in point has been produced.
I have already observed that a precise authority can
hardly be supposed to exist amongst the English cases,
and no case calling for the decision of this particular
point has occurred in our own country. I am, therefore, compelled to proceed very much upon principle,
but I think my decision is in accordance with the principles of equity, and supported by analogy, and, restricted as it is, the appointment of a receiver is not so
far as I can judge opposed to public policy or public convenience, while it advances the interests of justice by securing the application of property to the satisfaction of
debts, in place of its passing into the hands of the debtor.

The Attorney-General v. Lauder.

Rectory—Presentation—Demurrer.

By the Constitutional Act, 31 Geo. III., ch. 31, his Majesty and his successors were empowered to authorise the governor of the province of Quebec to erect parsonages or rectories therein according to the establishment of the Church of England; in pursuance whereof Sir John Colborne in 1836, then Lieutenant-Governor, erected and endowed the rectory of Kingston. By a provincial statute subsequently passed the Church Society of the diocese of Toronto was incorporated, and by a later statute the right of presentation was vested in such Church Society. Subsequently the legislature erected the Diocese of Ontario out of a portion of the Diocese of Toronto, and the bishop, clergy and laity of the diocese were incorporated under the name of the "Incorporated Synod of the Diocese of Ontario," who by a by-law passed in 1862, invested the then bishop with the right to appoint to all rectories during his incumbency. The bishop in pursuance of such authority afterwards, on the death of the incumbent, presented to the rectory of Kingston; whereupon an information was filed by the Attorney-General on the relation of certain of the parishioners against the bishop and the rector praying to have such by-law of the Synod declared void and set aside. A demurrer by the bishop and rector for want of equity was allowed, the court considering that under the several acts and proceedings which had been passed and taken the right of presentation was vested in the bishop during his incumbency. But, *quære*, if the Church Society of the Diocese of Toronto before the setting off of the Diocese of Ontario had passed a by-law similar to the one passed by the Synod of Ontario, whether the right to make such presentation did not remain with the Bishop of Toronto.

Statement.—This was an information filed by the Attorney-General at the relation of *William Rudston, Overton Smith Gildersleeve, Thomas Askew, Thomas Weeks Robison, Charles Smith Ross,* and *Archibald Hamilton Campbell,* against the Reverend *William B. Lauder,* the Right Reverend *John Travers Lewis,* Lord Bishop of the Diocese of Ontario, The Incorporated *Synod* of the *Diocese of Ontario,* and the *Church Society* of the *Diocese* of *Toronto* setting forth that by an act of the Imperial parliament, passed in the 31st year of the reign of his late Majesty, King George III., his Majesty and his successors were empowered to authorise the governor of the province of Quebec to erect parsonages or rectories, according to the establishment of the Church of England, and to endow them by grants of land. The right of presentation to the same was, by the same act, vested in the Crown, to be exercised through its representative in this province.   On the 21st January, 1836, Sir *John Colborne*, then Lieut.-Governor, by letters patent, reciting among other matters the regard that his Majesty had for the spiritual welfare of his subjects resident in the township of Kingston, erected and endowed the rectory in question.   Shortly afterwards he exercised the right of presentation vested in the Crown, by appointing as rector the Rev. Dr. Stuart, who occupied that position until his death in October, 1862; that by a provincial act, passed in 1843, the Church Society of the Diocese of Toronto was incorporated ; and by an act passed in 1851, and assented to by her Majesty in 1852, the Crown divested itself of the right of presentation, and transferred it to the respective dioceses in which the several rectories were situated; and consequently, Kingston being then in the Diocese of Toronto, the right of presentation to the Kingston rectory became vested in the Church Society of the Diocese of Toronto.   In 1862, the legislature by an act passed in that year, divided the Diocese of Toronto, by forming a portion of it into the Diocese of Ontario.   The bishop, clergy, and laity of the Church of England in the latter diocese were, at the same time, incorporated under the name of "the Incorporated Synod of the Diocese of Ontario."   This act further invested them with "the *like* corporal rights, powers, *patronage*, and privileges as by any acts of the parliament of this province are conferred on any church society incorporated in any diocese of the United Church of England and Ireland in the said province."   The powers conferred on the synod were to be exercised either through the synod or by boards or committees of that body, and powers as to framing by-laws and rules were also conferred upon the synod, and, unless otherwise ordered, the appointment of members of such committees was to be in the hands of the bishop.

On the 5th of November, 1862, the Synod met in special session at Ottawa, and passed a resolution, which

was afterwards confirmed by a by-law, to the effect
that during the life and incumbency of the present
bishop the appointment to all rectories within his diocese should be vested in him.

The information further alleged, that the incumbency or rectory of Kingston having become vacant by
the death of the Rev. Dr. *Stuart*, as before stated, and
being so vacant, on or about the 17th day of November,
1862, the defendant the Bishop assumed to present,
and did in fact present to the rectory or parsonage
the defendant *Lauder*, a Doctor of Divinity, and a duly
ordained minister of the Church of England, and he
thereupon entered into possession of and held the
same; and the defendant *Lauder* had no legal right
to the incumbency of such rectory, the right to presentation to the same being, under the provisions of
the first mentioned act, vested in her Majesty, to be
exercised by her as therein provided, and at the
time of the death of the Rev. Dr. *Stuart*, still
continued, and was in her Majesty, except in so far
as the same had been, and was legally and validly
vested in the Church Society of Toronto, by the act of
1851-2, above mentioned; and which society had not
delegated or assumed to delegate to or vest in any
person or body corporate whatever such right of presentation to the rectory of Kingston.

The information further alleged that neither the incorporated Synod of the Diocese of Ontario, nor the
Lord Bishop of Ontario, ever had any legal right of presentation to the said rectory of Kingston, and the exercise by the bishop of the right of presentation and
presentment by him of the defendant *Lauder*, was, under
the circumstances stated, illegal and void, and ought to
be so declared by this court: the legislature in conferring the like powers, patronages, and privileges as
were enjoyed by any incorporated church society of
England, etc., did not transfer to or vest in the incorporated Synod of Ontario the right of presentation to

rectories or parsonages held or vested in the Church Society of Toronto ; that even if the right of presentation did become vested in the incorporated Synod of Ontario by virtue of its incorporating act, yet it is expressly declared and enacted, that all of the powers of the said incorporation shall be exercised by and through the synod of the diocese, and by such boards and committees as might from time to time be created by the synod by a by-law or by-laws to be passed for that purpose, and that the resolution and by-law above mentioned (and which were set forth at length in the information), were illegal and void, inasmuch as the synod, otherwise entitled to such presentation, thereby attempted to delegate and vest in the defendant the Bishop the functions and powers which by the acts above mentioned the synod ought to have exercised and retained to itself, and which it is incapable of transferring to or vesting in any other person ; also, for that the attempted delegation and transference by the synod to the bishop of its alleged right of presentation was void and is excessive, in that it was and is not of a particular vacancy that had occurred, but was in respect of all the rectories in the diocese that in any future time during the life and incumbency of his lordship might become vacant, and was an attempt by the present members of the synod to bind their successors throughout the whole of such period.

The prayer was, that under the circumstances the said resolution and by-law of the incorporated synod might be declared void so far as it related to the rectory of Kingston : that the exercise of the right of presentation by the Bishop, and his presentment thereto of the defendant *Lauder* might be declared illegal and void ; that the defendant *Lauder* might be removed from such rectory and enjoined from acting or assuming to act as such rector, and from holding, enjoying, or receiving any of the lands, profits or emoluments belonging to such rectory ; that said defendant might account for such profits or emoluments as he had received from the same, and for further and other relief.

To this information the defendants the Bishop and *Lauder* put in, respectively, general demurrers for want of equity.

Mr. *Hillyard Cameron*, Q. C., and Mr. *Strong* for the demurrer.

Mr. *A. Crooks*, Q. C., and Mr. *Blake* contra.

In support of the demurrer counsel contended that by the express words of the statute all the powers conferred by any act of parliament on any church society in Canada are given to the Synod of Ontario. And that the word "patronage" which is used in the statute must be taken to confer on them the right of presentation to rectories, that in fact being the only patronage such societies have ; and it cannot be urged as any valid objection to the by-law that the patronage is vested in the Bishop during his life-time, for if deemed expedient the by-law could be rescinded.

They also objected that the Attorney-General has no right to interpose, there being no right of presentation in the Crown ; for if the by-law be decided to be bad, then the right to present is in the Church Society. *The Attorney-General* v. *Newcombe*, (a) *The Attorney-General* v. *Foster*. (b)

In support of the information it was contended that by the 31 Geo. III., his Majesty was empowered to set aside certain lands for rectories ; and during the vacancy of any incumbency the lands must be deemed to be in the Crown ; and as the author of the trust created by the grant the Crown has a right to see it properly

---

(a) 14 Ves. 1.   (b) 10 Ves. 395.

executed. The act incorporating the Synod of Ontario did not transfer to it the rights of the Church Society, but simply confers on the Synod the same powers as are enjoyed by the Church Society; and for all that is shewn it may be that the society still held the right of presentation here. If, as is contended by the defendants, the diocese of Ontario possesses the *"like powers"* as the Church Society of Toronto, then they ought to be at liberty to exercise control in the latter diocese. The Synod being merely a trustee ought to exercise its own judgment in presenting to vacancies: the act of incorporation does not give it power to delegate its authority. The Synod is in fact the mere agent of the incorporation, and at most can only act through committees.

Long v. *Grey,* (a) The *Attorney-General* v. *Fowler,* (b) *Attorney* v. *Cumming,* (c) The *Attorney-General* v. *Sitwell,* (d) *Perry* v. *Shipway,* e) *Clark* v. The *Panopticon,* (f) *Webb* v. *Byng,* (g) *Newsome* v. *Flowers,* (h) were with others referred to.

Judgment.—VANKOUGHNET, C.—By the act of the 31st George III., ch. 31, power was given to erect certain rectories, and under that power the rectory of Kingston was constituted.

By section 39 of the same act, his Majesty was empowered "To authorise the Governor to present to every such rectory an incumbent or minister of the Church of England, and to supply from time to time such vacancies as might happen therein." And it was provided, "That every person so presented to such rectory should hold and enjoy the same, and all rights and profits and emoluments thereto belonging or granted, as fully and amply, and in the same manner, and on the same

---

(a) 9 Jur. N. S. 805.
(c) 2 Y. & C. CC. 139.
(e) 1 Giff. 1.
(g) 2 K. & J. 669.

(b) 15 Ves. 85.
(d) 1 Y. & C. 559.
(f) 4 Drew. 26.
(h) 31 L. J. Ch. 29.

terms and conditions, and liable to the performance of the same duties as the incumbent of a rectory in England."

This right of presentation is, in England, familiarly known as an advowson, and is property. It is expressly recognised as such in terms in the 17th section of the Church Temporalities Act, 1841, of this province. It is given in the books as the most apt illustration of an incorporeal hereditament. It may be conveyed by deed or devise, in whole or in part.

By the act of the provincial legislature of 1852, this right of presentation was vested in, and was to be exercised by, the Church Society of the Church of England in the diocese within which the same was situate, or by such other person, bodies politic or corporate, as such church society, by any by-law or by-laws to be by them from time to time passed for that purpose, should or might think fit to direct or appoint in that behalf.

The rectory mentioned in this suit is situate within the diocese of Ontario, which has been recently erected by letters patent from the Crown. There is no society known as the church society within this diocese. By the act of 25 Victoria, ch. 86, section 1, a body corporate is created under the name of "The Incorporated Synod of the Diocese of Ontario," and "is to have and is invested with the like corporate rights, powers, patronage and privileges, as by any acts or acts of the parliament of this province are conferred on any church society incorporated in any diocese of the United Church of England and Ireland in this province," and to the said corporation, and the members thereof, the several clauses and provisions of the said acts are to apply, so far as they are not inconsistent with the act now in recital. Had a church society been erected in the Diocese of Ontario instead of the incorporated Synod, it was admitted on the argument that the right of presentation would

have been in that society. The words which gave to the
Synod certain rights, and which I have quoted, are not
very happily chosen, and are somewhat open to the
criticism to which they have been subjected on the
argument of this case. They are not that the Synod
shall have all the power that a church society would
have, and shall stand in the place of such church society, or shall have and exercise within the Diocese of
Ontario the right, &c., formerly exercised within the
limits thereof by the Church Society of the Diocese of
Toronto, but they are that they shall exercise the like
powers of any church society. What the legislature
meant is obvious enough. They never could have intended that the Church Society of the Diocese of Toronto,
within its abridged limits, should continue to exercise
jurisdiction in the Diocese of Ontario, and they intended to transfer those powers to the incorporated Synod.

The question is, whether the words used will effect
this intent? The first consideration that presents itself
to one's mind is, does the Church Society of Toronto
shrink with the limits of that diocese as they may be
fixed from time to time? There is nothing in any act
of parliament that I can find to say so. But the act of
22nd Victoria, ch. 65, incorporating a church society for
the Diocese of Huron seems to assume this; and must it
not necessarily be the case? The Church Society of the
old Diocese of Toronto had no territorial limits assigned
to it: it was merely the church society of the diocese.
Must it not take up its abode within that diocese where
ever it from time to time lies? Must it not shrink or
expand with it? Can it exist out of the diocese and
exercise jurisdiction out of it? I think not, though it
may, undoubtedly, hold property out of it, and the right
of presentation is property. Then if it cannot exercise
jurisdiction out of the diocese of Toronto, and is confined within it, it is not the church society of the diocese
of Ontario; and if it be not the church society of that
diocese, then there is no church society there to exercise

any rights or powers as such. If so, then the difficulty vanishes, for, when there is no church society in or possessing any power in the diocese, then the right of presentation cannot, of course, be exercised by a church society, and therefore the giving to any body corporate or otherwise within the Diocese of Ontario, " the like corporate rights, powers, *patronage* and privileges', conferred on any church society can have full effect, and would convey the right of presentation, which is in the strictest sense of the term *"patronage,"* and even if these were insufficient, the extension to the Synod "of the several clauses and provisions" of the acts relating to the church society would convey all the rights and powers which these societies had. To illustrate what I mean—if illustration be necessary—were certain powers given to the city of Hamilton (which, of course, had no jurisdiction in the city of Toronto) to exercise rights in regard to taxation, or harbour improvements, an act giving the " like" powers to the city of Toronto would plainly confer the same and the exclusive rights upon that city. But independently of this process of reasoning, I think, looking at what seems to me the plain intent and meaning of the legislature, I ought rather to hold, however doubtful the language employed, that the right of presentation passed to the Synod of Ontario. Even if it could be maintained that the Church Society of the Diocese of Toronto still held the powers and rights which they formerly possessed within the limits of the Diocese of Ontario, yet the Synod of that diocese is invested with the " like" rights and powers; and having exercised them, I take it the rectory must be treated as full, and that there is, therefore, no room for the action of the other body.

Difficulties, however, of another kind than those presented here may arise under these various enactments. The Crown is, by statute, deprived of the power of presenting. Suppose no church society existed in any new diocese which may be erected, or no body specially authorized by the legislature to exercise the patronage, where does it lie ? Supposing, as may have happened in this case, that the church society for the time being exercised the power given to it, and lodged their right of presentation for life in the Bishop of Toronto, within whose diocese Kingston then was, would he or not still retain the patronage, the society having, at the time it conferred it, the right to dispose of it ? These difficulties may require legislative interposition to remove them ; but they lead me to the consideration of the by-law under which the Bishop of Ontario has claimed to act. This by-law vests in him the patronage of all rectories during his life or incumbency. I suppose it meant his life *and* incumbency. I have had some doubts whether the legislature intended that the church society, or corresponding body, should make such an extensive disposition of this right. But, on reflection, I do not find anything to limit their exercise of it either in the language of the act or in the consideration of the public policy which led to it. We have only to read the act to see that the legislature intended to sever all connection between the Crown, or the government as representing the public generally, and the Church of England, and to leave to the latter the exclusive management of its own affairs of every description. The Crown surrenders all interference in them, and the legislature practically says this— " the connection between you and the Crown as representing the general public has been inconvenient and impolitic—we get rid of it—we do not interfere with any rights you have, but we give you the exclusive use of them—we have, or rather the Crown, subject to our right to interfere with and dispose of them, has the patronage of presentation to livings—we think it no longer expedient that the Crown should use it—and we are indifferent how you use it, but to enable you to do so in the manner most acceptable to your community, we place it in the possession of the body recognized by law as your representative and under your control. That body may do with it as it pleases, and we have no further concern in the matter; and it may deal with it by by-law," the usual mode of declaring the corporate will and act.

Taking this view of the statute, and treating the right of presentation as a right of property, it seems to me that however unwise or inexpedient such an exercise of it as has been made in the present case may be, the legislature has given to the corporation the power unconditionally of disposing of the patronage and that I must therefore treat the by-law in that behalf as valid. I do not think it can be repealed, as I think it vests the property, the advowson, in the Bishop for, at least, the period of his incumbency of office.

Demurrer allowed.

THE WESTERN ASSURANCE COMPANY v. TAYLOR.

Incorporated company—Mortgage to.

An insurance company was by its act of incorporation authorised to hold real estate for the immediate accommodation of the company, "or such as shall have been *bona fide* mortgaged to it by way of security, or conveyed to it in satisfaction of debts previously contracted in the course of its dealings, or purchased at sales upon judgments which shall have been obtained for such debts;" and having sold and conveyed a vessel, took from their vendee mortgages on real estate for securing the purchase money. *Held,* that this was a transaction within the act of incorporation the price of the vessel being a debt existing previously to the execution of the mortgage; but, *semble,* that under these words of the act it was not, as with banking institutions, necessary to the validity of such a mortgage that any previous indebtedness should exist.

This was a suit to foreclose a mortgage executed by the defendants to the plaintiffs, which was resisted under the circumstances set forth in the head-note and judgment.

The cause came to be heard before his Honour Vice-Chancellor *Spragge*, at the sittings of the court at Chatham in October, 1863.

Mr. *Blake*, for the plaintiffs.

Mr. *Fitzgerald* and Mr. *Douglas,* for the defendants.

Judgment—Spragge, V.C.—I think mortgages upon which the plaintiffs proceed are not open to the objection urged, viz, that they are against their act of incorporation. They were taken in security, or part security, for the purchase money of a schooner sold by the plaintiffs to *Taylor;* which vessel may have come into the hands of the plaintiffs in the course of their business of marine assurance, as to which no question is raised; and if so in their hands, it would be in the course of their dealings to make sale of such vessel.

The clause restrictive of the holding of lands by the company is the 7th. It first affirmatively authorises the company to acquire and hold real estate; and then in a proviso, defines the purposes for which only, real estate may be acquired and held, first, as is usual, for the immediate accommodation of the company; then come the words upon which this point turns, as follows, and with the following punctuation: "or such as shall have been *bona fide* mortgaged to it by way of security, or conveyed to it in satisfaction of debts previously contracted in the course of its dealings, or purchased at sales upon judgments, which shall have been obtained for such debts;" a subsequent part of the clause enables the company to make loans of its funds on bond and mortgage. Taking the words I have quoted as punctuated, the words, "debts previously contracted in the course of its dealings," apply only to lands conveyed to the company in satisfaction of debts, making four classes of cases—1st. Lands necessary for accommodation for transaction of business. 2nd. Lands mortgaged by way of security. 3rd. Lands conveyed in satisfaction of debts; and 4th. Lands purchased at sales upon judgments obtained for such debts; and moreover, as suggested by Mr. *Blake,* the sentence is not perfect if the words "debts previously contracted in the course of its dealings," are applied to mortgages, for it would read thus: "or such as shall have been *bona fide* mortgaged to it by way of security, * * * debts previously contracted in the course of its dealings." The word "for" after security would be necessary to make the sentence perfect. Further, taking the construction of the sentence as we find it, the words "debts previously contracted," &c., preceded by the word "for" would have followed the words "mortgaged to it by way of security;" then "or conveyed to it in satisfaction of" *such debts* as in the following member of the sentence, "or purchased at sales upon judgments which shall have been obtained for *such debts.*"

I think, too, looking at the whole clause, that it could not have been intended to incorporate the words "debts previously contracted," &c., with the next preceding member of the sentence. The office of the 7th clause is three-fold: 1st, to define the powers of the company as to holding lands; 2nd, to restrain the company from using its stock, funds, or moneys in dealing in merchandise; and 3rdly, to define how the funds of the company may be invested, and, among other things, in mortgages. There would have been some inconsistency in saying that the company might hold lands mortgaged only by way of security for debts previously contracted, and saying also that the company might invest its funds in mortgages, meaning, I have no doubt, mortgages of real estate.

There was, besides, an obvious propriety in restricting the taking of absolute conveyances of real estate, as it would be restricted if the clause be so read. The policy of the act appears to be to prevent the company from becoming large holders of real estate, and as one means of effecting this, not to allow the company to purchase it except for its immediate accommodation. The policy in relation to this company, and to banking corporations, is essentially different; as to the latter, it was to prevent their lending money upon mortgage; while this company is expressly authorized to lend money in that way.

But if I had found it expressly provided that the company might hold lands mortgaged to it by way of security for debts previously contracted in the course of its dealings, I should still have thought this transaction within the permission of the act. The sale of the schooner was, as I have observed, in the course of the dealings of the company, and the purchase money was a debt to the company. The debt was not contracted by or with the mortgage, as is the case upon a loan of money, where the advance of the money and the giving of the mortgage are contemporaneous acts. Here the mortgage was the stipulated way of securing the payment of the purchase money, (and it was probably part of the contract that it should be so secured,) but the contract of sale created the debt, which I think was a debt previously, that is previous to the execution of the mortgage, contracted within the meaning of the act.

I think, however, that the true reading of the act is, that it authorises the company to hold lands mortgaged to it by way of security, without restricting it to debts previously contracted. I think such a reading should be adopted, because debts then contracted, that is, at the giving of the mortgage, not previously, are obviously contemplated and authorised.

I disposed of the other points of the case at the hearing at Chatham.

LAWRENCE v. POMEROY.

Crown patent—Costs—Crown lands department.

It is the duty of parties dealing with the Crown lands department to be fair and candid in all their communications and statements; where therefore a bill was filed to set aside a patent which had been issued to a purchaser of a clergy reserve lot, on the ground that the same had been so issued in ignorance of the opposing claim of the plaintiff, upon the fraudulent misrepresentations of the patentee, and the concealment of the facts by him from the Crown land department; the court, although unable to afford the plaintiff the relief sought, dismissed the bill without costs as against the defendant who had thus dealt with the department.

This was a bill to have a patent issued to the defendant *Pomeroy* rescinded, and the cause came on to be heard before his Lordship the Chancellor, at the sittings of the court held at Cobourg, in October, 1863. The facts material to the point disposed of are stated in the judgment, which was delivered at the close of the argument.

Mr. *Roaf*, for the plaintiff.

Mr. *Cameron* and Mr. *Blake*, for the defendant.

Judgment.—VANKOUGHNET, C.—I think the plaintiff must fail. The only ground on which he, in his own right, could ask to have the patent rescinded is, that he had an equity to the consideration of the Crown, of which they were in ignorance when the patent issued, and which, if known to them, might have influenced their judgment in his favour. I do not understand any of the cases to carry further than this the right of a private individual to question the validity of a patent, and I am not disposed to carry it further, but rather to limit it, as I have a strong opinion that the Attorney-General is the proper party to invite the action of the court. Then was the Crown, when the patent here issued, ignorant of the plaintiff's alleged rights? It seems to me not; all that the plaintiff says here now was then known to the Crown. By petitions and affidavits furnished by the plaintiff and others, and by the report of the local Crown lands agent made some four months before the patent issued, the department of Crown lands was put in possession of all the facts connected with the plaintiff's claim. They knew that one *Julius Warner* was the original purchaser of the lot (a clergy reserve) in 1837; that he had paid but one instalment, one-tenth of the purchase money; that he had many years ago left the country and, apparently at all events, abandoned the lot; that he had never during a long series of years asserted any claim to it, and only at last by the execution of the assignment of it, in the October previously to the issue of the patent, to one *Barnard*, from whom defendant *Pomeroy* obtained an assignment : they knew of the plaintiff's long possession and improvements, and yet with a knowledge of this, the original sale never having been cancelled, and the assignee having paid up the balance of the purchase money in full, a patent was issued to him, and the plaintiff informed of it, and that his claim was rejected. There is no room in this state of facts to infer that the Crown has or may have been deceived, or that they overlooked the plaintiff's claim. Had the defendant desired to show this he should have produced direct evidence of it, as the facts furnished lead in the contrary direction. But the plaintiff insists and *Pomeroy,* the defendant, concealed from the Crown the fact that *Warner* said to him when he applied to purchase the lot that he had never intended looking after it and offered it to him for nothing, and then sold it to him for $30, whereas the assignment expresses $50, and the assignment from *Barnard* $500, though nothing was ever paid to him, he having been a mere go-between in the transaction. The Crown, however, knew from the report of the Crown land agent, and from the affidavits before it, that *Warner* had so far abandoned the lot, and knowing this, they recognised his assignment, the sale still standing in his name: they would have learned nothing further if *Pomeroy* had mentioned to them what *Warner* said. As to the statement of a false consideration in the deed, this I fear is a common, though a very improper practice. All dealings with the department, so much at the mercy of individuals, should be fair and above board, and I cannot too strongly condemn the conduct of the defendant *Pomeroy* in his attempt to embarrass the department, and keep open the question of the claim to the lot by asserting in a letter written to the department in the name of another party, one *Higgins* (though with his consent) that he *Higgins* had an assignment from *Warner's* heirs, when *Pomeroy* well knew that such an assignment never existed. If the statement of the false consideration could or would have influenced the department had they known the falsehood, I think the Attorney-General and not the plaintiff must seek relief, if any can be had on that ground. On the other head of equity on which Mr. *Roaf* sought to rest the plaintiff's case, viz., that the defendant *Pomeroy* had by means of knowledge derived in confidence from the plaintiff, secured the patent, I think the case is not made out. Even if the pleadings were so shaped (and they are not) as to sustain it, I do not see that the defendant derived any information from the plaintiff's papers of importance to him, or which he in any way used to his own advantage. Those papers merely shewed the plaintiff's case, and were in the possession of the government at the time of the issue of the patent. Nor do I see that the defendant put himself in the position of trustee as to the plaintiff. The plaintiff shewed him his papers, and left them with him to examine, asking (as he alleges) defendant for a loan of a few dollars on the security of them, and defendant returned him his papers, refusing the loan. The defendant learned this much, that the plaintiff was prosecuting a claim to the land; and he immediately sets to work to prevent its success by hunting up the original nominee and purchasing from him, though there is evidence to shew that he had been making some enquiries after him before he saw defendant's papers. There is evidence of a conversation, not the one referred to or stated in the bill, which shews that defendant acted a most disingenuous part towards plaintiff, who had consulted him as a friend upon the sufficiency of his claim. It is sworn that defendant said to plaintiff not to concern himself about his claim, that it was all right, and not to be in a hurry to pay the purchase money to the government, as they would call for it when they wanted it, and yet almost immediately after thus disarming the plaintiff, he sets to work actively to secure the lot for himself. This conduct, and his mode of dealing with the government, are so reprehensible that while I refuse the plaintiff any relief, I dismiss the bill as against the defendant *Pomeroy* without costs. The other defendant must have his costs, as no case whatever is made against him.

FORD v. PROUDFOOT.

Sale of land for taxes—Municipality—Costs.

The wild land assessment was unpaid for the years 1853, 4, 5, 6 and 7. On the 25th of February, 1858, the treasurer issued his warrant to sell for arrears of taxes; and on the 13th of July following a sale was effected by the sheriff. On a bill filed by the owner of the land to set aside this sale, *held*, that no portion of the taxes was due for five years, within the meaning of the act.

A municipality in proceeding to a sale of land for taxes is in the position of a trustee; and if it is afterwards sought to impeach the sale on the ground of any irregularity in directing such sale, and it is sought to make the municipality answerable to the purchaser for the purchase money paid, or the costs of the suit, the municipality must be made a party to the cause.

This was a bill to set aside a deed made by the sheriff of the county of Simcoe, upon a sale of land for taxes, on the ground of improper conduct on the part of persons attending the sale; and also, for that the sale was effected under a warrant issued before any portion of the taxes had been five years in arrear and unpaid.

Mr. *Blake*, for plaintiff.

Mr. *Strong*, Q.C., and Mr. *Crickmore*, for defendants.

Henry v. *Burness* (a), *Massingbird* v. *Montague* (b), were referred to by counsel.

Judgment.—SPRAGGE, V.C.—A short point raised at the hearing of this case is sufficient for its determination. I think the sale was premature.

The arrears of taxes, for non-payment of which the land was sold, were for the years 1853, 4, 5, 6 and 7. The treasurer's warrant for sale was issued on the 25th of February, 1858, and the sale take place on the 13th of July, in the same year. There were therefore five years' taxes due at the date of the warrant and of the sale. The question is, whether any portion of those taxes had been due for a period sufficiently long to warrant a sale under the statute. The following sections of the act, Consolidated Statutes of Upper Canada, ch. 55, bear more or less upon the point, 16, 19, 49, 50, 51, 59,

---

(a) Ante, vol. viii., p. 345.　　　(b) Ante, page 92.

61, 63, 70, 72, 76, 89, 91, 115, 123, 124. The last is the most material : " Whenever a portion of the tax on any land has been due for five years, or for such longer period, and for such amount as a by-law of the council prescribes, the treasurer of the council shall issue a warrant under his hand and seal, directed to the sheriff of the county, commanding him to levy upon the land for the arrears due thereon, with his costs." The 128th and subsequent sections prescribe the duties of the sheriff in regard to preparing lists, advertising and selling. Section 123 puts that in the negative, which section 124 puts in the affirmative : " No land shall be sold for taxes unless a portion thereof has been due for five years."

Section 16 provides that " the taxes or rates levied or imposed for any year shall be considered to have been imposed for the then current year, commencing with the first day of January, and ending with the 31st day of December, unless otherwise directed by by-law. If there had been no provision for the payment of taxes, a year's taxes would not be due until the end of the year ; they would only be accruing due in the meantime ; they would not be due, at least not in the sense of being payable, unless expressly made payable in advance.

It is clear from the sections to which I have referred, that no taxes for a year, or part of a year, are made payable until the collector's roll is placed in the collector's hands ; because until that is done there is no hand to receive them : this may be as late as the 1st of October. It is also clear that the year's taxes cannot be due, in any sense, until after the time for appealing from the assessment roll is expired, and the municipality has fixed the rate which shall be imposed. This must be done under the statute before the first of August ; it may be done before. It is quite impossible that it should be done so early in the year as the 23rd of February, the date of this warrant ; and taking the periods given for the different proceedings, the latter part of July would be the more probable time.

But it is said that a *portion* of the year's tax is due, after the first day of January, and that other portions grew due from day to day, until the whole is due, and that all that the statute requires is that a *portion* shall be due for five years.

I cannot accede to this view. The land is no doubt "liable to taxation," in the words of the statute, from the 1st of January, for such taxes as may thereafter be imposed for the current year; but it does not follow, nor can I see, that any taxes are *due* until they are at least ascertained. Besides, I think that the word "due," as used in sections 123 and 124 means *payable*, and the use of the words "arrears due" in the latter section confirms me in this view. The effect of these two sections as I read them is, that there must have been a default for not less than five years before lands are saleable. The use of the word "portion" was necessary to authorise a sale to cover the taxes due, up to and inclusive of the year before the sale.

To apply my construction of the act to this case, the taxes for 1853, the earliest year of arrear, were due and payable, say sometime between the 1st of August and the 1st of October in that year. The treasurer's warrant was issued a little more than four years and a half after the earliest of these dates, and the sale took place within five years, consequently the sale was premature.

The land having been sold before it was saleable, I have no doubt that the sale was invalid. It is in the same position as if taxes for only one year, or no taxes at all, were in arrear. The purchaser cannot support his purchase, upon the sheriff's deed alone, or upon that and the treasurer's warrant; but the sale must be one warranted by the statute. The statute authorises a sale only upon a contingency which has not happened, and the warrant, the sale, and the sheriff's deed are all nullities. I should hold this if there were no authority upon the point. But the question has been decided in several cases, Doe *Upper* v. *Edwards* (a), Doe *Me-Gill* v. *Langton* (b), and in *Munro* v. *Grey* (c), also in Doe dem *Bell* v. *Reaumor*, not reported.

I incline to think that the five years must expire before the giving of the treasurer's warrant, and that it is not sufficient if they expire before the sale. If, however, the defendants desire to argue that point, and can shew as a fact that the five years did actually expire in this case before the sale, dating from the delivery of the collector's roll, a thing not impossible, but very improbable, I should not refuse them the opportunity.

With regard to the objection, that if the sale be void, it is a case for law not for this court : the case is rested upon other grounds, beside that on which I decide, which are proper for the consideration of this court ; but inasmuch as the plaintiff may wholly fail upon these points —and I cannot say that he succeeds upon them unless I give judgment upon them in his favour—I must examine these grounds and decide upon them, unless the point upon which I do decide furnishes a ground for coming into equity. The bill prays that the purchaser may be ordered to re-convey, or it should be to convey, but I doubt that if that is a reason for coming into equity unless upon the ground that the sheriff's deed is a cloud upon the plaintiff's title, a point not expressly put by the bill. I doubt if it is necessary, though I think usual, to state that as the ground where it is so, where facts are alleged which shew a deed to be a cloud upon title. The plaintiff may take leave to amend, if as a matter of caution he desire it. I think the sheriff's deed in this case comes within the category of a cloud upon title.

The plaintiff by his bill offers to reimburse the de-

(a) 5 U. C. 694.   (b) 9 U. C. 91.
(c) 12 U.C. 647.

fendant what he has paid, with interest; I think that should be a condition of relief. He also offers (at the bar) to undertake to bring no action at law for the irregular proceedings, that is reasonable, probably; though I am not sure that I could properly have imposed it as a condition of granting relief.

The British America Assurance Company do not, I think, set up sufficiently that they are, *quoad* their mortgages from the purchaser, at sheriff's sale, purchasers for value without notice. But if the sale was invalid, as I hold it to be, no title legal or equitable passed, but remained in the plaintiff, and he cannot be called upon as a condition of relief to pay the mortgage created by the purchaser at the sheriff's sale.

I think the decree should be without costs. The purchaser had a right to presume that the official acts of the treasurer and sheriff were rightly done. I do not think it necessary upon the question of costs to go into the questions raised, in regard to the conduct of the sale, and of parties attending the sale, because assuming the plaintiff. to have proved his allegation upon these heads, I do not think it would have been a case for visiting the purchaser with costs.

After this judgment had been pronounced counsel drew the attention of the court to the objection which had been urged on the hearing, as to the necessity of having the municipality before the court.

After taking time to look into the authorities,

Judgment.—SPRAGGE, V. C.—In disposing of this case, I overlooked the question of parties. In my view of the case only one point is material, that is, taking the municipality to have had no power to sell these lands, they not being saleable at the time; whether the purchaser has not a right to require that the municipality be made a party.

There are two old cases recognised in modern text books which appear to be the same in principle as the one before me. One is *Harrison* v. *Pryse,* reported in *Barnardiston,* (a) in which it was said that "where a real estate is in the hands of a trustee, and the trustee conveys it over to another, who had notice of the trust, if a bill is brought by the *cestui que trust,* the trustee must be made a defendant." This however was a dictum only, and not the point decided.

In *Jones* v. *Jones* (b) the bill was to set aside a lease; and was filed as I gather from the facts stated, by *cestui que trust* against the lessee; the trustees not being made parties; and it was objected that they were necessary parties, they being parties to the lease and having been guilty, as it was alleged, of a breach of trust. Upon this Lord *Hardwicke* observed: "Now it is insisted by the defendant's counsel the trustees ought to be made parties, that if the plaintiff prevail the defendant may have relief over against them who have been guilty of a breach of trust, if they have not applied the £350 towards the execution of the trust. There is another point on the general head which entitles the defendant to have the trustees before the court; and that is, if the defendant should appear to have paid the trustees the £350, as he insists he did, and it is no answer to say that the defendant ought to have brought a cross-bill."

Greenwood v. *Atkinson* (c) was a suit by a surviving trustee, the other being one *Bolland,* (d) against the surviving partner of the other trustee; the defendant and the deceased trustee having been in partnership as attorneys and solicitors; and the two trustees having employed the law firm to invest certain trust moneys, the defendant and *Bolland* invested the moneys in a loan to one *Lee,* who was one of the several *cestuis que trust,* upon a security which the bill alleged was lost through the neg-

(a) Page 324.   (b) 3 Atk. 109.
(c) 4 Sim. 54,   (d) 5 Sim. 419.

ligence of the defendant and *Bolland*. The answer stated that *Lee* became bankrupt, and objected that his assignee should be made a party in order to his having his remedy over against *Lee's* interest in the trust estate. The objection was sustained, and the cause ordered to stand over to add parties.

There are other cases bearing more or less upon the point. The principles established by them seem to be that where a defendant has a remedy over in respect of the transaction brought in question by the plaintiff, the person against whom the defendant is entitled to his remedy over ought to be made a party; and this is in order to avoid multiplicity of suits, and to do complete justice between the parties.

The application of the principle is obvious in this case. The defendant *Proudfoot* purchased of the municipality, which assumed to have power to sell, but which in fact had not, and he paid his purchase money to the municipality. If the land is taken away from the defendant he ought to have back his purchase money, and ought not to be put to a separate suit to obtain it.

The objection should have been taken by demurrer or by the answer, but I apprehend the only consequence of its not being so taken is, that the cause must stand over to add parties without costs, or perhaps even upon payment of costs, where the defect appears upon the bill. Here it was only in one view of the case that the municipality was a necessary party; and the defendant making no objection by pleading, to the frame of the suit, the plaintiff might, not unreasonably, suppose that as a decree between the then parties could be made as the suit was then constituted, the defendant was content to contest the question in issue without the presence of the municipality. I think under the circumstances the order should be without costs.

CAHUAC v. DURIE.

Practice —Injunction.

A creditor having proved his claim in the master's office, afterwards proceeded to sell under his *fi. fa.* Upon the application of a co-defendant the sale was restrained with costs.

Statement.—The bill in this cause was filed for the foreclosure of a mortgage; the usual decree was made, referring it to the master to make enquiries as to incumbrances; among others *Twyne* and *Kempe* were made defendants in the master's office in respect of a subsequent mortgage ; and *Rigney, Brown* and *McDonald* were also made defendants having a *fi fa.* against lands in the sheriff's hands upon a judgment recovered by *Rigney* and *Brown* against the defendant by bill, which judgment was afterwards assigned to *McDonald.* *Twyne* and *Kempe* proved their claim under their mortgage, and *McDonald* his under the judgment. The master, by his report, found that as to a part of the judgment *McDonald* had priority over *Twyne* and *Kempe,* and as to the other part, that he was postponed to them ; the *fi. fa.* having two endorsements to levy, the second one being subsequent to the registry of the mortgage of *Twyne* and *Kempe.* Pending the making of the master's report, but after the claim had been proved and the priorities established, *McDonald* proceeded to advertise the lands in question for sale by the sheriff under his execution, whereupon the defendants *Twyne & Kempe* moved for an injunction to restrain the sale.

Mr. *Gwynne,* Q.C., in supoprt of the motion.

Mr. *Crooks,* contra.

Upon hearing the application, his Honour Vice-Chancellor ESTEN directed that the execution creditor should be at liberty to do what was necessary to maintain the writ, but not to proceed to a sale, he paying the costs of this application.

BARTELS v. BENSON.

Injunction.

In a proper case upon petition by defendant, the court granted an injunction against the plaintiff.

The facts of the case are set forth in the judgment.

Mr. *Gwynne*, Q. C., for petitioner.

Mr. *Sullivan*, contra.

Judgment.-SPRAGGE, V.C.-The defendant by his petition prays that the decree obtained by the plaintiff may be
vacated, and that he may be permitted to answer; or that
the report may be vacated, and for a reference back to the
master, with other alternative prayers. He also prays
that proceedings in a certain action of ejectment in
respect of lot six on East street, in the village of
Napanee (the second action of ejectment in respect of
that lot) may be stayed.

The defendant presented a similar petition in November, 1861, except the prayer for staying proceedings in
the above action, which has been commenced since.

The plaintiff filed affidavits in answer to that petition,
and the defendant took proceedings under the general
orders for the cross-examination of the deponents.
The cross-examination did not take place, in consequence of an unfounded objection on the part of the
gentleman attended for the plaintiff; and the result
was an agreement that certain costs should be paid by
the plaintiff; that untill they were paid proceedings
should be stayed; that upon payment the solicitors
should arrange between themselves a new day for such
cross-examination; and the defendant's solicitor should
have ten days thereafter for bringing on the petition.
The former petition as well as the present one sets forth
certain equities in relation to lot six; and also in relation

to one of the judgments upon which the plaintiff is proceeding.

The plaintiff instead of proceeding in accordance with the agreement made between the solicitors, brought the second action of ejectment to which I have referred; and this proceeding has induced the present petition; he now files affidavits in answer upon the merits, among them is one by the solicitor, in which he says that he was always ready and willing to pay any costs which might be agreed upon under the agreement, and to proceed with the cross-examination; and he denies what is alleged in an affidavit by the defendant's solicitor, that he was ever applied to, to proceed with the cross-examination. It is not necessary that I should decide upon this conflict of statement, it lay upon the plaintiff's solicitor to " arrange," as the agreement expresses it, with the defendant's solicitor, for the payment of the costs; and upon such payment the two solicitors are to " arrange " for the cross-examination. It was not open to the plaintiff, under the circumstances, to proceed at law for the recovery of lot six. I am told, and it is not denied, that the affidavits filed upon the merits in answer to this application, are substantially the same as those upon which cross-examination was to be had; this is obviously improper, and even if they vary in some unimportant particulars which are not pointed out, still the merits must be the same, and the plaintiff has concluded himself by the agreement, from any other mode of bringing the merits before the court than the mode thereby agreed upon. He must still proceed under the agreement. In the meantime he must be enjoined from proceeding in ejectment as to lot six, and must pay the costs of this application.

HENRIHAN v. GALLAGHER.

Lessor and lessee—Personal representative.

Where a lease for years contains an agreement for the sale of the
fee, the right to purchase goes to the heir-at-law, not the personal
representative, on the death of the lessee.

Statement.—This was a bill filed by *Eliza Henrihan*,
administratrix of *Michael Henrihan*, against *James
Gallagher*, setting forth that at the decease of the intestate he was possessed of certain leasehold premises
in the county of Hastings, as lessee of the Canada
Company, and the plaintiff being unable to cultivate
the same, had agreed to sell and convey it to the defendant for £150, payable by instalments, which agreement was completed by a conveyance to, and mortgage from, the defendant, securing the payment of
the purchase money in the manner agreed upon.

The bill then stated an agreement by which the
plaintiff released the mortgage given by the defendant,
under a promise to execute a fresh one, for the purpose of enabling him to procure the conveyance from
the Canada Company ; the fact of his having procured
such conveyance, and his refusal to execute such mortgage : also the commencement of an action of ejectment to turn the plaintiff out of possession of the property, contrary to the agreement between the parties.

The prayer of the bill was to restrain this action ; to
declare plaintiff entitled to a lien on the property for the
balance due of purchase money, and that the defendant
might be ordered to execute another mortgage according to his agreement.

The defendant suffered the bill to be taken *pro confesso* against him, and the cause came on to be heard
before his Honour Vice-Chancellor *Esten*.

Mr. *Hector Cameron*, for the plaintiff, asked that a
decree might be pronounced in the terms of the prayer,

but this the Vice-Chancellor refused, stating that the land was the property of the infant heirs, and that the administratrix had not any right to sell it. The plaintiff thereupon re-heard the cause before the full court.

Mr. *Brough*, Q.C., and Mr. *Hector Cameron*, for the plaintiff, referred to *Sampson* v. *McArthur*(a), as establishing the right of the plaintiff to the decree sought. They contended that the right of purchase was inseparable from the lease, so that the assignment of the lease carried with it the right of purchase. The Mayor, etc., of *Congleton* v. *Pattison* (b), *Vernon* v. *Smith* (c), were also referred to and commented on by counsel.

The judgment of the court was delivered by

VANKOUGHNET, C.—I think the judgment of my brother *Esten* in this case right, and that *Sampson* v. *McArthur* does not estop us from this conclusion. In that case the decree in the court below was in exact accordance with the judgment here, and that decree was affirmed by the Court of Appeal, which did nothing more than affirm it, and so far, and so far only, therefore, is the judgment of the higher court binding upon us. It is true that the eminent judge who delivered the judgment of that court in one passage of the judgment expresses the opinion as of the whole court, that the decree had gone too far, and that the assignee of the husband and wife of the lease took all the rights which the lessee under the Canada Company had, including the right to exercise the option of purchasing, thus treating this as personalty; but not only do I learn from at least one member of the court responsible for the judgment then delivered, that such was not the opinion of all the members of the court, and should be taken as the express l opinion of Sir *John B. Robinson*

(a) Ante vol. viii., p. 72.   (b) 10 East, 136.
(c) 5 B. & Al. 1.

alone, but the point involved in it never formed the subject of argument, and was in no way important to the decision of the question then before the court. Lord *Cranworth,* I think, more forcibly than any other judge, has remarked upon the danger of judges expressing opinions upon matters not material or necessary to the decision they are called upon to give—they are mere *obiter dicta,* and often create embarrassment.

The plaintiff here contends that the administratrix could and did sell not merely the term, but the right to purchase the fee, and yet admits that that right did not pass to the administratrix, but to the heirs-at-law. If the administratrix did not herself take the right, she could not give it to any one else, and we think she did not take it. For whose benefit could she exercise it? It seems clear on authority and principle that the heirs-at-law could not call on her to pay the purchase money out of the personalty, for the ancestor had not in his lifetime elected to purchase. If the heirs-at-law could not demand this who could? Could the administratrix by applying the personal estate of the testator convert it into realty? and would the next of kin take realty under the right of their ancestor, and if so, on what principle known to the law? Was the right of the ancestor to purchase and acquire realty a right that would go through the administratrix to his next of kin, and has it ever so gone? If it would not, then, how could the administratrix assign it? The term may well subsist in the administratrix, and the right to acquire the realty in the *heir-at-law,* even to the destruction of the term, when the latter exercises his option to purchase. But it is said that the right to purchase is contained in a covenant which runs with the term, *i. e.,* the land. If this were so, as the term passed to the administratrix, the right to purchase must have gone also; but I think I have shewn that it could not go to her, and if so, there is an end of that position. I do not, however, think that the right to purchase is in any way attached to the term—it is a right to the individual quite independent of the term, which may subsist without it or with it—or, as I think, is the proper construction of the instrument of lease, there was a contract on the part of the Canada Company to sell to the lessee at any time within ten years, at a fixed price, giving him in the meantime a lease. It is not like the case, as was argued, of a covenant for a renewal of a lease. The right to purchase—the purchase itself—is something outside and beyond the lease altogether: of a higher and totally different character, which the lease merely *as such* will not bear and carry with it. The covenant here gives the right to purchase to the lessee, his *heirs* and assigns.

WILSON V. DANIELS.

Vendor's lien—Sale of land chattels for undivided price.

B. having an interest in unpatented lands enters into partnership with D. and A., and each acquires an undivided one-third in the lands ; A. then conveys his third to D., who continues the partnership business with B., having an undivided two-thirds, and also owning chattel property in partnership with B.

B. afterwards agreed to withdraw from the partnership and sell all his interest in both land and chattels to D. in a "lumping bargain," for £350. Conveyances of the chattels, and also of the real estate were then executed, in which the considerations stated appeared to be merely nominal, and there was no means of distinguishing the price of the land from that of the chattels. Promissory notes were given to secure the purchase money, and possession of all the chattel property was taken by D.

On a bill filed by endorsees of the promissory notes against D. and purchasers under him, claiming a lien upon the land, *Held*, that the mode of sale and the circumstances shewed it to be the intention of the parties that no lien should exist.

Statement.—The bill in this case was filed on the 7th of February, 1863, by *Stewart Wilson* and *Charles S. Wilson*, against *Henry Daniels, Calvin Campbell, J. S. M. Wilsox, John H. Cronk,* and *Judah Cronk,* setting forth that in June, 1852, one *Edward Bateman* had interests as actual settler in certain lands in the townships of Bexley and Somerville, fronting on Gull river, and having valuable water privileges.

Soon after obtaining his location tickets for these

lands, *Bateman* entered into partnership with *Henry
Daniels* and one *Bartlett*, the agreement being that the
two latter should contribute towards completing the
purchase of the land, and aid with means and labour
in erecting a saw-mill on the premises, obtaining partnership stock, and generally in carrying on a lumbering
business.

The firm thus continued business till 1856, when
Bartlett sold his interest to *Daniels*, who remained in
business with *Bateman* till March, 1857, the firm being
styled, " *Edward Bateman & Co.* *Bateman* then agreed
to sell his undivided one-third of the lands, and also
a quantity of chattel property he had on the premises
to *Daniels* for the aggregate sum of £350, no division
being made in the price as to the lands or personalty,
but it being, as expressed by the parties, " one lumping bargain." Separate conveyances were executed
to *Daniels* of the chattels and real estate, but the considerations expressed in them were proved to have
been only nominal, and promissory notes were given
by *Daniels* to *Bateman* to secure the purchase money,
less a sum due *Daniels* in another transaction. The
plaintiffs are holders for value of three of the notes on
which they had recovered judgment at law against
Bateman and *Daniels* for £226 12s. 6d., and they also
have a formal assignment from *Bateman* of any lien
he had for the purchase money represented by these
notes. Since his purchase from *Bateman*, *Daniels* had
failed in business and made an assignment of all his
property to the defendants, *Campbell* and *Wilcox*, and
they had agreed to sell the lands in dispute to their
co-defendants *John H.* and *Judah Cronk*.

None of the defendants denied notice of the plaintiff's claims, but they insisted that under the circumstances no lien upon the lands existed for any part of
the purchase money.

Evidence was taken, and the cause heard before his

Honour Vice-Chancellor *Esten*, at Whitby, in October, 1863.

Mr. *J. C. Hamilton*, for the plaintiffs.

Mr. *John Bell*, Q.C., for the defendants.

Dixon v. *Yates*, (a) *Winter* v. *Lord Auson*, (b) *Withes* v. *Lee*, (c) *Grant* v. *Mills*, (d) *Hooper* v. *Ramsbottom*, (e) *Harrington* v. *Price*, (f) *Bell* v. *Phynn*, (g) *Hanson* v. *Myer*, (h) *Payne* v. *Shadbald*, (i) *Mitchell* v. *McGaffey*, (j) *Colborne* v. *Thomas*, (k) *Boulton* v. *Gillispie*, (l) *Helliwell* v. *Dickson*, (m) *Seton* on Decrees, p. 451, and *Cross* on Lien, p. 93.

Judgment.—ESTEN, V.C.—I have perused the pleadings and evidence and referred to the exhibits as far as was necessary. It does not appear to me that the circumstance of this land being partnership property, and therefore personal estate, would prevent the lien from attaching; or that the circumstance that *Bateman* had paid only one instalment of the purchase money to the government, and that the remaining instalments had been paid by the other parties, would have that effect: nor the circumstance that the lands were intended to be used in the prosecution of the business. It is quite clear that the law confers the right which is asserted in the present case independently of the agreement of the parties, and that in order to prevent its operation it must either expressly or by implication be extinguished. An intention of that nature may be, and often is, inferred from the circumstances, indeed almost always, when it is deemed to have become extinct, for it is seldom the subject of express stipulation. In the present instance *Bateman* disposed of his interest

---

(a) 5 B. & Ad. 339.
(c) 2 Jur. N. S. 9.
(e) 4 Cowp. 121.
(g) 7 Ves. 452.
(i) 1 Cowp. 427.
(k) Ante, vol. iv., p. 102.
(m) Ante, vol. ix., p. 414.

(b) 3 Russ. 488.
(d) 2 V. & B. 306.
(f) 3 B. & A. 170.
(h) 6 East 622.
(j) Ante, vol. vi., p. 361.
(l) Ante, vol. viii., p. 253.

in the partnership, that is,'his one-third share in the
debts, goods and lands of the partnership for one sum of
£350, without any severance or apportionment of the
consideration amongst the different subjects of sale. Part
of this sum of £350 was deducted by *Daniels* to satisfy
an individual debt due to him from *Bateman*, and for
the residue, several promissory notes were given; and
thereupon *Bateman* executed an assignment transferring
all his interest in the goods and chattels in consideration
of £500; also a conveyance transferring his interest in
lots 14, 15, and 38, in consideration of £100; and also
a conveyance transferring his interest in lot 16, in consideration of £125. These considerations, it is obvious,
were nominal, as they amount in the aggregate to £725,
whereas the whole consideration agreed to be paid by
Daniels was only £350. The difficulty presented by
the present case is, that the consideration has not been
apportioned. The chattels and debts were transferred
and delivered, and the lands conveyed. No lien could
exist *quoad* the chattels and debts, and never could be
intended to exist; for it is evident that on the delivery
of the notes they were to become the absolute property
of *Daniels*. The conveyance of the land, however, did
not destroy the lien, if any existed; but for what sum
would the law, under such circumstances, confer a lien—
for the whole amount of the consideration? Mr. *Hamilton*
contended for this result: but can his contention be supported? It is true that if cash were to be paid, *Bateman* might have refused to transfer the debts, or deliver
the goods, or convey the lands until it had been paid;
and if they had been partly transferred and delivered,
he might have refused to complete the transaction until
the whole consideration had been paid; but *Bateman*
having performed his part of the contract by transferring the debts, delivering the goods, and conveying the
lands, the law must give the lien on the lands, if any is
to exist; and for what sum can it give it? It cannot, I
think, for the whole, for part of the consideration belongs
to the other subjects of sale, and the lien is given by

the law only for the consideration for the land ; and if the rule were otherwise, and the subject of sale were goods worth, we may suppose, £500, and land worth £500, and one undivided sum of £1000 were agreed to be paid for the whole, and the goods were delivered, the land would be charged with a lien for £1000, or double its value, which would be impossible. If the parties had agreed that so much of the consideration should belong to the land, it is possible that the plaintiffs might have substantiated this claim; but if the lien cannot be established for the full amount, it cannot be established for any part, for it is impossible to say for what part it ought to be established, and the circumstance that the parties have not apportioned and defined the particular part of the consideration appertaining to the land, I may regard as evidence of their intention that no lien on the land should exist, and such I think is the correct conclusion,. and therefore I think that the bill should be dismissed with costs.

BANK OF MONTREAL v. HOPKINS.

Mortgagor and mortgagee—Trustee and cestui que trust.

C. H. being the owner of the equity of redemption in three distinct tenements, sold and conveyed one of them to J. T. K. by a deed in fee, with absolute covenants for quiet enjoyment, freedom from incumbrances, &c., taking from the purchaser a bond by which he covenants to pay £241 of the money owing on the outstanding mortgage; the purchaser afterwards went to the holders of the mortgage, concealed from them the existence of his bond, produced the deed to himself, and agreed with the holders of the mortgage for the release of his portion of the property, and a release was accordingly, for a valuable consideration, executed by them. J. T. K., having become insolvent, absconded from the province, and a suit to foreclose having been instituted against C. H., he sought to charge the plaintiffs, the mortgagees, with the amount payable by J. T. K. under his bond: but the court, acting on the rule established in Ford v. Chandler, reported ante, vol. viii., page 85, considered the plaintiffs warranted in treating the absolute covenants executed by the defendant (C. H.) as an undertaking by him to pay off the whole sum remaining due upon the mortgage, and, therefore, charged the portions still vested in him therewith.— [ESTEN, V.C., *dissenting*.]

This was a bill filed by The *Bank of Montreal* against *Caleb Hopkins*, seeking to foreclose a mortgage on certain freehold property in the city of Toronto.

The defendant resisted the suit so far as it was sought to make him liable for the whole amount due on the mortgage, on the ground that the plaintiffs had released a portion of the mortgage premises to *Joseph T. Kerby*, to whom defendant had conveyed it by a deed in fee, and which contained absolute covenants for title; freedom from incumbrances, &c.

James McCutchon, the agent of the bank in the transaction with *Kerby*, was examined as a witness in the cause, and in his evidence he swore as follows:

"I was the agent of the mortgagee in this matter I know the mortgaged premises, and sold them. I remember executing a release to Mr. *Patrick ;* he had then, I think, made two payments, that is, paid two instalments with interest, thereupon I executed a release to him. I don't know that Mr. *Kerby* made any payment; he asked me to give him a release. He shewed me a deed from Mr. *Hopkins*. I found no mortgage on the registry, which I searched, from *Kerby* to *Hopkins*. I first heard of an agreement between them about paying the mortgage when Mr. *Hopkins* came to pay me some money long after the release. Mr. *Patrick* is Mr. *Hopkins'* son-in-law ; Mr. *Hopkins* knew of the release to *Patrick ;* he never made any objection to me on the ground of it. I think *Hopkins* knew of the release to *Patrick* when he came to pay me £25, which must have been in 1858 ; he afterwards made a payment in 1859 ; he then spoke of the bond he had from *Kerby*. I received the money generally from the parties, and gave the receipt as for money coming from *Morphy* [the original purchaser.] I think there was a house at the time of the release on *Kerby's* portion, built or building, but I am not sure. I understood he wanted to borrow money to complete his building. He said he had paid Mr. *Hopkins* in full, and he shewed me the deed. I did not tell *Kerby* that there was any amount due or unpaid on the mortgage when I gave the release to *Kerby*. I did not stipulate for any other sum than £20, and he did not agree to pay any more. Mr. *Hopkins* made a payment of £46, and £40, and he may have paid £132 altogether, but I cannot say. I have had no correspondence with *Kerby* about this matter. I cannot say whether at the

time of the release *Kerby* was building on the part released. I think Mr. *Patrick* paid in one instalment
for Mr. *Hopkins*. I have received one instalment and
£40 and interest from Mr. *Hopkins*. The rest I received from Mr. *Patrick*, but whose money it was I
cannot tell.

At the hearing.

Mr. *Hodgins*, for the plaintiffs.

Mr. *Crickmore*, for defendant.

The point in issue appears in the head-note and
judgment of

Judgment.—ESTEN, V. C.—I apprehend that when a
mortgagor alienates the equity of redemption in part of
the lands, the rights and obligations of the mortgagor and
purchaser in regard to the discharge of the mortgage
debt as between themselves depend entirely on the terms
of the agreement between them. When the mortgagor
undertakes to discharge the mortgage wholly as between
themselves, the mortgage debt is thrown upon the remainder of the estate retained by him, and any one
purchasing part of such remainder must purchase it subject to this burden. It is only in this case that the
doctrine enunciated in the case in 5 *Johnson* (a) is true,
and it is only to such a case that the learned Chancellor
intended to apply it. Where it is part of the agreement
of purchase that the purchaser shall disharge a certain
portion of the mortgage as between him and the mortgagor, this portion is thrown on the part of the estate
purchased, and the rest of the estate becomes a surety
for its discharge. When the existence of the mortgage
is known, but the facts and evidence utterly fail to furnish any clue to the actual terms of the agreement, I
apprehend that the court will intend that the purchaser
is to pay a proportionate part of the mortgage debt as

_____

(a) C. C. 241.

between him and the mortgagor. A mortgagee of an estate is of course a mere trustee, beyond securing his principal, interest and costs, and I apprehend that a trustee is in no case justified in dealing with the trust estate without the knowledge of the *cestui que trust*.

The Court of Appeal did not, I apprehend, intend to contravene this doctrine in the case of *Ford* v. *Chandler*: they considered that the *cestui que trust* had there misled the trustee by having signed a writing which was shewn to the trustee, who drew a wrong conclusion from it. I should think it a safe rule to establish that the trustee should not, whatever he may see, however strong appearances may be, take upon himself to deal with the trust estate without communication with his *cestui que trust*, when such communication is possible. The safety derived from placing property in the hands of trustees will be in a great measure destroyed if a contrary doctrine should prevail.

The Court of Appeal thought in the case of *Ford* v. *Chandler* that the trustee was justified under the circumstances in acting upon the writing that was shewn to him without previous communication with his *cestui que trust*, which perhaps may not have been in his power. I do not recollect how the fact was in that respect. When the *cestui que trust* is within reach, nothing can be more easy than for the trustee to inform him that he is requested by a third party to make some disposition of the trust estate, and that he has seen documents which appear to authorize it, but to ask whether it is right that he should accede to the demand. Surely it is better for the trustee before he disposes of property which is not his own, but belongs to another, to perform such a simple act, rather than take upon himself without enquiry to decide what is proper for him to do, whereby, through drawing a wrong conclusion from the facts which appear, property placed in his hands for safe custody may be taken from those whose interests had been so anxiously guarded by the author of the trust. The utmost caution should, I think, be exacted from a trustee in dealing with the trust estate. It is not merely that it is not his estate, but that of another, but that it has been placed in his hands for safe custody, and entrusted to his care. In the present case, as I understand, the agreement between *Hopkins* and *Kerby* was, that *Kerby* should pay £241 of the mortgage debt; this obligation in fact formed part of the consideration of the purchase, and this portion of the mortgage debt formed a part of *Kerby's* purchase money. Undoubtedly as between him and *Hopkins* his part of the estate became *quoad* this part of the debt, the principal debtor, and bound to indemnify the residue of the estate retained by *Hopkins ;* in other words, *Kerby* might have redeemed the whole estate from the plaintiffs, but he must have conveyed to *Hopkins* the part not sold to himself, on receiving from *Hopkins* the balance of the debt after deducting the £241. The plaintiffs, by releasing the part of the estate sold to *Kerby*, from the mortgage, have deprived *Hopkins* of his rights ; that is, being subject to this mortgage, trustees, they have dealt with the trust estate without the sanction of their *cestui que trust.* Of the part of the estate sold to *Kerby*, the plaintiffs were, beyond the mortgage, trustees for *Kerby*, subject to the right of *Hopkins* to redeem the whole estate, and hold this portion of it until paid the £241. This estate of *Hopkins* they have disposed of without his sanction. They must be deemed to have known that by the general law if any particular agreement were made between *Hopkins* and *Kerby* concerning the discharge of the mortgage, certain rights would accrue to either according to the circumstances of the case, subject to their own security; they were bound to respect and preserve those rights, and before they ventured to deal with the estate to ascertain what they were. It is said that the absolute conveyance to *Kerby*, with receipts in the body of the deed, and on the back, for the purchase money, and a covenant that the estate was free from incumbrances, misled the plaintiffs. But they were misled because they did not choose to enquire. I think nothing of the receipts in the body of, and endorsed on, the deed. It is well known that in half the cases that occur, especially in this country, they are contrary to the fact, and are wholly unreliable. In England the receipt is seldom or never endorsed unless the purchase money is paid; in this country, I believe, it is nearly as much a matter of course as the receipt in the body of the deed; I think neither of them should have deceived the plaintiffs. Then the covenants might appear at first sight to indicate that *Kerby* was to hold the estate he had purchased free from the mortgage. But in this respect also it is well known that deeds are not accurately framed. If any agreement existed as to the discharge of the mortgage, the effect of it would not be precluded by a covenant that the estate was free from incumbrances in equity, and if an action were commenced at law on that ground, it would be restrained in equity. The plaintiffs therefore were not justified in considering the form of the deed as conclusive, or in determining for Mr. *Hopkins* the extent of his rights. Enquiry was easy, and should have been made, and I think it was gross negligence not to make it. It is contended that Mr. *Hopkins* should have made known to the plaintiffs the terms of the agreement he had made with *Kerby*, and no doubt it would have been an act of prudence to have done so, but he was under no obligation of duty to take that step; he knew that the plaintiffs ought not to deal with his estate without his sanction. Upon the plaintiffs an obligation of duty rested to inquire of their *cestui que trust* before they dealt with his estate, and Mr. *Hopkins* to make known his right to the plaintiffs, was an unnecessary, although, doubtless, a prudent act. It is true that if the *cestui que trust* does anything to mislead his trustee, and the trustee exercises reasonable diligence, he is discharged from responsibility for any disposition of the estate as to which he has been ensnared by the act of the *cestui que trust*. But in this case the mere form of the deed was not a safe ground on which to proceed, and enquiry was so easy that its omission was inconsistent with reasonable diligence.

I think the just order to make is to declare that so much of the mortgage debt as *Kerby* was bound by the terms of the agreement with *Hopkins* to pay has been discharged ; but *Hopkins* must transfer to the plaintiffs all his rights as against *Kerby* for the recovery of the purchase money.   It may be that he has a lien on the estate to compel the payment of this £241, and that this lien may not have been prejudiced by the release, but I think it must be at the expense and peril of the plaintiffs to enforce any such rights that may exist.

From this decision of his Honor the plaintiffs appealed by way of re-hearing before the full court.

Mr. *Roaf*, for plaintiffs.

Mr. *Strong*, Q.C., and Mr. *Crickmore*, for defendant.

The judgment of the court was delivered by

VANKOUGHNET, C.—After the most careful consideration I can give to this case I have formed an opinion opposed to that expressed by my brother *Esten* on the hearing before him.   The deed from *Hopkins* to *Kerby* is now produced, and it contains absolute covenants for title, and a covenant for further assurance in the usual form.   It was executed while the bank were holders of the mortgage now sued upon, and was produced to them when *Kerby* applied for the release of the portion of land covered by the mortgage.   This *Hopkins*, by his covenant for further assurance, undertook to procure for him.   I think the bank on seeing this deed were justified in assuming that *Hopkins* had assigned to *Kerby* all his interest in the land covered by it, and were under no obligation to ask *Hopkins* if his deed really meant what it expressed ; or if there was any secret trust by which he was still to have a lien on the land.   I think a person holding the position of *Hopkins* has no right to give another such a document, enabling him to use it, and then when it is used and acted upon by his trustee, turn round and tell the latter that he should not have believed it, but should have sought for information behind it.   I think he must be held bound by his own act, and abide the consequences of it.   He chose to part with his estate in the land trusting to the personal responsibility of the debtor, and if he meant that the latter should not deal as the owner of the equity of redemption with the mortgagee, it was at least his duty to have notified the mortgagee accordingly.   A *cestui qui trust* has duties and responsibilities as well as the trustee, and he cannot by his own act mislead the latter, and then turn round and hold him responsible. I think this case is governed by *Chandler* v. *Ford*, (in appeal,) and that in principle it is identical with it.

ESTEN, V. C., remained of the opinion expressed by him on the original hearing.

Per Curiam.—Defendant to pay amount remaining due on the mortgage together with costs.— [*Esten*, V. C., dissenting.]

THE GREAT WESTERN RAILWAY COMPANY v. THE
DESJARDINS CANAL COMPANY.

*Specific performance—Appointment of engineers to inspect work before
acceptance.*

Two incorporated trading companies agreed by writing under their
corporate seals, the one to construct certain works for the other,
which on completion were to be inspected by engineers on behalf of
each of the contracting parties, and upon the engineers approving
of the works, and reporting them as completed, they were to be
accepted as soon as completed by the party for whom they were
done, who were to be forever debarred from denying. or contesting
the due and proper execution, completion, and acceptance of such
works. The parties to perform the work having, as they alleged,
completed it, notified the others thereof, calling upon them to
appoint an engineer, as stipulated for, which request was not complied with, and subsequently a portion of the works contracted for
(a bridge) was destroyed. On a bill filed for the purpose of compelling an acceptance of the works, the court thought that the
delay of one of the contracting parties until after such destruction
to name an, engineer, as had been stipulated for by the agreement,
did not preclude the other from obtaining an inspection of the
works ; but that such inspection and approval must, under the
circumstances, be had by a reference to the master.—[VANKOUGH-
NET, C., *dubitante.*]

Statement.—The bill in this case was filed on the 25th
September, 1858, by *The Great Western Railway Company*, against *The Desjardins Canal Company*, setting
forth that after the construction of the defendants' work
had been completed the plaintiffs ascertained that it
would greatly conduce to the stability and permanency
of their railway if the defendants would close the chan-.
nel or outlet of the canal as then constructed and allow
a new channel or outlet to be made ; and accordingly
the plaintiffs and defendants made and entered into an
agreement under the corporate seals of the parties
respectively, dated the 7th June, 1852, which recited
that " whereas in the construction of the said railroad
it is found necessary to carry the same across the Desjardins Canal. And whereas the said canal company
for the improvement of the said canal desire to make
a new channel or outlet through Burlington Heights,
in the vicinity of the present natural channel or outlet.
And whereas the filling up of the present natural
channel or outlet would be an advantage to the said
railroad company. And whereas the said canal company has agreed that the said new channel shall be

opened at the place hereinafter indicated, and the present channel closed and filled up at the point at which the said railroad is now under construction, so that the said railroad may pass over the said filling up without a bridge or by any means the said railroad company may think proper to adopt. And whereas it has been further agreed by and between the said companies that the costs and expense of effecting the said change of channel shall be borne jointly by the said companies, but in the proportion and manner following, namely, the said canal company to contribute twelve thousand five hundred pounds, and the railroad company the residue, whatever the same may amount to. And whereas the said canal company are not in possession of funds sufficient to carry out so soon as the same are required to be effected the said changes and improvements, and it has therefore been agreed by the said companies that the said railroad company shall perform the same and advance that portion of the expense thereof which is to be borne by the said canal company as aforesaid, and that the latter company should give security for the repayment of the same at the time and in manner as is stated in such securities. And whereas the land on which it is proposed to make the said new channel is ordnance property, and it will be necessary to obtain leave to make use of the same, and these presents are, therefore, only to become operative and efficient in case the consent of the officers or persons competent to give such consent can be obtained therefor. Now these presents witness, and the said the Great Western Railroad Company, in pursuance and consideration of the premises, for themselves, their successors and assigns, hereby covenant, promise, and agree to and with the said the Desjardins Canal Company, their successors and assigns, in manner following, that is to say, that they, the said the Great Western Railroad Company, their successors or assigns, shall and will, with all due diligence, and with the use of all means within their power, well and sufficiently do perform, erect, execute and complete the excavations, bridges, and all and singular other the works, matters, and things mentioned and contained in the specifications and plans hereunto annexed, (signed by the respective presidents of the said companies,) according to, and agreeably with, the said specifications and plans, causing no unnecessary delay, and using all available means

that can or may be adopted for the completion of the
same,and furnishing and providing of good quality all
the materials therefor,and that they will not until the
first day of November now next ensuing,hinder or ob-
struct the navigation of the present outlet of the said
canal more than is reasonably necessary for the purpose
of doing and performing the hereinbefore mentioned
improvements and works, provided always, and it is
hereby expressly declared and agreed by and between
the companies parties hereto, that it shall be lawful
for, and the said the *Desjardins Canal Company* for
the consideration herein appearing hereby grant liberty
to the said the *Great Western Railroad Company,* their
successors and assigns, to close, fill up and throw an
embankment over and across the said canal or outlet
thereof after the said first day of November aforesaid,
at the place or point where the said railroad is to be
carried over, and to keep and continue the said canal
and outlet thereof (being the present natural channel
or outlet) closed, filled up, and embanked at all times
thereafter,and to use the same filling in or embankment
for the purposes of constructing the said railroad and
maintaining and using the same ; the said railroad
company to have the gratuitous use of the said canal
for the performance of the before-mentioned works,
subject to the foregoing stipulations : And whereas
doubts have been expressed as to whether it would be
safe to leave that part of the cut or new channel aforesaid, which is composed of cemented gravel, at the present elevation, as shewn upon the plan hereto annexed,
and signed by the presidents of the said respective
companies parties hereto : it is hereby agreed by
and between the parties hereto that the cutting and
finishing of that part of the work shall be decided and
determined upon by the chief engineer for the time
being of the said the Great Western Railroad Company,
and an engineer to be appointed by the Desjardins
Canal Company, who shall be authorised to visit and
examine that part of the said cut and works as they
proceed, and in the event of any disagreement between
the said engineers, they shall be at liberty to choose a
third engineer, whose decision shall be final, and the
said the Desjardins Canal Company shall then accept
and receive the works from the said Great Western
Railroad Company, as finished, irrespective and inde-
pendant of,and notwithstanding anything contained in,
the next following proviso and agreement; this proviso

expressly providing for the said cemented gravel work.
And it is hereby further provided and agreed by and
between the respective parties to these presents, that
upon the said the Great Western Railroad Company
notifying the said the Desjardins Canal Company, that
the said canal cut and works aforesaid are completed,
the said the Desjardins Canal Company shall appoint
a competent and experienced engineer,who,in company
and associated with the chief engineer for the time being
of the said the Great Western Railway Company, shall
visit and inspect the same, and in the event of these
failing to agree, then they shall call in another engineer
or person to act as umpire, or any two of them shall
report the said canal and works properly,and according
to the true intent and meaning of these presents,
executed and completed, the same shall be accepted by,
and shall belong to, the said the Desjardins Canal
Company ; and the said last named company, their
successors and assigns, shall for ever be debarred from
denying and contesting their due and proper execution,
completion, and acceptance.   In witness whereof the
said the Great Western Railroad Company have, by
their president, set the corporate seal of the said
railroad Company, and the said the Desjardins Canal
Company have, by their president, set the corporate seal
of the said canal company to these presents the day
and year first above written."

That after the execution of this agreement the plaintiffs proceeded with the construction of the works, in
accordance with such agreement, until the same were
finally completed, in compliance with the terms of the
contract; during the progress of which the defendants
paid to plaintiffs a large sum of money, on account of
their proportion of the expense incurred, according to
the terms of the agreement; and at the time that the
works were completed, a large sum of money was still
due and unpaid by the defendants, amounting to about
£3,000, which was still due : that after the completion
of the works the plaintiffs on several occasions notified
the defendants in writing that the said canal cut and
works in the said agreement mentioned were completed
and requested the defendants to appoint an engineer to

visit and inspect the works, in company with the chief engineer of the plaintiffs, as provided by the agreement, and in order to the final transmission to, and acceptance by, the defendants of the works. Notwithstanding which the defendants had not appointed any engineer, in accordance with the terms of the agreement, nor would they accept and receive the same as completed, or pay the plaintiffs the balance remaining due.

The prayer of the bill was, that defendants should be ordered to appoint an engineer to inspect the works; and should also proceed in the delivery and acceptance thereof, as provided by the agreement; and that they should be perpetually enjoined and restrained for commencing or prosecuting any suit or proceeding at law, in reference to these works; and that they might be ordered to pay such amount as might be found due to plaintiffs.

In April, 1859, the defendants put in their answer, disputing their liability to be called upon in this manner, on the ground, amongst others, that the works had never been properly executed; and setting up, also, the appointment of Mr. *Paige* a civil engineer, to act with the chief engineer of the plaintiffs, and the fact that *Paige* had reported against the sufficiency of the work; alleging that they, the defendants, had sustained great loss and inconvenience by reason of the non-performance of the agreement by the plaintiffs.

The cause was put at issue, and witnesses at some length were examined before the court in September, 1859, consisting entirely of the officers and engineers of the plaintiffs and defendants respectively, the effect of which sufficiently appears in the judgment.

The cause came on for hearing upon the pleadings and evidence before his Honour Vice-Chancellor *Esten*.

Mr. *Hillyard Cameron*, Q. C., and Mr. *G. D. Boulton*, for the plaintiffs, referred to *Walker* v. *The Eastern*

Counties Railway Company, (a) *Jackson* v. *Jackson,* (b)
Storer v. *Great Western Railway Cympany,* (c) *Sander-*
son v. *Cockermouth & Workington Railway Company,*
(d) *Gourlay* v. *The Duke of Somerset,* (e) *Rowe* v. *Wood,*
(f) *Gregory* v. *Mighell,* (g) to shew that where the
parties will not appoint an arbitrator or engineer the
court will ascertain the fact itself.

Mr. *Strong* and Mr. *Blake,* for the defendants, opposed the relief asked, on the grounds:

1st. That an inspection and certificate of the completion of the works were an indispensible condition to
the acceptance of them, in this court, as well as in a
court of law.

2nd. If this is not the rule, then the works are not
in fact completed.

3rd. The agreement is one such as this court will
not enforce; and,

4th. The appointment of an engineer will not be
decreed.

Here the defendants did in fact appoint an engineer,
who inspected the works, disapproved of and reported
against them; before another inspection was had the
bridge was destroyed without having been inspected: by
the agreement inspection of the bridge was stipulated
for, however, and this has now become impossible; that
the defendants had always objected to this portion of
the work as sufficient in its construction, and while
the bridge was not replaced no advantage could be derived by the defendants' engineer attending: the in-

---

(a) 6 Hare, 594.   (b) 1 S. & S. 184, 22 L.J. 873.
(c) 2 Y. & C.C.C. 48.   (d) 11 Beav. 497.
(e) 19 Ves. 429.   (f) 1 J. & W. 315.
(g) 18 Ves. 328.

spection being to take place after the final completion of the work. The bridge having thus been included in the agreement, and being also subject to inspection, it must, before acceptance will be enforced, be inspected; and as this has, under the circumstances, become impossible, this part of the agreement must remain the subject of an action at law under the contract. It was clearly the duty of the plaintiffs to keep up the works until completion, so that they could be produced in a state to be inspected.

That work constructed under a contract will be accepted by the person for whom the work has been performed, is an implied stipulation of every agreement, and if here the plaintiffs succeed in obtaining the interference of the court in their behalf—in every case a like application may be made. There was no mutuality in the contract, as the defendants could never have compelled the plaintiffs to perform the works. An acceptance of them would be a bar to all actions by the defendants. *Wilks* v. *Davis* (a) shews the court will not appoint an arbitrator.

They also referred to *Scott* v. *The Corporation of Liverpool*, (b) *Scott* v. *Avery*, (c) *Horton* v. *Sayer*, (d) *Milnes* v. *Gery*, (e) *Darbey* v. *Whitaker*, (f) *McIntosh* v. *The Great Western Railway Company*, (g) *Ranger* v. *The Great Western Railway Company*, (h) *Kemp* v. *Rose*. (i)

Mr. *Hillyard Cameron*, Q.C., in reply. In effect the contract between these parties stipulated for a release being given by the defendants to the plaintiffs. Had it in express words been so agreed then this court would have compelled it. An acceptance of the work will not

---

(a) 3 Mer. 507.   (b) 5 Jur. N. S. 105.
(c) 2 Jur. N. S. 815; S. C. 5 H. L. Ca. 811.
(d) 5 Jur. N. S 989.   (e) 13 Ves. 400.
(f) 4 Drew, 134.   (g) S & G. 146.
(h) 5 H. L. Ca. 72.   (i) 4 Jur. N. S. 919.

preclude the defendants from bringing any action for a non-performance of the agreement. He also contended that the bridge was not within the terms of the contract.

Judgment.—ESTEN, V.C.—I think the agreement was of such a nature that it ought if possible to be specifically performed. I think the plaintiffs stipulated to stand in a position of perfect immunity and security against all dispute and objection, and that they have a right to require that they shall be placed in this position, if the powers of this court enable it to grant such relief. It must be deemed that they would not have entered into the agreement unless this stipulation formed a part of it. True it is that the court might not be able to decree the specific execution of the works, and that therefore mutuality may be wanting; but I question whether this fact forms an obstacle to relief, and whether, if necessary, it would not give jurisdiction to the courts to decree the specific execution of the works. The nature of the case, however, precludes this question.

The facts of the case are these. It was desired both by the plaintiffs and defendants to alter the course and outlet of the Desjardins Canal. The plaintiffs in fact wanted to carry the road over the former channel. It was agreed between them that a new cut should be made through Burlington Heights by the plaintiffs at their own expense, that is to say that the defendants should pay £12,500 and the plaintiffs the residue of the expense. The two agreements were then duly executed, the second merely substituting a suspension for a wooden bridge, and the defendants agreeing in consequence to pay £500 more. I think this bridge was within the provision in the first agreement regarding inspection. The defendants executed securities to the amount of £13,000. The works were performed by the plaintiffs, but the defendants complained of the delay. On the 13th of September, 1854, they were inspected by Mr. *Reid*, the engineer of the plaintiffs, and Mr. *Paige*, of the board of works, on behalf of the defendants, and it would appear of the government also. Mr. *Reid* says that the works had all been performed according to the contract. Mr. *Paige* says that they were not then in a proper state according to the contract, but that he had no reason to think they had not been performed according to the contract originally, and suggested some additions which he said if performed would satisfy him. Mr. *Reid* undertook to recommend them to the plaintiffs, although, as he says, they were not required by the contract. They are said to have been afterwards performed. Mr. *Reid* says distinctly that the works had been performed according to the contract in 1853, that they were inspected in 1854, and Mr. *Paige* suggested some additions not in the contract, which were afterwards performed in a superior manner to what was undertaken, and that the cut was twice re-dredged by the plaintiffs.

Mr. *Paige's* evidence supports this statement to a considerable extent. On turning to his reports made about the time, they shew that the work was not then in a satisfactory state, although perhaps not inconsistent with an original execution of it, correct according to a somewhat strict and literal interpretation.

McCormick's report, dated November 21st, 1854, disapproves of the work as it was then, but is not inconsistent with an original performance of it according to the contract literally construed. I am inclined to think that by the original work, &c., and additions made to it, if the contract was not carried into effect entirely according to a fair interpretation of it, a close approximation was made to that result, although perhaps the delay may have been considerable, and may have caused loss to the defendants, it not appearing, however, whether it was greater than was necessary, or whether it could have been avoided. The objections to the work seem to resolve themselves into six points: the depth, the width, the course, the slopes, the bridge, and the facing.

Of these the objections to the width and course seem to be without foundation. With regard to the depth, the cut might have been originally excavated to the required depth, and afterwards have become of insufficient depth; the slopes may have been originally of the required inclination, and made according to the contract, and afterwards deranged by the rains; the facing may not have been required by the contract, and may have been added gratuitously, and may have been properly executed, although some complaints were made by some of the directors, not engineers. There is much reason to think that the works were originally executed according to the fair meaning of the contract. The points of enquiry are only three, in this respect on the first contract, which does not provide for the suspension bridge, namely, the depth, the slope, and the facing. The two former are clearly provided for, and were probably executed according to contract, but afterwards deranged. The contract does not seem to provide for any protection to the banks except through the marsh. The suspension bridge is provided for by the second contract. It must be remarked, however, that diagrams and plans were attached to the agreements which I have not seen. I have referred to a number of cases cited in the course of the argument, some of which were of doubtful applicability. It is well settled that this court will not decree the specific performance of an agreement to refer to arbitration. Such a decree would be inconsistent with the legal maxim that an agreement for arbitration shall not deprive the courts of jurisdiction ; moreover, although arbitrators may be appointed, the court cannot compel them to arbitrate, and it will not in the case of an agreement perfectly executory pronounce a decree which it may not be able to enforce. It is equally clear that the construction of an agreement must be the same at law, and in equity, and that where a provision for arbitration is incorporated with the agreement, and the party is only to pay what arbitrators shall award; or where the agreement is to pay when an engineer or architect shall have

certified what is due, and only what he shall so certify, as
no action can be maintained at law, so no suit can be instituted in equity until a breach of the agreement has
occurred, which cannot be the case unless and until
the arbitrators have awarded in the one case, or the engineer or architect has certified in the other. It is also quite
clear that where an agreement has been entered into for
the sale of property at a price to be fixed by arbitrators,
this court cannot decree the specific execution of this
agreement, unless the arbitrators have fixed the price,
although when the agreement is to purchase at a valuation the court will itself ascertain the value. These
propositions embrace, I think, most, if not all, of the
points involved in the cases cited by the learned counsel
for the defendants. The doctrines, however, which
they settle or recognise, admit of some important qualification. Thus, although the construction of an agreement must be the same at law and in equity, yet equity
does not always regard parts of an agreement as essential
which are so considered at law. This is familiarly ex-
emplified with respect to the time of performing an
agreement which is not generally regarded as essential
in equity, although it construes the agreement in this
respect in the same way as a court of law. Where also
the agreement provides for the intervention of a third
party, although it receives the same construction in a
court of equity as in a court of law, yet equity does not
always regard this provision as an essential part of the
agreement. This occurred in the case of *Gourlay* v.
The *Duke of Somerset*, (a) where the defendant agreed to
grant a lease to the plaintiff containing such covenants
and reservations as Mr. *Gale*, who was his steward,
should approve. The court referred it to the master to
approve of a lease, considering the intervention of Mr.
Gale as not an essential term of the contract. An important qualification, too, to the general doctrine with
respect to the intervention of arbitrators is established by
the case of *Gregory* v. *Mighell*, (b) which was before the

(a) 19 Ves. 429.   (b) 18 Ves. 328.

same able and distinguished judge who decided *Gourlay* v.The *Duke of Somerset*. This qualification is, that where the contract does not remain in *fieri*, but has been so far carried into effect that justice requires that it should be completely executed, the court will disregard the stipulation for the intervention of arbitrators, and will itself determine what they were intended to settle. In the case of *Gregory* v. *Mighell*, where the rent was to be fixed by arbitrators, and the defendant, after allowing the plaintiff to occupy the premises under the agreement during the whole term agreed upon of twenty-one years, and to make expenditure, at the end of the term refused to execute arbitration bonds, the court held that the defendant could not, after allowing the agreement to be acted on in that way, prevent its specific execution, by refusing to nominate an arbitrator, and referred it to the master to fix the rent. It was said in a late decision that this was a strong case, but that it had never been questioned. It is also settled that where no right of action accrues, until some act be performed by a third person, such as the furnishing a certificate by an engineer, and after the work has been performed, the engineer, by collusion with his employer, refuses to furnish the certificate, a court of equity will grant relief, and direct the necessary accounts, in order to ascertain what is due, whether the court has, in the abstract, jurisdiction over the subject matter or not. In the present case, if we suppose that the works have been faithfully performed by the plaintiffs, what can be more unjust than that the defendants should refuse to nominate an engineer to inspect them, in order to their acceptance. The plaintiffs, it must be intended, performed the work, and made the large expenditure necessary to that end, on the faith that when it was completed it would, after due examination and a satisfactory report, be accepted, and that they would be protected from litigation with respect to it for ever. The defendants permit the plaintiffs to make this large expenditure, and to complete the works, and then with-

hold that without which they never would have undertaken them, and insist that it cannot be enforced,
because a report must first be made by engineers, and
they refuse to nominate one on their own behalf.
Upon the hypothesis that the work has been faithfully
performed, no conduct can be more unjust, and it inflicts
great hardship upon the plaintiffs. But I think it is
the duty of this court to interfere under such circumstances.   If it were necessary, I should think it would
be right to compel the appointment of an engineer.
The court certainly refuses to compel the appointment
of arbitrators, but that is when the contract remains in
fieri, and it is better to refer the parties to their legal
remedy.   Here the agreement has been performed to
that extent that this court is bound to compel its
complete execution.   In the case of *Morse* v. *Merest*,(a)
where the defendant refused to permit the arbitrator
to enter on the land, the court compelled him to do
so.   But it does not appear to me to be necessary
to resort to this step, which might indeed be nugatory,
as the engineer appointed might refuse to act.   I may
remark, however, that if he should refuse to act in collusion with the defendants, the case would appear to be
within the principle of *McIntosh* v. *The Great Western*. (b)
The present case appears to me to be within the principle of the case of *Gourlay* v. *The Duke of Somerset*.
The report of an engineer appointed by the defendants
themselves does not appear to me to be essential.   All
that the defendants stipulated for is, that they shall not
be compelled to accept the work until it is ascertained to
have been satisfactorily completed; and being unskilled
in such matters, they stipulate that a skilled engineer
shall report upon the matter on their behalf, in conjunc-
tion with the chief engineer of the plaintiffs, and possibly
with an umpire, or that the umpire should decide.   It
appears to me that all that is required is, that a skilled
engineer shall exercise his judgment; it is not like fixing

(a) 6 Madd. 26.   (b) 3 S. & Gift. 146.

the price of land about which the judgments of different men may differ. It is true that a difference of opinion is contemplated by the agreement which provides for the appointment of an umpire; but whether a certain work has or has not been performed according to plans and specifications is not a question upon which a serious disagreement can be anticipated, or with respect to which confidence can be deemed to be exclusively reposed in the judgment of any particular individual. But however this may be, and whether the intervention of an engineer appointed by the defendants be considered essential, or the court will appoint its own officer to ascertain and report upon the completion of the work according to the rule followed in the case of *Gourlay* v. *The Duke of Somerset*, it appears to me that the present case is clearly within the principle established by the case of *Gregory* v. *Mighell*, and that the contract has been so far performed that it is the duty of this court to ascertain whether the work has been satisfactorily completed, and in that case to compel its acceptance on the part of the defendants, and thereby to place the plaintiffs in that position in which they stipulated that they should eventually stand, of perfect security against future litigation, and on the faith of occupying which position they entered into this agreement and have proceeded with the acquiescence of the defendants to carry it, as they allege, into execution. It appears that the plaintiffs, when they considered themselves to have completed the works, notified that fact to the defendants, and required them to nominate an engineer in terms of the agreement. They nominated Mr. *Paige* accordingly, and he and Mr. *Reid*, the plaintiff's chief engineer, inspected the works, when Mr. *Paige* suggesting some additions which he said if performed would make the works satisfactory to him, Mr. *Reid* undertook to recommend to the plaintiffs to make them. It is alleged that they have been made in a superior manner to what was suggested or undertaken. At all events it has become incumbent on the defendants again to nominate some engineer to assist in the inspection of the works. I do not doubt from the evidence that the plaintiffs consider themselves *bonâ fide* to have completed the works on reasonable grounds, of which they have given due notice to the defendants and required them to fulfil their agreement. Under these circumstances it has become incumbent, I think, upon the defendants to nominate an engineer to inspect the works. They contend indeed that they have not been satisfactorily performed, and that they are not bound to accept them, and in this contention they may possibly be right; but surely it is their duty under the circumstances to appoint an engineer in order to ascertain that fact. This duty they have failed to perform, and I think no course remained to the plaintiffs but to resort to their legal remedies for enforcing their rights, supposing the facts to be as they allege, of which the engineers are to judge. I propose therefore in default of the defendants' nominating an engineer and of his co-operating with the chief engineer of the plaintiffs and an umpire if necessary in inspecting and reporting upon the works within a month, to appoint one or more engineers for that purpose with instructions to examine the works, and with the aid of the present and of additional evidence if necessary to report whether at any time heretofore the works have been completed within the meaning of the contract between the parties; reserving further directions and costs. I may remark that any difficulty which might have arisen from want of mutuality has ceased to exist if the plaintiffs have performed their part of the contract, as it is clearly settled that where a party has performed his part of a contract he is entitled to the specific performance of the terms in his favour, although the acts which he has performed are of such a nature that this court would not in the abstract compel their specific execution.

The defendants being dissatisfied with the decree drawn up, in pursuance of this judgment, set the cause down to be re-heard before the full court.

·Mr. *Roaf*, for the plaintiffs.

Mr. *Strong*, Q.C., and Mr. *Blake*, for the defendants.

Judgment.—VANKOUGHNET, C.—Had I been called upon to decide this case originally, I think I would havé refused the plaintiffs a decree. My brothers, more familiar with such subjects than myself, think them clearly entitled to it, and I do not therefore absolutely dissent, though I have very grave doubts as to the propriety of interfering. I can find no authority for such a decree as alone the plaintiffs can have here, for I believe we are all agreed that the terms of the decree must be altered, and that the reference to ascertain whether or not the work which the plaintiffs contracted to do was or was not done according to contract, must be to an officer of this court, and not as the decree at present provides, to two strangers, to be chosen by the parties themselves. Indeed both plaintiffs and defendants contend for this alteration. That this can be the only decree to which the plaintiffs are entitled, seems to me a very strong if not an insuperable objection to their obtaining any relief here. What the ·plaintiffs and defendants agreed upon was, that an inspection of the works should be had by engineers, and that their finding upon them should be conclusive. This, I believe, is a very common stipulation among contractors; and one can at once see its value, for whether the finding be right or wrong it will not be thereafter open to question, unless indeed on the ground of fraud; but mere error in judgment or opinion will not vitiate it, and a manifest advantage is therefore gained by the one party or the other in such a tribunal. But this mode of decision is now impossible, for part of the subject matter of the proposed inspection has disappeared, viz., the suspension bridge. It is quite true that the inspection was not had through the fault of the defendants, and I quite agree that they had ample notice while inspection could have been had, and did not act upon it. But still it is one of those impossibilities—

one of those things of the past, which it seems to me almost out of the power of this court to remedy. If there were any contingent right or remedy depending upon it; if, for instance, the plaintiffs could not recover from the defendants their share of the money to be paid for the work till it was found whether or not the work was done, then I admit that the court would not allow the plaintiffs to suffer by the negligence or fault of the defendants, but would interfere and remove the difficulty out of their way; but such is not the case here; there is nothing to be gained by this reference more than can be obtained or ascertained in an action at law if the plaintiffs be attacked. The only question now can be, whether or not the work was done according to contract. The plaintiffs say it was. If so, why ask this court to declare it; they can shew this in any action brought against them. If it was not so done, why should they not pay damages? Suppose the defendants had sued them at law, would it not have been very difficult for this court to have interfered and removed the enquiry from a jury to the master of this court? What the parties stipulated for they cannot have—the tribunal of their selection is impossible. It cannot be that this court will always interfere because by some act or default of some of the parties a certain term of a contract has become impossible. Suppose an engagement for certain services by a celebrated engineer, or for the execution of certain work by him, or an undertaking by a party to procure his report on work as a final judgment thereon, and he dies without the engagement being performed; this court cannot make his executors do it for him, or do it through the master of this court: damages at law afford the only redress. I do not see my way to the relief sought for. Suppose the master to report that the work is not performed according to contract, what then is to be done? Can the court order the plaintiffs to complete them? Can they give the defendant damages? Will the parties not be left to law after all?

Judgment.—ESTEN, V. C., remained of the opinion expressed on the original hearing of the cause, with the variation proposed by his Lordship.

SPRAGGE, V. C.—I think that under the agreement the plaintiffs were bound to have their works in such a state at the time of their completion that the engineers could form their own judgment, upon inspecting them— could see that they were constructed and finished according to the contract : though they would not be liable to keep them in repair during any delay which might occur after default by the defendants to appoint an engineer.

At the inspection in September, 1853, the engineers, *Paige* especially, formed their judgment from what had been the case in relation to the completion of the works, rather than from what he found to be the case at that time. He refused to give a certificate, apparently because he considerad some of the works not executed according to the spirit of the contract, and he suggested further works ; which further works and more have been, according to the evidence of *Reid*, completed.

My brother *Esten's* judgment proceeds upon a failure of duty on the part of the defendants in not appointing an engineer after the completion of these further works, if they were completed. The evidence of the completion of the works is not precise as to time. The letter of the 6th of September, from the plaintiffs' managing director, states them to be then completed, and notifies the defendants that the plaintiffs' responsibility has therefore ceased, and asks for payment. It does not, it is true, call upon the defendants to name an engineer, but the letter from the same officer of the 9th of the preceding month, notified the defendants that the works would be completed by the end of the month, and suggested the appointment of Mr. *Paige*, the enginerr, to inspect the works on the 1st of September.

Under the contract it was the duty of the defendants upon being notified of the completion of the works to appoint an engineer, without any suggestion of the plaintiffs, and the defendants seem to have understood such to be their duty, for they requested Mr. *Paige* to act for them, but for some reason he did not do so; and I refer to both these letters to shew that the notification under the one of the 6th of September was in pursuance of the contract. I have no doubt that it thereupon lay upon the defendants to appoint an engineer; and if at that date the work was completed, the plaintiffs had, by such completion of work and notification of it, placed themselves right with the defendants; and that the defendants were bound thereupon to accept the work, and were thenceforth debarred from questioning its due execution and completion.

The chief difficulty, I understand, now is, about the suspension bridge. Mr. *Reid* swears that it was built according to the plans and specifications. Mr. *Paige* did not inspect it in September, 1854, not considering it within his instructions; but in one of his letters he expresses a general opinion that its structure both as regards cables and otherwise appeared to be light for the span, adding, that he had not examined it sufficiently closely to give any definite opinion on the subject.

This bridge is no longer in existence, so that the inspection contemplated by the parties is no longer possible, so far at least as the bridge is concerned. Still all the works which the plaintiffs were to perform were at one time in a state of completion and of readiness for inspection. Whether completed according to the contract, is another question.

The inspection did not take place, evidently as I think, through the default of the defendants. The bridge should have been inspected with the other works; but the defendants' engineer, either from want of instructions or from misconceiving his instructions, declined to

inspect it. Further, upon being notified by the letters
of the 9th of August, and 6th of September, the defendants again made default, and I do not think it can lie
in their mouth to say that the mode of ascertaining the
completion of the contract stipulated by the parties
has become impracticable, and therefore that it should
not be ascertained in any mode.

There is this difference, certainly, between the English
cases referred to and this case : that in the former, the
thing to be ascertained was auxiliary to the carrying out
of a contract upon which the parties were to act ; while
in this case it is only to set at rest the rights of the
parties, and then to stop. But looking to the nature
of the works to be performed by the plaintiffs, it was
of the highest importance to them, upon the cempletion
of the works, to have the fact of their completion established and settled, so as not to be open to future question.
It was a point expressly stipulated for, and we may
assume was part of the consideration for their contract.

I think the thing principally stipulated for was the
ascertainment of the fact of the completion of the works ;
that fact ascertained, could no longer be questioned,
and the prevention of future question was evidently
the object of the provision ; the *mode* of ascertaining it,
I think, was subordinate ; the mode agreed upon was
doubtless a good one, but still I think we can only
regard it as a means to an end, and I think if the end
is still attainable by any just mode which the machinery
of the court can provide, it will be right to aid the plaintiffs in attaining it, and not leave them to be disappointed
of the end stipulated for, because the means contemplated
have been frustrated through the default of the defendants. I think the English cases have proceeded upon
this principle, and in this spirit, and that it is only in
circumstances that they differ from the case before us.
I think this case is a proper one for relief ; what is
sought was expressly stipulated for, and is material to
the plaintiffs, I may add, though this may not be a

sufficient ground in the absence of express agreement, its tendency is to prevent litigation.

· I do not think the evidence is sufficient to enable us to make a decree declaring the works finished. The proper mode of ascertaining the fact, I think, will be by a reference to the master ; and the fact to be ascertained will be, whether at any time, and if so, at what time, the works were completed according to the contract.

On the question of returning the deposit : as the decree had been altered in a material part, the court said that the defendants failed in the main part of their contention, although it was true that they had succeeded in obtaining an important variation of the decree, though in a subordinate part, but yet one on which the learned Vice-Chancellor had exercised a deliberate judgment ; and therefore they would order the deposit to be divided ; but they expressed themselves strongly against any attempt to sustain an appeal because of a slip in some matter of consequential direction, or purely subordinate relief, which might have been avoided or corrected by a reference to the judge who ordered the decree, or by speaking to the minutes ; saying that in any such case, though the error was corrected on the re-hearing, they would subject the appellant to the costs of the appeal.

The Commercial Bank of Canada v. Cooke.

*Fraudulent assignment—Marriage settlement (setting aside)—Partie
—Pleading.*

Although the consideration of marriage is one of the most valuable,·
still a settlement upon the marriage, either of the settlor or a child
of the settlor is, like any other conveyance, liable to be impeached
as void under the statute of Elizabeth, on the ground of having
been made to hinder and delay creditors. Where therefore a person in embarrassed circumstances hastened the marriage of his
daughter, and made a conveyance of all his real estate to a trustee
for the benefit of his daughter and the issue of the intended marriage, having stated to the solicitor who prepared the conveyance
and to the trustee that his object in so doing was to prevent his
property from being seized by his creditors, and there being a
strong presumption that the daughter and her intended husband
had also been informed of the object of the settlor ; the court upon
a bill filed by a judgment creditor, against the husband and wife
and their infant children, to set aside such settlement, declared
the same void as against creditors ; notice by the trustee of the
fraudulent purpose of the settlor being sufficient to bind the issue
of the marriage. To such a bill the settlor is not a necessary party.
Where a bill was filed to impeach a deed as colourable, and the evidence shewed it to be fraudulent, if not colourable ; and the same
statements would have been necessary had the bill sought to impeach it on the ground of fraud ; the court refused to entertain an
objection at the hearing that the bill had not sought to set it aside
on that ground, or assigned fraud as an alternative ground of
relief.

Statement—The bill in this cause was filed by the *Commercial Bank* of Canada, against *Edward Fenelon Cooke*,
and *Mary Martha*, his wife, *James Grant, Edward
Fenelon, Donoghue Cooke, Jennette Cooke, Anson Gilbert
Northrup* and *James Wells*, setting forth that *John
Donoghue* had carried on business as a dealer and
manufacturer of boots and shoes in Belleville, and
that his brother *Florence Donoghue* carried on business
in the same town as a retail grocer, for whose accommodation *John Donoghue* had endorsed several notes,
many of which had passed into the hands of the plaintiffs and others, and were held by them when *Florence*
became insolvent, in the latter part of 1855, and made
an assignment to *John* of all his estate, real and personal, in trust to pay, first, what *Florence* owed *John*,
and what he was liable for as endorser for *Florence ;*
and on the further trust, to pay the residue, if
any, to the other creditors of *Florence : John*, at
the same time owing a large amount of debts

on his own account, besides his liability as such endorser ; and was at the same time the registered owner in
fee of several portions of real estate, and was also
possessed of a valuable stock of goods in his shop ; also
a large amount of debts due, and divers debts accruing to
him, but the whole was not sufficient to pay his liabilities.
Finding his affairs to be in this condition, and several
actions having been instituted against him by his creditors he applied himself to contrive a scheme for defrauding the plaintiffs and others, his creditors, by keeping
his property from them, and at the same time retaining
the use and benefit thereof for himself and his family,
and with this view took the advice of several persons as
to how such fraudulent object could be accomplished,
and put to his solicitor divers questions as to the legal
effect of certain proceedings he had thought of taking.

That the plan he ultimately formed was to persuade,
if he could, *Henry Swift & Co.*, of New York, creditors
of *Florence,* to assume his insolvent estate, and pay his
debts ;·and failing this, his plan was to hasten the marriage of his daughter, the defendant *Mary Martha*, to
the defendant *Edward Fenelon Cooke*, so that the same
might take place before creditors could recover judgment against him ; and by an *ante* nuptial deed to
settle on her nominally, but really for his own benefit,
all his real estate, which constituted the chief part of his
assets ; and to secure in like manner for his own benefit,
by placing in the name of other persons, his personal
estate through the means of a friendly creditor, and by
pretended sales or other dispositions thereof ; and then
to apply for his discharge under the statute relating to
insolvent debtors ; thereupon *John Donoghue* communicated to his family, and amongst others to *Mary
Martha*, the condition of his affairs, and the plans he
had formed for defeating his creditors, and she, well
understanding the same, gave her consent thereto ; that
the defendant *Edward Fenelon Cooke* some time before
this period had been a shop clerk in Belleville and other

places in Canada, but had afterwards gone to the
United States, where he had been employed as a sales-
man and travelling clerk in Baltimore and New York,
and in the summer of 1855 had paid a visit to Belleville, on which occasion he had engaged to marry the
said *Mary Martha*, without either of them stipulating
or applying for or expecting any *ante* nuptial settlement to be made. At the period of these negociations
John Donoghue had seven children, five daughters and
two sons.

In pursuance of such, his fraudulent scheme, *John
Donoghue* proceeded to New York, saw the defendant
Edward Fenelon Cooke, and explained to him the position of his affairs, and the plans he had formed of keeping his property from his creditors, and obtained the
consent of *Cooke* to marry the said *Mary Martha* at
once, and in other respects to aid him in carrying out
his plans in the way *Donoghue* desired. While in New
York *Donoghue* induced one *Fowler*, a creditor, to
appoint *Cooke* as his agent to accept of a bill of sale
of the stock in trade and furniture of *John Donoghue*,
and to act for *Fowler* in taking such proceedings as
might be necssary to protect such stock and furniture
from other creditors, and *Cooke*, in order to further such
designs, accepted the agency. That *Donoghue* and
Cooke immediately left New York and proceeded to
Belleville, and forthwith on their arrival *Donoghue*,
with the privity and consent of *Cooke* and *Mary Martha*,
gave instructions to his own solicitor to prepare the
documents he considered necessary for his purpose, the
solicitor before and at this time being aware, and
having notice, of the fraudulent intent and purpose of
the proposed settlement; but having first learned the
same through his confidential connection with *Donoghue*, he did not feel at liberty to refuse to prepare the
required instrument, and he acted in the preparation
thereof for all parties; no other solicitor having been
employed by any of them, and he had no actual

communication with any of them except *Donoghue*, who was allowed to arrange the matter as he thought proper. The solicitor accordingly prepared a marriage settlement and bill of sale, and the same were examined and approved of by *Donoghue*, but were not submitted to *Cooke* for his approval, his concern therewith, or that of his intended wife, or of *Fowler*, being merely nominal, and he saw them for the first time when engrossed and brought to the shop of *Donoghue* to be executed by him and the other parties thereto. The marriage settlement so prepared was expressed to bear date the 4th of October, 1855, and to be made between *Donoghue* of the first part, *Cooke* of the second part, *Mary Martha Donoghue* of the third part and the defendant *Grant* of the fourth part, and in consideration of such intended marriage purported to convey certain lands therein mentioned and described to *Grant*, in trust for the defendant *Mary Martha* and her heirs, the issue of the said marriage. the property so conveyed and settled being altogether out of proportion to the station and circumstances of *Donoghue*, and such as *Cooke* and his intended wife would not have expected *Donoghue* to make, and such as they knew he would not have made had he not been in embarrassed circumstances, and had not had a fraudulent object in making the same. That no such settlement was stipulated for or contemplated by either *Cooke* or his wife at the time they entered into the engagement to marry. Nor was such settlement a consideration with either for agreeing to marry.

The bill further stated that the defendant *Grant* refused at first to execute the settlement, but ultimately withdrew any objection and executed the deed, being urged to do so by the defendant *Cooke*, and assured by him that it was a mere matter of form, and would be all right in a short time when *John Donoghue's* affairs would be arranged. Immediately after the execution of the settlement the marriage between *Cooke* and *Mary*

Martha took, with a view of completing the fraud on creditors by thus giving a supposed legal validity to the deed
of settlement. That within a few daws after the marriage *John Donoghue*, with intent to effect his said fraudulent design, requested *Cooke* as agent for *Fowler* to
accept a bill of sale, which was not before executed, of
the goods and chattels, and which *Cooke*, to aid such
fraudulent object of his father-in-law, consented to do,
which was thereupon executed for the alleged consideration of £368, and *Donoghue* thereby professed to sell and
convey to *Fowler* all his stock in trade and household
furniture, as also the firewood and vegetables he had
provided for his family, subject to redemption on payment of £368, and *Cooke* in the capacity of agent for
Fowler, on the 13th day of October, made the necessary affidavit for the registration of the bill of sale,
which was registered in the proper office on that day.
On the 19th of October two other judgments were recovered against *Donoghue* for large amounts. Possession
of the real estate was not delivered to any of the
defendants under the deed of settlement, but on the
contrary *Donoghue* occupied and enjoyed the same as
before; he also with his family remained in possession
of the household furniture, &c., as before, using and
enjoying the same; selling his stock in trade and
appropriating the proceeds to his own use.

The bill, amongst other statements, also set forth that
John Donoghue had presented a petition for protection
against process to the judge of the county court, which
was accordingly afforded him, and the defendants
Northrup and *Wells* were duly appointed assignees of
his estate and effects: that the defendants *Edward F.
D. Cooke* and *Jeanette Cooke* were the only issue of the
said marriage, and prayed that the deed of settlement
might be set aside; that the judgment of the plaintiffs
might be declared to be a charge on the property
comprised in such deed of settlement in priorty to the
settlement, and for relief consequential thereon.

The defendants *Cooke* and wife and their children answered the bill, *Cooke* and wife asserting, amongst other grounds of defence, that their marriage would not have taken place had not the deed of settlement been executed: denied all knowledge of *Donoghue's* insolvency, or of any fraudulent intention on his part in executing the settlement, or that to their knowledge the solicitor who acted in the preparation of the deed by instructions from both parties had any notice thereof.

The plaintiffs having put the cause at issue by filing replication, evidence was taken before the court, when amongst others, *John Donoghue* was examined as a witness on behalf of the plaintiffs. His evidence was to the effect following:

"I have lived in Belleville for a number of years; about twenty-five; I kept a boot and shoe shop; in 1855 *Florence Donoghue*, my brother, carried on the grocery business; at that time I endorsed notes for him: in October, 1855, I was endorser on his paper at the Commercial Bank, and elsewhere, to the amount of upwards of £2,000, or I think it was about that amount; I had real property, the same as is comprised in the marriage settlement; I had no other; I was in possession of it; I had also stock-in-trade worth three or four hundred pounds, as I estimated it; I owed, of my own debts, to *Fowler*, of New York, £368 2s. 8d.; to *Lessin*, of Montreal, £103 16s. 0d.; *Smith & Cochrane*, of Montreal, £95 9s.; I owed no other debts: my book accounts due to me amounted to from four or five hundred pounds, I think; I had household furniture; nothing else that I recollect; I did not know in October, 1855, to what amount I was endorser for my brother; I supposed it was only to about half the amount; I ascertained the real amount about six months afterwards; suits were brought against me in the fall of 1855, I think in October; they were in respect of my endorsements, and I left it to my brother to attend to them; I became alarmed about my position when *Swift & Co.* of New York, came to my brother about his indebtedness to them. Mr. *James O'Reilly*, of Kingston, spoke to me about it, and about my endorsements for my brother; this was before I went to New York, some time before

the marriage settlement: at New York I went to *Cooke*
about his marrying my daughter; there had been correspondence between them; I told him that as there
had been such correspondence, I would make a marriage
settlement; he gave his consent after some time; he did
not object, but seemed to weigh the matter in his mind;
he mentioned his expecting some property from Ireland,
left him by his father or his mother; I told him that I
would settle my freehold property, my house and land;
it was agreed that he should return with me to Canada.
I asked him to do so for the purpose of getting married;
Cooke had been in Belleville the previous summer;
nothing passed between us then as to a marriage; not
a word; I recollect none; wrote to myself or my
daughter proposing a marriage; this was, I think, after
he had been here in the summer; there was no engagement between them that I know of; before going to New
York I spoke to my daughter about it; I asked her if
she would marry *Cooke* if I gave her a marriage settlement; she was on a visit to Kingston, and I went to see
her; she consented, and I then proceeded to New York.
I was going to New York to see *Swift & Co.*, to see if
they would accept *Florence Donoghue's* effects in satisfaction of their claim, and pay off his debts; my
daughter agreed to the proposed arrangement; I told
her what I proposed to settle; I gave no reason to her
for doing this; my object was to secure the property in
her, to prevent its being taken for my debts; I thought
it better to settle it on my daughter than to have it
sacrificed; I had then seven children; at New York I
do not know that I told *Cooke* about my endorsements
for my brother, and that he had failed; I may have
done so; I do not know what I said about this in the
insolvent court; *Cooke* went with me to *Henry Swift* at
New York; I told him *Florence* was in difficulty; I
proposed to *Swift* to take *Florence's* assets, and pay off
his liabilities; *Swift* declined; *Cooke* took part in the
discussion. After my return I instructed Mr. *O'Hare*
to draw the marriage settlement; he told me that if I made
the settlement, I could not get the property back again;
I said I wished to secure it for my children, that it should
not be sacrificed for my debts; I do not know that I
told *Cooke* at all of my difficulties until after his marriage; I gave Mr. *O'Hare* instructions to draw a bill of
sale to *Fowler*; *Cooke* acted for *Fowler* in the matter;
this was after the marriage; *Cooke* went to New York

about a week after the marriage, and remained there a month or two ; *Cooke* got a power of attorney from *Fowler*, which he got attested by the British consul ; this was done at New York; the marriage settlement and bill of sale comprised all I had, except my book accounts ; I did not tell my daughter about my troubles before her marriage ; about a week elapsed between my seeing my daughter at Kingston and her marriage; she did not ask the reason of the haste, and I gave her none; my daughter did not accompany *Cooke* to New York a week after her marriage, she continued to live in my family; I lived in the house five or six months after the settlement; I forget when I left; I forget whether I remained till the summer of 1857. At New York I first spoke of a settlement to *Cooke;* he did not mention it first; in his letter nothing was said about a settlement ; the marriage took place in October, I think on the day the settlement was executed: looking at the settlement, I say the signatures are those of the parties named ; it was executed by all of them; paper C. was executed by me as a memorial of the settlement for registration ; paper B. was executed by *Cooke* and myself; the signature to the affidavit is his ; it was given to secure *Fowler;* the debt stated was correct, I believe; the debt was afterwards paid, and I made payments in Montreal ; I made no payments to the plaintiffs ; my stock and furniture were sold ; *Cooke* bought in my furniture at sheriff's sale. After the bill of sale I went on selling the goods, and sent the money to *Fowler;* I used the wood and vegetables which were in the bill of sale; shortly after the settlement, I agreed with Mr. *Grant* to pay him rent; I asked what rent he would charge; he said £25 a year; I went to ask him; he did not ask me; I thought I satisfied the rent by Mr. *Cooke's* board ; when *Cooke* came to live in Belleville, he lived with me; the furniture was that included in *Fowler's* bill of sale; part of it was that purchased by *Cooke.* Since the settlement, *Grant* has acted as trustee in managing the property. I was in the insolvent court in the year after the marriage settlement; part of the debts upon which I was insolvent were due, I think, at the date of the marriage settlement; it is so stated in the schedule in the insolvent court, but I do not know how it is; there were debts of my own contracting before the marriage settlement, not exceeding £500 in all; I think my stock and debts, and other personal property, were amply

sufficient to pay it all; my book debts amounted to five
or six hundred pounds; my stock was worth five or six
hundred pounds; the nominal amount of my brother's
assets were £3,571 8s. 1d., consisting of real estate in
Kingston, his stock in trade, and book debts; my
liabilities on his account were about £2,000; my
daughter was about seventeen or eighteen when she was
married; she did not know about my business affairs, or
my responsibilities; my brother led me to believe at the
time that I was on his paper to only half the amount; I
thought some notes were renewals, which were not.
Cooke had lived in Belleville for a number of years
before he went to New York; he and my daughter
corresponded after he left; *Cooke* told me that the
marriage could not then take place but for the settlement; there are two children, issue of the marriage; I
thought before I went to New York that *Swift & Co.*
would take my brother's assets, and pay off his debts;
they had an agent here who agreed to do so; my
endorsements for my brother were for his accommodation only.

Argument.—Mr. *Mowat*, Q. C., and Mr. *McLennan*,
for plaintiffs.

Mr. *Blake*, (Mr. *Strong*, Q. C., with him,) for
defendants.

On the case being opened counsel for defendants took
a preliminary objection that *John Donoghue* was a
necessary party to the suit in order to being present at
the taking of accounts which were necessary to be
taken, his estate over and above the property settled
being liable to make good any deficiency. This case is
different from a bill against the assignee of a bankrupt.

Counsel for plaintiff insisted there was no authority
for this objection, an insolvent debtor being in a
position analogous to a bankrupt who, even before he
obtains his certificate, is not a necessary party. If
wrong in this contention, and it should appear that
Donoghue was a necessary party he could be added as
a defendant in the master's office.

As to the merits of the case, *John Donoghue's* own

statements shewed that at the time of the execution of the settlement he was not in a position to make any settlement, much less such as was made here which was totally disproportioned to the means and expectations of both the parties to the marriage. No one could read this evidence without feeling convinced that the marriage was brought about by *Donoghue* for the express purpose of shewing some colour for the assignment being made, which comprised the whole of *Donoghue's* real estate, and the bill of sale to *Fowler* covered all his personal effects, except such debts as were owing to him. *Donoghue* continuing in possession of the realty, and using the personal effects in the same manner as he had always done, was conclusive to shew with what intent the deeds were executed. As against creditors only a fair and reasonable settlement will be upheld.

They referred to *Campion v. Cotton, (a) Hardey v. Green, (b) Exp. McBurnie, (c) Doe Watson v. Rutledge, (d) Doe Parry v. James, (e) Harrison v. Richards, (f) Bott v. Smith, (g) Holmes v. Penney, (h) Taylor v. Jones, (i) Colombine v. Penhall. (j)*

The evidence shewed that both *O'Hare* the solicitor and *Grant* the trustee were aware of the fraudulent object *Donoghue* had in view in making this pretended settlement. And notice to them was sufficient to affect all parties—infants as well as adults—interested under the deed. On this point they referred to *LeNeve v. Le Neve, (k) Toulmin v. Steere, (l) Wise v. Wise. (m)*

The settlement here made was in reality a gift—not like the case of a settlement made on a settlor's wife.

(a) 17 Ves. 263.	(b) 12 Beav. 182.
(c) 1 D. McN. & G. 441.	(d) Cowp. 705.
(e) 16 East, 212.	(f) 10 Hare, 39.
(g) 21 Beav. 511.	(h) 3 K. & J. 90.
(i) 2 Atk. 600.	(j) 1 S & G. 228.
(k) 3 Atk. 646.	(l) 3 Mer. 222.
(m) 2 J. & La. 403.	

For the defendants it was contended that the grounds now insisted upon by the plaintiffs were not open to them upon the pleadings, the transactions being stated as colourable, both as regards the deed of settlement and the bill of sale.

It is probable a fraudulent intention did exist in the mind of *Donoghue*, but this not being a settlement on his intended wife, who it might be supposed would be likely to make herself acquainted with her intended husband's business, could not be disturbed on the grounds alleged, and proved the daughter was not *particeps fraudis;* on the contrary, she seems to have been entirely ignorant of her father's means as well as of the liabilites in respect of his endorsations for his brother. Apart from these, assuming her to have been at all conversant with his affairs she might reasonably suppose him to be worth a considerable sum over and above his debts—at least £1000 more. It is said to be impossible to estimate the consideration of marriage, and if this be so, then it is impossible to say that this settlement was extravagant. It may be that *Donoghue* at one time intended to retain the use of the property; but when told by his solicitor that he could not do so he made the settlement with full knowledge that in so doing he divested himself of all interest in the property; and the whole evidence goes to shew that the settlement here made was actual, not colourable merely. The acts of all parties are quite inconsistent with the view that the transaction was only colourable. The hastening of the marriage was only a matter of suspicion, and the court will require more than mere suspicion before it will act in setting aside the solemn acts of parties, particularly where, on the faith of such acts, the situation of others has been altered. Here the position of *Cooke* and his wife is irrevocably altered, and is very different from the case of *Colombine* v. *Penhall,* cited by the plaintiffs. No fraudulent intent is brought home to either *Grant* or *Cooke.* The most that is shewn is that *Donoghue* desired to defeat his creditors; not that the marriage was with that view by the parties to it.

The marriage it is sworn took place on the faith of the settlement being valid; and at all events the children, the issue of the marriage, are in the position of purchasers for value without notice. *Fraser* v. *Thompson*, (a) *Nairn* v. *Prowse*, (b) were cited in addition to the cases already referred to.

Judgment-SPRAGGE, V.C.-The settlement, which is impeached in this case, was made by *John Donoghue*, the father of *Mary Martha Cooke*, upon her marriage with the defendant *Edward Fenelon Cooke*. Most of the cases in the books have arisen out of settlements made upon the marriage of the settlor himself. Marriage is a valuable consideration: it is styled by Lord *Campbell*, in *Fraser* v. *Thompson*, (c) the most valuable of all considerations; and Lord Justice *Turner* in the same case speaks of the high value of the marriage consideration, which cannot be measured. It cannot be placed higher than this, whether the settlement be made upon a marriage of a child of a settlor, or a marriage with the settlor himself. I apprehend that they both stand upon the same footing, and the provision in the several successive bankrupt acts, avoiding conveyances to children or others *except upon the marriage of children*, or for some valuable consideration, indicates this.

But still such a settlement must be open to be impeached as void under the statute 13 Elizabeth, and upon the same grounds as any other conveyance for valuable consideration.

It is too clear upon the evidence to admit of a doubt, that the object of *Donoghue* in making the settlement

---

(a) 1 Giff. 49.   (b) 6 Ves. 752.
(c) 4 DeG. & J. 659.

in question, which was of the whole of his real property,
including his homestead, was to defeat his creditors, and
that the marriage of his daughter with *Cooke* was part
of his scheme.   The conclusion would be irresistible
without his proving it expressly by his evidence, but he
does state it in so many words: "My object was to
secure the property in her, to prevent its being taken for
my debts.   1 thought it better to settle it upon my
daughter than to have it sacrificed.   I had then seven
children."

   It is necessary, however, to affect the daughter and
Cooke with notice before their marriage of the object
and view which *Donoghue* had in making the settlement.   This I think is done by knowledge in Mr.
O'Hare, the professional gentleman who drew the
settlement, of its nature and object: he must be proved
to have had the knowledge, and to have been the
solicitor of *Cooke* and his intended wife.   As to the
solicitor having notice of the settlor's object, besides
the almost certain inference that he must have drawn
from the circumstances, *Donoghue* appears to have
told him his object.   *Donoghue* says, "I instructed
Mr. *O'Hare* to draw the marriage settlement.   He told
me that if I made the settlement I could not get the
property back again.   I told him I was content."   This
of itself could scarcely leave room for doubt—but he
was more explicit : "I said I wished to secure it for my
children that it should not be sacrificed for my debts."

   That Mr. *O'Hare* was solicitor for *Cooke* and his
intended wife, as well as for *Donoghue*, is expressly
stated in the answer of *Cooke* and wife.   They say
that they as well as *Donoghue* were parties to the
instructions given to Mr. *O'Hare* to prepare the
marriage settlement, and that Mr. *O'Hare* did act
in the preparation thereof as the solicitor for all parties
thereto, which they, the parties answering, believe is a
usual and customary practice in the preparation of such

instruments in Upper Canada. I see no reason why this answer should not be read. It is a voluntary and deliberate statement, and does not fall within the reason upon which my brother *Esten*, in *Pegg* v. *Stennett*, allowed an answer given by a mortgagee under oral examination to be withdrawn from the evidence, viz., that the párty so examined was *inops cansilii*.

It is settled law that notice to a solicitor in the transaction is notice to those for whom he is acting· This principle was applied in *LeNeve* v. *LeNeve*, where the solicitor of a. party to a marriage settlement had notice, and as was said of that case in *Toulman* v. *Steere*, the interest of the unborn children was not attempted to be distinguished from that of the mother. In the latter case there was a purchase of real estate, and a prior incumbrance was known to the agent of the purchaser; an infant was interested in the purchase; but Sir *William Grant* applied the rule, notwithstanding.

The admission in the answer of *Cooke* and wife, is, however, evidence against themselves only, not against the children, the infant defendants, and I do not find the fact sufficiently proved, *alivnde*, but *Grant*, the trustee of the marriage settlement had notice, and that, in the opinion of Lord *St. Leonards*, when Lord Chancellor of Ireland, in *Wise* v. *Wise*, affects all the *cestuis que trustent*. It is clear from *Grant's* own evidence that he had notice. *Donoghue*, when asking him to become trustee, told him that he was embarrassed through endorsing for his brother; that he would not have his property sold to pay the debts of his brother; that he wanted his property secured so that his creditors could not take it. There are passages to the like effect, some of which point to the settlement being colourable only.

If the defendants are to be affected with notice of *Donoghue's* object and view in making the settlement, as I think they must be, it is quite sufficient under the case of *Bott* v. *Smith* to avoid it. The marriage at that time, and the marriage settlement, are parts of a scheme in which they concurred to defeat the creditors of *Donoghue*.

I rest my decision as to notice upon the grounds that I have stated, but I am far from saying that there is not enough in the circumstances proved to show *Cooke* to have been *particeps fraudis*, if not also the young lady, who, under the extraordinary circumstances detailed in the evidence, became his wife.

It is objected that the case made by the bill is not the case proved—the case made being that the marriage settlement was only colourable. Upon reflection I think there is less in the objection than I at first thought. If it had been no part of the plaintiff's case that the settlement was colourable, the bill would have contained the same allegations that it does contain, omitting only to state the transaction as colourable; and it would not have been demurrable; or, if the bill had added to the allegations made, a submission to the judgment of the court, that if the transaction should not appear to be colourable the plaintiff was still entitled to relief, the bill would, I think, be unexceptionable. But that would not be putting the case upon a different ground, but submitting that dispensing with one ground, sufficient would still remain, and though a case is often so put, and it is good pleading, I think, to so put it, I am not prepared to say that it is necessary. At all events at this stage of the cause after evidence taken, and taken, as I judge, as it would have been offered and taken if the bill had been framed as it is suggested it ought to have been framed, I ought not, I think, to give effect to the objection. (*a*)

An objection was taken at the hearing that *Donoghue*

(*a*) Smith v. Kay, 7 H. L. Ca. 750.

is a necessary party. I do not see that he is so. The transaction as between him and the objects of the settlement is, of course, not affected and|no relief of any kind is sought against him.

The decree must be for the plaintiffs, with costs against defendant *Edward Fenelon Cooke.* I think the costs of this suit as well as the plaintiffs' debt, may properly be paid out of the settled estates.

HENDERSON v. WOODS.

Trustees—Authority of one to act without concurrence of his co-trustees.

A. and B., executors and trustees under a will with power of sale, sell and take a mortgage to secure purchase money, they being in the recital named as executors. B. without the knowledge or consent of A, assigns the mortgage and appropriates the consideration money to his own use. *Held,* that no estate passed under the assignment except so far as the trust estate might be found debtor to B.; and also, that as between the contending equities of the trust estate and the assignee, the maxim *qui prior est in tempore potior est in jure,* would apply in favour of the trust estate.

Statement.—This was a suit brought for the foreclosure of a mortgage made in November, 1852, by one *G. S. Massington* and wife, to *Oliver Barton* and *J. B. Preulx,* for securing the sum of £147 10s. and interest.

The mortgage moneys formed part of the estate of the late *Alexander Kennedy,* and the mortgage was made to *Barton* and *Preulx* as such executors, a recital to that effect being contained in the mortgage.

The bill alleged that *Preulx* declined to act as executor during the life of *Barton,* who accordingly was sole acting executor till his death; and that by an assignment dated the 15th of November, 1852, *Barton* conveyed the mortgage to the plaintiff, for the consideration of £150 then paid.

The defendant *Woods* had become entitled to the

equity of redemption of the premises, subject to the mortgage, and when applied to for payment of the amount
due, had raised the question whether, under the circumstances attending the assignment, the plaintiff or
Kennedy's estate were entitled to the money.

The answer of *Preulx* denied that he had declined
to act as executor or trustee jointly with *Barton* in
such matters as required their joint acts, and alleged
that he did not join in or consent to the assignment to
the plaintiff, but that such was made by *Barton* alone,
and any moneys received were appropriated to his own
use; and that he died a debtor to *Kennedy's* estate to
an amount exceeding that secured by this mortgage,
and without assets.

The terms of *Kennedy's* will, and the effects of the
evidence adduced, are set out in the judgment.

Argument.—Mr. *McDonald,* for the plaintiff, contended that under the circumstances the assignee had
received an absolute and effectual conveyance of the
mortgage *bonâ fide,* and that if there were a breach of
trust, the estate of which *Barton* was executor, rather
than the plaintiff should suffer the loss.   Consolidated
Statutes of U. C., ch. 90, sec. 9.

Mr. *Blain,* for *Woods,* consented to pay to the party
entitled.

· Mr. *Hector,* Q.C., for *Preulx,* contended that the assignment had not been effectually executed by *Barton* alone,
and that whether he held as executor or trustee, *Preulx,*
who had not renounced his office, should have joined with
him to make the conveyance effectual, citing *Denne* v.
Judge, (a) and the American decision of *Hertel* v.
Bogart. (b)   He argued that if one were allowed to alie-

(a) 11 East. 288.   (b) 9 Paige, 51.

nate the estate without the consent of the other, the objects of the trust may be often defeated by the malfeasance of one, and that in the present·case the estate being the prior creditor should have preference to the plaintiff. It is also proved that the plaintiff had full knowledge of the trust. *Leigh* v. *Barry* (a), *Ex parte Rigby* (b), *Williams* v. *Mattoch* (c), *McCrae* v. *Farrow* (d), *Lepard* v. *Vernon* (e), *Sinclair* v. *Jackson* (f), *Hill* on Trustees, 305 ; *Lewin* on Trusts, 265 ; *Williams* on Executors, ed. of 1856, p. 852.

Judgment.—SPRAGGE, V.C.—The will of the late *Alexander Kennedy*, after appointing *Oliver Barton*, since deceased, and the defendant *Preula*, his executors, and after devises of certain real estate, contained the following clause : " The residue of my property, either personal or landed, I hereby authorize my executors, or either of them (in the event of death or refusal to act), to sell and dispose of the same, and from the proceeds to pay any just and lawful debts, all the expenses of this my will, of whatever nature, and that no action or suit shall be instituted either in law or equity for any act or acts, deed or deeds, of these my executors ; and whatever balance, after such debt and expenses have been liquidated, I request the same to be equally divided amongst the above named my children." The will is dated the 12th of August, 1847.

The will was proved by both the executors, and in 1852 they concurred in a sale of a parcel of land part of the residuary real estate. By mortgage dated the 8th of November, 1852, the purchaser mortgaged the land purchased to both, to secure the sum of £147 10s., payable 1st May, 1860, with interest in the meantime. On the 6th of June, 1855, *Barton* alone, without, so

(a) 3 Atk. 582.   ·   (b) 19 Vesey, 462.
(c) 3 Vern. 189.
(d) 4 Henning and Munford, Virginia R. 443.
(e) 2 V. & B. 51.   (f) 8 Cowan, 543.

far as appears, or there is any reason to think, the concurrence of *Preulx*, assigned the mortgage to the plaintiff for the expressed consideration of £150. *Barton* appears to have died indebted to *Kennedy's* estate in a sum exceeding £200, and probably insolvent; and it is alleged by *Preulx* that the money paid by the plaintiff to *Barton*, if any money was paid, was appropriated by *Barton* to his own use, and that *Kennedy's* estate has not had the benefit of it.

There is some evidence of a roll of bank notes being in the possession of *Barton* at about the date of the assignment, which he stated at the time to be money which he had received from the plaintiff for a mortgage on the *Kennedy* land, which the plaintiff had bought from him. Under the assignment is a receipt for £150. The assignment was annexed to the mortgege, and both were delivered to the plaintiff. One of the witnesses to the assignment is called, who states that he saw the money paid. The other witness is dead. I think from the evidence that the roll of notes was in *Barton's* hands the day before the execution of the assignment. I think the evidence of payment is as much as could be expected under the circumstances. It is suggested that the assignment was made to pay a private debt of *Barton's*, being for board due to plaintiff; he did board with the plaintiff, but it was some time after the assignment.

Assuming for the present that the money was paid by the plaintiff to *Barton*, and that *Barton* appropriated it to his own use, the question is, whether the loss is to fall upon the plaintiff or upon the *Kennedy* estate.

The plaintiff must have known that the mortgage belonged to the *Kennedy* estate; for although the mortgagees are not therein described as executors and trustees, *Barton* in his assignment is described as executor of *Kennedy's* estate, and as such assumed to assign the mortgage; the necessary inference was, that *Preulz* also was an executor or trustee. The evidence shews that *Barton* managed the affairs of the estate, not exclusively, but principally; he was a resident in the neighbourhood, while *Preulx*, who was a Roman Catholic clergyman, only visited it occasionally, and intimated his intention of withdrawing from the trust; and I should think that if the assignment had conveyed a perfect legal title to the plaintiff that this court would not have interfered with it.

But there are opposing equities: the plaintiff's equity is to have his title perfected so as to enable him to recover the mortgage money, or to foreclose: on the other hand is the equity of the *Kennedy* estate to have the like benefit of this same mortgage, and it is an older equity. Again, in the eye of this court the mortgage debt is the principle thing, the land mortgaged only the accessory. So far as the assignment of the mortgage debt is concerned it is an assignment only of a chose in action, and consequently passed subject to the equities of the *Kennedy* estate in respect of it. What this bill seeks is, to divest the legal estate residing in *Preulx*, for the benefit of the *Kennedy* estate. I do not see my way to doing this in the face of the equities of the estate.

There are moreover some circumstances which militate somewhat against the plaintiff's equity. A mortgage made in 1852 payable in 1860 was sold by one of two executors in 1855, the testator having been dead at least a year before the mortgage was made (how much earlier does not appear). The offer to sell this mortgage might have created suspicion, or at least have called for explanation. Added to this, the assignment is made by one only of the mortgagees; the absence of the concurrence of the other was also a suspicious circumstance. Upon both these points a cautious man would have enquired of *Preulx*; and if

such enquiry had been made there is reason to think
from the evidence that the money would not have
been lost.

The case of *Lepard* v. *Vernon* is in some respects
analogous to this in principle : one of two executors
assigned to a creditor of the testator a claim which
the estate had upon the Board of Ordnance for work
done by the testator ; and the question was whether
the debt due by the Ordnance should belong to the assignees or to the general creditors.   The remarks of
Sir *William Grant* are apposite to this case, he said :
" It is said, as each of the executors has the power to
dispose of the assets, the assignment by one is good.
If he had parted with any portion of the property to
Goodacre or *Buzzard*, if by the assignment they had
obtained any legal advantage, it could not perhaps be
taken form them : but this is a mere assignment of a
chose in action by one of several executors, of which no
use can be made unless this court should act upon it,
and interfere to give the particular creditor an advantage against the other executors and the general creditors : that the court will not do, but will direct the
money to be paid to the other executors for the benefit
of the general creditors."

It has been made a point in this case whether the
mortgage was held by *Barton* and *Preulx* as executors
or as trustees.   I have assumed that they held it as
executors, and am inclined to think that they did hold
it in that character, because after raising money by sale
of real estate, the fund so raised was distributable by
them as executors, a distinction intimated by Lord
Ellenborough, in *Denne* v. *Judge*.   In the American
case referred to by Mr. *Hector* of *Hertel* v. *Bogart*, the
mortgage was held by trustees, who were also executors,
in their character of trustees.   Chancellor *Walworth*
held also, that the assignment of the mortgage was a
breach of trust, and that it was known to the assignees
that it was made to secure purchase money on the sale

of the real estate of the testator. This case would have
been stronger for the defendants if *Barton* and *Preulx*
had held as trustees, but taking them to have held the
mortgage as executors, I still think the plaintiff not
entitled to what he asks. He may take an enquiry, if
he desires it, whether any of the money paid by him
to *Barton* was applied to the purposes of the estate,
because to that extent he is entitled to hold his assignment, but I think not further. In any event the defendants are entitled to their costs. If this enquiry
be taken; further directions to be reserved; if not
taken, bill to be dismissed with costs.

MILLER v. McNAUGHTON.

Will—Defeasance clause—Practice.

A testator after appointing executors and expressing full confidence
in them, provided "that in case any of the legatees offer obstructions to the proceedings of my said executors in the fulfilment of
the powers hereby conferred," then that such persons should suffer the penalty of "being debarred of all claims to any part, or
portion, of my estate under any pretence whatsoever, in the same
manner as if he, she, or they had actually predeceased me without issue, and such shall be, and are hereby declared to be debarred therefrom accordingly, any law or practice to the contrary
notwithstanding."

Held, in an administration suit by one of the legatees against the
executors, on the application of other legatees, made parties in the
master's office, that an enquiry might properly be directed whether any of the legatees had forfeited his or her share under the
above provision.

The original decree not containing such a clause of enquiry, was
now amended in that respect on motion.

Statement.—The bill in this case was filed in September, 1862, by *Mary Miller*, a daughter and legatee of
the late *Graham Lowton*, who resided near the town of
Milton, and died on the 19th of March, 1861, having
first made his last will and testament disposing of all
his estate, bearing date the 20th day of September,
1859. By this will the testator, after providing in the
usual manner for the payment of debts and funeral
expenses, made several specific devises and bequests
to several members of his family, and directed the re-

mainder of his estate to be realized and divided among them in certain specified proportions. *John McNaughton* and *Ninion Lindsay* were appointed executors with ample powers to manage and wind up the estate. The executors were empowered to appraise, divide, and apportion among the members of testator's family such parts of the personal estate as they should think it "neither seemly nor advisable to bring any to public sale," and it was provided that any "legatee or legatees to whom such shall be apportioned shall be bound to accept the same at the valuation so placed thereon in part payment of the share of such residue hereby bequeathed to him, her, or them, under the penalty, should they refuse to do so, or should they in any other way offer obstruction to the proceedings of my said executors in the fulfilment of the power hereby conferred, of being debarred of all claim to any part, or portion of my estate under these presents, or under any pretence whatsoever, in the same manner as if he or she, or they had actually predeceased me without issue, and such shall be, and are hereby declared to be debarred therefrom accordingly, any law or practice to the contrary notwithstanding."

The original defendants to the suit were the executors and *John G. Scott*, a grandson and legatee of the testator.

The bill charged that *Scott* was indebted to the testator at his death on a promissory note for $700, which the executors refused to take any means to collect, under the pretence that the same was cancelled by the testator before his death, the contrary whereof the plaintiff charged to be the truth.

Evidence was taken at Hamilton, and the cause heard before his Honour *V. C. Spragge*. Evidence at great length was taken as to the state of mind of the testator when the settlement referred to with *Scott* took place, the result of which was to shew that, though the testator was bedridden at the time and in a very low state of health, yet the settlement had been previously contemplated, and was concluded in the presence of Mr. *McNaughton* and other witnesses with full knowledge of its contents, the testator signifying that he desired such to be a release of all his claims against his grandson.

The settlement was therefore sustained, and *Scott* dismissed with his costs. Various other matters were specifically charged against the executors, but their investigation was held properly matter of account, and the usual administration decree was made with reference to the master at Hamilton.

The master in considering the decree, ordered the other legatees to be made parties, and this being done Mr. *Blake* moved on their behalf, and on notice to the other parties, to vary the decree by inserting an enquiry such as is above indicated.

Argument.—Mr. *Proudfoot* for the plaintiff.

Mr. *J. C. Hamilton* for the executors.

The following authorities were cited by counsel: *Wheeler* v. *Bingham* (*a*), *Powell* v. *Morgan* (*b*), *Morris* v. *Burroughs* (*c*), *Wynne* v. *Wynne* (*d*), *Cook* v. *Turner* (*e*), *Williams on Executors*, page 1133, *Tattersall* v. *Howell* (*f*), and *Cleaver* v. *Spurling* (*g*).

After taking time to look into the authorities,

Judgment.—SPRAGGE, .V. C.—This is an application to vary the decree, made in an administration suit, by legatees not made parties before the hearing. The application is made upon grounds appearing upon the face of the bill.

(*a*) 3 Atk. 364.   (*b*) 2 Vern. 90.
(*c*) 1 Atk. 399,   (*d*) 2 Manning & Gr. 8,
(*e*) 14 Sim 293.   (*f*) 2 Mer. 26.
(*g*) 2 P. Wms. 526.

The will of the testator, after authorizing the conversion of the estate into money, by his executors, and the disposition of the proceeds, authorizes the executors, in their discretion, instead of bringing "certain parts," as the will expresses it, to sale, to apportion them in specie among the legatees, requiring them to accept the same "under the penalty, should they refuse to do so, or should they in any other way offer obstruction to the proceedings of my said executors in the fulfilment of the powers hereby conferred, of being debarred of all claim to any part or portion of my estate under these presents, or under any pretence whatever, in the same manner as if he or she had actually predeceased me without issue." The provision as to legatees dying without issue before the testator, is as follows :—" In case any of my said legatees, special or residuary, shall depart this life before me, and before the bequests hereby made shall vest, then his, her, or their interest herein shall accrue and belong and be paid to the lawful offspring of each such so predeceasing, if any, share and share alike ; otherwise the same shall go and be divided among the survivors of my whole children alive at the time of my death, equally share and share alike."

For the application, it is contended that the filing of the bill was an obstruction involving a forfeiture under the will, and that if not so, still there should be an enquiry as to whether the plaintiff has done any act to work a forfeiture. The filing of a bill for administration of the estate would certainly not necessarily be an obstruction, and I see nothing in this bill having that character, unless it be the prayer, "that the estate of the said testator may be administered, and the trusts of his will executed by and under the direction of this honourable court."

This, construed strictly, is, I think, asking the court to take into its own hands that which the will commits to the discretion of the executors, and so, offering an obstruction to the fulfilment by the executors of the powers conferred upon them. But none of the allegations in the bill are directed to this point. The bill complains of various acts of malversation for which it asks to bring the executors to account. Then follows the prayer I have stated. I incline to think this not an obstruction within the will, but rather that the pleader in framing the prayer has followed the general form, omitting, inadvertently perhaps, to except from administration by this court that which the testator had left to the discretion of his executors. I think the discretion was a matter of personal confidence not to be withdrawn from the executors and exercised by this court. I think so from its nature, and from the language of the will : " Finally, having full faith and confidence in my executors before named, and considering that circumstances may occur to make it in their judgments," &c. I incline to think too that the forfeiture is one to which the court will not refuse to give effect, if the obstruction be established, and as to that I think there should be an enquiry. It is true there is no answer raising the point, nor, of course, any evidence upon it. The course taken under the general orders has made it impossible for the parties making this application to do either, and I think it would be doing them less than justice, unless they were placed in the same position as if they had answered and given evidence upon the point. Further directions should be reserved. The costs of this application to be costs in this cause.

Malloch v. Pinhey.

*Mortgage by absolute conveyance—Statute of Limitations—Dormant
equities, 11th Clause of Chancery Act.*

On the 16th of January, 1831, an absolute conveyance was made in
fee to secure a loan of money, the alleged mortgagor remaining in
possession until the spring of 1841. On the 1st of March, 1841,
the alleged mortgagee wrote to a subsequent mortgagee, on the
same property, claiming £93, 12s, 8d. as due from the mortgagor,
and on the 7th and 21st of June, of the same year, he again wrote
to the same incumbrancer alleging that he had originally advanced
about £60, which with interest then amounted to £90 or £100 and,
suggesting that the land should be sold for the benefit of the alleged mortgagor ; and he kept an account in his books against the
alleged mortgagor of principal and interest in respect of the said
alleged debt up to the 1st of January, 1856. The subsequent incumbrancer purchased the mortgagor's equity of redemption.
Upon a bill filed by such mesne incumbrancer in February, 1861,
claiming a right to redeem the premises against the representatives of the alleged mortgagee, who had died in the meantime. the
court held that the letters written by the mortgagor were sufficient
to take the case out of the Statute of Frauds, and that the right
of the plaintiff was not barred by the provisions of the Statute of
Limitations ; that the act relating to dormant equities did not
apply to the facts of this case, and that the 11th clause of the
Chancery Act did not affect the plaintiff's right to redeem.

Statement-This was a bill filed on the 28th of February,
1861, by *Edward Malloch*, against *Charles Hamnett Pinhey, Constance Pinhey, John Hamnett Pinhey, James
Lewis*, and *Peter McVeigh*, setting forth, that in January,
1831, the defendant *McVeigh* was the owner in fee of
100 acres of land in the township of Goulbourn, and
being desirous of going to Ireland for a time, required
to borrow £40 for that purpose, applied to one *Hamnett
Pinhey*, the father of the defendants *Pinhey*, since
deceased, who agreed to lend that sum upon receiving
a mortgage on the 100 acres to secure £45, that sum
including £5 previously due by *McVeigh* to *Pinhey*.
Accordingly, by a deed of the above date, the land was
conveyed to *Pinhey* in fee, the same being in its form
absolute, and prepared by, or by the instructions, of the
said *Pinhey*, although it was intended and agreed to be
a mortgage only to secure payment of the said sum of
£45 ; and that *McVeigh* for many years afterwards believed that the deed had been drawn in the form of a
mortgage ; that *McVeigh* immediately after the execution

of such conveyance went to Ireland, but returned to this province in June of that year, and went to reside on the property, where he continued to reside until the latter part of the year 1841, when he removed to another farm in the neighbourhood ; but he then leased the mortgaged premises to tenants, and for some time thereafter continued to receive the rents thereof.

The bill further alleged a conveyance in fee of the mortgaged premises to the plaintiff by *McVeigh*, on the 29th of May, 1837, for securing £50, and that plaintiff had not any notice of the conveyance of these lands to *Pinhey*, and did not become aware thereof until some time after the execution of the deed to himself ; and that immediately on ascertaining that such was the fact the plaintiff spoke to *McVeigh*, when he informed the plaintiff that the conveyance to *Pinhey* was intended as a mortgage only, and that he had very nearly paid up all that was due on such security : that on the 10th of November, 1840, the plaintiff wrote and sent a letter to *Pinhey*, which was set out at length in the bill, and in which he stated that he had obtained from *McVeigh* a deed of the mortgaged premises, and that when putting the conveyance on the registry he discovered the deed to *Pinhey*, which, on mentioning to *McVeigh*, he asserted had been given by way of security, which had been nearly all paid, and that subsequently he (*Pinhey*) had advanced some more money to pay for other land, but not on the deed, and concluded by requesting *Pinhey* to "*pay him nothing on account of the lot, and will thank you to inform me by post, what sum you took the lot in security for, and what amount he paid you of that sum.*"

In answer to this letter, *Pinhey* wrote on the 14th of November, 1840, as follows :—"I have just received yours of the 10th inst., and note its contents, not without astonishment at the effrontery of *McVeigh*. There is so little truth in what he appears to have

stated to you, that if you see any prospect of being
'*victimised*' by him, send him forthwith to me, and
desire him to bring from me to you such a letter as
will extricate him from suspicion."

That shortly afterwards plaintiff again applied to
Pinhey to ascertain how much was due him by *McVeigh*
on the mortgage ; in answer to which on the 1st of
March, 1841, *Pinhey* wrote : " From *McVeigh* the
amount due me is £93 12s. 8d.," that plaintiff finding
a mortgage had been made on the said land to *Pinhey*,
on the 25th of May, 1841, wrote to him expressing
his willingness to accept the amount of *McVeigh's*
indebtedness to plaintiff, and to convey the land to
Pinhey, or to pay *Pinhey* his claim—he assigning his
title—at the same time charging *Pinhey* with having
in his letter of November, 1840, evaded answering his
enquiries respecting *McVeigh's* indebtedness. Whereupon *Pinhey*, on the 7th of June following, wrote to
plaintiff, saying.: "Your proposition is very fair　*　*
*　*　*　In the year 1831 or 1832, I lent him cash,
(about £60.)　Having received nothing from him, I
think you will find that with the interest to this date,
my claim will be between £90 and £100.　I have no
means of estimating the value of the farm, but by the
offers which have been made from time to time, which
were from £160 to £175."　And on the 21st of the
same month he again wrote to plaintiff, saying : " I
wrote about a fortnight since touching *McVeigh's*
affair.　Have the goodness to let me know at your
earliest convenience whether it will be agreeable to
you to pay me the sum due to me by him.　I am quite
sure it is for the interest of *McVeigh* that the property
should be disposed of, and the proceeds made available
to pay his debts."

The bill further alleged that *Pinhey* was in possession
from some time in the year 1841, until his death, and
had received the rents and profits during that time, and

in like manner the defendants *Pinhey* had been in receipt of such rents and profits since his death ; and that they had conveyed the premises to the defendant *Lewis*, part of the purchase being secured by mortgage on the property, and prayed the usual enquiries and accounts, and that the defendant *Pinhey* might be ordered to pay plaintiff his costs whatever might be the result of the account.

The defendant *Lewis* answered, disclaiming all interest in the property.

The defendants *Pinhey* answered, alleging their ignorance of the transactions between their ancestor and *McVeigh ;* claiming the conveyance to be intended as it is expressed to be an absolute deed of the premises : they also claimed the benefit of the Statute of Limitations, being ch. 88 of the Consolidated Statutes of Upper Canada, the Dormant Equities Act, and the Statute of Frauds and Perjuries.

The cause having been put at issue, evidence was taken before the court at Ottawa, in the spring of 1862, the effect of which is sufficiently stated in the judgment.

Mr. *Fitzgerald* for plaintiff.

Mr. *Strong*, Q.C., for defendant.

The points relied on by counsel appear in the judgment.

Judgment.—ESTEN, V. C.—I am clearly of opinion that the plaintiff is entitled to a decree. The lands in question were conveyed by *Peter McVeigh* to the late Mr. *Pinhey*, on the 14th of January, 1831, absolutely in point of form ; but as the plaintiff contends by way of mortgage. The defendants, who are the representatives of the late Mr. *Pinhey*, are unable to state how

the matter is ; but one of them, Mr. *Charles Pinhey*,
says that he believes from what he has heard his father
say, and from the manner in which he dealt with the
property, that the transaction in question was an absolute sale. I think the letters of the17th and 21st of June,
1841, combined with the accounts, and the other evidence in the cause clearly establish the plaintiff's title.
They shew beyond dispute that the consideration for
the deed of the 14th of January, 1831, was £45,money
lent. It necessarily follows that the deed must have
been intended as a security. This amount is treated
as a debt on the 1st of January, 1841, when a note is
taken by Mr. *Pinhey* from *McVeigh*, for money lent,
which includes the amount in question. It is treated
as a debt as lately as April,1855, in an account of that
date. The letters of the 7th and 21st of June, 1841,
contain the strongest recognitions of the title of*McVeigh*.
It cannot be contended that they do not refer to the
property in question,and they clearly shew that*McVeigh*
then had an interest in it. It is quite clear from the
documentary evidence alone, that the land in question
was conveyed to Mr. *Pinhey* in January, 1831, by way
of security : and it is not pretended that the nature of
his title underwent any change by reason of any new
agreement between the parties. This evidence is of
course strongly corroborated by the oral evidence of
McVeigh, which appears to be admissible and to be
entitled to credit. The case is clearly distinguishable
from the cases of *Howland* v. *Stewart* (*a*), and *Monro*
v. *Watson,* in which respectively no documentary evidence of any importance existed. The case of *Lincoln*
v. *Wright* (*b*), establishes that extraneous evidence is
admissible to shew that a deed absolute in form was
intended to operate as a security both on the ground
of part performance, and of equitable fraud. It was
objected that the case was within theStatute of Limitations, the Dormant Equities Act, and the 11th clause

---

(*a*) Ante vol. ii., 61.   (*b*) 5 Jurist, N. S., 1142.

of the act establishing the Court of Chancery. But I think it is not affected by any of these acts of parliament. It is clear that *McVeigh* was in possession after January, 1841, and therefore the Statute of Limitations does not apply. It has been settled that the 18th Vic; ch. 124, does not apply to mortgages, because they are governed by the clauses relating to them in the act establishing the Court of Chancery; and I should think it can make no difference that the mortgage is not in form a security, but an absolute conveyance; because the parties know the real nature of the transaction, and what their real rights are. But even if the 18th Victoria, could be considered as applicable to this case, I do not think it would affect it. *McVeigh's* title was recognised not only in 1841, but as I think to a much later period. I see no reason to doubt that the sales to *Cuthbert* and *Lewis* were in furtherance of the plan of paying both claims and the surplus to *McVeigh*. The letter of the 21st of June, 1841, but indicates such a plan. The sale to *Cuthbert*, which appears to have been with the co-operation of *McVeigh*, and the subsequent sale to *Lewis*, was probably in pursuance of this plan, and the accounts which have been produced favor this supposition. It cannot be doubted that these accounts and memoranda shew the real mind and intention of Mr. *Pinhey* with reference to these transactions. These circumstances form, I think, an answer to the objection founded upon both statutes. Supposing them to apply to this case, the plaintiff is entitled to a decree for redemption. I think the mortgage debt must be taken to be £45. This fact appears from Mr. *Pinhey's* own memorandum. There were nothing in the circumstance of obtaining the note for £93 12s. 8d., including the mortgage debt, the note for £10, and compound interest upon both debts, to indicate an intention to augment the mortgage debt, or to make the note and interest on it a charge on the lands. I think the defendants should have their costs with this exception, that if, through inadvertence or oversight, they failed to produce the accounts under the order for production, and so necessitated the examination before the master, they should pay the costs of the latter proceeding. The plaintiff went into evidence with full knowledge of all the documentary evidence. It is true that the defendants insisted upon three statutes as raising a bar to the plaintiff's claim, but they were mere legal points submitted to the court, and did not increase the costs of the suit.

MALLOCH v. PLUNKETT.

Fraudulent conveyance—Pleading—Purchase at sheriff's sale.

An execution creditor proceeded to sale of the lands of his debtor, and sold a property which was subject to a mortgage for £500; given, as the creditor alleged, to defeat creditors, but which property the creditor alleged was worth not more than £200, and became himself the purchaser thereof at the price of £10 10s.; whereupon he filed a bill setting forth these facts; or that the mortgage was given to secure a much smaller, if any debt, and praying alternate relief in accordance with such allegations. The court at the hearing *pro confesso* refused to set aside the mortgage, but gave the plaintiff the usual decree as a judgment creditor, not as a purchaser. The proper course for the plaintiff to have taken under such circumstances was to have come to this court in the first instance, and not to proceed to a sale of the property with such a cloud upon the title.

Statement.—The bill in this case set forth that the defendant *Plunkett* being owner of 75 acres in Nepean, on the 7th of March, 1859, conveyed the same by way of mortgage to the defendant *Caldwell*, to secure £500 without interest, payable in March, 1869, although the land was worth not more than £200, for which mortgage no consideration was given by *Caldwell* to *Plunkett*, and *Plunkett* was not indebted to *Caldwell* in the sum of £500, or any other sum, for which the mortgage was given, but the same was given for the purpose and with the intent of defeating and defrauding the creditors of *Plunkett*, and to prevent them from recovering their debts against him; that *Plunkett* was at the time of creating the mortgage deeply involved and unable to pay his debts; that plaintiff had since recovered judgment against *Plunkett*, on which he issued a *fi. fa.*

against lands, under which the interest of *Plunkett* in
this land was sold, and a deed therefor executed by the
sheriff to the plaintiff, who became the purchaser
thereof at sheriff's sale for £10 10s. ; since which time
he had offered *Caldwell* £150 to induce him to discharge the mortgage so held by him, although plaintiff
did not thereby mean to admit *Caldwell's* right to be
paid any portion of the amount secured by the said
mortgage ; but on the contrary, plaintiff only offered
that amount by way of preventing litigation, which
offer *Caldwell* refused to accept ; and the bill charged
that even if the mortgage to *Caldwell* was not given
to defraud creditors, yet the same was given for a
much larger sum than was owing by *Plunkett* to *Caldwell*, and plaintiff submitted that *Caldwell* was entitled
to no more than the amount actually advanced by,
and *bona fide* due to, him on such security ; that in
any event plaintiff was entitled to have the mortgage
discharged upon payment of what (if anything) was
due thereunder, in the event of its being ascertained
that any thing was due to *Caldwell ;* and that he was
entitled to have an account taken of what moneys
Caldwell had, or might have, received, and prayed a
declaration that the mortgage was void, as a fraud
upon creditors ; that *Caldwell* had not advanced £500,
or any part thereof, to or on account of *Plunkett*, and
that the mortgage might be discharged ; but if the
court should be of opinion that *Plunkett* was indebted
to *Caldwell* at the date of the mortgage, that an account might be taken ; and for the usual relief consequential thereon.

Both defendants made default in answering, and the
bill was thereupon set down to be taken *pro confesso*
against them. On the cause coming on to be heard

Mr. *Fitzgerald*, for plaintiff, asked a decree declaring
the mortgage to *Caldwell* void, and ordering it to be
delivered up to be cancelled ; but

Judgment.—SPRAGGE, V. C.—I think the case suffi-

ciently stated to bring it within the statute 13th Elizabeth, and should give plaintiff relief on that ground as
a judgment creditor, not as purchaser, but for the form
of allegation as to the amount due on the mortgage to
Caldwell. I cannot read the bill as alleging positively
that the mortgage was made without consideration.
There must therefore be an account; the plaintiff having the ordinary remedies of a judgment creditor, with
leave to add the expenses of sale to his claim.

The proper course for the plaintiff was to come to
this court in the first instance, not to sell at law with
an evident cloud upon the title, purchase at one-
twentieth of the value, and then come to this court as
purchaser.

MILLER v. ATTORNEY-GENERAL.

Jurisdiction—Remedy of subject against the Crown.

The defendant was surety to her Majesty on the bond of Á., a customs officer. A. became a defaulter and absconded. The defendant,being sued at law on the bond set up the equitable defence,
that when the bond was executed by him his principal was in
charge of the small port of Bruce Mines; that the bond was given
and executed only in respect of that office; that the government
had afterwards removed the principal to another port where
larger customs receipts were collected, and where consequently
the risk was greater, and where the alleged defalcation occurred.
The express terms of the bond were however in respect of the
office of collector of customs in Canada, without any reference to
Bruce Mines, and the plea was held bad on demurrer by the
Court of Queen's Bench. The defendant then filed his bill in
this court, setting forth the facts, and praying for a stay of proceedings at law, or similar relief against the Crown. *Held,* that
this court has no jurisdiction to grant relief in the premises, the
rights of the Crown being brought directly in question.

The bill in this cause was filed by *Daniel G. Miller,*
under the circumstances set forth in the head-note,and
in the judgment of his lordship the Chancellor. The
facts are fully stated in the action at common law (*a*).
The Attorney-General having demurred to the bill the
demurrer came on for argument.

Mr. *J. W. Gwynne,* Q.C., for the plaintiff.

(*a*) Regina v. Miller, 20 U. C. Q. B. 485.

Mr. *Hodgins*, for the Attorney-General.

The following authorities were referred to in the argument: *Priddy* v. *Rose*, (b) *Attorney-General* v. *Halling*, (c) *Attorney-General* v. *Sewell*, (d) *Rankin* v. *Huskisson*, (e) *Taylor* v. *Attorney-General*, (f) *Colebrooke* v. *Attorney-General*, (g) *Rogers* v. *Maule*, (h) *Attorney-General* v. *Lambirth*, (i) *Evans* v. *Solly*, (j) *Attorney-General* v. *Galway*, (k) *Barclay* v. *Russell*, (l) *Penn* v. Lord *Baltimore*, (m) *Pawlett* v. *Attorney-General* (n) *Reeve* v. *Attorney-General*, (o) *In re Holmes*, (p) *Holmes* v. *Regina*, (q) *Manning's* Ex Prac. p. 87 ; *Blackstone's* Commentaries ; *Chitty* on Prerogative of Crown, 340 ; *Broom's* Legal Maxims, p. 57 ; Imperial Acts, 33 ; Hen. VIII., ch. 39, sec. 55 ; 23 and 24 Vic., ch. 34 ; 5 Vic., ch. 5 ; Provincial Acts, 34 Geo. III., chs. 2 ; 7 Wm. IV., ch. 2, and Con. Stats. U. C., ch. 10 & 12.

After taking time to look into the authorities.

Judgment.—VANKOUGHNET, C.—This bill is filed by the plaintiff to be relieved from liability upon a bond executed by him as security for one *Acton*, for the proper discharge by the latter of his duties as a collector of her Majesty's customs.   Upon this bond the Crown has recovered judgment at law for actual default in paying over money, notwithstanding certain defences urged by the now plaintiff.   The bill prays for an injunction to restrain the Attorney-General from proceeding upon this judgment.   The Attorney-General demurs, among other things, to the jurisdiction of the

(b) 3 Mer. 86.

(c) 15 M. & W. 687.

(d) 4 M. & W. 77.

(e) 4 Sim. 13.

(f) 8 Sim. 413.

(g) 7 Price, 156.

(h) 3 Y, & C. 74.

(i) 5 Price, 386.

(j) 9 Price, 525.

(k) 1 Molloy, 95.

(l) 3 Ves. 425.

(m) 1 Ves. 446, & 3 W. & T. 467.

(n) Hard. 467.

(o) 2 Atk. 223.

(p) 2 J. & H. 527.

(q) 8 Jur. N. S 76.

court. No case is to be found in which such relief as is sought here has ever been given by the Court of Chancery. All the text books which treat of the subject negative the right of the Court of Chancery to decree direct relief against the Crown, when the contest is simply one between it and the subject. *Blackstone's* Commentaries, *Chitty* on Prerogative, *Manning's* Exchequer Practice, *Broom's* Legal Maxims, all speak broadly to this effect. In *Priddy* v. *Rose,* and *Brown* v. *Bradshaw,* (a) the same doctrine was admitted; and only in cases where the rights of the Crown have come incidentally in question, and the Attorney-General has been brought before the court to protect them; or in cases where the Attorney-General has submitted them to be dealt with by the court, has a decree ever been made by which those rights were impaired or interfered with. There are some cases in which decrees have been made against public officers discharging duties under the Crown, who have been rather in the position of stakeholders or trustees for the public, or individuals claiming to have certain rights and privileges with which these officers were interfering or permitting interference, as in the case of *Rankin* v. *Huskisson,* and the case of *Ellis* v. Earl *Grey.* (b)

The claim of the Crown against the plaintiff is one relating to the revenue, with which in England the Court of Exchequer, and in this country the Courts of Queen's Bench and Common Pleas have peculiar power to deal. The statute 33 Hen. VIII., ch. 39, sec. 55, directs in what courts (the Court of Chancery not being one) debts due to the Crown shall be sued for. Section 79 provides, " that if any person or persons of whom any such debt or duty is at any time demanded or required, allege, plead, declare, or shew in any of *the said courts,* good, perfect, and sufficient cause and matter in law, reason or *good conscience* in bar or discharge of the said debt," &c., then *the said courts* shall have full power to adjudge and

---

(a) Prec. in Ch. 7, 153.   (b) 6 Sim. 214.

discharge the person so impleded," etc.· ·Under the
authority of this section the Court of Exchequer in
England has frequently granted relief against the
strictly legal claims of the Crown. All the cases which
were cited to me in support of this bill were cases from
the Exchequer, and it seems reasonable and convenient
that the whole matter should be disposed of there when
on grounds of· equity the court can stay its legal process. The Court of Exchequer has long claimed and
exercised an equitable jurisdiction in matters of revenue, and while the Attorney-General was proceeding by
a *sci. fa.*, or an extent on the one side of the court, matter in equity might be shewn on the other side why the
legal process should not have effect. The history of this
jurisdiction is traced and its character explained in the
very interesting and elaborate judgment of *Pollock*,
C.B., in *Attorney-General* v. *Halling*. Much valuable
information on the same subject is to be found in the
case of the *Attorney-General* v. *Sewell*. A difference of
opinion has prevailed in England as to the effect of the
imperial statute, 5 Victoria, ch. 5. In the *Attorney-General* v. The *Corporation of London* the Master of the
Rolls thought that all the equitable jurisdiction of the
Court of Exchequer, as well in matters of revenue as
otherwise, was by that act taken from that court and
transferred to the Court of Chancery. Some observations favouring this view were made in the House of
Lords on the hearing of the appeal in that case, as reported in 1 H. Lds., 440; but neither then, nor on the
hearing in the court below, was it necessary to decide
that question; and Lord *Cottenham* expressly reserved
his opinion upon it. In the *Attorney-General* v. *Halling*,
the learned Barons of the Exchequer deliberately considered the subject, and came to a clear conclusion that
they still retained their equitable jurisdiction in matters of revenue; and, accordingly, in that case they
exercised it. I follow this decision in preference to the
view of Lord *Langdale*. I think it better considered, and
until overruled by a higher authority, binding; and,

moreover, the reasoning in support of it seems to me very strong. The consequence of this holding would be that the peculiar equitable jurisdiction of the Court of Exchequer in matters of revenue was not by that statute transferred to the Court of Chancery. If it was, it might be contended that under our act, 20 Victoria, ch. 56, sec. 1, the Court of Chancery in this province possessed the same powers as those transferred from the Exchequer to Chancery, under the imperial act of 5 Victoria. Even if this were so, it would not follow that the Court of Chancery here was the sole tribunal in which parties to claims by the Crown in respect of revenue could have relief, or would at all interfere if the court of common law had power to do equity. The statute 34 George III., ch. 2, which constituted the Court of Queen's Bench in Upper Canada, appears to me to have given to that court all the powers which the Court of Exchequer in England then possessed " in the matters which regard the King's revenue ; " although the language of the act, by which this power is, as I think, conveyed, is open to some criticism. The imperial act of 5 Victoria could not affect this jurisdiction. The matter in dispute here is one which specially regards the revenue, and in respect of which I think relief can only be obtained in the Court of Queen's Bench here, where the proceedings at law are carried on, or by petition of right. It is not for me to do more than to intimate to the plaintiff the mode of proceeding by which he may establish his equity, if any, to relief. The Court of Queen's Bench will judge of its own powers and jurisdiction, and settle the form by which, if at all, its equitable aid can be invoked.

Finding that I have no jurisdiction in the matter, I abstain from expressing any opinion upon the merits of the case as stated in the bill.

Demurrer allowed.

NORWICH v. THE ATTORNEY-GENERAL.

Jurisdiction of court—Remedy of subject against the Crown.

The municipality of Norwich became sureties to the Crown for moneys advanced to a railway company. The property and functions of the company were altered and interfered with by acts of parliament, and the company finally united with another. The completion of the railway through the township of Norwich was thus indefinitely postponed, and the advantage expected to be derived by the township, when its municipality became indebted to the Crown, was not realised. The government having taken proceedings for the collection of the sum secured, the municipality filed a bill to stay such proceedings. *Held*, (following the decision' in Miller v. The Attorney-General,) that this court has no juris-\diction in the matter, and that the equitable jurisdiction in matters of revenue in this province, at the suit of a subject, resides in the superior courts of common law, if at all, and not in this court.

Statement.—The plaintiffs in this suit were the Corporation of the township of South Norwich, the defendants were the Attorney-General for Upper Canada, the Corporation of North Norwich, and *James Carroll*, Esq., sheriff of the county of Oxford.

The bill set forth several acts of parliament established, and otherwise affecting various railway corporations, and from the matters at length alleged, it appeared that the provincial act 10 & 11 Victoria, ch. 117, after reciting in its preamble the expediency of constructing a railway from Woodstock to the shores of Lake Erie, at some point between Ports Dover and Burwell, provided for the erection of "The Woodstock and Lake Erie Railway and Harbour Company," with corporate seal, capability of holding property for the use of the company, power to lay a track, construct a harbour at terminus, &c.

The works of the company were to be commenced within five years, and completed in ten, or the chapter forfeited. That by statute 16 Victoria, chapter 239, it appeared that the works having been delayed, the time for completion was then extended to two years, the company allowed to carry the Road to Dunnville, and the capital stock authorized to be increased to £500,000,

and the company permitted to borrow money to build
the road. That the 16 Victoria, chapter 23, authorised
municipalities in Upper Canada to raise money by
debentures upon the credit of the municipal loan fund
to aid public works. Upon any municipality becoming
indebted under this act, provisions are made for requiring its officers to levy the amount due at the requirements of the Receiver-General. When default
was made for two months the Governor-General's writ
was to issue to the sheriff of the county, and the debt
levied as a tax upon the ratepayers. At the date of
the passing of these acts the township of Norwich was
undivided, and the proposed railway would have run
through it, and by a by-law made the 1st of December,
1852, the township council determined to lend £50,000
to the railway company, and that the same should be
raised on the credit of the municipal loan fund. Debentures to that amount were issued by the government
in favour of the company, who gave their bond to the
township to indemnify them, and the township became
the debtors of the government. The company agreed to
pay the township interest at the rate of six per cent. per
annum on the amount of the debentures, and the balance
due, at the expiration of thirty years. Other neighbour-
ing municipalities made similar arrangements with
this railway and the government, so that the directors
had £145,000 of debentures at their disposal.

Working was re-commenced, but the parties disa-
greeing it was abandoned, and the road was still unfinished. It was alleged that £350,000 would be required
to render it available, the money already expended had
become lost, the country through which the works
passed had been rather injured than benefitted by them
in their unfinished state. By 18 Victoria, ch. 179, the
company were conditionally allowed to extend their
railway to the Suspension Bridge, and from Port Dover
to St. Thomas. The capital was to be raised to the
sum of £1,000,000, and the company was authorised
to amalgamate with any other similar company.

The plaintiffs complained that this and some other alterations in the law of incorporation of this company then made were to their prejudice.

By 13 Victoria, chapter 192, another million of pounds was to be raised for the Amherstburgh and St. Thomas Railway Company, and the track was to run from St. Thomas to Amherstburg; that the township of Norwich was then divided into North and South Norwich, which were still held jointly liable to the government for the debt, but liable to contribution as between themselves; that by 19 Victoria, chapter 74, shareholders desirous of being relieved from their responsibility to the Woodstock and Lake Erie Railway Company, were allowed to relieve themselves on surrendering the stock they held, and many of the stockholders took advantage of this, and by this means the plaintiff's security against the company was materially lessened. This having been done with the consent of the government, the plaintiffs allege as a ground of equitable relief, that the Woodstock and Lake Erie Company, and the Amherstburgh and St. Thomas Company amalgamated in February, 1858, with a joint capital of two millions of pounds, and the title of " The Great South Western Railway Company " was then assumed ; which amalgamation was effected by written agreements between the companies, and one of the provisions of the agreement permitted a delay in the completion of the Woodstock and Port Dover road, which was prejudicial to the plaintiffs, and being done without their consent was also charged as a ground for relief. This arrangement was subsequently confirmed by the statute 22 Victoria, ch. 113, and by the 5th section of that act the capital was increased to $10,000,000; and that other clauses in this act worked still further damage to the plaintiffs, in effect postponing the construction of the Woodstock and Erie road indefinitely. That the 22 Victoria, ch. 90, incorporated the Niagara and Detroit Rivers' Railway Company, from which lines were to run in one direction to Fort Erie, and in the other, to Amherstburgh, covering thus the proposed line of the Woodstock and Lake Erie road. New regulations for the management of this company were enacted, and as these materially varied the terms of the agreements subsisting when the plaintiffs became indebted as such sureties, they were set forth as grounds for relief. The property, moreover, of several of the former companies, of which this was the successor, was vested in this company, and this included the revenues of the Port Dover Harbour. This railway was to be completed in five years. That thereby the company, to aid in which the township of Norwich incurred their present liability, in fact never came into practical operation—that its properties and functions were at various times altered and interfered with by the legislature, and its identity at length destroyed by incorporation of its privileges, remaining estate, and line itself with the last mentioned company.

That the Woodstock and Lake Erie Company paid the Crown only the first instalment on the loan, and now, notwithstanding that damage, rather than advantage, had accrued to the plaintiffs from the railway works, the Governor-General's warrant had been issued to the sheriff requiring him to levy by assessment, sums in the aggregate amounting to $8,700, and interest, this being for instalments due in 1859-60.

The bill prayed for a declaration that the sums claimed ought not in equity to be levied, and that the sheriff might be restrained from proceeding under the Crown writ.

The Attorney-General in this case, instead of demurring, as was done in *Miller* v. *Attorney-General*, put in an answer requiring proof of the facts alleged, and also raising the question of the court's jurisdiction as against the Crown. The other defendants raised no material questions in their answers.

Evidence was taken and the cause heard at Hamilton before his Honour Vice-Chancellor *Spragge*, at the fall sittings in 1863.

Mr. *Blake* and Mr. *Kerr*, for the plaintiffs.

Mr. *McGregor*, for the Attorney-General.

The same authorities were cited as are referred to in *Miller* v. The *Attorney-General*.

Judgment.—SPRAGGE, V. C.—The judgment of his lordship the Chancellor in *Miller* v. *Attorney-General* decides against the plaintiffs the question of jurisdiction raised by the answer and argued before me in this suit; unless the jurisdiction can be sustained upon the ground that the Governor-General, whose warrant to levy the rate upon the municipality is sought to be enjoined, fills the character, *quoad* this act, of an agent of the legislature, and not as representing the Crown.

I do not think the jurisdiction can be sustained upon this ground. It is the right of the Crown as representing the public revenue of the province that is brought in question. The warrant of the Governor-General is merely part of the machinery by which the revenue is, in such cases, to be collected, the Receiver-General and the Secretary of the province being also instruments used in the process of its collection.

The frame of the bill is also against the plaintiffs' position.

It is the Attorney-General that is made a party defendant, and, of course, as the proper officer of the Crown. The 78th and subsequent paragraphs of the bill, in terms state the equity as against the Crown, and the first branch of the prayer is, " that it may be declared that the said liability is no longer subsisting, and that the Crown is no longer entitled to levy any sum from your complainants in respect thereof." I think the bill is properly framed as it is, and that the Crown properly represents the public revenue, whether the mode of its collection be by warrant of the Governor-General or in any other mode.

I have not considered the general question of jurisdiction, as that point is *res judicata* by the decision of *Miller* v. The *Attorney-General*. It certainly is an anomaly that the equitable jurisdiction in matters of revenue at the suit of a subject in this province resides in a court of common *law, if at all*, and not in a court of equity.

Ross v. Mason.

Parol evidence—Wife's estate.

A woman possessed of real estate sold the same, her husband joining in the conveyance thereof, and receiving to his own use the purchase money ; in consideration of which he agreed to settle on the wife certain other property which he held under lease with the right of purchase, and the lease was accordingly assigned to a trustee for the use of the wife, the husband at the same time promising to pay the amount to be paid for the purpose of obtaining the conveyance of the fee; the husband having died and his estate being in the course of administration in this court, and his widow having brought a claim into the master's office for the amount necessary to procure the conveyance of the fee: *Held*, on appeal from the master's report, that the master had properly received parol evidence to establish such claim of the widow.

Statement.—This was a suit instituted to administer the estate of the late *Ezekiel F. Whittemore*, and the usual reference as to debts, &c., had been made to the master, who in taking the accounts had allowed a sum of £260 to the widow of the deceased, under the circumstances stated in the head-note and judgment. Against this allowance the *Commercial Bank of Canada* who proved as creditors on the estate appealed.

Mr. *A. Crooks*, Q.C., for the appeal.

Mr. *Roaf*, Mr. *Hodgins*, Mr. *S. Blake*, Mr. *McLennan* and Mr. *Taylor*, for other parties.

Judgment.—SPRAGGE, V. C.—The objections to the master's report, with the exception of the fourth, were disposed of at the hearing of the appeal. I reserved my judgment upon the 4th objection, and the papers have only lately reached me.

This objection is to the allowance by the master, as a debt due by the estate of the late *Ezekiel F. Whittemore* of the sum of £260: which is claimed under these circumstances. *Whittemore* was assignee of the lessee of a lot and house in Bay street, in Toronto, which lease gave to the lessee, as is alleged, the option of purchase at the sum of £200. His wife the present claimant, was seized in her own right, of a piece of land on Toronto street, which he was desirous of selling to the government. His wife objected to the sale unless the lease of the house on Bay street was assigned to trustees for the benefit of herself and children. *Whittemore* agreed to these terms, his wife joined in the sale to the government, and he received and used the purchase money: this was in 1850.

Whittemore did not execute his part of the contract until December, 1857, when he assigned the lease to Mr. *Rutherford* upon trust; among other things, that in the event of his wife surviving him, an event which happened, *Rutherford* should convey absolutely to her. This *Rutherford* did in December, 1859, after the death of *Whittemore*.

So far there is no question between the parties; her title as assignee of the lease is not impugned. But it is stated upon affidavit that it was part of the agreement between her husband and herself that the house was to be settled upon her in fee, free from all incumbrances; and that the purchase money to acquire the fee simple should be paid by *Whittemore;* the assignment and the agreement to pay the purchase money being the consideration to Mrs. *Whittemore* for the alienation of the

Toronto street lot. It does not appear that the agreement to pay this purchase money was embodied in the assignment to *Rutherford.* That assignment, the original lease, and the mesne assignments are not produced. Mr. *Hodgins* makes affidavit that he had some time ago in his possession the title deeds from *Whittemore* to *Rutherford,* which are mislaid; he speaks of the assignment to *Rutherford* only, and does not state that it contained any agreement for the payment of the purchase money; that fact, and the fact that the orginal lease gave an option of purchase rests upon parol evidence only. The objection is, that the facts are not supported by legal evidence, by which I understand that parol evidence to prove this is not receivable. Mr. *Crooks* may have intended to say further, that they are not sufficiently proved even if parol evidence is receivable.

The first fact, that the original lease gave an option of purchase, is in fact proof of the contents of a written instrument. This is not well proved by the affidavit before me (an affidavit of *John Ginty* was read upon the appeal, and may contain better evidence than the affidavit which I have). One of the affidavits before me, that of *Alexander Manning,* only states that it was well known to all the parties acquainted with the agreement between *Whittemore* and his wife, and that the house was held by *Whittemore* under a lease for 21 years, with the right to purchase the fee simple for £200. Mr. *Rutherford's* affidavit only states that the house was to be settled upon Mrs. *Whittemore,* free from all incumbrances, and in fee simple. There is also an affidavit of the book-keeper in the office of the bursar of the University of Toronto, which states that the estate of *Whittemore* is indebted to the University in the sum of £200 for purchase money of the Bay street property, and £60 for arrears of rent, the University being now, as appears by the report, the owner in fee, and lessor of these premises. It does not appear that any of these defendants has ever seen the original lease. I think they do not sufficiently prove the contents : it is not good secondary evidence, even assuming that the original cannot be had. I suppose Mr. *Hodgins* means to say that the original held by *Whittemore* is lost, but a counterpart would probably be, and for all that appears is, in the office of the bursar of the University.

The next fact is, whether *Whittemore* did as part consideration of the alienation of the Toronto-street lot agree to pay this alleged £200 purchase money. If that can be proved by parol, and is proved, I think it is sufficient for the disposition of the whole case.

In *Clifford* v. *Turrell*, (a) before Sir *J. L. Knight Bruce*, it was proved by parol, that the payment of an annuity, and the providing a house, formed part of the consideration for the assignment of a lease of a farm, and the purchase of farm-stock and furniture ; the assignment itself stating a consideration, but not stating the annuity and house as any part of the consideration ; and the Vice-Chancellor decreed specific performance as to the annuity and house. I think that case governs this. I have already stated what is proved by the affidavits; they are the affidavits of Mr. *Rutherford*, who was at that time partner of *Whittemore*, and afterwards a trustee under the assignment, and of Mr. *Manning*, and they establish the agreement.

If I thought it necessary I would allow proof to be given of the alleged provision in the lease for allowing the lessee the privilege of purchasing for £200, but I think the evidence upon the other point sufficient, and upon this ground, that *Whittemore* represented to his wife that he had such right of purchase, and agreed to exercise it ; and such representation and agreement was part of the consideration for an alienation, of which he got the benefit. If the representations were untrue he

---

(a) 1 Y. & C. Chy. 138.

would have been bound to make it good, and to make the purchase if he could. It was probably true, but whether so or not, it appears that the purchase can be made, and the sum necessary to make it, that allowed by the master is, I think, a proper charge against the estate.

But though a proper charge against the estate, I do not think it is properly allowed by Mrs. *Whittemore*. It is in evidence that she has made an assignment of the Bay street property to *John Ginty*, upon certain trusts, for the benefit of her children and herself. *John Ginty* is the proper person to claim and receive this money, and to apply it in acquiring the fee for the benefit of the trust, as indeed I have no doubt that Mrs. *Whittemore* would apply it if it were received by herself. The reference goes back to the master upon other points, and he can make the requisite alteration in this respect.

As to costs, this is a contest between two creditors of the testator, and the one failing should pay the costs. I mean of course only the costs upon this objection. The other objections are allowed without costs.

ROBINSON v. BYERS.

Mortgage—Assignment by executor.

The executor of a mortgagee has not, under the provisions of the statute in that behalf (chapter 87, Consolidated Statutes of Upper Canada, section 5) any power to sell and convey the legal estate held by his testator to a person purchasing the mortgage.

This was a suit instituted by the plaintiff as assignee of a mortgage which had been assigned to him by the executors of the mortgagee; alleging that the money secured thereby was due and unpaid, and praying a decree of foreclosure in default of payment of what might be found due on foot of the mortgage.

The adult defendant made default in answering, and the bill was set down to be taken *pro confesso* as against him. The infant defendants filed an answer. On the cause coming on to be heard,

Mr. *Hodgins*, for the plaintiff, asked that the usual reference might be directed to the master to take accounts, and make enquiries.

Mr. *T. Holden*, for the infants, did not object; but,

Judgment.—VANKOUGHNET, C.—The plaintiff claims to be the assignee of the executors of the mortgagee, and as such seeks foreclosure; neither the executors nor the heirs at law of the mortgagee are parties to the bill, but the plaintiff contends that the legal estate in the land passed to him by the assignment from the executors, and in support of this position he relies upon section 5, chapter 87, Consolidated Statutes of Upper Canada. Without the aid of this statute there could be no pretence for such a contention by the plaintiff. The language of this section is that " when any person entitled to any freehold or leasehold land by way of mortgage has departed this life, and his executor or administrator is entitled to the money secured by the mortgage, or has *assented* to a bequest thereof or has assigned the mortgage debt, such executor or administrator, if the mortgage money was paid to the testator, or intestate in his life-time, *or on* payment of the *principal money and interest due on the* said mortgage money, may convey, release, and discharge the said mortgage debt and the legal estate in the land." This provision does not give the executor any power to sell or assign the legal estate in the land; it simply gives him power to release or convey the legal estate in the land, or discharge the debt, on the money being paid, and as it authorises him to do this after the mortgage debt has been assigned by him or after he has assented to a bequest by his testator of it, I suppose we must assume that the legislature intended that he might discharge this duty where the money was paid to the party who would be so entitled to receive it, *i. e.*, either by bequest or assignment. This is an awkward and troublesome method of procuring the re-conveyance of the legal estate com-

pared with that which might have been had, had the
legislature, when they permitted the executor to assign
the security, *i. e.*, the legal estate in the land given in
security; but this, it seems to me, they have not
done; and it may be doubtful whether, even after
payment to the assignee of the executor, the latter can
re-convey the legal estate, though, I think, in my construction of the statute, he can. Of course the legal
estate, until released, remains in the heirs of the
mortgagee, and they can be compelled to convey, even
though the executors have that power under the statute.

MENZIES v. WHITE.

Setting aside will—Soundness of mind, evidence of.

The validity of a will established, notwithstanding witnesses swore
that the testator was not in a fit state to make a will when the
same was executed; the evidence of the medical attendants and
surrounding circumstances tending to shew that the testator
was of sufficiently sane and disposing mind to understand the
devises in his will.

The principle of what is a sufficiently sane and disposing mind and
memory treated of and acted on.

Statement.—The bill in this cause was filed by *William Menzies* and *Grace Menzies*, against *John White*,
Janet Lawson, *William D. Lyon*, and *Archibald Macnab*,
stating that *James Lawson*, in his life-time, of the
township of Esquesing, had died without issue on the
31st of July, 1860, leaving the defendant *Janet Lawson*,
his widow; and being at the time of his decease
seised of certain lands; (setting them forth;) and that
he had been induced to make a will the night preceding
his death, leaving all his property to his said wife, and
appointed the defendants *Lyon* and *Macnab* executors
thereof; that the defendant *White* had since purchased
a portion of the real estate with knowledge of the circumstances attending the making of such will, and
which are fully set forth in the judgment.

The prayer of the bill was, that under such circumstances the said will might be declared void and set aside. The defendants, other than *Macnab*, against whom the bill was taken *pro confesso*, answered the bill, denying the charges thereof, and evidence was taken in the cause, the material points of which appear in the judgment.

Mr. *J. Hillyard Cameron*, Q.C., and *G. D. Boulton*, for plaintiffs.

Mr. *Mowat*, Q.C., and Mr. *McLennan*, for the defendants, other than *Macnab*.

Judgment.—VANKOUGHNET, C.—In this case the question to be determined is one of fact, there being really no difficulty as to the rules of law applicable to it, and for that reason considering the importance of the case to the parties, and the mass and bearing of the evidence given in it, I should have been very glad of the aid of a jury in disposing of it, had either party suggested such a course; called upon, however, to pronounce a judgment, I proceed to examine the evidence, and to state the conclusion which I have arrived at upon it, first explaining what the question in dispute is, and what I conceive to be the principles of law by which it must be governed. This question then is whether or not the testator at the time of making the will, which the plaintiffs here impeach and seek to have set aside, was in a state of mind competent to perform such an act, and whether or not the act so performed was his own, freely and deliberately done, so that this testamentary paper really expresses his intention and decision as to the disposition of his property after his death.

Thinking it unnecessary in this case, and not desirable at any time, if it can be properly avoided, to add to the definitions of legal rules and principles to be found in the books I adopt as suited to this case, and I apply to the consideration of the evidence in it the dicta of the judges in *Combe's* case, reported in *Moore*, at page 759, and of Lord *Coke*, in the Marquis of *Winchester's* case, (a) "that sane memory for the making of a will is not at all times when the party can speak, read, or write, or had life in him, nor when he can answer to anything with sense, but he ought to have judgment to discern, and to be of perfect memory; that it is not sufficient that the testator be of memory when he makes his will, to answer familiar and usual questions, but he ought to have a disposing memory, so as to be able to make a disposition of his property with understanding and reason, and that is such a memory which the law calls sane and perfect memory."

The testator on the 10th day of October, 1836, being seised, as I take the fact to be, of lot 2, in the second concession of Esquesing, made a will whereby he devised all his property, real and personal, to his wife, for life, and such property as he then owned he devised at her death to the plaintiff *Grace Menzies*, and such property as he acquired after making his will he devised on his wife's death to the plaintiff *William Menzies*. This will the plaintiffs claim under, and ask to have established as the last will of the testator. It is not shewn from whose custody this will has come, nor where it was deposited during his life.

Subsequently to the making of this will the testator acquired 400 acres of land in Nassagaweya, worth at the time of his death about $3000. On Saturday, the 29th of July, 1860, the testator received severe injuries in the abdomen, chest, and legs, from the attack of a bull, by which he was gored, and at 5 o'clock in the afternoon of Tuesday he died of these injuries, at the age of 70 years. His wife was about the same age at the time. It is proved that the lot in Esquesing was at the testa-

---

(a) 6 Co. 23.

tor's death worth from $3000 to $3500 ; that it was in very bad order as a farm; that the house on it was scarcely tenantable ; that there was no barn; that the fences were out of repair, and the premises entirely neglected; that besides this lot and the land in Nassagaweya, which was in a state of nature, the testator owned but little, the personality being of trifling amount beyond a debt due from certain persons in Hamilton, which is considered worthless, though it does not appear that this was so at the testator's death, or that if it was he had been aware of it. The testator owed at the time of his death from $2000 to $2500. Besides the plaintiffs resident in Scotland, and who were cousins of the testator, his only known relatives were some cousins in this country, with whom he does not appear to have been on intimate or even friendly terms. One of the plaintiffs, *Grace*, the testator never saw, as she was born after he emigrated from Scotland, to which he never returned. His wife was also his cousin, and appears to stand in the same relation as he did to the plaintiffs. He had no children. In this position of things, and on the Monday night before his death, the testator made the will in dispute, at the instance, and I may say solicitation of the defendant *White*. Mr. *Cameron* the counsel for the plaintiffs, very properly at the close of the evidence admitted that there was no evidence to shew that *White* or the other defendants were actuated by any improper motive in procuring the testator to make his will, and the bill, so far as it attributes any such motive to them or any of them, fails. I think, as I stated on the argument, that the defendants *White* and *Lyon* were prompted by a neighbourly, friendly feeling to an old man living a somewhat desolate life, when in ignorance, as they were, of the first will, they repaired to his deathbed, and urged him to settle his worldly affairs before death, which was rapidly approaching, overtook him. It is proved that they had been intimate with him, and that he was in the habit of consulting the defendant *Lyon* in his business matters. The other

defendant the widow, took no part whatever in the procuring of the will, and indeed appears to have been
ignorant of its existenee till after the testator's death.
A great number of witnesses were examined, and though
many of them have been contradicted in certain matters by them deposed to, yet I think they all intended
and endeavoured to speak the truth, and that the variances in their testimony are to be accounted for by
defects in memory and misapprehension at the time
of circumstances in which they had no special interest,
and to which they did not suppose they would
be called upon to speak.

All the witnesses concur in stating that the testator
retained possession of his senses up to almost the moment of his death, but many of them swear that he
was at times, and particularly on the night when this
will was executed, in a very drowsy state, the result,
as they think, of the drugs or medicines administered
to him. But one witness, and he the principal one for
the plaintiffs, *Archibald Macnab*, one of the executors
named in the will, and acting under it, and a defendant in the suit, swears that in his opinion the testator
was not in a fit state to make a will on that night.
Besides this expression of his opinion he gives the
following evidence :

On Monday evening I saw defendants, *White* and
Lyon, at testator's house first about dark. *White* was
standing outside the door, which was shut. *Lyon* came
out there to him. *White* said, " Well, have you made
any thing out of him ; " *Lyon* said " No, you go in
and try him ; " *White* then turned round to me and
said, "You go in and try him ;" I said, "No, I will
have nothing to do with it." Before *Lyon* came out
White said to me, " They were wishing him the testator to make his will, as it was necessary he should."
By " they " I mean *White* and *Lyon*. After I refused
to try testator, I followed *White* into the room where
testator was lying; the door opened into that room ;
testator's wife was lying on the bed then, I think.
Lyon did not go in with us; came in afterwards.
White went to a settee on which *Lawson* was lying.

White called him by name two or three times, and said, "Have you made a will?" *Lawson* did not answer. *White* asked me if I knew if testator had made a will; I said I thought he had. *White* then turned to testator, and spoke loudly in his ear, trying to rouse him, and asked him if he had made a will. *Lawson* opened his eyes, and in a low voice said "No." *White* then asked him how he would like to have his property left; he made no answer. *White* repeated his question again, once or twice more. *White* asked him if he wished his honest debts paid; I understood him to say yes, in a low voice. *White* pointed to his wife, and said, "I want you to make provision for that old woman; you know, *Lawson*, one-third of this place won't support her. *Lawson* made no reply. *White* then said, "Do you think £50 a year will support her?" *Lawson* said nothing. *White* then said, "Will £75 ($300) be enough?" *Lawson* then said "Yes." *White* asked him what was to be done with the rest of the property;" *Lawson* gave no answer. *White* asked him again, but there was no answer. *White* then said, "Well, I suppose we had better leave it to go as the law directs;" I heard no answer, but I think testator by his look, assented. I cannot say he answered one word. I heard the answers to the other questions. While *White* asked these questions there were in the room *Robert Nunn*, *William Lyon*, and two of my daughters, *Margaret* and *Janet;* one *McKinnon*, in my employ, was about the premises, but I think not in the room. Immediately after *White* commenced to wake up testator these came into the room. *White* asked him "Whom he would have for executor;" he said nothing. *White* said "Will you have *Archibald McNab* (meaning me) and *William Lyon,* your old neighbours?" I at once said "No, I will have nothing to do with it, you are more capable yourself." I think *Lawson* said "Yes" in answer. *White* then asked if he might send down to Mr. *Dewar,* to draw the will; *Lawson* said "Yes." During all this time *Lawson* said nothing but "Yes" or "No." He made no remark of his own accord; suggested nothing; he appeared to be, as I considered, in a deep sleep, or sort of stupor. Mr. *White* and *Lyon* the defendant left the house together after the last answer; I think in a buggy. I omitted to state that after Mr. *White* had asked him to provide for his wife, *White* said to him, "*Lawson,* I wish you would send for a minister, to pray for you; he appeared reluctant. I then shook him, and asked him to do so; he assented then. I remained in the house till *White* came back with *Robert Lyon.* *White* was absent not long; I thought they had been very quick about it. When they came in, *Nunn*, and the old woman and myself were there. I had no conversation with the testator in their absence; he was not in a fit state for it. *White* went up to him, and said, "*Lawson*, we have got your will;" there was no reply. *White* called him loudly by name several times, but no answer. *White* then went out and got some cold water, and applied to his face; he then opened his eyes. *White* then said, "We have got your will, shall we read it;" he said "Yes." *White* then read the will in portions, asking him, at the end of each portion, if he understood it; testator said "Yes." I take it for granted *White* read the whole will. I found the will did not read the same as talked of with testator, before *White* left for Milton. I noticed that there was nothing about the £75 for the wife; I said nothing at the time; *Nunn* and I remarked it afterwards. *Lawson* was a good scholar; could not only write, but prepare papers. *Robert Lyon* and *Nunn* raised him up till his arms were as high as the table. *Lyon* held his hand, with the pen in it, and made the testator's mark. *White* asked him, at the time, if he knew what he was doing; he said "Yes." Saw *Lyon* and *Nunn* witness it. Never, all the time *White* was there, heard *Lawson* originate a word. I was not on the best of terms with testator; he was prejudiced against me. He was a very passionate man. I am sure he would not have chosen me for his executor. I say, that at the time of the execution of the will, testator was not in a fit state to make it.

On his cross-examination he says,

At the time *Lawson* signed the will I did not think he was in a fit state to make a will; I thought it doubtful if he understood all *White's* questions. I think so still. I think it doubtful if he understood most of them. He appeared to understand the question about the £50 or £75 for his wife. I think that was the only one he understood. While the doctors were operating on him on Monday he was more conscious than he was afterwards on that day. He fell into a sleepy and drowsy state, and more so at night at the time the will was made. The fore part of

Tuesday he was in a drowsy state, but from about noon he woke up and recognized from that time to his death all who came in.

The day after the will was made he says, " *Robert Nunn* said there would be trouble yet about the getting up of the will." *Macnab* is shewn the petition and affidavit which he signed and made in the surrogate office to obtain probate of the will, on the 14th of November following the testator's death, but he does not recollect either the one or the other, though he says he did sign one paper in the office, and perhaps more, but he does not recognize his signature (which is deposed to by the clerk of the court) to either the one document or the other. He says, " I am 62 years of age ; my memory is good ; it was never of the best."

The two daughters of *Macnab* who were present at the first interview between *White* and the testator on Monday evening, confirm their father's statement of what then occurred. They appear to be intelligent respectable young women. They speak of the testator as apparently in a very drowsy state. *Margaret*, one of the daughters, says she thought testator was sensible but sleepy. The other witness present at this interview was *Robert Nunn*, one of the witnesses to the will. He says that when *White* and *Lyon* came into the room on Monday night *Macnab* was there, and asked *Lawson* if he knew them, (*White* and *Lyon*,) and that *Lawson* replied that he did, naming each of them. He says,

About an hour after I went in I spoke to him ; asked him if he was not considerably injured ; he said he was. I asked him if he thought he would get over it ; he said he thought he would. I asked him if he felt better ; he said he felt better than he was through the day. About half-past nine, I think, Dr. *Hume* came in. I heard *White* ask *Lawson* if he had settled his affairs, saying to him, if he had not he had better do so, as the doctor said he was in a bad way. *Macnab* then spoke to him, saying the same thing, and that the doc.ors thought he could not live long. *Macnab* then asked him to have a minister ; Mr. *Ferguson's* name was

mentioned, and *Lawson* said "No," he did not want
to see him. Mr. *Macnab* then asked him if he would
not like to see a nice pious man like Mr. *Mitchell;*
Lawson said he might come. Mr. *White* then again
said to him if he had not settled his affairs he had
better do so, as the doctor said he could not live long.
Mr. *White* then said, "if he had not made a will would
he not like to do so;" he said he would. *White* then
asked him how he wished to have it done, and would
he bring up Mr. *Bastedo* or Mr. *Dewar* (both lawyers
in Milton) to do it. *Lawson* made no answer. *White*
then asked him how he wished to have his property
left; and what was to be done with his old woman, she
would soon not be able to take care care of herself; that
she was getting old and feeble. I then went out, and
Mr. *White* shortly came out and walked across to Mr.
Macnab's with his daughters. Mr. *White*, before I left
the house, asked *Lawson* if he thought £50 would
suffice to support his wife; he said he thought not. Mr.
White then asked him if he thought £100 enough; he
said he thought it too much. Mr. *White* then proposed
£75, and *Lawson* said he thought that would do; I then
left. I don't remember *William Lyon* asking *Lawson*
any questions, or speaking to him. *White* and *Macnab*
were the persons who conversed with him. After
White came back, on leaving *Macnab's* daughters he
went back to *Lawson's* house; I remained there then,
I think, half an hour. *Lawson* seemed sensible all the
time I was with him. *White* went away with *William
Lyon*. *McKinnon* and I were together a short distance
from the house while *White* was inside. *White* returned
to *Lawson's* in an hour, or an hour and a half after he
left, with *William Lyon;* came back with *Robert Lyon*
in a buggy. I did not see *William Lyon* again that
night. *White* and *Robert Lyon* went into the house,
and called me in with them; *Macnab* was there too.
I think *Lawson* knew them. *White* said to him, I have
brought your will; are you willing to have it read;
Lawson said, "Yes." *White* went in with *Robert Lyon*
before me, and after a minute or two came to the door
and called me in. *White* sat down beside *Lawson* and
began to read the will, stopping after every few words,
and asking *Lawson* if he understood it. I understood
it to give all his property to his widow, after paying his
just debts and funeral expenses. *White* read the will a
second time, and then asked *Lawson* if he understood it;
he said, "Yes." I don't remember his saying any
thing more. *White* then said to him it was his last will,

and asked him again if he understood it, and he said,
"Yes, I do." *White* then asked me and *Robert Lyon* to
sign the will. I don't know whether we or *Lawson*
signed first. *Lawson* was lying on his back; he could
not rise up; he made a movement with his hands as if
to take the pen, when *White* asked him if he was willing to sign. I raised him up a little from the pillow. I
put my mark to the will. I looked at it. My mark
was made something as appears there. Mr. *Macnab*
asked *Lawson* if he understood that he was leaving his
property to his wife *Jennie*. This was after the will was
read. *Lawson* said, in reply, "Yes I understand I am
leaving it to my old woman," or "to my wife," I don't
remember which. He seemed to have his senses; he
was drowsy by times. I think he had his senses all
night. I spoke to him during the night; * * *
he understood me when I spoke to him. Early on
Tuesday morning he got some chicken soup. I am sure
I spoke to him more than once or twice during the Monday night; when I asked him how he felt; if he was
warm, and so on, he answered. On Tuesday morning
after he had the soup, I said to him I was going away
to my work; he told me I need not be in a hurry for a
time; I remained. After the will was executed *White*
asked him if he should send the buggy for a clergyman.
I knew Mrs. *Lawson;* she and her husband, as far as I
saw, lived happily together. When *White* was first there
on Monday evening *Lawson* was rather drowsy. Neither
at that time nor at the time when the will was signed
did *Lawson* say anything unless spoken to; the first
that I heard about the will was when Mr. *White* was in
the house. I saw *Macnab* and his daughters about there.
Mr. *White* asked him if he had made a will. I understood him to say, "No." Mr. *White* then asked him
how he would like his property to be left. *Lawson* did
not say; he answered merely as *White* asked the questions about the provision for his wife; in answer to the
proposal for £50 a year, I can't say whether *Lawson*
said "No," or "I think not." After the arrangement
of £75 for the wife, *White* then asked him what was to
be done with the rest of the property, if it was to go as
the law directs. I did not understand what this meant.
I did not go for water to put on *Lawson's* face. I did
not see any water put on *Lawson's* face to rouse him up;
I saw his face wiped with a wet cloth more than once;
he was kind of drowsy all the time; when the will was
read I thought the £75 for the wife would have been

there. When Mr. *Macnab's* name as executor was read, he *Macnab*, said he did not care about being executor. I made no remark about the £75 provision being left out. I asked *Hiram Anderson* the next morning if it was not a strange way to get the will made ; he asked me how it was ; I told him he would hear of that after. I thought it strange that what I had heard spoken of as the provision for the wife and for the rest of the property was not in the will. Mr. *Lawson* did not ask me to witness the will ; Mr. *White* did. I did not hear *White* speak to *Lawson* about the witnesses. Mr. *Lawson* could not raise himself, nor be raised ; he put out his hand ; I think Mr. *White* steadied the pen like in his hand. I held up his head a little from the pillow. It was Mr. *Macnab* spoke of the property being left to his wife *Jennie.* What *Lawson* said in reply was,"Yes, I understand it." I did not mean to say that he added, "I am leaving it to my old woman ;" it was *Macnab* said this. I think *Lawson* was asleep the greater part of the time *White* was absent getting the will drawn.

On the second occasion of *White's* visit to the testator on the Monday evening, *Robert Lyon,*the other witness to the will, was present, and he deposes as follows :

I knew *James Lawson* well for ten years before his death; was very intimate with him. Saw him on Sunday morning, after the accident ; he was quite sensible; did not seem in much pain ; spoke of the accident ; said the bull had tossed him on its horns; he talked a good deal; I thought he would be well in a few days ; he was a strong man. Saw him next on Monday night. Saw the will in Mr. *Dewar's* office that night, before it was executed. Called in at *Dewar's* office on my way back from my brother's store to my house ; walked with him from the office. He gave the will to *White*. *White* and I then went up in a buggy to *Lawson's* about twelve o'clock at night. Mrs. *Lawson, Macnab,* and *Robert Nunn* were there. *Macnab* asked *Lawson* if he knew us, referring first to *White,* and then to me ; *Lawson* said he did,mentioning *White's* name, and then mine. *White* conversed with him for some time,asking him if he thought he would get better; *Lawson* said he thought so. He asked him if he had much pain. He was not drowsy ; no effort to rouse him was made. *White* did not go for water ; *Nunn* or I got some; there was water in a basin, for wetting a rag to place on his forehead ;

the rag was on his forehead when we went in. *White* took the rag off his forehead, and wet it in the fresh water, and put it on his forehead; this was some time after he had been talking to him. *White* then said he had the will. He then read it, paragraph by paragraph, to *Lawson*, and asked him, on each, if he understood it; he said "Yes;" he read it over twice to him, and asked him if he understood it; *Lawson* said he knew he was leaving his property to his old woman. *Macnab* then got up, and turning to the old woman, said to *Lawson*, "Whom could you leave it to, Mr. *Lawson*, if not to your old woman." I had no doubt at the time that *Lawson* quite understood the will. It was months after, before I heard the will questioned. Mr. *White* said, "The will is now ready for signing." Mr. *Lawson* then put up his hand, and tried to get up by aid of some boxes, near the lounge where he lay. Mr. *White* told him not to rise; he might hurt himself; he could do it where he was; Mr. *Nunn* then went round behind him, and supported him; *Lawson* put out his hand, and took the pen; Mr. *White* guided his hand to make his mark; I then witnessed it; so did *Nunn*; this was done in the presence of *Lawson*. I know Mrs. *Lawson*; she is not silly or weak-minded; she is old and frail, but has her senses. *Lawson* and his wife lived happily together, as far as I know. Have often heard testator complain of *Robert Menzies*, who lived on the hill; never of his relations in Scotland. After the will was signed, Mr. *Macnab* said he had a last request to make, and that was to send for a minister, as the doctors thought he would die. When Mr. *Ferguson's* name was proposed *Lawson* said no, he did not want him. He objected to Mr. *Gillespie*. Said something at that time when *Mitchell* was proposed. As I recollect *Lawson* owed, at the time of his death, from $2,000 to $2,500, including the mortgage to *Elliott*. Besides the land in Esquesing and Nassagaweya, I know of *Lawson* owning no property, except a debt due by *Spohn & Start*, of Hamilton. It is not considered a good debt. He had a share of the crop, I believe, on the land at the time of his death. I know *James Menzies*. *White* and *Lawson* were intimate with one another. After the will was executed, and not before, Mr. *White* asked me to witness the will. Mr. *Lawson* did not ask him to witness the will. *Lawson* did not, himself, commence or originate any conversation. Mr. *White* had spoken to him for some considerable time, before he put the wet cloth on his head. I do not know why *White* himself did not witness the will. *White* wrote *Lawson's* name in the house. I wrote *Nunn's*, the witness. I read the will in Mr. *Dewar's* office, before going to *Lawson's ;* the purport of it, I recollect, was leaving the property to his wife, after paying his debts. While the will was being read, the testator said nothing more than "Yes" to each paragraph. Can't say why the will was read over twice. After the will was executed *White* again wet the rag, and put it on his forehead. No attempt was made to get *Lawson* to write his name. *White* wrote *Lawson's* name to the will in his presence, before his eyes, on a box beside him. *Lawson* was not asked to write his name. He acknowledged the signature to be his hand and seal for the purposes therein contained. *White* asked him if he so acknowledged, and he said " yes." After the second reading of the will, *White* asked him if that was the way he wanted it ; *Lawson* said "Yes." *White* said, "Do you understand it ?" *Lawson* said, "I know I am leaving all my property to my old woman." Except this, he said nothing in regard to the will but " yes," as I have stated. No explanation was made why *White* was not one of the witnesses. *Macnab*, in my brother's store, one day asked me if my brother was in, and on my saying " No," told me to tell my brother that he had closed the sale of the land to *White*, for $2,500, and not to hold out any more.

The two doctors who attended deceased, and who were in partnership in their professional business in Milton, were examined, and swore positively that the testator retained perfect possession of his senses to the last moment they were with him, and on the occasion of their visits conversed with them sensibly. On Monday morning they found it necessary to perform an operation on deceased for the purpose of replacing the intestines, which had protruded, and told him of it, and he expressed his willingness to submit to it. They did operate upon him accordingly, he losing very little blood, and one of the doctors, *McNeil*, says, "his powers of endurance were most marvellous ; he was very strong and quite sensible when the operation was performed." This same doctor before the operation was performed, advised him to settle his affairs ; he said, " he had done so long ago." The doctor says, " When I spoke to him about his affairs he answered me in a peevish way, as if he did not want me to speak about them." The doctors stayed with him that day from 10 o'clock a.m. to 2 o'clock p.m., and left him quite composed and sensible. They had given him two anodyne draughts, which they say were calculated to soothe and stimulate at the same time, and were not intended to produce sleep, though indirectly they would promote it by the relief from pain they afforded. Dr. *Hume* says,

I saw him again on Monday evening between 9 and 10 o'clock, and found him comparatively quiet. I asked him how he felt, and about his wounds ; he gave direct straightforward answers ; he was awake when I went in. I had no difficulty in making him hear or understand my questions. I asked him if he had his affairs settled, and told him he had better do so ; he said nothing to this. I was about twenty minutes with him on this occasion. Mr. *White* was there, so was *Robert Nunn* and others ; on my coming out *White* asked me if *Lawson* would live. I told him distinctly not. Mr. *White* then went into *Lawson's* room for a few minutes and came out, and I then went back to *Lawson's* room. I then again told him he had better get his affairs settled ; he then said he had an old will but did not know whether it was in existence or not ; he spoke freely enough to me, and seemed quite sensible. I was only there then a few minutes when I left. I left a draught which we call a suporific or anoydne, to allay pain ; but it would act at the time more as a stimulant. It was not sufficient to make him drowsy or stupid. I consider his mind not affected up to the time I left ; his voice was quite strong ; can't say whether I administered the draught before I left ; saw him next Tuesday morning about 6 o'clock a.m. ; found him lying comfortably ; spoke to him ; he answered intelligently ; his mind seemed clear. I was with him from half an hour to an hour ; he asked me if I had told Mr. *White* the night before that he could not live ; I said I had. I asked him if he had had his affairs settled ; he said yes, they were settled the night before. He turned himself over to enable me to do to him what I required ; from what I saw of him on Monday evening and Tuesday morning I do not think he could, in the interval, under or from the influence of the medicine I left for him, have been in a drowsy state, so as to unfit him from understanding. I had attended him from 1856. His wife and he had lived happily together, to the best of my knowledge. I am attending Mrs. *Lawson* now; she is unwell; for the last two or three weeks she has been in bed the greater part of the time; I saw her on Monday night. She is not in a fit state to attend here. She is out of bed now. She is a woman of good strong mind, but eccentric.

Dr. *Hume* on his cross-examination varies as to the particular times on that day on which some of the conversations referred to in his examination in chief took place, but on subsequent reflection corrects himself. One *Isabella Elliott*, a respectable young woman, testifies that she was with the testator on the day of his death, Tuesday, and that he was quite sensible; that his wife twice asked him what was to become of her when he died; that to the enquiry when first made he gave no answer, but at the second time told her to go to *William Lyon*. A Mrs. *Chisholm* and Miss *McNab* swear that they heard the same question, but say that the testator's answer to her was to go away, and not bother him. *Elizabeth Elliott* says that neither of these witnesses was present when the question was put the second time; and *Janet McNab* says she does not think Miss *Elliott* was present when she heard the question put. It seems strange that the wife should have known nothing or heard nothing of the will of the night before, and that no one should have told her of it, though it was to provide for her that it was made.

This is the principal evidence upon which I have to determine whether the deceased was at the time of making this will competent to do so: and secondly, whether it expresses his intention for the disposition of his property. The testator is described as a man of vigorous mind and body, of determined will and irascible temper, though weakened of course on the Monday night by the sufferings caused by his wounds, and by the operation which had been performed upon him. That he had his faculties of mind unimpaired,seems clear from all the evidence; and the only cause for doubt as to his ability to use them was the drowsy state in which he appeared to be. That he was drowsy and inclined to sleep, is, I think made out by the evidence; but the degree and extent of dowsiness is not so clear. According to the testimony of Dr. *Hume* he was awake and conscious when he left *White* with him on Monday evening; and according to all the testimony, he heard and answered the questions which *White* at the first interview put to him. That he understood the subject of conversation is manifest,and that he was able to exercise a judgment upon it appears from the answers which he gave to the proposals for the provision for his wife. What seems strange, is, that he should have told Dr. *McNeil*, early in the day, that his affairs were all settled long ago, a statement he had made to another witness, a neighbour, a few months previously. That again on Monday evening he should have told Dr. *Hume* that there was an old will, but he did not know whether it was in existence; but yet again later in the same evening tell *White* that he had not made a will. Still there is no evidence that his mind wandered—that he laboured under any delusion, or was affected by any thing but drowsiness. This being so, it seems to follow that all that was requisite was to rouse the deceased from this state of drowsiness or stupor to consciousness, and this being done, that he was competent, and I think I must hold that he was competent on Monday night,to make a will.

The only other question, and that to my mind the most difficult one is, whether or not the testator thoroughly understood the effect of the will he executed, and deliberately intended it to have that effect. The consideration of this question is freed from the difficulties presented by those cases, in which a dying man,or a man of much weakened intellect, has made a will in favour of one who had procured the will to be made, or who had great influence with him, or stood in a confidential relation to him. It is also unlike those cases in which the testator has passed over persons who would naturally have been the objects of his bounty. There is here no improper influence exercised—no motive for any—no ground for suspecting it—no secrecy, no exclusion of friends or strangers from the dying man's presence. The disposition made is a natural one, and a proper one. It is to his wife, also his cousin, with whom so far as we have evidence, he had lived happily. It was half a lifetime, if not half a century, since he had seen his relatives in Scotland, and there is no evidence that he ever corresponded with them. Four and twenty years had elapsed since he had made the will in their favour, of the existence of which he seemed doubtful, and of the custody of which during that time we are ignorant, and it does not appear that he knew whether the relatives were living or dead. It is not suggested that he ever contemplated leaving anything to any of his two or three relatives in this country. Freed then from every and any circumstance calculated to arouse suspicion, we are to make this second enquiry; and first, what are the facts and circumstances which should make us doubt that this will was the deliberate well-understood act of the testator.

1st. The state of stupor or drowsiness in which he appeared to be all the Monday evening. That he was drowsy on that evening I find upon the evidence, but as to its extent or degree the evidence conflicts; all the evidence, however, shews that the testator could be roused from that state so as to understand questions, and answer them, and this appears from the evidence of Mr. *Macnab*, the principal witness for the plaintiffs, and particularly as to the choice of a clergyman to attend him.

2nd. The varying answers he gave about the previous settlement of his affairs, and particularly his answer to *White*. which has already been alluded to.

In reference to this it is to be observed that the testator prior to the operation performed upon him on Monday, evidently did not contemplate death as near at hand, and was apparently very reluctant to think of it. As he grew worse and weaker he would naturally think more of his future and of what he was leaving behind, and doubt if the disposition which he had so long before made of the property could be established; and finally, when urged by *White* to settle his affairs, and asked if he had made a will, might content himself with answering, "no," as the shortest reason for making another.

3rdly. The variance between the will as made, and the previous proposition and arrangement at the first interview on the same evening, to provide a yearly sum of £75 for his wife. It is proved that after the conversation at which this was arranged, *White* left the house with the Misses *Macnab*, and then returned and entered the house, and remained some time with the testator—the witness *Nunn* says half an hour—and then left. What passed at that interview we do not know. *White* was then alone with the testator, and he cannot be a witness on his own behalf. Now in weighing what subsequently occurred, and considering the change made in the will from what was at one time intended, it is all important to bear in mind that the defendant *White* is free from the suspicion of any improper motive, and that though he subsequently bought a portion of the property devised, he paid for it at least its full value, and thus evidenced his own faith in the validity of the will. Then, after being absent between one and two hours, *White*, about 12 o'clock at night, returns with the will prepared in the shape in which it was executed. While he was absent the deceased slept the greater part of, perhaps nearly all, the time; it is not too much to imagine that those who remained with him were also somewhat drowsy during that time—one was a farmer, *Macnab*, the other a labouring man. As to what occured on this occasion, I must refer to the evidence already quoted, of *Macab*, *Lyon* and *Nunn*. As already stated, we do not know what passed between testator and *White* just before the latter left to get the will drawn, but this much might naturally occur to *White*, (a clever buisness man of large property,) on a moment's reflection, and may or may not at that interview have been suggested by him to the testator, and may account perhaps for the change in the disposition of the property, as at first proposed; and it is how was the £75 to be raised for the widow? It is clear upon the evidence that the lot on which the testator lived would not at all events without considerable expenditure, yield it—the wild land would yield nothing yearly—there was no personalty of any amount and the testator owed a considerable sum, part of it, $882, being with interest charged on lot 8, 6th concession of Nassagaweya. How then was the £75 to be procured? only, apparently by putting the property in trustees, empowering them to sell or invest; or to improve and rent. For what might have appeared rather a complicated method to effect this purpose, there was not much time, It was either at this interview with *White* last referred to, or on the occasion of the execution of the will, proposed to the testator to leave his property absolutely to his wife, a devise under all the circumstances, not an unreasonable one, nor of itself calculated to produce suspicion or doubt. The material question is, did the testator, on this will being read over to him, understand its purport, and freely and deliberately assent to it? If he did it is of no consequence when it was proposed to him to make such a will. To ascertain this we must first again look at the evidence last referred to. That the testator knew what the parties about him had come for, seems clear upon the evidence. He was asked if the will should be read to him, and he said no. It is not alleged that he had grown worse or more drowsy between the first and second interview with *White* on that evening, and being of sane mind, the conclusion would rather be that the more he slept, and the greater the time elapsing the

more would the effect of any drugs he had taken and the
consequent drowsiness disappear.   The will was short,
and one not difficult to understand.   If he could understand any thing at all, and knowing that the business in
hand was his making a will, he could understand on
being distinctly told, as it is sworn he was, that he was
by his will leaving all his property to his wife.   The
will was carefully read over to him twice, in sentences
by times, and he was asked at the end of each if he
understood it, and he replied he did, and then its effect
was distinctly explained to him, when he answered in
the language attributed to him by the witnesses *Nunn*
and *Lyon*, at least so they depose, and I cannot reject
their testimony as false.   Then we have the positive
evidence of Dr. *Hume* that the following Tuesday morning the testator asked him if he, the doctor, had on
the night before told *White* he was going to die ; that
the doctor replied he had, and asked him if he had settled
his affairs, when testator said, "Yes, they were all
settled the night before;" and again the witness *Isabella
Elliott* swears that in answer to a second question by his
wife as to what was to become of her, and which she
thinks neither Miss *Macnab* nor Mrs. *Chisholm* heard,
the testator told her to go to *William Lyon*. *Lyon* was an
executor under the will.   I think it clear then that the
testator knew that on Monday night he was executing
his will.   Finding as I do that he was competent if
awakened to consciousness on that night to make a will,
looking at the circumstances attending his property, and
his former will; his necessary uncertainty as to his
relatives; his assent to the necessity or propriety of
providing for his wife; the near approach of death for
the first time, apparently, that night, impressed upon
him ; the softening influence it would have on the stern
old man; his confidence in the advice of his friends, and
his readiness to yield to that advice which perhaps in his
hour of strength he might have rejected or postponed;
the simple nature of the will proposed to him; the evidence which is furnished of his clearly understanding it

at the time, and of his memory of it the following day, I cannot take upon myself to say that it is not the last will of the testator himself, or rather, I think, I must find that it is. I have arrived at this conclusion after anxious consideration of the evidence—after much doubt and fluctuation of mind—but upon the whole, as the one in my judgment most satisfactory. That the testator was influenced by the advice of *White* there can be no doubt; that but for that advice he might have gone out of the world trusting to the old will appearing; or indifferent or ignorant as to what would become of his property in its absence, is very likely; but then is the influence of such advice, or any persuasion or entreaty, fairly and *bona fide* given without any object of profit, and without gain to him who gives it, sufficient to enable a court to declare that it has so completely overborne the mind of the deceased that the will made in pursuance of it cannot be treated as his own act? Certainly not, if the testator was in a state of mind which enabled him to apprehend that advice, and exercise a judgment upon it, even if he did no more than resolve this, "the advice is more likely to be right than what I myself had previously determined to do, and I will follow it;" or, if exercising less judgment than this, he felt careless and indifferent as to what became of his property, and resolved to do with it as his friend advised.

The solitary question in such a case is, all fraud and improper or interested motive being absent, did the testator understand what he was doing, and did he do it willingly or deliberately? It might not have been the will which he would have made if left to himself—if he had not had advice—nay, he might be making it against his own inclination, but being a free agent, if he adopted the advice, and made a will accordingly, it is nevertheless his will. Many a man in sound health is persuaded by friends to do or not do acts against his own wishes and intentions; and many a case could be put of a man on his death-bed, softened by the entreaties of his friends, to make provision for these whom from passion, caprice, or mistaken judgment, he had resolved to neglect. Such advice, and such influences exerted with a man in possession of his senses, are not by any rule of law excluded from his bed side.

I have noticed and considered the contradictions which have been given to some of the statements of many of the witnesses; these chiefly relate to conversations and to dates, or to times of occurrences, matters on which witnesses thinking nothing of them after they had passed, are most likely to be mistaken. They are not, in my opinion, sufficient to set aside the direct testimony which they are intended to affect.

The statute (a) under which this bill is filed, and the power and duty which it imposes upon the court are in these words: " The court shall have power and jurisdiction to try the validity of last wills and testaments, whether the same respect real or personal estate, and to pronounce such wills and testaments to be void for fraud and undue influence, or otherwise, in the same manner, and to the same extent, as the court has jurisdiction to try the validity of deeds and other instruments." As already stated, I cannot, in my opinion, pronounce the will in question to be void ; and the plaintiff having charged the defendants with fraud in the procuring the will, the bill must be dismissed with costs.

(a) Sec. 28, ch. 12, Con. Stats. U. C.

AN INDEX

PRINCIPAL MATTERS.

ABSCONDING DEBTOR.

1. When it is necessary for the purpose of settling the priority of incumbrancers to enquire whether a party who had been sued was or was not an absconding debtor within the meaning of the act, this court will do so; and that, too, although the defendant in the action may not have taken any steps to set aside the attachment issued at law.

Montreal Bank v. Baker, 97.

2. *Held, also,* [affirming the decree] that the *bona fides* of proceedings taken against a person as an absconding debtor with a view to obtaining a priority, could be questioned in this court at the suit of a creditor or third party.

S. C., 298.

ACCEPTOR AND DRAWER.
(OF BILL OF EXCHANGE.)
See " Principal and Surety."

ADMINISTRATION.

A testator devised his real estate to his widow, and in the event of her re-marriage to his children. The widow afterwards filed a bill against the executors, charging mal-administration, which was disproved ; and on the contrary, that they had benefitted the estate by their management of it; and the master having found that the personal assets were insufficient to discharge the remaining liabilities, the court directed the executors to receive their costs out of the estate; that a competent portion of the real estate should be sold, and that the testator's children should be made parties to the suit in the master's office for the purpose of retaking the accounts, if desired by the guardian, they not being bound by the accounts already taken ; and, under the circumstances, refused the widow her costs.

Norris v. Bell, 23.

See also "Parties," 3.

ADMINISTRATOR.

1. The principle upon which an administrator should be charged with interest on funds belonging

to the estate considered and acted on.

McLennan v. Heward, 178.

2. An administrator *de bonis non* having obtained a decree against the representatives of a deceased administrator for an account of his dealings with the estate: *Held*, that he was entitled to charge the representatives with interest, &c., in the same manner, and to the same extent, as one of the next of kin might have done.—*Ib.*

3. Where an administrator who had acted as agent for the intestate during his life-time, had, with the assent of the deceased, used moneys belonging to him, without any attempt at concealment as to his so using them, the court refused to take the accounts against the administrator with rests; and the master having allowed the estate of the administrator a commission of 5 per cent. on moneys passing through the hands of the administrator in his life-time, the court refused, on appeal to disturb such allowance.—*Ib.*

4. Where the agent, after the decease of the principal, intestate, had procured letters of administration to his estate, and subsequently the person who became possessed of the assets as the personal representative of the administrator refused to account, and a bill was filed to enforce it; the court, under the circumstances, there being no evidence of any improper dealing with the estate either by the administrator or those representing him, allowed the defendants a commission of

5 per cent. on on all mone received and paid over or prope expended by themselves or th testator, and two and a-half p cent. on all moneys received him or them, but not yet paid ov but refused the costs of the suit

S, C, 2'

5. This court will not refer it the surrogate judge to settle t amount of compensation or co mission to be allowed to an adm istrator or executor : but havi possession of the subject matter litigation will finally dispose the rights of all parties.—*Ib.*

6 Whether an administra *de bonis non* can call in quest: the administration of his pre cessor in office.—*Quære.*

Tiffany v. Thompson, 2

7. Were the plaintiff me charges of improper cond against the administratrix, wh were not sustained in eviden he was ordered to pay all cc other than of an ordinary adm istration suit.

Hodgins v. McNeil, 3

See also " Amendment."

ADVERSE TITLE,

(NOTICE OF.)

See " Parol Contract."

AGENT.

See " Administrator." 4.

AGREEMENT.

(TO DEVISE.)

See " Specific Performance,"

AMENDMENT.

In a suit instituted by an administrator with the will annexed, upon a mortgage, the defendant produced a release for the mortgage money, given by the testator in his life-time; thereupon the plaintiff sought to be allowed to proceed against the defendant as a creditor of the estate, but as this would involve such an amendment as would create an entirely different record, the court refused such permission and dismissed the bill with costs.

Barrett v. Crosthwaite, 422.

APPEAL FROM MASTER.

See "Practice," 5.

ARBITRATORS.

See "Award."

ASSIGNEE.

(OF MORTGAGE.)

See " Mortgage." 9.

ASSIGNMENT

(FOR BENEFIT OF CREDITORS.)
See " Insolvent Debtor."

(VOLUNTARY OF CHOSE IN ACTION.)
See "Chose in Action."

AWARD.

(SPECIFIC PERFORMANCE OF.)

1. The finding of an arbitrator when unimpeached is treated as *res judicata* between the parties to the submission.

Bell v. Miller, 385.

2. This court, when the relief given by the award of an arbitrator is of a nature proper to be specifically performed, will decree that relief, and that, too although the court cannot specifically perform some part of the award, which is for the benefit of the plaintiff but which portion the plaintiff consents to forego. *Ib.*

BANKS.

Semble.—The directors and managers of incorporated banks are *quasi* trustees for the general body of stockholders, and if any loss should accrue to the bank by their infringing the statute against usury, they would be liable individually to make good the loss to the bank.

Drake v. The Bank of Toronto, 116.

BIDDING.

(DETERRING PARTIES FROM.

See " Sale," 2.

BOND FOR DEED.

See " Parol Contract."

CERTIFICATE (OF JUDGMENT.)

The certificate for registration of a judgment given by the clerk of the Queen's Bench, expressed it to be under " my hand and seal," and it being objected that it should have been expressed to be under the seal of the court, leave was given to the judgment creditor to produce an affidavit to shew what seal was really affixed to the certificate.

Proudfoot v. Lount, 70.

2. A confession of judgment was executed in the name of "*Matthew Rodger*." The certificate for registration was of a judgment against "*Matthew Rodger*." *Held*, that the mistake vitiated the registration.

McDonald v. Rodger, 75.

3. *Semble*, that in a certificate of judgment it is sufficient to state the amount of the true debt. *Ib.*

(FORM OF.)

See " Registration."

CHANCERY ACT.

(11TH CLAUSE OF.)

See " Mortgage," 13.

CHOSE IN ACTION.

(VOLUNTARY ASSIGNMENT OF.)

The holder of a debenture issued by the trustees of a Methodist church, transferred the same without consideration, by signing an endorsement as follows : " pay to James Gott, or order." and delivered the same to the person named in such endorsement. *Held*, that such transfer did not vest the debt in the transferee so as to prevent the claims of the creditors of the original holder of the debentures attaching upon it.

Gott v. Gott, 165.

COMMISSION.

See " Administrator," 3, 4,5.

COMPOSITION DEED.

The rule that the terms of a deed of composition must be strictly complied with, considered and acted on.

Hill v. Rutherford, 207.

The creditors of an insolv[e] debtor, by deed, absolutely a[nd] unconditionally released th[e] claim against him ; but it appea[rs] by a memorandum on the [in]strument, that such release w[as] intended to be in considerat[ion] of the debtor delivering to th[e] certain endorsed notes, whi[ch] however, he stated he was una[ble] to procure, and in fact they w[ere] not delivered as had been agre[ed] upon. *Held*, that the credit[ors] were entitled in this court [to] enforce payment of their origi[nal] claim, notwithstanding that [the] debtor offered to pay the sum which it was stipulated by [the] deed of composition that the no[te] should be given, or to give [the] notes agreed upon ; and that [the] court of common law had held [the] right of the creditors to reco[ver] was gone—[SPRAGGE., V. C., d[is]senting.]—*Ib.* [Affirmed by [the] Court of Appeal.]

See also," Principal and Suret[y]

COMPUTATION OF TIM[E]

See " Lessor and Lessee,"

CONTINGENT ESTATE.

See " Statute of Frauds."

CONTRACT.

(RESCISSION OF.)

See "Vendor and Purchaser," 1

CONTRIBUTION.

See " Marshalling Securities.

CONTRACTORS.

(LIEN OF, ON DEBENTURES AUTH[OR]IZED TO BE ISSUED FOR C[ON]STRUCTING A RAILWAY.)

See " Railway Company," 1.

CORPORATION.

See "Railway Company," 1.

COSTS.

When the plaintiff's bill sought to enforce two judgments, one of which the court held him not entitled to enforce, no costs were given to either party up to the hearing: the rule seems to be that where costs are to be set off against other costs, the court will not give costs to either party.

Cameron v. Bradbury, 61.

See also "Administration."
"Administrator." 4. 7.
"Crown Patent.," 1, 4.
"Duress,"
"Mortgage." &c.
"Parties," 6.
"Practice," 6.
"Vendor and Purchaser" 2

CREDITOR.

See " Amendment."

CROWN (THE.)

(REMEDY OF SUBJECT AGAINST.)

See " Jurisdiction."

CROWN LANDS DEPARTMENT.

See " Crown Patent," 4.

•CROWN PATENT.

(MISTAKE IN ISSUING.)

1. A locatee of the waste lands of the Crown having settled thereon, in preparing a portion of this land for cultivation cleared a portion of the adjoining land. According to the usage of the Crown Lands Department any person even without settling up-on lands of the Crown, effecting a clearing thereon, was always allowed the privilege of purchasing the lot so cleared, at the price fixed upon the land by the agent of the government. Subsequently, the government employed a surveyor to inspect the lands in the neighbourhood of the land so cleared upon, who, in his return, reported the property on which the clearing had been made as vacant and unimproved, and valued it at twelve shillings and six pence per acre. The agent who had so inspected the lands afterwards applied for, and obtained a patent for this lot, at the rate of eight shillings an acre, and almost immediately after sold it to a person who had full knowledge of the clearing which had been made. Upon a bill filed by the person who had made the improvement on the land, the court, under the circumstances, ordered the patent to be revoked, as having been issued in error and mistake, without costs. But, *semble*, that had the agent of the Crown, whose conduct had created the difficulty, been joined as a party, he would have been ordered to pay costs.

Proctor v. Grant, 27.

2. The court, while affirming the general doctrine on which the decree was pronounced above, reversed the same on the ground of want of notice of the improper conduct of the grantee of the Crown in obtaining the patent. [*Spragge*, V.C., *dubitante.*]

S. C., 224.

(REPEAL OF.)

3. *Semble*, this court may, in a proper case, set aside a patent issued upon the finding of the Heir and Devisee Commission.

McDiarmid v. McDiarmid, 144.

4. It is the duty of parties dealing with the Crown Lands Department to be fair and candid in all communications and statements ; where, therefore, a bill was filed to set aside a patent which had been issued to a purchaser of a clergy reserve lot, on the ground that the same had been so issued in ignorance of the opposing claim of the plaintiff, upon the fraudulent misrepresentations of the patentee, and the concealment of the facts by him from the Crown Lands Department, the court, although unable to afford the plaintiff the relief sought, dismissed the bill without costs as against the defendant who had thus dealt with the department.

Lawrence v. Pomeroy, 474.

DAMAGES.

See " Practice," 3.
" Replevin."

DEBENTURES.

A person negotiating the sale of a municipal debenture is not answerable that the municipality will pay the amount secured by the debenture. Where, therefore, a township municipality in pursuance of the Municipal Corporation Act of 1849, passed a by-law for the purpose of granting a loan of money to the Bayham, Richmond and Port Burwell Road Com-

pany, and issued debentu[r]s thereunder, which were sub[se]quently declared to be illegal consequence of the road compa[ny] not having been properly cons[ti]tuted : the court, in the absen[ce] of any proof of fraud, refused order one of the directors of t[he] road company to refund t[he] amount paid to him upon the s[ale] of one of such debentures.

Sceally v. McCallum, 4[8]

DEED (ABSOLUTE.)

(GIVEN BY WAY OF SECURITY.)

See " Mortgage," &c., 13.

DEED.

(EXECUTED IN BLANK.)

1. A debtor being about leave this province for the pu[r]pose of raising funds to d[is]charge his liabilities, sign[ed] and sealed a printed form mortgage upon certain lan[d] without, however, having insert[ed] either the name of himself or t[he] mortgagee therein, which was a[lso] in like manner executed by t[he] wife of mortgagor, and by hi[m] locked up in his desk. Fr[om] Halifax he wrote to his age[nt] here instructing him to fill the blanks as he should find n[e]cessary, which was according[ly] done, and handed over to t[he] mortgagee. *Held*, that this w[as] a sufficient execution of the mo[rt]gage, and that the same was [a] valid charge upon the proper[ty] embraced in the instrument.

Montreal Bank v. Baker, 9

2. *Held* [affirming the foreg[o]ing decree], that whether t[he]

deed there mentioned as having been executed in blank, operated as a deed or as a mere parol agreement, it created a charge upon the equitable estate of the debtor; and that a registered judgment creditor having notice thereof before the registration of his judgment would be bound thereby.

S. C., 298.

See also"Specific Performance,"4

DEFECT (LATENT.)

See "Vendor and Purchaser," 3.

DEMURRER.

See " Rectory."

DEFECTIVE TITLE.

See "Vendor and Purchaser," 2.

DEVISE.

(AGREEMENT TO.)

See "Specific Performance,"6.

(VOID.)

Where a devise is made upon several conditions, one of which is void, the other, though good by itself, being coupled by the void one, will also be rejected.

Re Babcock, 427.

DIRECTORS & MANAGERS.

(OF BANKS.)

See "Banks."

DONATIO MORTIS CAUSA.

A testator having agreed to sell a portion of his real estate had taken the note of his vendee for a sum of $900, being the amount of interest accrued due on the purchase money. This note and the papers relating to the sale, the testator had been frequently heard to say he intended to give to his son, who was named as an executor of his will. Shortly before his death,and in anticipation of it, he directed the case containing his papers to be brought to him, and from amongst them directed certain notes to be selected, and delivered them to his wife for her own use; the rest of the papers, amongst which were the note for $900, and the papers relating to the sale, together with several notes and documents including his will, the testator handed to his son, with a direction that if he recovered they were to be brought back; but in the event of his death then that he(the son) should keep them. *Held*, that this did not constitute a good *donatio mortis causa* of any of the securities.

Blain v. Terryberry, 286.

DORMANT EQUITIES.

Per *Vankoughnet*,C.—The Dormant Equities Act is not a bar in cases of express trust.

Tiffany v. Thompson, 244.

See also " Mortgage, &c," 13.

" Statute of Limitations."

DOWER.

(CONTRACT FOR SALE OF LANDS SUBJECT TO.)

See " Specific Performance," 1.

(RIGHT TO, AT LAW AND IN EQUITY.)

See " Mortgage," 10.

DURESS.

A party having been arrested on a charge of obtaining money under false pretences, agreed in presence of the magistrates who had issued the warrant to execute a mortgage on his farm to secure the amount; whereupon he was discharged, and he, together with the complainant who had sued out the warrant, went to a conveyancer and gave instructions for the conveyances which he subsequently executed. Afterwards a bill was filed by the mortgagor to set the instrument aside as having been obtained by duress and oppression. The court, under the circumstances, refused the relief sought, but as the conduct of the defendant had been harsh and oppressive, dismissed the bill without costs.

Boddy v. Finley, 162.

ENGINEERS.

(APPOINTMENT OF, TO INSPECT WORK BEFORE ACCEPTANCE.)

See "Specific Performance," 8.

EQUITABLE ESTATE.

(SALE OF, UNDER FI. FA.)

See "Married Woman."

EQUITABLE PLEA.

Where, upon a motion for an injunction to restrain proceedings upon an execution at law, it was shewn that the facts upon which the right to the injunction was founded had been raised as a defence to the action at law by way of equitable plea, the court refused the application.

Boulton v. Cameron, 297.

EVIDENCE.

See " Mortgage," 5.
" Practice," 2.

EXAMINATION—OF A D FENDANT.

See "Practice," 1.

EXECUTOR.

(SALE OF REAL ESTATE AT STANCE OF.)

1. The lessee of land, with right to purchase, devised same to his son, if it could paid for, and if it could not, t one half should be sold, and purchase money paid for other half, which he gave to son, an infant; the executor vanced out of his own mon sufficient to pay the price of land, and the lessors conveyed the devisee. The personal est of the testator being small, exhausted in the payment of de and funeral expenses, so that executor had no means of re bursing bimself, whereupon filed a bill in this court pray a sale of the real estate, and p ment of his advances. Court, under the circumstan directed a sale to be made of t portion of the lot which the t tator desired should be sold, i should appear upon enquiry fore the master that the paym to the lessors was for the ben of the infant.

Lannin v. Jermyn, 1

2. The duties and responsil ties of trustees and executors c sidered and acted on.

Larkin v. Armstrong, 3

3. As a general rule an assignment for the benefit of creditors ll be taken as a declaration of solvency, and equivalent to nkruptcy in England ; where erefore, some of the legatees of ;estator filed a bill against his ecutor and two of the legatees, arging mal-administration,and leging that the executor, subquently to the death of the testor,had made an assignment for e benefit of his creditors, and at he was insolvent, the court, on the motion for an injunction d receiver, before answer, unr the circumstances granted ι interim injunction and a rever, notwithstanding the exutor denied any mal-administion of the estate, or that s insolvency was the reason ε his making the assignment his estate.

Harrold v. Wallis, 443.

SSIGNMENT OF MORTGAGE BY.)

See " Mortgage," 14.

FORECLOSURE.

See " Practice," 4.

FRAUDS (STATUTE OF.)

Semble, the purchase of a devie's contingent interest in real tate is a purchase of an interest lands within the Statute of auds.

cDiarmid v. McDiarmid, 144.

FRAUDULENT CONVEYANCE.

1. The agent of a bank having come indebted to his principals a large sum of money, proceedgs were taken to enforce pay- ment thereof; and when execution therefor was on the eve of being sued out, the agent absconded from the country ; and, with the avowed object of defeating the claim of the bank, but, as the agent alleged, for the purpose of paying his other creditors, conveyed away to a person to whom he was only then introduced, a large quantity of valuable lands to be paid for in goods at long dates, returning at night for the purpose of executing the conveyances, and which were executed without any investigation of the title to the property ; and the agent subsequently assigned the agreement for the delivery of the goods to his son, taking in payment his notes payable over a period of several years. The court, under the circumstances, set aside the sale as fraudulent against the bank.

The Bank of Upper Canada v. Thomas, 321.

2. Where a bill was filed to impeach a deed as colourable ; and the evidence shewed it to be fraudulent, if not colourable and the same statements would have been necessary had the bill sought to impeach it on the ground of fraud ; the court refused to entertain an objection at the hearing that the bill had not sought to set it aside on that ground, or assigned fraud as an alternative ground of relief.

Commercial Bank v. Cooke, 524.

3. An execution creditor proceeded to a sale of the lands of his debtor, and sold a property which

was subject to a mortgage for £500; given, as the creditor alleged to defeat creditors, but which property the creditor alleged was not worth more than £200, and became himself the purchaser thereof at the price of £10 10s.; whereupon he filed a bill setting forth these facts; or that the mortgage was given to secure a much smaller, if any debt, and praying alternate relief, in accordance with such allegations. The court at the hearing *pro confesso* refused to set aside the mortgage, but gave the plaintiff the usual decree as a judgment creditor, not as a purchaser. The proper course for the plaintiff to have taken under such circomstances was to have come to this court in the first instance, and not to proceed to a sale of the property with such a cloud upon the title.

Malloch v. Plunkett, 556.

GENERAL RELIEF.

See " Notice."

GIFT, (BY HUSBAND TO WIFE.)

After the death of a man and his wife, a sum of money was found deposited in a bank at the credit of the wife, which had been so deposited in the life-time of the husband, but it did not appear by whom. The wife survived the husband, and after her death a question being made to whose estate the fund belonged, *held*, that it belonged to the estate of the wife.

Ferris v. Hamilton, 362.

GOVERNMENT AGENT.

(NEGLECT OF.)

See " Crown Patent."

HEIR AND DEVISEE COMMISSION.

1. The Heir and Devisee Commission having reported that the heirs at law of A. were entitled to a patent of certain lands in the Indian reserves, Charlottenburg, the Governor in council afterwards, upon a report of the Solicitor-General in favour of B., a brother of A., issued a patent to B. for the lands. The heirs of A. thereupon filed a bill to have the patent set aside, and a new patent issued to themselves upon the grounds of the patent having been issued to B. under an error. The court having found there was no error of fact, *held*, that the patent was properly issued to B. notwithstanding the finding of the commission.

McDiarmid v. McDiarmid, 144.

2. *Semble.*—This court may, in a proper case, set aside a patent issued upon the finding of the Heir and Devisee Commission. *Ib.*

IMPROVEMENTS.

(PAYMENT FOR.)

See " Vendor and Purchaser," 2.

INCORPORATED COMPANY.

(MORTGAGE TO.)

An insurance company was by its act of incorporation authorised

hold real estate for the imme-
iate accommodation of the com-
any, "or such as shall have
een *bona fide* mortgaged to it
y way of security, or conveyed
ɔ it in satisfaction of debts pre-
iously contracted in the course
f its dealings, or puechased at
ales upon judgments which shall
ave been obtained for such
ebts;" and having sold and
onveyed a vessel, took from
heir vendee mortgages on real
state for securing the purchase
ioney. *Held*, that this was a
ransaction within the act of in-
orporation, the price of the
essel being a debt existing pre-
iously to the execution of the
iortgage: and, *semble*, that
nder these words of the act it
ras not, as with banking insti-
itions, necessary to the validity
f such a mortgage that any pre-
ious indebtedness should exist.

The Western Assurance Com-
any v. Taylor, 471.

NCUMBRANCE, NOTICE OF.

See "Purchaser for value without Notice."

INFANTS.

Sale ordered without requiring
eposit in a suit for foreclosure
f mortgage.

Lawrason v. Fitzgerald, 371.
See also "Specific Perform-
nce," 7.

INJUNCTION.

See "Equitable Plea."
"Executor," 3.
"Pratice," 9, 10.
"Replevin."

INSOLVENCY.

See "Executor."

INSOLVENT DEBTOR.

An assignment was made to
trustees for the benefit of creditors, to which was appended a
list of names who were to rank
as privileged creditors. One of
these parties subsequently applied to the trustees, who in concert with the debtor handed to
him several notes and bills, more
than sufficient to cover the claim
of his firm, which he took away
with him for the purpose of
negotiating them, his desire being, as he stated, to realize funds
at once. Certain of the makers
and acceptors of these notes and
bills having become insolvent, a
bill was filed by the firm against
the assignor and his trustees for
an account of the trust estate,
and payment of their claim: in
answer to this bill the defendants
alleged that the bills and notes
had been taken in payment of
their demand, not as collateral
security only. The evidence on
this point was contradictory: the
court, under the circumstances,
referred it to the master to take
an account of the claim of the
plaintiffs against the estate, and
to enquire as to the dealings of
the trustees under the assignment.

Wood v. Brett, 78.

INSTANTANEOUS SEISIN.

See "Mortgage," 10.

INTEREST.

(ADDING SAME TO PRINCIPAL.)

See "Specific Performance," 5.

JUDGMENT (REGISTERED.)

(SALE UNDER FI. FA. ISSUED THEREON.)

1. The ruling of the Court of Queen's Bench in Doe. Dougall v. Fanning, 8 U. C. Q. B. 166, and Doe Dempsey v. Boulton, 9 U. C. Q. B. 532, that the sale by the sheriff under a writ of *fi. fa.* against lands conveyed the estate held by the judgment debtor at the time of the registration of the judgment, were referred to and followed; Thirkell v. Patterson, 18 U. C. Q. B. 75, and Wales v. Bullock, 10 U. C. C. P. 155, remarked upon.

Bank of Montreal v. Thompson, 51.

2. Where a bill has been filed prior to the 18th of May, 1861, *all* judgment creditors who had their judgments duly registered, are entitled to be treated as parties to the cause, though not actually named in the bill, and not added as such in the master's office until after that date, without having placed *fi. fas.* against lands in the hands of the sheriff.

Bank of Montreal v. Woodcock, 141.

3. In order to retain the lien created by the registration of a judgment recovered at law it is necessary that the bill to enforce such lien should have been filed on or before the 18th day of May, 1861.

Bank of Upper Canada v. Beatty, 321.

4. When a judgment creditor files a bill to enforce his judgment against the lands of the debtor, it must be shewn that the creditor has sued out execution on such judgment. *Ib.*

See also "Deed."

JURISDICTION.

The defendant was surety to her Majesty on the bond of A., a customs officer. A. became a defaulter and absconded. The defendant being sued at law on the bond, set up the equitable defence, that when the bond was executed by him his principal was in charge of the small port of Bruce Mines; that the bond was given and executed only in respect of that office; that the government had afterwards removed the principal to another port where larger customs receipts were collected, and where consequently the risk was greater, and where the alleged defalcation occurred.

The express terms of the bond were however in respect of the office of collector of customs in Canada, without any reference to Bruce Mines, and the plea was held bad on demurrer by the Court of Queen's Bench. The defendant then filed his bill in this court setting forth the facts, and praying for a stay of proceedings at law, or similar relief against the Crown. *Held,* that this court has no jurisdiction to grant relief in the premises, the rights of the Crown being brought directly in question.

Miller v. The Attorney-General, 558.

2. The municipality of Norwich became sureties to the Crown for moneys advanced to a railway company. The property and functions of the company were altered and interfered with by acts of parliament, and the company finally united with another. The completion of the railway through the township of Norwich was thus indefinitely postponed, and the advantage expected to be derived by the township, when its municipality became indebted to the Crown was not realized. The government having taken proceedings for the collection of the sum secured, the municipality filed a bill to stay such proceedings. *Held*, (following the decision in Miller v. The Attorney-General,) that this court has no jurisdiction in the matter, and that the equitable jurisdiction in matters of revenue in this province, at the suit of a subject, resides in the superior courts of common law, if at all, and not in this court.

Norwich v. The Attorney-General, 563.

LATENT DEFECT.

See "Vendor and Purchaser," 3.

LEASE (VOID.)

One E. was left in charge of the estate of N., who promised to leave the same by will to E. N. afterwards left this country and died abroad intestate, and E., acting on the presumption that N. had died without heirs, made a building lease in his own name of a portion of the estate, and the lessee entered into possession and erected valuable buildings thereon. Afterwards the heir of N. established his right to the estate as such, and refused to recognise the validity of the lease; whereupon a bill was filed seeking to bind the heir with this lease, or that he should pay the value of the improvements on the ground of a ratification of the lease. The court refused to grant either branch of relief asked, and the fact that the heir had instituted proceedings in this court against the lessor, calling upon him for an account of the rents, &c., received by him from the estate of the intestate, was not such a proceeding as could properly be considered a ratification of E.'s acts.

Moffatt v. Nicholl, 446.

LESSOR AND LESSEE.

1. By the terms of a lease it was provided that the lessee should have the right of purchasing the leasehold property upon his desiring to do so, "within the period of two years after the date of the commencement of the term," (the 1st of April, 1852.) On the 1st of April, 1854, the desire of purchasing was declared, and a tender of the purchase money made. *Held*, that the tender was within time, the day of the commencement of the term (1st of April, 1852) being exclusive.

Sutherland v. Buchanan, 135.

2. Where a lease for years contains an agreement for the sale

39

of the fee, the right to purchase goes to the heir-at-law, not to the personal representative, on the death of the lessee.

Henrihan v. Gallagher, 488.

(LESSEE IMPROVING PREMISES.)

See "Lease."

LIEN.

See "Judgment," 3, 4.

LIMITATIONS, STATUTE OF.

1. A person seeking to invoke the aid of the Statute of Limitations against a claim in respect of lands, must shew that he and those under whom he claims, have been in possession of the land, or what in law is equivalent to possession.

Arner v. McKenna, 226.

2. In 1834 a contract was made for the purchase of the easterly fifty acres of a lot of land, but through mistake the deed covered the whole north half, thus conveying the legal title to the north westerly quarters, but the purchaser went into possession of the portion actually intended to be conveyed, and shortly after the vendee of the westerly portion went into possession of and occupied it without any disturbance of his title or assertion of right by the party to whom the conveyance had been made by mistake, (although all parties knew of the error that had occurred,) until the year 1857, when the assignee of the person holding the legal title instituted proceedings in ejectment, and recovered judgment;

the evidence of adverse possession not being sufficient to outweigh the legal effect of the deed which had been so erroneously executed. The court, upon a bill filed for that purpose, restrained the owner of the legal title from proceeding to recover possession, and ordered him to convey the legal title in the land to the plaintiff, who was equitably entitled thereto, and to pay the costs of the suit.—*Ib.*

See also "Mortgage," &c., 7, 13. "Trustee," &c.

LYNDHURST'S (LORD) ACT.

(5 & 6 WM. IV., CH. 54.)

See "Marriage with deceased wife's sister."

MARRIAGE SETTLEMENT.

1. By a clause in a marriage settlement it was stipulated that trustees should at their option during the life of the intended husband, permit him or the intended wife to take and use the rents, issues and profits of the trust estate to their own use; and by a subsequent clause it was provided that new trustees should be appointed in certain contingencies. Upon a bill filed by the wife to appoint a new trustee by reason of the residence of one out of the jurisdiction, *held*, that this trust was one of personal confidence, and could not be executed by a trustee appointed by the court. And it appearing that the husband had not been heard of for upwards of four years, the court, under the circumstances, ap-

pointed a new trustee, and directed him to pay one half of the rents to the plaintiff, and the other half to be invested for the benefit of the husband.

Tripp v. Martin, 20.

(SETTING ASIDE.)

2. Although the consideration of marriage is one of the most valuable, still a settlement upon the marriage, either of the settlor or a child of the settlor is, like any other conveyance, liable to be impeached as void under the statute of Elizabeth, on the ground of having been made to hinder and delay creditors. Where therefore a person in embarrassed circumstances hastened the marriage of his daughter, and made a conveyance of all his real estate to a trustee for the benefit of his daughter and the issue of the intended marriage, having stated to the solicitor who prepared the conveyance and to the trustee that his object in so doing was to prevent his property from being seized by his creditors, and there being a strong presumption that the daughter and her intended husband had also been informed of the object of the settlor: the court, upon a bill filed by a judgment creditor, against the husband and wife and their infant children, to set aside such settlement, declared the same void as against creditors; notice by the trustee of the fraudulent purposes of the settler being sufficient to bind the issue of the marriage. To such a bill the settlor is not a necessary party.

Commercial Bank v. Cook, 524.

MARRIED WOMAN.

(ESTATE OF.)

A married woman jointly with her husband conveyed her estate absolutely to a trading company, and at the same time the company executed a covenant that they would re-convey upon certain stipulations being complied with, which they accordingly did several years afterwards; but while the estate was vested in the company, and before the passing of the act for the relief of married women, a judgment was recovered against the husband, and duly registered. *Held*, that this registration bound the estate of the husband; and his interest being equitable, was not affected by a sale of his interest under an execution at law at the suit of other creditors.

Ferrie v. Kelly, 262.

MARRIAGE WITH DECEASED WIFE'S SISTER.

The intestate, H. M., was married in this province in 1850 to the sister of his deceased wife, by whom he had children, and died in 1856. *Held*, that the marriage, though voidable during the lives of both parties to it, yet that its validity not having been called in question till after the husband's death, it must be now treated as indissoluable, and that the issue thereof are entitled as heirs.

Hodgins v. McNeil, 305.

Held, also, that Lord Lyndhurst's Act (5 & 6 W. IV., cap. 54) does not extend to the colonies.—Ib.

MARSHALLING SECURITIES.

In 1849 G. being the owner of Whiteacre and Blackacre, contracted to sell half of the former to B. by a bond which was never registered. In 1852 G. executed a mortgage covering both lots to ?., which was immediately registered. In 1852 G. executed a mortgage covering both lots to ?., which was immediately registered, but the Christian name of the grantor's wife (who executed to bar dower) did not appear in the memorial. In 1853 ?. gave a mortgage of Blackacre to P., who also immediately registered his conveyance. In 1855 ?. sold the remaining half of Whiteacre to M., and in the following year B. conveyed his interest in the other half to S. In 1861 C. sold Blackacre under power of sale in his mortgage, and the sale realized fully what was due thereon. In 1862 P. filed his bill against M. & S. in order that he might be subrogated to the rights of C. as against Whiteacre for the amount due him on his security. S. & M. had previously paid all their purchase money. *Held*, that P. was not entitled to any relief against S., but that if C.'s mortgage was duly registered, P. was entitled to contribution against M.   Boucher v. Smith, 347.

MERGER.

(OF CHARGE.)

See "Mortgage," 10.

MISNOMER.

See "Certificate," 2.

Registration of Judgment," 3.

MISSING DEED.

See "Specific Performance," 3.

MORTGAGE, MORTGAGOR, AND MORTGAGEE.

1. The holder of a mortgage security assigned the same for value on the ninth day of October, (Saturday,) on the eleventh of the same month the mortgagor, without notice of the transfer which had been made, effected an arrangement with the mortgagee, one of the assignees of the mortgage being present, and concealing the fact of the assignment from the mortgagor. The mortgagor thereupon filed a bill claiming to have the mortgage discharged, alleging fraud in the transaction of the assignment. The court, under the circumstances, ordered the mortgage to be released, but refused the plaintiff his costs in consequence of his failure to prove the fraud charged.

     Engerson v. Smith, 16.

2. The owner of lands created two mortgages thereon, after which his interest therein was sold under a writ of *fieri facias*, issued upon a judgment registered prior to both the mortgages, for the sum of twenty shillings, all parties being under the impression that the lands were sold subject to the two mortgages; subsequently the purchaser at sheriff's sale bought up the first mortgage, whereupon the holders of the second mortgage filed a bill against him, praying a decree of redemption or foreclosure, on the ground that the purchase of the equity of redemption at sheriff's sale bound him to discharge both

rtgages. The court, at the aring, refused this relief and missed the bill : but owing to : uncertain state of the authori- s on the point as to the effect to given to the registering of a dgment, without costs ; and th leave to file a new bill im- gning the sale under the *fi. fa.* : a decree of redemption would pronounced upon the submis- n to that effect contained in the swer, if the plaintiffs desired it relief.

ank of Montreal v. Thompson, .

fterwards affirmed in appeal.]

3. A party foreclosure subject a prior mortgage cannot call common mortgagor, if he has equity of redemption, to give dence as to the amount due on the prior mortgage.

Warren v. Taylor. 59.

4. A second mortgagee, as such, not impeach a prior-registered rtgage as fraudulent and void ainst creditors, but a judgment ditor, having accepted a mort- ge, does not lose his rights as a lgment creditor. *Ib.*

5. Where the usual affidavit ving a mortgage debt is made, onus of reducing the amount upon the opposite party. *Ib.*

3. In taking the accounts in master's office it is improper charge a mortgagee in posses- n with annual rests on rents eived by him until he is paid in full.

Coldwell v. Hall, 110.

7. The Statute of Limitations ms no bar to a claim, against mortgagee in possession, for upation rent. *Ib.*

8. The principal upon which a mortgagee is liable to be charged with rents not actually received considered. *Ib.*

9. A mortgage set aside under the circumstances. The rule in equity is, that the assignee of a mortgage takes it subject not only to the state of the account between the mortgagor and mort- gagee, but also to the same equi- ties as affect it in the hands of the mortgagee.

McPherson v. Dougan, 258.

10. L. purchased from S., who conveyed to him, and immedi- ately took back a mortgage to secure the purchase money, in which L's wife did not join. L. after- wards conveyed his equity of re- demption to H., who subsequently conveyed to S., and S. then sold to another party. L. having died, his widow sued at law for dower. A bill filed, praying an injunction to stay the action, and for a declara- tion that the widow, was, under the circumstances, not entitled to dower, was dismissed with costs.

On re-hearing this decree was varied, by declaring that the mortgage was not extinguished as a charge on the purchase of the equity of redemption by S. from H., or merged in his legal estate : but the court restrained the defendant from proceeding at law for the recovery of her dower, and declared that the dower so to be allotted should be charged with the payment of one-third of the interest of the mortgage money unless the defendant chooses to pay off one-third of the mortgage debt ; and

Per Curiam, the right to dower being favoured by both common law and equity, will assist a dowress by removing out of her way a satisfied mortgage, and will allow her to redeem an unsatisfied mortgage.

Per *Esten*, V.C.—That the question of merger is one of intention; in the absence of evidence of intention, the court will consider that course selected by the purchaser which was most for his benefit, and that in this case the mortgage became merged in S.'s estate ; that plaintiff had no equity to restrain the action for dower, and that the bill should be dismissed ; and.

Per *Spragge*, V. C.—That L. had in him before his conveyance to H. the beneficial legal estate, being entitled to the value of the land, beyond the mortgage debt, and any other incidental advantage; that in the interval between the execution and conveyance and mortgage, L. was a trustee for S., but not a bare trustee.

Heney v. Low, 265.

11. The act giving to County Courts equitable jurisdiction in relation to mortgages when the sum does not exceed fifty pounds does not apply when the defendant is resident out of the jurisdiction.

Lawrason v. Fitzgerald, 371.

12. C. H. being the owner of the equity of redemption in three distinct tenements, sold and conveyed one of them to J. T. K. by a deed in fee, with absolute covenants for quiet enjoyment, freedom from incumbrancers, &c., taking from the purchaser a bond by which he covenanted to pay £241 of the money owing on the outstanding mortgage; the purchaser afterwards went to the holders of the mortgage, concea from them the existence of bond, produced the deed to h self, and agreed with the hold of the mortgage for the rele of his portion of the prope and a release was accordin; for a valuable consideration, e cuted by them. J. T. K., hav become insolvent, absconded fr the province, and a suit to f close having been institu against C. H., he sought to cha the plaintiffs, the mortgagees, v the amount payable by J. T. under his bond ; but the co acting on the rule established Ford v. Chandler, reporte 1 a volume viii., page 85, conside the plaintiffs warranted in treat the absolute covenants execu by the defendant (C. H.) as undertaking by him to pay off whole sum remaining due u the mortgage, and, theref charged the portions still ve in him therewith.—[*Esten*, V. *dissenting.*]

Bank of Montreal v. Hopki 495.

13. On the 16th of Janua 1831, an absolute conveyar was made in fee to secure a l of money, the alleged mortga remaining in possession until spring of 1841. On the 1st March, 1841, the alleged m gagee wrote to a subsequent m gagee, on the same proper claiming £94 12s. 8d. as due fr the mortgagor, and on the and 21st of June, of the sa year, he again wrote to the sa incumbrancer alleging that had originally advanced ab £60, which with interest tl amounted to £90 or £100, a

suggesting that the land should be sold for the benefit of the alleged mortgagor, and he kept an account in his books against the alleged mortgagor of principal and interest in respect of the alleged debt up to the 1st of January, 1856. The subsequent incumbrancer purchased the mortgagor's equity of redemption. Upon a bill filed by such mesne incumbrancer in February, 1861, claiming a right to redeem the premises against the representatives of the alleged mortgagee, who had died in the meantime: the court *held* that the letters written by the mortgagee were sufficient to take the case out of the Statute of Frauds, and that the right of the plaintiff was not barred by the provisions of the Statute of Limitations; that the act relating to dormant equities did not apply to the facts of this case, and that the 11th clause of the Chancery Act did not affect the plaintiff's right to redeem.

Malloch v. Pinhey, 550.

14. The executor of a mortgagee has not, under the provisions of the statute in that behalf, (chapter 87, Consolidated Statutes of Upper Canada, section 5,) any power to sell and convey the legal estate held by his testator to a person purchasing the mortgage.

Robinson v. Byers, 572.
See also "Deed."
"Power of Sale."
"Practice," 7.

MUNICIPAL DEBENTURES.
(LIABILITY OF PERSON NEGOTIATING.)
See "Debenture."

MUNICIPALITY.
See "Parties," 6.

NOTICE.
In a redemption suit, upon its appearing that K., a purchaser for value, with constructive, but without actual notice, held a registered title of the lands in question, as well as S., to whom he had sold; the bill was dismissed as against K., with costs; and the plaintiff praying specifically for a re-conveyance of the premises mortgaged, *held*, that he was not entitled to personal relief, under the prayer for general relief.

Graham v. Chalmers, 239.
See also "Deed."
"Marshalling Securities."

OCCUPATION RENT.
See "Mortgage," 7.

OFFICER OF COURT.
INJUNCTION TO RESTRAIN ACTION AGAINST.
See "Practice," 3.

PAROL CONTRACT.
(PARTLY PERFORMED.)
In 1858, a parol contract was entered into for the sale of one acre of land, the consideration for which was paid, and the purchaser was let into possession of the property, which he occupied, improved, and built upon. Afterwards, and in the same year, the vendor executed by way of security a life lease to another person of 50 acres, including the acre so sold. In 1860, a bond was executed by the vendor to the wife of the purchaser

for the conveyance of the acre to
her. In 1862, the lessee for
life purchased the fifty acres in
fee, and the conveyance to him
was duly registered; the bond
for the conveyance of the acre
never was registered. The purchaser of the acre having filed
a bill for a specific performance of the parol contract, the
court refused relief on that
ground, the parol contract having become merged in the written contract or bond; but offered
the plaintiff, at the risk of costs,
permission to amend by alleging
the written contract, and to give
further evidence to establish
direct notice of the bond, reserving the question of costs until
after the enquiry; if this refused,
the bill to be dismissed without
costs, the defendant having falsely
asserted his title under the lease
to have been absolute and not
by way of security merely.

McCrumm v. Crawford, 337.

PAROL EVIDENCE.

1. Parol evidence to vary the
terms of a written instrument
rejected, although the court considered it doubtful if the written
document contained all the terms
of the agreement between the
parties.

McAlpine v. How, 372.

2. An assignment of a bond
for the conveyance of land was
made from a debtor to his creditor, by a writing absolute in
form, but the creditor at the
same time executed a memorandum shewing such assignment
to be by way of security only.

Subsequently the debtor exec
ted another absolute assignme
without receiving back any su
memorandum from the credit
The court, under the circumsta
ces, refused to act upon pa
evidence that the assignor w
to be interested in the procee
of the land over and above
indebtedness to the assign
Ib.

3. A woman possessed of re
estate sold the same, her hu
band joining in the conveyar
thereof, and receiving to his o'
use the purchase money;
consideration of which he agre
to settle on his wife certa
other property which he he
under lease with the right
purchase, and the lease was a
cordingly assigned to a trust
for the use of the wife, t
husband at the same tir
promising to pay the amou
agreed to be paid for the purpc
of obtaining the conveyance
the fee; the husband havi
died and his estate being in t
course of administration in th
court, and his widow havi
brought a claim into the maste
office for the amount necessa
to procure the conveyance of t
fee: *held*, on appeal from t
master's report, that the mast
had properly received parol ev
dence to establish such claim
the widow.

Ross v. Mason, 56

PARTIES.

1. One of several joint co
tractors having died during t
progress of the work contract

for, and a bill afterwards filed by the survivors to enforce a claim under the terms of the contract, *held*, that the personal representatives of the deceased partner should have been made parties; the rule respecting the rights of surviving partners to sue alone not applying to suits in equity.

Sykes v. The Brockville and Ottawa Railway Co., 9.

2. Where a bill was filed by one of several creditors of a debtor, who had assigned his estate for the benefit of his creditors, against the debtor and the trustee, seeking an account of the estate and payment, without making any other creditor a party, the court overruled an objection for want of parties, on the ground of the absence of any such creditor.

Wood v. Brett, 78.

3. In a suit to administer the estate of a testator, the heir-at-law ought to be a party; but when the personal representative filed such a bill against the devisee, alleging that no lands had descended, as to which the answer was silent, and the objection was not raised at the hearing, the court, under the circumstances, made a decree in the absence of the heir.

Tiffany v. Tiffany, 158.

4. Where a trustee commits a breach of trust, the party participating in it is not a necessary party to a suit for the general administration of the trust estate.

Tiffany v. Thompson, 244.

5. One devisee of a truste against whose estate a suit brought, sufficiently represen these interested in the estate.- *Ib.*

6. A municipality in procee ing to a sale of land for taxes in the position of a trustee; an if it is afterwards sought to in peach the sale on the ground any irregularity in directing suc sale, and it is sought to make th municipality answerable to th purchaser for the purchase mone paid, or the costs of the suit, th municipality must be made party to the cause.

Ford v. Proudfoot, 47{

See also " Administration," 1.

" Marriage Settlement.

" Power of sale."

PAYMENT OF MONEY.

(TO MORTGAGEE AFTER ASSIGNMEN
OF MORTGAGE.)

See "Mortgage," 1.

PERSONAL CONFIDENCI

See " Marriage Settlement."

PERSONAL REPRESENT/ TIVE.

1. The personal representativ may file a bill *as a creditor simpl*; upon the testator's estate agains a devisee of lands under the wil after the personal estate is e: hausted, and obtain a decree a an ordinary creditor.

Tiffany v. Tiffany, 15{

2. The other creditors need
t be made parties to such a bill,
t the heirs-at-law must.—*Ib.*
e also "Lessor and Lessee," 2.

PLEADING.

The plaintiff in a bill to im-
ach a security held by an in-
rporated bank, stated that the
tes held by the bank, and in
spect of which the bank claimed
lien under their charter upon
rtain stock, had been "dis-
unted for the said G., R. & H.
on an illegal and corrupt agree-
ent, whereby and by reason
hereof the said bank should and
d receive from G., R. & H., upon
e discount of the said promis-
ry notes a much larger and
eater rate of interest than at
e rate of 7 per cent. per annum,
d that it was only through and
' reason of such discount upon
ch illegal and usurious consi-
ration that the said bank be-
me, and is now holder of the
id promissory notes." *Held,*
sufficient allegation of the usury
between a stranger and a
rty to the transaction to let
the evidence of the usury.

Drake v. The Bank of Toronto,
6.

e also "Fraudulent Conveyance," 2, 3.

"Marriage Settlement." 2.

POWER OF SALE.

(IN MORTGAGE.)

The owner of land sold and
nveyed one acre thereof: after-
ards, and before the registra-
on of the deed of this acre, he
executed a mortgage on the whole
estate, (200 acres,) which was
duly registered, and sub-
sequently the purchaser of
the acre registered his deed.
Default having been made in
payment of the mortgage money,
the assignee of the mortgagee
proceeded to a sale of the estate,
the whole of which, including the
acre, was sold and duly conveyed.
The purchaser of the acre filed a
bill against the person exercising
the power of sale, and his vendee
claiming a right to redeem by
virtue of his interest in the one
acre, and alleging want of notice
of the intention to proceed to a
sale under the power contained
in the mortgage. To this bill
the vendor under the power put
in a demurrer for want of equity;
and also for want of parties, on
the ground that the mortgagor
was a necessary party. *Held,*
that for the purpose of obtaining
the relief prayed by the bill, the
mortgagor was not a necessary
party, although if the bill had
sought for payment of the surplus (if any) of the purchase
money over and above the amount
due on the mortgage, it would be
necessary to bring him before
the court.

Daniels v. Davidson, 173.

PRACTICE.

1. The examination of a defendant after answer, or after the
time for answering has expired,
is a substitute for the discovery
by answer, and a plaintiff can at
the hearing read such examination, or parts of it, in the same
maner as a defendant's answer,

or passages from it, could be used against him at the hearing : for this purpose it is not necessary to examine the defendant at the examination of witnesses.

Proctor v. Grant, 26.

2. A party who had improperly obtained a patent for land from the Crown, and conveyed the property to another, with notice, was called as a witness on behalf of his vendee, in a suit to have the patent revoked as having been issued through error and mistake on the part of the Crown. *Held*, that although he might be subjected to an action at the suit of his vendee in the event of the patent being set aside, and the land granted to another, and therefore strongly interested in defeating the suit of the plaintiff, still that he was not one for whose immediate benefit the suit was wholly or in part defended ; and that the objection must be to his credit, not to his competency. *Ib.*

3. Proceedings under a *fi. fa.* at law having been set aside, and an action brought against the master, in whose name the *fi. fa.* had been sued out, an injunction was issued restraining proceedings. *Held*, the application for an injunction in the original cause in this court was regular ; and that the officer of this court was the proper person to whom should be referred the question as to the amount of damage sustained by the proceedings which had been set aside.

Fisher v. Glass, 46.

4. Where a decree is soug to be changed from a sale to foreclosure, the cause must set down to be re-heard, a notice served on the defenda and that, too, although the l had been taken *pro confesso.*

McClelan v. Jacobs,

5. Where an incumbran who objected to the order priority in which he was plac appealed from the finding of master, the court considered t the more convenient course adopt, although it was open have moved to discharge master's order.

McDonald v. Roger,

6. When a plaintiff, without p per enquiry into facts, and w undue haste filed a bill in tl court, to enforce a judgment law, in which he made charg of fraudulent practices agai the defendant, the court, wh granting him the relief to wh he was strictly entitled, refus him his costs of the suit, a ordered him to pay the costs the defendants. Neale v. Wint 261.

7. Where a reference is dire ed to take an account of whal due on a mortgage, it is comp ent to the parties to shew i real object for which it was ma if that is not apparent on t face of the instrument ; a when the bill has been taken *confesso* it is incumbent on master to require the mortga to shew how the money secui by the mortgage was advance

nd, *semble*, that such a course
rould be desirable in all cases.

       Sterling v. Riley, 343.

8. Where a cause is re-heard
y some of several defendants,
nd the court affirms the decree
s against them, the other de-
endants who did not re-hear
annot obtain any relief, although
hey appear on the re-hearing
nd ask it.

       Black v. Black, 403.

9. A creditor having proved
us claim in the master's office,
fterwards proceeded to sell
under a *fi. fa.* Upon the appli-
ation of a co-defendant the sale
ras restrained with costs.

       Cahuac v. Durie, 485.

10. In a proper case upon peti-
ion by defendant, the court
ranted an injunction against the
laintiff.

       Bartels v. Benson, 486.

See also " Will," 3.

PRESENTATION.

See " Rectory."

PRINCIPAL AND AGENT.

A person became surety for
nother for the due discharge of
us duty as agent in the purchase
f wheat for a mercantile firm.
fterwards the agent and his
rincipals entered into an agree-
1ent for partnership, and during
he continuance thereof he be-
ame indebted to his co-partners
1 the sum of £750, and the
urety having been called upon,
xecuted a confession of judg-

ment for the amount of his principal's indebtedness, in ignorance, as he alleged, of the fact
that the agency had ceased, and
a partnership been formed.
Upon a bill filed to enforce the
judgment against the surety, the
court, under the circumstances,
directed a reference to ascertain
what, if any, portion of the debt
for which the cognovit was given
arose in respect of dealings during the agency, reserving further
directions and costs ; or if the
plaintiffs should decline this reference, then that the bill should
be dismissed with costs.

       Gooderham v. Bank of Upper
Canada, 39.

See also " Specific Performance," 4.

PRINCIPAL AND SURETY.

The acceptance by a creditor
of part of his demand against his
debtor, and agreeing not to sue
him, with a reservation of the
creditor's rights against a surety
of such debtor, will not discharge
the surety : where, therefore, the
holders of a bill of exchange received from the acceptor a composition of the debt, and executed
a deed to that effect, but expressly reserved their rights against
the drawer of the bill, *held*, that
this had not the effect of discharging the drawer.

       Wood v. Brett, 452.

PRIORITIES,

See " Absconding Debtor."

PRO CONFESSO.

See " Practice," 7.

PRIVILEGED CREDITORS.
See "Insolvent Debtor."

PURCHASE (RIGHT OF.)
See " Lessor and Lessee."

(AT SHERIFF'S SALE.)
See " Fraudulent Conveyance,"
3.

PURCHASER FOR VALUE WITHOUT NOTICE.

Although the rule in equity is that a notice to be binding "must be given by a person interested in the property, and in the course of the treaty for the purchase," still where notice of an incumbrance to an intending purchaser was given by the son, and while acting on behalf of the incumbrancer in endeavouring to effect a loan upon the security of such incumbrance, the purchaser was held bound by such notice.

McNames v. Philips, 314.

RAILWAY COMPANY.

1. By the statutes 16 Victoria, chaps. 22, and 124, and the 18 Vic., ch. 13, certain municipalities were authorised to issue debentures under by-laws of the corporations to aid in the construction of a railroad. The contractors for building the road agreed with the company to take a certain amount of their remuneration in these debentures, and the work having been commenced certain of these debentures were issued to the company. The contractors afterwards failed to carry on the works, and disputes having arisen between them and the company, all matters in difference were left to arbitration, and an award thereunder was made in favour of the contractors for the sum of £27,645, payable by instalments. One of these instalments having become due, and been left unpaid, the contractors filed a bill to have the debentures delivered over to them in the proportion stipulated for according to the terms of the contract. *Held*, although the contractors would have been entitled to a specific lien on these debentures under their original agreement, the fact that they had referred all matters in difference to arbitration, and had obtained an award in their favour for a money payment, precluded them from now obtaining that relief; and a demurrer for want of equity was allowed.

Sykes v. Brockville and Ottawa Railway Co., 9.

2. *Held*, that a judgment creditor of a railway company with execution against lands of the company, lodged in the hands of the sheriff, is entitled to the appointment of a receiver of the earnings of the road, the profits thereof to be applied in payment of his demand.

Peto v. The Welland Railway Company, 455.

[Affirmed on re-hearing, 16th of February, 1864, *Vankoughnet*, C., dissenting.]

RECEIVER.

See " Executor," 3.

" Railway Company."

RECTORY.

By the Constitutional Act, 31 Geo. III., ch. 31, his Majesty and his successors were empowered to authorize the governor of the province of Quebec to erect parsonages or rectories therein according to the establishment of the Church of England; in pursuance whereof Sir John Colborne, in 1836, then Lieutenant-Governor, erected and endowed the rectory of Kingston. By a provincial statute subsequently passed the Church Society of the diocese of Toronto was incorporated, and by a later statute the right of presentation was vested in such Church Society. Subsequently the legislature erected the Diocese of Ontario out of the portion of the Diocese of Toronto, and the bishop, clergy and laity of the diocese were incorporated under the name of the "Incorporated Synod of the Diocese of Ontario," who, by a by-law passed in 1852, invested the then bishop with the right to all rectories during his incumbency. The bishop in pursuance of such authority afterwards, on the death of the incumbent, presented to the rectory of Kingston; whereupon an information was filed by the Attorney-General on the relation of certain of the parishioners against the bishop and the rector, praying to have such by-law of the Synod declared void and set aside. A demurrer by the bishop and rector for want of equity was allowed, the court considering that under the sev-

eral acts and proceedings wh[i] had been passed and taken [] right of presentation was ves[] in the bishop during his incu bency. But, *quære*, if the Chu[] Society of the Diocese of Tor[] to, before the setting off of [] Diocese of Ontario, had passe[] by-law similar to the one pas[] by the Synod of Ontario, w[] ther the right to make such p[] sentation did not remain w[] the Bishop of Toronto.

Attorney-General v. Lawder, 4

REGISTERED TITLE.

See "Notice."

REGISTRATION OF JU[]MENT.

(FORM OF CERTIFICATE OF.)

1. The certificate of judgm[] registered was entitled "In Queen's Bench," not "In Court of Queen's Bench," [] concluded with "Given under hand and seal," etc., instead "Given under my hand and seal of the said court," etc., [] omitted any form of action which the judgment was rec ered: *held*, a sufficient com[] ance with the form given in statute 9th Victoria, ch. 34.

Bank of Montreal v. Thompson

2. A judgment creditor omit[] to re-register within three yea[] *held*, that he hereby lost his l[] as to persons purchasing or coming incumbrancers after t[] time, and before a re-registrat[] was effected.

Warren v. Taylor,

3. A judgment was recovered against *"Charles Westley Lount,"* which was the correct name of the defendant. The registration was of a judgment against *Charles Wesley Lount."* *Held,* sufficient.

Proudfoot v. Lount, 70.

[But see McDonald v.Rodger,75]

See also " Judgment," 2.
" Marshalling Securities."
" Notice."

RE-HEARING.

The deposit on, divided under the circumstances.

The Great Western Railway Co. v. The Desjardins Canal Co., 523.

See also " Practice," 8.

REPLEVIN.

By the statute 23 Victoria, ch. 45, the courts of common law have power to impose such terms upon the party suing out a writ of replevin as will fully indemnify the defendant in the suit from all damages he may sustain by reason of the action. Under these circumstances this court will not interfere by injunction to restrain the plaintiff suing out such writ from taking possession of, and receiving the profits derivable from, the goods so replevied ; unless in a case where it could be shewn that complete security could not be obtained at law.

Bletcher v. Burns, 425.

REPEAL OF PATENT.

See " Crown Patent," 3.

RE-PURCHASE.

See " Sale."

RESCISSION OF CONTRACT.

See "Vendor and Purchaser," 1.

RESTS.

See " Administration."
" Mortgage," 7.

RIGHT OF PURCHASE.

See " Lessor and Lessee."

SALE.

1. *Held,* that the prior registration of a mortgage with a power of sale, enabled the mortgagee, in the proper exercise of such power, to sell free from the claim of a purchaser prior in point of time, but who had neglected to register his conveyance.

Daniels v. Davidson, 173.

(SETTING ASIDE.)

2. Where, out of an audience or attendance at a sale of twenty-five or thirty persons, three or four were induced to refrain from bidding, because they were informed that a person who was attending at the sale intended to buy the property for the family of the debtor ; the court refused to set aside the sale, which was made to such person at a small advance upon the upset price, although the person purchasing did so for the benefit of persons other than the family of the debtor.

Brown v. Fisher, 423.

(WITH RIGHT OF RE-PURCHASE.)

3. Where, after a treaty for loan on real estate, the owner thereof conveyed the same absolutely to the person to whom he

ad applied for such loan, receiving back a bond conditioned
to re-convey the property, on
payment of a certain sum at the
end of two years, and made default in such payment, a bill
filed, alleging the transaction to
have been one of loan and security merely, and praying redemption, was dismissed with cost.
On a re-hearing this decree was
reversed and the deed, declared
to have been made as security
only; the bond to re-convey containing an undertaking by the
vendor to pay the stipulated
amount, and it appearing that
the value of the property greatly
exceeded the sum paid for the
alleged purchase thereof; but
under the circumstances the
court charged the mortgagee with
such rents and profits as were
actually received, or an occupation rent, if in actual possession;
not with such rents as might
have been received, and allowed
him for repairs and permanent
improvements.

Renwick v. Barker, 202.

See also "Executor."

"Power of Sale."

"Practice," 4.

SALE FOR TAXES.

1. At a sale of lands for wild
land taxes, one of the sheriff's
officers conducted the sale, at
which he knocked down without
any competition to another officer of the sheriff a lot of land
worth about £350, for rather
less £7 10s., which lot was subsequently, with the assent of the
sheriff, entered in the sales book
in the name of the party who
had conducted the sale, for the
purpose of enabling the person
to whom it had been knocked
down to cheat his creditors.
Upon a bill filed to set aside the
deed executed by the sheriff, it
was shewn that by arrangement
amongst the persons attending
the sale it was understood a lot
should be knocked down to each
in turn, in pursuance of which
the sale in question was effected.
Under these circumstances the
court set aside the sale with
costs as against the person to
whom the conveyance was made.

Massingberd v. Montague, 92.

2. The duty imposed on sheriffs
at sales of lands for taxes is to
sell such portions of the lands
offered as the sheriff may consider it most for the advantage
of the owners thereof; where
therefore a sheriff so neglected
his duty in this respect that at
a sale for taxes very valuable
lots of land were knocked down
for trifling amounts of taxes, in
pursuance of an agreement to
that effect entered into amongst
the bidders, some of which lands
were purchased by bailiffs in his
employ, and with his knowledge; the court, in dismissing
the bill filed to set aside one of
the sales to the bailiff, as against
the sheriff, refused him his costs.
It is not sufficient that the sheriff
does not participate in such arrangements for his own benefit.
—*Ib.*

3. The wild land assessment
was unpaid for the years 1853,
4, 5, 6 and 7. On the 25th of

'ebruary, 1858, the treasurer ssued his warrant to sell for rrears of taxes; and on the 3th of July following a sale was ffected by the sheriff. On a ill filed by the owner of the nd to set aside this sale, *held*, nat no portion of the taxes was ue for five years, within the neaning of the act.

Ford v. Proudfoot, 478.

SEAL OF COURT.

See " Certificate."

HERIFF, (AND HIS OFFICERS), THEIR DUTY AT SALES FOR TAXES.

See " Sale for Taxes."

SHERIFF'S SALE.

(PURCHASE AT.)

ee "Fraudulent Conveyance," 3.

SOUNDNESS OF MIND.

(EVIDENCE OF.)

The principle of what is a ufficiently sane and disposing nind and memory treated of nd acted on.

Menzies v. White, 574.

PECIFIC PERFORMANCE.

1. The court refused to enorce a contract for the sale of and, which was subject to an utstanding claim for dower, ntil the title to dower was renoved; but the defendant in is answer having set up as a lefence charges of fraud which vere not established, withheld rom him his costs of the suit. *Chantler* v. *Ince*, reported ante

40

volume vii., p. 432, observed upon ; *Thompson* v. *Brunskill*, ante volume vii., p. 542, approved of.

Gamble v. Gummerson, 193.

2. A person being about to effect the purchase of land, stipulated verbally with another who had been accustomed to use a road over the property, that in the event of the purchase being completed he would be allowed to continue the use thereof, but afterwards refused to carry out such agreement, *held*, that this promise was merely voluntary, and, as such, insufficient to found a bill for specific performance.

Barr v. Hatch, 312.

3. On an enquiry as to title the vendor was unable to produce one of the title deeds, or to shew that a receipt was endorsed thereon for the purchase money, *held*, no objection to the completion of the contract. So also, that the non-production of a certificate of no taxes in arrear, was no objection to the title.

Thompson v. Milliken, 359.

4. The owners of several lots of land employed an agent to sell them, and for the purpose of enabling the agent to effect sales delivered to him blank forms of agreement, signed and sealed by them, leaving it necessary for the agent to insert only the name of the purchaser, the property sold, and the amount of purchase money to be paid; at the same time verbally instructing the agent to

reserve all pine timber fit for saw-logs upon effecting any such sales. The agent sold one of the lots, and after filling in the necessary blanks, delivered to the purchaser one of the agreements, without any reservation of timber, and the vendors subsequently refused to adopt the sale without such reservation being made; and commenced felling timber upon the land. Upon a bill filed by the purchaser for a specific performance of the contract before the time limited by the instrument for its completion, the court declared that the writing so delivered to the plaintiff contained the true agreement between the parties, leaving it to the vendors to enforce any claim they might have against their agent for having acted in breach of their instructions; and ordered the defendants to pay the value of the timber cut and removed by them, together with the costs of the suit.

Jury v. Burrows, 367.

[Affirmed on re-hearing, 16th of February, 1864.]

5. Where, by the terms of a contract for sale and purchase of land, it was stipulated that in the event of interest on the unpaid purchase money being unpaid at the end of each year, the same should be added to the principal, and the purchaser filed a bill praying for a conveyance upon payment of the amount of principal and simple interest only : the court refused to decree specific performance,

except upon the terms of payment of the interest, according to the stipulation in the agreement ; and, *semble*, that he would in like manner have been bound to pay this amount, if the bill had been filed by the vendor, seeking to enforce the sale.

Henderson v. Dickson, 397.

6. The owner of real estate having become greatly enfeebled, and unable to wait upon himself, offered to his son that if he would relinquish his own farm, and come to reside with the father, and take care of him during his life, that he would give the farm upon which he (the father) was resident, to his son. To this proposal the son acceded, and removed with his family to the residence of the father, who it was alleged subsequently made a will, devising the property to the son ; but after his decease no trace of the will could be discovered, nor was there any satisfactory account given of it. *Held*, that there had been a sufficient part performance to take the case out of the statute; and the court ordered the heir-at-law of the father to join in conveying the property to the son.

Black v. Black, 403.

7. The holder of a mortgage on real estate and of a judgment recovered against the mortgagor entered into an agreement, after the death of the mortgagor, with his widow and two of the heirs, for the release, on certain terms, of the equity of redemption in the mortgaged premises, and

also for the conveyance to him of another portion of the real estate in the discharge of the mortgage and judgment debts. On a bill filed to enforce this agreement, it appeared that other children of the mortgagor, who were infants, were interested in the estate, the court refused the relief prayed, but directed a reference to the master to enquire if it would be more for the advantage of the infants to adopt the agreement, or that a sale of the estate should be made under the decree of the court.

McDougall v. Barron, 450.

8. Two incorporated trading companies agreed by writing under their corporate seals, the one to construct certain works for the other, which on completion were to be inspected by engineers on behalf of each of the contracting parties, and upon the engineers approving of the works, and reporting them as completed, they were to be accepted, as soon as completed, by the party for whom they were done, who were to be for ever debarred from denying or contesting the due and proper execution, completion, and acceptance of such works. The parties to perform the work having, as they alleged, completed it, notified the others thereof, calling upon them to appoint an engineer, as stipulated for, which request was not complied with, and subsequently a portion of the works contracted (a bridge) was destroyed. On a bill filed for the purpose of compelling an acce ance of the works, the coi thought that the delay of one the contracting parties, ur after such destruction, to nai an engineer, as had been sti[lated for by the agreement, (not preclude the other from (taining an inspection of t works ; but that such inspecti and approval must, under 1 circumstances, be had by a : ference to the master.—V(koughnet, C., dubitante.]

The Great Western Railw Co., v. The Desjardins Ca₁ Co., 503.

See also "Award."

STATUTE.

(13TH ELIZABETH.)

See " Voluntary Conveyanc

SUBJECT.

(REMEDY OF, AGAINST THE CROW

See " Jurisdiction."

SURETY.

(UNDERTAKING TO BECOME.)

See "Vendor's Lien, 1."

SURROGATE COURT.

See "Administrator," 5.

TAXES.

See " Specific Performance."

TIME.

(COMPUTATION OF.)

See " Lessor and Lessee."
" Sale for Taxes," 3.

TITLE.

(ENQUIRY AS TO.)

See "Specific Performance," 3.

(LATENT DEFECT IN.)

See "Vendor and Purchaser," 3.

TRUSTS, TRUSTEE, & CESTUI QUE TRUST.

1. Where lands are devised to trustees to sell and divide the proceeds among residuary legatees, that is not a charge upon land within the meaning of the 22 Vic., ch. 88, sec 24, so as to be barred by the lapse of 20 years but it is the case of an express trust within the 32nd section of the same act. Following Watson v. Saul. 1 Giff. 188.

Tiffany v. Thompson, 244.

2. The duties and responsibilities of trustees and executors considered and acted on.

Larkin v. Armstrong, 390.

3. Trustees, with a power of investing in real estate, purchased at the instance of one of their number a lot of land for £1200, which upon enquiry before the master was found to be worth not more than £900; the master by his report charged the trustees with the full sum of £1200, refusing to give them credit for the £900, on the ground of collusion on the part of one of the trustees. The court, on appeal, considered that, under the circumstances, credit should be given for the value of the land, and referred the report back to the master.—*Ib.*

4. A. and B., executors and trustees under a will with power of sale, sell and take a mortgage to secure purchase money, they being in the recital named as executors. B. without the knowledge or consent of A. assigns the mortgage and appropriates the consideration money to his own use. *Held,* that no estate passed under the assignment except so far as the trust estate might be found debtor to B.; and also, that as between the contending equities of the trust estate and the assignee the maxim *qui prior est in tempore potior est in jure* would apply in favour of the trust estate.

Henderson v. Woods, 539.

(BILL TO CHANGE TRUSTEES.)

See "Marriage Settlement."

"Mortgage," 12.

USURY.

The rule of the court that a person seeking to impeach a security on the ground of usury, must offer to pay the amount actually advanced and interest, applies equally to the assignee of the debtor, although ignorant of the terms on which the security was effected.

Drake v. The Bank of Toronto, 116.

See also "Pleading," 1.

VENDOR AND PURCHASER.

1. The vendor recovered a judgment against his vendee for portion of the purchase money. Afterwards he wrote the vendee a letter cancelling the agreement. *Held*, that having cancelled the contract, he could not afterwards enforce his judgment.

Cameron v. Bradbury, 67.

2. A vendor who was unable to complete his contract for sale of real estate, by reason of his title being defective, had, notwithstanding, instituted proceedings at law to enforce payment of the purchase money. Thereupon the purchaser filed a bill alleging his willingness to perform the contract, if a good title could be made, but that a good title could not be made; that he had paid part of the purchase money and made improvements on the property. Upon a reference as to title it was shewn that the vendor was unable to make a good title. On further directions, the court ordered a perpetual injunction to restrain the action at law; re-payment of the amount of purchase money paid with interest, and that the same should form a charge on defendant's interest in the land, and that the defendant should pay the costs of the suit; but refused the plaintiff any allowance in respect of the improvements made by him. Kilborn v. Workman. 255.

3. in the year 1856 a purchase was effected of certain lands from one W. and a mortgage given back by the purchaser for the greater portion of the purchase money, such purchase being effected with the view of laying the property out into building lots for the purpose of sale ; which was accordingly done, and roads laid out running through the property. Several years afterwards a purchaser of one of the lots so laid out objected to complete his purchase on the ground that W. at the time he acquired his title from his vendors, the Bank of Upper Canada, was a director and the vice-president of the institution, and as such one of those entrusted to sell the real estate of the bank : which objection was sustained. W.'s vendee thereupon filed a bill to have the transaction set aside, his mortgage delivered up and discharged, and the money paid by him on account of the purchase, and expended for taxes and improvements, repaid to him with interest. There being no evidence of any act of the vendee confirmatory of the purchase after he became aware of this defect in the title, the court decreed the relief asked with costs.

Brunskill v. Clarke, 430.

VENDOR'S LIEN.

1. D. having been negotiating for the purchase of a large quantity of unpatented lands, and the vendee of the Crown requiring security for payment of the purchase money agreed upon between them, D. obtained from

his father a letter addressed to himself in the following words: "If you make the contemplated purchase from *Henderson* of wild lands, amounting to sixteen thousand acres, at six dollars per acre, and deducting all amounts due or hereafter payable on the same, I will become your security for the payment of the principal on the Crown lands, and interest: and the interest on all deeded lands.— *Walter H. Dickson.*" And in a postscript thereto added, "I will see you have two thousand pounds to pay in cash when all papers are signed.—*W. H. Dickson.*" *Held*, that this letter addressed to the son was not such a promise to provide for the payment of the £2000 cash as could be enforced by the vendor; and the vendor having conveyed the lands to the son, and taken the bonds of the father for payment of the price over and above the £2000, and without any reference to it, one of which bonds was subsequently delivered up to the father upon other security being given, and a large portion of the lands to which it referred having been conveyed by the son to the father, *held, also*, that under the circumstances the vendor was not entitled to enforce his lien against those lands in the hands of the father, for the portion of the £2000 remaining unpaid; but that his lien therefor would attach upon the lands remaining in the possession of the son, and to which alone the lien must be confined.

Helliwell v. Dickson, 414.

2. B. having an interest in u patented lands enters into pa nership with D. and A., and ea acquires an undivided one-thi in the lands; A. then conve his third to D., who continu the partnership business wi B., having an undivided tw thirds, and also owning chat property in partnership with B. afterwards agreed to wit draw from the partnership a sell all his interest in both la and chattels to D. in a "lun ing bargain," for £350. Co veyances of the chattels, and a of the real estate were then e ecuted, in which the conside tion stated appeared to be me ly nominal, and there was means of distinguishing the pr of the land from that of t chattels. Promissory notes we given to secure the purcha money, and possession of all t chattel property was taken D. On a bill filed by endorse of the promissory notes agaii D. and purchasers under hi claiming a lien upon the lar *held*, that the mode of sale a the circumstances shewed it be the intention of the part that no lien should exist.

Wilson v. Daniels, 4£

VOLUNTARY ASSIGNMEN
(OF CHOSE IN ACTION.)

See "Chose in Action."

VOLUNTARY AGREEMEN

See "Specific Performance,"

VOLUNTARY CONVEYANCE.

In a suit brought to set aside voluntary conveyance as void against creditors, it lies upon the parties interested in supporting the deed to shew the existence of other property in the debtor available to his creditors : but in such a case, the parties having omitted to give such evidence, the court, at the hearing, directed an enquiry before the master as to the indebtedness of the grantor at the date of the conveyance.

Brown.v. Davidson, 439.

WIFE'S ESTATE.

See "Parol Evidence," 3.

WILD LAND TAX.

See " Sale for Taxes,"

WILFUL DEFAULT.

See " Mortgage," 8.

WILL (CONSTRUCTION OF.)

A testator bequeathed to two of his grand-children the sum of £500 each; by a subsequent clause of his will, he directed certain bonds and securities to be realized and invested to meet two annuities charged on his estate, and after these annuities should cease " to exist then, and in that case, the money so to be invested to raise the sum to pay these annuities shall be divided equally among my children then living, share and share alike, or in case of any of their deaths, then to their children per stirpes, and not per capita." At the time of making his will, his daughter, the mother of the two legatees, had been dead for some time, held, that the children of such deceased daughter did not take any interest in the residuary estate.

Taylor v. Ridout, 356.

2. A testator by one clause of his will devised certain of his lands to his son absolutely, and in a separate clause provided : " And in case my son Henry shall die without issue, I hereby devise, &c., all my real and personal estate, hereinbefore devised to him, to the lawful issue of all my brothers and sisters ; whether said brothers and sisters be living or dead at the time of Henry's decease: " held, that the conditions had not the effect of cutting down the prior absolute devise to the son.

Re Babcock, 427.

(DEFEASANCE CLAUSE IN.)

3. A testator after appointing executors, and expressing full confidence in them, provided " that in case any of the legatees offer obstructions to the proceedings of my said executors in the fulfilment of the powers hereby conferred," then that such persons should suffer the penalty of " being debarred of all claims to any part or portion of my estate, under any pretence whatsoever, in the same manner as if he,

she, or they had actually predeceased . me without issue, and
are hereby declared to be debarred therefrom accordingly, any
law or practice to the contrary
notwithstanding."

Held, in an administration
suit by one of the legatees
against the executors, on the
application of other legatees,
made parties in the master's
office, that an enquiry might
properly be directed whether
any of the legatees had forfeited
his or her share under the above
provision.

The original decree not containing such a clause of enquiry,
was amended in that respect on
motion, after the master's report.

Miller v. McNaughton, 545.

4. The validity of a will esta
lished, notwithstanding witne,
es wore that the testator w
not in a fit state to make a w
when the same was execute
the evidence of the medic
attendants and the surroundi
circumstances tending to sh
that the testator was of suffi
ently sane and disposing mi
to understand the meaning a
effect of the devises in his wi

Menzies v. White, 5%

WRITTEN INSTRUMENT

See " Parol Evidence."

Lightning Source UK Ltd.
Milton Keynes UK
UKHW012226070119
334942UK00010BA/1714/P